BRITISH LABOUR HISTORY,
1815–1914

BRITISH LABOUR HISTORY
1815–1914

E. H. HUNT

Senior Lecturer in Economic History
London School of Economics

WEIDENFELD AND NICOLSON
LONDON

CONTENTS

Contents

Contents

Contents

PREFACE

This book was written because recent interest in labour history, and the proliferation of publications and courses, have increased the need for an introductory textbook that treats British labour history as a whole.

Labour history has always been one of the least respectable branches of the subject. Historians have concentrated on the history of organized labour, and much of what they have written presents the past rather as it might have appeared to a nineteenth-century trade union activist. The only other section of the working classes to have received much attention has been the very poor; those who were neither organized nor impoverished have been comparatively neglected. When, on occasions, discussion has shifted from working-class movements to other aspects of labour history the treatment has been very uneven. There are numerous books and articles on the 'standard of living' between 1790 and 1850, for example, but little attention has been given to wage movements in other periods and less still to the course of women's wages and comparisons between British and foreign wages. Even the literature on trade unions tends to be of the narrative kind, recording every detail of labour legislation and every skirmish with employers, yet affording little space to consideration of other influences upon trade union effectiveness and ignoring the fundamental question of the impact of unionism upon workers' incomes. Most historians of trade unionism, that is, have adopted the approach demonstrated in the Webbs' *History of Trade Unionism* (1894). Very few of them have taken the Webbs' more analytical *Industrial Democracy* (1898) as their model.

Critics have complained also that labour history is sometimes written as though the working-class experience can be understood without reference to the rest of history. Until recently there has been little attempt to incorporate the findings of historical demographers, business historians, and labour economists. Wage trends, for example, have been commonly described with hardly a mention of labour productivity or labour supply and housing conditions have sometimes been explained without reference to demographic pressures or to productivity in the building industry. Perhaps the most widespread criticism of labour history is that labour historians are too ready to display their political commitment. Kitson Clark's adage that honest indignation is a dangerous passion for historians is especially applicable to labour history.

In the last decade or so the study of labour history has advanced remarkably and several of the earlier shortcomings are being eradicated. Far greater attention is being given to once neglected areas of the subject. Most of what is said in the following chapters about the enormous importance of domestic service, for example, could hardly have been written fifteen years ago because at that time servants – unorganized, deferential, female, and not noticeably impoverished – were largely ignored. In addition, the work of social historians and historical demographers is now being incorporated within labour history and a start has been made upon the task of comparing the experiences of British workers with those of workers elsewhere.

The long-standing weaknesses of labour history and the more recent advances in the subject have together determined the broad pattern of the following chapters. Labour history of the traditional sort is well in evidence. But a conscious effort has been made to evaluate the importance and consequences of trade unions, rather than to merely chronicle their growth, and the farm labourers, domestic servants, and others who had little part in working-class movements have not been forgotten. The many anonymous Irish immigrants are included along with John Doherty and Feargus O'Connor, and workers of all kinds are considered as producers and consumers as well as in their role as members of working-class movements. Demand for labour, labour productivity, and labour supply are discussed at some length and I have attempted to provide points of comparison with labour in other countries so that the British working-class experience does not appear entirely in isolation.

In writing this book I have accumulated many debts. Before he died Professor Arthur John read and commented upon the early chapters. I am grateful to him for this and for many other kindnesses. D. E. Baines, Professor T. C. Barker, Dr L. A. Clarkson, and M. E. Falkus each took time from their own work to give me the benefit of their criticism and I am indebted to all of them. Those errors that remain are entirely my responsibility. I am grateful also to my wife for help and encouragement, to Weidenfeld and Nicolson for their patience, and to Mrs J. H. Lynas and Mrs J. M. Maxwell who typed a lengthy and much-amended manuscript.

LSE,
October, 1979   EHH

BRITISH LABOUR HISTORY,
1815–1914

The Diversity of Working-Class Experience

When the census enumerators had completed the great reckoning of 1861 they presented their findings in a table which distinguished the ten and a half million workers from the rest of the population and arranged them by their occupation. The table was headed by the Queen, other members of the royal family, and then over a thousand separate occupations arranged in alphabetical order and including, besides the commonplace, curious entries like the single executioner. Among the least curious and most commonplace of all occupations was that of farm labourer. The circumstances of one of these, Robert Walker, will serve to illustrate some aspects of the remarkable diversity of working-class life in the nineteenth century.

The census enumerators' books show that on 7 April 1861 Robert Walker was aged forty-five. He lived where he was born, at Badbury in Wiltshire, and on census night shared a cottage with his wife, five sons, and a daughter. We are given no details of how Walker spent the remainder of the day but we may reasonably assume that he was up and about before the enumerators had completed their special tally of those sleeping rough and long before they began collecting completed forms from respectable citizens. By six o'clock he would have been sitting down to breakfast. This meal was unlikely to contain meat, eggs, or milk. It could well have been 'kettle broth', bread and hot water flavoured with salt and perhaps an onion. Seven o'clock found him at work. Some twelve hours later he returned home for supper. This was the best meal of the day; it included potatoes, cabbage, tea, possibly cheese, and perhaps a little bacon. Fresh meat, or 'butcher's meat' as Walker would have called it, was not frequently seen on labourers' tables. When they could afford meat, Walker himself received the lion's share. He was the breadwinner and this was considered proper.

There was, in fact, more likely to have been meat that Monday evening than later in the week because as pay-day approached belts were tightened. Pay-day brought Robert Walker 9s or 10s for a working week of over sixty hours. Wiltshire farm labourers were among the worst-paid workers in Britain and it was Walker's meagre earnings, together with the number of his children, that largely determined the day to day conditions of his life – his cold and crowded accommodation, his miserable diet, and his shabby clothing. More than half of the expenditure on food went on bread and, with the notable exception of Walker's boots and his cherished Sunday suit, most of the family's clothing was purchased second-hand.

At eight o'clock that census morning, when Robert Walker was already well into his work, 300 miles away at Hartley in Northumberland John Bewick, a coal-miner, aged thirty-three, was getting up. Like Walker, Bewick was enumerated close to where he had been born. He was married and had five children between one year and ten years old living at home. His breakfast that morning and his evening meal later in the day were almost certainly superior to Walker's, particularly in the amount of protein they contained. A surviving budget from 1844 records a miner's wife buying 14 lbs of mutton and 14 lbs of bacon during one fortnight, and even Engels (visiting Britain that year) conceded that the miners' standard of living was 'reasonably good'.[1] Free or cheap coal was one of their advantages. Bewick's cottage was probably as crowded as Walker's, but it was neither damp nor cold.

There were also remarkable contrasts in the working day of the two men. Bewick worked a short day by any standards – if he began work at nine o'clock that morning he was back at the pit-head by four in the afternoon. Exactly how much he was paid for his work during the census week of 1861 is not known for another contrast between the miner and the farm labourer was that whereas a farm labourer's pay changed little from week to week and from year to year, the miner's pay varied with the price of coal and also according to the amount he hewed. But Bewick certainly earned substantially more than Walker for considerably fewer hours at work. If he received less than two to three times Walker's earnings, then April 1861 was an unusually bad month in the colliery villages to the north of Newcastle. Northumberland miners were among the best paid working men in Europe.

The contrasts in the lives of the two men extended far beyond pay and hours of work. Nowhere was it more evident that in the way they conducted relations with their employers. Trade unionism was no part of Robert Walker's world. He must have regarded the unions, if he thought of them at all, as urban phenomena, part of the world of the craftsmen and their like. Rather more than a decade later Joseph Arch's Agricultural Labourers Union made a fleeting impression on Badbury. But that brief excitement was soon over and more than thirty years passed before unionism was again of any consequence in the district. The miners of Northumberland and Durham, by contrast, had been the mainstay of the Miners Association in the 1840s and, had he lived, John Bewick would have seen the Northumberland and Durham Associations survive the crisis year of 1879 which put an end to miners' unionism almost everywhere else in Britain. He would also have seen a Northumberland miner, Thomas Burt, and another miner, Alexander

Macdonald, become the first working men to enter parliament, in 1874. At that time few farm labourers had even a vote.

Another contrast between the mining and the agricultural communities was their death-rates. The coalfields were distinguished by exceptionally high infant mortality, whereas children born in the cottages of farm labourers had a better than average chance of surviving the hazardous early months, despite their parents' poverty. The contrast in death-rates extended beyond childhood for mining was a dangerous occupation. In 1861 943 miners were killed at work: one life for every 90,000 tons of coal raised to the pit-head. John Bewick himself survived the census by less than a year. On 10 January 1862, shortly after the back shift had gone down, the beam of the pumping engine at the New Hartley Pit fractured and plunged down the shaft carrying with it a mass of masonry. By the time rescuers had hacked a way through the debris six days later the 214 men entombed in the mine were dead, among them John Bewick and James Bewick, his brother and next-door neighbour.[2]

Alongside these contrasts it is possible to find similarities in the lives of Walker and Bewick and some contrasts between their conditions and those of farm labourers and miners elsewhere in Britain. Neither of them lived in one of the fast-growing factory towns that symbolized new industrial society. Steam power helped Bewick to and from the coalface and kept the mine from flooding, but his tools and methods of work were as traditional as those of Robert Walker. Neither of them could count on their wives adding much to family incomes because neither rural villages nor colliery villages offered much work for women – a fact which probably helps to explain why miners' wives and farm labourers' wives were equally remarkable for bearing numerous children. At the same time there was a remarkable contrast between the wretched circumstances of Robert Walker and the modest prosperity of farm labourers in the north of England. Moreover, there were coal-miners elsewhere in Britain, in Somerset and the Forest of Dean for example, whose pay and hours of work were far inferior to those of John Bewick. Even among Bewick's neighbours there were great contrasts, most of all between the respectable, non-drinking, Methodist miners and the others. And the contrasts between (and among) factory workers, urban craftsmen, urban labourers, women workers of every kind, and the other occupational groups were no less remarkable.

PART I

THE LABOUR MARKET, INCOMES AND CONSUMPTION

1

WORK AND WORKERS

1 · *Size of the labour force; the activity rate*

Robert Walker, John Bewick, and the other ten and a half million people at work in 1861 were part of a labour force that had probably rather more than doubled since the beginning of the century. We cannot be sure of the size of the labour force in the early nineteenth century, nor of its occupational distribution, because the early occupational censuses were hit or miss affairs and the 'working population' and the 'normal occupation' of many workers were not well defined. Substantial numbers were self-employed and some of these were helped occasionally by members of their family. Many others pursued two or more occupations, and during the harvest many men and women became temporary farm workers. In the following half-century, that is between 1861 and 1911, the rate of increase in the labour force was probably a little slower. But it was sufficient to raise the number of workers to 18.6 million in 1911. This was not much less than the working population of France at the same date. The German labour force, however, was more than half as large again and the working population of the United States was by then 38 million.

The activity rate, that is the proportion that the labour force formed of the total population, appears to have changed very little in the second half of the nineteenth century. The slight fall from 46.6 per cent in 1851 to 44.1 per cent in 1881[3] may be entirely a consequence of retired workers being enumerated under their former occupation before the census of 1881. After 1881 the occupied proportion rose very gradually to 45.6 per cent in 1911. Evidence on activity rates during the first half of the century, for what it is worth, also suggests long-term stability. The ratio of workers to non-workers in the nineteenth century was therefore broadly similar to the ratio in recent years: the activity rate in 1971 was around 46 per cent. In several other respects, however, the composition of the nineteenth-century labour force was very different to that shown in the 1971 census. Although the majority of the working population were males aged fifteen and over at both dates, the proportion of this group that did not work was three times greater in 1971 (18.6 per cent) than it was in the second half of the nineteenth century. There was an obvious contrast too with respect to child employment. And while the activity rate of all females aged fifteen and over was not dissimilar to recent levels – it was 35 per cent in 1911 and 37 per cent in 1971 – married women were far less inclined to take employment in the nineteenth century than they are today.

II · *Beginning work and retirement*

We would expect the great majority of men aged twenty to sixty-five in the nineteenth century to have worked. We begin therefore by examining the employment of young people, old people, and women, where the more significant changes in activity rates have occurred. There are two main reasons why a substantially greater proportion of the total male population aged fifteen and over was at work a century ago. First, and most obviously, only small numbers pursued full-time education beyond the age of fifteen. Secondly, the retired proportion of the adult male population was then far smaller than it is now. This was partly because fewer men lived long enough to reach retirement age: in 1871 only 4.7 per cent of the population of England and Wales were aged sixty-five or over, in 1971 the proportion was over 13 per cent. And it was partly because very few workers looked forward to a pensioned retirement. In fact, before 1908, when the government introduced old age pensions, few workers were familiar with the concept of voluntarily retiring from work at a predetermined age. Some enlightened companies made limited provision before this date including many of the railway and gas companies and the Quaker firm of Cadbury. Admiralty employees could look forward to a pensioned retirement and some of the older and wealthier trade unions gave pensions to long-subscribing members. But the chief beneficiaries of pension schemes before 1908 were civil servants, other white-collar workers, and servicemen.

Most working men simply kept working for as long as they were able. Ageing was accompanied not by retirement and a pension, but by increased sickness and falling earnings. Unskilled labourers, who had little to offer but their strength, might see the beginning of this process in their forties. A change to lighter work – miners might move to less arduous work at the pit-head for example – stemmed the lengthening bouts of unemployment but at the cost of lower wages. Many workmen finished their days as messengers or night-watchmen. Some employers retained the services of ageing workers out of kindness; in this way considerable numbers of domestic servants and some farm labourers finished their lives virtually as pensioners. But most of those that survived suffered a gradual withdrawal from the labour market as sickness and senility gained the upper hand. Instead of a pension the more fortunate of them received sick benefits from a friendly society or trade union. The less fortunate relied upon their children, charity, and the poor rates. A time might come when extended benefits from one of these sources amounted to much the same thing as a retirement pension, but this was only achieved when the recipient was consistently too weak to work.

III · *Children's employment*

Just as the interval between work and death was far shorter in the nineteenth century than it is today, so too was that between birth and first employment. Far more of life altogether was taken up with the business of earning a living. In 1851 28 per cent of children between the ages of ten and fifteen were already at work and the census also recorded 42,000 workers under the age of ten. These figures are probably underestimates because it is likely that considerable employment of children who worked on a casual or part-time basis, particularly those who helped with their parents' work, was not declared to the census enumerators. Those who worked in contravention of the factory acts were also likely to have remained unrecorded. Even so, child employment, especially the employment of very young children, was almost certainly less extensive in 1851 than it had been fifty years earlier. It was probably also less extensive than it had been before the industrial revolution. Precisely how many children worked in pre-industrial England is not known and some historians have suggested that industrialization was in fact accompanied by increased employment of children.[4] What evidence we have, however, leaves little doubt that most children in pre-industrial England, and virtually all the children of the poor, were expected to contribute to their keep long before their tenth birthday. Early in the sixteenth century a Venetian nobleman described how English parents commonly put their children to work by the age of seven, or nine at the most, 'few are born who are exempted from the fate'.[5] Defoe in 1723 noted that in Norfolk children of four or five already earned their keep and in Yorkshire 'scarce any thing above four years old but its hands were sufficient for its own support'.[6] Later in the century the eldest son of Samuel Crompton recalled helping his mother clean cotton at the age of four.[7] Thus there was probably little scope for a general increase in child labour in the early stages of the industrial revolution, although in Lancashire and a few other places industrialization brought a rise in children's wages and the more intensive use of child labour, often outside the home where it was more likely to excite comment. During the course of the first half of the nineteenth century, child employment declined considerably, although to a level that was still high by later standards.

In the third quarter of the century there was little change in the overall proportion of children employed. There was far less employment of children under ten years old,[8] but the proportion at work between the ages of ten and fifteen fell only from 28 per cent in 1851 to 26 per cent in 1871. After 1871 a more general decline commenced which by 1911 reduced the proportion at

9

work between the ages of ten and fifteen to 14 per cent.[9] There is nothing particularly remarkable about the employment of children in nineteenth-century Britain. Child employment was commonplace virtually everywhere. Britain was poorer then than now, and therefore less able to support large numbers of non-workers. Moreover, the proportion of children in the population was considerably larger than it is today, so that the burden that would have been placed upon the rest of the community by completely withdrawing children from the labour force was very great indeed: in 1971 less than a quarter of the population was under fifteen, in 1851 the proportion was over one-third. The provision of mass education at the end of the nineteenth century, and the reduction in child employment at that time, were both made easier by the early stages of the reduction in the proportion of children in the total population.[10]

The reduction in child employment in the first half of the century was partly a consequence of legislation. An early step was the Health and Morals of Apprentices Act of 1802 which applied mainly to those pauper apprentices who had been taken north to work in the mills. This act attempted to ban the night-work of children and to limit their working day to twelve hours. But it was not accompanied by effective means of enforcement and in any event steampower was freeing the mills from thinly populated rural locations and opening the way to the greater employment of unapprenticed town children. In 1819 the employment of any child less than nine years old in a cotton mill was made illegal and those under sixteen were forbidden to work more than twelve hours a day, but again there was no effective enforcement and there was widespread evasion. The legislation of 1833, however, was of a different calibre. It extended the exclusion of children under nine to all textile factories except those manufacturing silk; it required a modicum of schooling for factory children aged nine to thirteen and limited their hours to nine a day; it prohibited night-work before the age of eighteen and, particularly important, it was accompanied by the appointment of factory inspectors.[11] There was further legislation in 1844 on the age at which children could enter the mills when, as part of an act that reinforced the legislation of 1833, textile print works were made subject to its provisions and the 'half-time' education system for children to the age of thirteen was introduced.

Outside the mechanized textile industry the only significant child employment much affected by legislation before the middle of the century was work in the mines. In 1842 Lord Ashley (Shaftesbury) introduced a bill intended to banish from the mines all females, whatever their age, and all boys under the age of ten. Nothing was done to prevent them working at the pit-brow, just as there was nothing to stop young children working in the domestic branch of the textile trades. Even so, it seems reasonable to suppose that these various legislative measures had some direct effect on the number of children employed.

But factory and mine legislation could not have been directly responsible for more than a modest part of the decline in child employment in the first half of the century because most children worked in areas unaffected by legislation. Some of the decline was probably a consequence of more enlightened recruiting policies on the part of employers who noticed that the competitiveness of the textile factories was not adversely affected by the statutory regulation of child employment. A further part was doubtless due to changing attitudes among parents who came to value education both for its own sake and as an investment in their children's future. Probably, too, attitudes of both employers and parents were influenced by the public debate on the regulation of cotton mills and mines and by the greater availability of school places as Anglicans and nonconformists competed to build schools where they might influence the young.[12] Another part of the explanation of falling child employment in the first half of the century may well be changing employment patterns. The decline of the domestic system removed work from the home where parents had complete control over child workers and where the employment of very young children was most extensive and least frowned upon.

Why was child employment in the cotton mills singled out for regulation? It was certainly not because the factory masters initiated the widespread employment of children or because they employed them at an especially tender age. Nor were the factory children exceptionally ill-treated, judged by the not very exacting contemporary standards. In fact, for a long time many of them continued to be engaged, supervised, and paid by adult operatives, in some cases by their parents.[13] The transport of pauper children to northern mills reflects little credit upon the London poor law authorities or the mill owners, but the essentials of the practice were not new. For over a century parish authorities had been aware of the advantage of placing young paupers where they, and their eventual dependants, would not fall upon the parish rates. And although there is abundant evidence of ill-treatment, some factory apprentices appear to have been well cared for.[14] Pinchbeck and Hewitt, after describing the widespread abuse of pauper apprentices outside the factory, concluded that factory apprenticeship 'could not have surpassed the evils of apprenticeship to scattered masters and mistresses'.[15]

What may have been more remarkable than the employment of children in the early cotton mills were the hours they worked and the unrelenting nature of the work.[16] But two other considerations are more important in explaining why the mills were singled-out for special treatment. First, factory children were working outside the home and sometimes, as was the case with pauper apprentices, without the presence of parents or other relatives and in such numbers that their employer could not possibly take a personal interest in their physical and moral welfare. On these particular grounds child

11

employment in the factory was more open to criticism than was domestic employment. Secondly, there was so much more that was novel about the factories than hours of work and working away from home. In Clapham's words, 'children were being overworked in a new and obvious way in new and unusually obvious institutions'.[17] The Lancashire cotton industry with its factories and machinery, its bewildering expansion and easy command of distant markets, was a prospect that could hardly fail to excite the imagination. Nowhere was the abuse of child labour less likely to be overlooked, and the shortcomings of factory employers were ruthlessly denounced by those whose economic and political ascendancy had been challenged. Similar attitudes were evident in Europe and the United States: in both child labour seems to have become a public issue only when children were employed in factories.[18]

In the third quarter of the century legal restriction upon child employment was considerably extended. In the early 1860s employment of boys under twelve in mines became conditional upon certain educational attainments; at the same time the pottery and lace industries, an assortment of textile finishing trades, and the manufacture of cartridges and lucifer matches were all made subject to existing factory legislation. A great many other industries and all places in which fifty people or more were employed were treated similarly in 1867. In the same year the Workshops Regulation Act restricted opportunities for children under eight years old to be employed in smaller establishments and required that those between the ages of eight and thirteen should not be employed on more than a half-time basis. The Workshops Regulation Act had an enormous potential influence because it applied to the places where employment of young children was most widespread. But legislation that applied to a multitude of small establishments proved less easy to enforce than the factory acts. The legislative pressure that most effectively delayed the entry of children to the labour market was now to come from a different quarter. Until 1860 compulsory education (other than of pauper children) had been limited to the half-time provision that applied to factory children between the ages of eight and thirteen. But the education acts of 1870, 1876, and 1880 introduced general compulsory education. At first these measures applied in their full rigour only to children under ten, but considerable obstacles were placed in the way of a child leaving school before he or she was thirteen. In 1893 the minimum age was raised to eleven and in 1899 (1901 in Scotland) to twelve. In this respect the children of the Lancashire and West Riding textile workers made less progress than most for there the half-time system persisted, all attempts to modify it being resisted by the children's parents through their trade unions.[19]

The occupational distribution of child labour in the early part of the nineteenth century is hardly less obscure than the proportion of all children at work. The legislation and literature of the period reflect contemporary preoccupations but provide uncertain guides to the importance of any particular group: far more children were employed than those up chimneys, down mines, and in the mills. The climbing chimney boys, like poor Tom in *The Water-Babies* (1863), are known to every schoolchild but their number never exceeded three or four thousand.[20] There were far more child miners. According to the rough estimates in the report of the Children's Employment Commission of 1842, children under thirteen accounted for 10 per cent or more of the labour force at a time when mining and quarrying employed some 194,000.[21] Many of these were employed by their father or other workmen; some began work when they were only four, although eight or nine was the more usual starting age.[22] The youngest were mostly 'trappers', whose task it was to open ventilation doors to let coal waggons pass. This was not hard work, but there were few other compensations: 'I'm a trapper in the Gauper Pit, [Sarah Gooder, aged eight] I have to trap without a light, and I'm scared. I go at four and sometimes half-past three in the morning, and come out at five and half past. . . . Sometimes I sing when I've light but not in the dark. I dare not sing then.'[23] When they were sufficiently strong they graduated to filling waggons and hauling or pushing them towards the surface.

More children still were employed in the textile factories.[24] These factory children performed a variety of tasks. The majority were piecers who watched the threads and tied together any that broke; some changed bobbins and kept the place tidy; and the smaller children were used for cleaning restricted spaces beneath machines.[25] But the factory children, the child miners, and the climbing boys together, could hardly have accounted for more than a quarter of all child workers in 1840.

As to the remainder, most of the girls were domestic servants. Dressmaking and assisting in domestic industry of various kinds probably came next in importance among girls' employment. Much of this work was also done at home, and it was in domestic industry that the employment of very young children was most commonplace. Children commonly began work at domestic industry when they were seven or eight and many started when they were much younger.[26] In a house at New Snenton near Nottingham, for example, three girls and their mother were discovered making lace. The youngest of these was four and had two years work behind her. She began in the morning at 6 a.m. or 7 a.m. and (as a concession to her tender years) stopped at 6 p.m. while her two elder sisters worked on into the evening.[27] Agriculture was another important employer of girls in the first half of the nineteenth century and considerable numbers were employed making pottery.

The employment of boys at this time was more important than that of girls and there was a greater variety of jobs which boys might enter. In 1851 boys under fifteen years old at work outnumbered girls under fifteen by almost two

13

to one. It seems likely that many more boys than girls worked in the coal-mines but the main contrast was the far greater employment of boys in agriculture. Textile employment, inside and outside the factories, provided work for nearly as many boys as girls and there were more boys than might be expected in the dress trade. Road and water transport (but not the railways) also employed a large number of boys as did building work, the metal trades, and dealing of various kinds. Many of these boy workers probably did little besides keeping watch, fetching beer, and running errands.

Table 1·1 *Main occupations of boys and girls under fifteen years in Britain (1851) (thousands)*

Boys		%	Girls		%
Agriculture	120	28.4	Textiles	98	41.3
Textiles	82	19.4	Domestic Service	71	30.0
Navigation and Docks	46	10.9	Dress	32	13.5
Mines	37	8.7	Agriculture	17	7.2
Metal Workers and Manufacture of Machinery and Tools	26	6.1	Metal Workers and Manufacture of Machinery and Tools	4	1.7
Dress	23	5.4	Navigation and Docks	4	1.7
General Labour	15	3.5	Earthenware	3	1.3
Dealing (various) incl. lodging and coffee houses	12	2.8	Dealing (various) incl. lodging and coffee houses	2	0.8
Building	11	2.6			
Domestic Service	9	2.1			
Earthenware	6	1.4			
TOTAL EMPLOYED	423		TOTAL EMPLOYED	237	

Source: Booth, *Journal of the Royal Statistical Society*, XLIX (1886).

The most remarkable change in child employment in the third quarter of the century was the substantial decline in the number employed on the land. The Gangs Act (1867),[28] greater use of machinery, the attraction of other jobs, and the introduction of compulsory education, were the main causes of this decline. Textiles and dress manufacture, particularly the domestic branches of textile manufacture, also employed considerably fewer children by 1881. During these years more boys than girls appear to have been withdrawn from the labour market. There was no occupation where boys' employment

14

increased by much, even in absolute terms, but domestic service by 1881 employed half as many girls again as were employed in 1851. Nearly half of all girls employed in 1881 were domestic servants and textile manufacture and dressmaking accounted for most of the remainder.

Table 1·2   *Main occupations of boys and girls under fifteen years in Britain (1881) (thousands)*

Boys		%	Girls		%
Agriculture	77	21.3	Domestic Service	107	45.3
Textiles	56	15.5	Textiles	76	32.2
Navigation and Docks	54	15.0	Dress	22	9.3
Mines	31	8.6	Education	6	2.5
Metal Working and Manufacture of Machinery and Tools	22	6.1	Agriculture	4	1.7
Dealing (various) incl. lodging and coffee houses	17	4.7	Dealing (various) incl. lodging and coffee houses	4	1.7
General Labour	14	3.9			
Building	12	3.3			
Dress	10	2.8			
Domestic Service	10	2.8			
TOTAL EMPLOYED	361		TOTAL EMPLOYED	236	

Source: Booth, *Journal of the Royal Statistical Society,* XLIX (1886).

After 1891 there was a dramatic fall in the number of young domestic servants. The occupational categories of the 1911 census prevent direct comparison with Booth's figures for earlier years, but there is some evidence that by 1911 the range of jobs which girls might enter had become somewhat less restricted, even if three-quarters of them were still engaged in the textile industry, dressmaking and domestic service. By this time agriculture was no longer the first occupation for boys: 'Education is doing away with children on farms,' complained a farmer in 1902, 'young people go into the towns and get situations they could not get unless educated.'[29] He was at least half right – education was one of the influences that encouraged boys to turn their backs on farmwork and look townwards – but many of the jobs in the towns required little education. In the occupational category that contained most boys in 1911, transport, the majority were messengers, porters, and 'watchmen'.

Table 1·3   *Main occupations of boys and girls under fifteen years
in Britain (1911) (thousands)*

Boys

		%
Transport	95	27.5
Textiles	46	13.3
Agriculture	39	11.3
Mines	36	10.4
Metals, Machines, Implements and Conveyances	29	8.4
Food, Tobacco, Drink and Lodging	16	4.6
Dress	12	3.5
Domestic Service	9	2.6
Commercial Occupations	8	2.3
TOTAL EMPLOYED	346	

Girls

		%
Textiles	68	34.0
Domestic Service	50	25.0
Dress	33	16.5
Food, Tobacco, Drink and Lodging	9	4.5
Paper, Printing, Books and Stationery	8	4.0
Transport	7	3.5
Metals, Machines, Implements and Conveyances	6	3.0
TOTAL EMPLOYED	200	

Source: *Census of 1911.*

The amount of child employment obviously varied from place to place. Even at the beginning of the century few children were at work in Newcastle before they were twelve,[30] while the colliery villages round about provided plenty of work for boys but little for their sisters. The textile towns provided work for both: Lancashire returned a higher proportion of juvenile workers than any other county in the 1911 census, and when the Poor Law Commissioners attempted to encourage migration to Lancashire and Cheshire in 1834 they had suggested that among the most suitable to go were widows with numerous children.[31] Many rural districts were among the most intensive users of child workers before the 1880s, employing them in agriculture, domestic service, and domestic industry. In Bedfordshire, Hertfordshire, and Buckinghamshire, for example, straw plaiting and lace making helped to make child employment as widespread as it was in the northern textile counties.[32] There was substantial variation too in the extent that children were used in agriculture. This was partly a consequence of farming patterns, but the main reason for such variations, according to the 1867 Commission on the Employment of Children, Young Persons, and Women in Agriculture, was the level of the father's wage: 'The counties where the fewest children under ten years of age are employed in farm work are for the most part those in which the total earnings of the agricultural labourers in permanent employment are high.'[33] Children in rural Northumberland, Cumberland and Westmorland were already being kept at school until they were twelve or thirteen at the time of this enquiry.[34] Rural Scotland had similar enlightened ideas on the importance of education. Scottish shepherds sometimes clubbed together to provide a tutor for their children, boarding and lodging him by turns.[35] Such attitudes were less apparent in the larger Scottish towns, but in Scotland as a whole a considerably smaller proportion of children than in England and Wales were at work in 1851, and in the following sixty years.

Table 1·4   *Proportion of children aged ten to fifteen employed:
England and Wales and Scotland*

	1851 (%)	1881 (%)	1911 (%)
England & Wales	30	19	14
Scotland	25	16	9

Sources: Booth, *Journal of the Royal Statistical Society*, XLIX (1886), and 1911 Census.

IV · *Women's employment*

Although the relative importance of children in the labour force was much greater in the nineteenth century than it is today, their contribution to total employment was far less than that of women. The censuses of 1851 and 1911 both show females aged fifteen and above accounting for slightly under 30 per cent of the labour force. The proportion of all females of this age who were occupied – 39 per cent in 1851 and 1881 and 35 per cent in 1911 – fell slightly over these years.[36] Whether women's employment was expanding or contracting before 1850, and whether it was then more or less than it had been in pre-industrial Britain, are difficult questions to answer because (as for child employment at that time) there is little hard evidence. The contemporary pre-occupation with factory employment, and the fact that men had for centuries dominated the gilds and all the more important occupations of a kind likely to leave records, have led some investigators to associate the industrial revolution with increasing employment of women. But they are probably mistaken. Industrialization created new opportunities for women, as it did for children, in new surroundings outside the home and more in the public eye: but the proportion of women at work in nineteenth-century Britain was probably not larger than the proportion that had worked before the industrial revolution.[37]

17

The extent of female employment was little influenced by legislation. After 1844, when women were classified as 'protected persons', those in trades subject to the factory acts had their working day regulated and were excluded from night-work. But apart from a very small number in a few insignificant occupations like glass-blowing, the only women prevented from working by legislation were miners. The Act of 1842 prohibited their underground employment, but the number of women thrown out of work was not great. Only 6,000 females of all ages were returned as mineworkers in the 1841 census and many of these worked on the surface. Among the other causes of the modest fall between 1881 and 1911 in the proportion of women occupied were declining employment opportunities in certain parts of the country and the changing age structure. Women were more likely to be occupied before their thirtieth birthday than subsequently, and in 1911 a greater proportion of all women were over thirty than in 1881.

Perhaps the greatest contrast between female employment in the nineteenth century and female employment today was in the participation of married women, 'the great bulk of whom', boasted the General Report of the 1911 Census (p. 161), 'are fortunately in this country free at all ages to devote their attention to the care of their households'. In 1911 90 per cent of wives had no paid employment: in 1971 over 40 per cent of them were at work. The percentage of all females aged fifteen and over employed at these two dates, however, was very similar (above, pp. 7–8). The smaller proportion of working wives at the earlier date was compensated by the comparatively large proportion of females who had left full-time education before they were fifteen, by a greater proportion of all women being in the fifteen to thirty-four age-group, and by the fact that a greater proportion of all women were then single. There were over one and a quarter million more females than males in 1911.

Wives had made a more substantial contribution to the labour force earlier in the nineteenth century. In 1851 almost a quarter of them were at work, and in 1800 the proportion at work may have approached, or even exceeded, today's level. One cause of this long-term decline in married women's employment during the nineteenth century was the transfer of work from the home to factories and workshops. Work outside the home was less easily reconciled with a wife's domestic duties. This was particularly true at a time when women married comparatively late in life and reared large families. The interval between marriage and motherhood, and that between the departure of the last child and a woman's death, were both shorter than they are today. In the nineteenth century, moreover, there were no electrical appliances and few convenience foods and other aids to housework. Another influence was the Victorian deification of home and family and the growing insistence that the home was a woman's rightful place. Married women who worked at any but the most home-orientated and undemanding tasks were increasingly regarded as objects of pity and disapproval.[38] Not least among the reasons why some contemporary observers were alarmed by the social consequences of early factory employment was that the mills employed numerous married women.[39] There was much talk of improprieties among the bobbins and shuttles, of dirty homes, unkempt children, and of how husbands thus neglected would seek comfort in drink. These fears were not entirely without substance. During the American Civil War, when the mills were sometimes idle for want of cotton and working wives stayed at home, infant mortality rates in the cotton towns declined.

The female occupational structure in 1851 suggests another reason why relatively few married women worked in the nineteenth century. Domestic servants, most of whom were required to live in, were easily the most numerous of female workers. In 1851 there were two domestic servants for each female textile worker and four of them for each woman that worked in a textile factory. Making the material for a shirt occupied the Lancashire mill girls for only thirty minutes – but its subsequent life required twelve hours or more of washing, starching, and ironing.

Table 1·5   *Main occupations of females (aged fifteen and over) in Britain, 1851 (thousands)*

		%			%
Domestic Service	1,027	37.3	Education	71	2.6
Textiles	508	18.5	Medicine	29	1.1
Dress	494	18.0	Metal Working and		
Agriculture	213	7.7	Manufacture of		
Dealing, various incl.			Machinery and Tools	25	0.9
Lodging and Coffee					
Houses	127	4.6	TOTAL EMPLOYED	2,752	

Source: Booth, *Journal of the Royal Statistical Society*, XLIX (1886).

After domestic service and textiles the main female occupations in 1851 were dressmaking and agriculture. How many women were employed at these, and at other occupations, in the first half of the century we do not know. The importance of domestic service may well have increased then as middle-class incomes rose. There doubtless was an increase also in the number of females employed in textile factories although this may have been more than offset by decline in the number employed in the domestic branches of the textile industries. Agriculture had perhaps employed fewer females in the twenty years or so after Waterloo than were employed by 1851 because some southern labourers had found it necessary to send their wives to work when the Poor Law Amendment Act of 1834 took away more acceptable supplements to their own earnings.[40] The other occupations that were of any consequence in 1851 are shown in Table 1·5. Education already employed 70,000 women, mainly as schoolteachers and governesses. Those classified under medicine were predominantly nurses – the census of 1871 was the first to show a woman doctor – and the largest single group among the 24,000 metal workers was the Black Country domestic nail-makers. Prostitutes should probably appear in the table but they escaped the attention of the census enumerators.

There appear to have been few changes of substance in female employment between 1850 and 1880, although in the 1881 census there are already signs of the important changes that were to occur by the end of the century. Perhaps the most notable development in these years was the fall in the number of women working in agriculture. One reason for this decline was that as their husbands' earnings rose fewer wives found it necessary to work on the land. Another reason may have been the greater use of farm machinery. In addition, education and the opportunities offered by domestic service were encouraging more country girls to set their sights on the nearest town.

Table 1·6   *Main occupations of females (aged fifteen and over) in Britain, 1881 (thousands)*

		%			%
Domestic Service	1,590	40.4	Education	138	3.6
Dress	649	16.7	Agriculture	109	2.8
Textiles	619	15.9	Medicine	41	1.1
Dealing, various, incl. Lodging and Coffee Houses	240	6.2	Food, Drink and Tobacco Mfg.	42	1.1
			Metal Workers and Manufacture of Machinery and Tools	40	1.0
			TOTAL EMPLOYED	3,885	

Source: Booth, *Journal of the Royal Statistical Society*, XLIX (1886).

There were some half million more domestic servants in 1881 than there had been in 1851, an increase of about 50 per cent. Of the other great female employments, dressmaking held its relative importance in the third quarter of the century but the importance of textile manufacture declined a little. Textile manufacture, however, was being rapidly concentrated in the factories and Booth's figures (Tables 1·5 and 1·6) conceal a rapid expansion of the number of females on textile factory pay-rolls and a rapid decline in the number who worked at home. Hardly more than half of the female textile workers worked in factories in 1850, thirty years later the proportion was over three-quarters. A similar transition was affecting those women in the category of 'metal workers and manufacture of machinery and tools', although in these occupations overall employment and the proportion working in factories both expanded significantly. Great changes were underway also in the commercial sector as women began to make inroads upon the City of London and similar male bastions. Booth's 'commercial' and 'administrative' categories contained only 2,300 females in 1851 but more than 15,000 in 1881. Female shop assistants had begun a similar advance, and the number of women teachers doubled in the same period.

Between 1880 and the First World War there was a far more substantial

Table 1·7 *Main occupations of females (all ages) in Britain, 1911 (thousands)*

The numbers in these categories in 1881 are shown in brackets.

			% 1911	% 1881
Domestic Offices and				
Personal Services	2,127	(1,756)	39.3	(45.2)
Textiles	870	(745)	16.1	(19.2)
Clothing	825	(667)	15.2	(17.2)
Professional Occupations				
and their Subordinate Services	383	(203)	7.1	(5.2)
Food, Drink, Tobacco	308	(98)	5.7	(2.5)
Commercial Occupations	157	(11)	2.9	(0.3)
Papers, Printing, Books				
and Stationery	144	(53)	2.7	(1.4)
Metal Manufacture, Machines,				
Implements, Vehicles, Precious				
Metals etc.	128	(49)	2.4	(1.3)
Agriculture, Horticulture				
and Forestry	117	(116)	2.1	(3.0)
Public Administration	50	(9)	0.9	(0.2)
TOTAL EMPLOYED	5,413	(3,887)		

Source: B. R. Mitchell and P. Deane, *Abstract of British Historical Statistics*, (Cambridge 1962), p. 60.

widening in women's employment opportunities. The more dramatic changes affected middle-class women. But there was also a considerable widening of opportunities for working-class females, not least in the fast-growing lower middle-class occupations. The number of women office workers rose particularly rapidly. By 1911 there were 121,000 female 'business clerks' (probably an underestimate) and 22,000 female 'officers and clerks' in the civil service. Women had only 8 per cent of all government and post office work in 1861, but they held more than half of it by 1911. There were still large areas of commercial life – such as banking – where they had made little progress. But whereas fewer than 1 per cent of all commercial clerks were female in 1861, and only 3 per cent of them were female in 1881, by 1911 women accounted for a quarter of the total.[41] Girls had benefited more than boys from the introduction of compulsory education and this doubtless was one reason for their progress in the white-collar occupations. They were helped too by male reluctance to master new techniques like typewriting, shorthand, and the operation of telephone switchboards. These decades after 1880 also saw a modest expansion in the number of female teachers and a rapid expansion in the number of shop assistants.* And as these three occupations grew they helped to reduce the former preponderance of domestic service, dressmaking and textile manufacture among female employment.

Towards the end of the century the proportion of women workers who were domestic servants was declining. This fall was partly due to the reduced size of middle-class families, to the greater availability of piped water, electricity, and the telephone, to higher wages for domestic servants, and to other pressures on middle-class pockets including taxes and the rising cost of their children's education. There were changes on the supply side also, including competition from other employment, a growing resentment of the restraints inseparable from service, and the relative decline of the rural population that was the source of most town servants. Textile employment and dressmaking also declined in importance between 1881 and 1911. The gradual increase in the share that females took of employment in textile factories ended by 1881[42] and those domestic textile manufacturing centres still surviving in 1881 were mostly gone by the end of the century. In several other industries, however, women were taking a larger share of the work. By 1914 they accounted for one worker in four in the new bicycle factories, and in engineering generally they had been encroaching rapidly upon the men's positions.[43] In a few places mechanization had led to their being displaced by men (as it did in laundry work) but in engineering, as in tailoring, boot and shoe manufacture, pottery,

---

* Neither occupation is separately distinguishable in Table 1·7. Shop assistants appear under several of the separate headings, and teachers appear with other occupations under the heading 'professional occupations and their subordinate services'.

printing, and many other industries, new techniques had far more often proved to be the women's opportunity.

Not all parts of Britain shared in the late nineteenth-century broadening of female employment opportunities. No more women were employed in agriculture in 1911 than had been employed thirty years earlier and in many rural districts employment opportunities contracted with the decline of domestic cloth making, lace making and the domestic manufacture of straw plait, gloves, buttons, pins, and similar items. One of the features of Rowntree and Kendall's investigation of rural poverty shortly before the First World War was how little wives were able to contribute to family earnings.[44] Other regions offering little female employment were the mining districts, the iron and steel towns, and other places with little light manufacturing or commercial activity and slight need of domestic servants. Rhondda, Aberdare, and Merthyr Tydfil occupied the last places on a table showing female employment that was included in the 1911 census. Middlesbrough, one of the few towns in Britain where females failed to outnumber men, was just above them, its iron trade offering 'absolutely no field for women in any part of it'.[45] The chief centres of women's employment were the textile manufacturing districts, especially the Lancashire cotton towns. In 1911 when some 26 per cent of females of all ages were at work in England and Wales, there were four Lancashire towns – Blackburn, Burnley, Preston, and Bury – where the proportion was above 50 per cent.[46] How many women worked depended everywhere upon local custom as well as the local employment structure. In the 1880s, for example, astonished East Anglians had watched the wives and daughters of migrant Scots farmers doing work that by then in East Anglia was only done by men. On the north-eastern coalfield women had ceased to work underground during the eighteenth century and none had worked below ground in Staffordshire, Shropshire, Leicestershire, or Derbyshire for some time before they were forbidden to do so by Ashley's act of 1842.[47]

These local customs on what work women might or might not perform operated within more general customary constraints that affected female workers in every part of Britain. Work was conventionally distinguished as either men's work or women's work. There were very few instances where men and women were engaged on identical tasks. What constituted women's work was determined partly by physiological characteristics: it was believed, for example, that certain work could be performed by none but nimble-fingered females and that various other tasks required physical strength beyond their capacity. Some occupations, including many of those that were well-paid, were barred to women because the likelihood that girls would cease work when they married made it unprofitable to give them extensive training and made the girls themselves reluctant to accept responsibility. But the greater part of both 'women's work' and 'men's work' was reserved exclusively to one sex not as a result of real or imagined physiological characteristics but by long-standing custom. Women were restricted to certain tasks because they always had been, because men were not anxious to yield any of their monopolies, and because few women felt strongly that there was much wrong with things as they existed.

Women understood the system and knew their place in it. For most of them it was in any case a matter of passing interest until marriage brought release from the labour market. Not all women were so minded. One Portsmouth mangle-woman took it upon herself to complete the household form in the census of 1851, placed her own name in the space reserved for the head of the household, and in the 'dependants' column entered the legend 'John – husband, turns my mangle'.[48] But such women, and the small number of (mainly middle-class) feminists who battled for women's rights, were very much exceptions, ahead of their time in what was emphatically a man's world. This was so at every stage of life: of those babies whose births parents did not bother to register, females considerably outnumbered males; similar discrimination when it came to schooling is reflected in rates of male and female illiteracy;[49] and a comment from Mrs Beeton to the effect that whereas anyone with pretensions to gentility employed a female domestic servant, 'to employ anything masculine, however diminutive, is the first sign of affluence' shows the same attitude at the workplace.

Men clung to their advantages for several reasons. They believed that a limited amount of work was available and suspected that allowing women to share work would cause some families to be without pay as a consequence of other families taking more than their share. They believed too that the introduction of women to a trade was usually accompanied by a fall in wages because women were prepared to work for less than men. This often happened, although men tended to forget that women were seldom introduced into previously male occupations unaccompanied by technical change (which altered the nature of the work) and that a major reason why they were prepared to work for less was because customary attitudes restricted women's labour to a handful of low-wage occupations. Working men also shared the widespread assumption that girls would find their greatest fulfilment as wives and mothers, and that their children's welfare, their husband's comfort, the very integrity of the family, all required that they devote themselves to the home. When females had to work, before or after marriage, they were considered best employed, not in competition with men, but at one of the traditional female occupations. Domestic industry or domestic service in homes of others who were concerned for their moral welfare were especially favoured. It was felt that at such work women might acquire domestic virtues, be relatively safe from assaults upon their modesty, and not be likely to become too independent.

Male exclusiveness was particularly evident among organized workers. A plea from the cotton spinners in 1824 illustrates several aspects of the male attitude:

> The women, in nine cases out of ten, have only themselves to support, while the men, generally, have families. . . . The women can afford their labour for less than the men. . . . Girls, many of them interesting ones . . . are thus rendered independent of their natural guardians . . . the reins of government are broken and the excited feelings of youth and inexperience let loose upon the world, a prey too often to pride, vice, and infamy.[50]

A petition from the potters in 1845, worried about losing work to machines operated by women, combined flattery with pathos in a reminder of where women should find their true vocation:

> To maidens, mothers, and wives we say machinery is your deadliest enemy . . . . It will destroy your natural claims to home and domestic duties, and will immure you and your toiling little ones in overheated and dirty shops, there to weep and toil and pine and die.[51]

In 1877 the TUC carried by an overwhelming majority a resolution that parliament should further restrict female employment, and in response to an outraged female delegate the secretary of the TUC Parliamentary Committee replied that one of the functions of trade unions was 'to bring about a condition . . . where wives should be in their proper sphere at home, instead of being dragged into competition for livelihood against the great and strong men of the world.'[52] By the end of the century male attitudes were becoming a little more relenting. Some trade unions were beginning to abandon protection of the male position by outright exclusion of women in favour of organizing women and attempting to raise their wages. But what was perhaps still most remarkable in 1914 was how little things had altered. For most of the previous century and certainly before 1890, males dominated all occupations of significance other than domestic service and the making of textiles and dress.

v · *The labour force as a whole*

We turn now to look at the labour force as a whole. At the beginning of the nineteenth century, so far as can be ascertained from the crude classifications of the early censuses, the labour force was divided between agriculture, industry (including mining), and all other occupations in approximately equal parts. The last category includes domestic service and most middle-class workers, so agriculture and industry probably each occupied more than a third of working-class males.

Table 1·8   *Estimated percentage distribution of the British labour force, 1811–1911*

	Agriculture, Forestry, Fishing	Manufacture, Mining, Industry	Trade and Transport	Domestic and Personal	Public, Professional & all other
1811	33.0	30.2	11.6	11.8	13.3
1821	28.4	38.4	12.1	12.7	8.5
1851	21.7	42.9	15.8	13.0	6.7
1881	12.6	43.5	21.3	15.4	7.3
1911	8.3	46.4	21.5	13.9	9.9

Source: P. Deane and W. A. Cole, *British Economic Growth, 1688–1959*, (Cambridge 1967), p. 142. *This work also gives details (pp. 137–40) of shortcomings in the early censuses.*

Agriculture was the largest employment for men and remained so throughout the first half of the century. But Britain was already closer to being a modern industrial society than any other nation. In 1850 when agriculture's share of the labour force was less than a quarter in Britain, it was one-half in France and more than a half in Germany and the United States.[53] There was no absolute decline in farm employment in the first half of the nineteenth century but farm productivity increased and the number of farm workers grew considerably less than farm output and less also than the labour force as a whole. Another feature of agricultural employment that was much noted by foreign observers, and usually regarded as one aspect of Britain's agricultural efficiency, was the very large number of landless wage-labourers. In England and Wales there were more than four times as many labourers as farmers in 1851.

Of the detailed composition of the industrial labour force in the early decades of the nineteenth century only a little can be said. We may be sure, however, that the great majority of industrial workers were not factory operatives. In 1815 cotton mills employed only some 114,000,[54] most of them women and children, and there were very few other factories. Most industrial workers worked for small employers and with tools that would have been readily recognizable by the artisans and labourers of Restoration England.

There were probably still fewer than 100,000 men factory operatives in 1830: far fewer, for example, than the number engaged in making and mending boots and shoes, and less than a third of the number working in the building industry, which was almost entirely unmechanized and the first employment for men after agriculture.[55] A second feature of industrial employment was the relatively minor importance of the heavy industries (coal-mining, iron making, and heavy engineering) before the railway construction of the 1830s. There were almost certainly more tailors than coal-miners in 1830, and in 1841 there were still three blacksmiths for every man engaged in the manufacture of iron.[56] There is little doubt, however, that industrial employment as a whole, inside and outside the factory, was increasing rapidly. According to the calculations of Deane and Cole (Table 1·8), between 1811 and 1851 industry (including mining) increased its share of the workforce from 30 per cent to 43 per cent. Farm employment fell from 33 per cent of the total to 22 per cent, while commerce, transport, administration, and the other service occupations, which economists call collectively the 'tertiary sector', maintained an approximately constant share.

The growth in industrial employment was experienced to some extent in many parts of Britain before 1840. Certain industrial areas grew especially rapidly and the investigator who measures industrialization by the density of blast-furnaces and factory chimneys might well conclude that the industrial revolution was yet to make its mark outside Lancashire, the West Riding, and a few other counties. But many industries grew without dramatic change in production techniques. London, for example, with its silk weaving, shipbuilding, clothing, and other miscellaneous trades, was the nation's chief industrial centre, but in 1830 boasted very few steam-driven factories. Here and there factory competition had quickly affected domestic and craft employment, but many old industrial centres using traditional techniques and forms of organization enjoyed a modest share of the increase in industrial employment well into the nineteenth century. By the 1850s, however, the eighteenth-century pattern of economic activity had been drastically altered. Different regions and different trades were affected at different times. In the struggle between the West Riding mills and the wool manufacturers of East Anglia and the West Country, for example, the bad years of 1837–43 may have been crucial: 'many old-established manufacturing centres which had, in the earlier 'thirties, still hoped for a revival of prosperity, now found themselves unable to battle any longer against the stronger forces of factory industry and power-driven machinery.'[57] Domestic industries suffered first and then local craftsmen and retailers – tailors, cobblers, thatchers, carpenters, bakers, blacksmiths, wheelwrights and the rest – as their services also came to be provided, directly or indirectly, from the new industrial centres. What was happening was that steam power, economies of scale, and specialization were giving increasing advantage to the factory towns. Productivity rose and prices fell sufficiently for the factory manufacturers to take markets that once had been the monopoly of local domestic workers and craftsmen. Low-wage and abundant small town and village labour no longer attracted capital because low-wage labour was no longer cheap. The outcome of this struggle was greatly accelerated by the railways, which reduced the cost of carrying goods and so eroded the protection that might otherwise have kept factory products from distant markets. Cheap transport and the advanced manufacturing techniques of the factories were thus together responsible for the deindustrialization of certain areas and for the remarkable regional variations in prosperity that became one of the outstanding characteristics of the nineteenth-century labour market.

After 1850 farm employment declined absolutely as well as relatively: sometime near mid-century British agriculture employed more workers than at any time before or since. During the 1860s and 1870s a quarter of a million men either retired and were not replaced or left for the towns and emigration ports. By the end of the century, when a change in the terms of trade between agriculture and industry brought a temporary respite, the farm labour force had declined by 450,000 from its mid-century peak. Agriculture was still a leading occupation, but whereas it had employed one in five in 1851, by 1901 it employed only one in twelve. In France, Germany, and the United States agriculture still employed one worker in three at the end of the century.[58] The fall in farm employment was obviously in part a consequence of the great inflow of foreign grain from the 1870s which caused prices to tumble, putting pressure on rents, profits, and wages, and encouraging a switch to less labour-intensive livestock farming. But the exodus was well underway before the early 1870s and it occurred in the livestock districts as well as in the corn counties. Men were clearly being attracted by the better opportunities of the towns, and labour productivity on the farms rose sufficiently to compensate for their absence. Many of those that left had been seriously under-employed.

The bulk of this labour, however, was no longer finding its way into industry. Early in the present century Alfred Marshall noted that although industrial output had increased many times, 'those occupied in manufacture of every kind were as large a proportion of the population in 1851 as in 1901'.[59] The more recent calculations of Deane and Cole show manufacturing accounting for about one-third of the labour force at both dates.[60] Most industries experienced a substantial rise in labour productivity. This did not occur in mining however and, in consequence, manufacturing and mining together slightly increased their share of the total labour force.[61] But the rate of transfer to manufacturing and mining was far slower than that which occurred in the first half of the century (Table 1·8).

Table 1·9 *Occupations: Britain, 1851, 1881, 1911 (thousands)*
M = Male   F = Female

		1851	1881	1911
Agriculture, Horticulture, and Forestry	M	1,788	1,517	1,436
	F	229	116	117
Textiles	M	661	554	639
	F	635	745	870
Metal Manufacture, Machines, Implements, Vehicles, Precious Metals etc.	M	536	977	1,795
	F	36	49	128
Building and Construction	M	496	875	1,140
	F	1	2	5
Transport and Communications	M	433	870	1,571
	F	13	15	38
Clothing	M	418	379	432
	F	491	667	825
Mining, Quarrying and Workers in the Products of Mines and Quarries	M	383	604	1,202
	F	11	8	8
Food, Drink, and Tobacco	M	348	494	806
	F	53	98	308
Domestic Offices and Personal Services	M	193	238	456
	F	1,135	1,756	2,127
Professional Occupations and their Subordinate Services	M	162	254	413
	F	103	203	383
Wood, Furniture, Fittings, and Decorations	M	152	185	287
	F	8	21	35
Commercial Occupations	M	91	352	739
	F	—	11	157
Bricks, Cement, Pottery, Glass	M	75	111	145
	F	15	27	42
Public Administration	M	64	109	271
	F	3	9	50
Armed Forces	M	63	114	221
	F	—	—	—
Paper, Printing, Books, Stationery	M	62	134	253
	F	16	53	144
Chemicals, Oil, Soap, Resins etc.	M	42	72	155
	F	4	9	46
Total Occupied	M	6,545	8,852	12,927
	F	2,832	3,887	5,413

Source: Mitchell and Deane, op. cit. p. 60.

There were, however, some significant changes within the manufacturing and mining sector. Mining itself, and the making and manufacture of iron, steel, and other metals (including shipbuilding) significantly increased their share of industrial employment. Building, another industry with a poor productivity record, increased its labour force rapidly until the first decade of the twentieth century. Relative decline of employment was particularly great in the numbers making textiles and clothing. Lancashire and the West Riding remained busy because textile output continued to rise and provided increased local employment in those trades that serviced the mills, but the north-west was no longer in the van of industrial change after 1850.

Three other trends in industrial employment became apparent during the second half of the nineteenth century. The first was that more work came to require at least a rudimentary degree of skill or literacy. Mechanization and the factory system, both expanding rapidly in the 1870s and 1880s, offered comparatively little employment for the completely unskilled. There was still a very substantial amount of totally unskilled employment outside the factories, but in this section of the labour market growth was slower than elsewhere. Secondly, by 1890 mechanization was also affecting the rate of increase in demand for highly-skilled workers. The most representative industrial worker by 1914 was one of the growing army of 'semi-skilled'. Thirdly, there was a marked expansion of employment in such occupations as the manufacture of confectionery, cigarettes, medicines, electrical goods, perambulators, and bicycles: Cadburys, Woodbines, Boots Cash Chemists, Beecham's Pills, Rudge, and Raleigh were all household words by the end of the century. Employment in these 'new industries', which were to grow rapidly in the interwar years when the staples declined or stagnated, was not spread evenly throughout the country and well before 1900 it is possible to trace the first signs of the massive redistribution of regional prosperity that occurred after 1918.

Most of the contraction in agriculture's share of employment after 1850 was taken up by expansion in the service, or 'tertiary', sector (Table 1·8). Until 1880 domestic service accounted for part of this expansion, but by 1911 domestic service was no more important than it had been in 1851. Of greater consequence in the long run were the rising numbers of civil servants and local government workers and those helping to provide professional, administrative, and commercial services to British industry and to much of the rest of the world. Commerce by 1911 employed eight times as many males as it had in the middle of the nineteenth century. Transport, already a major employment in 1851, also grew rapidly and on the eve of the First World War employed more workers than agriculture. Many of these tertiary workers were lower middle-class and many others could be equally well described as either middle-class or working-class. Their number grew for several reasons. One

30

was that much tertiary employment was essential to industrial production and labour productivity in the provision of services rose less rapidly than labour productivity in industry. Another was the increase in domestic and international trade. Tertiary employment grew also because rising real incomes generated employment in such occupations as those connected with education and health, entertainment, holidays, and the retail trade. The expansion was also partly a consequence of the fact that as industrialization progressed specialized service industries developed to supply needs that industrialists had previously supplied for themselves. To this extent the figures in Table 1·8 may slightly exaggerate the shift to the tertiary sector. But there is no doubt that a substantial change did occur.

Suggestions for further reading are on page 399.

2

POPULATION: BIRTHS AND DEATHS

I · *Labour history and population history; the three phases of population history*

We have already seen how demographic variables affected both the labour market and the circumstances of individual workers. The overall activity rate, the amount of child employment, and the number of working wives were all determined partly by the level of birth-rates and death-rates. Robert Walker's meals would have been more appetizing and his cottage less cramped (above, p. 1) had there been fewer children with claims upon his meagre wage. And his wage was low partly because farm labourers, as a class, fathered more than the average number of children and saw a relatively large proportion of them survive long enough to add to the over-large supply of rural labour. To study labour history some knowledge of population history is essential, for nothing else, except perhaps industrialization, so fundamentally shaped working-class existence.

Most west European countries have experienced three broad phases of population history. In the initial phase population increased slowly over the centuries but was subject to violent short-run fluctuations. Births considerably exceeded deaths in normal years but population growth was frequently interrupted by harvest failure and famine, by major epidemics, or war. The Reverend Thomas Malthus described these positive checks to population as 'nature's auditing with a red pencil'. In the second phase of population growth the threshold where nature's auditors intervened was lifted and population growth accelerated. The final phase saw a return to slow population increase but this time with birth-control as the chief check upon numbers. Britain had entered the second of these phases by the mid-eighteenth century and the transition to the final phase was underway at the end of the nineteenth century.

Two aspects of Britain's long-term population history need to be emphasized at the outset. The first is that the voluntary control of births within marriage, which is particularly evident in the third phase of population history, was a feature of the first and second phases also. It is sometimes suggested that the smaller families of the late nineteenth century were a consequence of the mass production of rubber sheaths. But the probable cause *median age of marriage vs date ?* [handwritten annotation]

of smaller families was more intensive use of traditional methods of birth-control, especially *coitus interruptus*, a form of control that had been used for centuries and one certain to reduce the birth-rate when practised by a large part of the population. There is some evidence, in the spacing of pregnancies, that *coitus interruptus* or some other form of birth-control was practised in the seventeenth century.[1] Birth-rate is influenced also by the age at which women marry, and in this way too British fertility had long been restrained. Gregory King estimated that in late seventeenth-century Lichfield only 15 per cent of women aged between twenty and twenty-four had married; in mid-twentieth-century India, by contrast, no less than 82 per cent of females aged fifteen to twenty-four had married.[2] The age at marriage in England continued to be fairly high during the second phase of population history: in 1851 70 per cent of women between the ages of twenty and twenty-four had not yet married.[3] The British birth-rate, that is, was subject to restraint both within marriage and by delayed marriage throughout the nineteenth century and for a considerable time earlier. Although the nineteenth century saw the most rapid sustained population growth ever experienced in Britain, the rate of increase remained well below what was biologically possible and also well below rates of growth in many parts of the world today.[4]

The second point which requires emphasis, and particularly in the context of labour history, is that while the timing of population 'take-off' and the later return to slower growth varied from country to country, and within countries, the broad pattern was experienced by most parts of north-western Europe. Thus, while it is conceivable that the causes of more rapid population increase in Britain were not felt elsewhere, it is highly probable that the main forces at work were those such as increased agricultural productivity, improved food distribution, and the reduction of plague and smallpox which were experienced throughout the whole area. It is also likely that influences felt only or mainly in parts of Britain – the eighteenth-century reduction in gin consumption, for example, and the supposed stimulus to population offered by factory employment – should be given less weight than they sometimes receive in accounts which consider Britain alone. The relationship between the demographic and the industrial revolutions would thus seem to be a tenuous one. Population rose not only in Lancashire but also in the 'Speenhamland' counties of rural southern England whose 'surplus' paupers so alarmed Malthus and the 1834 Poor Law Commissioners. Population rose too in the Scottish Highlands, where there was little increase of industrial employment of any kind, in Norway and Sweden, in Württemberg, Pomerania, Silesia, and also, of course, in rural Ireland.[5]

33

II · *Birth-rates in the nineteenth century; fertility differentials; the early birth-control campaign; the decline in birth-rate*

The more than threefold expansion of the labour force in the century after 1815 was due overwhelmingly to natural increase, the excess of births over deaths. From the 1830s when civil registration of British births began, until the end of the 1870s the crude birth-rate maintained a level around thirty-five births per thousand population. This was well above the death-rate, which was fairly steady at around 22 per thousand. In the 1880s the birth-rate fell. The death-rate fell also, but less rapidly, so there was a deceleration in the rate of population increase. The causes of this deceleration, however, were such that it exercised little influence on the number of workers entering the labour market until after 1914. Immigration contributed substantially to labour supply only at the time of the Irish famine, and even in that decade it accounted for less than a third of the increase. Before the 1840s, and throughout most of the 1850s and 1860s, immigrants were roughly balanced by Britons who went abroad. Subsequently emigration exceeded immigration.

The great watershed in the history of fertility between 1815 and 1914 is obviously the decisive fall in the crude birth-rate that began around 1880. A

Table 2·1   *Great Britain, population,*
1811–1921

	Population (millions)	Percentage increase in previous decade
1811	11.97	
1821	14.09	17.7
1831	16.26	15.4
1841	18.53	14.0
1851	20.82	12.3
1861	23.13	11.1
1871	26.07	12.7
1881	29.71	14.0
1891	33.03	11.2
1901	37.00	12.0
1911	40.83	10.4
1921	42.77	4.7

Source: Mitchell and Deane, *Abstract of British Historical Statistics*, p. 6.

Table 2·2 *England and Wales, crude birth-
and death-rates, 1841–1915*

	Average annual birth-rate (per 1000 population)	Average annual death-rate (per 1000 population)
1841–45	35.2	21.4
1846–50	34.8	23.3
1851–55	35.5	22.7
1856–60	35.5	21.8
1861–65	35.8	22.6
1866–70	35.7	22.4
1871–75	35.7	22.0
1876–80	35.4	20.8
1881–85	33.5	19.4
1886–90	31.4	18.9
1891–95	30.5	18.7
1896–1900	29.3	17.7
1901–05	28.2	16.1
1906–10	26.3	14.7
1911–15	23.6	14.3

Sources: Census of England and Wales, 1921, Preliminary Report,
p. 62; N. L. Tranter, *Population since the Industrial Revolution,*
(1973), p. 53.

great deal about fertility before the 1880s is obscure. Civil registration of births was not begun until 1837 in England and Wales, and not until 1855 in Scotland, and before the 1870s there was considerable under-registration of births. At present we cannot be sure to what extent the fall in fertility so evident in the 1880s was already occurring in earlier decades, nor can much be said with certainty on the differences between working-class and middle-class fertility before 1880 or on fertility differences among the working classes. However, more precise measures than crude birth-rate* suggest that some decline in fertility may well have occurred from the 1860s or even earlier.[6] And fragmentary evidence from parish registers, census enumerators' books and the first census of fertility (1911)[7] suggests that occupational differences in fertility of the kind clearly evident after 1880 were already in existence long before. Innes noted some signs of inverse association between fertility and occupational status in marriages contracted in the 1850s. Armstrong found a similar pattern in mid-century York, and Loschky and Krier have published

* Crude birth-rate takes no account of the proportions of females of child-bearing age in the population, their age structure, and their age at the birth of each child.

evidence of such differentials in rural Lancashire at the beginning of the century.[8] The mining population of the early nineteenth century was certainly believed to have been 'notoriously prolific',[9] and a more than average readiness to control family size would have been entirely consistent with the lifestyle of mid-nineteenth-century artisans. The Coventry watchmakers, for example, appear to have been dedicated self-improvers: 'The watchmakers generally are provident in their habits, do not marry early . . . send their children to school till the age of fourteen, belong to building societies, freehold land societies, and sick clubs.'[10] Thrift and delayed marriage were also among the distinguishing characteristics of Edinburgh skilled workers[11] and it was workers of this kind, prudent and calculating, who combined together in exclusive craft unions to maintain wages and social status by restricting labour supply. Men who believed that their collective security depended upon strict control of the number of apprentices and upon emigration might well have been inclined to exercise similar restraint in their procreative activities. It was, after all, partly on account of their Malthusian views that the artisans of the London Working Men's Association, who began the Chartist movement, came under attack from more radical working-class leaders.[12]

Two other groups of workers who may have been distinguished by below average fertility long before crude birth-rate fell were domestic servants and the Lancashire textile operatives. Most domestic servants stood to lose their posts if they married, which encouraged late marriages, and birth-control literature circulated extensively in the mill towns[13] where plentiful work for women made the opportunity-cost of child-bearing especially great. There is literary evidence which suggests that mill wives had smaller than average families and which mentions contraception, abortion, and even infanticide.[14] Opponents of the factory system claimed that familiarity with birth-control practices prevented 'factory immorality' from resulting in a high illegitimacy rate:

Q. 'Do you mean that certain books, the disgrace of the age, have been put forth and circulated among the females in factories . . .?'
A. 'Yes.'
Q. 'And you attribute the circumstances of there being fewer illegitimate children to that disgusting fact?'
A. 'Yes.'[15]

The literature under attack here was part of a campaign that was initiated in the 1820s by Francis Place and others – including John Stuart Mill, Robert Owen, his son Robert Dale Owen, and Richard Carlile, the radical publisher – with the intention of raising living standards by encouraging workers to have fewer children. The working classes had been on the receiving end of advice of this kind from the time when Malthus had first drawn attention to the relationship between incomes and numbers. But the conventional message had been that the poor were poor largely as a consequence of their own recklessness and that the remedy was delayed marriage and abstention within marriage. This exhortation may have won some converts, particularly among skilled workers, but for the most part it met little working-class enthusiasm. It was the more unwelcome because Malthus's name was inextricably linked with proposals to curtail poor law expenditure and to separate pauper husbands from their wives within the workhouse. Place's campaign, however, was of a far more positive nature. He saw birth-control not merely as a means to reduce poverty, but as an instrument of broader working-class advancement. And he proposed that families should be limited, not by onerous abstention, but by contra-ception. Meetings were held, and tens of thousands of handbills were distributed with instruction in contraceptive techniques and emphasis upon higher wages, a shorter working week, an end to child employment, and the other advantages birth-control might bring.

Whether this early birth-control campaign had any influence upon working-class fertility and living standards is another of the questions about pre-1880 population history to which only tentative answers can be offered. The evidence available does not preclude the possibility of some fall in fertility having occurred, but there was almost certainly no significant decline and it seems probable that the campaign was a failure. One of its weaknesses was that the contraceptive techniques it recommended were complicated and demanded considerable foresight and self-control. Greater success might have been achieved by combining emphasis upon the harmful consequences of large families with encouragement of more intensive use of traditional forms of birth-control that the poor were not so likely to regard as indelicate and unnatural.[16] The reluctance of the working classes to make much use of mechanical constraints was reinforced by opposition to Place's campaign from certain working-class leaders who thought his proposals tainted by Malthusian dogma and a distraction from the struggle for political reform. Some even argued that the hunger and misery Place hoped to dispel were a necessary precondition of social change.[17]

There was powerful opposition too from influential sections of the middle classes, in particular from clergymen and doctors. Middle-class concern was for public morality. In the public mind contraceptives were regarded primarily as accessories to prostitution and promiscuity. They had been used, above all, as a means of reducing the danger of venereal infection. Thus the birth-control movement was seen as a challenge to Christian morality and fiercely resisted. Doctors saw the issue as one that fell naturally within their sphere of professional responsibilities and upon those that used the various 'lustful', 'selfish', and 'immoral' practices they forecast a variety of undesirable consequences.[18] Both doctors and clergy continued to oppose all restraint, other than late marriage and abstention, into the twentieth century.[19]

There is far less doubt about the course of working-class fertility in the last decades of the century. Although fertility may have started to fall long before 1880, its decline was subsequently far more pronounced. Whereas the marriages of the 1860s produced, on average, just over six children, those contracted in 1915 produced, on average, a little under 2.5 children.[20] The decline was due to fewer and later marriages, as well as to control of births within marriage, although the latter was the more important influence. The decline was also more pronounced among some occupational groups than among others. There was a general correlation between income levels and the time when fertility began to decline significantly. First affected were the more wealthy urban middle classes. The life of Beatrice Webb, who married in 1892, illustrates the experience of this group in dramatic fashion. She was one of ten children of Richard Potter, industrialist and director of the Great Western Railway. Her marriage to Sidney Webb produced definitive histories of trade unionism, local government, the poor law, and the co-operative movement, but they had no children. The last group to significantly reduce family size were urban and rural labourers, whose fertility fell very little before 1900. This pattern of change had important consequences. Not least, it meant that some of those who stood to gain most from smaller families were among the last to be affected. Moreover, it led to a general widening of class differences in average family size: by 1911 the average miner or labourer supported almost twice the number of children that were dependent upon the average doctor or solicitor. The fall in fertility thus had the effect of accentuating class differences in living standards and may have had some part

Table 2·3   *Average number of children in 1911*
according to social class

Upper and Middle Class	2.77
Textile Workers	3.19
Skilled Workers	3.53
Semi-Skilled Workers	3.59
Unskilled Workers	3.92
Agricultural Labourers	3.99
Miners	4.33

Source: Census figures, cited by D. Glass, *Population Policies and Movements in Europe*, (Oxford 1940), p. 69. Standardized for age of wife at marriage and duration of marriage.

in explaining the high level of labour unrest before the First World War (see below, p. 322).

Table 2·3 shows the broad relationship between fertility and social class and also two occupational groups whose fertility levels deviated from this relationship. Although their husbands were relatively well paid, the wives of miners produced more children than the wives of rural and urban labourers. The textile workers were equally remarkable for exceptionally low fertility. A number of suggestions can be offered to explain these patterns. Whatever forces had initially motivated the middle classes, it is not remarkable that skilled workers were among their closest followers. Artisan attitudes and living standards had as much in common with lower middle-class attitudes and living standards as with the attitudes of the unskilled. Shared experiences were reinforced by the natural tendency to imitate the fashions of those immediately above them in the social hierarchy. For obvious reasons, unskilled workers and farm labourers would be among the last to reduce family size in response to fashions initiated by the urban middle classes.[21] Miners, more than most other workers, lived with their own kind, protected from outside influences of any type. This is perhaps one reason why their fertility was initially high and fell relatively slowly. It has been suggested too that demanding manual work leaves men disinclined to read or think when work is finished and thus less susceptible to outside influences.[22] In addition, the miners' work, like the work of labourers and in contrast to that of skilled workers, required little formal education but much physical strength. Thus they quickly earned full wages, which removed an impediment to early marriage. Particularly important was the shortage of female employment in colliery districts, which provided daughters with an incentive to marry early, and the relative abundance of young men which meant that there was no shortage of partners. Once married, the conflict between children and a wife's earnings seldom arose and the inability of wives to add to family income appears not to have acted as an incentive to limit children. Glass demonstrated that throughout the country there was an inverse correlation between county fertility levels and the amount of female employment.[23] The chief causes of the low fertility of textile operatives, as we noted earlier, were probably the unparalleled opportunities for women to work in the mill towns of Lancashire and the West Riding and the opportunities such employment provided to learn about birth-control techniques.

While it may tell us a great deal about fertility differences between occupations, the extent of women's employment throws no light on the overall fall in working-class fertility in the last quarter of the nineteenth century because in these years there was no increase in the proportion of all women who were employed or in the proportion of married women who were employed. In fact, it is far easier to offer explanations of why fertility declined more or less than average in any particular occupation than it is to explain the fall as a whole. Some suggested explanations of the general fall can be discarded at the outset. From what has been said already it should be clear that the fall was not to any significant extent a consequence of the sudden availability of contraceptives. Sales of rubber sheaths increased, but *coitus interruptus* remained by far the most favoured form of control up to 1914 and for long afterwards.[24] Nor should much weight be attached to those factory and education acts which raised the age when a child could work, and thus made children a greater economic liability. The children of those whose fertility fell significantly before 1890 were hardly affected by this legislation, while the fall in fertility of the less-skilled working classes, who might be expected to have been most sensitive to the loss of child earnings, was not very great for two or three decades after the more important of the factory and education acts. The contribution of children's earnings to high fertility at any time in the nineteenth century is easily exaggerated because in several of the areas where many children were employed there was also plentiful work for women outside the home. In these circumstances the advantage of children's earnings was offset by the higher opportunity-cost of pregnancy and childcare. The textile factory districts, in particular, came to be noted equally for above average rates of child employment and below average fertility.

Rather more weight should probably be given to the consequences of increased emigration. More men than women emigrated and thus fertility was affected by a reduction in the marriage prospects of females left behind. There was certainly an increase in the proportion of women who were still unmarried at the end of their child-bearing span, and in some areas, the Scottish Highlands and islands for example, emigration had a considerable influence on fertility.[25] But in the country as a whole the greater contribution to reduced fertility came from control within marriage. Moreover an increase in later marriage and non-marriage was evident among males as well as females, which suggests that the development was a consequence of more than just emigration. The influence that is generally given most emphasis in accounting for falling fertility is economic and social pressures that were felt especially by those classes whose fertility fell most decisively. Educating middle-class children was proving increasingly costly, and there was also an increase in the level of domestic comfort considered necessary to respectable middle-class existence. More servants were required; there were more things to buy, and more things to do, including taking the occasional 'change of air' and an annual seaside holiday.[26] Thus there was pressure to delay marriage until a family could be maintained in these more comfortable circumstances and to avoid jeopardizing that comfort with numerous children. The less stable economic conditions that began around 1873 exacerbated the struggle for security and social advancement and strengthened the case for family limitation. H. J. Habakkuk has suggested that a further influence that may have affected the middle classes was a reduction in child mortality (age one and over) starting in the 1850s and 1860s. In time, middle-class infant mortality (up to one year) also fell, and both developments may have necessitated greater control of births to maintain traditional family size.[27]

Some of these influences affecting middle-class fertility, including (eventually) the fall in child mortality and infant mortality, were felt also among the working classes and combined with social emulation to bring about a more general fall in fertility. House ownership, for example, was expanding among the artisans and some of the classes beneath them. Skilled workers may also have been conscious of an increase in the cost of child-rearing consequent upon the expansion of technical education, and workers of every kind felt the influence of rising expectations and the expanded range of entertainment and consumer products that rising incomes were bringing within reach. In Elderton's survey there are numerous observations of 'the growing desire for pleasure and excitement', of a taste for 'expensive and gaudy' clothes evident from about 1880, and of the opportunities for amusement opened up by cheap railway excursions, the bicycle, the electric tram, and the new cinemas.[28] These new tastes tended to be self-generating and they made workers increasingly conscious of the material costs of early parenthood and large families. Working-class incomes were not much affected by the 'great depression' but by 1910 a number of surveys had drawn attention to the extent of poverty and to the association of family size and destitution. These surveys increased 'felt poverty', and may have influenced working-class attitudes towards family size in the way that the 'great depression' influenced the middle classes. Attitudes must have been affected too by the introduction of state pensions (1908) which lessened dependence upon children in old age. In the background were developments favourable to birth-control that affected all classes: urbanization and education awoke ambitions, sharpened materialistic instincts, and encouraged the questioning of traditional practices. The late nineteenth-century occupational changes described in Chapter I are also a part of the explanation of falling fertility. There was a relative fall in the number of farm labourers and others in high-fertility occupations and a relative increase in the number of white-collar workers and others in low-fertility occupations.

There was also another birth-control campaign which, indirectly, caused the greatest disturbance of all to traditional attitudes.[29] In 1876 a Bristol bookseller had been prosecuted and convicted for selling an indecent pamphlet. The pamphlet in question, Charles Knowlton's *Fruits of Philosophy*, was first published in Britain in 1834, towards the end of the early birth-control campaign. Charles Bradlaugh and Annie Besant, two neo-Malthusians, resolved to make an issue of the right to publish. They

41

ostentatiously re-published Knowlton's pamphlet and were duly prosecuted. Their trial (1877–8) and its repercussions advanced the birth-control cause beyond all their expectations by providing for a lengthy and well-publicized discourse on the disadvantages of large families and the case for limitation. Sales of Knowlton's pamphlet leapt from 700 each year to 125,000 in the three months between the new edition and the trial.[30]

III · *Working-class mortality; occupational mortality and its decline; mortality from other causes*

The crude death-rate, which had been fairly stable from the start of civil registration in 1837 (Table 2·2), began to fall at about the same time as the crude birth-rate.[31] There are a variety of opinions on the probable course of mortality between 1800 and 1838, but no one can be certain of what happened. We can be reasonably sure, however, that mortality was unlikely to have been rising in rural areas and that it was unlikely to have been falling in rapidly-growing towns. And there is no doubt at all that the working classes, and particularly the urban working classes, were at all times in the nineteenth century far more familiar with death than we are today. In Liverpool, a particularly unhealthy town, working-class life expectancy (at birth) in 1841 was only fifteen years* and about half the children of the poorer classes died before they reached their fifth birthday.[32] In mid-century Preston, another unhealthy town, two out of every five who survived their first twenty-five years died before they were fifty.[33] Statistics like these give some impression of the enormous costs in lost employment and lost output, in poverty, and in physical suffering which must have been consequent upon sickness and death. They also suggest one reason why so few working men bothered to make adequate provision for old age (above pp. 8–9).

It would be quite wrong, however, to suppose that nineteenth-century Englishmen were more familiar with death than their ancestors or than contemporaries abroad. Horrific as it was, child mortality in the factory cities during the 1840s and 1850s represented a considerable improvement over the rates in London a century earlier when (according to the bills of mortality) as many as three out of every four christened died before their fifth birthday.[34] Rickman's rough estimates suggest that total deaths in London were around 48 per thousand in 1750 but that they had fallen to about 25 per thousand in 1821.[35] In the 1840s Germany (26.8), Holland (26.2), Belgium (24.4), and Russia (about 40) all had higher death-rates than England and Wales (22.4).[36]

---

*This figure, of course, refers to *all* working class deaths, including those of infants and young children whose mortality was exceptionally high. Those who survived the early years could expect to live well beyond their fifteenth birthday.

The rates in France (23.2), Switzerland (22.8), and Finland (23.5) were about the same as that of England and Wales.

Deaths from industrial accidents and occupational disease did not account for a very large part of total working-class mortality. But the slightest acquaintance with the statistics suggests possible links between mortality and occupation, and it is this aspect of working-class mortality that is perhaps of greatest interest to the student of labour history. Some occupations were notoriously more dangerous than others. For the miners who were always conscious of the possibility of maiming or sudden death, for men like the Sheffield grinders who knew the risks and waited for the signs of 'grinders' lung',[37] and for the matchgirls wondering how long they dare work without fear of contracting 'phossy jaw', safety at work was of considerable consequence. As late as 1900 mortality among tin miners, file-makers, and potters was well over double the mortality of farm labourers.

Table 2·4   *Comparative mortality (occupied males) 1900–02: high and low mortality occupations*

All Males	1,000		
All Occupied Males	925		
Tin Miner	2,169	Lace Manufacturer	831
General Labourer	1,987	Domestic Servants (Indoor)	815
Innkeeper, Publican, Spirit,		Shipbuilding	765
Wine, Beer Dealer	1,669	Coal Miner	
File-Maker	1,602	(Northumberland and	
Seaman	1,547	Durham)	763
Cutler, Scissors Maker	1,460	Barrister, Solicitor	739
Potter, Earthenware		Paper Manufacturer	684
Manufacturer	1,420	Teacher	599
Lead Manufacturer	1,365	Railway Engine Driver, Stoker	582
Chimney Sweep	1,240	Farm Labourer, Farm Servant	572

Source: Supplement to the Sixty-Fifth Annual Report of the Registrar-General, Pt. II, (*Parl. Papers* xviii, 1905), p. clxxxii.

The figures in Table 2·4, like most available figures on occupational mortality, have several shortcomings. These give no information on those who had 'retired' from their normal occupation, and tell us nothing about age at death or the extent to which occupational categories like 'general labourer' were swelled by ailing refugees from more demanding work. But they serve to illustrate the diversity of experience among workers. They show too the lack of any general association between industrialization and high-mortality occupations. Farm labourers were long-lived, but industrial occupations like shipbuilding, paper manufacture, and lace manufacture were decidedly more healthy than average, while some occupations hardly touched by the industrial revolution, like chimney sweeping and innkeeping, were decidedly unhealthy.

The more dramatic aspects of occupational mortality – children mangled in factory machinery, miners buried in pit explosions – were undoubtedly more common before 1914 than they are today. In the early twentieth century one miner in every 750 was killed each year and the miner's chance of violent death at work was more than twice the average. In 1966 it was only one-third greater than average and only one miner in 3,000 was killed at work.[38] There were more hazardous occupations than mining such as the merchant marine or working in railway shunting yards.[39] But miners, merchant seamen, and shunters are somewhat exceptional and considerably fewer workers were affected by accidental death or serious injury than by occupational diseases that killed or incapacitated slowly. The Sheffield grinders illustrate this point: some met a nasty and well-publicized end when a grindstone shattered, but deaths of this kind are only a small part of the explanation of why in the 1860s a fork grinder of twenty-one could expect to live only another fourteen years.[40] The main hazard was the stone and metal dust that entered the grinders' lungs. Dust-laden or otherwise contaminated air was a hazard to many other workers. For this reason certain friendly societies specifically excluded men in occupations like flour-milling, and even at the end of the century potters and cutlers were dying from respiratory diseases four to five times as fast as farm labourers.[41] Even in mining more men died of respiratory diseases than in explosions. And legislation governing the ventilation of mines that was introduced primarily to reduce the danger of explosions did more to reduce mortality by cleansing the air of dust.[42]

The mortality of chimney sweeps illustrates again the relative importance of violent and non-violent occupational deaths. Some sweeps died in falls and a few, possibly, were roasted alive, but their greatest menace was 'sweeps' cancer' caused by soot that was inhaled, scratched into the flesh, or consumed with food. At the end of the nineteenth century sweeps were eight times more susceptible to cancer than males generally.[43] Sweeping chimneys must have been thirsty work too if sweeps' mortality from alcohol-induced disease is any guide.[44] Alcohol, in fact, was one of the most lethal substances encountered at the workplace, and by no means solely on account of accidents consequent upon drinking. Publicans, innkeepers, and dealers in beers, wines, and spirits were near to the top of the table of occupational mortality in 1900–2 (Table 2·4). Their death-rate from alcohol poisoning was almost seven times greater

44

than the average.[45] Lead was another occupational hazard. The mortality rates of file-makers, plumbers, painters, and potters handling lead-glaze all reflect its influence. A Sheffield doctor described in the 1860s how workmen cutting files on a bed of lead consumed lead particles by their habit of licking the finger and thumb with which they held the chisel. He also noted a workman dipping his fingers, 'blackened and covered with fine lead dust', into a paper containing the salt for seasoning his beef.[46]

There was improvement in virtually every aspect of safety at work during the second half of the nineteenth century. By 1900 Sheffield medical men in search of pathological specimens were complaining, with relief no doubt, that it was becoming increasingly difficult to obtain good examples of 'grinders' lung'. From Stoke there were similar reports of the scarcity of examples of 'potters' rot'.[47] By this time workers who handled lead were less likely to take meals where they worked: some were precluded from doing so by legislation, others were dissuaded from poisoning themselves by works' rules and the provision of canteens and places to wash. By this time there were also few Sheffield grinding shops without mechanical fans to remove dust and there was less dust because there was less dry-grinding. The mortality rates of sweeps, file-makers, potters, and others in hazardous occupations had all been falling faster than the average.[48] Improvement is most easily traced in the statistics of violent death in the mines that have already been mentioned. Early in the century an estimated 8 miners per thousand met violent death at work each year; by the middle of the century the toll had been halved; and between 1903 and 1912 it averaged 1.33, or only one-sixth of the rate a century earlier.[49]

The reduction in occupational mortality and ill-health was the consequence of numerous reforms. In the background there were improvements in education that made men less tolerant of avoidable risks, more sensitive to dangers that were not readily apparent, and more amenable to safety discipline. Another general influence was rising standards of personal cleanliness; in the early nineteenth century chimney sweeps had infrequently bothered to wash at the end of the day and some of their climbing boys slept on bags of soot.[50] Among other background influences were innovations like the Davy Lamp, beneficial alike to productivity and mine safety,[51] the fall in consumption of beer and spirits towards the end of the century, the shortening working week which reduced accidents caused by fatigue, and the raising of the minimum age of employment.

More specific than these changes, and perhaps equally important, was legislation designed to reduce dangers at work. In coal-mining the landmarks were the beginning of state inspection of mines in 1850;* the first general

---

* Inspection of mine workers began in 1843.

measures for mine safety in 1855, which included the requirement that ventilation should be by mechanical means; the act of 1860 whose main concern was explosives and accidents in shafts; that of 1862, prompted by the New Hartley disaster (above p. 3), which required mines to have two access shafts; and the great amending and consolidating acts of 1872, 1881, and 1887 which covered virtually everything from the construction of safety lamps to the requirement that ambulances or stretchers be provided in case of accidents.

Some of the early factory acts touched upon safety, and the first factory act concerned solely with safety came in 1844. Its most important provision was that mill shafts and gearing should be safely fenced – a measure improved upon in 1856 and many times subsequently. There were important acts in 1864, 1866 and 1867 which extended legislation beyond textiles to a number of other trades, took measures to control dust and fumes by improved ventilation, and prevented those most obviously at risk from taking their meals at the workplace. In 1878 a consolidating act extended the law's protection into some of the many trades previously unregulated. From this time the gaps were closing rapidly as inspectors, medical men, and the trade unions called for further reforms in an atmosphere increasingly favourable to state intervention. Merchant seamen were among those who had been comparatively neglected, but Plimsoll's loading-line act of 1876 and the Merchant Shipping Act of 1894 helped to make amends, and a further act in 1906 gave them protection equivalent to that afforded by the great consolidating Factory and Workshops Act of 1901.[52] Making employers liable to pay compensation for injuries at work, a measure with an enormous potential influence, had also been somewhat neglected, despite considerable pressure from trade unions. The first Employers' Liability Act (1880) was weak and easily evaded. The Workmen's Compensation Acts of 1897 and 1906, however, were far more effective.

Gaps in the safety code still remained and the introduction of new techniques was always attended by new hazards whose control required recognition, investigation, and additional legislation. But looking back to the early nineteenth century, when safety legislation had been virtually non-existent, the Edwardians were understandably more impressed by what had been accomplished than by what remained to be done. Possibly they had less reason for satisfaction than they believed because in certain spheres – the regulation of chemical processes for example, workmen's compensation, and the thoroughness of factory inspection – Germany had recently come to set the pace.[53] Elsewhere, however, in temperature control and the regulation of poisonous processes for example, Britain retained her lead, and in 1914 none of her industrial rivals could claim a better all-round record in reducing danger at work. At the beginning of the new century the coal-mine mortality rate in Prussia was almost twice that in Britain.[54]

However dangerous were workplace conditions, they influenced health far less than the amount a man's work provided for the purchase of necessities, and whether or not it required him to live in a crowded city. For this reason the mortality rates of most workmen were not very different from those of their non-working wives. Chadwick illustrated that mortality was higher in larger towns and in those with the greatest number of inhabitants per acre: in the mainly rural county of Rutland the average working-class age at death in 1842 was thirty-eight years, at Truro (population about 10,000) it was twenty-eight years, and at Leeds it was only nineteen years. [55] Village labourers, in spite of doing similar work for lower wages, could expect to live considerably longer than town labourers.

Another indication of the peripheral importance of occupational hazards was the enormous proportion of all working-class mortality that occurred among children too young to work. At the end of the nineteenth century deaths of children under one year old accounted for a quarter of all mortality and those of children aged up to ten years for about 40 per cent of the total. [56] Infant mortality (deaths in the first year) in the nineteenth century compares particularly badly with late twentieth century mortality levels: in 1875 it stood at 158 per thousand (England and Wales), in 1975 at 15.7 per thousand. At the earlier date a newly-born child had less chance of surviving the following ten years than a man aged sixty-five, [57] and parents who were anxious that a particular name should remain in the family sometimes found it necessary to bestow the same christian name upon a succession of luckless infants. So many died, in fact, that in some places infant life was not valued highly: a Middlesbrough woman being offered consolation on the death of a child replied to a slightly shocked Lady Bell, 'It would not have mattered so much in another week, as by then the insurance would have come in.' [58]

There were enormous differences in infant mortality rates among the working classes. To some extent these reflected the father's earnings and perhaps also the inverse relationship between fertility and income levels that we noted earlier: the more children there were the greater the pressure on family income, on space, and on the mother's attention. But these influences operated alongside others that in many places were far more powerful. In 1910, for example, a government investigator whose responsibilities included both the relatively prosperous South Wales mining district of Maesteg and parts of low-wage Wiltshire noted that infant mortality in the first of these areas was over twice the level in the second. [59] Infant mortality rose steeply with housing density and was at its highest where crowded housing was accompanied by primitive methods of scavenging and sewage disposal. The farm labourer's great advantage in this respect was his uncrowded surroundings outside the home. The miner's great disadvantages were that the standard of his accommodation did not match the level of his wages and that the deficiencies of local government services were particularly evident in the mining districts.[60] Industrial Lancashire was another area notorious for high levels of infant mortality. The cotton towns were not poor nor were families there particularly large. But a considerable proportion of mothers were likely to be at the mill both shortly before they gave birth and (more important) not long after delivery. Several investigators noted the adverse influence upon infant mortality of married women's employment: one survey, the work of a doctor at Clithero, drew attention to the way infant deaths rose and fell in step with the trade cycle.[61] The mother's early return to work left the baby in the often indifferent care of relatives (sometimes young children) or paid baby-minders,[62] and encouraged early weaning which enormously increased the risk of infection.[63]

The chief causes of death of those who survived infancy and childhood were infectious diseases, especially before 1880. Cancer and heart disease, which now account for a high proportion of adult deaths, were less important causes of death in the nineteenth century because fewer lived long enough to succumb to cancer and heart attack.[64] Among males aged twenty-five to forty-four, tuberculosis, typhus, and other infectious diseases were responsible for almost half of all deaths between 1848 and 1872.[65] The relative importance of infectious and non-infectious diseases, and of the various infectious diseases, varied over time. After 1880 typhus was of little consequence, but tuberculosis remained by far the chief cause of adult mortality.[66] Tuberculosis killed slowly and undramatically. It was familiar and therefore accepted. Thus it received less attention in contemporary inquiries than its importance warranted. Among the working classes it was caused chiefly by poor diet and crowded housing and was carried by coughing, sneezing, spitting, and also by infected milk.[67] There were some links between work and tuberculosis – dust made the lungs vulnerable to attack – but the particular prominence of tuberculosis among the causes of female deaths in the third quarter of the century, and the subsequent greater than average reduction in female tuberculosis mortality, both suggest that working conditions and their improvement were not very important in accounting for its incidence.

Cholera is perhaps the most interesting of the other infectious diseases. It appeared only in four short epidemics and rivalled tuberculosis as a killer only in 1848–9, but its importance was much greater than the number of its victims might suggest. Cholera killed nearly half of those it affected, it killed them quickly, and its movements were alarmingly unpredictable. For no discernible reason certain towns which suffered grievously in the 1831–2 epidemic escaped almost unscathed in the greater onslaught of 1848–9. But at Pollokshaws (Lanarkshire) the first victim of the 1848–9 epidemic died in the same room and the same bed as the first victim of the 1831–2 epidemic.[68] Another reason for the excitement provoked by Asiatic cholera was that it was new to Britain. Long before it arrived its progress across Asia and Europe was watched with mounting apprehension. By 1826 it was into Russia, by the summer of 1831 it was in Berlin, having eluded the soldiers stationed on the Prussian frontier to bar its path, and in October it appeared at Sunderland. Wherever it occurred there was fear, hysteria, and social disorder. For a time fear of cholera was sufficient to overcome the working-class preference for delaying burial long enough to ensure a decent funeral and that life was quite definitely extinct. Cholera victims were despatched unceremoniously and buried extra deep. Another feature of its coming was religious and moral revival: church attendance rose, drunkenness declined, and in the Black Country in 1832 there was a rush to sanctify common law marriages.

But the most important consequence of the special fear cholera inspired was the frantic endeavour to contain the disease and discover how it was transmitted. Even before cholera first appeared in England it had stimulated the establishment of local boards of health, a hand-out of blankets and clothing to the poor, and a good deal of frenzied whitewashing and cleaning of privies. The main agent of infection was contaminated water although this fact was not established until 1854 and was doubted by some authorities long afterwards. It is sometimes suggested that the increase in sanitary activity brought on by cholera occurred because cholera is no respecter of rank, but this view is only partly correct. There were well-to-do victims of course, but the most affected areas were those where conditions were least wholesome: in fact, the suspicion that cholera was a Malthusian conspiracy to reduce the over-numerous poor was the cause of severe disturbances in parts of Europe. Typhoid and typhus fever also took most of their victims from among the working classes. Piped water and impure milk could carry infection far and wide but the most distinguished victim of typhoid, Prince Albert, should not be regarded as representative.[69] Typhoid, like cholera, is a waterborne disease. Typhus is transmitted by body lice and in the early part of the nineteenth century it appeared most often in winter when the poorest classes were least inclined to wash themselves and their clothing. It appeared too during trade slumps, when food was short, and was one of the diseases that ravaged Ireland and the Irish quarters of British cities during and after the great famine.

That the overall death-rate did not fall before 1870 does not indicate that Chadwick and other early-Victorian reformers laboured in vain. As we have seen, mortality was higher in large towns than in small towns, and during the nineteenth century more and more people came to live in large towns. It was therefore a considerable achievement to have kept the death-rate steady until the 1870s. Unhealthy as they were, the towns never were allowed to devour people as they had done before 1750[70] and as several French cities were still doing in the 1870s.[71] British cities were the healthiest in Europe and among the healthiest in the world. In 1880 the death-rate in Manchester compared favourably with New York's, Liverpool's was lower than Berlin's, London's was lower than that of Paris. The death-rate in London's Clare Market, where the London School of Economics now stands, was twice the national average but less than that of the city of St Petersburg taken as a whole.[72]

How was the death-rate contained and eventually reduced? Medical advances appear to have made surprisingly little impact upon any of the more significant causes of mortality except smallpox, whose virtual elimination was mainly due to vaccination.[73] Towards the end of the century infectious diseases came to be far better understood – but the laboratory breakthroughs that identified the tubercle, typhoid, and cholera bacilli had little practical influence upon working-class mortality until long after. The most important element in the overall fall was the reduced incidence of tuberculosis. This improvement was probably underway by the middle of the nineteenth century and was due chiefly to changes in working-class living standards, particularly to improved nutrition. Rising living standards contributed also to the reduction in typhus and other diseases and were by far the most important cause of the overall fall in mortality. Changes in living standards will be discussed in Chapter 3.

The other main cause of falling mortality was public health improvements, and the shortcomings of the medical profession in the strictly clinical sphere were at least partly redeemed by its contribution to this advance. Doctors worked alongside other reformers fired by compassion for their fellow men, with administrators in search of efficiency, and sanitary engineers armed with cheap iron and earthenware piping and Victorian hydraulic know-how. Besides the removal of filth and provision of clean water, public health embraced a multitude of lesser activities such as the paving and widening of streets and the isolation of victims of infectious diseases. It also embraced administrative activity such as compiling statistics of death and disease, the preventing of food adulteration and overcrowded housing, and regulating new building and the disposal of corpses. Not least there was the mundane but important business of impressing upon the lowest classes the value of personal and domestic hygiene. The expansion and improvement of charity dispensaries and poor law medical services, and the growing membership of friendly societies and other sickness insurance clubs, brought medical advice of this kind to an ever increasing proportion of the working classes. Cleanliness, of course, was one of the chief ingredients of Victorian respectability, and the almost universal quest for respectability must have prevented considerable ill-health.

A certain amount had been done to advance public health before 1800 and during the early decades of the nineteenth century. But the more impressive advance came after 1830. Reforming doctors like Neil Arnott, James Kay, and Thomas Southwood Smith drew attention to the extent of disease, its association with filth, and its preventability. Increased concern for public health owed a great deal also to the growing awareness of the enormous poor law burden arising from the death or illness of wage earners. Chadwick's nose for financial economy, his appreciation that where there was muck there was loss of money, led him naturally from poor law reform to public health.[74] There was an awareness too that the combination of insanitary conditions and poverty was an ideal breeding ground for working-class discontent. Cholera itself may have made a net positive contribution to the control of mortality because it killed relatively few and its arrival was a powerful stimulus to improved public health.[75] The first cholera epidemic, Chadwick's Report on the Sanitary Condition of the Labouring Population of 1842, the subsequent Report on the State of Large Towns and Populous Districts (1844), and the 1848 Public Health Act are landmarks in the early history of the public health movement.

Before 1850 reformers knew little of how disease was spread. Above all, they did not appreciate the importance of contaminated water. Illness was more often ascribed to the stench arising from burial grounds and cesspools than to the water that percolated through them to adjacent wells. But that filth and disease were linked was not in doubt and by tackling filth only good could ensue. In the 1850s and 1860s the importance of pure water came to be more appreciated. The turning-point in this respect was probably the investigations of John Snow (another doctor) during the 1854 cholera outbreak in Soho. He discovered that those who had drunk from the Broad Street pump perished in far greater numbers than their neighbours and that workers at a brewery in the heart of the afflicted area, who drank little water from any source, escaped unscathed – the cholera bacillus can survive only eight hours in beer. The marked discrepancy in cholera deaths between those areas served by the Lambeth Company, which drew its water from the Thames at Thames Ditton and filtered it before distribution, and those areas served by the Southwark and Vauxhall Company, which tapped the more polluted Thames at Westminster, endorsed Snow's findings. So too did the distribution of cholera victims in the 1866 epidemic when three-quarters of those struckdown in London lived in parts of the East End served by the indifferently purified supplies of the East London Water Company.

By this time the capital's two great sewerage schemes – the largest in the world – were nearing completion. Some other towns had been pressing ahead with equal enthusiasm. Liverpool was among the most dynamic. The Liverpool Sanitary Act of 1846 giving the council power to initiate sanitary improvements and appoint inspectors served as a model for other towns. In the following year Liverpool appointed the first medical officer of health, and some indication of subsequent progress there may be gauged from the more than threefold increase in *per capita* water consumption between 1846 and 1861.[76] Manchester too had a fairly good record and Glasgow secured an adequate supply of pure water in time to face the last cholera epidemic in 1866. At the same time there were a great many towns whose authorities did no more than they were obliged to do. Merthyr Tydfil was particularly noted for its failures and Birmingham's record was little better until the 1870s when Joseph Chamberlain set about creating 'the best governed city in the world'. Local authorities enjoyed a large measure of autonomy in sanitary affairs. Permissive legislation could be ignored and a great deal of what needed to be done waited upon by-laws that had to be initiated by the authorities themselves. There were water companies and other vested interests to be overcome, there was reluctance to spend, and resentment of central government interference. But opinion was changing and local government was gradually improved. Even the most laggardly towns were eventually forced to accept some of their responsibilities, and up and down the country a great deal had been achieved by 1870.

When cholera reappeared in north-western Europe – 8,000 died in Hamburg in 1892 – there were small outbreaks at many places in Britain but the standard of public health proved sufficient to forestall an epidemic. Around the turn of the century hospital facilities were expanded considerably and in this and other ways medicine began to contribute rather more substantially to the fall in death-rate. But the contribution from public health was still far greater. The major breakthrough at this time was the reduction in infant mortality. Why infant mortality had failed to fall earlier, when mortality at other ages was falling, is not yet understood. Perhaps it was held up by an increased resort to abortifacients, including poisonous abortifacients that resulted in the births of more unhealthy babies: 'six out of ten working women take something', claimed a woman in York just before the war, 'sometimes . . . it does no good . . . the child comes just the same, but it's puny, it's half starved.'[77] A change from breast-feeding to bottle-feeding may have been another development offsetting favourable influences upon mortality.[78] It may even be that late nineteenth-century statistics are more gloomy than they ought to be as a consequence of improved registration of babies who died at birth or soon after.[79] No one knows. A start to tackling infant mortality was made with legislation in 1891 and 1901 compelling mothers to remain from work for four weeks after delivery, and in the new century a determined campaign was begun. Local authorities in the least healthy areas were made uncomfortably aware of their defaults.[80] The training of midwives was commenced, there were renewed efforts to ensure the purity of milk, and health visitors were mobilized to educate the poor in the fundamentals of childcare.[81] The relative contribution of such measures and of other

52

influences like the decline in the number of town horses (whose dung was the favourite breeding place of the flies that infected infant food) are not known. But between them infant mortality was at last reduced.[82]

IV · *Population and working-class living standards*

Before examining working-class living standards in detail (Chapter 3) we need to consider the influence upon living standards of the demographic changes described in this chapter. Was the rate of population change usually conducive to maintaining and improving welfare, or would either a slower or a faster increase have been preferable at certain times? Was Britain in this respect similar to the American west, where rapid population increase was almost certainly an asset and where a more rapid increase could have been comfortably accommodated, or did it perhaps have more in common with parts of Asia and Africa today, where population presses upon resources and prevents rising output from increasing incomes? These questions and others that involve the concept of optimum population are not easily answered. One problem is that the rate of population change likely to maximize economic growth is by no means necessarily identical to the rate that will maximize working-class welfare.

The Reverend T. R. Malthus believed that population was definitely growing too fast in late eighteenth-century Britain and his views have influenced all discussion of questions concerning optimum population since the publication of his first *Essay on Population* in 1798. Malthus believed that population has a constant tendency 'to increase beyond the nourishment prepared for it'. In a revised version of his treatise, published in 1803, he conceded that the rate of population increase in Britain was affected by the 'preventive checks' of delayed marriage and restraint within marriage. But these and other qualifications detracted little from his essential pessimism and in the minds of his numerous disciples, who were inclined to grasp the essence of the thesis but not its qualifications, the message lost none of its severity. It was popularly believed that population normally grew too fast, and growing pauperism and rising bread prices reinforced this belief. Malthus, of course, was obsessed by the supposed 'bounty to population' offered by the old poor law and by his belief that rising incomes were almost invariably accompanied by increased fertility. He overlooked a great deal and a theoretical apparatus somewhat more complete than that he used can now be brought to bear on the question. But compiling a list of propositions on the relationship between population and incomes is altogether easier than determining which influences were important at any particular time.

A Malthusian situation is obviously less likely to arise if population growth is accompanied by plentiful capital and a willingness to invest. Malthus gave insufficient thought to the possibility that investment in agriculture might enable food supplies to keep pace with population and that industrial investment, which was often characterized by increasing returns, could provide a surplus of manufactured goods to exchange for imported food. A rising population, moreover, might increase total effective demand and thus provide an incentive to invest. It can also supply the labour necessary for industrialization and might open up opportunities for building roads, bridges, canals, and other projects whose *per capita* cost falls as population increases. On the other hand, it is obviously true that rising population may exert pressure on incomes, as Malthus suggested, and perhaps to an extent that provision of food and shelter leaves little income to provide a market for manufactured goods. Physical efficiency also may be restrained when labour is plentiful, cheap, and badly fed, and there will be less incentive to invest in labour-saving machinery and greater resistance to mechanization.

In the century after 1815 population and employment grew together, agricultural efficiency rose, abundant food and raw materials flowed into Britain from overseas, and for much of the period incomes rose also. It can safely be said that Malthus was mistaken in believing that population was growing far too fast. But the total population increase was comprised of the increase in each of Britain's diverse regional economies and that of every social class, and examination of these separate increases reveals that in many respects the rate of population change was clearly not optimal.

We noted earlier that the rapid population increase that began in the eighteenth century affected Ireland as well as Britain, and that parts of Britain heavily dependent upon agriculture had shared in the demographic revolution although they had scarcely more need of rapid population growth than Ireland. In most of the rural south and East Anglia, in rural Wales and in highland Scotland, age-specific fertility rates were not significantly below rates in areas like Lancashire and Yorkshire where demand for labour was buoyant. And death-rates were lower in the areas where labour was least in demand.[83] Thus in much of Britain population grew faster than demand for labour and faster than was good for the working classes. This combination of falling or slowly rising demand for labour and its rapidly increasing supply, unless neutralized by extensive out-migration, had in it the makings of a Malthusian crisis. In the Scottish Highlands, as in Ireland, a series of lesser disasters was crowned by famine when the potatoes failed in 1845 and 1846. The working classes of the rural south and rural Wales were spared famine, but they were well acquainted with hunger, unemployment, chronic under-employment, and low wages. High poor rates were another symptom of over-population in these areas.

Problems also arose because population tended to rise most among the poorest classes of society, particularly after the 1870s when fertility among the middle classes and skilled workers fell significantly. Consequently the supply of labour rose most rapidly in the most crowded occupations. Unskilled urban labourers and farm labourers suffered particularly from this unhappy conjunction: one observer commented in 1914 that town employers never had any difficulty finding 'practically at a moment's notice all the labourers they required'.[84] Another had noted (in 1875) how farm labourers 'do not abstain from marrying early and having large families because they know that employment cannot be found for their children . . . the result is that as they must work to live, so they must migrate in order to work.'[85] Furthermore, the poorest-paid workers had the largest number of dependants to support. Rowntree and other investigators of poverty attributed substantial distress to this cause (below, p. 125).

In these two important respects population growth was far from optimal. If rates of increase had been somewhat slower overall, and more in harmony with market requirements, there would have been fewer paupers, less inequality in incomes, and a greater proportion of all wages would have been available to spend on commodities more conducive to economic growth than food and shelter. There would also have been less pressure upon town space, water supply, and housing. Rents would not have risen as much as they did, and fewer town administrations would have been overwhelmed by the pace of urbanization. Working-class women, exhausted by repeated pregnancies and the struggle to raise large families, would have benefited particularly, because they suffered most of the cost of excessive child-bearing.[86]

These conclusions suggest some further points. First that for all the shortcomings of the Malthusian thesis, a great deal that was unpleasant about working-class life at the time when Malthus wrote, and for long afterwards, can be partly explained in terms of the pressure of numbers. It is easy to understand why he took such a despairing view of the possibilities of social progress and to understand why, at a time when population was growing more rapidly than ever before, so much importance was attached to the consequences of unlimited multiplication. Secondly, that the failure of the attempts of Francis Place to reduce working-class fertility (above, p. 37) is of some consequence in labour history. The hostile middle-class attitude towards birth-control demonstrates a considerable insensitivity towards the problems of the working classes. The middle classes recognized the crucial importance of birth-control in preventing poverty yet they vigorously opposed every means of control except an unnaturally lengthened celibacy followed, after marriage, by 'moral restraint'. And as if to make certain that the working classes would ignore their pleas, they allowed birth-control to become inextricably associated with the harsh new poor law regime that was inaugurated in 1834. Indeed, in one respect the new poor law may have *encouraged* fertility. The hope that offspring might care for elderly parents was among the reasons for large families, and the act of 1834 made the prospect of old age without filial help that much more daunting.

The problems associated with population growth were caused more by high birth-rates than by difficulties consequent upon the pattern of death-rates. Death-rates, especially infant death-rates, were highest among those with the lowest wages and this pattern both reduced the number who had to be fed and clothed on small incomes and eased the pressures of supply upon demand that caused low wages. There were exceptions to the pattern, the farm labourers in particular, but to a considerable degree differential death-rates moderated the tendency for population to rise most where it was least wanted. There were some favourable consequences too in the way that the fall in death-rate affected different age groups: the reduction was least among the aged and the very young, where it was likely to have an unfavourable effect on the activity rate, and it was greatest and came soonest among those age groups at which death was least predictable and where it caused most loss of output and most distress and hardship to survivors. Expenditure upon public health that reduced sickness and mortality among wage-earners may well have been among the most profitable of all Victorian investments.

Suggestions for further reading are on pages 399–400.

3

WAGES AND LIVING STANDARDS

I · *Nineteenth-century wages in perspective*

Working-class living standards in early nineteenth-century Britain were higher than those elsewhere in Europe. There is no doubt of this advantage or of its existence long before the nineteenth century. In 1704 Defoe spoke of 'the dearness of wages which in England outgoes all nations in the world' and a few years earlier Gregory King had judged living standards to exceed those in France by about one-fifth. In the course of the eighteenth century England's advantage over other nations became greater and more frequently noted.[1] Whereas Europeans made do with cheaper cereals, a large part of the English population fed on wheaten bread. Poor relief in many places was assessed according to the price of the wheaten loaf. White bread was also the staple diet inside the workhouse and when wheat prices soared during the French Wars the poor in southern England resisted less palatable substitutes, 'they had lost their rye teeth' they explained, 'oats were fit only for horses and potatoes for Irishmen'.[2] The Englishman was also well dressed by the standards of the time: he wore more woollen garments and less of the cheaper textiles and he was likely to wear leather shoes when the European wore clogs or went unshod.[3] Moreover, he dressed with greater style because England's wealth allowed quite ordinary men to follow the vagaries of fashion.

Average incomes in early nineteenth-century Britain also compare favourably with recent income levels in parts of Africa, Asia, and Latin America,[4] but they were less than a quarter of the level of British wages in the 1960s.[5] That wages have risen a great deal in the last century and a half will surprise no one. Indeed, the popular conception of living standards in the England of Peterloo and the 'hungry forties' is of a working class sunk in dire and unrelenting poverty. It is because anachronistic suppositions of this kind are so often encountered that the relative prosperity of the British wage-earner in the nineteenth century needs to be emphasized. Historians must bear a sizeable responsibility for the confusion. G. D. H. Cole, for example, wrote that the French Wars reduced living standards to the 'lowest possible point',[6] and another historian has advanced the improbable claim that 20 per cent of the Black Country working classes 'lived almost perpetually below the minimum level necessary to maintain life'.[7] This last conclusion was a consequence of measuring living standards against a 'minimum' which included 2 lb of meat, ½ lb of bacon, and a dozen eggs each week for two adults and two small children, three hundredweights of coal, a gallon of beer, an ounce of tobacco, and provision for expenditure on newspapers, postage, entertainment, holidays, and saving. A survey of 1836 in a country where talk of 'minimum' incomes is tragically more appropriate found that the 4,000 inhabitants of West Tulloghbegly (Donegal), including the priest, had between them five beds and two watches, that half the parish went unshod, and that all the homes of the poor contained a total of ten square feet of window glass.[8] Poverty of this intensity was very exceptional in nineteenth-century Britain. There were certainly some occupations where wages were insufficient to keep a family alive without help from charity or the poor law authorities, but the wages of the great majority of Englishmen were far above subsistence level. The wages of Englishwomen are another matter, of course, and one to which we shall return later in this chapter. The very poor, most of whom were not wage earners, are discussed separately in Chapter 4.

II · *The debate on the standard of living, 1800–50, (a) the course of real wages*

No period of wage history has been so much investigated as the years between 1800 and 1850. The debate on the standard of living at this time is probably the best known of all controversies in economic history. Given our woeful lack of knowledge on wage trends in the eighteenth century, when what happened to incomes is crucial to understanding the origins of the industrial revolution, and given that most reasonable men have long accepted that there was no dramatic change in real wages during the first half of the nineteenth century, the attention lavished upon these years may seem surprising. Historians have been attracted to this particular period mainly because the debate on what was then happening to living standards embraces the highly controversial question of the effect of the industrial revolution upon the working classes. Attention has focused upon living standards in the early industrial towns, especially the cotton towns. Among migrants to these towns were many who previously had worked on the land or at domestic industry and their migration, in effect, was from pre-industrial England to industrial England. Was this a comparatively painless transition from a society where squire, parson, farmers, and the harvest exercised a patronizing and not over-benevolent despotism to one where high wages and greater freedom outside the mill gate more than compensated for urban squalor and mill discipline? Or was the more typical experience an exchange of independence, security, and modest prosperity – such as might be afforded by the combination of farmwork, domestic industry, and cottage garden – for an urban existence in which work was more onerous and more frequently interrupted and the threat of cholera or typhus eclipsed whatever attractions the town might offer?

These questions were much debated at the time. Variations upon the first, more optimistic, school of thought were heard most often from Whig employers, politicians, and political economists. Confronting them were many Tories, alarmed lest the traditional society they still dominated should be undermined, and resentful of the growing class of thrusting manufacturers with their new money and disturbing priorities. Among the pessimists were also many novelists and poets who had been aroused by the effusion of smoky mill towns and the unsavoury disclosures of the first enquiries into factory employment. Mrs Gaskell, Disraeli, Dickens, and the rest of the 'condition of England' novelists did much to mould contemporary public opinion and have continued to exercise a considerable influence. More or less on the same side were many radicals, working-class and middle-class, who had little love for the Tories and their deferential society but who abhorred the new industrial environment and yearned for the life of independence and simple virtues conjured up by Feargus O'Connor's vision of a society where each man had three acres and a cow. Karl Marx and Friedrich Engels occupy a special place alongside these early radical pessimists. Conditions in early industrial England shaped their understanding both of economic and social trends before this time and the cataclysm they expected soon to follow. England was the first country to industrialize; where England led others would follow. And industrialization, according to Marx and Engels, had created an immiserated proletariat, united in interest and purpose and increasingly alienated from the plutocracy of millowners and coal-masters it would eventually displace:

> With the development of industry [Marx, *Communist Manifesto*, 1848] the proletariat not only increases in number; it becomes concentrated in greater masses, its strength grows, and it feels that strength more . . . . Machinery obliterates all distinctions of labour and nearly everywhere reduces wages to the same low level.

Besides helping to account for the intensity of debate, the emotional and political overtones endemic in contrasts between 'merrie England' and the 'dark satanic mills', and inseparable from the work of Marx and Engels, help to explain why the best-known economic history controversy is distinguished also by a low level of academic objectivity.

After 1850 Britain was committed irrevocably to further industrialization and the 'condition of England' was no longer so much discussed. By the 1880s the debate had been taken over by historians. At Oxford Arnold Toynbee damned the industrial revolution as 'a period as disastrous and terrible as any through which a nation ever passed'. The pessimist interpretation predominated for the next half century: the Hammonds followed the Toynbee tradition and so did G. D. H. Cole with his references to 'history's blackest day' and 'the long agony of the industrial revolution'. Then, in 1926, Clapham commenced a counter-attack armed with Silbering's price index and Bowley's wage statistics. Far from being a period when wages fell towards subsistence, he claimed, in the sixty years after 1780 the real wages of most urban workers increased. Other historians, notably Ashton, built upon this foundation, some casting further doubt upon the flimsily supported assertion of falling wages that featured prominently in the pessimist account and others claiming to show that conditions in industrial England were not nearly so bad, and conditions in pre-industrial England not nearly so good, as the pessimists believed. So successful was this reinterpretation that E. P. Thompson in his *Making of the English Working Class*, published in 1963, attacked what he called 'the new anti-catastrophic orthodoxy'. More recently, however, the optimists' advance has been checked.[9]

For the moment we will ignore mill discipline, urban diseases, and the other less quantifiable parts of the debate and concentrate upon changes in wages and what wages represented in purchasing power. Even now, more than fifty years after Clapham first confronted the literary tradition with the sober testimony of wage and price statistics, this part of the debate abounds with bold and contradictory claims. These arise partly from the difficulties encountered in compiling indices of real wages for a period during which their general direction was not readily apparent and one punctuated by hectic booms and severe depressions. Prices fluctuated dramatically, particularly at the beginning of the period. By selecting appropriate starting and finishing dates it is perfectly possible to construct indices which illustrate any of a range of increases or decreases in real wages. Any index that uses 1800 as its base, for example, will contain an upward bias, because in that year real wages were depressed by exceptionally high food prices. There is an enormous quantity of scattered and unsystematic evidence, but there are few long runs of wages in single occupations in specific areas, and this is an important omission at a time when wages varied extensively from one occupation to the next and between different parts of the country. Factory wages, based often upon piece-rates that were subject to frequent revision, present especial problems. There are also the difficulties raised by fines for unpunctuality, spoiling raw material, and other misdemeanours, and by the fact that some workers were expected to employ, and to pay, their own assistants. Moreover, the early censuses of occupations are so hazy that it is impossible to be sure how much average wages were raised by the movement of workers to better-paid employment and to parts of the country where wages were relatively high.

Ascertaining how workers spent their wages also presents formidable problems. Ideally the historian should use only retail prices but most surviving series are of wholesale prices and little is known of the weight that should be ascribed to different items or of the way that expenditure patterns responded to price changes and the introduction of new commodities – to the reduced cost of coal and cotton clothing, for example, and to the increased availability of potatoes. Some workers were affected by the impositions of the 'truck' system whereby employment might be conditional upon the purchase of goods from employers or their agents, but how many is not known. We do know that rent made onerous, and possibly growing, inroads upon the earnings of urban workers and that workers who migrated townwards had always to pay more for accommodation. Yet several of the earlier investigations, including all those that used the Silberling price index, made no allowance at all for changes in rent. As Professor Ashton pointed out some time ago, Silberling-man was hardly representative:

> He did not occupy a house, or at least he was not called upon to pay rent. He allowed himself only a moderate amount of bread and very little porridge, and he never touched potatoes or strong drink. On the other hand, he got through quite considerable quantities of beef and mutton and showed a fondness for butter. Perhaps he was a diabetic.[10]

More difficulties arise from the need to adjust hourly or weekly earnings to compensate for periods of unemployment. In the mid-1830s, for example, Lancashire was hard at work. So scarce was labour that some mills stood idle for lack of operatives and in 1834 the poor law authorities were persuaded to organize the migration of families from the low-wage south. These migrants at first flourished in their new surroundings, enjoying meat every day, new clothes, and coal fires without stint.[11] In 1836, however, the trade cycle turned downwards, the poor law migration scheme was soon abandoned, and some of the hapless migrants returned south. When unemployment is rising and prices fall, the real wages of those still at work may well improve, and the obvious questions arise of the extent to which unemployment reduced average real wages in the first half of the nineteenth century and whether unemployment was increased by industrialization. There is also the related question of employment within the family: according to some reports employment for women in the manufacturing districts increased faster than men's employment. Women's and children's earnings may also have risen considerably, and both developments would have tended to raise family earnings. But such gains may have been partly at the expense of adult males. In other places, by contrast, men's wages may have benefited by reduced competition from their wives and children, and in such cases rising real wages for men and falling family earnings could have occurred together.

Given all these various and formidable obstacles to the construction of reliable indices of real wages it is not surprising that some investigators have tried a quite different approach to the problem – that is, to estimate change in living standards from consumption or output totals. Duty was levied upon tea, sugar, coffee, tobacco, and other goods and there are output figures for some items that were not taxed. By dividing the number in the population into the total quantity of any commodity a crude index of prosperity may be calculated. However, an index of this kind is very crude indeed. When duties were high, as they were in the early decades of the nineteenth century, smuggling was widespread. Thus by no means all goods that were imported were recorded. In the second quarter of the century, when Britain adopted a policy of free trade, smuggling became less worth while and so the official statistics recorded an increasingly greater proportion of goods that entered the country. For these reasons an index that relies much upon imported commodities will contain an upward bias. Secondly there is the obvious problem of distribution. *Per capita* consumption of coffee for example, according to the official statistics, increased enormously between 1790 and 1840. But even if we could be sure that the rise does more than reflect a decline in smuggling, it is not clear how much of the increase was consumed by wage earners. Another difficulty with this approach to determining changes in living standards is that output figures do not record articles produced and consumed within the home. In the early stages of industrialization, when factory-made goods could be purchased as substitutes for goods once made at home, output statistics might indicate rapidly rising consumption per head when consumption was actually rising slowly or not at all.

What then of the actual wage trends? In a recent article that students of the standard of living debate will find extremely useful M. W. Flinn has drawn together all the most frequently used price and wage series and considered what generalizations can be deduced from the mass of evidence.[12] He took care to minimize distortion caused by a short-run price fluctuations and, among other things, indicated the strengths and weaknesses of each item of evidence. His calculations suggest that from about 1790 until near the end of the French Wars, wages of most workers kept pace with rising prices. Between 1813 and the early 1820s prices fell sharply and to a greater extent than wages so that those fortunate enough to remain in work (a significant qualification) appear to have enjoyed an increase in living standards of as much as 25 per cent. These gains seem to have been generally retained (although not much increased) in the second quarter of the century, and with unemployment perhaps by then less severe, a greater proportion of the labour force may have benefited from the earlier gains.

These conclusions provide little comfort either for those who follow the gloomy generalizing of Marx and Engels or for light-hearted optimists. On balance, they are perhaps more damaging to the pessimists' case, since there is nothing that suggests a general and sustained fall in real wages at any time between 1790 and 1850. There were two long periods when wages changed very little, separated by a short interval of improvement. If wage rates could be accurately weighted to allow for the diminishing importance of employment in agriculture and domestic industry, and for the migration of labour from low-wage to high-wage areas, the conclusions might provide more comfort to the optimists. But when all this is said, it remains that over some sixty years average real wages are unlikely to have improved by more than a quarter.

These generalizations hide an enormous diversity of experience. By a combination of migration and change of occupation some workers doubled or tripled their earnings, others enjoyed substantial rises without such moves, and some were immiserated. Prominent among the more fortunate groups were the 10 to 15 per cent of wage earners who are conventionally labelled the 'labour aristocracy'. These were skilled men: compositors, building craftsmen, engineers, coach-makers, watchmakers, boiler-makers, and the like. A sizable proportion were trade unionists and at a time when prices were more often falling than rising any effective union resistance to wage cuts was an especial advantage. A few occupations, like the woolcombers, lost 'aristocratic' status as a consequence of industrialization, but these were more than offset by others, like the engineers, whose work was created or greatly expanded by the same process. As E. P. Thompson has remarked, 'if we were concerned only with the skilled "society men" in regular employment, then the controversy as to living standards would long ago have been settled on the optimistic side.'[13]

Another occupational group that had little reason to regret the day when Arkwright put the first waterframe in the first cotton mill were the factory cotton spinners. They too might be considered a part of the labour aristocracy. G. D. H. Cole (using, admittedly, Silberling's suspect price index) shows the real wages of Manchester mule-spinners more than doubling in the first half of the century.[14] Many of the less well-paid cotton mill operatives also enjoyed rising real wages and it may be significant that industrial unrest in the mills arose far more often from workers' attempts to reduce the working day than because they considered themselves ill-paid. Moreover, mill operatives perhaps suffered rather less than other wage earners from unemployment because manufacturers who had sunk capital into mills and machinery were anxious to keep their capital busy and often continued operating in slack periods. Domestic workers, on the other hand, could be laid-off at any time with little cost to their employers. To this list of workers whose real earnings increased in the first half of the century we can confidently add the majority of farm workers in the Scottish Lowlands, most domestic servants, and perhaps also building workers.[15] And when the course of coal-miners' real wages is eventually known it may well be found that they too belong in this category.

These more fortunate workers were increasing in relative importance during the first half of the century. At the same time, or from the 1830s at the latest, there was probably a relative decline in the number whose real incomes were falling. In one sense these changes add weight to the optimists' case. But the decline and disappearance of groups like the handloom weavers is, of course, the essence of their tragedy. Handloom weavers were not factory workers but their plight is hardly less attributable to the industrial revolution than is the engineers' and spinners' prosperity. There were other reasons why their wages fell: they suffered from the overcrowding of their trade and from the competition of more badly-paid European weavers. But it was the mechanization of cotton spinning and the increased output of machine-spun yarn that had initially raised handloom weavers' earnings to as much as 40s a week and persuaded large numbers to take up the loom, and it was the effective mechanization of weaving after 1820 that most decisively forced down wages. By 1826 a lad of fifteen supervising two power looms produced as much as six handloom weavers and there were few times after this when handloom weavers averaged more than 7s a week.[16] From a peak of nearly 250,000 in 1820 their numbers fell to some 40,000 in 1850. A decade later they had virtually disappeared. The broad outlines of this tragedy were repeated in several other occupations: among the Black Country nail-makers, for example, whose decline began with the introduction of machine competition about 1830. The midland framework knitters and a great many of the London workers mentioned by Mayhew owed their plight to a similar combination of circumstances, although in these cases the trouble was at least as much unrestricted entry to their occupations as competition from factories. This was obviously true also of southern farm labourers, many of whom had no share in the modest general gains of the first half of the century and some of whom almost certainly suffered a fall in earnings.

III · *The debate on the standard of living, 1800–50, (b) non-wage aspects of living standards; the alternatives to industrial England*

Standards of living have to be judged on more than relative movements in wages and prices. Although the contention that wages fell was for long a mainstay of the pessimists' case, many of them, recognizing the weight of adverse statistical evidence, have now retreated to a less assailable position. The neo-pessimist case rests upon the allegedly soul-destroying nature of factory work, the changed relations between rich and poor, urban squalor, and other variables of a similarly less quantifiable kind. Thus E. P. Thompson writes:

> Over the period 1790–1840 there was a slight improvement in average material standards. Over the same period there was intensified exploitation, greater insecurity, and increasing human misery. By 1840 most people were

'better-off' than their forerunners had been fifty years before, but they had suffered and continued to suffer this slight improvement as a catastrophic experience.[17]

At work there was the alleged loss of freedom to labour and to cease labour at will. The 'irregular cycle of the working week' and 'the larger irregularity of the working year' with its seasonal rhythms, festivals, holidays, and fairs were replaced by unremitting, machine-dictated toil. The factories meant discipline and fines, confinement, and the relentless oppression of the clock.[18] The pessimist case against the mills includes also the alleged extension of the obnoxious 'truck' system and many novel occupational hazards. It includes too, of course, the urban workers' intense vulnerability to the trade cycle: in the pre-industrial world, it is claimed, a man's garden and his right to the produce of woods and commons were a cushion against industrial slump. But in the towns he lacked friends and depended too much upon his cash income. When that income was interrupted independence was lost, and with it status and self-respect.

Another part of the pessimist view concerns the consequences of industrialization for the family. Some historians have claimed that industrialization was accompanied by an extension of women's and children's employment but this, as we saw in Chapter 1, was probably not generally the case. However, the factory did remove work from the home and if women and children followed the work, family bonds were loosened. Some families were able to work together at the mill but many could not and thus each morning, 'roughly torn apart by the factory bell', its members departed their various ways. At worst this left the home and younger children woefully neglected, or perhaps in the charge of an unemployed husband. Contemporary pessimists made much of such influences upon the family and were particularly concerned about the moral consequences for wives and elder daughters working outside the home. To Richard Oastler, author of the famous letters on 'Yorkshire Slavery', this 'violation of the sacred nature of the home' was 'the greatest curse of the factory system'. Gaskell, in *Artisans and Machinery* (1836), wrote of 'the general immorality of town populations', of the 'almost entire extinction of sexual decency', and of mills as 'emporiums of profligacy', These assaults upon the integrity of the family were seen by pessimists as taking place within the broader catastrophe of a disintegrating traditional society in which the poor had once enjoyed customary rights and protection and the rich had honoured their responsibilities. Industrialization and its handmaiden *laissez-faire* brought harsher attitudes, 'an abdication on the part of the governors' (Carlyle), a world of each for himself in which poverty came to be regarded as a consequence of moral failings that relief could only aggravate. Such attitudes were epitomized by the juxtaposition of growing wealth and abject pauperism, by increased residential segregation,[19] by the insensitivities of the new poor law of 1834 that set out to reduce the living standards of able-bodied paupers, and by the middle-class Mancunian who listened patiently while Engels remonstrated against conditions in the working-class districts and as they parted remarked, 'And yet there is a great deal of money made here. Good morning, Sir'.[20] The pessimists attribute also to industrialization much of the blame for the other evils that so disturbed Engels – the barrack-like towns, the wretched living quarters, the smoke, squalor, and disease.

These, in brief, are the reasons why many historians maintain that industrialization was a catastrophe for the poor far greater than could be compensated by modest additions to real wages. As testimony to the consciousness of immiseration they can point to the difficulty of manning the early mills, which depended heavily upon casual labour and innocent children, and to the works' rules and onerous fines that were necessary to shape the worker to the factory regime. So reluctant were the silk weavers of Coventry to enter the factory, so determined to preserve their respectability and independence, that when mechanization became inevitable they erected steam engines at the end of their rows of cottages and conducted the power to each home with belting. There is further evidence of the consciousness of present or imminent distress in the anti-industrialism that was a part of the Chartist protest, in Methodism with its consoling disregard for earthly miseries, and in the number who sought escape from industrialization in the American wilderness or through the Chartist land scheme and other new Jerusalems.[21]

Some of these points are conceded, or partially conceded, by the optimist school. Human progress, they argue, rarely means more than a surplus of gains over losses, and a discontinuity so great as the industrial revolution inevitably was attended by social costs. But other points they dispute. The assertion that the factory system tragically weakened family ties, for example, is countered by the conclusions of recent work on family structure in the cotton towns which suggests that separation of home and workplace was more than compensated by the likelihood that industrialization made it easier for children, their parents, and grandparents to live in the same house or neighbourhood.[22] Preston in 1851 contained a larger proportion of households with relatives beyond the nuclear family than was usual either in pre-industrial England or in the England of the mid-twentieth century. Whereas a great many country-born youths left their birthplaces to find work, and many of those that stayed either could not afford to look after aged parents or did not care to, towns like Preston offered ample local employment and grandparents earned their keep by child-minding and similar chores while others were at the mill. Although working men may have resented the undermining of their authority as wives and children moved to paid employment beyond their protection and discipline, those thus partially released from patriarchal authority probably saw things differently. Lancashire mill-girls gained an enduring reputation as being among the most independent of all working-class women.[23] Removal of work to the factory must also have left the home cleaner and less cramped, and so long as the family slept under the same roof and shared at least some of their meals and recreation the 'rough tearing apart each morning by the factory bell' was probably not felt as much of an imposition.[24] After all, no such importance is attached to the dispersive influence of the school bell when education moved outside the home.

With regard to work itself the optimists have made much of the disproportionate weight allegedly accorded to evidence of the very worst factory conditions. These, they argue, were no more typical than those created by model employers like the Gregs, the Oldknows, the Ashworths, and the Strutts. The Strutt workers were provided with houses, shops, schools, a library, a swimming-pool with a swimming instructor, and a room for dancing. In reply to evidence of working-class distaste for factory work, optimists can note that the difficulties of recruiting labour for the early spinning mills arose in part because so many mills were located where population was sparse and also because the mills themselves had made non-factory work more attractive by boosting handloom weavers' wages. By the 1830s, when factories were less novel and handloom weavers less scarce, some categories of mill employment were coveted and from the cotton districts came numerous complaints of the difficulty in finding domestic servants because working girls preferred to enter the mills.[25] There is no doubt of the dominant townward direction of population movement in the first half of the nineteenth century. For every worker who sought refuge abroad or among O'Connor's toiling peasantry there were many more who could hardly wait to shake the mud of the fields from their boots. And while reactions to the new environment must have varied enormously, it seems reasonable to suppose that migrants were heavily weighted with those who were resentful of the monotony and oppressions of rural life and who put the greatest premium on the higher wages, excitement, and greater independence of town life.

Factory work required no more exertion than much other work. Several contemporaries who were hostile to industrialization conceded this point.[26] Rather than a slave to the machine, the worker was its overseer. His task was boring and he had to walk about a great deal, but the water-wheel or steam engine did the exhausting physical labour.[27] The optimists can hardly deny that factory hours were initially long. But they can point out that even longer hours were commonplace in some non-factory occupations and that after 1830, with legislation curbing the working day, the cotton towns gradually lost their reputation for excessive hours. They can point also to progress in other aspects of industrial and urban life during the latter part of the period covered by the standard of living debate. The mills became safer, less crowded, better ventilated, and less dependent on very young children. Gaskell, in 1836, conceded a recent 'vast improvement' and Engels spoke of the 1833 legislation (above, p. 10) as having removed 'the most blatant evils of the factory system'.[28] A start had been made towards curbing 'truck' abuses (with acts in 1831 and 1842) and the factory towns benefited from the early public health reforms described in Chapter 2. Cheap iron and earthenware pipes and steam-driven pumps, quintessential products of the industrial revolution, had a vital part in the latter advance. Education and literacy were both improving long before 1850, and a considerable expansion in charitable activity of every kind (below, pp. 127–8), an awakened public conscience, and the new spirit of enquiry and reform, were all evidence that the 'abdication of the governors' (above, p. 65) was never more than partial.[29] Alongside the harsh individualism of *laissez-faire*, paternal and humanitarian attitudes had survived and in some respects had grown stronger.

This heightened social consciousness and new determination to investigate social evils have an important part in optimists' claims that the traditional association of industrialization and deterioration in the quality of life is founded upon a too rosy interpretation of pre-industrial conditions. Attention is drawn to many abuses that had long existed but which later commentators often blamed upon those that made them public. Professor Ashton put the case succinctly:

> a generation that had the enterprise and industry to assemble the facts, the honesty to reveal them, and the energy to set about the task of reform has been held up to obloquy as the author, not of the Blue Books, but of the evils themselves.[30]

Industrialization created some new evils and intensified some old ones. But Professor Ashton's point contains a great deal of substance.

Those alarmed by the proliferation of mills, mines, and urban squalor too easily slipped into believing that all things unpleasant were a consequence of industrialization: 'Everything in this district that arouses our disgust and just indignation . . .' wrote Engels, 'is of relatively recent origin and belongs to the industrial age.'[31] Thus many long-standing problems came to be attributed to industrialism, together with certain others that had appeared more recently but whose chief cause lay elsewhere. These assumptions were nurtured by the belief, instinctive in many men and especially in town-bred middle classes, that rural pursuits are natural and healthy and that city life is unhealthy and corruptive. Purged of its blemishes, pre-industrial England came in many men's minds to assume a benign countenance. Nostalgia for this imaginary past inspired the romantic poets and 'condition of England' novelists. Frances

Trollope rushed to Manchester on one of the first trains and, after a hasty survey, wrote *Michael Armstrong* (1840) for a readership anxious to hear the worst of the industrial north. It also inspired Peter Gaskell, the Tory radical, who wrote wistfully of the sturdy yeomanry still happily ignorant of trade unionism or 'clubs for raving politicians', and of 'the golden times of manufacturers' when each community was 'one great family' guided by the squire, 'a kind and indulgent master . . . loved and reverenced by his tenants'.[32] Engels copied those parts of Gaskell's work he found most to his taste and Cobbett, with his talk of the 'hell-hole northern manufacturing towns', was in the same tradition.

'Merrie England', of course, never existed. Gaskell's kindly squires had probably been common enough, but so too were those who resembled more the grasping villains of Victorian melodrama. The independence and status that landownership conferred, and which loom large in 'merrie England', were far from universally enjoyed: there were already two hired hands for every farmer by the early eighteenth century and one Englishman in four lived in a town. And the slightest acquaintance with eighteenth-century urban death-rates, or a glance at Hogarth's prints, will leave no doubt that the absence of modern industry provided no immunity from urban squalor. Information on the extent of pre-industrial poverty is scanty, but it is generally agreed that the work of Gregory King and others indicates a considerably greater proportion of the population in chronic want than Booth and Rowntree discovered two centuries later. The economy was already sufficiently dependent upon trade and manufacture to suffer serious trade crises and harvest failures then had far more serious consequences than in the nineteenth century. Nor were pre-industrial working conditions as idyllic as some have suggested. The domestic workers' supposed freedom to work as they wished often amounted to no more than the freedom to trade leisure at the beginning of the week for overwork at its end; employment of very young children was widespread, and women were expected to do a great deal of dirty and backbreaking work. Women's employment as miners, for example, certainly did not begin with the industrial revolution. Indeed, those women highlighted in the 1842 report (above, p. 18) may well have been the remnants of a once larger number: the last woman to work below ground on the Northumberland and Durham coalfield came up about 1780 when the industrial revolution was just beginning.[33] The bonding of Scottish miners, a system often compared with serfdom and sometimes with slavery, was coming to an end at about the same time.[34] Some part of the belief in an earlier 'golden age' probably originated in tales of the prosperous fifteenth and early sixteenth centuries. What we know of prices and wages does suggest comparative prosperity at that time. But it must be borne in mind how much this owed to the unwelcome easing of population pressure by plague. Moreover, if roast beef featured more prominently in the lives of the English poor then than it did during the period of the industrial revolution, so did other things that were less often remembered and less romantic, such as bubonic plague and the whipping and branding of pauper vagrants.

The pessimist case, then, relies too much upon romanticized notions of pre-industrial England. But this reservation, and the other 'optimist' arguments, by no means completely dispose of the claim that improvement in real wages may have been more than offset by deterioration in aspects of living standards that cannot be quantified. And the pessimists, for their part, can no more prove this claim than the optimists can disprove it. Each side may claim priority for whatever arguments suit its case but as it stands, and as it is most usually specified, this part of the standard of living debate is inconclusive. But is it correctly specified? Whether the people of industrial England were more or less contented than their rustic forebears cannot be determined – but the effect of industrialization on their lives is less indeterminable than commonly supposed. The debate entails a comparison between England as it was and the non-industrial alternative. Most of those who have taken part in the debate, and virtually all of the pessimists, have assumed that the best guide to England as it would have been without industrialization is England as it was before industrialization. Engels, for example, claimed that pre-industrial workers 'vegetated happily and but for the Industrial Revolution would never have left this way of life'.[35] But industrialization is not the only force able to disturb income levels and traditional ways.

By far the greatest of the other disturbing influences was demographic change. During the eighteenth century the restraints on population growth were lifted and population rose rapidly. At first population increase brought no significant pressure on living standards because improved food supply was among the influences that allowed the population to rise. But before 1800 there were signs in several parts of Europe that the breathing-space permitted by agricultural improvement had been largely taken up, that living standards were coming under pressure. To some extent, and in certain places, industrialization itself was among the causes of population increase: without it the acceleration would have been slower. But, as we noted in Chapter 2, this relationship was not evident at all in most places where population rose and even in Britain it was only of secondary importance. It seems reasonable, therefore, to suppose that the idyllic life depicted by Engels, if it ever existed, would sooner or later have been disturbed by demographic change even in the absence of industrialization. Likewise, those who seek some idea of what England might have become by 1850 without the industrial revolution should look initially, not to the England of 1740 but to areas which had experienced demographic change without industrialization – to Ireland in the 1840s perhaps or to parts of Britain itself, like Wiltshire or Sutherland, that were still largely unblemished by mine or mill. Ashton made this point long ago and some others have taken up his theme.[36] But for the most part the debate has continued to disregard the sobering question of what happens to those who increase their numbers without passing through an industrial revolution. What happened to English standards of living in the first half of the nineteenth century may be in doubt, but there is little doubt about what happened in Ireland. On several occasions, in 1816–17, 1821–2, and 1845–6 especially, demographic pressures inflicted upon Ireland misery far exceeding anything that industrialization brought to Britain. And within Britain counties like Wiltshire and Sutherland, with their low wages and endemic under-employment, experienced their own milder version of Ireland's problems. Money wages doubled in Lancashire and the West Riding between 1770 and 1850 but in Wiltshire they were the same level at both dates.[37] And poor rates per head of population in Wiltshire at mid-century were over twice the level in Lancashire.[38]

That Britain was largely spared the pressure upon living standards felt by Ireland and much of Europe was due mainly to the industrial revolution. Enclosure, which has been condemned by the Hammonds and others as second only to industrialization in causing hardship, helped also because it increased food supply without land fragmentation of the kind that occurred in Ireland. Enclosure also encouraged mobility of labour by loosening the ties that elsewhere bound poor men to the land. But enclosure could not provide sufficient employment to absorb more than a very little of the increase in population. Industry met this need in a manner that had about it none of the terrifying prospects associated with the division of land-holdings and a swelling, impoverished peasantry. The industrial population was employed efficiently: it produced cheap coal and numerous manufactured articles for the home market, it produced also an exportable surplus that paid for the food imports that became necessary as population outstripped farm output, and it produced the ships and railways that brought this food to British tables and opened up new markets abroad and new destinations for British emigrants. And eventually, after 1850, industrialization raised the standard of living of a vast and still growing population far beyond the levels of pre-industrial Britain.

In this way, which is after all among the remedies that economists prescribe for under-developed and over-populated countries today, Britain largely, although not painlessly, escaped the worse consequences of population increase unaccompanied by industrialization. Some of the pain, it is true, might have been avoided. It was not necessary that the state should have abandoned so much of its regulative function, and far more might have been done to protect victims of change without too much undermining the individual enterprise that was the mainspring of growth. But keeping things as

71

they had been was not a practicable alternative. From this standpoint the whole debate over the consequences of industrialization upon the working classes, and the division of historians into hostile camps, is absurd. It is as if two teams of doctors were discussing the case of a man kept tolerably alive by blood transfusions with one team arguing that the transfusions must be beneficial because they detect improvement in his condition and the other arguing that the transfusions must be harmful because they can detect no such improvement.

Industrialization is not the only possible means of escaping population pressure of course. Another possibility is that in the absence of industrial employment surplus population emigrates in sufficient numbers to prevent living standards falling. But emigration is attended by its own social costs and mass emigration is seldom initiated until it has become a dire necessity. The Irish endured indescribable miseries before sufficient numbers fled to effect a significant easing of demographic pressure. A fall in fertility is another possible response to a reduction in mortality. Fertility was controlled to some extent in pre-industrial England and in the absence of industrialization some response from this quarter might have occurred. But no country, not even France, significantly reduced fertility until long after population pressure was manifest. Of those areas within Britain that suffered demographic pressure the Scottish Highlands certainly provide evidence that emigration prevented living standards falling as far, as fast, and as often as they might otherwise have done. Even so, there was insufficient emigration to prevent famine occurring at times in the Highlands, and the overcrowded counties of rural southern England were certainly not distinguished either by high rates of out-migration or by low fertility.

The adverse consequences of population pressure were not felt only in the rural parts of Britain. The towns suffered too, and they suffered not least because they were a refuge for the surplus population of rural Britain and Ireland. In this respect also the consequences of industrialization and of population increase are often confused: investigators have attributed to industrialization a great many urban problems whose chief cause was rising population. Léon Faucher did this when he visited Manchester in 1844; Engels did the same, and so, more recently, has E. J. Hobsbawm who seems to blame the industrial revolution not only for the mounting pressure of people upon space, but also for the introduction of the cholera epidemics that reached Britain after decimating the population of many parts of pre-industrial Europe and Asia.[39] Had Faucher and Engels investigated Edinburgh, Dublin, or any other large city at that time still largely unaffected by modern industrialism, they would have found most of Manchester's problems already in existence and they would perhaps also have realized how tenuous were the links between population increase and industrialization. Some of the most

[handwritten marginalia: deterrent of real wages? Buying power?]

crowded housing, the least adequate sanitation, and the highest mortality were to be found in the factory towns it is true, but this for the very good reason that migrants seeking escape from the consequences of rural over-population very sensibly went to those towns where unemployment and low wages were least in evidence. Thus because they offered the most certain relief from the *economic* consequences of population pressure, the industrial cities, in their housing and their death-rates, and in the way their administration was overwhelmed, exhibited some of the most acute *social* consequences of that same pressure.

IV · *Real wages, 1850–1914*

There is less controversy concerning living standards between 1850 and 1914 and wage movements in this period can be described more briefly. The years up to the mid-1890s saw remarkable progress although there are different views on when the improvement in real wages began and on its overall magnitude. According to some authorities the rise was already underway in the 1850s, others detect no significant progress before the late 1860s, and some place the upturn even later.[40] By 1860 some of the least acceptable aspects of early industrialism had gone and a second or third generation of town-bred workers was becoming increasingly reconciled to industrial society. In G. D. H. Cole's words, the 'period of looking back' was over, 'the call of the fields had grown fainter; the clanking and puffing of the engines had deadened their ears'.[41]

Cole, relying as we must still on the statistical labours of G. H. Wood and A. L. Bowley, estimated the likely increase in real wages between 1850 and 1900 at between 70 and 80 per cent.[42] Bowley had calculated that real earnings doubled but Wood thought Bowley's index allowed too much weight to items whose price fell by more than the average.[43] Until wage historians re-work the estimates of Wood and Bowley or, pending that formidable task, until someone does for the second half of the century what M. W. Flinn has done for the first, Cole's estimate is as good as any. This increase took the wages of Wood's 'average operative' from 20s a week in 1850 to around 35s in 1900. The cost of living was much the same at these two dates. Improvement at this rate is now so commonplace that it is easy to forget how slow progress had been before the industrial revolution. The only previous increase in real wages comparable to that in the second half of the nineteenth century was the long rise induced by falling population in the sixty or seventy years following the Black Death (1348–50).

The nineteenth-century increase may have been significantly above or below Cole's estimate of 70 to 80 per cent and less of it may have come between 1880 and 1896 than Cole suggests. G. J. Barnsby has gone so far as to question the existence of significant increases of any kind during the nineteenth century.[44] His suggestion, however, discounts the pioneering work of Wood and Bowley too much, ignores the corroborative evidence of consumption trends, and is based upon evidence from a region where wages undoubtedly rose less than the average.[45] Better figures of unemployment and more knowledge of the extent of short-time working might, however, lead to a downward revision of Wood and Bowley's estimates, especially for the years of falling prices after 1873 when rising real wages occurred alongside pressure on profits, diminishing business confidence, and a higher level of unemployment. Among those trade unionists for whom figures are available, average unemployment was 4.5 per cent between 1851 and 1873 and 5.3 per cent or more between 1873 and 1896.[46] On the other hand, J. W. F. Rowe has shown that the statistics used by Wood and Bowley considerably underestimate the rise in miners' wages, and their indices make no allowance for the spatial redistribution of the labour force in favour of high wage areas.[47]

One point that needs to be brought out clearly is how much of the rise in average real wages was attributable to the changes in occupational structure described in Chapter 1. Employment rose fastest where pay was relatively high: in mining for example, and in many semi-skilled occupations. Demand for unskilled labourers rose less fast and the number of farm workers, whose pay was very low, fell absolutely. This redistribution was effected partly by workers moving from one occupation to another and some of those that did so increased their pay handsomely, especially when they combined the transition with movement to a higher-wage district. If Robert Walker (above, pp. 1–3) for example, had left his native Wiltshire in 1850 to enrol as a London constable his earnings would have immediately almost doubled from some 9s or 10s to 17s a week.[48] But much of the redistribution was achieved by the expanding occupations recruiting a disproportionate share of lads and girls entering their first job, and for many of those who remained in the same occupation the increase over the second half of the century was well below 75 per cent: printing compositors, for example, and workers in the Sheffield trades, received increases of only 25 to 30 per cent.[49] Some workers who remained at the same occupation obviously did far better than this: those who spent these years doing the same work on a Scottish farm, for example, or in one of the building trades, probably enjoyed increases of two-thirds and upwards.[50] But for the labour force as a whole something like one-third of the overall increase in real wages between 1850 and 1900 is attributable to changes in occupational structure.

Shortly before the end of the century the great rise in real wages came to an end. Whether real wages subsequently fell, stagnated, or rose slightly we cannot say. The indices most often used are not above suspicion, particularly with regard to the allowance they make for changes in the level of unemployment and the increased importance of better-paid occupations.[51] Bowley, in fact, suggested that his figures were subject to a possible error of as much as 5 per cent in either direction. His index, that compiled by G. H. Wood for the years up to 1902, and the Phelps Brown and Browne index (which leans heavily on Bowley and Wood) are shown in Table 3·1. The indices are not fully in agreement even on the direction of change. The findings of the Board of Trade's comparison of prices and wages between 1905 and 1912, which are

Table 3 · 1   *Real Wages 1895–1914*

	Bowley	Wood		Phelps Brown and Browne
		Full work	Allowing for Unemployment	
	(1914 = 100)	(1850 = 100)		(1890–99 = 100)
1895	100	174	163	103
1896	100	176	170	103
1897	98	176	169	103
1898	99	174	169	101
1899	104	180	176	106
1900	103	183	177	104
1901	102	181	174	105
1902	101	177	169	103
1903	99			102
1904	97			101
1905	97			100
1906	98			103
1907	101			105
1908	101			106
1909	100			104
1910	98			104
1911	97			102
1912	97			102
1913	97			101
1914	100			

Sources: A. L. Bowley, *Wages and Income in the United Kingdom since 1860*, (Cambridge 1937), p. 30; G. H. Wood, 'Real Wages and the Standard of Comfort since 1850', *Journal of the Royal Statistical Society*, LXXII (1909); E. H. Phelps Brown and M. H. Browne, *A Century of Pay*, (1968), p. 445, col. 3, index of wage earnings in composite units of consumables.

more gloomy than any of the series shown in Table 3·1, are also worth noting: they show building, engineering, and printing wages rising in these years by 2 per cent, 4 to 5 per cent, and about 4 per cent respectively, while the cost of living increased by as much as 11 per cent.[52] It seems reasonably safe to say that there was no marked overall rise or fall in real wages during the whole period 1896–1914. There was, as always, a considerable diversity of experience. The real wages of some occupational groups, like the railwaymen, some building workers, and coal-miners in certain parts of the country certainly fell. At the same time some other workers, those employed in Sheffield's heavy trades for example, almost certainly enjoyed rising real wages.

With the benefit of hindsight we can see that the mid-1890s was a turning-point of some consequence. But it is as well to remember that the ending of the rise in real wages was far less obvious to contemporaries, who had very little statistical information by which to judge movements in wages and prices, and also that the gains of the previous half-century were not lost. Some historians, impressed no doubt by the grim findings of the numerous poverty surveys of this period and by the bitter industrial conflict of 1908–13, have allowed themselves to believe that the setback was more decisive that it was and more resented. Asa Briggs, for example, argues that 'throughout the whole Edwardian period the pressure on real wages was the main fact of working-class existence'. Marghanita Laski has even suggested that the fall in living standards among the poor was such that breast-feeding declined because the mother's diet became inadequate to produce a sufficient flow of milk.[53] Just how conscious were workers of pressure on real wages, and when this consciousness emerged, are points obviously relevant to the question of what caused the great pre-war labour unrest and they are mentioned again in Chapter 9.

v · *Non-monetary changes in living standards, 1850–1914; changes in working hours, 1815–1914; the worker as consumer, 1815–1914, changes in leisure, diet and housing*

The great increase in real wages after 1850 was powerfully reinforced by numerous non-monetary improvements in living standards. There were notable advances in public health and the urban environment, in education, in medical services, in safety at work, in the status of trade unions, and (particularly after 1900) in child and infant welfare and the provision of old age pensions and insurance against sickness and unemployment. There were substantial political advances too, not least the franchise extensions of 1867 and 1884. Some of these changes have been discussed already and others will be discussed in later chapters. At this point we need only note their existence alongside the changes in real wages and also that progress in all these spheres continued, and increased, during the years of stagnating real wages and industrial unrest before the First World War.

Working hours and leisure

Another significant non-monetary advance in living standards during the second half of the century was the reduction in hours of work. What happened to working hours before 1850 and how the working week at that time compared with the pre-industrial regime, are questions that were touched upon earlier. The answers to these questions are not altogether clear. There was, almost certainly, an increasing regularity of work. In the eighteenth century many workers took time off on fair days and for elections and similar occasions. If they had sufficient money left after the Sunday break, and if the week's stint was not too pressing, 'Saint Monday' might be honoured. At that time many tasks were also liable to be interrupted by the weather and the changing seasons. Much of this pattern endured into the nineteenth century and in some places, among the domestic and workshop trades of Sheffield and Stourbridge for example, it persisted well after 1850.[54] But the new, gas-illuminated, steam-driven mills were oblivious alike to darkness, Saint Monday, and the vagaries of weather. Their owners, moreover, as we noted earlier, were especially anxious to keep costly industrial plant at work. At the same time a sharpened awareness of the links between idleness and public disorder, and the new enthusiasm for encouraging 'rational' (improving) recreation among the working classes, led to the suppression of some of the traditional fairs and sporting occasions that had encouraged irregular working. Bull baiting, cock fighting, public hangings, and other lusty sports and entertainments were each the subject of increasing moral disapproval. It was in the early nineteenth century, for example, that London journeymen ceased to habitually down tools for public hangings. So although there was still an enormous variety in working hours, and still many occupations where there was not yet a 'normal' working week, by the 1830s the number of establishments that worked a regular six-day week throughout the year (excepting only Easter and Christmas) had increased significantly.

Whether more regular work also meant a longer working week is more debatable. An extremely long working day was commonplace in many non-factory occupations both at this time and in pre-industrial England. Sheffield silversmiths, for example, in 1680 announced that they would in future refuse to begin work before 6 a.m. or continue after eight o'clock in the evening; the ordinary working day in the indoor trades of early eighteenth-century London was said to be from 6 a.m. to 9 p.m.; and in the first half of the nineteenth century many domestic workers, including the Stourbridge nailers, worked as many as fourteen hours a day.[55] But most of these workers enjoyed longer and more frequent breaks than factory operatives, their work was less intensive, and some of those who worked such long hours after 1800 did so in an attempt to maintain their incomes against factory competition. Moreover, by 1800, when the factories worked twelve hours or more, many town artisans worked only ten, or ten and a half, hours a day.[56] Given this, and taking into account that factories worked a full six days, it seems likely that in the early part of the century their working week was longer than average.[57] After 1830, however, legislation brought the factory working day into line with the average in other occupations. By the 1850s factory workers probably worked fewer hours each week than the majority of workers, and the factory children probably worked considerably fewer hours than most child workers. There were still no legal limits to the time that men might work in the mills. But in practice, as the 'ten hour' campaigners and employers were both well aware, legislation on women's and children's hours affected the working day of men also.*

At mid-century the average working week was probably between sixty and seventy-two hours with large numbers working considerably more or less than the average. Between then and the First World War the working day was reduced substantially, although the gains were neither so great nor so continuous as the gains in real wages. Much of the reduction in hours was concentrated in the busy years of the early 1870s. By the time that boom was spent the engineering trades, the builders, the cotton workers, and many others had an average working week of between fifty-four and fifty-six and a half hours. There were similar, if less substantial, advances in the years of low unemployment around 1890 when the trade unions' eight-hour day campaign was in full swing. The London gas workers' bloodless victory of 1889 (below, p. 304) put them among those who worked an eight hour day. Those coal hewers who still worked more than eight hours were brought into line in 1908, and by 1914 building workers in many towns had reduced their summer week to fifty hours. Each of these groups had a short working week by the standards of the time. The average working week of all full-time workers on the eve of the War was some fifty-six to fifty-seven hours – a reduction, that is, of between 10 and 20 per cent on the working week of 1850. Actual hours worked had probably fallen less than the amount by which the normal working week was reduced because one consequence of the reduction in nominal working hours was greater opportunity of 'overtime' working at a higher rate of pay. The marked discontinuity in reductions in hours is explained by Bienefeld as a consequence of employers placing more importance upon maintaining the long working day than workers attached to its reduction. In normal times, he argues, workers gave wages higher priority than hours. But at times of

* The campaign to reduce factory hours is discussed in Chapter 6, below.

exceptional union strength, like the early 1870s, money-wage increases were won fairly easily and the unions, with the possibility of imminent unemployment in mind, gave far more attention to shortening the working week.

The unions certainly assumed a more prominent place in attempts to reduce hours after 1850 than they had done earlier. But legislation continued to be important, and the indirect influence of both unions and legislation, in setting examples and preparing the way for change elsewhere, was at least as significant as their direct influence. Many workers gained some reduction in hours in the 1860s as factory regulations were extended beyond the cotton and woollen mills, and the Coal Mines Act of 1872 limiting boys (up to sixteen years) to ten hours work a day and fifty-four hours a week was in many places the occasion for a general reduction in miners' hours. It was the government too that eventually put limits on the excessively long working day of young shop assistants (1886) and railwaymen (1893). The latter intervention, which sprang more from fears for passenger safety than concern for the railwaymen, was significant in that it was the first direct government regulation of the working hours of grown men, who had always been considered capable of looking after themselves. The granting of an eight-hour day to underground colliery workers in 1908 was another early example of this kind. In South Wales and some other fields the act of 1908 brought a substantial reduction in the working day. But the Northumberland and Durham hewers, who had long worked less than eight hours, walked out on the day the act became law. The government, and local government, also influenced hours of work by being prominent among the more enlightened employers who kept working conditions well ahead of statutory requirements: much of the Admiralty labour force, the men at Woolwich Arsenal, most municipal gas workers, all those employed by 'independent labour'-administered West Ham, and many other public sector workers had an eight-hour day by the end of the century.

The factory acts of 1850 and 1853 which set the mill week at sixty hours and stopped the engines at 2 p.m. on Saturday had a special significance. The short Saturday was by no means unknown before this, especially in the textile towns of Lancashire and west Scotland. There were, moreover, those workers, miners and domestic workers especially, who observed Saint Monday and thus worked only five days each week. For some of these the introduction of a Saturday half day was combined with a new insistence that they be present on Mondays, and in such cases there was no gain so far as working hours were concerned. But most factory workers, and a great many non-factory workers, had worked a full six-day week and for these the Saturday half day was a welcome change in working arrangements. The statutory establishment of a short Saturday in the textile mills set the scene for its more widespread adoption: in the 1850s and 1860s it was spreading through the building trades and to those occupations coming within the ambit of the factory acts. Many other occupations came to enjoy the five and half day week in the following decade and although some had to wait far longer – most shop assistants, for example, and farm labourers – the great majority of industrial workers had it by 1880. By the time of the Royal Commission on Labour (1891–4) workers of any kind who worked a full six days were in a minority.

That the French labelled the short week '*la semaine anglaise*' is indication enough that the same could not be said of workers there. Nor could it have been said of workers elsewhere on the continent. Working hours in Europe, in fact, were generally in excess of those in Britain and had been throughout the century. A report of 1833, for example, gave the average weekly hours in cotton mills as 69 in England, 72–84 in France and Switzerland, and 72–90 in Prussia.[58] Forty years later two English factory inspectors, Alexander and Jasper Redgrave, visited France and Belgium and commented repeatedly on the very rudimentary legal limitations to hours of work there and the long working day.[59] Lancashire cotton workers hesitated to demand further reductions of hours in the 1890s from fear of giving too much advantage to Germany 'where they worked between 60 and 70 hours', and in the following decade a Board of Trade enquiry (1905) showed again the British workers' advantage.[60]

The Saturday half day and the Bank Holiday Act of 1871 – another case of government intervention in working hours – were essential ingredients in the great expansion and enrichment of working-class leisure that occurred in the last quarter of the century. Cheaper transport played a part too: the excursion trains, trams (horse-drawn and later electric. Richard Hoggart's 'gondolas of the people'), bicycles, and the London Underground. The changes may be traced in a variety of spheres – organized sport, football in particular, was one of the most important. Football of a kind had been played for centuries, but the game that we know today with its competitions, mass following and standardized rules is not much more than a century old. Until the 1870s football was dominated by gentlemen amateurs from London and the Home Counties. Working-class participation, as players and as spectators, grew first in Lancashire where the Saturday holiday had made most headway. By 1890 the game had been taken over by the industrial north and midlands. No northern or midland team had won the F.A. Cup before 1883: that year's final between the Old Etonians and the plebeian Blackburn Olympic (whose team included five mill workers) was therefore a symbolic occasion and Blackburn's winning goal was a small watershed in working-class history. Between then and the First World War the cup only once went to a club from south of Birmingham.[61]

There was a similar northwards expansion of the seaside industry, due largely to greater numbers of working-class people having the time and means to visit the coast. The majority of working-class visitors to the coast were on excursions, but some were taking an annual holiday. The beginnings of the working-class holiday are as obscure as the beginnings of the short Saturday. In pre-industrial England apprentices and domestic servants periodically returned to their parents, there was much general visiting to friends and relatives, and there were holidays of a kind in the hayfields and hopfields and at times of slack trade, particularly around Christmas. But the annual family holiday away from home was almost entirely confined to the middle and upper classes until the third quarter of the nineteenth century. Working-class holiday-making of this kind began first among the workers of those same northern industrial towns that pioneered the Saturday half day and working-class football. Their favourite destinations were the nearby coasts, especially Blackpool. By the end of the century holiday-making had spread more widely among the working classes: Charles Booth quoted London witnesses to the effect that holiday-making among all classes was 'one of the most remarkable changes in habits in the last ten years'.[62] So accepted had the practice become that there were a number of charities devoted to providing holidays for the needy. An early twentieth-century survey of poverty in Edinburgh, for example, noted the activities of the 'Mothers' Rest Organization', the 'Holiday House', and the 'Children's Holiday Fund'.[63] Charity was necessary partly because few among the working classes, and especially among the poorer of them, were paid for the time they took in holidays. Some enlightened employers like Levers and Brunner Mond, some of the railway companies and larger shops, and a number of municipal authorities (including West Ham), gave holidays with pay, but in 1914 such employers were still the exception. Holiday-making, that is, should be regarded not as part of the non-monetary increases in working-class incomes so much as one of the ways in which workers disposed of their increased real wages.

Diet

The most significant changes in working-class consumption were those affecting what there was to eat. Before 1850 approaching three-quarters of all wages went on food and the proportion was still over 50 per cent on the eve of the First World War. There were, of course, enormous variations in diet that owed little or nothing to long-term movements in real wages: those, for example, that reflected occupational wage differences or the relative prosperity and dietary eccentricity of particular areas. The size and earnings of a workman's family also affected diet and we noted earlier a weekly cycle in which less and worse food was eaten as pay-day approached. To avoid problems of this sort we will confine our attention initially to the long-term experience of farm labourers in southern England – it must be borne in mind

81

that they ate far less well than most workers and spent a greater part of their wages upon food. Robert Crick, a Suffolk man with five children, will serve to illustrate their general position in the 1840s:

Table 3·2   *Weekly budget of Robert Crick, farm labourer, Lavenham, Suffolk, c. 1842*

	Earnings		Expenditure
Robert Crick (42 yrs)	9s 0d	Bread	9s 0d
Wife (40 ,,)	9d	Potatoes	1s 0d
Boy (12 ,,)	2s 0d	Rent	1s 2d
,, (11 ,,)	1s 0d	Tea	2d.
,, (8 ,,)	1s 0d	Sugar	3½d
Girl (6 ,,)	—	Soap	3d
Boy (4 ,,)	—	Blue	½d
		Thread etc.	2d
		Candles	3d
		Salt	½d
		Coal and wood	9d
		Butter	4½d
		Cheese	3d
	13s 9d		13s 9d

Source: *Reports on the Employment of Women and Children in Agriculture,* (*Parl. Papers* XII, 1843), p. 233.

For those in Crick's circumstances the list of purchases would probably have looked much the same at any time in the first half of the century: the main features of his budget resemble those shown in D. Davies's, *The Case of Labourers in Husbandry* (1795) and F. M. Eden's, *The State of the Poor* (1797). There were some gains in the first half of the century – in particular the increasing use of potatoes and reductions in the price of coal and fish brought about by the railways. But there were losses too. The railways were beginning to take milk to the towns, making it dearer at the farm-gate. And there had been a fall in the number that 'lived in' the farmhouse, a change almost certainly to the labourer's disadvantage so far as his stomach was concerned. Also on the debit side must be put increasing adulteration of food and drink. The rural labourer was obviously not the worst affected by this development, but a surprisingly high proportion of his requirements were shop-bought, the more so as he substituted tea, the publican's beer, and ready-made bread for brewing and baking at home. The growing complexity of food supply, difficulties in enforcing traditional controls on manufacture, the increased impatience with controls of any kind, and urbanization, were together responsible for a serious general deterioration in food quality. In this respect 'free trade' had done the working man no good at all. His bread became adulterated with alum, chalk, and other more harmful ingredients, and his beer was polluted with such noxious substances to hide its weakening that those who drunk it were sometimes drugged by additives before the alcohol had a chance to take effect.

The two outstanding features of Robert Crick's budget are, first, that food accounted for as much as 80 per cent of income and, second, that no less than four-fifths of this was spent on bread, enough in fact to buy about 50 lb of bread each week. Farm labourers ate more bread than most, and farm labourers in the south (where fuel was costly) were less likely than were northern workers to bake their own. The southern population, moreover, ate mostly expensive wheaten bread whereas that of northern England, Wales, and Scotland at this time still consumed considerable quantities of oats and other alternatives to wheat.[64] But bread formed an immensely important part in most nineteenth-century working-class budgets – the term 'breadwinner' and prayers for the granting of 'daily bread' once had a far more than symbolic importance. The non-farinaceous food in the Crick diet, in fact, amounted to hardly more than flavouring to help the bread go down. Sweet tea did this with less benefit than the home-made beer it was displacing, but tea had become fashionable from the time when its use was confined to superior classes, and was doubly welcome for bringing warmth to an otherwise cold meal. A third point to be noted in Table 3·2 is the absence of any outlay on meat. In this respect, however, Crick's expenditure may be misleading because it was unusual for even farm labourers to be entirely without meat. It is true that those in the south were lucky if they often tasted fresh meat; the mid-century *Morning Chronicle* survey reported the labourers of north Essex 'strangers to butcher's meat' and Joseph Arch remembered how in his youth fresh meat 'would come like Christmas, once a year'.[65] But most families could afford some bacon, if only at the week-end. Like many other farm labourers Robert Crick probably kept a pig, and he may have fed it, and helped to feed his family, from a cottage garden or rented potato patch. Bacon was highly regarded by the poorest classes because it went further than any other meat; it had no equal for flavouring bread or vegetables, it kept well, was easily prepared, and could be eaten in minute quantities.

In accounts of diets during the 1860s and 1870s some support may be found for those who place the start of the great rise in real wages as early as the 1850s. An annual budget of a Somerset labourer (Table 3·3), published in 1874, is worth recording because it affords some useful comparisons with Robert Crick's budget and provides several insights into the minutiae of rural working-class life.

Table 3·3   *Annual budget of John —, farm labourer, Somerset 1871–2*

Rent	£5 4s 0d	Candles	7s 6d
Poor rates and tithes	9s 0d	Butter	17s 4d
Coal (1 cwt. per week)	£2 12s 0d	Treacle	6s 6d
Shoes and shoe repair	£2 5s 0d	Matches, thread, tape	3s 6d
Bread	£11 14s 0d	Broom and salt	2s 0d
Potato ground rent &		Cups, saucers, plates	1s 8d
potato seed	£3 0s 0d	Schooling for 4 children	17s 4d
Club pay (i.e. insurance)	12s 0d	Tools and tool repairs	£1 18s 1d
Soap	10s 10d	TOTAL EXPENDITURE	£31 13s 9d
Tea	13s 0d	TOTAL EARNINGS	£31 16s 6d

Source: F. G. Heath, *The English Peasantry*, (1874), pp. 41–2.

For these years we also have a Norfolk labourer's own account of how his wage was distributed in the last week of January, 1873 (Table 3·4). He was paid 12s and had, as he put it, 'a wife and three childrin to maintian out of that':

Table 3·4   *Weekly budget of farm labourer,*
Norfolk, January 1873

Coles	1s 9d
Bred	6s 6d
Rent	1s 3d
Close	1s 0d
Baken	4d
Shop	1s 2d

Source: L. M. Springall, *Labouring Life in Norfolk Villages, 1834–1914*, (1936), p. 138.

The absence of milk and meat (other than 'baken') in these two budgets is again significant, but there are also signs consistent with some improvement from the budgets of the 1840s, most notably the smaller proportion of total income spent upon food and, in particular, upon bread. There is corroborative evidence from Joseph Ashby's Tysoe where by the 1870s, it was said, the men more often had a bit of cheese to accompany an onion and more suet puddings with bacon, 'times were not so bad as they had been'.[66] The quantities of the more costly foodstuffs – bacon, fresh meat, and cheese especially – shown in the numerous budgets collected by Dr E. Smith (1863) and Robert Hutchison (1869) are also consistent with some modest improvement in diet during the 1850s and 1860s.[67]

The more marked changes, however, came in the following decades. Here is T. E. Kebbel writing of the farm labourer's diet in 1887:

> He was never so well off as he is now. From Northumberland to Wiltshire, from Essex to Yorkshire, this is the uniform report. . .. A joint of meat weighing six or seven pounds, with a Yorkshire pudding of goodly dimensions underneath it, goes from the cottage to the bakehouse every Sunday . . . . Broiled ham . . . figures on the breakfast table, and reappears at supper. When the labourer's tea is taken out to him in the hayfield by his wife she often carries with it a tin of preserved salmon.[68]

Kebbel's account is probably a little optimistic even for Northumberland and Yorkshire, the more prosperous of the counties he mentions. But that significant progress had occurred there is no doubt at all. A. Wilson Fox, who conducted two official enquiries into farm labourers' conditions early in the twentieth century, compared diets at the time of Dr E. Smith's 1863 survey with those in 1903: the average labourer consumed only two-thirds as much bread and rather less potatoes by 1903; he had one-third as much again of butter and other fats, twice as much sugar and more than twice as much tea; he ate less bacon but far more beef and mutton.[69] Bread and flour accounted for less than a third of all food expenditure in the rural south by this time and an almost equivalent amount was spent on meat.[70]

The budget of a labourer's family at Corsley (Wilts.) for two weeks in January 1906 (Table 3·5) gives a more detailed impression of the changes that had occurred and may be usefully compared with those shown in Tables 3·2 and 3·3 (above).

One change apparent from this budget is the far greater variety of food appearing on the labourer's table: sardines and bloaters, corned beef, tinned milk, rice, Quaker oats, currants and raisins, jam and pickle, cakes, eggs, cocoa, and fresh fruit each appeared rarely or not at all before 1860 but were commonplace by 1900. There were more hot meals and these more often were followed by 'puddings' of one kind or another. What this meant to the labourer can be appreciated by comparing typical Suffolk meals of 1903 (Table 3·6) with those of the kind that might be prepared from the food shown in Robert Crick's budget (Table 3·2).

Table 3·5   *Budget of farm labourer, Corsley,*
Wiltshire, January 1906

Purchases – first week

Tea, ½ lb.	8d	Suet, ¼ lb.	2d
Sugar	7¾d	Baking powder	1d
Butter	1s 10d	Papers	2d
Bacon	1s 4d	Soap, 1 lb.	3d
Quaker oats	5½d	Oranges	2d
Tobacco 2 oz.	6d	Currants, ½ lb.	1½d
Cheese	9d	Beer, 1 pint	2d
Lard ½ lb.	2½d	Coal	1s 2½d
Bread	3s 4½d	Milk	6½d
Oil	2½d	Stockings	6½d
		Total	13s 4¾d

Purchases – second week

Tea, ½lb.	8d	Oranges	3d
Sugar, 3 lb	5½d	Coal 1 cwt.	1s 2½d
Butter, 2 lb	1s 0d	Milk	7d
Bacon, 3 lb.	1s 6d	Flannelette	1s 4¼d
Beef	1s 0d	Matches	1½d
Quaker oats	5½d	Sweets, ¼ lb.	1d
Tobacco	6d	Pepper	1½d
Cheese, 1½ lb.	9d	Biscuits	1d
Lard	2½d	Fish	4d
Bread	2s 6d	Sprats, 2 lb.	2d
Oil	2½d		
			13s 6¾d

In addition rent cost 1s 6d a week, a friendly society
subscription 2s 5d per month, and a rented allotment 5s per
annum. The husband's wage was 15s 0d and there were five
children.

Source: M. F. Davies, *Life in an English Village*, (1909), pp.
196–7.

By late twentieth-century standards these meals lack variety and are not
enticing. They may not have appealed to many people in 1903 either, for
Suffolk labourers ate badly even by contemporary standards.[71] But to those
like Robert Crick and Robert Walker (above pp. 1–3, 82–3) they would
have represented very good eating indeed.

Table 3·6   *Farm labourer's meals, East Suffolk about 1903*

Breakfast: porridge, milk, a little fat pork or bacon, cheese, bread, dripping, tea.

Dinner: boiled pork (sometimes a rabbit), potatoes, cabbage, swedes, turnips or
           other vegetables, boiled rice and treacle or dumplings. On Sunday, beef or
           mutton, vegetables, baked batter pudding, milk pudding or plum pudding
           or fruit pie.

Tea and   bread, butter, cheese, tea, occasionally a meat pudding.
supper:

Source: *Wages, Earnings, and Conditions of Employment of Agricultural Labourers,*
(*Parl. Papers* XCVII 1905), p. 233.

The farm labourers' progress reflected that of the working classes generally. Successful retailers like Liptons and Sainsbury, Chivers the jam manufacturers, and Rowntree's, Cadbury's, and Fry's, purveyors of cocoa to the masses, all grew and flourished on the basis of rising working-class expenditure in the last third of the nineteenth century. Charles Booth noted that the largest groups in his London East End survey (*c.* 1889) expected four meals a day, including meat and vegetables at midday, and that even the poorest classes usually ate at least one meal containing meat, bacon, or fish.[72] By 1906, it has been calculated, the average working-class diet, 'stodgy and monotonous but . . . certainly substantial', provided rather more calories than the statutory rations of the years after 1945.[73] Average meat consumption by this time (1909–13) was as high as the level in the 1950s.[74]

Nevertheless, the diets of farm labourers and many poorly-paid urban workers were still nutritionally inadequate in several respects, as the medical records of Boer War and First World War recruits and several contemporary studies testify.[75] Their diet was restricted not only by their incomes but also by the shortcomings of their wives, whose culinary achievements have often been compared unfavourably with those of thrifty French and German women who were said to do wonders with less promising ingredients.[76] Some country wives did all their cooking on one or two days in the week, and ignorance of the value of different foods was a considerable handicap to adequate nutrition. Consumption of fresh fruit, for example, was held back before 1900 by the conviction (perhaps not entirely unfounded in an age of gastric disorder) that it could easily be harmful, especially to children. A very large part of the additional fruit consumed after 1880 reached the working classes via the jam factory. Wives were not helped, of course, by the rising price of fuel and poor cooking facilities. Many cottages, particularly rural cottages, lacked even a primitive coal oven and cheap gas ovens with penny meters were rare before 1890 even in the towns.

Another problem was that despite the very significant reduction in food adulteration during the second half of the century, the quality of the food consumed by the working classes deteriorated in other ways after 1880.[77] First there was the spread of roller-milling which provided a finer flour and a whiter loaf much esteemed by the consumers. Unfortunately, this was achieved by removing from the flour the dark wheat germ that provides protein, mineral salts, fats, and vitamins. The danger was quickly appreciated and there were attempts to supply an equally palatable wholemeal loaf. But most of the working classes – oblivious to the blandishments of Hovis, Daren, and the rest – preferred their bread with the most nutritious part removed. Second, margarine was introduced and partly substituted for butter. At first margarine was made from beef fat, but in time it came to be composed increasingly of vegetable oils deficient in vitamins. The last of this trio of retrogressive technical advances was canned condensed and skimmed milk which was cheaper than fresh milk, easier to store, and gave children no protection against rickets.

Housing

Rent was next in importance to food in the working-class budget. But whereas food prices fell in the second half of the century, rents increased, and improvement in working-class housing was less impressive than that in diet and real wages. There is no easy way of representing long-term changes in the overall quality of working-class housing. There is, from 1801, an index of numbers of persons per house, but its value is very limited because the average number per house was never much above average family size. Discussion of housing standards is complicated also by the enormous variation in house design and in housing standards throughout the country.

For the moment, therefore, we will concentrate upon housing in England and Wales up to the middle of the century. Most unskilled town workers had a house to themselves with their own door opening on to a street or courtyard. Tenements, or 'flats', of the kind that accommodated the poor in many European cities were less common in England. The most typical town house was of two stories with a modest cellar for coal and lumber. It was built of brick, roofed with slate, and stood among numerous similar houses in a terrace or court. In Leeds, Liverpool, Nottingham, Birmingham, and other northern and midland cities it could well have been a 'back to back'. Inside there was likely to be one sizable living-room, or perhaps two smaller rooms, floored with brick or flags. There might be a kitchen also and upstairs two, or perhaps three, bedrooms. Houses with three bedrooms and those where the family was small or impoverished in many cases accommodated one or more lodgers besides the family. There was not likely to be much of a garden and 'back to backs' lacked even a yard of their own for storage and drying clothes. The lavatory, if there was one, was outside. Many poor families had a lavatory for their exclusive use, others shared with neighbours and this was the general rule in the early 'back to backs'. Sharing generally involved no more than one or two other households but the sanitary reports of the 1840s cite numerous instances of lavatories that served a dozen or more families. The lavatory was unlikely to contain a water closet. Before the 1840s, in fact, very few houses of the poorer classes were supplied even with water for drinking. Water came from a communal standpipe or, less generally, from a pump or well, and it might be available for only a few hours each day when women and children queued to fill all the buckets and basins they could lay hands upon.

A great deal of this town housing was relatively new, especially in the fast-growing industrial towns. Newness was no guarantee of good repair or sound construction, but housing of the kind described here was generally better than surviving cottages from the seventeenth and eighteenth centuries or the dilapidated and divided houses once occupied by the middle classes. Typical rents were of the order of 1s 9d to 3s 6d a week, or between 10 and 25 per cent of an unskilled town worker's wage. It is not known for certain whether rent took a greater part of incomes over the course of the first half of the century, but given the press of population upon land in the towns, and the absence of either considerable rises in unskilled wages or falls in the cost of building, a rise seems likely. We may be reasonably certain that there were very few places where the burden of rent significantly fell.[78]

The average artisan paid more for his accommodation than labourers paid, but rent accounted for a smaller part of his income and his wage was more likely than the labourer's to have kept pace with any increase in rent during the first half of the century. Artisans were more frequently found occupying the newest housing on the outskirts of towns, they moved house less often than unskilled workers, and in some places a sizable minority owned their own homes. At Leeds and in other northern towns artisans sometimes built a pair of adjoining 'back to backs', occupied one themselves, and paid off their mortgage with the help of rent from the other. A 'back to back' in Sheffield, with one proper bedroom and an attic bedroom, cost only £60–75 to buy outright at mid-century, no more than a skilled man earned in a year.[79] As a rule, however, artisans were found in the better sort of four- or five-roomed terrace house with a garden behind it and something more than a step between the front door and the road. Their front door opened upon a hall of some kind, and most had a separate kitchen, a main living-room, and a parlour reserved for Sunday-best, for family reunions, laying out corpses, and similar important occasions. An under-used parlour was the surest hallmark of working-class gentility. The lavatory at the back was for the family's exclusive

89

use and there was a fair chance by the 1840s that a house of this kind would have an inside water tap. A few, but very few, had flushing water closets.

Country labourers at this time were very unlikely to have been acquainted with flushing water closets or even with piped water. If, as some claim, they were better housed than town labourers it was certainly not by much. The conventional view of typical farm labourers' housing has been much distorted by middle-class romanticizing about their rose-clad thatched cottages and lives of fulfilling toil and simple pleasures. Their main advantage of course, as we noted in Chapter 2, was uncrowded surroundings. They had no piped water, but there were fewer neighbours to pollute their wells and country cottages had space for a barrel to collect rain-water. There was enough space too for most cottages to have a lavatory of their own and for a garden. Moreover, there was the great advantage of low rents: Robert Crick (above p. 82) who paid in rent 1s 2d a week in 1842, or about 12½ per cent of his wage, was not untypical. Against all this there were two great disadvantages. First, space indoors. Contemporary reports suggest that the average town labourer's house was larger than the rural labourer's cottage and the rural labourer, of course, was likely to have more surviving children to accommodate. Concern about the moral consequences of husband, wife, adolescents, and younger children of both sexes sharing one or two bedrooms (and in many cases only one or two beds) is a recurring theme in nineteenth-century inquiries on rural housing. Secondly, there was the condition of the building itself. The average cottage was older than most town houses, probably in worse repair, and it was likely to contain more of the features that early-Victorian builders had for the most part learnt to avoid – low ceilings, tiny windows, and floors of pounded earth that were impossible to clean. The countryside had more houses of wattle and daub and other inferior substitutes for brick and stone, and their picturesque thatched roofs let in rain and harboured vermin. Shortly after Joseph Arch inherited his father's cottage in 1862 he replaced its thatch with slate.[80]

There were numerous exceptions to these typical housing patterns of the first half of the century, only the more important of which can be mentioned here. The main exceptions to what has been said of rural housing were, first, the rural slums that developed in parishes adjacent to those where landlords restricted building in order to reduce the number of inhabitants with a claim on the poor rates. This practice was found most in parishes dominated by a small number of substantial landowners. Labourers might have to walk several miles to work in these 'closed' parishes from the neighbouring 'open' parishes which were distinguished by exceptional overcrowding, high rents, and high poor rates. Second, there were the model cottages built for farm labourers by enthusiastic and philanthropic landlords such as those erected on the estates of the Duke of Bedford. There were model houses for industrial workers too, many of them in rural areas to which industry had been directed by water-power or some other advantage and where company housing was necessary to attract labour. At Egerton (Lancs.) the Ashworths built a complete village. Most of their houses had three or four bedrooms, a living-room, kitchen, pantry, a walled backyard with a lavatory to themselves, and (from 1835) piped water.[81] Saltaire, perhaps the best-known model industrial community, was begun in 1851 amid pleasant surroundings on the River Aire because the enterprising Titus Salt (Congregationalist and Bradford wool manufacturer) saw it as his duty to provide labour with decent accommodation. His houses each had a kitchen, scullery, pantry, cellar, their own gas and water supply, and at least three bedrooms.[82] Among other well-known examples of model industrial housing are the fine Wedgwood cottages (£7 10s per annum plus rates, stuffed with handsome furniture and eight-day clocks) that so delighted the *Morning Chronicle* investigator in 1850,[83] and the accommodation erected by railway companies at Swindon, Crewe, and elsewhere. Housing of this kind was unlikely to provide much direct return on capital. The main returns came indirectly; there was satisfaction in fulfilling a christian duty, and the unquantifiable but possibly substantial benefits that accrued from contented and co-operative employees.

These happy consequences of perceived mutual advantage were far less evident on the coalfields. Here too there was a great variety of standards: some colliery housing was very good indeed, but there was a considerable amount that was exceedingly bad. Why was this? In the first place colliery housing was erected in a hurry because when a pit was sunk men were needed at once.[84] And although pits were generally in rural districts, so that space for housing might appear to present no problems, the necessity for every man to begin and end the day at the same place made it convenient as well as cheaper to crowd them into terraces around the pit-head. Some employers made married tenants take a single miner as a lodger. Building standards were affected also by the transient nature of mine operations. Some colliery land was held upon leases too short to encourage sound building, there was always a danger of subsidence or of housing made suddenly worthless by a flooding of the pit, a major accident, a crippling strike, or simply by exhaustion of the best seams. The miners for their part, when deciding how much they could set aside for rent, were influenced by the enormous fluctuations in their pay. They considered a 'reasonable' rent to be one they could afford when times were bad; thus their accommodation fell far below what might be expected for such a comparatively well-paid occupation. But these extenuating circumstances are not the whole story. Too many owners were neglectful of what Titus Salt would have called their christian duty, too ready to put immediate profits above the health and comfort of their workers, and too slow to see that decent housing and reasonable long-run profits were not incompatible. And too many miners, and their wives, accepted standards of accommodation and cleanliness far worse than the average in Britain and far worse than they could afford: 'The earnings of these men were, at the time of my visit, probably greater then those of any equally large body of workmen in the kingdom', wrote a school inspector in South Staffordshire in 1846, 'These men and their families, nevertheless, live in more squalid and miserably dirty and worse-furnished abodes . . . than I have observed in respect to any other labouring population.'[85]

There was some exceptionally bad housing also in the crowded and expensive centres of most large cities. Part of the city centre problem was competition for scarce land from commercial and industrial undertakings that pushed up rents. Another part was the large amount of casual work to be had there: casual workers, like the miners, were inclined to take worse accommodation than they could have afforded from their average earnings. Moreover, their need to be on call when work became available prevented them from living in the better, and cheaper, suburban houses. In a number of towns there were also pockets of handloom weavers, framework knitters, and other impoverished remnants of once prosperous trades. Men from rural districts in search of work, the unemployed and the unemployable from smaller towns up and down the country, and refugees from Ireland's Malthusian crisis all flocked to the centres of the larger cities, adding to the pressure on crowded accommodation. This shifting population occupied the worst urban accommodation: the crumbling tenements, cheap lodging-houses, and the damp, ill-ventilated, fever-ridden cellars.

Exceptionally poor and overcrowded housing of this kind could be found in almost every town, especially at times of severe unemployment when families might move to cheaper accommodation or share their house with another family, 'huddling' as this was called. But in most places, including many of the larger towns, the number in this category was not great. It was said of mid-century Sheffield for example that 'it is the custom for each family among the labouring population to occupy a separate dwelling, the rooms in which are furnished in a very comfortable manner'.[86] Similar claims were made for Birmingham and Leicester at this time, and for Bradford 'except among the Irish'.[87] The same could not be said of Nottingham with its framework knitters and the unenclosed common-fields that prevented building on the town boundary before the 1840s, nor of Leeds, and certainly not of Manchester with its 'Little Ireland' and 20,000 inhabited cellars (1832). But the two greatest concentrations of bad housing in England were London and Liverpool. Numbers per house in London increased from 7.03 in 1801 (when the average for England and Wales was 5.6) to 7.72 in 1851; in Liverpool there was a rise from 6.78 to 7.32.[88] Neither town had a major factory industry to provide high wages and relatively steady employment, both were ports and commercial centres with a great deal of casual employment. London, with its riches and reputation, was the destination of numerous migrants and so was Liverpool because of its accessibility from Ireland. A tenth or more of Liverpool's population lived in cellars in the 1840s and another 10 per cent in lodging-houses.[89] London, where rents were well above the level in any other city, had two special difficulties: its size, which was an effective bar to workmen walking in from the suburbs, and the unparalleled commercial competition for space at the centre.

The worst housing in Glasgow and Edinburgh was as bad as anything south of the border. These two cities felt some of the same pressures as affected London and Liverpool, but their housing – particularly the number of one- and two-room tenements of the European kind – reflected also a generally lower standard that was evident in every Scottish town.[90] And not just in the towns: Scottish colliery housing, especially in the west, was exceptionally bad even by coalfield standards and so was the housing of the Scottish agricultural population. One-room rural cottages, cottages without ceilings or proper floors, and cottages where the family was barely separated from horses and cattle were all more common north of the Tweed. The lowland 'bothies' – spartan, barrack-like, farm accommodation for single men – were another feature of Scottish rural housing. There were at least three main reasons for Scotland's poorer housing. First, relative to its population Scotland had more Irish immigrants than England and Wales. Second, the Highlands suffered a demographic crisis not dissimilar to that in Ireland and there was a consequent flight of impoverished migrants to the towns. Third, for long before the nineteenth century Scotland had been decidedly poorer than England. Incomes were no longer so clearly below English levels after 1800, but earlier poverty was still reflected in poorer housing and a preference for low rents over better accommodation. These characteristics were also evident for some distance on the English side of the border: housing conditions in Newcastle, South Shields, and Gateshead were distinctly worse than those in most other English provincial towns.

Whether or not there was any general improvement in working-class housing during the first half of the century is as indeterminable as most other aspects of the standard of living debate. In the war years before 1815 interest rates were high, timber was scarce, and there may well have been a general fall in standards. Before 1800 there had been fewer 'back to backs', not nearly so many inhabited cellars, and less sharing with lodgers. In certain places, including London and Liverpool, conditions for the majority probably deteriorated up to the 1840s. On the other hand a number of local studies have reached tentatively optimistic conclusions: in Nottingham for example numbers per house fell from 5.7 in 1801 to 4.1 in 1841, despite the city's peculiar disadvantages (above p. 92), and a probable 'striking advance' has been claimed. Optimistic claims have been advanced also for Leeds and Sheffield.[91] And in most places, including those where housing had earlier deteriorated, growing awareness of the links between crowding, dirt, and disease, and the early public health campaign (above pp. 50–1) brought certain improvements in the urban environment before 1850. Several towns had forbidden the occupation of cellars and Manchester (in 1844) had put an end to building 'back to backs'. Liverpool was a pioneer in housing reform as in other aspects of public health: between 1842 and 1850 it introduced regulations covering the amount of space around new buildings and the dimensions of rooms and windows; it required courtyards to be paved and drained and each new house built around a courtyard to have its own lavatory.[92]

In the following half-century working-class housing definitely improved. Lord Shaftesbury, near the end of a lifetime devoted to helping the poor, spoke in the 1880s of the 'enormous' improvement during the previous thirty years.[93] Not long after this, 'overcrowding', defined as more than two to a room, was first recorded in the census. The proportion of the population 'overcrowded' was 11.2 per cent in 1891, 8.2 per cent in 1901, and 7.8 per cent by 1911, by which date four-fifths of families of three persons or more occupied at least four rooms.[94] Most urban houses had gas lighting by the end of the century, many had a gas cooker too and the spread of piped water – four-fifths of Manchester houses had their own tap by 1876 – had brought a proliferation of sinks and sculleries. A few working-class houses were already being built with bathrooms and hot water systems.[95] There were still numerous shared lavatories, but each house erected after 1875 was required to have its own, and by 1911 about half of all towns in England and Wales could boast that 96 per cent or more of their lavatories were of the water closet kind.[96] A few towns, including Liverpool, were already 'largely water-closeted' in the 1880s.[97] The worse lodging-houses had been forced to close long before this and those authorities that had not already barred inhabited cellars and the building of 'back to backs' were brought into line in 1909.[98] Another notable development towards the end of the century had been the great expansion of working-class commuting by tram (and in London by train also) which made possible far more building on cheap suburban land. The rural population did not benefit so much from sanitary reform and falling agricultural rents after 1873 diminished landlords' enthusiasm for building model cottages. But the 1865 Union Chargeability Act removed the greatest incentive to create 'closed' parishes (above, p. 90 and below p. 140), and the drift of labourers to the towns eased pressure on existing housing stock and also helped to maintain employers' interest in its improvement.[99]

There is no doubt that English working-class housing compared well with most housing in Europe. Rowntree found little to choose between English and

Belgian housing but drew attention to the contrast between the proportion of one-room dwellings in Berlin (44 per cent), Stockholm (49 per cent), and Oslo (37 per cent) and the far lower proportion in London (18 per cent).[100] European rooms were generally rather larger than English rooms, but whereas the English census defined overcrowding as more than two to a room, in Austria and several German cities 'overcrowding' was considered as beginning only when a room was occupied by more than five. Even so, at the end of the century no less than one-fifth of the Viennese and 17.5 per cent of the population of Breslau fell within their own definition of overcrowding.[101] Breslau still had 15,000 cellar-dwellers and three-quarters of French families in those towns investigated by the Board of Trade in 1909 had fewer than four rooms.[102] That the initials 'WC' were understood throughout Europe is evidence of Britain's lead in sanitary standards, and American sanitary-ware manufacturers, when attempting to win a little of their home market in the 1870s, found it necessary to emblazon their products with a lion and unicorn and the legend 'Best Stafford Earthenware'.[103]

Despite all this there was much concern about housing towards the end of the century. When the rate of housing progress is compared with achievements in other aspects of working-class welfare it is not really difficult to understand why contemporaries were concerned. Moreover, progress had been dearly bought. Rents rose steadily, they rose faster than could be explained by improvements in accommodation and they continued to rise through the long period of falling prices after 1873. Between 1845 and 1910 urban rents rose by about 85 per cent; food and raw material prices, by contrast, were a little lower in 1910 than they had been in 1845.[104] Not all rents increased at this rate. In rural districts rents hardly rose at all, but the level of rural rents was of diminishing relative importance as more and more people lived in the towns. The worst housing was still to be found in Scotland, on the coalfields, and in the larger English and Welsh towns. And the obstacles to improvement, by and large, were still those described earlier although by 1900 Scotland's poorer housing could no longer so plausibly be regarded as the expected consequence of recent poverty (above, p. 93). Glasgow's overcrowding approached that in the great cities of Europe. Over half of Glaswegians were 'overcrowded' in 1901, measured by English standards, and ten years later the figure was somewhat higher.[105] Colliery housing remained comparatively neglected by housing reformers until the infant mortality campaign early in the twentieth century. It was less often the subject of local legislation than housing in the great cities, less visited by sanitary inspectors, and more under pressure from in-migration and a high birth-rate. Provision of piped water, gas, and water-borne sewage disposal to relatively isolated colliery settlements was comparatively expensive and so the miners (like the farm labourers) benefited less than urban workers from such developments.

Several provincial English cities still struggled with formidable difficulties in the second half of the century, but they struggled with increasing success. In 1892 Liverpool and Manchester both returned lower rates of 'overcrowding' than the average. London experienced no such relief and as the northern cities came to grips with their problems attention focused on the capital. There had been some progress in London too, of course, but it was not much in evidence in the poorest quarters near the centre. The chief difficulties remained London's size and the great commercial demand for land and buildings that pushed up rents. Trams and workmen's trains helped eventually, but until the 1880s the railways' influence was probably on the debit side because most of the 75,000 or more 'dishoused' by railway building in the second half of the century were working-class Londoners.[106] By the 1890s a room near the centre cost upwards of 4s a week and rent was taking more than one-fifth of income in about 85 per cent of London working-class families.[107] London was distinguished too by its ubiquitous lodgers, by towering blocks of flats – still a rare sight in provincial England in 1914 – and, of course, by overcrowding. In 1891 overcrowding in London (19.7 per cent) was almost double the England and Wales average (11.2 per cent). In Finsbury over half the population was 'overcrowded', and in several central districts the average number of persons to each house increased at every census between 1841 and 1881.[108]

It was of London therefore that most was heard in the 1880s when deepening economic depression, increasing crowding, and Andrew Mearns's *Bitter Cry of Outcast London* (1883) stirred middle-class consciences and re-awakened fears of the association between slums, crime, disease, and disorder. This new interest in working-class housing was distinguished also in three other ways: first, improved housing was now seen as an end in itself and not primarily as a means to contain disease; second, there was a growing inclination to emphasize poverty among the causes of bad housing; and third, doubts were increasingly voiced concerning the appropriateness of what was being done to remedy the situation. Regulation of private building was commonplace by this time, but there had been very little building by local authorities and virtually no interference with market-determined rents. One aspect of the change in attitudes evident in the 1880s was a new willingness to consider government intervention of this kind. Another was the spreading realization that building regulation could easily raise the rents of new housing to levels beyond what the poor were prepared to pay, and that when sanitary inspectors closed unfit accommodation they tended to intensify overcrowding and insanitariness in adjacent houses. For some time, in fact, the great slum clearances and street improvements that featured prominently in city housing policy after 1875 had probably done as much harm as good because the authorities had in many places simply demolished housing with no thought of replacement.[109] And where demolished housing had been replaced the new building often incorporated all that was considered desirable in the way of minimum standards and thus was rented out at far more than those who had been displaced were accustomed to paying. In these circumstances 'improvements' could easily result in slums being replaced with fine housing for the artisan and lower middle classes at the expense of those who had inhabited the slums and of the adjacent slum areas to which they dispersed.

The chief attempt of private philanthropy to provide a solution to the housing problem was the model dwellings movement. This movement began in the 1840s and had its heyday between 1860 and 1890. It was most active in London, and some of its tangible achievements (the blocks of flats erected by Waterlow, Peabody, and the rest) can still be seen in and around the city centre. Model dwelling companies took various forms. Some aspired merely to accommodating well-paid artisans. But most were more ambitious and their importance lies in their attempt to demonstrate the feasibility of housing the poorer classes of London, decently and at a profit, by providing 'models' that speculative builders might be eager to imitate. Their flats showed how to economize on expensive city centre land without causing overcrowding and their accommodation was good by the standards of the time. By 1905 the nine largest associations housed 123,000 people.[110] But in two important respects they failed to achieve their main ambitions. First, their returns on capital were not sufficient to make similar ventures attractive to speculative builders; second, such modest financial success as they achieved was not derived primarily from housing the poorer classes. Even those companies that kept standards to a minimum found that they had to charge more than most low-wage tenants were prepared to pay. Clerks, artisans, policemen, and the like comprised at least half their tenants. Those of lower occupational status were the more sober and steady of their kind – those, that is, who attached most importance to decent accommodation and who were not disposed to quarrel with irksome regulations about noise, cleanliness, and taking in others' washing. Some of the poor were repelled by regulations such as these and by the barrack-like exteriors and awesome dimensions of the buildings.

Among the other attempts to improve working-class housing in the second half of the century were those of the building societies, employers' tied housing, and local authority building. Rowntree found 6 per cent of working-class houses in York owned by their occupiers in 1899[111] and in places more prosperous than York – the cotton towns for example and parts of artisan London – the proportion was higher.[112] Woolwich Arsenal workers were well represented among the leaseholders who occupied a third of Plumstead houses in 1887 and in 1873 they had demonstrated against the poor rate burden on house owners.[113] But building societies obviously could do little to ease the worse housing problems because owner-occupancy required good wages and a steady job. There was also some excellent tied housing erected in the second half of the century, including that at William Lever's Port Sunlight (begun 1888) and Cadbury's Bournville (1890s). But these latter-day Saltaires, splendid as they were, accommodated only a tiny proportion of the working-class population. And subsidized local authority building, which was eventually to play a very important part in providing working-class housing, made little progress before 1914. The 1890 Housing of the Working Classes Act which required local authorities to clear slum housing and rebuild, increased the tempo of local authority activity, but in 1914 London and Glasgow, two of the most active authorities, housed fewer than 2 per cent of their populations.[114] The main contributions to the slight easing of London's housing crisis between 1890 and the war were increased working-class commuting, the great (private) house-building boom that commenced in the mid-1890s, and (after 1900) reduced in-migration, increased emigration, and the falling birth-rate.

The whole housing problem, it is worth noting, was one that perhaps worried the middle classes more than the workers. It was middle-class reformers who began to talk of a housing crisis in the 1880s; workers themselves appear to have been remarkably indifferent to the 'problem' until after 1900.[115] And while there were some workers everywhere, and a great many in rural districts and in central London, whose wages were simply insufficient to pay for reasonable accommodation, there were many others whose accommodation failed to satisfy middle-class expectations partly because middle-class priorities and working-class priorities were different. The Royal Commission on the Housing of the Working Classes (1884–5) drew attention to 'the inability of the workmen to appreciate the comforts of better dwellings',[116] and a colliery manager giving evidence to the Royal Commission on Labour in 1892 claimed that Lanarkshire employers who offered well-paid miners nothing smaller than two-room cottages had difficulty recruiting labour. He also claimed that one company had reluctantly built single-room cottages after finding that families in its two-room cottages (renting for only 2s to 3s a week) were moving into one room and sub-letting the other.[117]

Perhaps the most fundamental obstacle to better working-class housing was one that is often overlooked: low productivity in the building industry. As one percipient contemporary observed, what the building industry needed was an Arkwright. Sadly, it did not find one. Building was not entirely by-passed by the industrial revolution: cheap window glass and iron piping, powered sawing, and the fall in transport costs that brought cheaper imported raw materials and access to suburban land all helped to offset rising land prices and rising building wages. But these benefits were mainly peripheral: the overall increase in building productivity – some 17 per cent between 1850 and

1910 – was very low indeed.[118] So neither costs nor rents fell, and so far as workers' homes were concerned the evidence of half a century of rising living standards was to be seen less in the house itself than in its far more abundant and comfortable contents: in the curtains, clocks, pictures, and ornaments commonplace in ordinary working-class houses by the end of the century, and in the papered parlour, stuffed sofas and chairs, sewing machines, and pianos of the better-paid.

VI · *Wage differentials – occupational, spatial, sex, and international differentials*

Wage differentials of one kind or another have already been sufficiently mentioned to demonstrate the great variety in working-class living standards. The extent and causes of wage differentials can now be examined more systematically.

Workers were probably most conscious of the differentials which distinguished their occupations from others. The great difference was between the unskilled workers and the craftsmen. 'In passing from the skilled operative of the West End to the unskilled workman of the eastern quarter of London', wrote Mayhew, 'the moral and intellectual change is so great that it seems as if we were in a new land and among another race.'[119] But this dichotomy is itself a gross simplification. There was great diversity within the craft and labour categories. And there was far more between them than Mayhew's words imply – the cab-driver who carried Mayhew to the East End, for example, and numerous other 'semi-skilled' workers. Among labourers the navvy held pride of place and most kinds of specialist labourers, coal-porters for example, were paid more than general labourers. Any labourer who worked alongside a craftsman acquired thereby a little of the craftsman's status, including greater job security, and a small differential in pay. Thus an engineer's labourer ranked above a bricklayer's labourer and both were inclined to regard unattached labourers in the same condescending way that a duke's scullery maid might regard one who scrubbed in a middle-class kitchen. The *Morning Chronicle*, where Mayhew made his distinctions between artisans and the unskilled, recorded the wages of various workmen in a South Wales ironworks in 1850: labourers were paid 10s 6d a week, puddlers' labourers were paid 11s, the puddlers themselves nearly twice this, and those who rolled the iron as much as 40s or 50s.[120] The enormous gap between the puddler and his assistant was not exceptional – most labourers received only between 50 and 70 per cent of the craftsman's rate. In the building industry, for example, craftsmen were paid about half as much again as their labourers, and this ratio had prevailed for over four centuries.[121] Differentials like these were the cause of another differential noted by Rowntree at the end of the century: at thirteen years the sons of the poorest workers at York were three and half inches shorter and 11 lb lighter than the sons of labour aristocrats.[122]

For much of the nineteenth century, especially between 1840 and 1880, there was a slight increase in the craftsmen's differential.[123] This trend ceased well before the 1914–18 war and in some trades had begun to be reversed: average unskilled building rates, as a proportion of skilled rates, were 64 per cent in 1885, 67 per cent in 1913, 75 per cent before the end of the First World War, and 85 per cent in 1954.[124] The persistence of wide occupational differentials before 1914, and their long-term stability, reflect both the abundance of unskilled labour and the enormous influence of custom in the labour market. Craft trade unions also helped to maintain differentials. The subsequent erosion of differentials was due to several causes: there was the growth of semi-skilled work that blurred the divisions between the labour aristocracy and the unskilled; at the same time education was equipping more to enter the better-paid jobs, and after 1890 family limitation and trade unionism were spreading downwards into the unskilled classes. A growing egalitarian sentiment, of which the Fair Wages Resolution of 1891 and the Trade Boards Act of 1909 were evidence, worked in the same direction. After 1914 wartime inflation, with 'across the board' cost of living increases, tended to freeze customary differentials in money terms and thus greatly reduced their relative importance.

The differential between working-class incomes and those of the professional classes was greater before 1914 than it has since become. Civil servants of executive grade, for example, were paid two and a half times as much as post office engineers in 1879: in 1950 they received only 50 per cent more.[125] However, the difference between working-class incomes and lower middle-class incomes was not great. Three hundred pounds a year was often mentioned as the smallest sum necessary to support middle-class standards in the middle decades of the century, but relatively few white-collar workers even approached this amount.[126] Clerks, teachers, curates and, in fact, the greater part of all the 'middle classes', kept up appearances on salaries that were about the same as, or not much above, the earnings of skilled workmen.[127] It was the supposed iniquity of being paid no more than those they regarded as inferiors that featured most prominently among the grievances of Liverpool clerks.[128] The difference between average middle-class incomes and average working-class incomes, like that between the incomes of skilled and unskilled workmen, was probably increasing gradually for much of the time before 1880. In the third quarter of the century particularly, it has been argued, 'the whole scale of income distribution was being stretched'.[129] The proportionate increase in the number of domestic servants is also often cited as evidence of growing middle-class affluence.[130] By 1880, however, and in the case of the lower middle classes perhaps well before 1880, middle-class differentials were under pressure. After a respite between 1900 and 1914 this pressure increased. Routh has shown how civil service pay rose less than average between 1875 and 1950 and describes a 'pronounced depreciation of clerical labour in terms of manual or technical labour'.[131] The more affluent of the middle classes felt this pressure particularly: many senior civil service salaries actually fell in real terms between these dates. White-collar differentials were eroded by mass education, which increased the supply of clerical workers, and by trade unionism. In the twentieth century these influences were reinforced by inflation and increasingly progressive taxes upon income.

Another important differential, although one of which workmen were less conscious, was in wages paid for the same work in different places. There were remarkable variations of prosperity within nineteenth-century Britain. Between the highest and the lowest wage districts the difference in wage rates was as great as the difference between average British wages and average United States wages.[132] The wretched southern farm labourers, for example, demanding 2s or 2s 6d a day during the Swing riots of 1830 were asking for no more than was actually paid to farm labourers around Manchester. Twenty years later James Caird noted that Dorset labourers were still paid only half the Lancashire rate. The same kind of comparisons could be made for most occupations: the official rates recognized by the Amalgamated Society of Carpenters and Joiners in 1908 varied from $4\frac{7}{8}$d per hour in Falmouth to $10\frac{1}{2}$d per hour in London.[133] These differences were not offset by compensating differences in the cost of living: there were some spatial price differences but for the most part the cost of living was not noticeably higher in high-wage towns and it did not vary much between high-wage and low-wage rural districts. Money-wage differentials, that is, were generally reflected in standard of living differentials. Caird, around mid-century, noted that in the north 'the labourers are enabled to feed and clothe themselves with respectability and comfort, while in some of the southern counties their wages are insufficient for their healthy sustenance'.[134] Towards the end of the century an official report described conditions in Northumberland as 'nearly all that an eastern counties labourer ever hoped for in his wildest dreams', and a 1903 enquiry calculated that northern agricultural labourers consumed each week over 40 per cent more meat than labourers in the eastern counties.[135]

This pattern of spatial differentials was not of long standing. It was largely a function of the relationship between industrialization and population growth which had redistributed national income in favour of industrializing areas. In the northern counties, London, and parts of the midlands as far south as Birmingham, most wage-rates were high. But where population growth had not been accompanied by industrialization, wages were low. During the second half of the century South Wales and much of southern and central Scotland joined the high-wage areas and the Black Country, where

101

industrialization had begun early and plant and raw materials by 1870 were nearing exhaustion, suffered a relative decline. There was also some overall reduction in spatial differentials in the second half of the century, although the extent to which differentials persisted until the end of the century was perhaps more remarkable than the reduction that occurred. The erosive influence of labour migration was largely offset by the locational advantages of high-wage centres (capital was not attracted to low-wage labour), by trade unions pushing up wages in the more prosperous areas where their membership was concentrated, and by the continuing high rate of natural increase in those parts where wages were low and labour plentiful. After 1900 the reduction in spatial differentials accelerated – falling fertility reduced population pressure in low-wage areas, the trade unions expanded geographically and became less tolerant of long-standing inequalities and low wage areas had begun to take a greater share of economic activity. During the 1914–18 war across the board cost of living increases eroded spatial differentials, as they eroded most other wage differentials, and after 1920 the collapse of the nineteenth-century staple industries brought about a fundamental change in the regional pattern of demand for labour.

Women had always been paid considerably less than men no matter where they worked. And the sex differential in wages, like occupational and spatial wage differentials, was far greater in the nineteenth century than it is now. We saw earlier (Chapter 1) how much the level of women's wages owed to the conventional division of employment into men's work and women's work that confined women to certain limited and badly-paid areas of employment. In so far as men and women did different work, differences in their pay are just a part (although a distinct and interesting part) of the hierarchy of occupational differentials that has already been described. There were, however, a number of cases in which women worked alongside men at identical tasks and their respective wages in these situations can be examined. It is also possible to assess, very roughly, the difference between average pay for men's work and for women's work and to examine how, and why, the gap between them altered.

The most important category of work done by men and women alike was factory weaving. Women were also to be found working alongside male printers in certain towns and sharing the same tasks in the production of nails, clothing, brushes, and miscellaneous other articles. There was no uniform pattern in the relationship between men's and women's wages in these occupations. Most women weavers were paid the same piece-rates as the men so that a given amount of work gave them equivalent wages, but in some branches of weaving, the West Country worsted trade for example, there was a man's rate and a, lower, woman's rate.[136] In non-textile occupations the more usual practice appears to have been that women doing the same work as men were paid an inferior rate.[137] Women compositors in London, for example, did for 5½d work that earned a man 7½–8½d, and in Perth and Bungay print shops their pay was calculated on the men's scale and then divided by two. Female brush-makers in Bristol were reported earning only a quarter of what men were paid for similar work, female nail-makers and post office clerks also toiled at discriminatory rates, and the first Senior Lady Inspector of Factories was appointed at half of the man's rate.[138]

Two other points are worth noting about these instances where men and women did the same work. The first is that the female weavers who worked with men for identical rates were among the highest-paid women workers in Britain whereas male weavers were badly paid compared with men. If the women gained from doing work that was not unequivocally women's work, the men (particularly the men of the West Riding) clearly lost something by competing in an occupation where pay was affected by the prevailing level of women's wages. The second point is that when men and women were on the same piece-rate the men's earnings were usually higher because they did more work in a day.[139] There were various reasons for this. It was said that the majority of men were spurred by family responsibilities while a great many girls looked forward to marriage and early retirement – 'You work harder than others according as you want the money or not', explained a girl cigar-maker to Eleanor Rathbone. 'Married women often work quick. Men always do and the men's work is better. They have families to keep but we like to lark a bit.'[140] Lancastrian women weavers, working with men and affected by a spirit of competition, produced far more in a day than the Scottish women who had cotton weaving to themselves.[141] Another reason why men could do more was because they are naturally stronger. Men also took more expert care of their machines and were said to cope better with minor breakdowns and non-repetitive tasks, 'male weavers will often tune their own looms rather than lose time in waiting for the tuner. The women weavers have apparently never learnt this art.'[142]

These points suggest that the lower overall level of women's wages for similar work was not entirely a matter of custom and prejudice. And there were other, longer-term, advantages on the men's side. Females were generally not as well educated as males, they absented themselves from work more frequently, and in many occupations their hours and working conditions were restricted by factory and workshop acts: there were good reasons for paying less to a newspaper compositor who could not work at night or after 2 p.m. on Saturday. The women could offer employers one or two compensating advantages: they drank less and they were more docile (a double-edged 'advantage'). But the balance of advantages was obviously with the men. All this, however, still leaves the greatest part of the difference between men's and women's wages for similar work to be explained in terms of custom and

103

prejudice and the influence of prevailing wage levels for work that was exclusively women's. After all, women had been paid far less than men for similar work long before the factory acts, and female typists in government offices were paid less than male typists although their productivity was higher. Women's pay in those occupations where they did not compete with men was low for two main reasons. Firstly because the greater part of all female labour was forced to crowd into only those occupations that the men abandoned to them and, secondly, because of the long-standing and generally accepted assumption that women ought to earn less.

We know far less about women's wages than we know of men's wages. All estimates of the average for women before 1914 are deficient in one or another respect: the wages of women and those of girls are not always distinguished; full-time and part-time workers are thrust together; weighting by occupation is inadequate or non-existent; and earnings in the most important of all women's occupations, domestic service, are sometimes omitted. The average for women full-time workers was probably somewhere between one-third and two-thirds of the men's average. Surviving figures for several industries in 1883 and those shown in the 1886 and 1906 wage censuses are all within these limits.[143] The proportion naturally varied a great deal from industry to industry and in every case, of course, the work for which men's wages were paid overlapped little, if at all, with the work at which women earned their wages. Figures of textile wages in the 1830s show the women earning less than half as much as men, in the mid-century Leicester hosiery trade and in Leeds woollen mills around 1886 the proportion was about half, and in the 1906 wage census average textile wages are shown as 15s 5d for women and 28s 1d for men.[144] Those male and female weavers who worked at the same task for the same pay were obviously exceptional even among textile workers. In the metal trades the 1906 wage census averages were 12s 8d (women) and 33s 11d (men).[145]

The best-paid women were the Lancashire cotton workers.[146] In 1906, when the women's average was about 14s, they averaged 18s 8d or about as much as the average male farm labourer. At the other end of the scale were those who worked on the land or at homework of one kind or another: the Dorset button-makers and the Bedfordshire pillowlace-makers, for example, the straw plaiters who occupied last place in the 1891–2 wage census, and the sweated needlewomen and matchbox-makers of London's East End among whom Booth's investigators found women working for as little as 1d per hour.[147] There was another women's wage differential that is worth mentioning: the average earnings of married women (who accounted for a high proportion of home workers) were well below the average for all women. If their husbands were alive and brought home a reasonable wage these low earnings might not be accompanied by hardship. Indeed, two of the assumptions underlying the relationship between men's and women's wages were that men should be paid more because they required sufficient to support a family and that female earnings were a marginal bonus to the husband's, or father's, wage. These assumptions were obviously generous to bachelors who had no dependants, but their greater shortcoming was that they overlooked those who had to provide basic food and shelter from their 'auxiliary' female earnings. As we shall see in Chapter 4, women without male support, especially widowed mothers, were prominent among those of working age who needed help from charities or the poor law authorities.

What was the long-term trend in the relationship between men's and women's wages? There is no certain answer to this question – the estimates of men's and women's earnings at different dates already cited are not comparable with each other and cannot be used as a guide to chronological change in the differential. G. H. Wood presented a collection of rather vague and incomplete figures in his 1903 survey which suggest some narrowing of the differential between 1820 and 1870 but not subsequently.[148] There are several reasons, however, for thinking that the average women's wage was in fact becoming a greater proportion of the average man's wage throughout the second half of the century, and probably at a rather faster rate after 1870 than before. Women stood to gain more than men by the withdrawal of competition from child labour, and the introduction of compulsory schooling affected girls' education (and potential earnings) more than it affected the education of their brothers. Women must have gained disproportionately also from the reduction in the differential for skill after 1880, and the legal minimum wages established by trade boards shortly before the First World War almost certainly affected their wages more than men's wages.[149] The less belligerent trade union attitude toward women workers apparent by 1890 (below pp. 259, 300) is perhaps another reason for supposing that the differential was narrowing. Occupational changes worked in the same direction: after 1880 women were increasingly finding employment in the new semi-skilled manufacturing occupations, as teachers, and as office workers. Pay in each of these occupations was above the woman's average. At the same time, and before this, there was a substantial fall in the proportion of women workers dependent upon farmwork and domestic industry where pay was exceptionally low. Schoolteachers, clerks, farm workers, and many domestic workers are all excluded from Wood's index of women's wages. Had they been included (on a weighted basis) his index might well have shown a definite narrowing in the sex–wage differential throughout the whole of the second half of the century. This trend probably continued up to the war. During the war it definitely accelerated.

Another female employment that does not appear in Wood's index is domestic service, by far the most important female occupation. Domestic servants' wages present special problems: there were numerous grades of servants, and board and lodging, allowances for tea and sugar, the 'cook's dripping', cast-off clothing, and other perquisites accounted for a high proportion of total income. One point on which virtually all are agreed, however, is that taken as a whole and compared with other women the domestic servants were fairly well paid.[150] At the end of the century a woman out of her teens could expect £18–£20 per annum clear of her bed and board. Those who lived out received another 12s to 14s per week, which indicates a total, in cash and kind, approaching £1 a week.[151] This was comfortably in excess of the average of all women's wages and on a par with the pay of Lancashire mill workers. Many farm labourers' daughters who entered service must soon have earned as much as their fathers. A second point about which little doubt exists is that the wages of domestic servants had risen faster than wages in most occupations during the nineteenth century. Figures compiled by W. T. Layton show an increase of over one-third in their money wages between the mid-1820s and mid-century,[152] a period when prices were falling and when most workers' real wages improved very little. In the third quarter of the century, according to his figures, their wages increased more slowly than wages in industrial occupations, but after 1870 they again advanced rapidly. Layton's and Wood's statistics in combination suggest that the money wages of (a) domestic servants, (b) women industrial workers, and (c) all industrial workers (men and women combined) between 1823–7 and the end of the century rose respectively by 138 per cent, 66 per cent, and 54 per cent. Clearly indices like Wood's that omit domestic servants will tend both to exaggerate the size of the overall sex-wage differential and underestimate the rate at which the differential was being eroded. 'What could be said in favour of all the ceaseless fetching and carrying?' asks J. F. C. Harrison.[153] These figures of domestic servants' wages, if nothing else, suggest that a full answer to his question would perhaps be less gloomy than he expects.

There was, of course, much to be said against domestic service. Not least among its non-monetary disadvantages were the very long working day and the need to maintain 'constant watchful respect'. Even when work was done (and before it started) servants were still 'on call', their time not entirely their own. In some respects these disadvantages increased during the nineteenth century: a greater insistence upon the wearing of uniforms, for example, was probably symptomatic of a more formally subservient status, and the impositions of service were doubtless felt more as greater freedoms were introduced elsewhere. But there is also a great deal that can be said in favour of domestic service. Without it the consequences of Malthusian pressure and of the decline of cottage industry in rural districts would both have been far more serious. Service provided country girls with a surrogate home and family, it eased the transition to urban life, reduced the number to be fed on farm labourers' wages, and left a little more space in their cramped cottages. At mid-century some two-thirds of servants were the daughters of rural labourers.[154] Servants' food and accommodation were in most cases far better than what they could have expected in their parents' home[155] and there were few workers so likely to receive medical attention paid for by their employers, pay during sickness, and regular paid holidays. Their employment was also comparatively uninterrupted by the trade cycle, adverse weather, or technological unemployment and its hierarchy of ranks provided the socially ambitious with a well signposted route towards the middle classes. Service also offered improved prospects in the marriage market because servants acquired a modicum of middle-class polish, habits of order and cleanliness, and savings – all of which were much esteemed by the higher ranks of working men.[156] Some of the demographic consequences of so large a part of the labour force being 'in service' have already been mentioned (above, pp. 36, 39n) and other consequences will be noted in later chapters.

The last of the wage differentials to be examined – that between British and foreign wages – is another part of labour history that has been relatively neglected. So far as it is possible to tell, the advantage that English wage earners enjoyed over those on the continent in 1800 (above p. 57) was well maintained throughout the first half of the century. J. Thomson, a Clithero cotton manufacturer, crossed the Channel in 1817 and again in 1824 to ascertain whether low-wage Frenchmen constituted a threat to Lancashire, and when Edmund Ashworth did the same in 1833 he came back with figures showing wages in France and Switzerland as much as 50 per cent below English rates.[157] An American visiting Europe in 1825 estimated the wages of carpenters as equivalent to 97 US cents a day in England and between 55 and 75 cents in France, and those English navvies who helped build the Rouen to Paris railway were paid twice the local rates.[158] Mulhall cites figures for 1835 showing wages in England to be 25 to 50 per cent higher than those in France; French wages, in turn, were as much or more above wages in Italy, Holland, Spain, Portugal, Russia and Ireland.[159] We have too J. C. Symon's calculations from the 1830s, showing real wages in France, Belgium, Austria-Prussia, and Switzerland to have been 88, 72, 71, and 67 per cent respectively of the English level.[160] As may be expected with a subject so emotive as living standards, it is possible to find several contradictory claims. Engels, for example, claimed that English farm wages were well below the German level;[161] but such claims are at odds with all the statistical evidence. The figures we have suggest that most English workmen, far from living at 'subsistence' level in the years covered by the standard of living debate (above, p. 57), enjoyed incomes well above those that provided subsistence of sorts for millions of Europeans. They also suggest, however, that wages in areas of recent settlement outside Europe, where population pressed lightly upon resources, were well above English levels. A number of sources for the 1820s and 1830s indicate a very substantial money-wage differential between England and the United States that was perhaps equivalent to a real advantage of between 20 and 40 per cent.[162] All of these international differentials vary according to which occupations and which parts of each country are compared, and according to the state of their trade cycles.

Better information is available for the second half of the nineteenth century: Phelps Brown and Browne have calculated that United Kingdom real wages in the 1860s were between a third and a half greater than the levels in Germany, France, and Sweden, and that average American real wages, once they had recovered from the effects of the Civil War, were about 25 per cent above the British level.[163] Several other sources confirm this general impression. There are, for example, the numerous reports from HM Diplomatic and Consular Agents that were compiled partly as a guide to intending immigrants.[164] Hamburg wages were reported higher than wages elsewhere in Germany yet 'low when compared . . . with the wages paid in England'; food there was 'far inferior, both in quantity and quality, to that which an English workman is accustomed to'.[165] Lord Brabazon, from France, advised the English workman that he was 'infinitely better off' at home; a Swiss report put wages at 33 to 40 per cent below the English rate; the workmen of Antwerp were at an even greater disadvantage; and the position of the Danish operative was adjudged 'decidedly inferior' to that of his fellow in England.[166] Similar evidence is available in the 1873 enquiry by Alexander and Jasper Redgrave, in T. Brassey's *Foreign Work and English Wages* (1879), and in a collection of United States consular reports on 'Labor in Europe' (1884–5) which describe English wages as 'generally speaking the highest in Europe'.[167] There is also A. Fryer's interesting attempt to calculate the cost of living in Stockport and twenty-three foreign cities, from which a Stockport railway porter and a Stockport housemaid (contemplating marriage perhaps) could calculate that they were about twice as well off where they were than they would have been in Italy, Greece, Portugal, or Russia, but that he might increase his income by about half if they emigrated to Missouri or South Australia.[168] Although Britain's economic lead over other nations diminished between 1860 and the end of the century, the relative level of British real wages, it seems, was not reduced. Swedish wages rose relative to those in each of the other four countries analysed by Phelps Brown and Browne, but the margin between average British and average American wages remained at about 25 per cent and the gap between British wages and wages in France and Germany was well maintained and may have slightly widened.[169]

After 1896, there was some erosion of the British workman's advantages. The change in trend that is such a marked feature of British wage history at this time (above, pp. 74–6) was less evident abroad. Even so, on the eve of the war real wages remained comfortably above the levels of the most prosperous parts of Europe and the relative position of the British workman, compared to workmen elsewhere, was still considerably more favourable than it is today.[170] Board of Trade investigations put the level of money wages per hour in Germany and France in 1905 at about three-quarters and two-thirds respectively of the English rate with rent, food, and fuel prices exceeding English levels by 20 per cent in Germany and by 14 per cent in France.[171] The average amounts of meat consumed per head at about this time were: in the United Kingdom 122 lb, in Germany 99 lb, and in France 80 lb.[172]

VII · *Quality of the labour force and the causes of changes in real wages, 1815–1914*

The main cause of high real wages in Britain, compared with wages in Europe, was that labour productivity in Britain was high. Free trade, after 1850, was another cause of relatively high wages because the British workman, unlike the German and the Frenchman, was denied none of the benefits of cheap imported foods. His advantages might possibly have owed something also to the way that national income was distributed between wages, salaries, profits, and rent. But we know insufficient of how national incomes were divided to do more than note this as a possibility.

Output per worker in Britain had almost certainly compared well with that in Europe before the nineteenth century. A relatively high proportion of the labour force was already occupied at trade and industry and by the late eighteenth century British agriculture had no equal. British workmen were as willing as any to respond to cash incentives, to accept change, and to take up new employment. Moreover, they were better nourished than any others. They were not on the whole better educated, but Scottish education was not far short of the best in Europe, and the literacy rate in mid-eighteenth-century England was already at or near the 30–40 per cent level that economists have suggested is necessary for significant rises in incomes to occur.[173] Certain skills were in short supply, but elsewhere they were even scarcer and there is no other evidence which suggests that the quality of British labour was a significant barrier to economic growth and rising wages. The industrial revolution then increased most of these advantages and Britain's lead over Europe was not significantly diminished until towards the end of the nineteenth century.

High labour productivity in the nineteenth century was obviously the consequence of diverse influences. But the separate contribution of labour force characteristics can be roughly distinguished from the contributions of inventors, entrepreneurs, and others. The anxious Clithero manufacturer we noticed visiting France early in the century (above, p. 107) returned to

England satisfied and his comments afford one illustration of the labour contribution to productivity: 'the labour of Alsace', he reported, 'the best and cheapest in France, is dearer than the labour of Lancashire . . . the energy of the English workman surpasses that of every other manufacturing country I have visited.' Léon Faucher, who crossed the Channel in the other direction in 1844, found the Lancastrian 'indisputably the best workman on the face of the earth; the best spinner and the best mechanic.'[174] The skill and energy of British navvies was such that their labour was cheaper than that of Frenchmen working alongside them at half their pay,[175] and in 1870 the British Consul at Nice noted both that French wages were low and that the amount of work done by the average Frenchman in a day was 'certainly not two-thirds of that done by an average English workman'.[176] Lancashire operatives, and the shipyard workers of the Clyde, Tyne, Tees, and Wear, were still considered to be more than the equal of any in the world at the end of the century.[177] By this time there were increasing complaints that at many other tasks the workmen of Germany or Belgium had become at least the equal of British workmen. These complaints, however, were new ones; there had been few grounds for unfavourable comparisons with European labour until the 1880s. American labour productivity on the other hand, and American wages, had long been above British levels in most occupations.

A major achievement of the first half of the nineteenth century was the creation of an efficient industrial labour force – disciplined, reliable, diligent, and prepared to work full-time at the same task throughout the year. This was not done without anguish, but there was never sufficient working-class resistance to seriously delay the new order. The transition would have been more difficult, of course, had Britain not had so many workers who were familiar with pre-factory industrial employment, or if more of its agricultural population had been peasants instead of landless labourers. It was eased also by the rapid increase of population which allowed expanding sectors to recruit additional labour without necessarily contracting the number in traditional occupations. To a population well accustomed to wage labour and cash incentives, higher wages and plentiful employment were powerful inducements to abandon existing work patterns. High wages were supplemented by works rules and fines, by piece-rates, bonuses, and sundry other devices. 'Long pay' and truck, for example, were intended partly to curb drunkenness.[178] Child labour probably helped too by conditioning workers to the factory regime at an early age.

Conditioning in various ways favourable to labour productivity extended far beyond the workplace. The churches, Methodism most of all, preached piety, respect, thrift, and sobriety. Their congregations were encouraged to endure suffering without protest and to seek salvation through hard work. Schools taught similar virtues including, in particular, concentration, punctuality, and regular attendance. The same lessons were passed from mistresses to servants, and thence to servants' spouses and children. To deal with those who somehow remained oblivious to all this indoctrination, the new workhouse deterrent was introduced in 1834. It would be quite wrong, however, to give the impression that the work ethic was invariably accepted with reluctance, or that conditioning all flowed from above. Many workers (and their wives) were keenly aware of the rewards that might accompany thrift and hard work. They took an active part in the Methodist and Sunday school movements and their friendly societies, co-operative societies, and trade unions were among the institutions that propagated the Smilesian virtues.[179]

It is sometimes suggested that the quality of British labour was severely affected by shortcomings in the education system. But the great majority of working men needed no more academic training than the schools were quite capable of supplying. Teaching children to attend on time and do as they were told was perhaps the most important contribution of education in the first half of the century. And the more exacting economic requirements of the second half of the century did not extend much beyond requiring a greater proportion of recruits who could read, write, and perform elementary calculations. These demands were met. The proportion of working-class children receiving more than the very minimum of schooling rose from about a quarter in 1815 to around half at mid-century, and to 100 per cent before 1900.[180] The railway companies, the police, the retailers, and the rest had no difficulty finding sufficient literate recruits.[181] If a serious educational weakness existed at the level we are concerned with here[182] it was Britain's rudimentary facilities for vocational training. After 1850 the mechanics institutes declined and the late nineteenth-century expansion of evening classes and other part-time teaching in technical subjects left Britain still considerably behind Germany in the provision of formal vocational training.[183] Germany, however, and other countries, lacked Britain's enormous reservoir of skilled workmen and for this reason they needed more formal instruction. In Britain the supply of skill appears to have been adequately maintained by 'on the job' training. And the shortcoming that was becoming evident by the 1880s was not in the numbers being trained, but rather that at a time of accelerating technical change 'on the job' training was less likely than formal vocational training to keep abreast of new developments and more likely to produce workmen who would be unsympathetic to technical change.

The other main influences upon labour productivity have either been discussed already or will be considered in later chapters. Labour mobility (Chapter 5 below) was generally high: the rate of occupational change and the spatial redistribution of population in response to changes in demand for labour were both impressive. The trade union influence upon productivity is more debatable but in Chapters 6, 8, and 9 it will be argued that the generally high quality of British labour was not seriously impaired by adverse union influences before the very end of the nineteenth century. With regard to nutrition there is no doubt of Britain's advantage over her European rivals. By providing the means to obtain enough energy for efficient working and to sustain physical health and mental vigour, higher wages increased labour productivity and thus helped to pay for themselves. At the end of the century there were still many British workers who earned 'insufficient to obtain the minimum necessaries for the maintenance of merely physical efficiency', but the proportion below Rowntree's poverty line must have been considerably greater in Germany and France. The British workmen's relatively short working day was perhaps another cause of high labour productivity because it meant less fatigue and less boredom. And Britain's pioneer investment in public health, as was suggested in Chapter 2, almost certainly more than paid for itself by reducing absence from work through sickness and death and by reducing the number whose work suffered because they were only partially fit. Towards the end of the nineteenth century, however, the German government and German employers showed themselves to be far more aware than their British counterparts of the value of social insurance and similar investment in human capital.

In chronological terms the influence of the developments that have been described was a continuous rise in labour productivity until the 1880s and distinctly slower improvement between 1880 and 1914. This increase was one of the two main determinants of the chronological changes in real wages that were described earlier and remain to be explained. The other was the rate of population change. Change in the way national income was distributed and in the terms of trade also had some influence upon the course of real wages, but economic growth was by far the most important variable. Between 1815 and 1850 industrialization was occurring, labour was moving into high productivity occupations, there was less disguised unemployment, more division of labour, work was less interrupted by the weather and the seasons, and output grew rapidly. But in the 1840s there were still many occupations, and many parts of the country, barely touched by the industrial revolution. Most of the cost-reducing benefits of railways and steamships, and the most significant expansion of the factory system, were still to come. At the same time population had increased rapidly and in those areas that had not felt the stimulus of industrial and commercial change rising numbers tended to depress local wages and to swell the number of migrants available to supplement labour supply in the higher wage districts. The net effect of these influences was that output increased by no more, or not much more, than was sufficient to hold average wages steady in the face of rising numbers.

There were also two secondary reasons for the failure of wages to rise decisively before 1850. One was the long deterioration in the terms of trade. Prices of imports, that is, fell less than prices of British exports. This was to be expected at a time when industrial productivity was rising but it meant, nevertheless, that some part of Britain's increased output went in payment for relatively dearer imports and thus was not available to raise living standards. It seems likely also that a more than proportionate share of the increase in Britain's wealth went to the middle and upper classes. Tax and profit statistics and the evidence of consumption patterns, not least the employment of servants, all point in this direction.[184] This does not mean that income was being transferred from poor to rich. But so long as the biggest gains from industrialization went to those who were most directly responsible for its progress, the amount available to raise workers' living standards was proportionately less than their existing share of the national income.

When more is known of changes in the incidence of taxes, and of changes in the proportion of central and local government expenditure that benefited the working classes, it is possible that we may find further developments unfavourable to wage earners in the first half of the nineteenth century.[185] We know, of course, that taxation was borne disproportionately by the working classes and that the greater part of central government revenue went upon servicing the national debt. Taxation, that is, almost certainly transferred income from the workers to other classes. But it had done so before 1815. What we need to know is whether taxation became *more* regressive and, if it did, whether by sufficient to offset the favourable influence upon wages of the tendency for tax revenue *per capita* (in real terms) to fall. It is sometimes suggested that wages may also have been retarded because industrialization perhaps required a considerable increase in the proportion of the national income that was set aside for investment. But this argument carries little weight in the context of the British industrial revolution. When a poor country industrializes quickly wages may be held down in this way. Britain's industrial revolution, however, was not of this kind. Capital was abundant in Britain, industrialization occurred gradually, and there was no significant rise in the proportion of national income invested until large-scale railway building commenced in the 1830s.

In the second half of the century output decisively outstripped population growth. Increased productivity came from many sources: from the changes in occupational structure and the other improvements in labour productivity that have been described, from greater specialization and economies of scale, and from numerous technical advances that raised the amount that could be produced in a day and the amount that could be commanded with a day's wages. Improvements in transport were prominent among these advances. Transport improvements abroad, and on the oceans, were partly responsible also for the more favourable trend in the terms of trade from the late 1850s which is another part of the explanation of rising real wages. In particular, they helped to make possible the abundance of cheap food that cascaded into Britain after 1870. The change in terms of trade was not dramatic – net barter terms improved by only some 15 to 20 per cent in four decades.[186] But the working classes probably gained more than others from this improvement and the less well-off among them, who spent the highest proportion of their incomes upon bread and other cheap foodstuffs, gained most of all. The advantages of the lower wage earners in this respect were probably sufficient to offset the slight widening in the differential between skilled and unskilled wages that was noted earlier.

Further relief came with changes in commercial and fiscal policy. Besides allowing British workers to reap the full advantages of the opening of new land overseas, free trade also entailed a reduction in a form of taxation that had fallen disproportionately upon the working classes. And income tax, which was re-introduced in part to make good the loss of customs revenue, left them largely untouched. Excise duties came to be levied rather more upon luxuries, and less upon necessities, and this too must have been welcome to wage-earners even if many among them felt that drink and tobacco were wrongly categorized. There were gains too in the way governments disposed of revenue. The proportion allocated to servicing the national debt, over half of the total before 1850, was less than 20 per cent by the end of the century, and expenditure on items like education and public health had risen considerably. The national debt still took as much as local authorities spent on sewerage, refuse collection, water supply, hospitals, and poor relief combined – but the changes that had occurred were mainly to the advantage of the working classes.[187]

Another possible contribution to rising real wages may have been an increase after 1873 in the share of the national income that accrued to labour. Until the onset of the 'great depression' its share was probably either stationary or falling.[188] Between 1873 and 1896, however, the combination of pressure upon profits, falling prices, and falling agricultural rents probably retarded the rate of increase in non-wage incomes while money wages seldom fell and more often were advancing despite falling prices. It was because they felt their incomes under pressure that the middle classes labelled these years the 'great depression'. Marshall, in evidence to one of the enquiries into the causes of 'depression', spoke of 'a depression of prices, a depression of interest, and a depression of profits . . . the employer gets less the employee more'. The statistics we have are equivocal on this subject – those calculated by Deane and Cole, for example, show very little change in distribution over these years while Saul cites figures to the effect that between 1870–4 and 1890–4 labour's share of the sum of pay and profits rose from 52 per cent to 62 per cent.[189] The latter estimate is more consistent both with what contemporaries believed the situation to have been and with what might be expected to happen to relative shares at a time of falling prices.

If one reason for the rise in real wages before 1896 was change in the distribution of the national income, the same mechanism may perhaps help explain the less favourable trend in real wages between 1896 and the war. The evidence is again less certain than it might be.[190] But no one claims that labour's share rose and in this respect there is a contrast with the years before 1896. There was a similar contrast between the two periods with regard to the terms of trade – after 1900 their improvement ceased. This change was not very great, but there remains the contrast between a period when the terms of trade worked for higher wages and one in which they did this no longer.[191] Part of the trouble was that the empty lands of the world, from whose settlement and cultivation Britain had gained so much, were filling up. The increasing demands of the home population curbed United States food exports and raised their price. And the vast territories recently acquired in Africa and Asia, while they may have afforded satisfaction of some kind, did little to fill British stomachs or British pockets. These changes in income distribution and in the terms of trade may have more than offset continuing working-class gains from changes in taxation and government expenditure.

But the chief explanation of the change in real wage trends after 1896 is again the relationship between numbers and output within Britain. There is general agreement that sometime in the last quarter of the nineteenth century the rate of increase in productivity declined and that between 1900 and 1914 it grew very little and may have fallen absolutely.[192] The debate on the timing, causes, and extent of this 'climacteric' need not delay us: most would agree with Phelps Brown's general diagnosis of a pause in the availability of great cost-reducing innovations: 'By 1900 the application of steam to power and transport, and of steel to equipment, had been largely worked through. New techniques, in electricity, chemicals, the man-made fibres, and the internal combustion engine . . . were being developed, but . . . their impact would not be massive until after the First World War.'[193] This 'pause' was felt to some extent by other industrializing countries, but for several reasons Britain was most affected. Sweden, for example, had still to exploit innovations whose potential Britain had exhausted, and the United States had rich deposits of coal and other minerals whereas British mine productivity was falling steadily because the most accessible coal had long been taken. Britain was perhaps at a further disadvantage in that a relatively high proportion of its labour was organized and organized labour at this time was increasingly uncooperative over the adoption of labour-saving innovations, increasingly resentful of managerial authority, and given to downward revisions of what constituted 'a fair day's work'. These developments are discussed in Chapter 9. Among other suggestions that have at different times been put forward to explain the failure of productivity to maintain its advance are poor entrepreneurship, the transfer of labour into service occupations in which productivity was not easily improved, the slower rate at which labour left agriculture, the high level of British capital exports at this time, long-standing weaknesses in the education system, a reduction in the working day and the working week beyond the point where hours reductions paid for themselves in higher productivity, and increasing expenditure upon the armed forces and upon social welfare projects whose immediate economic returns were low. Whatever the relative importance of each of these contributions some substantial decline in the rate of productivity advance towards the end of the nineteenth century seems beyond doubt. This decline was largely responsible for the setback to real wages.

Suggestions for further reading are on pages 400–1.

4

POVERTY

1 · *The extent of poverty*

Chapter 3 discussed wages and wage earners' living standards. This chapter is concerned with the very poorest among the population, many of whom depended more upon charity and poor relief than upon wages. How many fell below the 'poverty line'? What were the chief causes of their plight? And what was done about it?

It was not until near the end of the nineteenth century that poverty was first measured in any systematic fashion and most of our evidence of the extent and causes of poverty is from around the turn of the century. The number of 'paupers', those receiving assistance from the poor law authorities at any particular time, had long been known. They amounted to almost 9 per cent of the population in the 1830s and to less than 3 per cent of the population at the end of the century.[1] But it was also known that far more suffered from poverty than ever applied to the boards of guardians. Thus it was possible for quite contradictory estimates of the extent of poverty to circulate at the same time. In 1883 Andrew Mearns in his *Bitter Cry of Outcast London* claimed that as much as a quarter of the population of London received insufficient income to maintain physical health. Claims such as this, based more upon impression than upon scientific investigation, encouraged Charles Booth, a merchant shipowner and philanthropist, to begin, in 1886, his celebrated survey of the London poor. Booth employed seven assistants and their findings eventually filled seventeen volumes with a wealth of information on the people of London. Booth discovered as much as 30 per cent of the population of the world's wealthiest city, and 38 per cent of its working-class population, living below the poverty line.[2] This line was judged to be at an income of 21s a week, the amount that Booth calculated was sufficient for a family to both obtain the minimum food, clothing, and shelter necessary for physical health and industrial efficiency and to make adequate provision against the possibility of sickness, accident, and unemployment in the future. About 10 per cent of London's working-class population earned insufficient to provide merely for their current needs.

A decade after Booth's first results appeared, B. Seebohm Rowntree, a member of the Quaker chocolate manufacturing family, began a similar survey of his native York. He advanced Booth's methods by drawing upon nutritional science to determine the calorific requirements of working men, wives, and children. To maintain physical efficiency a family of two adults and three children was calculated to require by this time (1899) a weekly income of 21s 8d. Rowntree also distinguished between 'primary poverty' and 'secondary poverty'. Primary poverty was a condition where income was insufficient even if every penny was spent judiciously. Secondary poverty occurred when those whose incomes were theoretically sufficient to maintain physical efficiency suffered poverty as a consequence of 'inefficient spending'. 10 per cent of York's population, and 15 per cent of its working-class population, were found to be in primary poverty.[3] A further 18 per cent of the whole population, and 28 per cent of the working classes, were living in secondary poverty.[4]

Rowntree also emphasized the changing incidence of poverty at the different stages of working-class life. Young children increased the demands upon their father's wage and so the first experience of poverty often came early in life. Adolescence and the opportunity to start earning eased this pressure but marriage, and their own children, soon pushed young workers back towards the poverty line. Relief came as their children became self-sufficient, but in time earnings began to reflect the onset of old age and declining strength. These alternating periods of want and comparative plenty came to be known as the 'poverty cycle'. The chief practical implication of the cycle was that a considerably greater proportion of the working classes were likely to experience severe poverty at some time during their lives than the 10 to 15 per cent calculated by Booth and Rowntree. Numerous other surveys followed the work of Booth and Rowntree. The most notable of these was the investigation in 1912–13 of poverty in Stanley (Co. Durham), Northampton, Warrington, and Reading by A. L. Bowley and A. R. Burnett-Hurst, the first poverty survey to make extensive use of sampling techniques.[5] These four towns were selected with the intention of discovering how much poverty, and the causes of poverty, reflected different economic conditions: 6 per cent of the working-class population was found to be in primary poverty at Stanley, 9 per cent in Northampton, 15 per cent in Warrington, and as much as 29 per cent in Reading.

By illustrating such variety Bowley and Burnett-Hurst undermined the assumption, based on the conclusions of Booth and Rowntree, that similar levels of poverty might be found in most British towns.[6] In fact, the diversity of labour market conditions was reflected by great variety in the levels and causes of poverty. London, of course, was deficient in well-paid female employment and factory work. In 1890 there was perhaps nowhere else still so dependent upon casual employment and upon low-productivity domestic industry that was vulnerable to factory and overseas competition. London also attracted more migrants from Ireland and the English provinces than any other town, including more than its fair share of the foot-loose, idle, drunken, or simply unfortunate. The capital's numerous charities and those of its workhouses with a reputation for open-handedness were a constant attraction for the social wreckage of the provinces.[7] Poverty in London, moreover, attracted particular attention because it existed alongside the relative affluence of the majority of workers and the conspicuous consumption of the wealthy.

How much reliance can be placed on the results of the early poverty surveys? Few of the results can be accepted with complete confidence. Booth relied heavily upon information from school attendance officers and families with children of school age (a cause of poverty) were over-represented in what he supposed to be a cross-section of the population. Rowntree's estimates of food requirements were later considered by nutritionists to be over-generous and at the time of the second survey of York (1936) he conceded that his 1899 poverty lines were 'too rough to give reliable results'.[8] Working-class respondents, confronted by middle-class investigators, were notoriously liable to underestimate incomes. School attendance officers were unwelcome visitors at most times, and as one of their duties was to investigate claims for means-tested remission of various school fees they were particularly likely to be left ignorant of income from lodgers and odd jobs and from the work of wives and children.[9] Most poor law and charity assistance was also means tested and the poorer respondents, suspecting that investigators might have some influence in the disposal of relief, took care not to jeopardize future claims. Income acquired illegally was particularly likely to remain undisclosed. The poor sensed also what was expected of them, 'we had a goose for dinner last Sunday, and a giblet pie on Monday, and you can't put that down in those sort of books'.[10] These are each reasons for suggesting that the early surveys may have exaggerated the extent of poverty. Worth noting also is that poor law and charitable assistance ensured that the number suffering the physical consequences of poverty was far less than the number whose other income was insufficient to keep them above the poverty line. On the other hand, however, Rowntree's survey was undertaken at a fairly prosperous time, his definition of the family's minimum necessary expenditure on items other than food was austere even by contemporary standards,[11] and the proportion that suffered poverty in the low-wage rural districts was certainly greater than the proportion that suffered in London and York.[12] We can probably be reasonably sure that the proportion of working-class people in primary poverty up and down the country at the end of the nineteenth century was not much (if at all) less than the 15 per cent suggested by Rowntree. This, of course, was far greater than the proportion of the population who were officially designated as paupers and far more also than most informed observers had expected the surveys to reveal.

How do these levels compare with poverty levels at other times? For earlier periods impressions must suffice because there were no investigations sufficiently scientific for their results to bear comparison with those of Booth and Rowntree. Gregory King's estimates for the late seventeenth century certainly suggest that poverty was then considerably in excess of late nineteenth-century levels. And the recent attempts of Anderson, Armstrong, and Foster to assess the approximate numbers that lived below Rowntree's poverty line in mid-nineteenth-century Preston, York, and Oldham all suggest poverty levels higher than those at the time of Rowntree's investigation.[13] That, of course, is what we should expect. Rowntree's poverty line budget would have cost at least as much in 1850 as it did in 1899, and over the same years money wages rose considerably and many more insured themselves against sickness and other contingencies.[14]

Changes in poverty levels since 1900 can be described with greater certainty. There was probably little significant improvement in the Edwardian era. Any gains from reduced expenditure upon child-rearing and drink are likely to have been offset by pressure upon real wages and, in particular, by higher food prices. After 1914 the upward trend in earnings resumed. Unskilled workers' wages rose rapidly in the war years and the unskilled were the chief gainers also from the introduction and extension of state pensions, unemployment pay, and health insurance. A second survey of London poverty, in 1928–9, found that the proportion that Booth would have designated as living within his two categories of poverty had been reduced, despite the depression, by over half.[15] Rowntree's second survey of York, in 1936, found that the proportion of the working classes in primary poverty there (judged by the standards of 1899) had fallen since 1899 from 15.5 per cent to 6.8 per cent.[16] By this time expectations, and the amount of poverty that society was prepared to tolerate, had so changed that Rowntree adopted a revised poverty line based upon 'minimum human needs' far in excess of what he had considered adequate in 1899. After 1945 the revised standards of the 1930s were in turn dismissed as anachronistic.

II · *Causes of poverty*

The causes of poverty revealed by the early poverty surveys were as surprising and disturbing to most contemporaries as the calculations of its extent. Poverty was revealed as less a consequence of idleness, drinking, and other personal shortcoming than had been commonly believed. These findings had an important part in strengthening demands for less parsimonious poor relief, for old age pensions, health and unemployment insurance, and other positive measures. Booth calculated that only a quarter of his 'submerged one-tenth' were impoverished chiefly by drink, idleness, and 'excessive children'. More than half (55 per cent) were in poverty as a consequence of insufficient earnings, and a further 10 per cent due to sickness and infirmity.[17] Rowntree found that over half of primary poverty at York also arose from insufficient earnings. There, about one-fifth of primary poverty was due to the illness, old age, or death of the chief wage-earner and a rather larger proportion than this to 'largeness of family' (over four children).[18] These causes were each ascribed different weights in the explanation of secondary poverty and Booth's lists of causes are not directly comparable with Rowntree's. Rowntree's definitions, for example, precluded expenditure on drink appearing among the causes of primary poverty. The crucial point, however, was clear enough: a very considerable part of poverty was not 'self-inflicted'. Rather, it derived from low wages and other circumstances over which the poor themselves had little control.

At York low wages were mainly a consequence of low rates per hour for regular work. Rural poverty probably also arose more from low weekly wages than from unemployment. In London, however, hourly rates of pay were relatively high and low wages were mainly a consequence of irregular employment. Low wage rates and unemployment must both have been even more serious causes of poverty earlier in the century when real wages were lower, when more men and women were engaged in declining domestic industries, in arable farming with its erratic labour requirements, and at casual work and occupations liable to be disrupted by the weather, by uncertain transport, or loss of power. Before 1850 moreover, when Britain produced most of its own food, trade cycle slumps were often accompanied by high food prices and fewer workers could then afford to make provision against unemployment. But the working of the trade cycle was still a major source of poverty in 1900: school medical reports from this time show significant variety in the height and health of poor children that reflect the amount of work that had been available during their vulnerable early years.[19] The long-term average rate of unemployment in the second half of the century – according to the only figures available, those of trade unionists – was between 4.5 and 5.5 per cent.[20] In 1879 average unemployment exceeded 11 per cent, and at Sheffield only a few of the city's normally prosperous enterprises worked more than two days each week.[21] Whenever the average was over 8 per cent a fifth or more of unionists were likely to draw unemployment benefits at some time during the year. There were also severe localized slumps such as the Lancashire 'cotton famine' during the American Civil War and that which impoverished Coventry when the silk ribbon trade was opened to European competition in 1860. After 1890 major strikes and lock-outs, especially those of miners, were another cause of unemployment. At such times personal savings were exhausted, trade union and friendly society benefits dried up, and many who normally lived comfortably above the poverty line were forced to seek relief.

121

Old age was not as important a cause of poverty as low wages at the end of the nineteenth century, but it was more important than Booth and Rowntree at first suggested. Booth ascribed only 10 per cent of poverty to illness and infirmity combined, but his reliance upon school attendance officers had caused him to pay insufficient attention to families in which the chief wage-earner was elderly. At York, according to Rowntree, only 5 per cent of primary poverty resulted from the old age and sickness of chief wage-earners.[22] But, like several other investigators, Rowntree measured poverty in working-class households and omitted the numerous elderly inmates of workhouses and poor law infirmaries. In 1890 it was calculated that well over a third of the working-class population aged 65 and above were paupers, and almost half of all paupers in 1906 were aged 60 and above.[23] The high proportion of elderly people among paupers is not really surprising: state pensions were not paid until 1909, very few workers received occupational pensions, and as late as 1890 half of them were still either too poor, too reckless, or too uncertain of reaching old age to make adequate provision against eventual loss of earnings. Earlier in the century even fewer provided against old age and at that time it was also quite common for trade unions and friendly societies to collapse, leaving their ex-members without immediate prospects of benefits and perhaps already too old, or too sick, to be welcomed by another society.

Sickness was still among the important causes of poverty in 1900. But it had probably been even more important earlier in the century. We noted above how Chadwick and other early public health campaigners underlined their humanitarian appeals by directing attention to the enormous economic cost of preventable illness. They emphasized in particular how poor rates were swollen by the deaths of working men and by the vicious circle of sickness, loss of strength, reduced earnings, and consequent low-feeding that delayed recovery. The Chadwickian reforms, improved medical services, legislation on health and safety at the workplace, and (after 1850) rising wages together reduced the amount of poverty attributable to ill health. The government health insurance scheme (introduced 1911, operational 1913) came too late to make much impression before the war but by this time most workers were already covered by sickness insurance of one kind or another. Many more had joined friendly societies in the second half of the century, some employers had established sick clubs to which workers made a weekly contribution, and a few had introduced paid sick leave.

Perhaps the most obvious poverty consequent upon sickness and death was the poverty of widows and orphans. A half or more of pauper children were fatherless, and women and children together generally comprised some three-quarters of all paupers.[24] Women, in fact, were the chief sufferers from most of the causes of poverty and there were always more women than men below the poverty line. Their prominence among elderly paupers was mainly a consequence of wives outliving their spouses at a rate (assessed in the 1911 census) of two to one. Women suffered also, of course, because the female surplus compelled so many to spinsterhood, and because working widows and spinsters were paid at rates which reflected the assumption that all females were dependants. Working-class wives deserted by their husbands almost invariably became paupers, as did the majority of unmarried mothers.[25]

In addition to their considerable share of recorded poverty, women endured further hardships that investigators were unable to measure. Working-class tradition paid exaggerated heed to the wage-earner's food requirements, and the share he received of the more costly foods was especially disproportionate. The breadwinner, in fact, was most often also the meat-eater.[26] If there was anything extra to buy, such as a pair of boots, the man seldom did without, 'me and the children goes without dinner – or mebbe only 'as a cup o' tea and a bit o' bread, but Jim ollers takes 'is dinner to work, and I give it him as usual; 'e never knows we go without, and I never tells 'im.'[27] Men also benefited most from expenditure on health insurance and were thus far more likely than their wives to receive prompt and adequate medical attention. This uneven distribution of income within the family was beneficial to productivity at the workplace but it was obviously detrimental to the health of wives and children.[28]

Women, as we shall see, were almost certainly also the chief sufferers from the considerable poverty caused by what Rowntree called 'inefficient spending'. For every family in poverty because their income was absolutely insufficient, there were almost two other families whose suffering might have been averted by better management. In fact, not all 'inefficient spending' was as easy to avoid as Rowntree implied. Uncertain and fluctuating earnings made budgeting a nightmare and led too easily to dependence upon pawnbrokers and retail credit to smooth the fluctuations. Pawnbrokers, who charged 2 per cent on loans against items deposited for up to a month, were an expensive alternative to saving. Retail credit incurred no interest charges, but it tied poor families to expensive corner shops and denied access to the co-operatives and multiple stores, most of which did not allow credit.[29] Lavish expenditure upon funerals – a hardwood coffin, plumed horses, a ham tea, and plenty to drink – perhaps also falls within the category of unavoidable 'inefficient spending'. In the 1840s (when few unskilled workers earned as much as £1 a week) it was calculated that the average outlay on the funeral of a working-class adult was over £5 and that on a child's funeral was 30s. The combination of a high birth-rate and low life expectancy meant that such expenditure occurred comparatively frequently.[30] When the deceased had been the family breadwinner an elaborate funeral might appear to have been foolish as well as unnecessary. But such expenditure was conventional[31] and those who flouted the conventions were made aware of communal displeasure.[32]

Some of the more avoidable 'inefficient spending' was a consequence of housewives' indulgences – of a fondness for gin, or the unnecessary use of money-lenders, hire-purchase, and ready-cooked convenience foods. But the chief cause of avoidable secondary poverty was the substantial proportion of family income that was kept back for the husband's use. The proportion withheld obviously varied from household to household and according to the custom of the district. The Methodist miners of County Durham, for example, were said to 'tip-up' their entire earnings.[33] A Second World War inquiry estimated that the average working man kept about a quarter of his pay for pocket money[34] and the average proportion kept back before 1914 almost certainly was not less than this. What many husbands decreed sufficient for domestic needs was determined largely by what was sufficient for their own spending outside the home. And their priorities must often have imposed a poverty-line existence upon wives and children.[35]

At the time of the poverty surveys the husband's pocket money went mainly on drink, tobacco, and gambling. Booth and Rowntree showed that drink and other working-class indulgences were not the main causes of poverty but their findings left no doubt that the contribution of drinking to poverty was substantial. At York in 1899 drink was the greatest single cause of secondary poverty. The average working-class family spent an estimated 6s to 6s 10d each week upon drink, a sum equivalent to a third of a labourer's earnings and more than one and a half times their average rent.[36] Fifty years earlier London coal-porters interviewed by Mayhew – one of whom boasted that he limited himself to a pint an hour while working – cheerfully admitted both that they spent over a third of their earnings upon drink and that most of them had some item in pawn.[37] Drink was also indirectly responsible for some of the poverty ascribed to low wages, unemployment, and sickness. Much working time was lost in drinking and in recovery from its effects; habitual drunkards risked dismissal and prolonged unemployment; and some drank themselves into ill health and an early grave. Heavy drinkers claimed that beer was necessary to their strength. But drink was an extraordinarily expensive way to obtain nutrition.[38]

Some men could not easily avoid drinking. Wages might be paid in public houses,[39] and public houses also served as unofficial labour exchanges. Publicans knew of local vacancies and foremen might be found at the bar with jobs at their disposal for whoever paid the rounds. To some extent also drink was obviously a consequence of poverty as well as one of its causes. The public house, warm and cheerful, and the company of friends were the more attractive if a man's work was unrewarding, his home squalid and overcrowded. Those demoralized by lack of work, and those experiencing the cultural shock of transition to industrial life, might equally seek solace in drink. But for many working-class males the pub was, by choice, their centre of life out of work. Many other working men, and the great majority of working-class wives, managed to cope with the difficulties of working-class existence without alcoholic support.[40]

One sign of the enormous importance of drink among the causes of working-class poverty was extensive temperance activity. The temperance movement is sometimes described as if it was an overwhelmingly middle-class phenomenon, concerned to impose bourgeois virtues upon an unregenerate proletariat. But, as we noted in Chapter 3, the middle classes had no monopoly of the Victorian virtues: temperance was as much a working-class trait as drunkenness. The Order of Rechabites (total abstinence) was one of the largest friendly societies at the end of the century; 'new model' trade unionists (sober in every sense) moved their branch meetings from the public house; and a temperance hotel was among the initial objectives of the Rochdale co-operative pioneers in 1844. Henry Vincent led a teetotal Chartist movement and numerous other working-class leaders had a part in the abstemious tradition. John Burns, for example, boasted that Battersea's new Latchmere Estate (1903) would 'not be tainted with an off-licence or degraded by a beer shop'.[41] Keir Hardie at one time prescribed lessons on temperance and thrift as the remedy for poverty and proclaimed the reason why so much poverty existed after decades of material progress to be self-evident, 'The people are pouring it down their throats in intoxicating drink'.[42]

Large families were also shown by Booth and Rowntree to be less important among the causes of poverty than many had believed. Nevertheless they were important. And, like drink, they were indirectly responsible for some of the poverty ascribed to low wages and other causes. Rowntree calculated that almost a quarter of those in primary poverty at York would have escaped poverty had they not burdened modest incomes with five or more children.[43] Bowley and Burnett-Hurst touched upon another aspect of this relationship when they noted that in the towns they surveyed 16 per cent of the working-class population, but 27 per cent of the child working-class population, lived below the poverty line.[44] Drink and the unequal division of family income may have had some responsibility for this demographically-induced poverty. Had working men suffered equally with their wives the consequences of devoting so much income to raising children they would probably have been less indifferent to its cost. As it was they often had sufficient when the rest of the family went hungry, and the public house provided a more than acceptable escape from overcrowded accommodation. Thus protected, men felt less incentive to limit their families to what their income could comfortably support, or to emancipate their wives from a lifetime of pregnancy and child-minding.

125

III · *Treatment of poverty, (a) charity*

There were two main agencies of poor relief: charity and the poor law. For a number of reasons, perhaps most of all because the poor law reform of 1834 has generated so much controversy and because it has become customary to look first to the government to treat poverty, historians have always devoted far more attention to the poor law than to charity. Of the two, however, charity almost certainly dispensed the greater amount in poor relief during the century after 1815. In the 1860s the annual expenditure of the charities of London alone was roughly equivalent to the combined expenditure of all the poor law authorities of England and Wales.[45] At Edinburgh private charity was still distributing well over twice as much as the poor law authorities in 1911.[46] Some charitable spending was only tenuously related to relieving poverty – much of the sum earmarked for educational purposes for example – but there was also a very considerable flow of personal charity that passed unrecorded.

Charitable activities appeared in numerous forms and to further a bewildering variety of worthy causes. Informal charity embraced the grateful pension to long-serving domestic servants, the bedding and beef tea bestowed upon the rural poor during sickness and childbirth, and the impromptu 'whip-round' of workmates and neighbours for victims of a pit or factory accident. Prominent among medical charities were the voluntary hospitals where the poor were treated gratis upon production of a subscriber's letter of introduction or for a nominal fee. Employers whose workmen suffered many accidents were generally generous subscribers to these hospitals, some trade unions also subscribed, and so did many poor law authorities. Until the second half of the nineteenth century most poor law authorities had only rudimentary hospital facilities of their own. There were also voluntary dispensaries providing advice and medicine to out-patients, voluntary asylums (many of them housing poor law clients), voluntary 'lying-in' charities with their voluntary midwives, and (in the second half of the century) the 'medical missions' that dispensed a concoction of medicine and religion to the urban poor. The relative importance of voluntary medical assistance declined after 1860 but a survey of Norwich in 1910 found voluntary medical expenditure still equivalent to the combined expenditure of the poor law authorities and town council.[47] Housing charities included those engaged in the 'model dwellings' movement after 1840 (above, p. 97) and those concerned with providing almshouses for the elderly. There were charities whose mission was to alleviate poverty by distributing surplus population throughout the Empire, and numerous others whose character was determined either by what they offered – bread, coal, blankets, soup, etc. – or by whom they relieved. Each fever epidemic and hard winter gave rise to numerous *ad hoc* appeals[48] and major crises and disasters were matched by voluntary efforts on a commensurate scale. The appeal on behalf of the dependants of victims of the Hartley Colliery explosion (1862), for example, raised £82,000[49] and well over £1 million was collected to relieve Lancastrians during the cotton famine.

There was a voluntary response, in fact, to virtually every social need. Until near the end of the nineteenth century charity was widely believed to be both capable of treating the whole range of social problems and to be almost invariably the most appropriate agency for this task. This belief was natural at a time when society was more integrated than it has become and when the role of government was far more circumscribed. Help for the distressed, particularly for those nearby, was an unwritten but widely accepted responsibility of the propertied classes. And assistance far more often entailed the personal involvement of donors than is possible when mandatory aid reaches the poor via anonymous civil servants and salaried social workers. There can be no denying the impressive achievement of nineteenth-century charitable agencies. In the comprehensiveness of their endeavours, and in the sheer volume of their assistance, they exceeded both what was accomplished by public relief and what had been accomplished by charity in the past. Charities were less inhibited than governments by dread of spending, by the necessity to await consensus approval before introducing innovations, or by bureaucratic inflexibility. In many areas of social welfare voluntary activity appears to have been a useful, almost an essential, preliminary to collective activity. Charities, that is, showed what needed to be done and what was possible. They also established a great deal of what became the accepted theory and practice of social administration.

For a number of reasons charitable activity increased substantially in the first half of the nineteenth century. 90 of the 119 voluntary hospitals, dispensaries, and infirmaries serving London in 1862 had been founded since 1800, and well over half of all the capital's 640 charities had come into existence between these dates.[50] The increase was primarily a consequence of the heightened social consciousness, the greater readiness to recognize and tackle social problems, that was mentioned earlier (above, p. 68). The churches, the Church of England especially, vigorously set about making amends for their previous semi-neglect of the urban poor. There was a conscious redeployment of effort from the heathen overseas to the heathen at home whose material deprivation came to be regarded as no less a matter of concern than his spiritual poverty. Charity was also extended as population growth and industrialization intensified social problems, and because of the new awareness of the relationship between poverty and disease. In addition, the threat of social unrest reminded the wealthy that charity was conducive to social stability as well as being good for their souls. Voluntary help demonstrated self-sacrifice and sympathy and its acceptance implied a degree of obligation and willing subordination. The contribution of insurrectionary fears to the increase in charitable activity is easily exaggerated, however, because there was no noticeable slackening of charitable endeavour for several decades after the last Chartist threat.[51] Another part of the explanation of expanding charitable activity is the unparalleled opportunities it offered for social climbing. Industrialists and businessmen (and their underemployed wives) were eager to establish their qualifications for social advance by emulating, or out-bidding, established leaders in their devotion to good causes. This early nineteenth-century expansion in charitable activity is not least remarkable for occurring in the face of the same dire warnings of the consequence of impulsive benevolence that drastically curbed poor law expenditure. Whether the expansion was sufficient to entirely offset the reduction in poor law expenditure is not known. But charity doubtless softened the blow.[52]

Even so, the charities failed to achieve their long-term ambitions and by the early twentieth century their relative importance in the relief of poverty was rapidly declining. Several serious shortcomings in the charity movement had been apparent long before 1900. One was the very uneven availability of relief. Londoners, East Enders most of all, were exceptionally well endowed with charities as were inhabitants of once prosperous towns like Norwich and Canterbury.[53] But the fast-growing industrial towns had fewer long-established funds to draw upon and a relatively small proportion of wealthy inhabitants. There was unevenness too in the management of charities. Some were well administered and dispensed their funds with maximum effect. The cotton famine relief, for example, was considered to have been handled competently. But certain charities were notorious for the scandalously large part of their income which was swallowed up in administrative expenses. Moreover, the warnings of the political economists were not entirely alarmist. Indiscriminate relief unaccompanied by attempts to tackle the cause of poverty was of little lasting benefit and discouraged self-help. A Canterbury wine merchant described how on the day of distribution of 10s gifts he was inundated by over-the-counter orders amounting to exactly that sum, and the chaotic distribution of the Mansion House Fund of 1886 was said to have brought numerous provincial rogues to London and to have induced working men to abandon their employment.[54]

It was to reduce such dangers that the Charity Organization Society (cos) had been founded in 1869. The cos was intended to co-ordinate charitable activity and to act as an initial clearing-house through which every applicant for relief would be required to pass. Its sponsors represented that part of the charity movement most sympathetic to the spirit of the reformed poor law of 1834 and most prepared to accept the charge that indiscriminate charity was undermining the remedial work of the poor law authorities. Many charities resented this charge and others were not prepared to yield any jurisdiction over the distribution of their funds. So the COS never enjoyed as much influence as it desired. But it gained sufficient influence to become accepted as the mouthpiece of voluntary poor relief. Its first priority was to curb indiscriminate benevolence of the kind that was alleged to degrade and demoralize recipients. This meant substituting for merely palliative assistance, help that was remedial and tailored to meet the particular circumstances of each distressed individual. It meant also a thorough vetting of applicants for relief, including visits to their homes, and a great deal of personal advice and guidance. The essential characteristics of the COS approach were the 'caseworker-client' relationship and the belief that material assistance combined with sympathetic interest and guidance was far more valuable, and more appreciated, than anonymous hand-outs. Assistance might be conditional upon the recipient joining a friendly society, attending temperance classes, sending his children to school, or some similar course of action designed to stimulate prudence and self-respect. The COS method was designed also to confound the professional scrounger who might be drawing upon several charities and poor law outdoor relief at the same time. One of its aims, in fact, was to secure a drastic reduction in poor law out-relief as part of a clearer division of responsibilities between public and voluntary activity, in which charities (and charities alone) would assist 'deserving' cases who were not in need of institutional care while the unregenerate able-bodied poor would be left to accept relief inside the workhouse.

The COS can fairly claim to have reduced some of the inefficiency of unorganized charity and it was largely responsible for several positive advances in the development of social services. These included the extension and formalization of 'casework' technique, social work training, the introduction of hospital almoners, and the beginnings of a social work literature.[55] But the COS was inclined to exaggerate working-class immorality and to underestimate the volume of unavoidable poverty. Its heavy paternalism and inquisitional preliminaries to assistance caused much resentment. As the nature and causes of poverty were reassessed and intellectual opinion moved toward accepting greater collective responsibility COS attitudes came under attack. Booth and Rowntree demonstrated the failure of charity and the existing poor law to provide adequate solutions to poverty and implied a need for radical preventive measures of the kind only governments could undertake. The COS reaction to the surveys was to dispute their methods, their results, and their implications. Proposals for non-contributory old age pensions, for free school meals, for sick and unemployment insurance, all met the response that they were likely to undermine incentives and working-class self-respect. Such unbending attitudes appeared increasingly old-fashioned and the COS lost influence and a good many of its more distinguished supporters. After 1906 it saw the state and local government agencies move purposefully into areas that once were the prerogative of voluntary agencies and the wholesale introduction of exactly the kind of welfare legislation it had so vehemently opposed.

IV · *Treatment of poverty, (b) the poor law; the old poor law and the 1834 Poor Law Amendment Act*

The legislative framework of poor law relief as it existed at the beginning of our period had been established in the seventeenth century. The main provisions were that the parish was the unit of administration; that relief was paid from a tax upon property within the parish; and that it was administered by unpaid 'overseers' of the poor whose duty it was to assist, whenever necessary, all those with a legal 'settlement' in the parish.[56] The 'impotent' poor (children, the aged and sick) were entitled to maintenance, the able-bodied poor were to be found work. This legal right to either employment or maintenance, a guarantee that although a man might be destitute he need not starve, was the chief distinguishing feature of the poor law in England and Wales until near the end of the nineteenth century.[57]

Within this broad framework the 15,000 parishes enjoyed considerable discretion. What became of applicants for relief under the old (pre-1834) poor law thus varied enormously from place to place. Most parishes managed without a workhouse, but some had built one in the eighteenth century and some 'unions' of neighbouring parishes shared a workhouse between them in the fashion that all parishes were compelled to follow after 1834.[58] Some of these early workhouses were primarily shelters for sick and elderly paupers who were unable to care for themselves, but in others the able-bodied poor were put to work at tasks designed, according to parish policy, either to be as unpleasant as possible, to bring the parish the maximum return, or to impart useful skills. Some parishes simply leased the entire workhouse to a private contractor. Certain of the parishes with no workhouse also hired out the able-bodied poor to the highest bidder, others put them to work mending the roads, and some dispensed outdoor relief without requiring work in return. There was similar variety in virtually every other aspect of poor relief. There was also great variety in standards of administrative efficiency. The average level was not high and corruption was commonplace. In some places, however, the part-time and unpaid overseers achieved standards that even the commissioners of 1834 were unable to fault. Some of the best administered districts were parish unions where the overseers had delegated part of their duties to salaried, full-time, officials who were able to exercise close control over day-to-day administration. Among the urban districts of Lancashire and

Yorkshire, in particular, reform was well advanced long before the great reform act of 1834.

Most of what has so far been said of poor law relief in the early nineteenth century does not apply to Scotland. North of the border the poor enjoyed no right to support from the rates, and taxation played a comparatively minor role in their relief. For the most part they were assisted from what was raised by church-door collections and other voluntary subscriptions. In rural Scotland local taxation was seldom levied other than in times of exceptional distress and at such times, during highland famines for example, central government aid generally far exceeded what was collected in local taxes. The larger Scottish towns levied poor rates on a more regular basis, but there too the poor had no rights to public assistance, the rates contributed comparatively little to their relief, and their lot was generally inferior to that of paupers in England and Wales.

Amid this confusion of poor relief practices and attitudes certain trends are apparent. Perhaps the most important was mounting demographic pressure upon the system of poor relief. So long as population had grown slowly and was roughly matched by the expansion of local employment the poor law arrangements coped adequately. But the population increase of the second half of the eighteenth century was only in a few places accompanied by a comparable expansion of employment; elsewhere, unemployment and the poor rates increased together. The corn-growing counties of the south and east, where the harvest peak demand for labour discouraged out-migration of surplus population, suffered most of all. The need of these areas to shed labour, and the need of the industrializing districts to attract labour, greatly increased the significance of the restraints upon labour mobility that were inseparable from the existing system of parochial relief. The old poor law had been designed for a relatively static society.[59] But now the need was for greater mobility, and a system that guaranteed a man subsistence where he was born, whether work was available locally or not, and which encouraged other parishes to receive him with unkindly suspicion, was an obvious impediment to mobility.

Although these pressures were felt in the eighteenth century, there was at that time no noticeable attempt to curb expenditure. The trend rather was to make relief more easily obtainable. And when in 1793 war with France increased bread prices and swelled applications for relief the parish authorities responded generously. They were moved both by compassion for the poor and by their anxiety to contain discontent during wartime. Rural overseers knew also that wartime grain prices would help ratepayers to meet the cost of additional relief. In 1795 the justices of Speenhamland in Berkshire announced that they would henceforth grant out-relief to all in need – sick or able-bodied, employed or unemployed – on a declared scale that took account of the price of bread, the number of a man's dependants, and his income. This expedient was widely adopted throughout much of the rural south and midlands. Some versions of the Speenhamland system were far from generous, but in most parishes its adoption meant that relief was easier to obtain and that the pauper population came to include many more able-bodied men whose wages were supplemented from the poor rates. It meant too that a smaller proportion of all relief was granted inside parish workhouses.

Peace, in 1815, brought an end to exceptional farming prosperity and the swollen poor rates were then regarded with greater concern. The poor were helped by lower grain prices, of course, but rapid population increase had continued during the war and a quarter of a million discharged soldiers and sailors now swelled the ranks of unemployed and semi-employed labour. After the war poor law expenditure per head of population – about 12s per annum or between one and two weeks' wages for a southern farm labourer – was (in real terms) 50 per cent or more above the level of the mid-1780s.[60] This might appear to have been not too onerous a burden when servicing the national debt was costing four times as much. But whereas interest on the national debt was paid out of central government funds, each parish was separately responsible for its poor and in places the poor rates were several times as high as the national average. Sussex, with a population only slightly greater than Northumberland, in 1831 spent between three and four times as much on poor relief, and some Sussex parishes were supporting well over a third of their working population.[61]

The current cost was not the only reason for concern. The second census, taken in 1811, had shown that population was growing as fast as Malthus had feared. His gloomy prognoses now commanded greater attention and his views on the poor law were unequivocal. Poverty, and the fear of poverty, he believed to be among the 'preventive checks' against early marriage and over-population. Poor relief removed this check and the increased relief offered at marriage and at the birth of each additional child was alleged to act as 'a bounty upon population'. In other ways, too, the poor law was believed to be sustaining the poverty it was attempting to alleviate. Generous out-relief, it was said, reduced the incentive to seek work and so men grew accustomed to a tolerable idleness. Employers, knowing that the parish would provide the necessary supplement, were alleged to be progressively reducing wages, and thus accelerating the pauperization of the labour force and leaving no place for the self-respecting labourer who was eager for work at a living wage. Generous parish relief was said also to be encouraging relatives to neglect their obligations towards the sick and elderly.

For all these reasons poor relief was tightened-up after 1815. There was no sustained decline in real expenditure (prices were falling) but the rate of increase was definitely curbed. Even so, critics were far from satisfied. The canker of demoralization, as they saw it, was contained, but they sought its complete removal by a drastic reform of the whole mechanism of public relief. Most critics urged a form of public assistance that would dispense relief less liberally and under conditions that offered no incentive to idleness, improvidence, early marriage, or large families. The more positive critics – the Benthamites or utilitarians – were anxious also to sweep away the corruption, inefficiency, and irritating untidiness of the existing parochial administration. They envisaged a system that would be more uniform and more subject to central direction, one in which the idle, the sick, the aged, and every other category of pauper would be classified, separated, and accorded their appropriate treatment. Certain features of existing administration in the better-managed towns and parishes were held up as examples: the enlightened treatment of the sick poor at Manchester for example, and the strict application of the deterrent workhouse test at Southwell and elsewhere in Nottinghamshire. Inspiration came also from Scotland where the poor were afforded very few opportunities to become demoralized.

This was the background to the Royal Commission on the Poor Laws that was appointed in 1832 to report on the operation of the poor relief and how it might be improved. Edwin Chadwick and Nassau Senior were the leading influences among the nine commissioners. Detailed questionnaires were sent to every parish in England and Wales and some 3,000 parishes, about one-fifth of the total, were visited. The commissioners' report, completed in only two years, endorsed every major criticism of the existing system of relief and its main recommendations were incorporated in the Poor Law Amendment Act of 1834 that was to serve as the legislative basis of public relief until after the First World War. One of the two principal recommendations was that relief should be subject to the overall direction of a central poor law board with the power to combine parishes into larger, more efficient, 'unions' and whose task it would be to ensure that the poor laws were administered correctly, and uniformly, throughout the country. The 1834 Act accordingly established the Poor Law Board consisting of three commissioners with Edwin Chadwick as their secretary. It provided also that the new poor law unions were to be managed by elected 'boards of guardians' who were responsible for implementing the instructions of the Poor Law Board. These changes introduced an unusual degree of central influence in local affairs and represent a major landmark in administrative history. The other principal recommendation of the Royal Commission, and one of greater concern to the poor, was that the able-bodied poor and their families should henceforth be assisted only within a workhouse and under conditions that were 'less eligible' than those of the lowest-paid independent labourer outside. The Act that followed made no specific regulation on this point but it was quite clear that in reforming the system of relief the new Poor Law Board was to be guided by the

Commission's recommendation. Among other recommendations similarly accepted were that children, the sick, and the elderly should be treated separately from the able-bodied poor, and that parishes should be encouraged to use the poor rates to subsidize the emigration of surplus population.

The new poor law reflected several contemporary philosophies. Promoting emigration, discouraging early marriage, and the separation of husbands and wives in the workhouse all show the influence of Malthusian thought. Liberal individualism was evident in the harsh incentives to self-help and the underlying assumption that poverty was normally the consequence of personal shortcomings. The purposeful state interventionism and the search for order and efficiency were purely utilitarian. What the new law conspicuously lacked, however, was the softening influence of humanitarianism whose effect upon the volume of voluntary poor relief has already been described. To the poor this omission was its most conspicuous feature. Henceforth, or so it seemed, they were to be more punished than pitied and this hardening of the spirit was understandably resented.

The new attitude towards the poor, and the new poor law itself, derived in part from certain incorrect assumptions that the Royal Commission failed to notice. The Commission had been appointed in response to insistent demands for retrenchment and reform and was dominated by leading critics of the old poor law. They had no doubt of what the inquiry would discover and their findings and recommendations reflected more the situation as they imagined it to be than the situation that existed. Only one parish in ten returned the Commission's questionnaire, and the parishes that were visited appear to have been selected on no scientific basis. Indeed, they may have been selected, consciously or unconsciously, because they best illustrated the commissioners' preconceptions.[62] Chief among their misapprehensions was a grossly exaggerated notion of the extent of unemployment and under-employment among able-bodied men. This category of pauperism offered the most tangible evidence of the demoralizing effect of liberal out-relief. It was most common in the rural south, but even there the greater part of the pauper population consisted of old people, children, and the sick, most of whom had no choice between work and pauperism.[63] In the northern industrial districts, moreover, there was little permanent unemployment of the kind that obsessed Chadwick and his colleagues. Industrial unemployment was largely cyclical and the old poor law was well adapted to its treatment.

Recent research suggests that the allegedly rising expenditure upon wage supplements, the supposed 'snowballing' effect of Speenhamland payments (above, p. 132), was also largely imagined.[64] The commissioners erred too in their understanding of the relationship between wage rates and the level of poor relief. Their prejudices led them to conclude that the main reason why poor rates were highest where wages were low was not that low-wage districts needed most relief, but rather that high poor rates in these districts had reduced wages.* They were correct in assuming that population pressure was prominent among the causes of rural poverty, but wrong in assuming that the poor law had much responsibility for this pressure through its supposed encouragement of early marriage and large families. Population growth probably owed more to falling mortality than to rising fertility and was by no means confined to the Speenhamland counties. Poor relief, in fact, may have affected death-rates as much as birth-rates, both by providing poor families with sufficient extra income to reduce infant mortality and by encouraging people to remain in parts of the country where mortality was lowest. But neither its influence upon birth-rate nor its influence upon mortality were of much significance.

There are at least three other general criticisms of the Royal Commission on the Poor Laws. The first is that it too easily assumed that most of the working classes fell naturally into idleness and improvidence if given the opportunity, and that many of the unemployed were therefore idle by choice. Secondly, the commissioners were far too sanguine in their calculation of how much central direction in local affairs would be tolerated. And, third, they failed to include among their administrative reforms any provision to ease the financial burden of the poorest parishes. Each separate union, and each parish within each union, was to remain entirely responsible for the cost of maintaining its own poor.

As most of the false assumptions and false remedies of the Royal Commission were echoed in the Poor Law Amendment Act of 1834 it seemed inevitable that some of those deterred from applying for relief by the workhouse regime would suffer not from the trauma of having to work, but from unrelieved poverty. It seemed likely too that a workhouse regime sufficiently harsh to deter the idle would also be the lot of many deserving poor who were forced to apply for relief. Moreover, its operation in the northern manufacturing districts, where the trade cycle was a major cause of unemployment, appeared to require an enormous initial expenditure upon workhouse accommodation, most of which would stand empty in normal times. The same act, however, offered solutions, or partial solutions, to several problems. It promised to curb administrative inefficiency and corruption, to introduce improved and more specialized treatment for children, the sick, and

* To some extent poor relief doubtless did influence wages in the way the commissioners supposed, but influence of this kind was probably offset (or more than offset) by its tendency to reduce labour supply (and thus raise wages) as a consequence of inducing some men, and allowing many wives and children, to withdraw from the labour market. The old poor law, in fact, may well have had a far more unfavourable influence upon wages than Mark Blaug and other critics of the 1834 report have recognized. But it influenced wages mainly by discouraging labour mobility, not by wage subsidies.

the elderly, to remove at least some of the impediments that the poor laws imposed upon labour mobility, and to reduce poor rates in the hardest pressed districts. It promised also to take away poor law incentives to idleness and improvidence, of which there were certainly sufficient to provide a plausible basis for the commissioners' exaggerations.

v · *The new poor law; the poor law under attack*

Thus the amended poor law was a mixture of necessary reform and misconceived innovation. It was fortunate therefore that local opposition, the commissioners' own second thoughts, and their feeble powers of enforcement, combined to prevent the law ever being applied in its full doctrinal rigidity. Unfortunately, some of the more welcome reforms were also stillborn. Local opposition was fiercest in Lancashire and the West Riding where there had been considerable piecemeal reform before 1834, where ratepayers and the poor were fairly satisfied with existing arrangements, and where the inappropriateness of the new remedies for industrial areas was underlined by the onset of trade depression in 1836. Establishing the new poor law unions, the election of boards of guardians, and the erection of workhouses were all delayed by the organized resistance of the local population that will be described in Chapter 6. In 1850 many Lancashire and West Riding unions were still making do with what workhouse accommodation they had inherited from the old regime and no union had built sufficient accommodation to fully enforce the workhouse test. By bending the law, by exploiting its obscurities, by procrastination, obfuscation, and outright defiance, much of the spirit and practice of the old poor law was successfully preserved within the administrative framework of the new. Surprised at this response, and lacking the means and the will to impose their wishes, the Poor Law Commission retreated. Uncompromising dictation gave way to consultation and hopeful persuasion; breaches of the law and enormous variation in administrative practice were tactfully overlooked.

Lancashire and West Riding authorities were particularly successful in maintaining their preference for out-relief. Maintaining a man upon out-relief was far cheaper than maintaining him inside the workhouse. Workhouses yielded economies only if their higher *per capita* costs were offset by a more than proportionate drop in applications for relief, and the Lancashire and West Riding guardians believed that the great majority of their charges deserved relief and were not to be confused with the demoralized pauper population that allegedly existed in the rural south. They had no objection to imposing the workhouse test upon the workshy: this had always been their policy. But its extension, they claimed, would impose unnecessary suffering upon the respectable poor and risk demoralizing them *inside* the workhouse by contact with professional scroungers. There was the possibility too that the workhouse separation of husband, wife, and children might break-up marriages (and thus further burden the poor rates), and it was obvious that a man forced into the workhouse was badly placed to find work when the trade cycle recovered. The proportion of paupers relieved inside workhouses rose very little in these two counties. In the 1840s over 90 per cent of West Riding paupers were still being assisted by outdoor relief and the main workhouse function remained the provision of hospital facilities and accommodation for needy children and the elderly poor.[65] Some unions compromised with the new regime by introducing the 'labour test' whereby out-relief was combined with daily taskwork at the workhouse or on the roads. Others dispensed out-relief as freely as they had done before 1834.

On Tyneside and in some other parts of the north the concessions won in Lancashire and the West Riding were conceded without a fight.[66] There were also more than thirty towns up and down the country where existing local acts provided partial immunity from innovation.[67] Poor law practice changed most in the rural south where the old poor law had most needed reform and where the commissioners faced little overt or organized opposition. Even in the south, however, there was far less dis-continuity than the statute book implies. There was a general tightening-up, more workhouses were built, and systematic out-relief of the Speenhamland kind virtually disappeared. But in time the southern guardians also learnt to bend the rules. They retained a great deal of their autonomy, they continued to grant far more out-relief than the Poor Law Commission thought desirable, and thus they afforded the southern poor considerable protection from the insensibilities of the new law. One of the most exploited weaknesses in the regulations was the clause permitting out-relief to able-bodied men in the event of sickness or accident. Expenditure under this heading in Norfolk and Suffolk was twice the national average between 1842 and 1846 – a level that reflected not local epidemics but the continuation of traditional means of relieving surplus population without violating the letter of the law.[68] In England and Wales as a whole the great majority of able-bodied adult paupers continued to be relieved without being made to enter a workhouse.[69]

There was sufficient overall change, however, to substantially reduce total poor law expenditure, despite an increase in the workhouse population,[70] and to reduce the proportion of the population seeking aid. The proportion of the total population assisted from the rates fell from 8.8 per cent in 1834 to 5.7 per cent in 1850, and to only 3.2 per cent in 1880.[71] How were these savings achieved and at what cost to the poor? Not all came from denying what had been given readily before 1834. Some came from more professional administration, economies of scale, and reduced corruption. It was to be expected also that rising real wages after 1850 would reduce demands upon poor relief irrespective of poor law policy. And among those who might have received more assistance under a less deterrent system there were many who did not suffer much under the new regime: some of those who were encouraged by the new poor law to move to well-paid work elsewhere, for example, and some of those whose response had been to enrol in friendly societies.[72] Of the rest, it is probably safe to assume that reduced help from the poor law authorities was in many cases offset by greater assistance from relatives (as the poor law commissioners had intended) or out of the ever-increasing sums dispensed by charities. Some others – how many we cannot tell – suffered deprivation in one form or another.

Perhaps the greatest sufferers from increased stringency were not those deterred from applying for relief but those who received it, especially those relieved in the workhouse. Just how cruel were the new poor law workhouses is a question once obscured by considerable myth. The most typical post-1834 workhouse was a less pleasant institution than the most typical of its predecessors, but it was not nearly so bad as those workhouses portrayed in the propaganda of the anti-poor law movement and in the caricatured accounts of 'condition of England' novelists. The new workhouses were in many cases less crowded and insanitary than the workhouses built before 1834. Some of the very worst workhouse conditions, in fact, were to be seen in those places successfully resisting the Poor Law Commission – preference for the old ways was in several places 'prompted as much by a desire for economy as for humanity'.[73] And certain of the much publicized workhouse scandals, including the notorious Andover affair of 1845,* arose less from innovations introduced in 1834 than from the inability of the commissioners to enforce their regulations. The reformed workhouses provided accommodation that was rather cleaner and certainly no more overcrowded than the worst urban housing, and workhouse food – monotonous, none too plentiful, and badly cooked as it often was – compared not unfavourably with what the poorest classes were accustomed to at home.[74] Accommodation and diets much 'less eligible' than those of the worst-paid independent labourers would have meant a greater risk of sickness and malnutrition than the authorities dared contemplate. It remained true also that English and Welsh paupers were still, on the whole, better fed, better housed, and less harshly treated than the majority of paupers elsewhere – in Europe.

The mainstay of the poor law deterrent, and the most resented contrast with the old regime, was strict workhouse discipline and the increased stigma that was successfully attached to pauper status. The typical workhouse accommodated men, women, and children (and thus husbands, wives, and their offspring) in separate wings. The inmates rose early and took their meals

* Half-starved inmates of the Andover workhouse were discovered to be fighting over the marrow in putrid bones that they were crushing to use as fertilizer.

in enforced silence, they were deprived of most of their personal possessions and wore a distinctive uniform that was intended both as a constant reminder of their fall from respectable independence and as a warning to others. Permission to go outside the workhouse, to receive visitors, to smoke, were each beset with grudging restrictions, and workhouse labour – stone breaking, oakum picking, and similar tasks – was of soul-destroying monotony. All paupers, indoor or outdoor, lost the right to vote and faced a prying investigation into their personal circumstances. In 1836 Chadwick even attempted to ban the tolling of church bells at pauper funerals.

One of the most unfortunate aspects of the new regime was that children and the elderly and sick workhouse inmates, whom Chadwick and the rest had never intended to suffer the deterrent workhouse regime, were in many places treated little differently from the 'undeserving' able-bodied poor. The 1834 report recommended that sick and aged paupers should normally receive outdoor relief, and that those admitted to the workhouse should be housed separately and 'granted their indulgences'. It was intended, for example, that elderly couples should sleep in married quarters rather than in segregated dormitory accommodation. But these good intentions were costly and they conflicted with the overriding desire to reduce expenditure. Moreover, special treatment for the old and sick conflicted with other tenets of the new poor law. Some guardians considered that the expenses of age and sickness should be met from savings, and in this light those who had neglected to join friendly societies and sick clubs were not entirely 'deserving': to treat them kindly was to provide an incentive for others to be similarly improvident. They argued also that too many workhouse 'indulgences' would encourage sons and daughters to neglect their duty towards aged parents. So while in some places treatment of the old and sick improved noticeably in the 1830s,[75] in many other places plans for their special treatment were quietly shelved.

In time, however, the Poor Law Commission and its successors, the Poor Law Board (1847) and the Local Government Board (1871), gradually succeeded in enforcing better treatment for the non-able-bodied poor. More unions built separate workhouse infirmaries, some of a commendably high standard; more poor law dispensaries were established; and in appointing poor law doctors guardians began to give greater consideration to medical qualifications and rather less to filling the post at the least cost. Poor law doctors, traditionally resentful of the guardians' niggardliness, had always been inclined to regard their charges more as patients than as paupers. Mindful also that their own status advanced with improvements in poor law medical services, they campaigned for further reforms. There was a major breakthrough in 1867 with the Metropolitan Poor Law Act providing for the establishment of purpose-built and professionally staffed institutions for the sick and insane. From this time onwards, in London first and then throughout the country, indoor medical services for the poor began to assume the appearance, and some of the spirit, of a general hospital service for the working classes. The new hospitals were physically separate from the workhouses, trained nurses gradually took the place of untrained female pauper assistants, and medical considerations came to take priority over concern for the rates. In 1885 the stigma of disenfranchisement was removed from those whose only call upon the rates was for medical assistance. By this time approaching three-quarters of all hospital beds were administered by the poor law authorities.

Treatment of pauper children and the elderly also improved. The original new poor law policy for child paupers was that they should be educated in workhouse schools rather than being put out to 'apprenticeships' at the first opportunity, a policy that had too often meant simply off-loading orphans as cheap labour. By the 1860s, however, thinking was moving in favour of removing children from the workhouse atmosphere by placing them either with suitable foster parents or in small 'children's homes' where conditions were as close as possible to family life and from which they could attend local schools with non-pauper children. Less was done to provide separate accommodation for elderly paupers. The majority of these, of course, received out-relief and a substantial proportion of those receiving in-relief were sick. But most of the remainder continued to live within the main workhouse. Their conditions, however, were made increasingly distinguishable from the harsh regime that was originally intended for the able-bodied poor. In 1847 boards of guardians were instructed not to separate elderly couples. Later injunctions attempted to free the old from the more onerous restrictions upon visiting and absences from the workhouse. Some unions were not in need of such instructions – others, however, were still separating elderly couples after 1900. As with most other aspects of poor relief, there was still a great diversity of practices and standards.

Among other notable developments in poor law practice during the second and third quarters of the century were the changes in the settlement law that are described in Chapter 5, the changes in poor law financing initiated by the 1865 Union Chargeability Act which ended the system whereby each parish in the union was separately responsible for the cost of maintaining its own poor, and significant changes in Scottish poor law administration. The effect of the changes in Scottish poor relief was gradually to reduce the contrast with English practice. As urbanization and industrialization advanced, and as migration filled Scotland's towns with newcomers unknown to the kirk officials and subject to trade cycle unemployment, the strain on the voluntary relief agencies had increased. A growing proportion of poverty was relieved from the rates and there was increasing pressure for reform. In 1843 a schism deprived the Church of Scotland (the chief source of voluntary relief) of a large part of its membership and soon after a Royal Commission was appointed to enquire into Scottish poor relief and suggest improvements. Its main findings were that relief was inadequate and ill-organized. The subsequent Poor Act of 1845, 'for the amendment and better administration of the laws relating to the relief of the poor in Scotland', required each parish to give 'adequate' help to the poor and set up a central board of supervision to direct their activities. The able-bodied poor were specifically excluded from any rights to relief, the parishes were still not combined into unions, and they were not obliged to erect workhouses, or even to have poor rates at all if adequate voluntary help was forthcoming. Nevertheless, this legislation was a significant step towards the English system and as the Board of Supervision used its powers to raise relief towards English levels more parishes were compelled to levy a poor rate. By the 1890s some 95 per cent of Scottish parishes levied poor rates and both expenditure per head of population on public poor relief and the proportion of the whole population in receipt of relief had moved close to levels in England and Wales.[76]

In the mid-1860s the proportion of the English and Welsh population on relief had begun to rise after falling for three decades.[77] Relief expenditure rose too[78] and fears were expressed that poor law practice had moved so far from the 'spirit of 1834' that the workhouse threat was no longer a sufficient deterrent. In fact, the rise in the pauper population was to prove short-lived and increased expenditure was mainly a consequence of better treatment for non-able-bodied paupers. But there had been a general softening of the workhouse regime[79] and an increasing willingness to grant out-relief – and there was now a campaign to reverse these tendencies by re-imposing the principles recommended in the 1834 Report. Out-relief to the able-bodied came under particular attack: in certain unions widows and deserted wives in receipt of out-relief were deprived of their children so that they might find employment, elderly paupers were threatened with the workhouse in the hope of provoking filial aid, and charities were entreated to avoid blunting the workhouse deterrent by ministering to the 'undeserving'. In the following decades the long-term retreat from the harsher aspects of the 1834 regime was periodically interrupted by similar attempts to stiffen poor law administration. They erupted whenever the number of paupers or the level of poor law expenditure appeared to rise unduly, and they were concentrated particularly in London where the persistence of poverty and failure of the workhouse deterrent were most obvious.

Not long after the first of these campaigns the poor law began to be criticized from quite different quarters. From Oxford T. H. Green and his disciples mounted a scholarly attack on *laissez-faire* liberalism. Their 'new liberal' alternative looked less towards self-help to keep men out of poverty and more towards government preventive measures. And at a time when growing overseas competition was eroding middle-class confidence and faith in economic individualism, such ideas had a better reception than would have seemed possible in the third quarter of the century. Socialists, whose voices were beginning to be heard in the 1880s, joined the attack upon the poor law and were particularly critical of the assumption that poverty was largely a consequence of moral weaknesses. Parts of the trade union movement, suddenly strengthened in the late 1880s, added to the criticism. The franchise expansion of 1884 had made politicians more willing to listen to working-class complaints and in 1894 the property qualifications for membership of boards of guardians were abolished, which enabled some of the more articulate working-class critics of the poor law to attack the system from within. The poverty surveys showed both that there was more poverty than there ought to have been if the workhouse deterrent functioned effectively and that poverty was less the consequence of character defects than poor law thinking assumed. They showed too that many independent workmen lived below the level necessary to industrial efficiency, a finding supported by the alarming proportion of Boer War recruits found unfit for service.

At a time of mounting economic competition and competition for tropical territory, of war in South Africa and threat of war in Europe, evidence that poverty was making men unfit to be either efficient workmen or efficient soldiers created a considerable stir.[80] Germany meanwhile had introduced old age pensions and state health insurance. All these developments helped to change attitudes to poverty. In particular they made the case for switching policy emphasis from relief to prevention. Charles Booth himself epitomized the change in attitudes. In the 1880s he was a liberal individualist of the traditional kind, anxious to repudiate socialist claims concerning the extent of poverty. Profoundly influenced by his own discoveries, he became a leading campaigner for non-contributory old age pensions and a convert to what he described as 'limited socialism'.[81]

The call for positive measures to prevent poverty met a fruitful response. Joseph Chamberlain's circular of 1886 encouraging local authorities to schedule public works so as to provide employment during trade depressions;[82] the 1891 Fair Wages Resolution; the Workmen's Compensation Acts of 1897 and 1906; the extension of public health activity concerned to prevent disease; the 1905 Unemployed Workmen Act; school meals and medical services; non-contributory old age pensions (1908); trade boards and labour exchanges (1909); and the introduction of health and unemployment insurance (1911) were all measures that afforded satisfaction to critics of the poor law. Each of these reforms was concerned at least as much with the prevention of poverty as with its relief, and most of them intruded upon areas of policy and administration that were traditionally regarded as falling within the jurisdiction of the poor law authorities. Old age pensions

(5s a week to those over 70) proved particularly effective in reducing the number of applicants for poor relief.

The position of the poor law authorities by 1900 clearly had a great deal in common with that of the COS (above, pp. 129–30). They had not been entirely unresponsive to pressure for change. But their critics were convinced that the poor law system was too unyielding, too permeated with the 'spirit of 1834', to serve as the framework of more radical policies. They argued too that the poor themselves, conditioned by more than half a century of 'less eligibility', would never look favourably upon welfare services administered by the guardians. For these reasons reformers endeavoured to place new welfare services outside the poor law administration. Old age pensions, for example, were met from central government funds and paid out at post offices. When Beatrice Webb called for the poor laws to be entirely abolished and their functions distributed among other local and state authorities (in her Poor Law Commission minority report of 1909) she was asking for something that had been effectively in the making since the 1880s. Her demands were not to be entirely satisfied, however, until after the Second World War.

Suggestions for further reading are on pages 401–2.

5

MIGRANTS, EMIGRANTS, IMMIGRANTS

1 · *Changes in population distribution; costs and benefits of labour mobility; British labour mobility, 1815–1914*

George Ewart Evans in one of his delightful books on East Anglian life (*Ask the Fellows Who Cut the Hay*) tells of John Edmunds, a Benhall man, who left his parish only once, to take corn to Wickham Market six miles away. Once safely back on his own side of Farnham Bridge he lit up his pipe and was heard to say 'Thank God I'm back in good owd England'. From another Suffolk village (Monk Soham) there is an account of a woman who received a letter from her son in Hull and sought comfort from the curate, 'That did me a tarn at first', she said 'for I thought that came from the *hot* place' (*Suffolk Times and Mercury*, 5 Oct. 1894). Some among the population of nineteenth-century Britain were obviously very parochial. Others, however, were equally remarkable for their readiness to uproot themselves and re-settle in distant places, or to move continually around the country and overseas in response to shifting economic opportunities. There were, for example, Scots miners who every summer when Scottish wages fell departed for the United States: 'Many of them have their return passage tickets', Alexander Macdonald (president of the National Miners Association) told an official enquiry in 1873, 'and whenever the wages come [down] to 4s or 5s or 6s a day they will not be found here but will be off.'[1] Cornish miners provide a similar example – so many of them moved to the Scottish coalfields that public libraries there took the Cornish newspapers.

The broad outlines of the distribution of population as it was in 1914 were already discernible a century earlier. For some time before 1815 the towns, and particularly industrial towns, had accommodated a fast increasing share of all people. This trend accelerated in the nineteenth century. In 1801 one person in six lived in a town of 20,000 and upwards, most of them in London; by 1851 more than a third of the population lived in towns of this size, and by 1911 considerably more than one-half. More than three-quarters of the population of Manchester, Bradford, and Glasgow aged twenty and over at the time of the 1851 census had been born elsewhere. And at the end of the century as many as 70 per cent of London policemen and over three-quarters of the staff of the London General Omnibus Company were country born.[2] As well as moving towards the towns Britain's centre of gravity had shifted northwards, although London more than maintained its impressive share of the total population. By the end of the nineteenth century the grandsons and great-grandsons of early nineteenth-century rural labourers were likely to be hewing coal in Durham or Glamorgan, tending machines in Manchester, Birmingham, or Leeds, or building houses to accommodate yet more new arrivals in almost any British or North American city. Their sisters had abandoned the farms for the factories and exchanged rural domestic industry for urban domestic service. Migration was not the sole cause of population redistribution. There were also spatial differences in the rate of natural increase. But, as we noted in Chapter 2, these differences were themselves largely a consequence of the fact that there was a more than proportionate number of young adults among migrants.

Migration contributed to the housing shortages and administrative difficulties of towns like Manchester and Bradford in the first half of the century. For the most part, however, migration within Britain and the accompanying changes in occupation were economically and socially beneficial. People moved from low-wage areas to high-wage areas, from areas where employment was declining or growing slowly to others where demand for labour was increasing and labour productivity was higher. High rates of out-migration can obviously give rise to labour shortages, especially of young workers. But migration in Britain did not often, or in many places, reach such levels that the losing areas would have benefited by a diminished outflow. Areas of out-migration were characterized by relatively low wages, high fertility, and surplus labour. In these circumstances migration was advantageous both to those that moved and to those that were left behind.[3]

The same could probably be said of emigration although it too brought costs as well as benefits. Without emigration several of the consequences of over-population noted in Chapter 2 would have been more in evidence: farm workers' wages would have been even lower and the towns would have been more crowded. Unemployment too, and the social tension conjured up by un-employment, would probably have been greater because emigration rose when the trade cycle moved downwards and slackened when demand for labour recovered. British emigrants also helped to increase overseas demand for British products. But we cannot be certain that the net influence of emigration was beneficial. On the debit side there are the disadvantages consequent upon a disproportionately heavy loss of adult males. Emigration probably also drew more than proportionately upon the more enterprising, more able, and more materialistic of the British population. Moreover, the easing of demographic pressure by emigration was achieved partly at the cost of increasing the number of unmarried women that the Victorians found so troublesome. The costs and benefits of immigration, from Ireland and eastern Europe, are even more debatable and will be discussed at some length later in the chapter.

How does labour mobility between 1815 and 1914 compare with mobility in the eighteenth century and since 1918? And how mobile were British workers compared with workers in other countries? The fragmentary evidence available, mainly comparisons of net migration flows across county boundaries, suggests that the overall level of mobility in the nineteenth century, and especially between 1840 and 1890, was relatively high. Information on inter-county mobility before the census of 1851 is particularly unreliable. For what it is worth it suggests no long-term increase in mobility in the eighteenth century, although between 1781 and 1830 the level seems to have been distinctly above that of 1701–50 (Table 5·1). After 1830 mobility almost certainly began to rise (below, pp. 149–51) and by 1870 its level was not only well above eighteenth-century rates but also exceeded the level between 1921 and 1931 and that between 1951 and 1961.

Table 5·1   *English counties: Average annual rate of migration, 1701–1830*

Sum of county migration gains and losses (per cent)

1701–50	1751–80	1781–1800	1801–30
174	169	223	208

Source: P. Deane and W. A. Cole, *British Economic Growth 1688–1959*, (Cambridge 1967) Table 26. On these figures and their shortcomings see ibid. pp. 106–22. Some demographers consider them of very little value.

Table 5·2   *Counties (England, Wales, and Scotland): decennial net migration, 1861–1961*

A Sum of country migration gains and losses (per cent)

1861–71	1871–81	1881–91	1891–1901	1901–11	1921–31	1951–61
772	803	812	639	570	652	508

B Number of counties with a migration gain or loss of 8 per cent or more

1861–71	1871–81	1881–91	1891–1901	1901–11	1921–31	1951–61
49	45	51	34	26	35	19

Source: Census Reports. The figures in Table 5·1 are not comparable with those in Table 5·2.

Certain other aspects of labour mobility in the nineteenth and twentieth centuries reinforce the impressions conveyed by the figures in Table 5.2. The movement of population into the London area for example, the 'south-east drift', was absolutely greater in four of the six decades between 1851 and 1911 than it was between 1951 and 1961.[4] And the losses of the three Welsh counties most affected by rural depopulation in the 1950s (Merioneth, Montgomery, and Radnor) were exceeded in five of the six decades between 1851 and 1911. The decline in farm employment, moreover, was about 16 per cent of the 1921 labour force between 1921 and 1951 but about 22 per cent of the 1861 farm labour force between 1861 and 1891. Emigration rates are also consistent with mobility having been at a historically high level in the second half of the nineteenth century. There had been some emigration from Scotland before the 1830s but little of significance from England and Wales. In the 1880s, however, 150,000 or more were leaving Britain every year, a figure equivalent to the population of Leicester at that time and not far short of half of the total excess of births over deaths.[5] There was very heavy emigration again between 1900 and 1914, but emigration proportions as high as those of the 1880s have not re-occurred since the First World War and legal barriers to emigration today are very much greater than they were a century ago.

Such comparisons as are possible between labour mobility in Britain and in other parts of nineteenth-century Europe are similarly consistent with the impression of high rates of mobility: the French farm labour force – inefficient and immobile[6] – is often cited among the causes of slow economic growth in nineteenth-century France and in Prussia and several other German states serfdom survived well into the nineteenth century. A. F. Weber, in his *Growth of Cities*[7] (1899), concluded, 'the English are apparently the most mobile people of Europe'. A much more recent comparison suggested the same conclusion.[8]

The geographical variations in wages, employment, and poverty that were such prominent features of the nineteenth-century labour market should not be regarded as significantly detracting from what has been said of high labour mobility. They existed not because labour was immobile, but because other labour market forces, whose influence was to widen geographical differences in prosperity, were exceptionally strong at the time. We saw in earlier chapters how demographic changes caused labour supply to increase in all parts of the country whereas for most of the nineteenth century industrialization, and increasing demand for labour, were concentrated in a few regions. Substantial regional differences in income were an inevitable consequence of this combination of circumstances. Today governments would act to moderate market forces causing such wide differences in income, probably by directing capital to low-wage areas, but little thought was given to such possibilities before 1914. During the century and a quarter or so when population was everywhere rising rapidly while demand for labour was concentrated upon the factory districts, the coalfields, and London, very high levels of labour mobility were required merely to prevent spatial disparities from continually widening. Mobility was equal to this task: rural Britain avoided the full Malthusian fate of rural Ireland. Migration was sufficient also to ensure that economic advance was seldom slowed for want of labour. There were occasions when labour was difficult to obtain – when a mill was first erected on some remote riverside, when mines, reservoirs, or railway works were started in sparsely populated districts, and even in more populous centres during hectic trade cycle booms. But there were always plenty of unemployed, under-employed, and badly-paid men and women at no great distance and it was seldom long before higher wages persuaded sufficient of them to move.

II · *Changes in labour mobility, 1815–1914*

The most typical nineteenth-century Briton appears then to have been closer to the foot-loose Scots miners than to those Suffolk rustics who trod warily over their parish boundary. But any talk of the representative migrant is misleading and the enormous differences in mobility at different times, between the sexes, and among different age and occupational groups, must now be examined in more detail.

It is perhaps as well to begin any disaggregation of overall mobility by stating two rather important asides: many migrants were not motivated by economic considerations, and the most typical probably did not cross county boundaries and so are not represented in the statistics shown in Tables 5·1 and 5·2. All detailed studies of mobility have indicated both that net gains or losses by migration represent only a fraction of a far greater movement in both directions and that most moves were over very short distances. In a substantial minority of cases the prime reason for moving was neither employment nor higher wages. Some became migrants upon marriage, others moved to be close to relatives, to occupy better accommodation, or in search of fresh credit and unexploited charity. Movement of this kind was in all directions, so that even the least prosperous areas had a substantial inflow of population. For the most part, however, (and fortunately for the labour historian) movements not predominantly motivated by economic considerations tended to cancel each other out. So the statistics of net migration, the visible part of a far greater turbulence, reflect fairly well the mainstreams of movement in search of work and higher wages.[9]

The statistics of migration before the mid-nineteenth century (Table 5·1) are too unreliable to bear much comment. The quickening of economic activity in the second half of the eighteenth century may in fact have been accompanied by a more definite increase in mobility than Table 5·1 suggests, and the slight reduction in mobility in the first third of the nineteenth century shown in the table, although compatible with the thesis that the Speenhamland system of outdoor poor relief retarded mobility, may also be illusory. Between 1830 and 1860 mobility almost certainly increased. The increase is not apparent in Tables 5·1 and 5·2 because the estimates for the pre-registration period (Table 5·1), which refer only to England and measure migration over two decades or more, cannot be compared with the far better figures of decennial migration rates for the whole of Britain after 1861 (Table 5·2). However, some local studies draw attention to sharp increases in mobility in the 1840s[10] and there were significant changes in the labour market whose influence was undoubtedly in that direction. In particular, there were important changes in the poor law, in attitudes to emigration, in industrial location, and in transport.

The old poor law, as we have seen, restricted mobility in two ways. First, and most important, many parishes dispensed relief fairly liberally and thus provided an acceptable alternative to migration in search of employment. A contemporary claimed that

> the chief cause which has prevented English in distant counties from availing themselves of the vast demand for labour in such thriving . . . towns as Birmingham, Liverpool, Manchester, Leeds etc. is the operation of the poor laws, by which the unemployed poor has been chained to the soil . . . . Where the parish is bound to maintain a man at home, it is natural that he should not go abroad to seek for work . . . he will prefer the certainty of a scanty maintenance on idleness among his own friends.[11]

The other poor law restraint on mobility was the settlement laws, by which a migrant out of his own parish might be refused relief and could be forcibly removed to his parish of settlement if he needed assistance. The proportion of all migrants that suffered removal was not large and unmarried mothers and widows with young children were more likely to be moved than those who normally could earn their living. Many country parishes willingly forwarded relief to migrants in need of help, and poor law overseers in the manufacturing centres often granted relief to those without a local settlement both because removal procedures were expensive and because they appreciated the convenience of a labour supply to hand when trade recovered. The influence of the settlement acts upon mobility, therefore, was less the actual returning of migrants to their parish than that the possibility of removal they contained, however slight, strengthened the identification of the parish with security and provided potential migrants with another reason to stay put.

In 1834 the more formidable of these poor-law barriers to mobility was partially removed by the Poor Law Amendment Act. More stringent administration, the curbing of outdoor-relief, and the new workhouse regime made dependence upon the parish no longer such a comfortable alternative to finding work. As we saw earlier, the act was nowhere applied with as much thoroughness as the poor law commissioners had intended. But enough was done, particularly in the south where the old poor law had most restricted migration, to raise mobility significantly. The settlement laws were not much affected by the Amendment Act of 1834 but between 1846 and 1865 they too were changed in various ways that encouraged labour mobility. In 1846 migrants resident five years in a parish were deemed exempt from removal, in 1861 the period was reduced to three years, and in 1865 to a year.

A further aspect of the new poor law that might at first seem likely to have encouraged greater mobility was the organization and subsidy of emigration overseas and migration to the manufacturing districts. In fact, these activities did little to stimulate movement and so great was working-class dislike of the new poor law that their influence may have been in the opposite direction. Richard Oastler and William Cobbett drew analogies between poor law emigration and criminal transportation and denounced what they alleged were plots to transport the southern poor into factory slavery and to weaken northern trade unions. There were not more than 26,000 poor law emigrants between 1834 and 1860, when those leaving by their own means often exceeded 20,000 per annum.[12] The internal migration schemes of 1835–7 (see above, p. 61) involved fewer than 5,000, many of whom returned south at the onset of depression. But that the poor law authorities became so involved in such schemes at all is indicative of changing attitudes to emigration that were widely shared. In the eighteenth century Britain's economic and military power was believed to depend upon a large and growing population and emigration was not encouraged. As Malthusian thought gained acceptance, however, rising numbers were viewed with alarm and attitudes to emigration changed. Emigration soon became a panacea for a great variety of social ills: here, it seemed, was the answer to the plight of the handloom weavers, the surplus spinsters, and the victims of potato famine and numerous other disasters. And emigration was far from merely an official, or middle-class, response to social problems. The great majority of emigrants went without subsidy or sponsorship. During the cotton famine the Lancashire operatives were reported 'unanimous' in their wish to be gone, 'Mr. Lincoln can make a clean sweep of Lancashire if he will.'[13] Many trade unions encouraged emigration for a time as a means of maintaining wages and reducing unemployment: the Staffordshire potters, for example, in 1846 set up a 'Mutual Assistance Society for the Removal of Surplus Labour'. Not far behind the initial enthusiasm for emigration came the means to put enthusiasm to increased effect. The railway began to open up the North American interior for settlement and improved shipping services on the Atlantic, especially the introduction of steamships by mid-century, made the crossing cheaper, quicker, less hazardous, and less uncomfortable.

An accelerated change in the location of economic activity, another cause of increasing labour mobility between 1830 and 1860, was noted in Chapter 1.

Employment in small market towns and old established manufacturing centres was succumbing to factory competition. At the same time the expansion of the farm labour force, and of the total rural population, slackened and ceased. Associated with the first of these developments was the spread of railways whose influence upon mobility was probably very great.[14] It should not be thought, however, that the early railways much affected labour mobility by providing migrants with faster, cheaper, and more comfortable travel. Britain is a small country, it had long been reasonably served by coach and wagon transport, and few migrants moved very far at a time either before the railways were built or subsequently. There had been considerable migration between highland and lowland Scotland long before the railways, Welsh harvesters had worked their way right across England, and the Nottingham framework knitters had walked to Scotland each year when their own trade was depressed. A very great deal of working-class travel still took place on foot and by wagon, slowly but cheaply, after the railways were built. William Blades, for example, described how in the 1860s he walked from his East Riding village across Yorkshire to Coniston and Grassington for the haymaking, 'most journeys in those days were made on foot by the working classes'.[15] When Thomas Wood was sacked by Platts of Oldham in 1847 he walked to Huddersfield looking for work and then on to Leeds and York.[16] The railways probably increased the proportion of long distance migration, they influenced mobility too by the amassing of labour for their construction, and their very existence, symbolizing as they did an acceleration in the rate of progress, must have made men less reluctant to accept change. But for the majority of migrants their advantages in speed, comfort, and cost were of marginal consequence, just one factor among many to be considered when contemplating the exchange of what was familiar for uncertain advantages elsewhere. Their main stimulus to migration came indirectly. It came from the assistance railways afforded those forces which favoured the expansion of employment in large towns and manufacturing districts. By reducing freight rates the railways allowed factory-made goods to compete with the products of craftsmen and domestic workers, they reduced employment in coaching and water transport, and they brought American corn to compete with the produce of British farms. As a consequence they made migration far more necessary.

Another influence probably conducive to rising mobility between 1830 and 1860 was that an increasing proportion of children attended school for long enough to have their expectations significantly raised and to learn something of opportunities elsewhere. Education was still an influence making for greater mobility at the end of the century. After the 1880s, however, the rate of mobility appears to have declined. The fall, in fact, was perhaps not as great as Table 5·2 suggests because emigration took a greater part in the total movement after 1880 and whereas a migrant from one British county to another appears twice in the figures, an emigrant appears only once. Moreover, emigration from the towns was disproportionately high, and because the towns were the destination of most internal migrants the statistics of emigration tend to mask those of internal migration. There is one other respect in which the fall in migration suggested by the figures in Table 5·2 needs to be qualified. Transport changes in the second quarter of the century encouraged people to move home in search of employment, but the effect of two of the most significant changes that occurred towards the end of the century, the introduction of the bicycle and of better and cheaper tram and train services, was to encourage working-class commuting. Farm labourers from the Cambridge and Lincolnshire clay country, for example, bicycled long distances each day to jobs in the Fens, and M. K. Ashby describes how in rural Warwickshire men living near railway stations left the district less than others by the 1890s because 'they could travel a few miles to work without leaving their homes'.[17] By increasing the number of jobs a man could reach from his home, developments of this kind lessened the need for migration. Thus labour mobility of a kind not reflected in Table 5·2 was increased and to some extent acted as a substitute for longer-distance mobility.

But there is not much doubt that mobility fell. The migration figures of a single county that normally lost population are free of the distortions that increased emigration introduces into aggregate figures of county gains and losses. Wiltshire was such a county: in the decade after 1871 it had a net loss of 29,000, in the following decade 25,000, between 1891 and 1901 the loss was down to 18,000, and between 1901 and 1911 it was only 13,000. How are we to explain such reductions in migration? One reason, probably the most important reason, is that migration at the level of the 1880s, when Wiltshire lost over 10 per cent of its population, was not easily sustainable because the exodus drew heavily upon young people. Their children, who might otherwise have been the migrants of the 1890s and 1900s, were being born in the towns. A second reason was the revival of agricultural prosperity. The changing terms of trade between agriculture and industry (above, p. 115) reduced pressure on British agriculture (especially the grain sector) and thus also on agricultural employment. The expansion of market gardening, a relatively labour intensive form of farming, was another development that helped to curb the loss of rural employment. Whereas between 1881 and 1891 the farm labour force fell by some 8 per cent, between 1901 and 1911 it rose for the first time since the 1840s.[18]

Economic revival in the south of England was not confined to agriculture. By 1890 there were already signs that the south, and the south-east in particular, would in future be at less of a disadvantage in competition for industrial employment with the manufacturing north and midlands. At

Chelmsford, for example, the Marconi radio company established its first factory in 1898 and Cromptons (another electrical manufacturer) and the Hoffman ball-bearing company followed soon after. This revival, which obviously reduced the necessity for migration, arose from a variety of sources. One was the growth of the new industries that were to come into prominence in the inter-war years. As we noted in Chapter 1, these industries were not particularly attracted towards the coalfields; electrical power was diminishing the pull of the industrial revolution areas. Electricity also had a revivifying effect on what was left of the south's traditional manufacturing industries. Most industrial employment that could profitably be transferred to the industrial cities had already gone by the end of the century, so some respite from that quarter was due in any event. In a few trades where congestion costs and high city-wages were especially pressing there was even a trickle of employment away from the great towns – some printing work, for example, was moved from London to Tonbridge in Kent and to Beccles and Bungay in Suffolk. The south, especially the Home Counties, benefited also from the late nineteenth-century growth of employment in the tertiary sector (see above, pp. 30–1) as middle-class commuting and the growing holiday and ex-cursion trades spread London's wealth out to its satellite towns and along the Essex, Kent, and Sussex coasts. The flow of migrants to the coalfields was well maintained but employment in manufacturing was growing less fast by the end of the century (above, pp. 28–31) and the northern and midland manufacturing centres were no longer such an attraction for migrants. After 1891, in fact, the northern towns grew no faster than towns in the south. For a century after 1750 Britain's centre of gravity had moved northwards, by 1900 the drift back had begun.

III · *Age, occupational, and spatial variations in labour mobility*

Young people were always prominent among migrants. One reason for this was that young country workers who moved townwards could expect to gain larger proportionate increases in earnings than migrants who were entitled to the full adult wage.[19] For village-girls, faced with declining employment prospects at home and a clamourous demand for their services in the towns, migration was particularly attractive: 'It is this opening for early employment [domestic service] that strips the rural districts of their young girls, and causes . . . the lads exceptionally to outnumber the girls in country places.'[20] So much was this the case that the overall level of internal migration among females usually equalled or exceeded that among males;[21] in Flora Thompson's 'Lark Rise' 'there was no girl over twelve or thirteen living permanently at home'. And the urban non-monetary advantages – greater freedom and independence, the fewer hours of work and infinitely more fascinating ways of filling the rest of the day, 'the difference between the Mile End Fair on a Saturday night, and a dark and muddy country lane with no glimmer of gas and nothing to do' – were an especial inducement to village adolescents.[22] Once a man was married, and especially if he had children, migration became less attractive and a more formidable undertaking; there was less time or money for town amusements, the cost of moving was less easily raised, and the implications of not finding work were more serious. The longer migration was delayed, moreover, the greater the wrench if it also entailed changing occupations: some degree of adaptability was required for a youth merely to enter a different occupation from his father's or to take up new work after a year or two, but ten or more years in the same employment considerably enhanced the 'psychological' cost of change.

It was partly because the 'psychological' cost of moving was so great for them that farm labourers were less mobile than most other occupational groups: 'though of all classes . . . agricultural labourers are under the greatest necessity to leave their birthplaces, and have the greatest inducement to do so, no class is so hard to move away.'[23] Unless they went overseas farm labourers could seldom contemplate migration without being prepared also to change occupations. Young men, who were not yet settled into farmwork, figured far more prominently than adult labourers in the rural exodus. Unfortunately, however, the rate at which agricultural employment was contracted by 'wastage', that is by young men not replacing those who died, was slowed by the fact that boys finished school before they were old enough to leave home. This left little alternative to finding work, usually farmwork, in the village. And although many lads were able to make the break after a few years, too many others were trapped. Their sisters, as we have already noted, were both more fortunate and more mobile because domestic service provided young girls with bed, board, and a substitute for parental care. Once he was engaged on a regular basis a farmworker was unlikely to be sacked. This, one of the advantages of his work, was also another impediment to mobility, and it was paid for in under-employment and low earnings.

There were other aspects of the farm labourers' life that helped to put them among the least mobile groups. Most workers in the nineteenth century found changing accommodation no great impediment to moving because they were used to paying market rents and because accommodation to rent was fairly readily available. But farm labourers were reluctant to leave their low-rent 'tied' cottages, and particularly so if leaving jeopardized a parent's tenancy. Their low wages afforded limited scope for saving to finance migration and the rural districts, of course, were most affected by the immobilizing influences of the old poor law. In addition their knowledge of opportunities elsewhere reflected their geographical remoteness and the solitary nature of farm work:

mid-century labourers were reported to have 'no distinct notion of Canada
. . . their only idea seemed to be that it was very far off. . . . Some had heard of
New Zealand, others had not. With the name of Australia they almost
exclusively associated the idea of transportation.'[24] Income comparisons were
obscured by payments-in-kind and by the labourers' ignorance of town prices:
at 'Lark Rise' (the village of Juniper Hill, about nineteen miles from
Oxford) it was said (incorrectly) that Oxford 'was "a gert big town" where a
man might earn as much as five and twenty shillings a week, but as he would
have to pay "pretty near" half of it in house rent . . . he'd be a fool to go
there'.[25] Rents were certainly higher in the towns but there was precious little
else to be said of the rural cost of living 'advantages'. A labourer who migrated
from Oxfordshire to take unskilled work in London in the 1880s would have
had to pay three times as much for rent, but two days work at London rates
more than made good this difference and by the end of the week, and having
paid his rent, he would have had twice as much money in his pocket.[26]

These various impediments to the mobility of farm labourers were reflected
in their migration patterns. They were especially likely to move to the same
towns, to the same districts, and even to the same streets, as those to which
earlier migrants from their village had made their way. From the village of
Netherbury, for example, deep in rural Dorset, a considerable exodus to South
Wales occurred in the 1890s after one brave individual settled there and found
it good.[27] In the Booth survey there is an account of how poor migrants from
an East Anglian village who travelled to London made first for the home of a
successful ex-villager.[28] Farm labourers were prominent also in that part of
total migration which took place in short stages. Moving in this way – from
the village to a local market town, then to a larger provincial centre and
perhaps after that to London, overseas, or to one of the great manufacturing
towns – allowed gradual acclimatization to new work and surroundings and
eased the break with traditional society.

After the first wrench subsequent movement was less difficult and in most
cases the further a migrant travelled from his rural starting-point the more
conducive was the environment to mobility. A rising income was a part of this
process, another was the company of fellow migrants, increasingly from areas
other than his own, and a third part was better knowledge of market
conditions. The urban skilled workers were more mobile than the unskilled;
they were better paid, better educated, better informed, and more likely to
move over long distances. Their trade unions, in particular, were an important
source of market information. Many unions reported on the 'state of trade' in
all the major British centres and some, particularly those like the Engineers
and Carpenters with branches on both sides of the Atlantic, provided similar
information on conditions abroad. This advice was a great aid to mobility,
and not least when it drew attention to adverse conditions because there were

few more powerful reinforcements to inertia than disappointed returned migrants. The union sponsorship of emigration that we noted earlier was paralleled within Britain by the 'tramping system' whereby unemployed society men could travel from branch to branch in search of work, sure that wherever they went they could depend upon a bed, food, and advice on local employment. Union policy was by no means always conducive to mobility: after 1880 their emigration schemes and the tramping system both fell out of favour[29] and their restrictions on entry at all times curtailed the occupational mobility, and thus also the geographical mobility, of workers outside their ranks. For their own members, however, and especially between 1840 and 1880, the unions were a considerable encouragement to mobility. Union contacts and the tramping system were important adjuncts to another aspect of mobility that was associated most of all with artisans, the tradition that young men before they married should move about a bit to broaden their experience, what E. J. Hobsbawm has called 'the artisan equivalent of the grand tour'. Oxford building workers considered a man 'wasn't a tradesman' until he had been to London,[30] and so many provincial workers made for the capital that the London building trades found it scarcely necessary to train apprentices.

Distinctions of the kind described in the mobility of rural and of urban workers, and between the skilled and the unskilled, could easily be carried much further. There were, for example, variations in the level and pattern of labour mobility between different parts of the country. At certain times South Wales, whose fortunes depended particularly upon exports, was a substantial net gainer of migrants while industrial districts more dependent on the home market were depressed and experiencing heavy emigration. Another such variation introduces an important qualification to what has been said about the less than average mobility of farm labourers. Most of the impediments to rural mobility applied particularly in the south of England. The immobilizing influences of the old poor law, for example, were obviously of less consequence in the north, where the Speenhamland system was scarcely known, and of even less consequence in Scotland where the unemployed poor were encouraged and assisted to move to where work was available. A report of the 1830s contrasted England (it would more accurately have said 'southern England') with its unemployed poor 'chained to the soil', and Scotland where 'circulation of labour has not been impeded by an ill-administered system of poor laws'.[31] The farm employment contract in the north, where men were generally engaged for six months or a year at a time and customarily discharged themselves at the end of their contract and made for the hiring fair, also favoured mobility as did long familiarity with seasonal migration and the north's superior schooling.[32]

One interesting aspect of southern migration is the overwhelming attraction of London. The number of natives of Wiltshire enumerated in the London area and in the industrial counties of Staffordshire, Glamorgan, and Lancashire illustrates the general pattern: Wiltshire is as near to Staffordshire as it is to London and nearer to South Wales.

Table 5·3   *Enumeration of Wiltshire-born in 1871*

Enumerated in London and	Middlesex	47,161
	Lancashire	1,524
	Staffordshire	950
	Glamorganshire	1,859

Source: Census of England and Wales, 1871.

London's attraction was probably due partly to accessibility – road and rail links focused upon the capital – and must have owed something also to the combination of London's dominance in pre-industrial Britain and the tendency of migration streams to perpetuate themselves. The propaganda of the 'merrie England' school (above, pp. 59, 68–70) may also have had a part in turning southern labourers away from the mining and manufacturing north. Southern farm labourers and their offspring were in any case unlikely to be particularly attracted by factory employment. They preferred to seek work with which they were at least partly familiar. Outdoor work, especially working with horses, and domestic service met their needs far better than the factories, and there was ample employment of this kind in London.

Patterns of the kind evident in the mobility of farm labourers can be traced in many other occupations. By no means all coal-miners were as mobile as the Scots miners who were mentioned above (p. 144); the semi-independent 'free-miners' of the Forest of Dean and the peasant-miners of Pembrokeshire, for example, content with their low incomes and scraps of land, were both slow to respond to high wages on the main South Wales coalfield. There were curious rigidities too in the movements of some of the most mobile classes: in the Cornish tin-mining and china clay working village where A. L. Rowse was raised all the men knew about conditions in South Africa, many had worked there, and Rowse recalls the *Cape Times* as one of the first newspapers he read regularly. Yet his uncle and aunt were held in great esteem because they had visited London, 'nobody else in the village had been to London'.[33] But enough has now been said to show that migration patterns, like most other aspects of working-class life, admit of few simple generalizations.

IV · *Irish immigration – rate of immigration and pattern of settlement*

One aspect of greater mobility in the second quarter of the nineteenth century not mentioned earlier was the quickened influx from Ireland at that time. Lacking urban skills and yet persuaded to move by the flimsiest prospect of employment, the Irish were also another exception to the generalization that the rural unskilled were less mobile than average. The Irish, of course, were exceptions to many other generalizations and their distinguishing characteristics comprised one of the great demarcation lines within the working classes. Contemporaries with as little in common as Engels and Dr Arnold agreed broadly on the distinctiveness of Irish immigrants. The working class, wrote 'Engels, 'degraded by industrialization' was 'still further degraded by having to live alongside and compete with the uncivilized Irish'; Dr Arnold spoke of 'the tremendous influx of Irish labourers . . . tainting the whole population with a worse than barbarian element'.[34] Irish workmen, 'hot blooded, passionate, excitable', had a crucial role too in Engels' forecast of imminent social disintegration. He expected them to reduce native wages towards subsistence level and to overcome the 'stolid, patient, and sensible character of the English'.[35] Another issue of particular interest in the history of Irish immigrants is the claim by a number of historians, including E. P. Thompson, that Irish labour was indispensable to Britain's industrial revolution. For these and other reasons the Irish in Britain deserve more attention than they commonly receive. Doherty and O'Connor, of course, are well enough known for their part in trade union and Chartist affairs. But the ordinary Irish workmen (who comfortably outnumbered trade unionists for much of the nineteenth century) have been largely neglected. Their neglect is the more remarkable in the light of the considerable interest in the economic and social consequences of recent immigration into Britain, and when set against the considerable attention that scholars have devoted to American immigrant history.

There was an Irish presence in Britain long before the nineteenth century. Until the end of the eighteenth century, however, immigration was slight and permanent settlement was of little consequence outside London. Its pace then increased as Ireland was afflicted by the demographic pressures described in Chapter 2. In those parts of Ireland where the potato was adopted with most enthusiasm these pressures operated with especial vehemence. Ireland had no poor law until 1838, its charities were insufficient, and when crops failed many faced either flight or starvation. A secondary influence at work both there and in much of rural Britain was the decline of workshop and domestic industry as mechanization, falling transport costs, and (in Ireland) the removal of protective duties concentrated output in the factory towns. At the same time spade husbandry was being displaced by less labour-intensive techniques and land was being converted to grazing. In the 1820s the combination of famine (in 1821–2), agricultural depression, and the introduction of steamships on the Irish Sea[36] greatly increased the pace of Irish immigration. The greatest influx of all occurred in the years immediately following the catastrophic potato failures of 1845–6: the population of Ireland then fell by some 2 million. At least three-quarters of a million perished, about as many left for America, and nearly half a million settled in Britain.

This famine influx raised the number of Irish-born in Britain to approaching three-quarters of a million, about 3.5 per cent of the population. Immigration continued after the famine and until the 1880s there were sufficient arrivals to maintain this number, although not to increase it nor, of course, to maintain its relative importance. By 1911 the number of Irish-born had fallen to 550,000 or about 1.3 per cent of the population. These figures, however, underestimate the significance of Irish immigration in two important respects. First, among those who arrived adults of working age were over-represented and there were usually more males then females. This was true even of the famine years when migration was probably less age-selective than usual, and it was particularly true of certain occupational groups like the seasonal harvest workers.[37] Second, and more important, the Irish community comprised far more than those born in Ireland. Children born to immigrants in the Irish quarters of British cities were hardly less Irish than their parents, and the same could be said of many born into families several generations removed from Ireland because the immigrant communities were well defined and within them Irish nationalism, Irish culture, and the Roman Catholic faith were carefully nurtured. In his history of the Irish in Britain John Denvir wrote of the London Irish, either native or London-born 'for one is often quite as good as the other', and of the Liverpool Irish seemingly 'on a piece cut from the old sod itself'.[38] Although the proportion of Irish-born in the population fell after 1850, the relative strength of the 'effectively Irish' was better maintained and from the 1840s to the First World War the overall Irish contribution to the British labour force must have been some 4 to 6 per cent of its total.

In Liverpool, Manchester, and Glasgow, in most other northern manufacturing cities, and in London, the Irish contribution to the labour force was far above the average. The census of 1851 showed that 22 per cent of Liverpool's population, and 18 per cent of Glasgow's, had been born in Ireland and in both cities the 'effectively Irish' proportion must have been a third or more. Bootle, Widnes, and some of the west of Scotland manufacturing towns were at least half 'Irish'.[39] Immigrants made overwhelmingly for London and for the great northern manufacturing centres (those near the west coast especially) where employment prospects were favourable and wages relatively high. The three main areas of settlement in

1841, containing together over half of the Irish-born, were Lancashire and Cheshire, Lanarkshire, and London. This broad pattern persisted until 1914.[40] In the south-west of Scotland there was considerable Irish settlement in country districts and a few Irish farmworkers were employed on a permanent basis in Lancashire but, these exceptions aside, Irish immigration was part of the great movement to the towns. The Irish harvesters of course were not permanent settlers. As many as 50,000 of them were said to have visited Britain annually in the 1840s, but harvest machinery and other influences reduced their number to 20,000 by 1880 and to only 8,000 in 1913.[41] Harvesters went mainly to the English north and midlands and to southern and central Scotland; few sought work in the low-wage and labour-surplus counties south of Cambridgeshire and north of Perthshire where the relationship between the demand for labour and its supply was closest to that in Ireland.[42]

v · *Social problems associated with Irish immigration*

Wherever they settled Irish immigrants were distinguished by the extraordinary wretchedness of their quarters: 'The worst accommodation is good enough for them', wrote Engels, 'The majority of cellar-dwellers are nearly always Irish in origin.'[43] Their streets were said to be the worst and filthiest in London and there were numerous similar accounts of Irish districts in other British cities and in North America.[44] Much working-class housing was poor, of course, and it was to be expected that unskilled immigrants who made for the fastest growing cities would occupy some of the very worst. But their homes appear to have been more wretched than could be explained by low incomes: 'They do not live equally well with the English on equal wages', an Irish Roman Catholic priest admitted in 1834, 'An Englishman who earns 18s a week is found to have his children neatly clad, and his house comfortable; whereas an Irishman on the same wages has his children ill-clad, and his room or cellar filthy.'[45] Another priest noted that many among his Liverpool flock who earned good wages were living in cellars, and Dr Kay believed that the minimum standards in new building were determined by what Irish immigrants were prepared to tolerate.[46] Some of the Irish, it seems, rejected the housing standards of the native poor just as many of the native poor rejected those standards the middle classes sought to impose. Immigrant expectations were set by what was commonplace in Ireland and Ireland was much poorer than Britain. Ireland was also less crowded and practices such as the raising and slaughtering of pigs and the dumping of household waste in and about the home were far less a menace to health there than they were in British cities.

Numerous reports suggest that what was saved on rent very often was spent on drink and this preference was another trait the middle classes found disturbing. The 1834 Report on the Irish Poor in Britain generalized in terms of immigrants aiming at an existence little above that in Ireland and spending on drink 'everything beyond the sum which enables them to live in this manner'.[47] Discussing Irish immigrant living standards towards the end of the nineteenth century John Denvir, the Liverpool-Irish editor of the *Catholic Times*, conceded that 'drink, more than poverty, has been the curse of the Irish'.[48] Excessive drinking might be expected to accompany a substantial increase in real income and the transition to British cities where family and community restraints were slackened. Aspects of Irish culture may also have encouraged drinking because in America, where the Irish were one immigrant group among many, no other nationality surpassed them in the consumption of alcohol.[49]

Overcrowded and insanitary housing, and links with Ireland where diseases under sporadic control in Britain remained endemic, gave rise to another social problem: the Irish enclaves were a health hazard. Immigrants, 'pestilence on their backs, famine in their stomachs', periodically overwhelmed the medical facilities of the western ports. 'The districts of Liverpool where we have seen fever to be most prevalent', ran a report of 1844, 'are exactly those where the Irish are congregated';[50] in 1847, 750 of the 1,150 patients in the Glasgow fever hospital were Irish.[51] Typhus, sometimes called the 'famine disease' or 'Irish fever', took its greatest toll in the year after the potatoes failed. Leeds lost all five of its Roman Catholic priests at that time and Liverpool lost eleven priests, ten Roman Catholic and one protestant.[52] The immigrant population was notorious too for its strong prejudices against smallpox vaccination and for its 'wakes'. 'Wakes' entailed not merely keeping a corpse for some time before burial but also bringing into its close proximity friends and relatives from near and far who might take infection away with them. A Mrs Sullivan of Saffron Hill (one of London's Irish districts) whose daughter had died in the workhouse persuaded the parish to let her have the body, 'to bury her decently' – three successive collections among the neighbours were spent on drink by which time a fever broke out in the house and six more perished.[53]

Sickness, death, and perhaps drink too, were among the reasons Irish immigrants were so often applicants for public assistance: 'Out of a given equal number of English and Irish in the same circumstances', claimed a Manchester poor law overseer in 1834, 'there will be a much greater number of applicants among the Irish'.[54] In Liverpool two-thirds of those granted casual relief in 1824 were Irish and in 1847 an official of the city declared that many ratepayers were in danger of being 'pauperized by the increase of rates', that the working classes were 'exasperated at the supposed preference of Irish to English poor'.[55] Claims of a similar kind were heard from many other towns.[56] There were other reasons why immigrants might be expected to have made heavy demands upon the poor rates. They suffered more than average rates of unemployment and many had arrived in Britain penniless. It was said also that they were recklessly improvident,[57] and this shortcoming was compounded by what E. P. Thompson calls their 'cheerful, predatory attitude' to the poor law. Among the harvesters, for example, were those notorious for leaving their wives and children in Liverpool to get what they could from the poor rates and by begging until they all returned to Ireland. Some charitable help reached the immigrants from the native Roman Catholic population and some from the embassies of Roman Catholic European nations. But native Roman Catholics did little to welcome their pauperized co-religionists – the divisions of class, culture, and nationality proved greater than the bonds of shared religion. And even had they been more forthcoming there were probably insufficient wealthy Roman Catholics in Britain to do for the Irish what the Jewish community later did for the alien poor.

Given all this there seems likely to have been substance in the numerous complaints about the Irish share of poor relief, although there are no national figures to support such complaints.[58] Nor are there figures on the total Irish share of charity although here too there are many reports of their prominence among the population of beggars, vagrants, and applicants for relief. Glasgow citizens, for example, complained to the 1834 enquiry that 'when . . . large sums were raised by voluntary subscription for supporting the unemployed, we were visited by immense numbers of the poorer class of Irish, who came here in order to get a part of the subscription.'[59] Immigrants also took a sizable share of employment designed to aid the native poor – the building of the Edinburgh–Glasgow canal for example, and also the Caledonian Canal which it was hoped would help distressed Highlanders but in the event employed a greater number of Irish.[60] Emigration schemes and other charitable endeavours were apt to founder on the objection that any easing of pressure upon the poor would merely encourage greater immigration.[61]

Two other supposed social consequences of immigration that gave rise to concern were the allegedly high crime rate among immigrants and their fertility. From 1860 to 1890 Irish immigrants comprised less than 8 per cent of Bradford's population but they accounted for between 14 and 24 per cent of those brought before the city magistrates.[62] Engels talked of Ireland supplying England and America with 'pimps, thieves, swindlers, beggars, and other rabble.'[63] Their allegedly high birth-rate aroused fears of eventual religious domination and racial deterioration. Some within the Roman Catholic church, confident of the steadfastness of their own flock, welcomed the late nineteenth-century fall in working-class fertility with pleasurable anticipation, and in her 1914 study of the English birth-rate E. M. Elderton (of the Francis Galton Laboratory for National Eugenics) contemplated

Liverpool's birth-rate with apprehension, 'There can . . . be little doubt that the Irish element is the source of the unique position of Liverpool among the Lancashire towns . . . in the one big town where the birthrate is stationary, the population appears to be inferior in skill and intelligence'.[64] There was too, of course, the ever-present fear that the supposed immigrant characteristics would prove contagious, that the native poor would be demoralized and reduced to Irish levels.

For all these reasons Irish immigration was regarded as little short of a social disaster. How much of the criticism heaped upon the Irish population was deserved in unknown. Doubtless immigration aggravated many social problems. But these problems had existed before many Irish came to Britain and would have persisted to some extent in their absence. We can be reasonably certain that the immigrants' shortcomings were seldom minimized. Their prominence in the criminal statistics, for example, was mainly for offences of a comparatively minor kind – drunkenness, petty theft, and crimes against the person committed in mitigating circumstances.[65] Thrift and foresight were probably far more common virtues among the immigrants than native critics supposed. Some sent cash regularly to help relatives in Ireland and others were carefully hoarding pennies towards the price of a ticket to America. Thrift must have been second nature to people of peasant stock, some of whom had been accustomed to accumulating an annual rent.[66] Comment on Irish housing and domestic habits naturally tended to dwell upon the worst examples and tended also to discount those immigrants who made most progress towards British standards. Despite what contemporaries believed there is far more evidence of immigrants adopting British standards than of natives falling into the ways of the 'low Irish'. There was, in fact, something of 'Catch 22' in the popular conception of what were typical Irish conditions. The least respectable of the native population were sometimes assumed to be Irish, and those immigrants who acquired a measure of respectability and the Smilesian virtues were likely to be regarded as honorary English or Scots – 'I have one Irish plasterer', boasted a Birmingham employer, 'a very civil, steady man, you would hardly think he was an Irishman'.[67]

Perhaps the charge that future research on Irish immigrants may prove least sound is that concerning their allegedly vast families. Immigrant reproduction rates were almost certainly above the average: a high proportion of them married and they probably married younger than the average.[68] But this was probably no less true of natives who were in the same occupational classes as those where the Irish were concentrated. When E. M. Elderton attributed Liverpool's high birth-rate to the Irish she overlooked the probability that any city with Liverpool's occupational structure would have been among the last to record a fall in fertility, whatever its racial and religious composition. There is also the crucial difference between gross fertility and effective fertility. Even if Irish mothers had given birth to an exceptionally large number of babies it by no means would follow that they reared exceptionally large families because their housing and sanitary standards, although not as bad as some reports alleged, were certainly bad enough to cause exceptionally high infant mortality.[69]

VI · *Irish immigrant employment; occupational immobility; effect of Irish immigration upon wages, employment, and trade unionism; segregation and integration*

Closely associated with the social problems that have been described was the nature of immigrant employment. In the towns where they settled Irish immigrants did much of the least desirable work. They did those jobs that were badly paid and most frequently interrupted, work of the 'roughest, coarsest, and most repulsive description . . . requiring the least skill and practice'.[70] Most of the men were labourers of one sort or another'. In Manchester, Liverpool, and Glasgow the great majority of building labourers were Irish. Many Glasgow and Liverpool dockers were Irish also and they were well represented among those doing the work of the other great ports. They were prominent too in the more arduous and hazardous occupations, in the sweltering sugar refineries, for example, and about the St Helens and Clydeside chemical works. Some of the less skilled mill work in Lancashire and Yorkshire also fell to them, although Irishmen were said to dislike the tedium of machine-minding. Before 1850 those inside the Lancashire and Yorkshire mills were heavily out-numbered by handloom weavers. Used to Irish living standards and content therefore to take up the handloom long after its decline had begun, immigrants were among the reasons its demise was so protracted. Their abhorrence of routine and the blandishments of London employers, whose letters to Ireland would always bring fresh labour, led them also into other depressed domestic industries and the London sweat-shops. Two other male immigrant employments of some consequence were the armed forces and the lower branches of retailing. Those of their working wives and daughters who were neither millgirls nor in the domestic textile and needle trades were mainly domestic servants of the poorer sort, taking those least sought-after posts from which they were not excluded by religious prejudice and their lack of social graces.

There were some exceptions to this pattern of mainly unskilled and low-paid urban work. These included those Irish who settled in the rural south-west of Scotland and the seasonal harvesters (above p. 160). There was also a minority of skilled or semi-skilled immigrant workers, tailors, shoemakers, carpenters, and others; and in industrial Scotland considerable numbers of immigrants appear to have secured work of a kind elsewhere barred to them. Whereas there were said to be less than a hundred Irish among the 'aristocratic' spinners of Lancashire (1835), in the Scottish mills they accounted for most operatives at every grade.[71] There were also far more Irish miners in Scotland than there were in England and Wales. This less rigid confinement to the lowest rungs of the occupational ladder in industrial Scotland was a consequence of the combination of extraordinary rapid growth of industry there during the years of heavy immigration, the reluctance of Scots to work in mills and coal-mines on terms that immigrants accepted willingly, the tradition of textile employment (including mill work) in the north of Ireland, and the extensive use of immigrants to break strikes. Even so, in Scotland, as in England and Wales, Irish workers remained 'largely confined to the lowest ranks of the industrial army'.[72]

That they remained so much confined to the lowest ranks is perhaps the most remarkable aspect of immigrant employment. Most came without skills or capital so it is not surprising that they began at the bottom, but the pattern that has been described is hardly less applicable to those long resident in Britain, and to their sons and grandsons. There was a certain amount of movement into artisan and white-collar occupations.[73] But the progress that has been detected was slight and there is little doubt that the overall level of occupational mobility was extremely low: 'The Irish seldom get any better', reported a Birmingham employer in 1834, 'they are born bricklayers' labourers and they die bricklayers' labourers.'[74] At Merthyr Tydfil, some time after this, immigrants were described as providing much of the manual labour in the ironworks but little of that which required skill, 'Such a wonder as an Irish puddler was never heard of'.[75] Observers who were decidedly sympathetic to the immigrant community said much the same. The *Dundee Catholic Herald*, as late as 1920, lamented 'Among our Catholic boys and girls there is a great dearth of social and educational ladder-climbing'.[76]

Some of the more sympathetic commentators ascribed this lack of progress, or most of it, to discrimination, 'with a fair field and no favour the Irishman is bound to come to the front'.[77] Discrimination there certainly was and a great deal of it, both from employers (despite the obvious advantages of cheap Irish labour) and, even more, from native workers. But discrimination is only a part of the explanation. After all, the Jewish immigrants who came later in the century and faced at least as much hostility made far more progress. These later immigrants to Britain perhaps had some advantages over the Irish.[78] But Irish immigrants in America, in control of the cities of New York and Boston, might be considered to have enjoyed considerable advantages over several other immigrant groups by the 1880s, and comparative studies show that they (with the Italians) were the outstandingly poor performers among America's immigrants: 'the mobility of the [New York] Jews . . . was exceptionally rapid that of the Irish . . . was exceptionally slow' (Oscar Handlin).[79]

All this suggests that the occupational immobility of Britain's immigrant Irish cannot be explained as entirely a consequence of discrimination. Of the other causes that must be added to the account inferior education, both in Ireland and in Britain, is probably one of the most important. At Greenock in 1855 64 per cent of the Irish-born who married were unable to sign their name in the register, whereas among Scots the proportion was only 24 per cent.[80] Priests and parents were anxious that if Roman Catholic children were to be educated at all it should be in Roman Catholic schools. But the Irish community could not provide financial support comparable with that given to protestant schools and the state at first did nothing, and for long after not enough, to make good this handicap. Catholic parents moreover, poorly educated themselves, were inclined to attach slight importance to schooling.

Education was just one element in a complex of interrelated social and cultural characteristics that were inimical to material success. Some of the others were mentioned earlier, a propensity to drink for example which was probably among the reasons so many of those Boston Irish who advanced up the occupational ladder eventually fell back among the labourers.[81] Low expectations and high leisure preference worked in the same direction and reflected an acquired or inherited indifference to the philosophy of 'getting on'. The Roman Catholic church was a major source and reinforcement of these qualities: it diverted thought from worldly aspirations and worldly responsibilities and was the nucleus of those cohesive and introspective enclaves within which immigrants sustained their national identity by conforming to traditional cultural values and rejecting the more materialistic priorities of the wider community. The cohesiveness of the Roman Catholic Irish enclaves, and contact with countrymen recently arrived or soon to return to Ireland, also helped to keep alive the belief that their residence in Britain was temporary. Those who looked forward to returning home or moving on to America were particularly unlikely to commence the long haul to respectability, with all the short-term sacrifices that entailed.

Yet another impediment to progress and one that applied especially to those Irish who came to Britain (it was probably mainly a consequence of centuries of British domination) was the quality Engels set such store upon, a national disposition to be 'agin' the government or, indeed, almost any secular authority. This contempt for authority, and especially British authority, was not easily reconciled with the pursuit of status and acceptability. The church, Roman Catholic schools, and Irish folklore all instilled attitudes likely to sharpen national animosity and increase a sense of alienation from British society. Not least, of course, was the widespread belief that Ireland's manifest troubles owed nothing to Malthusian pressure and everything to British oppression.[82] The contrast with the attitudes of Jewish immigrants in Britain, refugees from persecution in eastern Europe and hoping never to return, is obvious and important.

How did native workers react to Irish immigration? The animosity that immigrants felt towards Britain was fully reciprocated. Very few native workers were Roman Catholics. Most were not participating members of any church, but protestantism and the national interest were closely identified, and patriotism and anti-Catholicism were traditional aspects of working-class culture. Thus the massive intrusion of clannish and anglophobic Irish was felt as an affront to national dignity and a threat to traditional liberties. Immigrants were disliked too, and feared, for their poverty and ignorance, their squalor, their competition for charity and poor relief, and, of course, because they were seen as a threat to native living standards.

Cobbett put the possible economic consequences of immigration in his usual forthright way: of the three countries ruled from Westminster, he said, one had 'meat and bread and knives and forks', another had 'oatmeal and brose and horn spoons', and the third 'only potatoes and paws'.[83] The danger was that immigration would reduce England to 'potatoes and paws'. Engels, as we have seen (above, p. 158), had no doubt that immigration reduced living standards and several historians, including Redford, have come to the same conclusion, 'the main social significance of the Irish influx lay in its tendency to lower the wages and the standard of living of the English wage-earning classes'.[84] There were three ways in which immigrants were thought to reduce living standards: by taking work, by reducing wages, and by weakening trade unionism. Sometimes immigrants took work simply because they were there first. Moreover, they were generally willing and uncomplaining, prepared to accept conditions that natives thought intolerable. In other cases they were employed simply because they were prepared to work for less. Natives sometimes worked alongside immigrants at a higher wage,[85] but more usually they had either to work for what immigrants would accept or abandon that particular employment.

The supposed immigrant influence upon wages was particularly obvious, and particularly resented, when it occurred during a strike, as quite often happened in the first half of the century. During the prolonged mining strike of 1844, for example, Lord Londonderry attempted to coerce the Durham miners by bringing over men from his Irish estates.[86] Immigrants also helped the employers to victory in the famous Preston cotton strike of 1853–4 (below, p. 255).[87] Some unions specifically excluded Irish immigrants[88] and it was well known that immigrants were not much interested in the political aspirations of native workers except when these aspirations happened to touch upon Irish affairs. Immigrant loyalties were primarily to Ireland and the church and there were times when these allegiances conflicted directly with the interests of native workers. For a decade after 1833 the Roman Catholic church waged a vigorous campaign against trade unionism. This campaign was provoked by the secrecy and ritualism that were associated with unionism and by links between certain immigrant union activity and the agrarian terrorist societies that were challenging clerical authority in Ireland. Union membership was forbidden under threat of denial of the sacraments and during the campaign Irish participation in unionism diminished.[89] Immigrant attitudes to Chartism, as we shall see, were dominated by a similar division of loyalty and by a preoccupation with Irish politics. General Napier, who was in charge of military precautions during the early Chartist campaigns, relied especially upon Irish detachments in the army, trusting that mutual animosity would preclude any fraternization with native workers.[90]

However, the Irish contribution to industrial relations was by no means always on the employers' side. Those long settled in Britain were less frequently strike-breakers than new arrivals and the main era of immigrant strike-breaking was over by 1860. Some among those from Dublin and Cork, where there was a tradition of trade unionism, brought their experience with them and others had participated in factional feuding or agrarian terrorism and could put their experience to effect against blacklegs and recalcitrant employers. A ready resort to violence when aggrieved was perhaps the most distinctive Irish contribution to industrial relations. In Liverpool, among the Lancashire and Scottish handloom weavers, in the Scottish cotton mills and elsewhere in the west of Scotland, Irish trade unionists were almost as prominent leading strikes as breaking them. These union activities, 'unscientific' and ephemeral although they often were, helped to offset the anti-union activities of other immigrants. With hindsight it is clear that the long-term effects of immigrant anti-union activities were in any case very slight because for a variety of reasons (among which immigration was not important) stable and effective trade unionism was not established in the occupations where the Irish were competitors for employment until long after their competition and blacklegging had ceased to be a significant obstacle to organization.

It will be argued below that contemporaries also misjudged the probable influence of Irish immigration upon native employment and wage levels. But neither hindsight nor a judicious balancing of advantages and disadvantages could be expected from workmen made unemployed by immigrants or forced to take a lower rate. At the point where Irish labour was substituted, or seemed likely to be substituted, hostility frequently erupted into violent clashes. In 1845, writes Terry Coleman, 'there was near civil war among the railway navvies'. But for the ruthless opposition of English and Scots navvies Irishmen would undoubtedly have taken a far greater part in railway building:

> Notice is given that all the Irish men on the line of railway in Fife Share must be off the grouwnd and out of the countey on Monday th 11th of these month or els we must by the strength of our armes and a good pick shaft put them off. Your humbel servants, Schots men.[91]

There were several other occupations where repeated physical clashes occurred and where employers gave work to Irishmen at risk to their own lives and property: rival harvest gangs, for example, often came to blows[92] and at the time of the Swing disturbances every farmer in Kent and Surrey who had ever employed an Irishman was said to be in fear of native retribution.[93] The Airdrie miners struck work in 1854 'until all the Roman Catholics should be expelled'.[94] In their part of Scotland immigrants were believed to have reduced both the wages and the status of the Scots collier and native trade unionism was closely associated with Orangism.[95] Economic grievances had some part too in much of the fighting and rioting whose ostensible and initial cause was simply differences in religion – in the disturbances that followed the Pope's restoration of the English Roman Catholic hierarchy in 1850, for example.

The strength of mutual animosity and the extent of Irish segregation changed during the course of the century. Both were high in the early decades when immigrants were described as 'a separate and rejected caste' that seldom mixed with the English, 'it is like oil and water' (1834).[96] In the late 1840s and the 1850s differences were reinforced by the landing of the famine immigrants who were more numerous, more destitute, and a greater threat to health than previous arrivals.

E. P. Thompson has attempted to play down the divisions between natives and immigrants in the early nineteenth century: 'If they were segregated in some towns,' he says, 'the Irish were never pressed back into ghettos.'[97] He claims that there was 'a great deal' of inter-marriage and considers the clashes that occurred less remarkable than the 'relative ease' with which immigrants were absorbed into working-class communities. But his emphasis has the appearance of a bold attempt to obscure one of the more obvious divisions among the working classes. The significance of his distinction between being 'segregated' and being 'pressed back into ghettos' is not clear, and his unsubstantiated claims about inter-marriage and ease of absorption are clearly contradicted by most studies of Irish immigrants in Britain. J. Werly begins his article on the Irish in mid-century Manchester by refuting Thompson's account; 'Irish Town and Little Ireland existed both as physical ghettos geographically separated from the English living-quarters, and also as institutional ghettos culturally apart from the English.'[98] In Leeds at this time, according to T. Dillon, the Irish were 'an isolated minority', and C. Richardson describes 'the evolution of homogeneous ethnic quarters' in Bradford where the Irish preference for living together was facilitated by native exodus from the streets where they settled.[99] At Greenock there was a marked contrast between the easy integration of Highlanders and the far slower and more difficult assimilation of the Irish: whereas the cultural institutions of the Highlanders might have been designed to transform their members into ambitious and respectable lowland Scots, the schools, churches and other institutions of the Roman Catholic Irish served to strengthen and perpetuate their distinctiveness.[100] And whereas 80 per cent of the Roman Catholic Irish in Greenock who married in 1855 married other Irish Roman Catholics, the rate of intra-group marriage among Highlanders was 60 per cent.[101] The Irish were similarly distinguished in mid-century Boston where their inter-marriage rate was less than that of any other group.[102]

By the 1860s the divisions between the two communities were beginning to be eroded. Those entering Britain from this time were in less desperate straits than the 1840s immigrants and the rate of inflow had declined so that an increasing proportion of the Irish community were either British-born or had been long resident in Britain. By the 1880s improved Roman Catholic education and the temperance crusades were also contributing to assimilation. Cardinal Manning undertook temperance work among the Roman Catholic poor with the expressed intentions of reducing the distinctiveness of immigrant social habits.[103] The dock strike of 1889 was something of a watershed in this process of gradual assimilation. Half or more of the London dockers were of Irish extraction and the strike, together with Cardinal Manning's sympathy and successful intervention, helped to reduce differences between Irish and native workers. The arrival in the 1880s of another wave of immigrants who were distinctly stranger than the Irish had a similar effect. The British-Irish joined native workers in deploring Jewish competition just as the Irish in America acquired some degree of identity with more established groups by their animosity towards negroes and the late nineteenth-century 'new' immigrants.[104] When Ben Tillett told Jewish immigrants disembarking at London that he wished they had not come he must have been echoing what many had said or implied to his Irish ancestors.[105]

Integration, however, was frequently interrupted and still very far from complete in 1914. The continuing tendency of natives to identify themselves by reference to the qualities that set them apart from the less respectable newcomers was touched upon by Marx in 1870 when he suggested that the British worker 'feels himself a member of the ruling nation. . . . He cherishes religious, social, and national prejudices against the Irish worker'.[106] Physical violence involving the immigrant community still erupted from time to time. In 1867, for example, a Fenian bomb outrage killed 50 Londoners, setting off a series of anti-Irish incidents. There were serious riots and looting in Tredegar and Birkenhead in 1882, each ostensibly initiated by Irish insults to Salvation Army bands, and 'orange and green' violence continued to be almost as prominent a feature of working-class life in Glasgow and other Scottish cities as it was in Belfast.[107] It was as late as 1892 that John Denvir was boasting of the Irishness of Britain's Irish, and residential segregation, although less rigorous than it had been in mid-century, remained very marked.[108] The Liverpool Irish were still regarded as synonymous with social problems;[109] at Greenock the overwhelming majority of Irish Roman Catholics continued to find marriage partners from among their own community;[110] and in the slums of Edwardian Salford it was said that any daughter who married 'some low Mick from the Bog' brought disgrace to her family, 'such unions seldom occurred'.[111]

VII · *Irish labour and British economic growth*

The suggestion that Irish immigrants conferred substantial benefits upon the British economy, sufficient perhaps to offset the social and economic problems that accompanied their arrival, remains to be examined. The case, in short, is that immigrants were a mobile and adaptable source of labour, that they promoted economic growth by being ready to work wherever and whenever hands were required, and that they took up a variety of backbreaking, dangerous, and disagreeable, but absolutely essential, tasks that natives would not touch. Variants of this argument have been advanced many times, J. A. Jackson, for example, writes that immigrants found their way as casual labourers 'into a wide variety of employment which effectively mirrors the changing needs and rapid expansion of the country. . . . The existence of a large pool of cheap labour at a time of national expansion proved an essential ingredient to the rapid industrial advance.'[112] To J. E. Handley immigrants were 'indispensable adjuncts of the expansion of industry and agriculture', and E. P. Thompson considered them 'essential for the Industrial Revolution. . . . By the 1830s whole classes of work had passed almost entirely into the hands of Irishmen since the English either refused the menial, unpleasant tasks or could not keep up with the pace.'[113] There is no lack of contemporary opinion that supports such interpretations. In particular there is the evidence of employers to the 1834 inquiry on the Irish in Britain: 'The boundless coalfields beneath us, and the boundless mines of labour, so to speak, existing for us in Ireland, form together one of the great secrets of the almost unparalled prosperity of this part of Scotland' (Paisley cotton manufacturer).[144] In the same inquiry another cottonmaster said that had the Irish not come to Lancashire manufacturers might have found it necessary to move to Ireland to use their labour.[115] Other employers alleged that native labour regarded certain occupations as beneath their dignity, that

171

the immigrants did work 'which the national pride of an Englishman will not allow him to do'. 'Carrying the hod' (bricklayer's labourer) was said to be one such task, working in sugar refineries was another, 'only the Irish could stand the heat'.[116]

But the employers who argued this case did so to further their own interests, and historians who have repeated their arguments have allowed themselves to be confused by a fairly blatant piece of special pleading. Manufacturers found Irish labour a convenience and the advantages it offered them over available alternatives obviously helped to offset whatever social and economic costs immigration imposed. But such advantages were certainly not sufficient to sustain the claim that Irish labour was indispensable.

The argument can be examined in its two main parts. First there is the supposition that in the absence of immigration there would have been an absolute shortage of labour. Industrialization clearly required labour, but to suggest that it required immigrant labour is to postulate a labour-scarce economy whereas Britain was a labour-surplus economy. Irish immigration occurred against a background of a rapid natural increase in labour[117] and Malthusian fears of over-population. It occurred at a time when emigration was encouraged and subsidized by central and local government, by charities, friendly societies, and trade unions. Immigrants were matched by native departures in the first half of the century and after 1850 those leaving far outnumbered those who came. Besides those who left Britain in search of work and higher wages, some of them specifically to avoid Irish competition,[118] there were other great reservoirs of under-utilized labour in the declining handicraft trades like handloom weaving and in all the rural districts. The clashes that occurred between natives and immigrants are one indication of how much newcomers competed with, rather than complemented, indigenous labour. And the class of labour that Britain needed least, that of which there was a veritable super-abundance, was precisely that unskilled kind which Ireland supplied so copiously.

The existence of a general labour surplus obviously does not preclude temporary labour shortages in parts of the country and one of the chief advantages immigrants offered to employers over native unskilled labour was their more rapid response to any sudden need for labour. The greater mobility of immigrant labour was probably most obvious before the poor law reforms of 1834 when, as we saw earlier, fairly liberal poor relief enabled parts of Britain's great reservoir of under-utilized rural labour to remain where it was. But even in the first half of the century, when the immigrant contribution to the British economy was probably greatest, Irish recruitment was often at the expense of native workers. The Highlanders, for example, were in direct competition with immigrants for harvest work and for industrial employment in the west of Scotland and some of the heaviest immigration of all occurred during the 1847–8 slump when native unemployment was high almost everywhere. Highlanders, like other Scots, were obviously unaffected by the immobilizing effects of the English poor law, and these effects were of significant influence within England and Wales only in the 'Speenhamland' counties of the rural south. There was a great deal of under-utilized native labour far closer to Lancashire and Yorkshire than that in the Speenhamland counties. There were the handloom weavers, for example, and the surplus of nearby rural areas. It was said in 1834 that the farm labourers of west Cheshire and Flintshire were fully employed only at harvest time and one response to the question of how Liverpool would manage if Irish immigration ceased was that 'being so near to North Wales, where there is an over-abundant population, there would be no difficulty in finding porters etc. for the work of the town'.[119]

Labour mobility in fact, both before and after poor law reform, was far greater than is implied by suggestions that Irish labour was crucial to British industrialization. Some figures help to make this point clear and also to put the size of the Irish contribution in perspective. The 1851 census shows that well over half the population of Birmingham aged twenty and above had been born elsewhere. Of these, under 7,000 were born in Ireland and over 63,000 were born elsewhere in Britain.[120] In Bradford at the same date native migrants aged twenty and above were more than five times the number of Irish migrants.[121] There were too, of course, other possible alternatives to imported labour that are not mentioned among the speculations of those who argue that no immigration would have meant far slower economic growth. For example, a tighter market for labour might have encouraged greater substitution of capital for labour. There is the possibility too that had immigrants not proved such a convenience to northern employers more would have been done to stimulate labour mobility within Britain, perhaps by an earlier removal of the poor law obstacles to mobility.

Thus the argument that immigrant labour was essential to economic growth because Britain had absolutely insufficient labour of its own, or because native labour was insufficiently mobile, rests upon false assumptions. The second part of the 'indispensability' thesis: that the Irish did essential work which natives shunned as too dirty, too dangerous, or too degrading, is also unconvincing. It is not entirely without substance – there was difficulty in manning the early textile mills and Irish labour helped to overcome that obstacle. We noted earlier how immigrants willingly accepted certain categories of dangerous and uncomfortable work. Had they not been available employers would probably have been forced to rely more on women and children, they might have had to pay rather higher wages to attract labour, and they would probably have been forced to give higher priority to safety and to making the workplace more attractive in other ways to

173

indigenous labour. Such resorts might have resulted in marginally less economic growth than occurred, but the difference would hardly have been substantial.

The suggestion that immigrants undertook whole categories of essential labour that natives would not do is undermined in the first instance by the fairly obvious fact that a great deal of dirty and backbreaking work in the building of turnpikes, canals, docks, and harbours was completed in the eighteenth century before Irish settlement was of much consequence. E. P. Thompson acknowledges this but claims that religious revival, 'the imprint of Baxter and Wesley', had raised the self-esteem of native workers to a level where they would no longer undertake brute force physical labour.[122] Such an argument, besides grossly exaggerating the influence of Baxter and Wesley, founders upon the fact that most work of this type was still done by natives in the 1840s and, indeed, throughout the century. Thompson and others have wrongly assumed that the Irish take-over of certain categories of less desirable work in Liverpool and Manchester, and in a few other towns that were highlighted in the 1834 inquiry on the Irish poor, occurred also throughout the rest of Britain. This was far from the case. The report, reasonably enough, concentrated on just those few areas of Britain where the Irish were a substantial part of the population. Whereas the bricklayers' labourers of Manchester and Liverpool were all Irish, in the smaller southern towns such work was done almost entirely by Englishmen.[123] The building of railways too, surely as dirty and backbreaking as any work, was completed without much help from immigrant labour.[124]

The usual course of events in occupations where the Irish became strongly represented in certain towns was that immigrants first secured a foothold by their readiness to work for less than natives, as strike-breakers, or by their extraordinary quick response to changing labour requirements. A contemporary (1834) account illustrates the process in one occupation: 'Formerly the harvest work of Scotland and the North of England was chiefly performed by the Scottish Highlanders; but the . . . comparative speed and cheapness with which the Irish labourers can come into the market have enabled them to keep the field against the Highlanders. The latter having accordingly been obliged to follow other occupations or emigrate to America.'[125] Once a strong presence was established native competition could be excluded in two ways. First, by discouraging them from entering the work and harassing any that remained. A Manchester builder explained how an Englishman who tried to work as a bricklayer's labourer 'would be so annoyed by them that he would be forced to give it up'.[126] Another Manchester builder occasionally took on an English labourer, 'but he is always driven off; they sometimes play him malicious tricks, and sometimes work unusually hard for a couple of days in order to tire him'.[127] If an

Irishman became a ganger or foreman then their monopoly was soon assured.[128] The second, more passive, way in which natives were excluded by Irish workers was by the stigma that became attached to Irish work – natives seldom worked willingly as equals alongside immigrants.[129] A number of the jobs where immigrants were able to establish themselves in these ways were those of the less desirable kind that natives were least reluctant to surrender. But the fact that in a few towns immigrants secured a monopoly of certain unpleasant tasks does not mean that natives would not do such work. It was the incumbent workers they considered beneath their dignity, not the work itself. Even in a city with as many Irish immigrants as Liverpool the natives retained some very menial work, including their monopoly of nightsoil removal.[130]

The effect of Irish immigration upon the pace of British industrialization was therefore not great. It doubtless had some effect and quite possibly a positive effect, especially in the early decades of the century. But immigration was far from crucial to growth. Had the Irish not come the work they did would have been taken up by natives, although perhaps a little more slowly, and under less disagreeable conditions. There would have been greater internal labour mobility as a consequence of population moving into the towns to do the work that in fact was taken by immigrants, and there would probably also have been rather less native emigration. The handloom weavers and similarly distressed handworkers would have been absorbed somewhat faster. Wages in the poorer parts of rural Britain would have been higher as a consequence of more of their surplus labour moving to the towns and rural unemployment would have been less.[131] Because the alternative to immigrant labour in the cities was labour from elsewhere in Britain, the immigrant influence upon wage levels where they settled was neither as bad as native workers and several historians have suggested nor as favourable as might be inferred from those who argue that immigration was essential to economic growth. The main influence of Irish immigration upon wages and employment fell upon the less prosperous parts of Britain that the immigrants themselves shunned.

One further consequence of no Irish immigration, although not a very important one, would have been a certain amount of inconvenience to northern employers who would then have needed to be rather more conciliatory towards local labour and less indifferent to the existence of badly-paid and under-employed labour elsewhere in Britain. These northern employers exaggerated the importance of Irish labour to the British economy because they were anxious to avoid the inconvenience that would accompany restrictions on immigration or the establishment of an Irish poor law. The argument that Irish labour was indispensable to industrial growth leans far too much on their exaggerations. The economic advantages of immigrant labour, such as they were, accrued mainly to them: a considerable part of the economic costs of immigration, and most of the social costs, fell upon native workers.

VIII · *Alien immigrants in Britain – their numbers, location, and occupations*

Ireland was by far the most important source of immigrants. Others came, of course, and from all corners of the world, but considering Britain's relatively high wages and minimal obstacles to entry their number was remarkably low. The 1901 census showed only 165,000 foreign-born workers in England and Wales and many of these, like the 17,000 seamen, were obviously birds of passage. Besides the seamen there were over 4,000 merchants, some 2,500 artists and musicians, and 14,000 in the catering trades and domestic service. Scotland gave employment to a mere 13,000 foreigners at this time; they included navvies from Scandinavia helping to construct the railway between Fort William and Mallaig and a few thousand Polish metal workers. The only settlement that in any way approached the importance of Irish immigration was that of Jews from eastern Europe after 1880. Their coming, like the coming of the Irish before them, caused alarm and much heated debate on the likely consequences for housing, employment, wages, and working conditions. Historians, however, are more agreed about these issues than were contemporaries and Jewish immigration has not given rise to marked differences of opinion such as those on the economic influence of Irish immigration or the rate of Irish assimilation.

Of the 60,000 or so Jews already resident in Britain in 1880, most had been born here and fewer than half could be described as working class. There had been a trickle of poor Jews from Germany, Holland, and eastern Europe before this time (10–20,000 between 1850 and 1880)[132] but it was only after 1880 that immigration became substantial. Between then and the First World War Britain gained some 120,000 Jewish settlers. They were mostly from Russia and Poland and the great majority arrived poor. The immediate cause of increased immigration was the assassination of Tsar Alexander II in 1881 which provided an excuse for greatly intensified persecution of Russia's long-suffering Jews. Shortly after this, in 1886, Polish Jews were expelled from Prussia and in 1900 substantial numbers of Rumanian Jews joined the exodus. The Jewish population of eastern Europe was affected too by population pressure, by factory competition with their employment, by the reduced cost of moving westwards, and by the economic opportunities and religious and political freedoms of the United States. Although Britain took more Jews than any other European nation, a far greater number went to America. By 1910 there were well over a million Jews in New York City. Those who came to

Britain were largely responsible for a four- or five-fold increase in the Jewish population between 1880 and 1914[133] and for a greater increase in the number of Jewish workers.[134] Even so, they never accounted for as much as 1 per cent of the labour force and there were many years after 1880 when native emigration exceeded the whole of Jewish immigration between 1880 and 1914.

A further consequence of this immigration was an increase in London's already substantial share of Jewish workers. More than half of the total Jewish population in 1850 was in London, perhaps two-thirds of it was there by 1880, and the great majority of those mainly working-class immigrants who came in the following decades also went to London. Estimates put the London Jewish population in 1900, native and foreign-born and the prosperous as well as the poor, at about 140,000. The number of Jewish workers was probably about the same as the number of London Irish workers.[135] The Jewish labour-force, however, was less spread about the capital, the great majority lived within a couple of miles of the junction of Commercial Road and Whitechapel Road and the foreign-born population of Whitechapel in 1901 (a third) exceeded the proportion of Irish-born in mid-century Liverpool. Outside London the two great centres of Jewish settlement were Manchester and Leeds where there were some 25,000 and 15,000 Jews respectively in 1900 and considerably more by 1914. Then came Liverpool, Glasgow, and Birmingham, each with 5,000 to 7,000.[136] The other great cities each had a Jewish settlement but nowhere else did Jewish workers exercise a significant influence in the labour market. London's chief attractions were, first, that it was the main seat of those trades the immigrants had followed in Europe and, second, the presence of a substantial earlier settlement with the social and religious infrastructure necessary to Jewish existence. There, not far from London docks, were Jewish employers and Jewish employment and, quite often, relatives or friends who had departed earlier. There too were synagogues, kosher shops and Jewish clubs, Jewish banks, Yiddish newspapers, and even a Russian post office. Accommodation could be rented from Jewish landlords and nearby were Jewish voluntary schools and board schools with so many Jewish pupils and teachers that they finished early on Fridays and observed the Jewish holidays. There were few things that could be had in the Warsaw ghetto that were not also available in Whitechapel. Some natives complained that it was difficult to distinguish between the two.

The most important Jewish employment was ready-made tailoring, an industry characterized by small workshops, slight mechanization, extensive division of labour, and a considerable 'outwork', or purely domestic, sector. Tailoring supported a quarter or more of London's working-class Jews after 1880 and not far short of half of the new arrivals.[137] It was also the most important provincial employment for poor Jews. At Leeds, where the Jewish tailoring trade was an adjunct to the clothing factories, workshops were distinctly larger than the average in the East End. Of the other immigrant occupations the most important were hawking and dealing, and the manufacture of boots, shoes, slippers, and cheap furniture. All of these, and most other immigrant occupations, shared with tailoring the characteristics of small production units, labour intensiveness, and continuity with traditional Jewish employment.

There were a number of reasons why immigrants were largely restricted to this narrow range of occupations, besides the obvious one that they preferred to take up in England work that was already familiar. Most new arrivals could not speak English and therefore had little choice but to work with their co-religionists. There was also the hostility of native workers to be taken into account and sundry religious obstacles to entering other employment, particularly the need to observe Jewish religious holidays and to live not far from a synagogue. More positively, tailoring, hawking, and similar small-scale and lightly capitalized trades, were attractive to Jews because they offered the best chance to a poor man hopeful of achieving employer status and with it independence, respectability, and possibly prosperity. These aspirations were highly developed in the Jewish immigrants and, as we noted earlier, Jewish social mobility contrasted with that of Irish immigrants. The 'strongest impelling motive of the Jewish race' wrote Beatrice Webb, was 'the love of profit as distinct from other form of money-earning'; 'As soon as they are in work (Factory Inspector, 1887) they live hard . . . save up every penny . . . the height of their desires is to set up for themselves as employers of labour.'[138] Many merely aspired to employer status but many others reached their goal and avoided slipping back. The more successful of these moved out of the ghetto and into middle-class suburbia.

IX · *Social and economic consequences of alien immigration*

Britain was a traditional refuge for the persecuted refugees of less liberal European regimes and as such Jewish immigrants received much sympathy. But there was a world of difference between the trickle of romantic and well-connected foreign radicals seeking asylum and the post-1880 Jewish immigration. The Jews were numerous and they were poor. They were refugees but they were also competing for work and accommodation. For these reasons their arrival gave rise to concern. Before long working-class resentment was being voiced and middle-class sympathizers took up the workers' protests. These sympathizers were moved by various motives. Most obviously they felt compassion for the native poor but some Conservative politicians were also strongly motivated by a desire to win working-class votes and to attack free trade at one of its weakest points. Unrestricted immigration was a part of the free trade citadel not easily defended as beneficial to the working classes. And if measures were taken to protect natives from the competition of foreign labour within Britain then some further protection against foreign labour abroad would be a logical progression. The defenders of free trade reacted accordingly and these tangential issues dominated the political debate on alien immigration and what, if anything, was to be done about it.

The various problems associated with Jewish immigration can be divided into mainly social problems and mainly economic problems. The greatest of the social problems was probably housing. As we saw in Chapter 3, the East End of London was overcrowded and rents there were high. By going there and by their determination to live in certain districts the immigrants were believed to push up rents and displace Londoners: 'The feeling is that there is nothing but the English going out and the Jews coming in' (witness to the Royal Commission on Alien Immigration). Bethnal Green was said to be in danger of conversion, 'not into the new Jerusalem of which they sung, but into the Jerusalem which they knew to exist in Whitechapel, St. George's and Stepney – street upon street of overcrowded houses filled by a foreign population' (*Eastern Post*, 1901).[139] Lord Brabazon became involved in the 'aliens question' because he feared that immigration was undoing his attempts to relieve congestion by sponsored emigration and Joseph Arch, the farm labourers' leader, was one of many others who thought similarly, 'Several thousands of our best men emigrate every year . . . but instead of this relieving the congested state of the population, we get in about three times as many worthless pauper aliens.'[140]

Associated with competition for housing was the claim that immigrant overcrowding, and the transition to London of the sanitary standards of Warsaw and Kiev, were a potential menace to the capital's health. It was feared too that all manner of infectious diseases long since controlled in Britain might accompany the newcomers to London and be carried far and wide on the jackets and trousers put together in Jewish workshops. The reappearance of cholera in Europe in 1892, and the terrible epidemic at Hamburg where many Jews took ship, was especially worrying: the TUC Parliamentary Committee report of that year drew attention to 'a new argument [that] has arisen in the last fortnight . . . the community has been seriously threatened with a cholera plague through the unrestricted immigration of these destitute aliens' (p. 29). Another charge sometimes heard was that immigrants were a public burden, 'a heavy charge upon the rates'.[141] It was well known that most of them arrived with few possessions and in contemporary literature references to alien immigrants were as often as not preceded by adjectives like 'pauper' or 'destitute' – Arch's reference to 'worthless pauper aliens' and the reference to 'destitute aliens' in the 1892 TUC Parliamentary Committee report were entirely typical. Yet another complaint was that among the immigrants were numerous criminals and political extremists. One rumour suggested that synagogues were being hastily built in all the prisons and the Conservative MP for Tower Hamlets claimed that 'the vast majority of these foreign Jews are nihilists and anarchists of the very worst type'.[142] The notorious Houndsditch Murders (1910) by a gang of alien anarchists disturbed while robbing a jeweller's premises, and the subsequent Sidney Street siege, did nothing to lessen the popular association of alien immigration with criminals and political extremists. Finally, the alien immigrants were castigated for their allegedly high fertility, a shortcoming that was highlighted by the contemporary fall in native fertility and the growth of an eugenic movement. Sidney Webb was one of those who drew attention to high Jewish fertility and he expressed fears that the difference between immigrant and native fertility would result in either 'national deterioration or . . . this country gradually falling to the Irish and the Jews'.[143]

Some of these social problems were, in fact, by no means as serious as contemporaries supposed, and others were far less the consequence of Jewish immigration than contemporaries claimed. The alleged influence upon East End housing was the charge with most substance. Wherever immigrants settled rents increased especially fast and natives were displaced. According to one estimate, when a street 'turned Jewish' rent rose by 50 to 60 per cent.[144] Immigrants accepted worse overcrowding than was usual in London and landlords profited accordingly, sometimes openly discriminating in favour of alien tenants. A few wealthy members of the Anglo-Jewish community did something towards housing new arrivals and displaced natives. In particular there was Rothschild's Four Per Cent Industrial Dwellings Company, part of the 'model dwellings' movement, but the 4,600 or so he housed by 1901 was far short of sufficient to offset Jewish settlement.[145] Much of the East End had a serious housing problem before Jewish immigration became substantial of course, and the problem doubtless would have persisted without immigration. Even so, immigrant settlement considerably aggravated the situation in certain districts.

Fears that the immigrant quarters would constitute a health hazard proved almost entirely unfounded. Although they came from cities far less sanitary than London, and although they were crowded both at home and at work, the Jewish immigrant population was at least as healthy as its native neighbours. In fact, they were probably healthier – mortality among Jewish immigrants in Manchester (1901) was below the rate of the city as a whole for every age-group except those over sixty-five years, and this despite their low incomes and their concentration in the least healthy parts of the city.[146] Among children under five years, Jewish immigrant mortality was more than 20 per cent below the city average. Perhaps one reason why Jewish immigration proved so much less of a threat to public health than some expected is that most Jews were accustomed to town life.[147] They knew far better than the Irish the awful consequences of uncleanliness in crowded cities. Other reasons may include the attention customarily bestowed upon Jewish infants and a tradition of cleanliness whose roots were in part religious – the regulations surrounding the raising, slaughter and distribution of meat, the ritual ablutions and change of clothing, the sabbath feasts, the Passover house-cleansing, and Jewish burial customs all had a more than religious significance. Particularly important was a remarkable improvement in sanitary standards shortly after arrival. This improvement owed a great deal to the work of the (voluntary) Jewish Board of Guardians which set up its sanitary committee in 1884 and encouraged newcomers towards native standards by a combination of inspection and health propaganda. The constant influx kept the Jewish sanitary authorities busy but the improvement in new arrivals and the good reputation of Jewish streets is attested not only in their mortality rates but also by contemporary investigators. Some of the streets which in Charles Booth's famous map were coloured black (the most notorious) by 1900 had been taken over by Jews and become respectable.[148]

The main concern of the Jewish Board of Guardians was the co-ordination of Jewish charity and the moral and material welfare of poor Jews. The substantial flow of financial and practical assistance from wealthier Jews to their needy co-religionists is one important way in which Irish and Jewish immigration differed and also the main reason why talk of Jewish imposition upon the rates was largely misconceived. There were sufficient prosperous Jews in Britain to bear the cost of Jewish poverty, and although the newcomers were of a different nationality the Jewish community willingly undertook this burden. In part it was done because the Anglo-Jewish establishment was sensitive to latent (and often not so latent) anti-Semitism and wished to avoid the ill will that would fall upon all Jews if newcomers drew heavily upon public funds. Institutions to care for destitute Jewish immigrants had been established long before 1880 and as immigration rose their activities were expanded. As the 1894 Report on the Volume and Effects of Recent Immigration from Eastern Europe stated clearly, 'in the strict legal sense of the term . . . hardly any of the alien Jews are "paupers" '.[149] A few of the least deserving applicants for Jewish charity were allowed to experience the public workhouse regime and considerable numbers of Jewish immigrants made use of poor law medical services. But by far the greater part of the burden of relieving the able-bodied Jewish poor fell not upon Gentile ratepayers as was alleged, but upon Jewish charity. There was some taking of Gentile charity, but this was mostly thrust upon the Jewish districts in the hope of winning converts. Indeed, the fear that poor Jews might fall into the clutches of Christian missionaries, and that any who entered the workhouse might not be able to obtain their proper food or to observe Jewish holidays, were other reasons why the Jewish establishment so carefully looked after its own.

There was not much more substance in the other charges that associated Jewish immigrants with contemporary social problems. Contrary to what some of their detractors claimed the Jews were, by and large, 'a peaceful and law-abiding community', with a crime rate less than the general rate.[150] It seems that they were guilty of at least their share of commercial crime (fraud, adulteration etc.) and some of them dabbled in prostitution, but they were very much under-represented among convictions for robbery and violence.[151] Those who spread the rumours that came close to triggering anti-Jewish riots at the time of Jack the Ripper could hardly have picked a less likely milieu for the assassin.[152] There were, it is true, a number of socialists and anarchists among the immigrants but never so many as the Conservative member for Tower Hamlets supposed (above, p. 180) and the great majority of the Jewish community had little sympathy for political extremists. Some of their activities they considered offensive: the Yom Kippur Anarchist Balls, for example, that were preceded by the provocative consumption of ham sandwiches outside Spitalfields Great Synagogue. Others, such as the anarchists' talk of class war and attempts to create fraternal alliances between poor Jews and anti-Semitic dockers,[153] they found either irrelevant or naive. Moreover, the Jewish anarchists (whose short and interesting history W. J. Fishman has described with great sympathy) were not much given to antisocial outrages of the kind perpetrated by anarchists on the continent. Rudolf Rocker, their (Roman Catholic) leader, was profoundly distressed by the Houndsditch murders. Eugenists were probably right in supposing that Jewish fertility was high, but there were hardly sufficient Jewish immigrants to justify Sidney Webb's fear of their successors taking over the country. Such fears appear out of place anyway in the eugenist case because the immigrants possessed many of the laudable characteristics of the native middle classes whose falling fertility the eugenists deplored.

Of the social problems for which Jewish immigrants were blamed, only one – high rents and overcrowding – had been significantly worsened by their arrival. Industrious, ambitious, frugal, sober,[154] law-abiding, self-sufficient and devoted to their homes and children, Jewish immigrants positively brimmed with the Smilesian virtues. Economic problems, of course, were another matter. The main charges against the immigrants in this sphere were that they took work and increased unemployment, that they depressed wages, that they were substantially responsible for the long hours and poor working conditions characteristic of the East End sweating system, and that they impeded trade unionism. Keir Hardie claimed that 'every foreigner throws one British workman out of employment', and John Burnett charged them with bringing 'thousands of native workers to the verge of destitution'.[155]

There was something in each of these allegations but less than Hardie and

Burnett supposed. What critics of immigration commonly overlooked was that unemployment, low wages, sweating, and weak trade unionism were each present in the East End in similar degree before many Jews arrived. As Beatrice Webb observed in correcting John Burnett's exaggerated account of immigrant responsibility for sweating, 'if every foreign Jew resident in England had been sent back to his birthplace, the bulk of the sweated workers would not have been affected'.[156] Trade unionism had never made much headway in the East End – it flourished most among well-paid males who worked for large organizations with impersonal industrial relations, whereas East End workshops were small and had always employed many women. Numerous East End 'employers' were scarcely distinguishable from their workers. Wages, employment, and trade unionism each suffered also from the great fluctuations in demand for labour that afflicted the London workshop trades, and from the thousands of wives of dockers and casual labourers who were anxious for work at almost any price. Shortly after the increase in Jewish immigration all of these problems were highlighted as a consequence of the greater concern for the poor and the new enthusiasm for going among them to count and classify their problems that were described in Chapter 4. It was the Jewish immigrants' misfortune to come to Britain shortly before this frenzied investigation began and to make for those parts of the capital that already had more than their share of problems and were soon to have more than their share of sociologists. Seeing the association of distress and alien settlement, certain newspapers and much of the public and trade union world too readily assumed that they had arrived together. But for the most part the late nineteenth-century East End surveys were simply rediscovering the problems that Mayhew had described, less scientifically, over thirty years earlier. So much had Mayhew's work been forgotten that some newspapers presented idealized accounts of a carefree pre-immigration East End life that had something in common with earlier romantic accounts of pre-industrial England. With the coming of the Jews, it was implied, 'merrie Whitechapel' was gone forever.

Exaggerated accounts of immigrant responsibility for East End economic problems arose partly from certain misconceptions. First, the number of Jewish immigrants was exaggerated. There were for a long time no controls on immigration and no reliable figures of how many came to Britain. In the 1892 edition of Whitaker's *Almanack*, for example, the rate of inflow was stated to be as much as 140,000 each year. The Board of Trade report of 1894 showed that this and many other estimates were far too high – in particular, insufficient allowance had been made for those who left for America soon after landing. A second misconception arose from the tendency to ascribe to all immigrants the very low, but transitory, earnings of 'greeners' just off the boat. Judging wages by piece-rates also led to confusion because the Jews extended the practice of sub-dividing tasks, made more use of simple machinery, and usually concentrated upon the cheaper end of the market. Thus comparisons of their piece-rates with those that had prevailed when productivity was lower, or with piece-rates paid in the better-class, and less sub-divided, end of the market, inevitably, but wrongly, suggested that immigrants worked for below the going rate.[157]

Assessing the effect of Jewish immigration upon employment and incomes as Keir Hardie did (above, p. 182), simply by judging the likely impact of additional labour upon existing levels of wages and employment, was another way in which the adverse consequences of immigration came to be exaggerated. Jewish immigrants affected demand for labour as well as its supply, and in more significant ways than via their own purchases. There is little point in examining the thesis that alien immigrants made a strategic contribution to British economic growth after the fashion that some claim for the Irish (above, pp. 171–4) because there were no labour bottlenecks in the East End and the occupations they entered were on the periphery of the economy. But whereas Irish immigrants contributed little but unskilled labour the Jews brought also qualities that were less abundant in Britain – enterprise, drive, and technical expertise. Their industry and ingenuity raised productivity and expanded markets. Thus they created employment in London, Manchester, and Leeds and affected workmen's living standards all over Britain by reducing the cost of clothing and furniture. Without Jewish enterprise the miners' delegates who became so indignant during the 1895 TUC debate on immigration when they were accused of wearing the results of sweated labour would have paid more for their suits, and the name of one poor Jewish immigrant who landed in 1901, Montague Burton, later became synonymous with the working man's 'Sunday best'. Besides raising tailoring productivity by extending division of labour and making greater use of the sewing-machine, Jewish enterprise can claim credit for the expansion of the Manchester waterproof garment trade and the manufacture of ladies' jackets and mantles. These jackets and mantles had at one time been imported from Germany but by the 1890s the Germans were importing them from Leeds. Similar successes were recorded in the tobacco trade and the manufacture of cheap furniture.[158] Although these achievements were overlooked by opponents of immigration they were acknowledged in several official inquiries,[159] and they went at least some way towards offsetting the adverse consequences of the Jewish immigrant increment to labour supply.

When all this has been said, however, it remains that for native workers alien immigration almost certainly made a bad situation somewhat worse. Immigrants added their labour to an already over supplied market and their eagerness to work made them willing victims of sweating. Their industriousness, and the number that became small employers, probably intensified both price competition and pressure on wages in the East End and helped also to sustain declining hand-trades which otherwise would sooner have succumbed to factory competition. And while they worked in parts of the labour market that were unconducive to effective unionism whatever the faith or nationality of the worker, there can be little doubt that immigrants set back the day when the East End workshop trades would cease to be an organizer's nightmare. Their language and their consciousness of themselves as a separate ethnic and religious group, their easy tolerance of poor wages and conditions, their individualism, and their ambition all made them eminently improbable recruits to trade unionism. But the sum of all their unfavourable influences, social and economic, was by no means as serious as many contemporaries alleged. It was also considerably less than the social and economic costs of Irish immigration.

x · *Segregation and anti-alienism*

There is no doubt that the Jews remained a community apart. Assimilation had not proceeded far by 1914 and that which had occurred was offset by the arrival of new immigrants who were very poor and quite ignorant of English ways and the English language. Alien immigrants were never involved in so many physical clashes with natives as the Irish immigrants had been, but this was largely a consequence of their being more segregated than the Irish. Instead of competing directly for unskilled manual employment they worked in a limited range of occupations, within limited areas, and in most cases for Jewish employers. They were fortunate too that by 1880 Britain was less vicious and better policed than it was at the time of the main Irish influx. Physical violence was largely confined to attacks on Jews who ventured outside the ghettos or who had not yet gained its sanctuary. Walking from the London docks to the ghetto, for example, meant passing through dockers' territory and the chance of a stoning.[160] A similar fate awaited 'sheenies' who entered Robert Roberts's Salford slum and the extensive anti-Jewish rioting of August 1911 was directed against shopkeepers and other propertied Jews who had settled among the Monmouthshire miners.[161]

The intensity of working-class anti-alienism probably did not change much between 1880 and 1914. It fluctuated with the trade cycle and unemployment, and was increased by the Boer War, by the Houndsditch Murders, and by the political tension that preceded the First World War. On the other hand reports of exceptionally cruel persecution in Russia at the time of the Russo-Japanese War and following the 1905 revolution increased sympathy for refugees, and the easing of London's housing shortage by the end of the century took some of the pressure from one particularly explosive issue. For the most part, however, the political battles that led to the imposition of controls on immigration in 1906[162] (a minor victory for the protectionist lobby) were fought over the heads of working-class people and we know far less of their feelings than we know of the views of politicians and union officials who tended to be preoccupied with the way that immigration affected bigger political questions.

Trade union attitudes towards alien immigrants changed markedly in the mid-1890s. Their initial reaction was hostile, chauvinistic, and a little hysterical. The bootmakers, tailors, and others directly affected were the most vociferous but union anti-alienism spread far beyond the East End. In his 1892 plea for restriction W. H. Wilkins was able to list forty-three unions and trade councils that had condemned unrestricted immigration, among them the Amalgamated Society of Engineers, the Durham Miners Association, the Amalgamated Society of Railway Servants, and many others who were not much bothered by alien competition.[163] The TUC passed motions deploring the entry of alien labour in 1888, 1892, 1894, and 1895 and Keir Hardie (who seconded the 1888 motion) remonstrated strongly about the alleged effect of the handful of foreigners in Scotland in evidence to the 1889 Select Committee on Emigration and Immigration (Foreigners), 'Dr Johnson said God made Scotland for Scotchmen, and I would keep it so.'[164] In 1891 a London Trades Council resolution supported by Tom Mann and Will Crooks went so far as to blame Jewish immigrants for the failure of trade unionism to make headway among farm labourers.[165] Shortly after this, however, union attitudes were moderated; the London Trades Council rejected an anti-alien resolution in 1895–6 and, like the TUC, never raised the subject again; Leeds Trades Council passed its last anti-alien resolution in 1895.[166] Some East End unions remained hostile and so did Blatchford's *Clarion* (below, p. 310), but their attitudes were no longer typical. The timing of this change is partly explained by trade recovery after 1895, but other influences sustained it. The unions had come to realize that the volume of immigration was insufficient to justify their earlier outbursts. They were a little ashamed of the fuss they had made and now gave rather more heed to those on the left who were conscious of the incompatibility of anti-alienism with socialism and anxious that racial animosity would impede the fostering of class animosity at home. Unions were also reacting to what some among them regarded as unprincipled exploitation of working-class xenophobia by Conservatives anxious to undermine free trade. By 1903 Keir Hardie had so revised his ideas that he firmly denied immigration caused unemployment and when Ben Tillett came to write his account of these times (in 1931) he censored all references to his own anti-alien activities.[167]

The attitude of the Anglo-Jewish establishment to immigration control and to assimilation was more constant than the union attitude but also more ambivalent. Jewish authorities were not insensitive to the consequences of immigration upon native housing and employment nor unaware of native xenophobia and the dangers this posed. As we saw earlier, the charitable activities and sanitary work of the Jewish Board of Guardians both sprang partly from a desire to contain native hostility. For the same reasons, and because they wished to keep immigration at a level that would not overwhelm their resources, the Jewish authorities were far from unequivocally in favour of unrestricted entry. They advised European Jews of the congested labour market in the East End, they emphasized the dearness and scarcity of accommodation, and drew attention to the relative advantages of emigration to America. Those who landed in London and could be persuaded to move on were helped across the Atlantic. Part of the same policy was the avoidance of relief on a scale that might itself encourage immigration. The Jewish Board of Guardians gave very little relief at all to newly-arrived immigrants and when a dissenting group opened the Poor Jews' Temporary Shelter in 1885, partly to cater for new arrivals, it was at once closed by the Jewish Board of Guardians on the grounds of insanitariness. The Jewish community also attempted to encourage Jewish youths to take up work outside the usual ghetto trades and to direct new arrivals towards Jewish communities in provincial towns where anti-alienism was less evident than it was in the East End.

In one sense most of these activities might be regarded as parts of a policy of anglicization. The provision of classes in English and the considerable pains taken in Jewish schools and orphanages to inculcate English manners, civic responsibility, and a pride in the Empire could be similarly regarded. Immigrants were willing recipients of this conditioning. They had no wish to return to their old homes and they took a grateful pride in British institutions. Besides, they were ambitious and a knowledge of English and the ability to move easily in English circles were aids to social and material success. But the desire for anglicization was highly qualified. Assimilation, or some assimilation, was regarded as necessary primarily because it was an insurance against attack upon those religious and cultural freedoms that preserved the Jewish identity. Complete absorption into English society would have been considered a fate not much preferable to full-scale persecution. Thus Hebrew was taught as well as English, and the measured steps in the direction of anglicization were accompanied by strong communal pressure against conversion and against marriage to non-Jews. The extent to which the community succeeded in doing sufficient to avoid unwelcome attention, and yet not so much as to jeopardize its identity, is perhaps as remarkable as the absorption of approaching 100,000 poor Jews in the congested East End at so little cost to the host community.

Suggestions for further reading are on page 402.

PART II

WORKING-CLASS MOVEMENTS

6

WORKING-CLASS MOVEMENTS, 1815–1850
I · TRADE UNIONISM AND OTHER MOVEMENTS

I · *Introduction: the growth of working-class movements*

Workers sometimes combined together: to seek or avoid changes in their wages and working conditions, to effect insurance against unemployment and other hazards, to bring pressure to bear upon parliament or increase their representation there, and for a great many other reasons. These various working-class movements are the subject of Part II. Chapters 6 and 7 cover the eventful years up to the decline of Chartism. Chapter 8 takes the story to the beginning of the 'new unionism', and Chapter 9 completes the survey up to the First World War. This chapter discusses trade unions before 1850, Owenism, the agitation that preceded the 1832 Reform Bill, the factory movement, and the campaign against the new poor law. Chartism, the first great working-class protest movement, is considered separately in Chapter 7 together with the prospects of working-class revolution in these years and the extent of working-class consciousness, two issues that are closely related to the history of working-class movements.

The number of working-class institutions, and their membership, increased spectacularly from the late eighteenth century. This increase was in part a consequence of urbanization. Town dwellers were more vulnerable to cyclical unemployment and they were less likely to have relatives and friends nearby to help out during crises. Membership of friendly societies, trade unions, and clubs was therefore to some extent a defensive reaction to changing circumstances, a substitute for more traditional, and less institutional, communal activity. It was a consequence also of a larger proportion of the labour force working alongside others for employers they hardly knew, circumstances that underlined the differences between master and men and encouraged working-class organization. Town workers were also more likely to be able to afford to join friendly societies and similar institutions.

There was considerable overlapping of functions among the early working-class institutions: most trade unions, for example, had some friendly society activities, some were little more than friendly societies. Unions pursued political as well as economic aims, sometimes by highly unconstitutional methods. Luddism, and the 'Rebecca' and 'Captain Swing' protests, have each been described as a kind of informal trade unionism, as 'collective bargaining by riot', and Chartism embraced virtually every contemporary working-class movement and most forms of protest and 'self-help'. Only the more important of these various institutions and activities can be considered in any detail and some of them – including, for example, the Anti-Corn Law campaign in which workers joined forces with other classes – are treated very briefly. Trade unionism, the movement that eventually came to be considered the most representative and most powerful of all working-class movements, will receive the greatest attention.

II · *Extent and characteristics of early trade unionism*

Although trade unionism was encouraged by town growth and industrialization, it began long before the eighteenth century. The Webbs were inclined to belittle their own evidence of very early trade unionism by insisting that unionism began only when there existed 'a continuous association of wage-earners for the purpose of maintaining or improving the conditions of their working lives'. Even so, they traced the movement's 'origins' back as far as the late seventeenth century.[1]

This question of the timing of trade union origins is more than a semantic matter. For the Webbs' pioneering work has greatly influenced succeeding scholars, and their emphasis upon the 'continuity' of association – which amounts to an emphasis upon formal, institutionalized association – has led historians to underestimate the strength and importance of informal combinations and, more importantly, to exaggerate the significance of certain formally constituted trade unions whose achievements and market strength failed to match their grandiose pronouncements and elaborate rules and procedures.[2] At a time when effective combinations of workmen on more than a local basis were extremely difficult to organize, and when most unions were composed of men who worked and lived together, formal organization was less necessary to effective unionism than it became later. Workmen without formal organization had their acknowledged, if unofficial, leaders and their unwritten trade practices that might be effectively protected by informal combination. Informal collective pressures were used to exclude women and other 'outsiders'; coal-miners consciously adjusted output (and thus their wages) by regulating their working day, and H. A. Turner argues that the beginning of 'continuous association' in the cotton industry was much earlier than has been suggested by interpretations that equate unionism with formally constituted organization.[3] Continuous trade unionism in this sense probably began long before the eighteenth century.

Nevertheless, trade unionism cannot be said to have affected more than a small proportion of workers by 1815 and it was still a minority movement at mid-century. For 1842, a very bad year, the Webbs estimated membership at under 100,000[4] or about 1½ per cent of the labour force. For 1834, a good year for the unions, membership has been estimated at a million or more.[5] But even this was less than one worker in five and the greater part of the million were only trade unionists so long as their supposed powers of combination were not put to the test. Until the end of the century, in fact, the great majority of British workers had no part in trade union history.

Who then were the unionists? In exceptional and short-lived bursts of expansion, such as that of 1829–34, the movement touched workers of every kind including even farm labourers and women. Such episodes, however, were unusual and added far less to union strength than they added to membership. The effective unions of the first half of the century, those that could withstand counter-attack and cyclical depression, were overwhelmingly composed of well-paid and skilled male workers. Most of these unionists – the carpenters for example, the masons, printers, coopers, coachbuilders, and watchmakers – were in traditional handicraft occupations. Some others, notably the engineers and mule spinners, were in occupations that were created or vastly expanded by industrialization. Even in these relatively well-paid occupations combination was much affected by the condition of the labour market. In bad years membership slumped, and in the smaller towns and the less prosperous parts of the country, where labour was always plentiful, there was little effective unionism of any description.

These effective unions were not large. Their basis was craft loyalty and shared craft interests; therefore they were mainly unions of men in one occupation. There were at times loose associations between craftsmen in different towns which facilitated the tramping system (above, p. 156) and activities like parliamentary lobbying, but most union business was conducted locally. The extremely fragmented labour market, the expense and slowness of communications (especially before the railways), the absence of great combinations among employers, and artisan pride in self-government were all restraints on size. Union policy was concerned mainly with practical matters, with trade affairs and members' welfare. Unions endeavoured to maintain craft customs and artisan independence, to protect wages and differentials, and to provide sick and unemployment pay, medical care, and other friendly society benefits. The welfare benefits they met from high subscriptions and their other ends they achieved by carefully segregating unionists from the mass of workers and prudently exploiting the strength derived from skill and relative scarcity. Scarcity was maintained by the regulation of labour supply – in particular, by restricting the number of apprentices taken on, by denying union membership to those who had not served apprenticeships or who were incapable of earning the union rate, and (where they could) by refusing to work with non-union men. Controls upon overtime and piece-rate working, the tramping system, emigration schemes, and high entry fees played a supplementary role in maintaining labour scarcity. Certain skilled occupations, several in the Sheffield trades for example, were effectively closed to all but the sons and nephews of existing workers.

It is significant that these various policies were directed as much, or more, against the less-skilled as against employers, and that they tended to relegate direct bargaining and open confrontation to a secondary role. Part of the strength of the craft unions was that they generally remembered their limitations. They knew that employment and earnings fell in trade depressions and at these times adopted a patiently defensive stance and awaited better conditions. Employers were by no means necessarily hostile towards unions of this kind. They were accustomed to craft unionism and craft union privileges were a small part of their total costs. Moreover, skilled men were not easily replaceable and if challenged they were likely, sooner or later, to counter-attack. Most craft unions combined their conciliatory attitudes towards employers with lack of enthusiasm for radical politics. The Manchester printers were particularly circumspect: they declined any part in John Doherty's National Association for the Protection of Labour (1830), they condemned the violent and revolutionary tendencies of Robert Owen's Grand National Consolidated Trades Union (1833–4), and refused even to celebrate the 1832 Reform Act.[6] Later they deplored the 'futility' of militant Chartism and denounced Feargus O'Connor as an unfair employer who used too many apprentices to print the *Northern Star*.[7]

There were exceptions to each of these generalizations about those who were able to practise effective unionism. The factory spinners, for example, especially in the Glasgow area where many were Irish, combined craft union tactics with cruder, overtly aggressive, measures. Their early history was punctuated by riots, frequent strikes, and threatened and actual acts of terrorism against employers and other workers. They were also, compared with the older and more decorous craft societies, more inclined to look for increased strength in broad geographical associations or in combination with other occupations and less preoccupied with purely trade concerns. There was also a radical element that operated at all times within many craft unions; among the tailors, shoemakers, and some of the other skilled workmen of London its presence was especially marked. At certain times, exceptional demand for labour or the heady rhetoric of men like John Doherty and Robert Owen encouraged a significant proportion of all skilled workers to believe that almost anything was possible, even the creation of one big union that would include workers of every kind.

What of the great majority of the labour force that lacked the skills and scarcity value of the craftsmen? These for the most part simply could not practise effective unionism. This too is a very broad generalization and must be qualified at once. Between the labour aristocrats with their strong formal

194

unions and those like the farm labourers and sweated needlewomen there were many degrees of skill, and in London and the great industrial centres substantial numbers of semi-skilled workers could practise unionism of a limited and intermittent kind. The coal-miners are an obvious example. Most miners lived in close-knit colliery communities where workplace grievances were communal grievances and group loyalty was reinforced by a shared consciousness of mining hazards. The considerable size of some individual collieries, and the social chasm this opened-up between employers and workers, were further encouragements to organization. The hewers, moreover, were well-paid and in many places graduated to hewing through an 'apprenticeship' of less well-paid and less highly regarded work. They also enjoyed a considerable measure of 'independence' – one of the hallmarks of the craftsman – because close supervision of their work was impossible. Although there was no continuous, formal, miners' unionism before 1850 there was much informal combination and the Miners Association of Great Britain, which survived from 1842 until 1848, at one time had 100,000 members.[8]

Even the farm labourers could engage in 'collective bargaining by riot'. Such tactics were not often employed by those able to practise orthodox unionism, and whereas orthodox trade unionism advanced when economic conditions were good 'collective bargaining by riot' was far more likely to occur in economic depressions. But it was not confined to workers desperately resisting the inevitable, and it was sometimes practised shrewdly and with effect. Luddism (1811–17) was the outstanding example of this form of proto-unionism. Luddism occurred chiefly among the midland framework knitters and was at its height in 1811 and 1812.[9] The status and earnings of framework knitters had been eroded by unrestricted entry and wartime trade disruptions and changes in fashion had reduced employment. There was also bad feeling about truck payments and frame-rents. Systematic frame breaking began in response to wage reductions at a time when food prices were high, and was focused upon those employers who had adapted frames to make the cheaper 'cut-up' hosiery for which demand was relatively strong.[10] Luddite strategy was short-sighted and largely ineffective, but machine breaking and other tactics were carried out with remarkable efficiency on a large scale and they caused great alarm.[11]

Two rather more effective examples of collective bargaining by riot were the 'Scotch Cattle' activity of 1820–35 and the 'Captain Swing' episode of 1830. Scotch Cattle was the name taken by bands of South Wales miners and ironworkers whose 'midnight visits' and other quasi-terrorist activities disciplined unorganized workers and won concessions from powerful employers. They were concerned in disputes over wages, hours, 'truck', and the exclusion of English and Irish workmen. Captain Swing was the reputed, but probably mythical, organizer of the agrarian riots, rick burning, and machine smashing that occurred in southern and eastern England in 1830 and which were partly responsible for the disuse of the threshing machine whose threat to winter employment had been the chief cause of discontent.[12] As orthodox trade unionism developed, however, tactics of this kind became more exceptional: it is significant that Yorkshire Luddism scarcely affected Leeds where the croppers' union was strongest, and that the Scotch Cattle were quiescent in the prosperous mid-1820s when trade unionism advanced.[13] Violence in industrial relations declined also because violence of most kinds became less tolerated by the authorities. There were fears that in the new industrial towns rioting of the traditional kind might become uncontainable and collective bargaining by riot, even in its milder forms, came to be regarded – like bull baiting and public hangings – as an unseemly remnant of a more rumbustious age.

Most attempts at formal unionism among the less skilled workers were short lived. Such unions grew fast from small beginnings. Often they began in response to some single grievance but they inclined to quickly adopt far grander aims. Lacking market scarcity, the unskilled aspired naturally towards large general unions that would embrace all workers and thus eliminate their greatest weakness. These aspirations came closest to being fulfilled in the early 1830s, but even at that time the difference between what was planned and what was achieved was very wide. The basic weakness was that there was usually a great abundance of unqualified labour eager to find work. Manufacturing centres were crowded with migrants from the country, with handloom weavers and others made redundant by technical change, and with Ireland's rural surplus. Many of these were first or second generation industrial workers. Most of them, the women and child workers in particular, were easily pleased and notoriously difficult to organize. Irish immigrants were perhaps less deferential than the rest but, as we noted earlier, they were for a long time too ill-disciplined, too preoccupied with other matters, and too easily disheartened to make sound trade unionists. There were times when even unskilled labour was scarce, but never for long, and the periodic trade depressions strengthened employers and put unbearable strain on nascent unions. Employers also had the law and government on their side whereas the unskilled lacked even the vote. Thus even the most circumspect unskilled trade unions were vulnerable and their lack of market strength, and the ease and frequency with which employers substituted 'blackleg' labour during strikes, inclined them towards the more desperate forms of activity that few employers were willing to tolerate. The employers were confident, self-made men. They were soundly backed by prevailing political and economic theory, their voices were increasingly heeded at Westminster, and they were not lacking in the will to exploit their strong market position.

The tactics dictated by weakness – mass unionism, mass demonstrations, and similarly flamboyant gestures directed as much at local and central government as at employers – raised other obstacles to unionism among the unskilled. There was first the fundamental problem of communication to be overcome if the scattered protests of workers throughout the country were to be effectively combined. Secondly, there was the formidable, probably insuperable, task of reconciling interests that varied between occupations and from one part of the country to the next, of persuading the impatient to subordinate immediate grievances to the long-term general interest. Funds were another problem: poor workmen were deterred by high subscriptions, and inadequate funds made unions vulnerable to any opposition. For the same reason, and because they hoped for more radical solutions to working-class problems, the general unions largely ignored the provision of friendly society benefits. Thus their members were not bound to them by accumulated subscriptions and they could not be disciplined (as craftsmen could) by threatening to revoke benefit rights. Finally there was the problem of leadership. It would have required quite outstanding leadership to do much with such unpromising raw material in such hostile circumstances, and none appeared. Indeed, poor leadership and squabbles at the top were not least of the weaknesses of the general unions. Among those who came to the fore were some whose extremist views repelled potential members and invited repression. Others pursued anachronistic fantasies – 'merrie England' or co-operative socialism. Some were simply inefficient or dishonest. Doherty's National Association of United Trades for the Protection of Labour and Owen's Grand National Consolidated Trades Union both lost substantial sums to absconding officials.

III · *Unionism under the Combination Acts*

Until the repeal of the Combination Acts in 1824 most forms of union activity in England and Wales were illegal. This legislation, however, was of less consequence than is sometimes suggested. The Hammonds, for example, grossly exaggerated its importance when they claimed that without the Combination Acts the course of English history 'would have been very different for many generations'.[14] There was considerable union activity throughout the years when the Acts were nominally in operation. There were strikes of weavers, for example, in 1808, 1818, and 1819. Spinners, miners, building workers, dyers, hatters, and weavers in the Manchester district were all on strike in 1818, and in Nottingham at least fifty unions operated at one time or another between the introduction of the Acts (1799) and their repeal.[15] A pamphlet of 1823 described the legislation as a 'dead letter' for several classes of artisans, 'namely the shoemakers, printers, papermakers, shipbuilders, tailors, etc. who have had their regular societies and houses of call, as though no such Act was in existence'.[16] Other workers made a cursory pretence that their unions were friendly societies, and there was also, of course, a great deal of informal combination among craftsmen of a kind that could not have been eradicated even if the law had been vigorously enforced.

But it never was rigorously enforced – Nottingham with its fifty illegal unions saw only five prosecutions in twenty-five years.[17] The Combination Acts were introduced by a government that was inclined to frighten itself by exaggerating the extent of revolutionary trade unionism and at a time of national crisis when Britain was at war with revolutionary France. Unions that pursued economic ends openly and without violence were generally tolerated.[18] Employers could instigate legal action without official support but for the most part they too left the law unused. Convictions were not easily obtained and could be expensive. A prosecution, moreover, embittered industrial relations. There were, in any case, over forty earlier acts against combination at the disposal of employers and the government. The Combination Acts were intended to deal with combinations more surely and more quickly than existing legislation, but nothing that was illegal under the Acts of 1799 and 1800 had previously been lawful. It is hardly surprising, therefore, that Scottish workers, who were exempt from the legislation of 1799 and 1800, seem to have enjoyed no especial advantage in the following decades over workers in England and Wales.[19]

Another reason why the Combination Acts were largely inoperative was the existence of an ill-defined area where combination was still legal. There was a very fine distinction between a possibly illegal combination and one established to call upon the authorities to enforce or change the law. The reform meeting at St Peter's Field, Manchester, that preceded the abortive march of the Blanketeers in 1817,[20] for example, was not illegal when it began. Nor was the fateful meeting two years later, also at St Peter's Field, that ended in the 'Peterloo Massacre'.[21] And the notorious 'Six Acts' that were introduced shortly after 'Peterloo' were designed to curtail some of the forms of combination still permissible under the Combination Acts.[22]

An upsurge of union activity occurred at the time the Combination Acts were repealed which has helped to foster the belief that the Acts were a significant obstacle to trade unionism. But the expansion was short-lived and much of it was due to a brief trade boom that coincided with repeal and provided conditions conducive to union expansion. Some of this advance was doubtless also a consequence of workers being confused by the publicity surrounding repeal into believing that their wages had been kept down by the Combination Acts, that repeal would make combination easy, and that combination would at once raise wages. But the euphoria soon dissipated, and when the trade cycle turned down in 1825 many learnt the hard way how inconsequential was the law in determining wage levels and who might organize.

The Combination Acts, in short, were of little significance. They probably did induce some extra caution in union affairs, including a more overtly circumspect avoidance of political issues. The number of unions who considered it prudent to assume the form of friendly societies or to operate without formal organization is evidence of this. At the same time, by implying a conspiratorial nature in even the least objectionable forms of combination, the government may also have unwittingly provoked some additional support for the violent methods of the secret unionism it feared. The Combination Acts probably had some significance also in the way the great expectations aroused by their repeal helped to prepare the way for the radical general unionism of 1829–34. But their greatest significance was perhaps the symbolic one that they showed clearly how unfairly the retreat from paternalism could bear upon the working classes. The repeal of apprenticeship regulations and of wage fixing and similar protection was accompanied by the strengthening of a repressive aspect of paternalism whose intent was to deny workers an alternative means of defence. This is not to say that government policy on industrial relations was entirely negative or invariably on the side of employers: they too were subject to the Combination Acts (a few were prosecuted) and additional measures to facilitate arbitration were introduced in 1800, 1803, and 1824. On the specific issue of the right to organize, however, changes in the law, largely inoperative although they may have been, were designed to operate against working-class interests.

IV · *The general unionism of 1829–34; cautious progress, 1834–50; trade unionism and working-class welfare before 1850*

The chief developments in trade union history between the repeal of the Combination Acts and mid-century were a number of unsuccessful attempts at general union and a probable long-term expansion in the number able to organize effectively. This quarter-century is distinguished also by increasing class-consciousness and the existence alongside trade unionism of several other movements in which many working men, and in some cases the unions themselves, took an active part. Robert Owen's co-operative philosophy was taken up in the 1820s; in 1830–2 there was the great campaign that led to the Reform Act; at about the same time the organized factory movement was established, and an anti-poor law campaign began in 1836. There was also substantial working-class backing for the Anti-Corn Law League (formed 1839) and, of course, for Chartism.

The sharp economic downturn of 1825 dashed for a time the high aspirations that had been conjured up by prosperity and the repeal of the Combination Acts.[23] In these less auspicious circumstances the trade union world contracted and its prudent and elitist characteristics were again dominant. There were moves towards wider association, but for the most part they took the form of craftsmen uniting (none too successfully) with others of their kind elsewhere. The Journeymen Steam Engine and Machine Makers and Millwrights Society (1826) lasted longer than most such amalgamations and its establishment was to prove an event of some significance. The same cannot be said of the quaintly mis-entitled 'Philanthropic Hercules', established shortly before the Combination Acts were repealed and probably the first attempt at a union with no occupational restraints upon membership. Another general union, begun at Manchester in 1826, was abandoned 'before it was so much as known to a large majority of the operatives in the neighbourhood'.[24]

However, the expectations aroused in 1824–5 had been suppressed, not forgotten, and by 1830 another, more exciting, advance was underway. Unlike most union advances, this one owed little to favourable economic conditions. Far more important was the initiative of John Doherty, the heightened expectations generated by Reform agitation, disappointment at its outcome, and, of course, Owenism. Robert Owen's quasi-socialist references to 'the productive class' ('the source of all wealth'), and his intolerance of the unemployment inseparable from capitalistic competition, became more widely known after the publication of his *Report to the County of Lanark* in 1821. His ideas, often simplified and made more anti-capitalist than he would have liked, struck a responsive chord in many trade unionists. The possibility that earnings might be enhanced by the omission of profit-taking intermediaries had an obvious appeal, while co-operative production appeared to offer both a means of safeguarding artisan independence and a constructive occupation for members who were unemployed or on strike. Many unions experimented in co-operative production, operated co-operative stores, subscribed to Owenite periodicals, and filled their own newspapers with co-operative propaganda. When he returned from America in 1829 Owen found that working-class support for co-operativism had developed in his absence and, despite his aversion to change 'from the bottom up', he determined to turn it to his advantage.

Also in 1829 John Doherty, the leader of the Lancashire spinners and a keen co-operator, succeeded in bringing together most of Britain's unionized cotton spinners in one organization, the Grand General Union of all the Operative Spinners of the United Kingdom. This union can perhaps claim to be the first truly national trade union although the allegiance of the Scots and Irish spinners proved very fragile and by 1831 the Grand General Union had disappeared with very little to show for its existence. But Doherty had already moved on to a more ambitious project. In February 1830 he called together delegates from twenty different trades with the intention of forming a union open to all occupations.[25] The National Association of United Trades for the Protection of Labour (NAPL) was launched a few months later, the first of the projected general unions to achieve substance. Its chief strength was Doherty's own cotton spinners but the union succeeded also in enrolling other textile workers, some building and metal workers, miners, potters, and engineers. In all, as many as 150 separate societies joined the NAPL and Doherty claimed 100,000 members. But this union too had a short and unsuccessful life. A few strikes were won by its constituent parts (who each continued their separate existence as single-occupation unions) but the NAPL never mobilized its united strength and in 1832 it collapsed in the face of financial and administrative difficulties, apathy, and, above all, the tendency of each society to give first priority to its sectional interests. Although partially inspired by Owenite socialism, Doherty's creation was equally remarkable for the extent to which its short life was shaped by traditional attitudes. It did not recruit directly and never amounted to much beyond a very loose association of independent, self-centred, craft societies whose leaders were far less anxious than Doherty was to pursue broad class interests. Most of his own spinners saw the association as simply a means to consolidate their trade interests. They were reluctant to commit their strength to others' battles, and when they realised that the NAPL had little to offer them they withdrew, accusing Doherty of neglecting his own occupation.

The Operative Builders Union, which came into prominence about the time the NAPL disappeared, was a more significant departure from craft union traditions. It was confined to building workers and initially organized on a federal basis with separate sections for each trade. But it admitted building workers of every kind, including labourers; it exercised more power over its members than the NAPL; and it was far more influenced by Owenism. Numerous workers who were previously unorganized, or organized on a town basis, were brought together into a national society that at one time was 60,000 strong. Owenism made a particular impact upon building workers because the system of general contracting for building work was spreading from London into the provinces and threatening the independence of craftsmen who were accustomed to making their own bargains with customers. At the 'Builders' Parliament' of 1833 a programme of action drawn up by Owen and a handful of his disciples was adopted wholesale. A suitably impressive Gild Hall was planned, to be designed by Owenite architects, and the union resolved to seek building work on its own account and to supply no more mere proletarian labour. By this means it hoped to force the great contractors either into bankruptcy or into the union. The Builders

Union, that is, planned to take over and operate the building industry. That an organization composed mainly of normally sober artisans could contemplate such a far-fetched scheme indicates clearly the raised expectations and general excitement of the early 1830s and says much for the persuasive influence of Robert Owen. But like most who attempted to put his ideas into practice the builders soon ran into difficulties. Few customers put work their way and their pretentious demands provoked several major disputes, the usual outcome of which was a return to work on the understanding that those re-engaged would have no more to do with the Builders Union. These difficulties strengthened the 'exclusives' within the union, those who were not inspired by Owenite socialism and who resented the loss of local autonomy to the 'Builders' Parliament'. So sectionalism and disintegration accompanied and accelerated industrial defeats. By late 1834 the union was shattered and its half-completed Gild Hall was sold to become a warehouse.

Brief, but unprecedented, advances occurred in a number of other occupations at this time: the potters' union established by Doherty in 1830 for example, the semi-secret Yorkshire Clothiers Union which the Webbs likened to the Operative Builders Union, and an attempt in 1831 to unite the various miners' unions of Lancashire, Cheshire, the West Riding, Staffordshire, and North Wales. Tommy Hepburn's union of Northumberland and Durham miners (1831) succeeded for a time, caused great anxiety to the coal-masters and local authorities, and then succumbed after a hard fought struggle in which troops and 'blacklegs' figured prominently.

Best known of all the 1829–34 unions was the Grand National Consolidated Trades Union. The GNCTU, in fact, was none of the things its title proclaimed. Its fame derives from Owen's leadership, from its vast claimed membership, from the Tolpuddle Martyrs, and from the way its collapse effectively ended the Owenite episode in trade unionism. A large general union intended to take over employment of every kind in the way that the Builders Union hoped to absorb the building industry was launched at a conference in October 1833. Robert Owen was there, inspired by his success at the 'Builders' Parliament'. There was strong support from London craftsmen, especially the tailors and shoemakers. Several of the societies that had participated in Doherty's NAPL were also among the first to join and an appeal from the silk-workers of Derby, who were locked-out and seeking funds to begin co-operative production, inspired more general support. A second conference, in February 1834, adopted the title 'Grand National Consolidated Trades Union' and drew up a constitution. Delegates sought pledges of help from trade unions, co-operative societies, and even from friendly societies. Where no organization existed, lodges of the union were established on either a single- or multi-occupational basis; there were also lodges of female workers. The union ultimately claimed to have 800,000 members. But a leader's pledge of support committed his membership to very little, and although there was doubtless much enthusiasm and sympathy for the GNCTU its effective strength was very slight. Only some 16,000, almost half of these London tailors and shoemakers, carried their commitment as far as paying a subscription.[26]

The considerable enthusiasm aroused by the GNCTU is indicated most obviously by the Tolpuddle affair. Agricultural labourers and particularly those in Dorset, were normally beyond the margins of the trade union world. Yet it was for swearing a secret oath, part of the GNCTU's elaborate ritual, that the six 'martyrs' were convicted and sentenced to be transported to Australia. An impressive protest campaign followed, organized by the GNCTU.[27] It was at this point that Owen himself took over the union's direction. He attempted to curb strikes and other displays of class militancy, and confidently predicted that if his programme was followed society would be peacefully transformed within weeks as capitalists, managers, and workers of every kind became aware of the benefits of co-operation and flocked to join the union. But by midsummer 1834 the Grand National had disintegrated, despite improving trade conditions. It collapsed because of the defeat and withdrawal of the London tailors, and from a combination of virtually all of the weaknesses that could afflict general unions. Thoroughly disillusioned by his attempts to reform society with the help of the workers, and probably more than a little relieved at the collapse of a union whose class-divisive activities he could not control, Owen retired to pursue his co-operative campaign by other means.

The disappearance of the GNCTU ended five exciting years that had begun with Doherty's Grand General Union of Operative Spinners. Besides attempts at national and general unions these years saw also the turbulent Reform campaign, the 'Swing' riots, and the beginning of the factory movement. The significance of events at this time has a fairly prominent place in trade union historiography. Some interpretations have suggested that unionism of the kind epitomized by the GNCTU was more effective, more radical, and more representative of trade unionism generally in the first half of the nineteenth century than was the case. The Webbs rightly emphasized the feebleness of the general and industrial unions but they also exaggerated union radicalism by labelling these years 'The Revolutionary Period'. And their talk of the trade union movement falling into 'a period of general apathy' after 1834 (even if 'not absolutely left for dead') grossly inflates the significance of the preceding events.[28] H. A. Turner has done the same more recently by generalizing in terms of a period of 'mass labour movements' followed by a 'retreat' into craft exclusiveness that 'cut off the infant general labour movement . . . and postpone[d] its substantial reappearance for half a century'.[29] There is little to be said for such views. So far as their effectiveness in the labour market is concerned the NAPL, the GNCTU, and the others amounted to little more than strings of pretentious initials. And they were characterized far less by revolutionary zeal, or working-class solidarity, than by the persistence and pervasiveness of sectional interests.

On the other hand, these developments cannot be simply dismissed as a temporary aberration by a small part of a movement that otherwise retained all its elitist and conservative characteristics. Despite their weaknesses the unions of 1829–34 represent a move in the direction of working-class consciousness. Parts of the labour aristocracy stood aloof, but it is quite obvious that significant numbers of craftsmen forgot for a time the limitations of their strength and how much it depended upon segregation from the unskilled. A. E. Musson, in correcting the errors of the Webbs and others who gave too much prominence to these events, has perhaps gone a little too far in the direction of emphasizing the continuity of trade union history and its fundamentally conservative and sectional nature.[30] The provincial printers (whose history Professor Musson has written) appear to have been more 'aristocratic' in their outlook than most craftsmen and less easily seduced by Owenism and other diversions.

Thus the return to normal in the autumn of 1834, although it was neither a collapse nor a retreat, does represent something of a change of course. Long after this there were still occasional outbursts of 'collective bargaining by riot' and some unions were involved in militant Chartism, but for the most part the elusiveness of the Owenite millennium and the proven futility of attempts to create general unions seem to have left a sobering and lasting influence. There was one further attempt to launch a general union – the National Association of United Trades for the Protection of Labour (1845) – but it received very little support and soon became transformed into a modest pressure group seeking better industrial relations through conciliation. 'Past experience', wrote a member of the Manchester Stonemasons, 'has taught us that we have had general union enough'.[31] Most of the craft unions, as we shall see, took care not to become closely embroiled with Chartism, and the more Chartist rhetoric inclined towards physical violence the more aloof craft unions became. Branches of the Steam Engine Makers Society were suspended for putting funds in the Chartist Land Bank and two branches of the Stonemasons Society proposing to do the same met indignant protests against their 'absurd political speculation'.[32]

There were other signs that unions were coming to recognize the permanency and potential of the new industrial order. There was, in particular, the great enthusiasm for education of every kind: for reading rooms and elevating discussion, for mutual improvement societies, and for the mechanics' institutes that did so much to instil orthodox liberal economic philosophy. The more earnest unions ceased to meet in pubs and instead of devoting fines to drink applied them to defraying the costs of lectures and recitals. Trade policy emphasized again the desirability of harmonious industrial relations, the mutual interests of masters and men, and the need to protect friendly society benefits by avoiding costly strikes. The appearance of union emigration schemes in the 1840s, in part a recognition of Malthusian pressure and the primacy of demand and supply in determining wages, is often taken as yet another illustration of union acceptance of orthodox economic thinking.[33] The Liverpool stonemasons, for example, in 1849 proposed that emigration should be encouraged as a substitute for striking, and the Carpenters at one time referred to emigration as the 'natural outlet' for the 'surplus labourers and mechanics' produced by the 'prolific character of the Anglo-Saxon race'.[34]

So progress after 1834 was of an unspectacular kind. There was a prolonged period of bad or indifferent trade between 1836 and 1842 when many unions were hard put to maintain their ground and some went under. Thereafter membership rose steadily and a series of amalgamations took several occupations a long way towards national union. There was also further co-operation between trades on a town basis along lines that anticipated the trades councils set up in the 1850s and 1860s. The engineers' societies came through the depression better than most and made considerable progress in the 1840s. The financial affairs of the Journeymen Steam Engine Makers were already firmly controlled from head office, they appointed a full-time general secretary in 1843, and were soon pursuing the amalgamation that led to the foundation of the Amalgamated Society of Engineers in 1851. Another significant development about this time was the Miners Association of Great Britain which in 1842 drew together several of the smaller unions that had survived the depression. The Association overcame a series of set-backs in 1844, it engaged W. P. Roberts, the 'miners' attorney-general', to defend its members' interests in the courts, and survived until the 1848 depression. Like many of the craft unions the Miners Association avoided radical politics and stressed its mutual interests with employers: Feargus O'Connor was refused permission to address a national delegates' meeting in 1844 and in the same year one delegate declared that 'Hitherto it has been a battle between masters and men about wages. Now the miners are determined that it shall be a battle between masters and men on the one side and the public on the other.'[35]

What was the influence of all this trade union activity upon working-class welfare before 1850? Craft union membership brought considerable benefits: by controlling entry to the trade and regulating working practices the unions protected wages and artisan independence. In addition, craft unions performed many of the functions of a labour exchange. They also provided a wide range of welfare benefits and, of course, conviviality. To belong to one of these craft societies was itself a desirable status symbol, a sign of respectability. Certain of the less respectable and less enduring unions also helped their members in various ways. The Miners Association, for example, was partly responsible for the scrapping of the annual bond in the north-east and for advances in colliery safety legislation. However, only a small proportion of the labour force were members of successful unions and large general unions like the GNCTU were short-lived and almost entirely ineffectual. Moreover, at least some part of craft union achievements was obtained at the expense of the less privileged workers who were excluded from membership. The overwhelming impression, therefore, is that the net contribution of the unions to working-class welfare as a whole was not great. Other movements (some of them with middle-class leaders) probably brought equal or greater benefits: the friendly societies in particular, which had nearly a million members as early as 1815,[36] the public health movement, the temperance campaign, Methodism, and perhaps also the factory movement and the campaign against the amended poor law.

Even craft unions did hardly more than reinforce the benefits that would have accrued to their members from the operation of more powerful forces. Compared with the trade cycle, the harvest, demographic variables, and the levels of invention, innovation, and enterprise, the unions were not a very important influence in the labour market. Contemporary claims that their blind and selfish pursuit of short-term gains had a significant long-term effect upon wages and employment, that they exercised a 'tyranny' over employers and endangered Britain's competitiveness, can be largely discounted. And at this time, when unions were too weak to entirely disrupt production of any commodity, and when work was insufficiently specialized and insufficiently capital-intensive for a small number to throw many others out of work by withdrawing their labour, strikes did little harm to other workers. Unionism did accelerate the decline of certain occupations like the Norwich weaving trade and shipbuilding on the Thames, but in these cases it was only one influence among several working in the same direction. Technical change was seldom delayed for long by union resistance: the unions knew that the usual outcome of uncompromising resistance was that their members were replaced by outsiders. It is arguable, in fact, that Britain's cautious and pragmatic unions were less of an impediment to technical advance than unorganized labour whose reaction to new technology was inclined to be more volatile and more destructive.

v · *Owenism; the Reform campaign of 1830–2; the Factory Movement; the Anti-Poor Law campaign*

Owenism

Robert Owen's early life is perhaps most notable for his remarkable social mobility. The son of a small-town ironmonger and saddler, and a draper's apprentice at the age of ten, he became manager of a spinning mill with five hundred employees when he was hardly out of his teens. In 1800, still not thirty, he moved to New Lanark as part owner and sole manager of the largest cotton spinning establishment in Britain. He proved to be a highly competent entrepreneur and New Lanark, its workers, and its profits all flourished together.

Owen the industrialist is remembered most for his management of labour. Like other early factory masters he had to create a disciplined and reliable labour force from recruits that included many who were foot-loose, drunken, unused to machinery, and resentful of the clock. And like other employers Owen overcame these difficulties by a combination of the carrot and the stick and by special attention to children whose education and everyday routine could be organized to produce habits of order and industry. But more than most factory masters he relied upon kindness firmly applied and the conditioning influence of education. His workers were well housed and adequately provided with shops, schools, and other amenities. His mills and village were kept clean and tidy and the labour force was given every encouragement to follow this good example. Thus New Lanark became a model factory community that was much visited by enlightened travellers.

By 1812 Owen was acquiring a wider reputation as he began to publicize the lessons of managing New Lanark and to recommend their general application. His fundamental message concerned the tractability and perfectability of human nature. Man's character, he believed, was a function of education and environment. It followed that proper conditioning, unassisted by physical punishment or the harsh discipline of competition, could create a community without selfishness, indolence, intemperance, or dishonesty. The reform of society, that is, was but a logical extension of the transformation of dissolute Highlanders into respectable factory spinners. Education had a crucial place in this philosophy: in moulding character, in revealing the shortcomings of existing society, and in making known the virtues of the co-operative alternative. Owen's critique of society did not extend to anti-industrialism. His experience at New Lanark made him appreciate far sooner than most contemporary observers the prospects of relative plenty that industrialization made possible. What grieved him was that industrialization was often attended by waste and misery, by technological and cyclical unemployment. Why, he asked, should a society so rich and ingenious tolerate such poverty and unemployment? The solution he proposed was the creation of mixed farming and industrial communities of 300–2,000 people with property held in common and co-operative production. These 'villages of co-operation' were intended to eliminate unemployment and poverty and to serve as microcosmic 'new moral worlds'. They were to be the beginnings of an alternative to competitive capitalism and models for others to follow.

Owen's philosophy has earned him a place in the history of economic and political thought. Many have regarded him as the father of British socialism and his recognition that industrialization opened up optimistic alternatives to Malthusian orthodoxy was in marked contrast to the response of other radicals who looked firmly backwards to pre-industrial England. Some of his proposals for preventing poverty anticipated Keynes by over a century. He is remembered too for his criticism of religion, of education as it existed, and of the family – he believed religion, education, and the family conditioned people in the selfish ways of the immoral world. Owen has some claim also to a place among the early feminists. His criticisms of the family included its role in preparing females to accept a subservient position, and he supported the early birth-control movement partly because he saw birth-control as a means to female emancipation.

The initial response to Owen's proposals was not encouraging. The government showed little enthusiasm and neither did the county of Lanark. Some wealthy individuals were interested but far less was subscribed to establish villages of co-operation than Owen had anticipated. This is not really surprising because once removed from running New Lanark the practical man of affairs became something of a dreamer. His philosophy required a considerable suspension of disbelief concerning the perfectibility of human character and his unorthodox views on religion, the family, and private property alienated the wealthy classes to whom he looked for help. Working-class support was also not great initially, and the more orthodox radicals of the day were either indifferent or hostile. Many radicals did not share Owen's abhorrence of class conflict and they resented his insistence on the absolute necessity of character reform as a preliminary to other improvements. They also resented his paternalism, for Owen was by no means a democrat. He regarded democracy as ultimately desirable but most sensibly postponed until all classes were ready to embrace the co-operative ideal. At the time of 'Peterloo' and again in the reform agitation of 1830–2 he opposed universal suffrage and appealed to radicals not to seduce the ignorant poor into the ways of violence and class hatred.[37] Class-conscious radicals like James Morrison and J. E. Smith, who made much of Owen's declaration that 'labour' or the 'productive class' was the source of all wealth, either misunderstood or deliberately distorted what he meant by the 'productive class'.[38] They also disregarded the caveat that manual labour must be 'properly directed'. If Owen was indeed 'the father of British socialism', filial relations were sometimes strained. On several occasions he came close to disowning his contentious offspring.

In 1824 Owen left for America hoping to find a social climate more receptive to his proposals. But New Harmony, the co-operative community he founded in Indiana, proved an expensive failure. He returned home in 1829, much poorer but encouraged by growing trade union support for co-operation. The contrast between the successful factory manager and the visionary who learnt nothing from failure, and who expected to find utopia in each successive communal venture, was by this time very apparent. A little later he began the brief liaison with trade unionism that has already been described, and it was at this time too that co-operative stores first appeared in any numbers. The main purpose of the co-operative stores was to accumulate funds that would be used to establish villages of co-operation. They served also as a source of cheap, unadulterated, goods and as outlets for co-operatively produced articles. The 'labour exchanges' of 1832 and 1833 pursued similar ends to these but on a much more ambitious scale. They were intended to avoid capitalist employers and capitalist shopkeepers and had the additional refinement that workers were paid for their products in 'labour notes' representing the value of their work plus the cost of raw materials. These notes could then be used in exchange for goods of comparative value. Two major labour exchanges were opened, the famous one at Grays Inn Road in London, and a second at Birmingham. The London exchange, housed in an elegant assembly room sufficient to hold two thousand persons, was opened with characteristic Owenite flair and great expectations. But it proved to be yet another Owenite failure. Labour notes could not be forced into general circulation. There were squabbles over occupational differentials, goods whose production required considerable plant and capital could not be supplied, and the expensive offerings of workmen who were determined to continue their traditional employment in the face of changing technology accumulated unsold. Within two years the exchange closed with huge losses.

Co-operative enthusiasm was at its height in these years before 1834. By 1832 there was a flourishing co-operative press and some 500 co-operative societies with over 20,000 members. There was also the Owenite Builders Union and the Grand National Consolidated Trades Union, although most of their members probably had little understanding of Owen's philosophy. The co-operative societies themselves contained many besides those looking forward to establishing villages of co-operation: there were those who looked no further than the 'mere retailing' that Owen deplored, and others who were mainly motivated by the desire to avoid industrial change or to indulge in agrarian escapism. In 1834 most of these co-operative enterprises collapsed together. Owen then coolly announced that a new organization, the British and Foreign Consolidated Association of Industry, Humanity, and Knowledge, had supplanted the GNCTU. He reaffirmed his belief in the futility of seeking social change by industrial action, and together with his more dedicated followers continued the moral crusade by way of education, propaganada, and further villages of co-operation.[39]

With its church-like 'halls of science', its communal hymns, its baptismal and marriage ceremonies, its messianism and its millenarism, Owenism after 1834 came to resemble a religious sect. This pure Owenism is to be distinguished from sundry other more utilitarian co-operative activities that continued at the same time. Many unions continued to experiment with schemes of co-operative production – sometimes with aspirations towards higher things but more often merely to regulate labour supply and relieve their unemployed members. There were also a few co-operative building societies and there were co-operative stores that took no trouble to disguise their purely utilitarian purpose. The Rochdale Pioneers' store in Toad Lane, Rochdale, was the most famous of this kind. It was established in 1844 by twenty-eight flannel weavers who at first looked forward to founding an Owenite community. But they soon lowered their sights and became absorbed in buying and selling without thought of escape from capitalist society. The decision to distribute the trading surpluses by paying dividends on purchases ended any pretence that retailing was a route to the 'new moral world'. This was co-operativism truly secularized and Owen, not surprisingly, took little notice. But unlike almost everything which he attempted after leaving New Lanark, the Rochdale-style shopkeeping, the basis of the consumers' co-operative movement, proved enormously successful. It spread rapidly and eventually made a considerable contribution to working-class welfare.

What Owen would probably most wish to be remembered for is his compassion and his intellectual vitality. His most enduring legacies – increased working-class consciousness and the co-operative stores – were achieved despite himself. And his practical pursuit of the 'new moral world' through community building, labour exchanges, and co-operative production was almost wholly unsuccessful. Owen never succeeded in finding a practical means of combining worker participation and full employment with economic efficiency. He, and some among his followers even more so, overestimated the contribution of profits among the causes of poverty and underestimated the ability of capitalist efficiency to increase the national output by more than enough to meet the share taken by profits. That later generations of working-class consumers should see no reason to prefer co-operative stores over Marks and Spencers to him would have been incomprehensible. The brief and reluctant attempt to recreate society with the help of the trade unions was likewise unsuccessful. Owen's belief at that time that the middle and upper classes were likely to fall in with his plans was typical of his naive optimism.

The reform campaign of 1830–2

The Reform Act of June 1832 that brought direct representation for the first time to cities like Manchester and Birmingham (and which Robert Owen considered of little consequence) was preceded by almost two years of intermittent tumult. The campaign was dominated by middle-class interests, but there was significant working-class participation and the course and outcome of events hastened the development of working-class consciousness and had an important place among the origins of Chartism.

There had been considerable pressure for political reform at the time of the Blanketeers' march and 'Peterloo' but the agitation of 1830–2 was on a far greater scale. Pressure for a redistribution of parliamentary seats to give greater and more direct representation to the new industrial towns had become an important issue in the 1820s alongside traditional demands for secret ballots, an extended franchise, and curbs upon aristocratic and corporate privilege. By 1829 the 'political unions' that were to play an important part in mobilizing public opinion were being established and reform was the major issue in the election that followed the death of George IV (1830). Meanwhile, news from France that Charles X and his reactionary government had been deposed was further encouragement to British radicals. Bread prices were high too: Rostow's 'index of social tension' for 1829 is higher than that for any other year between 1790 and 1850.[40] Wellington's government fell in November 1830 and the Whigs introduced a reform bill in the following spring. This soon came to grief and another (and more riotous) general election resulted in a great majority for reform. The House of Lords' rejection of a second reform bill in October 1831 then provoked what were probably the most serious disturbances to occur in nineteenth-century Britain. Yet another bill was introduced in December 1831 and in June of 1832 it was carried.

Most working-class support for reform probably went to the middle-class dominated National Political Union, to Thomas Attwood's Birmingham Political Union 'of the lower and middle classes of the people', and to similar organizations. The National Union of the Working Classes (NUWC) that had been established by the London carpenters in 1831, which rejected each of the proposed reform bills as inadequate and put particular emphasis on working-class political advance, failed to win majority working-class support. The main working-class role in the campaign was a passive one, assigned to them by middle-class reformers. Were reforms not granted, the Whigs threatened, then working-class discontent might erupt into insurrectionary activity. A measure of reform, that is, was claimed to be necessary to preserve constitutional stability. Working-class leaders could hardly fail to be impressed by this successful exploitation of working-class grievances. And the outcome of the campaign, which left workers with very little to show for their support of the middle classes, must have caused many of them to regret their rejection of the NUWC. Disappointment in 1832 also caused workers to look to the unions as a more likely means of progress and thus strengthened the trade union advance that had begun a few years earlier.

The rioting that accompanied the campaign was itself significant because on a few occasions it was far more class-conscious than traditional 'collective bargaining by riot'. None of these disturbances spread far beyond where they started, but serious rioting alarmed Whig reformers for whereas talk of potential insurrection might secure reform, anything approaching actual insurrection was more likely to bring repression. In October 1831 Bristol was at the mercy of rioters for three days – at least twelve died and the Mansion House, the Bishop's Palace, the Customs House, the Excise Office, and many other buildings were destroyed. Nottingham Castle was burnt down and at Derby rioters stormed the city jail and released prisoners. What began as a reform disturbance at Merthyr Tydfil in June 1831 became a major riot dominated by working-class demands for higher wages and cheap provisions and resulting in more deaths than occurred at 'Peterloo'. On this occasion there was a disastrous attempt to disarm a detachment of regular soldiers and a party of the Swansea Yeomanry Cavalry was successfully ambushed. Merthyr's Whigs, thoroughly alarmed at having initiated a disturbance so much greater and more plebeian than they had intended, for a while lost all interest in reform.[41]

The factory movement
There are obvious parallels between the reform campaign and the factory movement. Both were well organized. They each had middle-class and working-class support with working men more prominent in the rank and file than among the leaders. And both sought change by constitutional means but at the same time brandished the threat that working-class violence might be unavoidable if all else failed.

Pressure for factory regulation had begun with the first factories, but Richard Oastler's famous 'Yorkshire Slavery' letter to the *Leeds Mercury* in September 1830 is usually taken to mark the beginning of the organized factory movement. The campaign concentrated upon shortening the factory working day and especially the working day of children and women. Robert Owen and Robert Peel, whose Health and Morals of Apprentices Act of 1802 was mentioned earlier, were among the pre-1830 factory compaigners, and so was John Doherty who had joined a spinners' 'short-time committee' when he first arrived in Lancashire from Ireland in 1816.[42] After 1830, however, pressure was more co-ordinated, more institutionalized, and on an altogether greater scale.

To a considerable degree the factory campaign was a part of the greater struggle over the 'condition of England' question. On one side were those whose reaction to industrialization was comprised of equal parts of nostalgia for the pre-industrial past, dread of the future, and horror at what they believed to be presently occurring within the mills. On the other were those staunch believers in the iniquity of government interference, most of whom were indebted to industrialization for their wealth and influence. This contest was mentioned in Chapter 1 and Chapter 3 and what was said there needs little elaboration. The chief opponents of factory regulations were Whigs, many of whom were also factory masters and non-conformists. The middle-class supporters of regulation were mainly Tory and Anglican: Oastler, for example, was a self-proclaimed 'Church and King Tory' and George Stringer Bull (the 'ten hours parson') was one of several Anglican clergymen active in the movement. The thesis that the factory movement was primarily a Tory response to Whig attacks upon the power and assumptions of the landed classes has been criticized as simplistic. And so it is. But when all the Tory manufacturers, the land-owning manufacturers, the reforming manufacturers, and the free trade squires have been noted, and due allowance made for the factory inspectors, medical men, and others whose main motivation was uninterested humanitarianism, it remains that there is much about the factory movement that is only understandable within the context of conflict between the land-owning and manufacturing classes.

Working-class support for reform came mostly from the factory districts themselves. Cotton spinners had first set up short-time committees during the French Wars: they lobbied and petitioned for government regulation and they sought reduced hours also by industrial action. Restricting the working day of all those aged less than twenty-one was among the aims of the Grand General Union of Operative Spinners (1829) and spinners dominated the Society for the Protection of Children Employed in Cotton Factories (1828). The factory workers' case was taken up also by other workers; by domestic workers hoping that regulation would reduce the burden of factory competition in particular, and by the unemployed.

Richard Oastler's 1830 attack upon 'infantile slavery' in the Bradford worsted mills set off a fierce debate that polarized opinion and brought a number of prominent reforming Tories into open alliance. The debate also lent impetus to working-class endeavour – especially among the Yorkshire operatives, who until this time had been less active than those in Lancashire. Agitation came to focus upon demands that the working day of factory children should not exceed ten hours and during 1831 middle-class reformers and operative reformers joined forces. Before long Oastler, Fielden, Bull, Doherty, and the operatives themselves were organizing short-time committees throughout all the factory districts. The committees collected and collated information and pursued the campaign by means of pamphlets, petitions, the newspapers, and numerous public meetings. At Westminster, Michael Sadler and Lord Ashley were the chief spokesmen of factory reform and in March 1832 Sadler introduced his 'ten-hour' bill. Later that year Sadler stood for re-election at Leeds and factory reform was the main issue in the riotous campaign that followed.

Sadler's bill and his candidature at Leeds were both unsuccessful and early in 1833 Ashley took over the parliamentary leadership of the ten hours campaign. In the spring a royal commission was appointed to examine the question, somewhat to the dismay of reformers who considered the case was not in need of further enquiry. Wherever they went in the north the commissioners were confronted by hostile demonstrations in which the factory children themselves were given a prominent part. But the outcome was favourable to reform and the important Factory Act of 1833 set a maximum nine hours working day for children under thirteen years and prohibited night-work for those under eighteen. The movement was perhaps never again as cohesive as it was before this legislation. Some were content that their main demands had now been met and soon afterwards transferred their zeal to contesting the new poor law. Others, Robert Owen most noticeably, began to agitate for greater concessions but the Owenite collapse of 1834 weakened these more militant campaigners. The operatives were perhaps less satisfied than middle-class reformers with the 1833 act because children's earnings fell as their hours were reduced and an extension of child shift-working dashed hopes that the new legislation would result (indirectly) in a shorter working day for adults.

In 1836 interest mounted again. The main objective by this time was to obtain the ten-hour day for women and young persons (13–18 years) and to ensure if possible that men also would benefit from any legislation. Shortly after this the factory movement became overshadowed by the poor law agitation and Chartism, but it never entirely died and following another revival in 1844 an act was introduced that began the 'half-time' system for children and set the maximum day for women at twelve hours. In 1847, a year when heavy unemployment strengthened working-class resolve and undermined employers' claims that hours reductions might leave them short of labour, John Fielden, who had recently taken Ashley's place at Westminster, successfully piloted a ten-hour bill through parliament. The results, however, were not all that reformers had hoped for. By using protected workers in relays employers were able both to prevent men benefiting from the act and to obscure the over-working of protected persons. This ploy left the reform movement deeply divided. Ashley and other moderates favoured a compromise Act (1850) by which the maximum working day of women and 'young persons' became ten and a half hours that had to be worked between 6 a.m. and 6 p.m. Less accommodating reformers were displeased by this and even more displeased when manufacturers discovered that they could exclude adult males from the consequences of the act by working shifts of children alongside men after 6 p.m. in the evening, as children had not been included in the compromise act. Their anger was short-lived however, because by 1853 a maximum working day of ten and a half hours and a 'short Saturday' for all factory workers were effectively established. But a saddened Ashley (who had become Lord Shaftesbury in 1851) had already retired to spend his compassion on less contentious issues and at this point the organized, crusading, factory movement virtually ceased to exist.

The campaign had achieved a great deal. The government became heavily involved in regulating factory hours and factory conditions while most other occupations were still unregulated. And whereas in 1820 the factory operatives had probably worked a longer than average day, by 1850 their working week was almost certainly less than that of most other workers. By no means all of this advance was due to the factory movement, but its contribution had been significant.

The anti-poor law campaign

Organized protest against the amended poor law began in 1836 when the factory movement was pushing hard for the ten-hour day. The two movements were closely associated. Poor law protest was strongest in the same northern towns where the factory movement had its strength, and several of the organizers of the factory movement, including Oastler, Bull, and Fielden, put themselves among the leaders of the poor law protest when the new poor law regime was first introduced in the industrial districts. Designed as it was to eradicate idleness, corruption, and parochial inefficiency, the amended poor law provoked great resentment. The act was based upon the assumption that much poverty was the consequence of individual moral failings and it was clearly intended that less help was to be forthcoming in future. The able-bodied poor were to receive little help at all outside the workhouse. A customary minimum standard of comfort, regardless of unemployment and other hazards, was regarded by the poor as an entitlement. Its threatened removal therefore – and by a parliament they had helped bring into existence – was felt as a betrayal. Some radicals, Joseph Raynor Stephens for example, argued that this unilateral revision of the unwritten 'social contract' justified the poor seeking redress by every means at their disposal, 'I will fight to the death sooner than that law shall be brought into operation . . . I and the northern men with whom I act will shake England to the centre.'[43]

Not all of the working classes, or those who spoke for them, were opposed to the amended poor law. Francis Place, for example, welcomed the new law because he thought it would ease Malthusian pressure, and some among the labour aristocracy felt it would do no harm if the lower orders were encouraged to follow their example by making provision against hard times through friendly societies. But trade unionists had their own reasons for not welcoming the new poor law because they anticipated that one of its consequences would be greater mobility of labour that would weaken unionism in high-wage districts. Many middle-class (and upper-class) Tories disliked the new law for more or less the same reasons that gave rise to working-class resentment: they were conscious that wealth entailed obligations and felt that the revised poor law was an attempt to deny the poor a customary right. In addition, they had a natural affection for the existing parochial system with its paternalism and explicit bonds of dependence. Middle-class opposition was by no means exclusively Tory. All shades of political opinion resented interference from London and in many districts Whigs, Tories, and the working classes stood together in defence of arrangements they considered appropriate to their needs.

In the south, however, where the new arrangements were imposed soonest and most rigorously, neither working-class opposition nor middle-class opposition was strong. There was some resistance from London parishes and several brief riots in rural areas, including Cornwall and rural Wales where interference from London was particularly resented. There was Cobbett too, a vigorous parliamentary opponent until he died in June 1835, and *The Times* campaigned on a national scale. But none of this seriously disturbed the poor law authorities and in most of the south the new arrangements were introduced without incident or overt opposition. There were various reasons for this. Two good harvests that brought employment and cheap food helped considerably, and railway building helped in certain districts. Financial and other considerations prevented the law being applied in the way the commissioners had intended and, as we saw in Chapter 4, local officials often bent the rules to favour the poor. The rural south, moreover, had little tradition of organized social protest. Remembering the futility of 'Swing' and the fate of the Tolpuddle Martyrs, the labourers were in no mood for a fight. Trade unionism was exceptionally weak in the south and there was no factory movement or any other movement that might have co-ordinated resistance. Above all, the south had a serious crisis of poverty. It was there that under-employment and the poor rates showed most the pressure of rising population and it was to deal with this regional problem that the amended poor law had been drafted. Ratepayers' reservations about the new law were quietened by their belief that action of some kind, and fairly drastic action, was unavoidable.

The north, as we noted in Chapter 4, was far less in need of the solutions offered by the new poor law. There industrialization had prevented a quasi-Malthusian crisis of the kind that swelled southern poor rates and at the same time had increased the problem of cyclical unemployment that the new poor law was singularly ill-designed to treat. A very considerable expansion of poor law accommodation would be required if all those thrown out of work in industrial depressions were to be forced into the workhouse and the deterrent function of the workhouse could hardly operate at such times because no work was available. Strict application of the new poor law in the north would obviously be both monstrously unfair and grossly inefficient. Moreover, there was little hope of much saving from the eradication of inefficiency and corruption because many northern towns had already conducted their own reforms. For these reasons, and because the commissioners began their work in the south, the north believed it would be left alone. And when an assistant commissioner arrived there in October 1836 there was alarm and indignation. Well-organized resistance quickly followed. The north, of course, had a strong tradition of social protest. In particular, there was the factory movement with its experienced leaders, its short-time committees, its funds, and its propaganda. Supporters of the factory campaign, almost to a man, joined in the poor law protest and their resolve was stiffened by the trade depression that began shortly after the commissioners turned their attention northwards.[44]

To some extent the anti-poor law protest followed a similar pattern to that of the factory movement. There were numerous mass meetings and petitions, a vigorous press campaign, and parliamentary pressure. But whereas the purpose of the factory movement was to abstract legislation from distant Westminster, the anti-poor law movement had to resist changes imposed from without and thus resorted sooner to direct action. Administrative obstruction and mob coercion of the commissioners and those willing to co-operate with them were a major part of anti-poor law activity. From the day he arrived in the north, and at every town he visited, the unfortunate assistant commissioner Alfred Power was barracked by hostile crowds. Board of guardians elections offered more subtle ways of thwarting his schedule. They could, for example, be boycotted: no candidates presented themselves for election at Oldham and there were partially successful boycotts at Todmorden, Bury, and Burnley. Elsewhere anti-poor law candidates were nominated, some of whom resigned immediately upon being elected while others used their office to impede the appointment of officials and in other ways obstruct the introduction of the new regime. Guardians who tried to implement the law faced massive popular hostility and in some places were terrified into resignation or ineffectiveness. At Huddersfield in July 1837, for example, the board of guardians, meeting in the workhouse to elect a clerk, was surrounded by a crowd 10,000 strong led by Oastler. When Oastler was refused admission to the meeting the building was stoned and the guardians fled to a nearby tavern where they were again besieged while part of the crowd set about wrecking the workhouse. No clerk was elected that day and soon after several of those guardians who favoured the new poor law resigned or ceased to attend meetings. Todmorden, Fielden's home town and a particular thorn in the side of the poor law authorities, was for a time virtually under military occupation as a consequence of the strength of poor law protest.[45]

In its very early stages Chartism helped to mobilize working-class support for the poor law campaign. Chartist leaders were interested most of all in parliamentary reform, but such was the strength of popular feeling on the poor law issue that O'Connor initially offered the movement his full support and the *Northern Star* (first published in November 1837) gave the poor law priority over all other issues. By the middle of 1838 however, after Fielden's failure to reverse the 1834 legislation in parliament, Chartist leaders began to urge the prior importance of political reform. By the autumn working-class radicals were coming to regard poor law agitation as a diversion. The middle classes, of course, felt little enthusiasm for the Chartist programme and were not inclined to embrace Chartism as an alternative to poor law agitation. But middle-class agitation also slackened at this time, in their case in response to concessions by the authorities. This combination of events brought about a considerable reduction in poor law protest. The campaign did not cease,[46] but it lost much of its momentum and working-class participation in its activities diminished significantly.

The ultimate purpose of the anti-poor law movement was repeal of the legislation of 1834 and this it failed to achieve. But the movement was by no means a failure. First, it considerably delayed the introduction of the new regime in the north. Secondly, and more important, several permanent concessions were extracted. Nothing approaching the statutory rigour of the amended poor law was ever seen in the northern counties. Certain concessions had been willingly conceded as the commissioners came to understand the irrelevance of parts of the new poor law to industrial districts. But others were hard won, and without the propaganda and active resistance of the poor law movement it would have taken far longer for practical considerations to prevail over doctrinaire zeal.

Suggestions for further reading are on pages 402–3.

7

WORKING-CLASS MOVEMENTS, 1815–1850
II · CHARTISM, REVOLUTION, AND THE MAKING OF CLASS

I · *Chartism and its origins*

Chartism, the greatest of all nineteenth-century working-class protest movements, began in May 1838 with the proclamation of the 'People's Charter' and in the following five years eclipsed all other working-class movements. The declared purpose of the Chartist campaign was political reform. That is, to induce parliament to pass an act containing the famous 'six points': manhood suffrage, annual parliaments, a secret ballot, equal electoral constituencies, payment of MPs, and the abolition of their property qualifications. But Chartism embraced also many demands that arose from economic grievances and these usually took precedence over the political campaign. The 'six points' in fact, manhood suffrage especially, served mainly as a popular rallying cry that could command support from working men with grievances of almost any kind and give their demands the appearance of concerted protest. The importance of economic protest in Chartism is immediately apparent in a much-quoted speech by J. R. Stephens [Lancashire, Sept. 1838]: 'This question of universal suffrage', he declared, 'is a knife and fork question . . . by universal suffrage I mean to say that every working man in the land has a right to a good coat on his back, a good hat on his head, a good roof for the shelter of his household, a good dinner upon his table.' Chartism also offered (or at least promised) practical answers to a whole range of working-class needs and aspirations: those in search of sobriety or club conviviality, secular education or Chartist christianity, cheap groceries or a return to the land, were each accommodated.

Another sign of the importance of economic protest in Chartism is that support fell away whenever economic conditions improved, even though parliamentary reform remained as distant as ever. Chartism was strongest between 1839 and 1842 – a time when jobs were often scarce, bread dear, and trade unionism least able to offer hope of alternative protection. These were years of mass meetings and torchlight processions, secret drilling, clashes with police and soldiers, and talk of revolution. With the onset of economic recovery those whose Chartism was little more than a symptom of temporary distress began to fade away. Many of the leaders and their more dedicated followers stood firm, and the Chartist co-operative stores and some other social reformist activities actually flourished in the good times. But the movement as a whole was significantly diminished. Then, in the depression that set in towards the end of 1847, Chartism became a mass movement once more, capable of frightening the middle classes and compelling the government to call the elderly Duke of Wellington from retirement to defend London. Two years later the economic barometer was again set fair and as a mass movement Chartism was finished.

The origins of the movement, as we have already seen, stretch back far before the publication of the Charter. At least five of the 'six points' featured in eighteenth-century reform campaigns and some of the banners carried at Chartist meetings had seen earlier service at 'Peterloo' and other meetings during the troubled years after the French Wars. There are obvious parallels too between Chartism and the reform agitation of 1830–2 that was also described earlier: Attwood, Lovett, O'Brien, and many others were active in both movements. In this sense Chartism was merely the third major instalment in a tradition that began before the nineteenth century. But Chartism was different from earlier reform movements, and from protests like the poor law and factory movements. Whereas they were all campaigns in which workers participated alongside other classes and under middle-class or aristocrat leadership, Chartism was consciously and overwhelmingly a working-class campaign. The suspension of class co-operation was, of course, temporary, and far from complete. It is true also that class consciousness of a kind was evident in the earlier Owenite episode and that Chartism was distinguished in many other ways than by class consciousness. But in the context of what had gone before, and of events after 1850, class consciousness was the movement's outstanding characteristic.

Chartism emerged then in the late 1830s when economic depression revived interest in long-sought political reforms. Hopes that the reformed parliament would introduce favourable legislation, and perhaps extend the rights recently granted to the middle classes, had been disappointed. Disappointment was followed by a sense of betrayal and heightened awareness of conflicting class interests. The obvious lesson for the future was that workers should look more to themselves. These sentiments for a time were muted and diverted by initial uncertainties and the prospect of advancement via mass trade unionism. By 1835, however, the Owenite unions had collapsed and by 1837 the bitter memories of 1832 were being revived by rising unemployment. Shortly before this the new poor law was first introduced to the north of England, another development of great significance to early Chartism. Feargus O'Connor and other radicals saw the strength of poor law resistance in the north and in time succeeded in detaching the working-class poor law protesters from their middle-class leaders and bringing them within the Chartist movement.

Some of the more class-conscious Chartists regarded poor law reform as a part of systematic repression by the newly dominant industrial middle class.

Urban police reform, the use of metropolitan police to quell provincial disorder, plans to establish county constabularies, what looked like callous indifference to the handloom weavers, and the supposed conspiracy by the Anti-Corn Law League to subvert Chartism and reduce wages, all contributed to the consciousness of repression. What was seen as systematic repression was in fact mainly a hotchpotch of Benthamite reform and applied *laissez-faire*. But these fears were felt and articulated, and are another element in the origins of Chartism and class consciousness.

II · *Early Chartism*

Few of the characteristics of Chartism that have been mentioned were much evident in the body that actually drafted the Charter in 1838: the London Working Men's Association. Its members were not much given to imagining repression, nor were they particular critics of the amended poor law. They certainly were not aggressively proletarian. The LWMA had been founded in 1836 by men active in the various radical associations that maintained a fitful existence after the collapse of Owenism. They were, for the most part, artisans. A few among them suffered competition from factories or sweated labour but none of them were among the more obvious victims of industrial change. LMWA policy emphasized moral reform and education as well as the 'six points', and its preferred tactics – meetings, petitions, and propaganda – were moderate and gradualist. There was a clear understanding of the differences between working-class interests and those of other classes but none of the doctrinaire objections to class co-operation that later characterized some parts of Chartism. Towards the lower classes – the less skilled, less intelligent, and less sober who were specifically excluded from membership – the LWMA was decidedly paternalistic. The LWMA, in short, represented 'moral force' Chartism which is to be distinguished from the 'physical force' Chartism of those less patient and more ready to threaten violence. William Lovett, the secretary, was the model 'moral force' Chartist and Francis Place, who helped Lovett draft the Charter, who deplored attacks upon the middle classes and gave qualified support to the new poor law, embodied its more conservative traits. At no time, of course, did the LWMA have a monopoly of London working-class reform agitation and in January 1837, long before the Charter was announced, a disaffected minority inaugurated a divisiveness that was to be an enduring Chartist weakness by breaking away to form the East London Democratic Association. This rival body, led by the young George Julian Harney, was less cautious and more class conscious. It sought support from working men of every kind and castigated the LWMA for its elitism and moderation, for its alleged Malthusianism and Whiggish ways.

Birmingham was the other main centre of early Chartism. The Birmingham

Political Union, which had played an important part in the 1830–2 reform agitation, was successfully resurrected in 1837. It was less exclusively artisan than the LWMA, drawing more upon both the middle classes and the unskilled, and its leaders were more enthusiastic advocates of the advantages of class co-operation. Thomas Attwood (a banker and MP) was particularly interested in proposals to stimulate the economy by currency manipulation. But in other respects the two movements were similar. A national petition for reforms almost identical to those in the LWMA's Charter was begun in Birmingham in the same year. Speakers were sent to other areas from both Birmingham and London and local political associations and working men's associations were established throughout the country.

But as the movement spread, as it was taken up in localities resisting the new poor law and those with more distressed hand-workers and sharper class distinctions than Birmingham and London, its temper altered. The gradualism and elitism associated with the artisan world of the LWMA were pushed from the foreground and Chartism became a mass movement: less patient, more threatening, more plebeian, and increasingly contemptuous of other classes. Feargus O'Connor had considerable influence in Lancashire and Yorkshire. His two great strengths were his popular appeal and his newspaper, the *Northern Star*. O'Connor's fiery speeches could move poor men upon whom the reasoned arguments of Place and Lovett would have been wasted, and he worked particularly upon the bitterness generated by poor law reform and the smouldering discontent of handloom weavers and other victims of machine competition. Initially he pretended a loyalty to the 'moral force' Chartists of London and Birmingham who found his methods and his talk of physical force so disturbing. But in the autumn and winter of 1838, as his personal following increased, O'Connor turned upon the 'moral force' leaders, by openly supporting the East London Democratic Association and by fanning the tension that existed between Birmingham's cautious leaders and their less fastidious rank and file.

When the time came to do more than talk and collect signatures these differences among the leaders became crucial. Towards the end of 1838 it was agreed to hold a convention in London that would be in session when Attwood and Fielden (above, pp. 213–15) introduced the Charter to parliament, and whose business it would be to decide the next move should the Charter be rejected. Delegates were selected to represent different localities and the convention assembled in February 1839. Meeting before the collection of signatures in support of the Charter was completed was probably a mistake. The initial excitement and high expectations could hardly be sustained over a long period of inactivity, and the longer the delegates debated the more obvious would be the differences that divided them. Weak organization and tactical miscalculation proved to be as much a characteristic of Chartism as dissension among the leaders. In the event the petition was not ready until May, the Charter was not debated in parliament until July, and in the meantime the convention fully exploited its opportunities for disagreement. The 'physical force' delegates argued that other means must be employed if constitutional methods proved fruitless – a national strike, for example, the withholding of rents and taxes or, in the last resort, armed insurrection. 'Peacefully if we can' said O'Connor, but 'forcibly if we must'. O'Connor himself usually took care to avoid an unambiguous call to arms but others, including Julian Harney who compared himself to Marat and waved daggers before his audience, were less careful, 'Your country, your posterity, your God, demand of you to arm, arm, arm!'[1] Talk of this kind naturally loomed large in newspaper accounts of the convention. Holding the convention at all was generally regarded as provocative because it claimed to be a 'people's parliament' and because the more militant delegates lost no opportunity to make comparisons with what they liked to pretend was a rival and less representative assembly at Westminster.

The promptings of the 'physical force' delegates did not go unheeded: from the industrial districts reports reached London of workers accumulating arms and drilling. The government made its own preparations. Torchlight processions had been banned in December 1838, drilling was outlawed in May 1839, authority was given to arm special constables, and troops were placed in readiness. Meanwhile the 'moral force' delegates warned of the futility of unconstitutional action and began to dissociate themselves from the militants. Delegates from the Birmingham Political Union were among the first to leave the convention and several moderate Scots soon followed them, 'the people of Scotland', said one, 'were too calm, too prudent and too humane to peril this cause upon bloodshed'.[2] Several radical MPs (upon whose support the Charter depended), other middle-class sympathizers, and sections of the working-class rank and file were also repulsed by talk of violence.[3] With the departure of the moderates the balance of the convention moved in favour of the 'physical force' delegates. In May 1839 the convention moved to Birmingham where the moderate Attwoodites were no longer dominant. A clash between police and Chartists occurred there early in July and in a sequel to this incident the unfortunate Lovett (who had issued a note of protest) was arrested. The lack of response to Lovett's arrest was a pointer to what would happen when parliament rejected the Charter (by 235 votes to 46) on 12 July 1839.

Although the convention had been deliberating its response to such an eventuality since February, the rejection of the Charter found the movement unprepared and its leaders in disarray. After two days of debate it was decided to call a limited national strike, a 'sacred month', to commence on 12 August. This was another mistake: economic conditions were unconducive to a successful strike and the support of the unions, or indeed of much of the rest of the labour force, was by no means certain. Moreover, it was not clear whether or not the strike was to be the starting point for more radical measures. As these difficulties were appreciated there were attempts to call off the strike, by O'Connor himself among others. Despite angry opposition, these second thoughts prevailed. No alternative course of action was substituted and the convention finally dissolved amid bitter recriminations and continuing talk of violence from a small minority who now realized that when it came to the point many of the supposedly 'physical force' delegates were not prepared to fight.

In many ways the rejection of the Charter in July 1839 is the major turning-point in Chartist history. Before then expectations were high and the movement retained a superficial cohesion. The weaknesses were there of course, and were already becoming apparent. But the extent to which the Chartist threat was comprised of bluff and self-delusion was not yet clear; bold claims to mass support were still untested. The crisis came, however, and Chartism wilted before it. The more realistic and constructive of its supporters had been forced into the background and 'physical force' Chartism proved to be a paper tiger. Chartism was never again so confidently militant and never again so menacing.

III · *Chartism after the first petition*

The Newport incident occurred in the aftermath of the failed convention. A force of miners, led by John Frost and under the impression that they were participating in a general rising, marched upon the town. When soldiers returned their first shots the Chartists turned and fled, leaving a number of dead behind them.[4] Another uprising, planned for 12 January 1840 to avenge Newport caused a few anxious moments for the authorities of Dewsbury, Bradford, and Sheffield, but proved hardly more substantial. O'Connor, who may not have known of the Newport plan (and who, in any event, was on his way to Ireland at the time) was shrewd enough to realize that fresh adventures were likely to be as futile and had unsuccessfully urged restraint. The main outcome of these incidents was further erosion of middle-class support, a deeper division between 'physical force' and 'moral force' Chartism, and the imprisonment or flight of many activists. All this left the 'physical force' element considerably weakened. Failure also caused some of the erstwhile militants to renounce violence and class hostility. Those who were imprisoned, like Bronterre O'Brien, had ample opportunity to ponder the implications of repeated failure. In 1837 O'Brien had declared that he was only disposed to petition after the fashion of the man who presented a petition to his victim with one hand while pressing a gun to his head with the other.[5]

But in prison he concluded that violent revolution was impossible and not long after he turned to supporting the moderate Complete Suffrage Union in its quest for 'reconciliation between the middle and lower classes'.[6]

By mid-1840 there were signs of a modest Chartist recovery, not least the establishment of O'Connor's National Charter Association. O'Connor was imprisoned in York Castle from May 1840 until August 1841 but he was able to maintain his overall command and from this time until 1849 he dominated the movement's more militant parts. In May 1842, however, parliament rejected a second petition and again there were no repercussions beyond renewed protests and talk of violence. Shortly after this Chartist hopes revived again when they succeeded in capturing a series of desperate strikes in the mining and textile districts of Lancashire, Cheshire, Yorkshire, and Staffordshire. But the extent of these strikes, the so-called 'plug plot',[7] exaggerates Chartist strength in 1842. The strikes were not begun to further Chartism. Indeed, O'Connor (like Engels) initially declared that they were engineered by the Anti-Corn Law League. And although Chartists succeeded in winning control, in extending the strikes, and in linking workmen's grievances to the Charter, wages and hours of work remained the prime issues to most of the workers involved. Attempts to keep them out 'until the Charter be conceded' were unsuccessful and the Chartists gained no lasting benefits from their intrusion. On the contrary, the failure of the strikes was a further blow to Chartist prestige and displayed again divisions in the leadership. Many Chartists were arrested and forced to shoulder more blame for the unrest than they deserved.

As unemployment fell during 1843, O'Connor found it impossible to sustain popular support. Besides economic recovery there was the rival expansion of trade unionism and renewed interest in factory reform. There were also the discouraging lessons of repeated disappointment. The government, moreover, did not pursue its advantage with sufficient ruthlessness to reinforce fears of a coming repression. In fact, Chartist decline was accompanied by a quickening of social consciousness, by popular enthusiasm for social enquiry and social reform, by the Factory Acts of 1844 and 1847, and by corn law repeal, all of which helped to reduce the class tensions upon which militant Chartism flourished. A *Manchester Guardian* report of May 1846 described how the one-time Chartist stronghold of Mossley (Lancs.) had become a centre of corn law agitation and its Chartist Assembly Room converted to house pigs.[8]

But to say that Chartism languished after 1842 is misleading in one sense because it underestimates both the continuing strength of 'moral force' Chartism and how much the movement had been divided by the attempt to transform its founders' moderate reformism into militant proletarianism. Many who had been repelled by talk of violence, or sobered by a spell in prison, took up (or returned to) 'moral force' Chartism. Lovett devoted himself to educational reform. Others threw themselves into Chartist co-operative activities, the Chartist Churches, or the Chartist temperance campaign. Chartist temperance hotels, Chartist coffee houses, and other means of furthering the conspicuous non-consumption of alcohol were politically inspired to the extent that they were designed to avoid taxes on drink, but in other respects they were far removed from what O'Connor considered to be true Chartism.[9] There was also considerable Chartist political activity that was unashamedly class co-operative, most notably in the municipal politics of several northern cities and within Joseph Sturge's Complete Suffrage Union (1841) that attempted to unite moderate Chartists with the middle-class reformers of the Anti-Corn Law League. The 'municipal Chartists' were mostly artisans and members of the lower middle classes. They were moderate and pragmatic, far more interested in town drains than the pursuit of political utopias. Moral force Chartism flourished particularly in Scotland. Other than in exceptionally bad times, or when O'Connor or his disciples ventured northwards on missions of conversion, Chartism there was opposed to violence and class conflict. The Scots had not shared in the anti-poor law agitation that brought so much militant support to English Chartism and after the quarrels of 1839 they organized their own separate convention.

O'Connor continued to carry the banner for political reform by the workers, for the workers, and without compromise. He denounced Lovett and the others who stood aloof from the National Charter Association, condemned the 'Religious, Knowledge and Temperance Chartism *Humbug*', mocked the establishment radicalism of municipal Chartism, and in 1841 went to Scotland determined, as he put it, 'to clip the wings of the rotten leaders of Glasgow'.[10] But even O'Connor was not oblivious to the lessons of failure and the possibilities of liberal reform and social harmony. In 1842 he proposed union with 'the industrious portion of the middling classes' whose interests, he acknowledged, had much in common with those of working men.[11] Two years later, after unsuccessfully engaging Richard Cobden in public debate, he described the leader of the Anti-Corn Law League as 'decidedly a man of genius, of reflection, of talent, and of tact'.[12] O'Connor's scheme to convert the British workman into a peasant smallholder was implicit recognition of the difficulty of sustaining interest in militant Chartism in normal times.[13] The Chartist 'land-plan' (which took much of O'Connor's energies after 1843) was, paradoxically, perhaps the most ambitious deviation of all from that quintessential Chartism O'Connor had in mind when he upbraided the church-goers, educationalists, and temperance campaigners.

The revival of militant Chartism in 1848, caused mainly by economic depression, received added impetus from events overseas. That year there were risings, or the distinct likelihood of risings, all over Europe. In particular there was the overthrow of Louis Philippe of France. These excitements aroused Chartist expectations, especially among the radical artisans of London who were more interested in international affairs than O'Connor and the mass of British workmen. London also harboured many European radicals, some of whom were active Chartists. Ireland too had been affected by the enthusiasm for revolution and the Irish immigrant population, hopeful of reinforcing whatever diversionary effect an uprising might afford their countrymen at home, added their support to Chartism for the first time. Besides illustrating again the dependence of militant Chartism upon hard times, this revival also demonstrates its tenacity. A core of activists had kept the movement alive through the lean years after 1842 and they were sufficiently numerous, and well enough organized, to provide the basis for a mass movement when the opportunity arose. There is no doubt that many among the middle classes were alarmed by this late-flowering Chartism. And the government did not take it lightly: Chartist limitations had been clearly exposed in 1839–40, but economic conditions were particularly bad in 1848 and the situation in Europe and Ireland was additional cause for anxiety.

The third Chartist petition was presented on 10 April 1848 after a period of rising tension. Preparations for its delivery were accompanied by the maximum of drama and intimidation: the Chartists boasted of six million signatures and a likely escort of hundreds of thousands to accompany the petition from Kennington Common to Westminster. Numerous rallies paid tribute to events in Paris. If Britain was to go the way of France, then the presentation of the petition, it seemed, would provide the occasion. The authorities took appropriately grandiose counter-measures. They decided to prevent a confrontation at the Houses of Parliament by banning the procession from Kennington and by guarding the Thames bridges. Troops, artillery, and more than 150,000 special constables were made ready under the Duke of Wellington. The outcome of all this preparation is well known. Far fewer Chartists assembled on Kennington Common than had been anticipated[14] and their leaders, almost pathetically anxious to avoid trouble, agreed to cancel the procession. The petition left in three humble cabs for parliament where its six million signatures proved to be as exaggerated as most other aspects of the occasion. It was rejected, light-heartedly and without much fear of the consequences.

This was not quite the end of Chartism. The West Riding, the Black Country, and some other provincial centres were not disheartened by the fiasco at Kennington. And although the leadership was as divided as ever, with O'Connor now warning against violence and making renewed overtures to middle-class reformers, some among them were anxious for revenge. Several serious clashes occurred long after the petition was rejected. But Kennington ranked prominently in the way Chartism was regarded by the middle classes. Many had been taken in again by the Chartist bluff and at Kennington the bluff was called. The authorities had been less gullible and less frightened. They had prepared massively it is true, but less because they accepted Chartist estimates of their own strength than because they were anxious to avoid bloodshed and eager to demonstrate that Britain was in no danger of following the revolutionary path.

Within a year it was obvious that support was falling fast: in October 1848 the *Northern Star* complained that 'popular indifference was never more clearly manifested than at the present time' and in 1849 Bronterre O'Brien declared that Chartism had failed.[15] The militancy after Kennington led to arrests and imprisonments, including the arrest of Ernest Jones (poet, lawyer, and godson of the Duke of Cumberland) who had entered the movement in 1845 and quickly joined its leaders. O'Connor by now was preoccupied with Irish politics and the remnants of his land scheme and soon began to display symptoms of the madness that led to his detention in 1852. No one had been so able to arouse popular enthusiasm and his demise when Jones and others were in prison was a serious set-back. But more important than this was economic recovery which soon restored working-class indifference to a level where even O'Connor in his prime could have made little impression. In the 1850s Ernest Jones and Julian Harney, with assistance from Karl Marx, directed what was left of the movement away from the Charter and 'knife and fork' issues towards socialist ideology and working-class internationalism. They laboured valiantly to regain support, but they laboured in vain because prosperity had removed the only basis on which Chartism had ever flourished and socialism was no substitute. Indeed, the transformation of Chartism into an ideological sect was made far easier by the absence of the rank and file to whom abstract ideas had never much appealed. By 1857 Jones himself at last recognized the futility of continuing to struggle against the apparently irresistible combination of economic progress, liberal reforms, and working-class apathy.

IV · *Occupational and regional differences in Chartist strength; Irish immigrants and Chartism; trade unions and Chartism*

Some indication has been given already of the diversity of Chartist activities and the varying responses from workers in different occupations and localities. Recent research, much of which has investigated Chartism in particular districts, has emphasized these diversities. Indeed, it has become hazardous to venture any but the most guarded of generalizations about the movement.

There seems little doubt that 'physical force' Chartism drew much of its support from distressed domestic workers like the handloom weavers, the framework knitters, and the Yorkshire woolcombers. We now know, however, that the cotton handloom weavers had a less crucial role than was once claimed for them, that the Spitalfields silk weavers were not active in the early years, and that some similarly depressed workers (like the Norwich and Trowbridge weavers) took little part in the 1848 revival.[16] Some factory workers, particularly those employed by large firms in one-industry towns, should be mentioned also among the supporters of militant Chartism although they resorted less quickly to violence than workers in domestic industry, were quicker to leave the movement when the trade cycle turned upwards, and some of them could look to trade unionism as an alternative protection. Coal-miners took part in two of Chartism's most militant episodes – the Newport rising and the 'plug' strikes – but their support was neither extensive nor consistent. During the 'plug' strikes the miners who had marched on Newport in 1839 refused to help and the Miners Association of Great Britain was at all times careful to avoid association with 'physical force' Chartism.

There were also some important exceptions to the relationship between militant Chartism and economic distress. Irish immigrants did much of the worst-paid work in several northern cities and yet were largely indifferent to Chartism before 1848, and the wretched southern farm labourers never took much part in the movement. It is perhaps safer to generalize in terms of an association between 'physical force' Chartism and declining economic status, although some of the most militant Chartists were prosperous artisans and one of the more interesting recent discoveries is how much Chartist strength in any district depended upon the energy and charisma of local leaders.[17]

The pattern of support for 'moral force' Chartism was rather different. 'Moral force' Chartists were less likely to abandon the movement when the trade cycle turned upwards and most of them belonged to the upper and middling ranks of the working classes. Chartism of this kind was strongest in towns with a diversity of occupations, a tradition of middle-class and working-class co-operation to secure reforms, and no great number of depressed domestic workers: in Birmingham and the more prosperous parts of London, for example, in Leeds and Sheffield where 'municipal Chartism' flourished, and, of course, in Glasgow. 'We may not be producing great effects upon the government', announced the *Scottish Patriot* in 1840, 'but we are forming a character for the people which they have never before possessed – making them intelligent by instruction, and moral by inculcating the principles of total abstinence.'[18]

Many occupations, and many parts of the country, gave little support to Chartism of any kind. In 1849, when the movement was almost finished, Julian Harney confessed sadly that 'multitudes of men . . . are yet ignorant of, or indifferent to, the Charter'.[19] The peak membership of O'Connor's National Charter Association, about 50,000 in 1842,[20] was fewer than 1 per cent of the working population. When the last petition was presented considerable numbers of working men – some railwaymen, for example, and most of the London coal-whippers – helped to maintain law and order as special constables. By no means all of them had been coerced into enrolling.

Among others who did not commit themselves even so far as signing petitions was a very high proportion of the rural population.[21] Small towns like Glossop which had paternalistic employers and few depressed hand-workers were never much affected by Chartism, and neither was Coventry with its easy class relations, liberal charities and poor law, and moderately prosperous freemen. Among other places where Chartism made little headway were most of the Wesleyan Methodist strongholds. In the Cornish mining districts, for example, Methodist and temperance leaders combined to exclude Chartist influence.[22] London was the scene of many Chartist processions and meetings but could never be considered a Chartist stronghold, least of all a stronghold of militant Chartism. In the early years O'Connor sneered at London's 'rottenness' and its 'superior' leaders and concentrated his campaigning where the poor law resistance was strongest. It was partly because enthusiasm in London was so slight that the first convention moved to Birmingham. Militant Chartism gathered strength in the capital after 1840 (in contrast to what happened in many other areas) and in the 1848 revival it was probably as vigorous there as at any time earlier. But the level of commitment still did not compare with that in the northern centres.

Part of the explanation of London's more significant part in the 1848 revival was that its substantial Irish population, which had previously been hostile or indifferent to the movement, in 1848 joined the Chartist ranks.[23] The main reason why the Irish marched with the Chartists in 1848 was mentioned earlier: they hoped that a Chartist diversion might increase the possibility of successful revolution in Ireland. Their earlier indifference[24] had its origins in the 'Irish question' and long-standing quarrels between Daniel O'Connell and Feargus O'Connor. Daniel O'Connell dominated Irish politics from long before Chartism began until he died in 1847. The Whigs had shown themselves less unyielding than the Tories on the 'Irish question' and this encouraged O'Connell to join them in informal alliance. Politically, he stood far to the right of O'Connor. Both worked for an independent Ireland, but O'Connell gave independence the higher priority. And whereas O'Connor dreamt of an Ireland transformed in the way that he hoped Britain would be transformed by the Charter, O'Connell and his clerical supporters were little interested in radical change beyond the transfer of government to Dublin. O'Connell was at one time associated with the moderate Chartism of the LWMA but he did not share O'Connor's passionate concern for the British working classes nor his hopes of an alliance between them and the Irish peasantry. He also joined with the Roman Catholic church in deploring Chartist violence. The immigrant population, far more interested in what became of Ireland than in the fate of the native poor, remained loyal to O'Connell. They ignored O'Connor's blandishments and resented his attacks upon their leader. Their physical presence, and their readiness to repay violence in kind, freed the (Whig) Anti-Corn Law League meetings in Manchester from Chartist disruption, and in March 1842 they broke-up a Chartist meeting at which O'Connor was speaking. It was therefore O'Connell's death in 1847, as well as the prospects of revolution in Ireland, that brought the Irish into Chartism in 1848.[25]

Another aspect of Chartism whose interpretation has been revised by recent research is the relationship with trade unions. The Webbs found 'no reason to believe that the trade unions at any time became part and parcel of the movement',[26] and their emphasis upon union aloofness has been repeated many times. If the Webbs had in mind craft trade unionism and O'Connorite Chartism then they were largely correct, as the haughty attitudes of the printers, engineers, and stonemasons clearly indicate (above, pp. 194, 204). Some trade unionists supported 'physical force' Chartism as individuals, but there is no doubt that the overall trade union commitment fell far short of O'Connor's expectations. The call to support the 'sacred month' (August–September 1839) met a tardy response, and union indifference to the fate of those arrested after the Newport raid was in marked contrast to their spirited protests at the sentencing of the Tolpuddle Martyrs: 'Never was there more criminal apathy than that manifested by the trades of Great Britain to the sufferings of those men' (O'Connor).[27] In 1845 O'Connor tried again to make common cause with the unions but again he was rebuffed: 'the pompous trades and proud mechanics', retorted the *Northern Star* (Nov. 1845), 'were now willing forgers of their own fetters.'[28]

But the labour aristocracy was not the whole of trade unionism and O'Connorite Chartism was not all of Chartism. The weaker and less proud unions were more willing to engage in radical politics, and in slumps especially, when their bargaining power was undermined, many of them turned to Chartism. The Webbs were not unaware of this and mentioned societies like those of the shoemakers, 'thoroughly permeated with Chartism'.[29] But there were more such societies than they imply, especially in London.[30] And unions of all kinds were never so hostile to moderate Chartism of the kind associated with Lovett. This aspect of Chartism is often overlooked in accounts that stress trade union aloofness. Some of the strongest union support for Chartism had come in the early stage of the movement when the LWMA and the Birmingham Political Union were influential and before their differences with the O'Connorites were consummated at the first convention.[31] 'Trade unions are for botching up the old system', complained one delegate in 1839, 'Chartists are for a new one'.[32] What was said here of the unions applied hardly less to 'moral force' Chartism.

v · *Chartist achievements*

'What have we gained?' asked Julian Harney in 1848, 'Is the reward proportionate to the toil expended?' The answer is inescapable: none of the six points was conceded and Chartism's other achievements were unimpressive and dearly acquired. Chartism probably hastened the expansion of charity and other measures to ameliorate the suffering upon which it flourished. The government was certainly mindful of the probable effects upon the Chartist rank and file when they prepared to reduce the duties on corn and other goods, and after the 'plug plot' strikes an official enquiry considered the mining abuses that were among the causes of the unrest.[33] Chartism also quickened interest in education, for ignorance as well as poverty were considered essential for it to flourish.[34] Class consciousness was increased too, and this was one of the things Chartism set out to achieve. It could claim in addition to have been the first independent working-class movement with substantial support and the *Northern Star* was infinitely more influential than any previous working-class newspaper. Chartism also played some part in the early history of female emancipation: there was much well-intentioned discussion of sexual equality, there were female Chartist associations, and only fear of ridicule prevented the original Charter including a demand that women too should have the vote.[35] The movement brought intermittent release from despair for the handloom weavers and other distressed workers and the satisfaction of purposeful common endeavour. To this list can be added the fellowship of the Chartist clubs and the good works of the Chartist temperance societies, Chartist shops, and municipal Chartism. All this was not inconsiderable, but it fell far short of Chartist ambitions.

Two other claims are sometimes advanced. First, that Chartism helped to moderate the imposition of the new poor law in the north. This may have been its influence for a time and Edsall found some evidence that supports the claim.[36] But the autonomous poor law campaign had resisted the commissioners more actively and with greater success, and it has been argued that Chartism helped the commissioners by splitting the anti-poor law movement and appropriating its support. Several anti-poor law leaders were of this opinion: Oastler, Stephens, and Fletcher went so far as to denounce Chartism as a Whig-Malthusian conspiracy to divert poor law resistance into futile political campaigning. The other claim is that although Chartism failed to secure its main objectives it brought nearer the eventual achievement of most of the Charter. This too is highly debatable. The government showed no sign of being prepared to offer concessions in response to Chartist threats. Daniel O'Connell believed that 'physical force' Chartism retarded reform and he may have been right. When Lord John Russell later considered the possibility of extending the vote he explained how in taking up the question he had been greatly influenced by the popular rejection of Chartist violence in 1848.[37]

There were also, of course, some notable Chartist failures. O'Connor's land scheme was one of the biggest. Misconceived and mismanaged, it quickly dashed most of the hopes it raised. Many of the small proportion of subscribers who were settled on the land soon returned to the cities. Some of them suffered great hardship and eviction by O'Connor's bailiffs. This painful lesson in the impracticability of the agrarian alternative to industrial society was one of Chartism's unsought consequences.[38] The acceptance that open confrontation was unlikely to succeed, and the strengthening of rural and city policing that Chartism encouraged, fall into the same category.

Chief among the costs of Chartism was the diversion of so much time and energy into a largely futile crusade. Had there been no militant Chartism the gains that accrued from the Chartist temperance movement, co-operative stores, and the other moderate Chartist activities that O'Connor denounced would probably have occurred anyway and in far greater measure. Because it was with successful reform and self-help movements of this kind – with the factory and poor law movements, the Anti-Corn Law League, the public health movement, the temperance campaigns, the friendly societies, and trade unions – that militant Chartism competed. Besides effecting immediate improvements in working-class life some of these alternatives to militant Chartism were undoubtedly also hastening the day when governments would feel able to safely extend the franchise. E. J. Hobsbawm has written that 'the historian of Chartism . . . can hardly fail to be saddened by the extraordinary feebleness of this greatest of all the mass movements of British labour'.[39] When its costs and failures are considered alongside its achievements sadness seems inappropriate: a stronger Chartist movement would in all probability have been accompanied by more missed opportunities, by less social reform, by greater class bitterness, and by more victims like those who died at Newport.

These enormous opportunity costs are the more regrettable because there was never much chance that O'Connor's strategy would succeed. Chartist demands were far more radical than those of either the 1830–2 reformers or the Anti-Corn Law League, and they were presented in more uncompromising fashion: if granted, said Engels, the six points 'would undermine the whole English constitution'.[40] Success at Westminster depended upon the support of middle-class MPs but the militants indulged in the rhetoric of class hatred and thus alienated middle-class sympathizers. Those MPs who had originally championed the Charter withdrew their backing and many other potential supporters – Disraeli, for example, whose sympathy for the poor and for moderate Chartism is so evident in *Sybil* (published in 1845) – were among the large majority of MPs that rejected the first petition. Asking for so much, and in such threatening fashion, virtually ensured that there would be no constitutional victory.

VI · *Chartism and revolution*

What chance was there of the Chartists carrying their case by force? Their leaders were certainly not prepared for such an eventuality. The possibility existed, however, and this of course is among the reasons why the Chartist era holds such a fascination for historians. In 1839–40, 1842, and in 1848 some of the ingredients of a 'revolutionary situation' could be seen in Britain, and there were only two or three other such occasions in the nineteenth century.

But there was never much likelihood of large-scale armed insurrection. Much was heard of the violence that might follow if the Charter was rejected, but these threats were not matched by a readiness to act. They were, in fact, largely bluff. The Chartists, that is, were following a strategy that had been employed successfully by the reformers of 1830–2. But whereas in 1830–2 a government of the landed minority had been presented with limited demands by the influential middle classes backed by considerable working-class support, the Chartists, with little middle-class support, presented more radical demands to far stronger and more representative governments.

Not all their threats were bluff, of course. But when events logically required that threats be made effective – when the Charter was first rejected in particular, and at Kennington – most Chartist leaders showed no willingness to fight. The real militants were isolated, left able to instigate only small-scale incidents such as that at Newport. They almost certainly did not intend that the Monmouth miners should march alone, but diligent searching by historians has failed to unearth any evidence of well-organized preparations for rebellion on a scale that would have taxed the government's resources. O'Connor's behaviour at moments of crisis illustrates clearly the essential moderation of 'physical force' Chartism. We noted earlier how he urged that the 'sacred month' (August–September 1839) should be abandoned; that he probably was unaware of the planned seizure of Newport and certainly did not encourage it; how he opposed the 'revenge rising' of 12 January 1840 and called off the 1848 march upon parliament. We know too that he had no contingency plans ready when the Charter was rejected in July 1839. Talk of violence was mere bluster. At one time O'Connor's caution provoked accusations that he was a government spy. This seems unlikely, but a government agent among the Chartist leaders could hardly have defused explosive situations more effectively. Besides overestimating the possibility of revolution, some of those historians who have taken Chartist threats at face value have exaggerated O'Connor's shortcomings. Fickle and eccentric he certainly was, but his repeated last minute pleas for moderation indicate not cowardly reversals of policy so much as sensible recognition that the government would not be panicked.

The limits to rank and file support must also be remembered when assessing the possibility of successful revolution. The main reason why O'Connor retreated each time he saw that the government would stand firm was because he appreciated that physical confrontation would not only be bloody but also futile. The stronger unions held aloof from 'physical force' Chartism and the planned general strike of 1839 had to be abandoned for lack of mass support. Very little evidence has been found in local studies that workers were prepared to take up arms in any numbers.[41] It is true that in some of the more ungoverned and violent localities, such as parts of east London and in some of the mining and metal-working areas, there was an ignorant and unruly population easily moved by demagogues. But its revolutionary potential was unpredictable and unpolitical. Such men were almost as likely to turn upon agitators as to follow them and they responded quickly to patriotic appeals, to slight concessions, and to any improvement in the economic climate.

The authorities could have provoked a revolutionary reaction. If fears of coming repression had been given substance, the government almost certainly would have faced determined resistance. But such fears, as we noted earlier, were largely unfounded. And although some magistrates and employers demanded vigorous repression, governments were generally reluctant to move against what they judged to be mere talk of violence. For the most part they stood aside until there was an immediate threat to the peace. Russell, the Home Secretary during the movement's early stages, boasted of his reluctance to put down Chartist meetings: 'So long as mere violence of language is employed without effect, it is better, I believe, not to add to the importance of these mob leaders by prosecutions.'[42] Lifting the death sentences upon the Newport leaders, the government's restraint at that time and the quickening pace of social reform, all helped to diminish the possibility that more than a tiny minority of workers would ever be ready to move from protest and petition to armed revolt.

While carefully avoiding unnecessary provocation, the government was usually ready to act decisively if its authority was seriously threatened. Throughout the Chartist period the army proved entirely dependable and highly competent. In the early years when the danger was greatest there were no external threats to disperse military strength. Later, in 1848, the situation in both Ireland and in Europe gave rise to anxiety, but these fears proved unfounded and by this time Chartism was less of a menace and the government better prepared. General Napier, who had been in command of the northern district at the crucial period, proved to be an inspired appointment. He was a known radical, opposed to the new poor law and sympathetic to parts of the Chartist programme. He refused to commit his men until intervention was absolutely necessary and frequently imposed restraint on panicky magistrates. At the same time he left Chartist leaders in no doubt that 'physical force' would be firmly resisted.

The regular army was the most efficient means of law enforcement: at Bradford, in May 1848, two troops of dragoons quickly put to flight a large force of Chartists who were having the best of a pitched battle with the city's regular police and a thousand special constables.[43] The army was backed up by the yeomanry, whose strength and efficiency varied from place to place, by the London police, who were effective and often drafted to provincial trouble-spots, by provincial police forces of variable quality, and by special constables. In the early stages of Chartism, and still to some extent in 1848, large areas of the countryside and some sizable towns were very poorly policed. The army could not be present in every potential trouble-spot and such places were vulnerable to sudden disturbance. Chartists might then gain control of whole districts. But they never held their ground for longer than it took regular troops and yeomanry reinforcements to reach the area. And throughout the Chartist era the developing railway system increased military efficiency. Soldiers could be kept concentrated in garrison towns, safe from attack and from Chartist propaganda, and then rushed by rail to put down any disturbance. The electric telegraph system which came with the railways also helped the deployment of troops. At times of crisis, as in 1848, the government reserved the telegraph system for its sole use. There was always the chance that Chartist success in one town would inspire others. The army could never have coped with simultaneous uprisings throughout the country, but trouble on this scale never occurred and was never very likely to occur. The forces available were adequate to deal with such threats as the Chartists were capable of mounting.

The authorities also appear to have been well informed of Chartist intentions. The government no longer employed its own spies as it had done before 1821, but magistrates, the police, and the army, were not similarly impeded. When militant Chartist leaders met secretly at Manchester after the Newport incident, police spies (admitted by an irate landlady to whom the Chartists owed £15) took down everything that was said. There were spies out drilling with the Birmingham militants in 1839, among those spreading the 'plug plot' strikes in 1842, and indeed on most occasions when violence was being planned or executed.[44] Spies had a considerable part in the actual instigation of several abortive Chartist 'conspiracies'. Their desire not to arouse suspicion, and the natural consequences of being paid on piece-rates, made them among the most active promoters of 'physical force' Chartism. A number of naïve would-be revolutionaries were enticed into 'conspiracies' of this kind and then arrested before they could do any harm.

The few quasi-insurrections that occurred were put down with little bloodshed and often simply by a display of military strength. Clashes were mostly of a kind in which Chartists openly confronted police and soldiers and in these circumstances a small force of trained men was more effective by far than when dealing with clandestine activity such as Luddism. At Newport, John Frost's Chartist 'army' ran for the hills when they were first fired upon by a detachment of only thirty-one soldiers. The disorder that accompanied the 'plug plot' strikes of 1842 was quickly ended when the government moved in troops by rail. There is every indication that more determined attempts to challenge the government would have met equally determined resistance. Napier invited Chartist leaders to military demonstrations and made clear the likely outcome of a large-scale rising: 'armed, starving and interspersed with villains, they must commit horrid excesses. . . . I would never allow them to charge me with their pikes, or even march ten miles, without mauling them with cannon and musketry and charging them with cavalry.'[45] In 1848 London was defended by the Duke of Wellington, 8,000 soldiers, the metropolitan police, and 150,000 special constables. The intention was that the army was to be used only if the police were overwhelmed, which was very unlikely. Had it proved necessary to use the army the outcome would not long have been in doubt: 'the troops are instantly to appear and the cannon to open with shell and grenades, infantry and cavalry are to charge – in short, they are to be made an example of' (Lord Malmesbury).[46]

VII · *Prospects of revolution before Chartism*

If working-class revolution was unlikely during the Chartist era how close was it in earlier decades? There was much talk of revolution during the 1830–2 reform agitation; similar hopes and anxieties had been evident in the post-war years; some commentators have detected revolutionary intentions in Luddism; and certain of the ingredients necessary to a revolutionary situation were present in the 1790s.

The 1790s fall outside the compass of this survey but the contrasts between Britain and France at that time can tell us a great deal about the chances of revolution in Britain during the following century. The example of the French Revolution and Tom Paine's critique of English society made traditional artisan radicalism more militant and more impatient. Paine's *Rights of Man* appeared first in 1791–2, the artisan London Corresponding Society was established and began to agitate for parliamentary reform in 1792, war with revolutionary France commenced in 1793, and in the hungry mid-1790s traditional food riots assumed a more menacing significance. At times the authorities were clearly worried: they had in mind the possibility of insurrection as well as foreign invasion when the yeomanry was established in 1794, there were naval mutinies and a French landing in 1797, in the following year there was an attempted rising in Ireland and another French landing, and 1799–1800 saw the panic introduction of the Combination Acts. According to E. P. Thompson, 'something like an "English Revolution" took place'.[47]

But British radicalism was far from transformed by revolutionary philosophies. The initial stages of the French Revolution may, in fact, have done more to reinforce British social equipoise than to bring revolution closer, because Britons were inclined to regard the French crisis as a predictable consequence of making do with a constitution so unlike their own. Their constitutional monarchy, parliament, the hustings, free speech, and a free press set them apart from continentals. British radicals were as conscious of these 'liberties' as any others. 'We were men', said Thomas Hardy, secretary of the London Corresponding Society, 'while they [the French] were slaves'.[48] Pride in the constitution was accompanied by a consciousness of material well-being and a chauvinistic contempt for all foreigners, for 'papish' foreigners especially who in the popular imagination wore wooden shoes and never ate roast beef. 'No popery and wooden shoes' was a cry often heard at eighteenth-century protest meetings and cartoon Frenchmen were always emaciated.[49]

These beliefs, and they were far from entirely fanciful, made an important contribution to the preservation of British social stability throughout the 'age of revolutions' (1789–1848). For the 'English revolution' had occurred (or rather, begun) a century before the fall of the Bastille and many of the liberties that Europeans sought by insurrection has long been the 'rights' of 'freeborn' Englishmen. The social contract between the nation and its rulers was sometimes felt to be threatened and might then be defended vigorously. But it is the belief in a social contract worth defending that is crucial. The English radical tradition, that is, was conservative and reformist. It was concerned not to sweep all away and begin afresh, but rather to preserve and extend the constitutional gains of the late seventeenth century.

At first, therefore, the French Revolution was widely welcomed in Britain. Led by their middle classes the French people seemed to be embarking upon their own belated version of the English revolution of 1688. Before long, however, it was clear that France had deviated from the gradualist example of the English revolution. By 1793 revolution had become synonymous with terror and counter-terror. Paine, moreover, had linked Britain with France as hardly less in need of reform and the French were talking of carrying their revolution abroad. By February 1793 Britain and France were at war. Had events in France continued to command widespread admiration then the government would have had ample reason to be alarmed. But radical opinion was repulsed by French excesses – by 1793 several of the heroes of 1789 had gone to the guillotine, trade unions and strikes had been outlawed,[50] and Paine himself was a prisoner of the Revolution. That the government could declare war upon revolutionary France sure of the support of the British people, and indeed on a great wave of popular loyalist enthusiasm, illustrates how slight was support for revolutionary change at home. When their material grievances had been settled the mutineers of Spithead clamoured to be at the French and in 1798 the London Corresponding Society, debating what to do in the event of invasion, heard its secretary denounce revolutionary France and propose that members should join the Volunteers.[51] Those who favoured an English revolution were weak and isolated.

Their number was probably increased by the government's exaggerated fears of revolution, which led it to turn upon radical reformers and revolutionaries alike. But the number of radical reformers was not great either, and there was little popular opposition to government repression. Even when enthusiasm for the French Revolution was at its height demands for reform had come mainly from small masters and shopkeepers and from craftsmen of the kind that founded the London Corresponding Society. The lower classes, deferential and loyalist for the most part, maintained their customary parochialism except to take passing comfort from the plight of the traditional enemy. E. P. Thompson's claims for 'something like an "English Revolution"' in the 1790s are, in fact, highly qualified in his own work[52] and he has subsequently conceded that throughout his account the centre stage is occupied by a minority of radical artisans and impoverished outworkers, and that the views of most of those beneath the artisans, those who manifested the 'flag-saluting, foreigner-hating, peer respecting side of the plebeian mind', are too much ignored.[53]

Despite spasmodic war weariness and occasional radical revivals, revolution was never more than an extremely remote possibility while Britain and France were at war. Luddism created near panic in some districts in 1811 and 1812, but recent studies suggest strongly that in the midlands, where the disturbances were greatest, the unrest was hardly more than traditional 'collective bargaining by riot' on an unprecedented scale.[54] There is rather more evidence of links between Luddism and revolutionary politics in the northern counties, but there too the revolutionary impulse was neither formidable nor sustained.[55] Even such unpolitical protests as Luddism contained revolutionary potential of course and a sizable and competent revolutionary movement might have exploited and extended the disturbances, especially in their early stage when the authorities were caught unawares. But no such revolutionary cadre was on hand to exploit the situation. When General Maitland took command of the affected districts he soon realized that the alarmist reports of local magistrates had little substance.[56] One consequence of Luddism, however, was that the government took care that the army would never again be so unprepared to deal with large-scale disturbances.[57]

In the post-war years revolution was probably closer than it had been in the 1790s. Britain was becoming more urbanized and more industrialized, wartime ultra-loyalism had ended, economic conditions were again very bad, and the authorities were still inclined to over-react when confronted by demands for constitutional reform. These were the years of the Hampden Clubs, the Spa Fields reform demonstrations (1816), the Blanketeers' march and Pentrich rising (1817), Peterloo (1819), and the Cato Street conspiracy (1820). Revolution, however, remained a very remote possibility. The greatest growth of factory towns was still to come and working-class consciousness was still in its infancy. Cobbett, Cartwright, and Hunt (then at the height of their influence) were no revolutionaries. Cobbett – devoted as he was to Anglicanism, the monarchy, and the constitution – caricatured the British reformist tradition. There were revolutionaries in Britain during these years, as there were at most times, but they were few, uninfluential, and closely watched. The authorities were also better prepared for trouble than they had been in 1811–12.

The Spa Fields meetings and the Blanketeers' march were protest demonstrations. The first passed off peacefully enough despite some rioting, the other was forcibly dispersed. The Pentrich rising began with a few hundred men intent upon capturing Nottingham. On their way their numbers and morale dwindled and the remnants of the uprising fled at the appearance of twenty hussars. This uprising, 'one of the first attempts in history to mount a wholly proletarian insurrection' (E. P. Thompson),[58] fell short of being wholly proletarian in one important respect: the notorious 'Oliver' (a government spy) had a large part in its execution. 'Peterloo' was preceded by violent talk and drilling and some demonstrators came to St Peter's Field armed with sticks. All of this alarmed the Manchester magistrates and was a part of the tragedy that followed. But 'Peterloo' was far from a revolutionary gathering. Hunt had issued strenuous appeals for 'quietness and order'. Most of those present were unarmed, many wore their best clothes and were accompanied by women and children.[59] The extent of violent reaction to the 'massacre' is also significant. In a revolutionary situation 'Peterloo' would have been inflammatory. The Cato Street conspiracy of the following year consisted of a handful of romantics, accompanied and encouraged by an *agent provocateur*. Those involved believed that they could plunge the country into revolution by assassinating the cabinet, but there is no evidence that they were a part of any wider insurrectionary movement capable of raising the country.

The government knew of their intentions and they paid for their naïveté on the gallows.[60]

Reform protest in 1830–2 was of a different calibre. It was probably at this time, the only occasion in the nineteenth century when a substantial proportion of the middle classes confronted the government, that Britain came closest to revolution.[61] The recalcitrant middle classes were well organized, they enjoyed considerable working-class support, and both groups were by then far more formidable than they had been in the 1790s or at the time of 'Peterloo'. The tumult too was on a far greater scale. But none of this necessarily implies that Britain was on the brink of civil war. And the kind of revolution that might have materialized was one instigated and directed by the middle classes. There was some autonomous working-class protest in the early 1830s; Owenite trade unionism, 'Swing', and the National Union of the Working Classes. But these activities were neither revolutionary nor a serious threat to the authorities. The Grand National Consolidated Trades Union and the rest were too ineffectual to successfully threaten anyone; the 'Swing' campaign was defensive, non-political, and unconnected with other disturbances;[62] and when serious rioting occurred at Bristol the National Union of the Working Classes appears to have shared the general feeling that things had gone too far.[63]

The middle classes probably could have organized a substantial revolt,[64] but it seems very unlikely that they were willing to press their case to the point where lives and property were endangered. Why should they have done this? Their economic and constitutional status was far superior to that of the French middle classes who revolted in 1789. They had gained more from the English revolution of the seventeenth century than other classes and they were hardly likely to risk plunging the country into bloody conflagration over the postponement of further concessions. They were aware too, of course, of the uncontrollable consequences of the revolution that the French middle classes had unleashed. We noted earlier how quickly middle-class reformers called for moderation when disturbances that had been stage-managed to frighten the government got out of hand. What happened at Bristol was especially sobering: 'though it was nearly another six months before the Reform Bill was finally carried . . . there were virtually no further popular disturbances . . . since Bristol the major parties to the dispute had seen the red light.'[65] The 1830–2 agitation, in short, was in all probability not much more than middle-class 'collective bargaining by riot' with the working classes doing their rioting for them. And like much other collective bargaining by riot it had the enormous advantage that its accommodation would strengthen the authorities at no great cost. The reformers naturally made much of this argument and there were sufficient on the government side shrewd enough to appreciate its truth. And so the authorities yielded. They yielded partly because the forces arrayed against them were very formidable and partly because the cost of yielding was not sufficiently great to justify whatever risk was entailed in putting threats of revolution to the test.

VIII · *British social stability; historians and revolution*

So working-class revolution was never close at any time between 1790 and 1850. The circumstances that favoured revolution before 1830 – the external threat to stability, the rudimentary policing arrangements, the unreformed parliament, and the repression of working-class agitation for reform – were more than offset by wartime patriotism, by the primitive state of working-class consciousness, and by the strength and persistence of class relations based upon paternalism, deference, cherished legal and political freedoms, and a long tradition of living together in reasonable harmony. By the mid-1830s working-class consciousness was stronger. But the reforms that regained and reinforced middle-class loyalty enormously strengthened the government. Many of those who had clamoured for reform in 1831 joined with the government in 1839 to oppose militant Chartism. The police and the army were more efficient by this time, the authorities had learnt far greater subtlety in handling working-class protest, and the new enthusiasm for social reform and the expansion of organized charity went some way towards making good the shortcomings of traditional paternalism in the growing industrial towns.

There were some slight doubts about the reliability of the army in 1830–2 but in practice, and against working-class opposition, it was as dependable in the early decades as it was when confronting Chartists. At Merthyr (1831) a rioter heard urging the crowd forward with assurances that the soldiers were but 'gooseberries' to be crushed in the workmen's hands, was shortly afterwards shot dead with seven others.[66] Not many died like this, despite deficient policing that compelled rapid resort to the military when trouble threatened. The infrequency and small scale of such confrontations, and the prominence in textbooks and folklore of comparatively minor outrages like 'Peterloo', are further illustrations of Britain's low revolutionary potential.[67] There were parts of Britain, some factory towns like Oldham, for example, where class tensions were close to the surface. But even in these places there was very considerable class co-operation and the unrest that occurred was short-lived and seldom contagious.[68] David Landes drew attention to another indication of Britain's social stability when he noted how the insurrectionary potential of urban workers retarded industrialization on the continent. Manufacturers there were 'never sure when labour unrest . . . would turn into political revolution', but Britain 'took social order for granted'.[69] Others have noted how in Europe cholera could excite class hostility, wild talk of conspiracies to kill off the poor, and political instability.[70] The presence in Britain of numerous political exiles allowed entry from more turbulent and less tolerant European countries is also significant.

Why then has so much been said here of an event that did not occur and was at no time very close? Partly, of course, because long-term stability of the kind enjoyed in Britain was not usual and the features that inhibited continental-style revolution are among those that distinguish British labour history from that of other nations. Partly because several historians have suggested that Britain narrowly avoided revolution. And, not least, because it was conditions in England that Engels and Marx had in mind when they forecast that industrialization would lead to class polarization, to working-class immiseration, and then to revolution: 'the wrath of the workers must very soon – one can almost fix the date – lead to revolution' (Engels, 1844). Their views alone would guarantee considerable interest in such issues. But what led Engels to these prophecies, and why have other historians followed him in suggesting that revolution was sometimes close?

Engels came to England in 1842 to see advanced industrialization at first hand. In 1844 he began his collaboration with Marx, and in the following year he completed *Condition of the Working Class in England*. His forecast of imminent revolution was obviously wrong but it was less naïve than critics sometimes allow. First, it must be remembered that Engels came to Britain from revolutionary Europe. Secondly, he came with only superficial knowledge of England. Thirdly, he was very young,[71] very angry,[72] as intent on producing political propaganda as scholarly analysis,[73] and in far too much of a hurry to adequately investigate England's history, institutions, and class relations – *Condition of the Working Class* was begun in the autumn of 1844 and finished the following spring. Moreover, Engels went to Manchester where classes were more polarized, unrest more commonplace, and individualism more rampant, than almost anywhere in Britain: 'If Engels had lived not in Manchester but in Birmingham his conception of "class' and his theories of the role of class in history might have been very different. In this case Marx might have been not a communist but a currency reformer.' [Asa Briggs][74] The consequences might have been equally pedestrian if he had delayed his visit; for Manchester soon afterwards lost its reputation as the 'shock city of the age' and his arrival in 1842 had coincided with perhaps the worst 'crisis of capitalism' in the nineteenth century. A more careful and less selective use of sources might also have led Engels to different conclusions because he relied heavily on the Chartist press and out-of-date government reports, and seems not to have realized how much was already being done to improve urban conditions.

Some historians have been encouraged to accept Engel's interpretation by their own assumptions about working-class living standards and the likely response to falling standards. If conditions were very bad and getting worse, as some historians believe they were, and if revolution is the natural response to immiseration, then a revolutionary situation must have existed. Such claims derive also from focusing attention upon a minority of political activists and either patronizingly discounting the views of the politically 'unconscious' lumpenproletariat or else assuming them to be identical to the views of activist 'spokesmen'. Finally, of course, they owe something to the tendency of historians to become obsessed with their interest of the moment – what better way of emphasizing the importance of almost anything than by suggesting that it alone stood between Britain and revolution? R. N. Salaman's claims for the insurrection-quenching powers of the potato ('What was the alternative, surely nothing but bloody revolution?') fall into this category as do R. Boston's wistful speculations about the possibly far more turbulent course of working-class history had his fleeing Chartists stayed at home.[75]

Several other events have at one time or another been charged with preventing working-class revolution in Britain. Some centre on the early years: it has been suggested for example that subsequent events might have been very different if only 'Oliver the Spy' and all his treacherous colleagues had not filled incipient revolutionaries with such fatal irresolution. A number of other speculations emphasize the greater likelihood of revolution had the upper and middle classes engaged in confrontation instead of sharing power and adopting so many of each other's values and interests. Then there are claims that revolution was very near when the depression that greeted Engels began to lift and might have occurred but for the mid-1840s railway-building 'mania' or the activities of the Anti-Corn Law League. The League was itself fond of claiming sole responsibility for preserving public peace. But revolution was never so close that some comparatively minor difference in the way events unfolded would have dramatically increased its likelihood. And the more fundamental suppositions necessary to make revolution seem at all probable are themselves so unlikely that little is gained by their introduction.

The supposition that Methodism prevented revolution is not often advanced now although at one time it had a considerable currency. This thesis is associated particularly with Elie Halévy who was naturally interested in why Britain's experience was so different from that of his native France. That Methodism had an enormous influence on working-class life is beyond question. Most would agree also that it was among the obstacles to revolution. Methodism encouraged deference, discipline, and quiet acceptance of the hardships of this world in preparation for a better life in the next. It raised living standards by encouraging temperance, hard work, and education; it provided compensation for lost communal activities; and its training in self-government and public speaking made Methodists prominent among the leaders of those sober and cautious trade unions that were to dominate organized labour. There is no doubt of the direction of its influence. What is in doubt is that Methodism was ever sufficiently influential to have filled the crucial role claimed for it by Halévy. In 1795 there were fewer than 100,000 Methodists and in 1851 they could claim no more than, at most, a quarter of the working classes.[76] Over large parts of the country, including some areas that featured prominently in disturbances, Methodism had very little strength.[77] Without Methodism the working classes would have been poorer, more drunken, less organized, and probably also more revolutionary. But they would have been by no means sufficiently more revolutionary to overcome the numerous other obstacles that made working-class revolution improbable.

IX · *The making of class, 1815–50*

Working-class consciousness emerged and became stronger during the first half of the nineteenth century. So evident is this that E. P. Thompson and others have suggested that a British working class already existed by the 1830s. 'Class' in this context has a special meaning: 'class' exists when men 'feel and articulate the identity of their interests as between themselves, and as against other men whose interests are different from (and usually opposed to) theirs' (E. P. Thompson).[78] The poorer people that is, although they may be described as 'working class' and although they may be aware of interests shared with their immediate neighbours and with others of like occupation further afield, do not form a 'working class' until sufficient of them are conscious of their collective interests as workers and until they are prepared to make common cause against other classes. There was no 'working class' of this kind in pre-industrial England. Rather, there were numerous, disparate, working classes that were more commonly termed 'ranks', 'orders', or 'degrees'. At that time loyalty and consciousness of mutual dependence and shared interests extended not so much horizontally towards workers in other occupations and other places as vertically towards the upper ranks of society in the same trade or locality.

There were few legal obstacles to mobility between these different social classes and the comments of foreign visitors in the eighteenth century suggest that there may have been more mobility of this kind in Britain than in most parts of Europe. But how social mobility was affected by industrialization is far from clear. Industrialization made it more often necessary to possess substantial capital to become an employer and for this reason some have suggested that it was accompanied by reduced social mobility. But industrialization occurred alongside an expansion of elementary education and Methodism that might be expected to have had some favourable effect upon social mobility. Industrialization also entailed massive occupational change. In particular, it required a sizable reduction in the proportion of low-wage agricultural labour and an expansion of relatively well-paid urban employment. Moreover, most businesses could still be commenced with very modest capital,[79] economic growth multiplied opportunities to begin businesses that might grow rapidly from small beginnings, and those businesses that became large capitalist organizations increased the opportunity for advancement into white-collar occupations. The mechanics' institutes were understandably proud of their numerous working-class members who became supervisors, foremen, and clerks.[80]

These changes in social mobility seem not to have influenced the intensity of class consciousness in any simple fashion. There is certainly too much evidence of continuing social mobility after 1790 to argue that working-class consciousness was much encouraged by reduced opportunities of social advance. In fact, increased social mobility of one kind – the flight from low-wage rural areas – was crucial to the making of class because urbanization and industrial employment spurred the establishment of trade unions and similar working-class institutions. Urbanization became associated also with social segregation as the better-off moved out to escape the smoke and congestion of city centres. This exodus left large areas with diminished middle-class patronage and overwhelmingly proletarian in character. Thus the ties between rich and poor were weakened and the likelihood of misunderstandings and animosity was increased. There was a paralleled development at the workplace: in the new mills a single capitalist employed scores of workmen. Such employers could easily become a focal point of working-class discontent and their anonymity denied them the full measure of customary loyalty. It was developments of this kind that Engels had in mind when he wrote that 'the history of the English working classes begins in the second half of the eighteenth century with the invention of the steam engine and of machines for the spinning and weaving of cotton'.[81]

These were the more important of the influences that had affected class relations sufficiently for E. P. Thompson to claim that by 1832 most English working people 'came to feel an identity of interests as between themselves, and as against their rulers and employers'.[82] Working-class consciousness was advanced too by many of the separate developments that were mentioned earlier. The French Revolution and Paine's *Rights of Man* laid the foundations of a working-class radical philosophy and the corresponding societies of the 1790s are often described as the first working-class political organizations. Resistance to attempts to introduce fresh anti-union legislation after the Combination Acts were repealed was important also and by the end of the 1820s Owenism had been adopted in a form that contributed to the language and philosophy of class. The following years were the most significant in the making of class. In the early 1830s the trade union movement came closer to leading a working-class movement than at any time before the 1890s. At the same time reform agitation and the subsequent sense of betrayal prepared the way for independent political protest, and Tolpuddle and poor law reform brought together workers of every kind in mass protest. Chartism was the culmination of all these developments: it embraced many more people than the unions and was more class conscious than any previous movement. The peak year of Chartism, 1839, was probably the high-point in this first approach to a British working class. Class consciousness existed by then, it was felt by a considerable proportion of working people, it was institutionalized, and the authority of the ruling classes was under challenge.

But was all this enough to create 'a working class'? A number of historians, including F. C. Mather, H. M. Pelling, A. E. Musson, and R. M. Hartwell, have suggested that the advance ceased before 'class' existed: 'a single working-class . . . did not as yet fully exist, and the forces which had been building it previously seemed to be set in reverse during the thirty years after 1848' (F. C. Mather).[83] The very nature of the reform campaign is perhaps good reason for doubting that working-class consciousness was much advanced before 1832: the middle-class manipulation of working-class support that occurred during the campaign was possible only because working-class consciousness was still in its infancy. The poor law protest too was directed by middle-class radicals. And although the Owenite union advance doubtless increased working-class consciousness, the failure of every attempt at general unionism was due not least to the fact that the single working class they assumed did not yet exist. Chartism overshadowed all these earlier developments but it was a weak and fragmented movement. Its more class-conscious elements were scorned by the stronger trade unions and it never had sufficient hold upon working-class opinion to maintain support when the trade cycle turned upwards.

There were numerous working-class people whose attitudes remained emphatically those of the old deferential society and there were many others who were neither sycophantic nor rebellious: most farm labourers and domestic servants, for example, who together accounted for over a third of the labour force in 1830, and the unskilled labourers of London, 'as unpolitical as footmen' (Mayhew).[84] Domestic servants adopted their employers' political views as willingly as they adopted their manners, advice, and cast-off clothing. They reckoned their 'salary' in annual instalments and when they became mothers passed-on their deferential attitudes to the next generation of workers. These genteel proletarians, in frequent close contact with the middle and upper ranks of society and willingly exchanging labour and loyalty for livelihood and protection, constituted a vigorously surviving part of the old organic society and a major obstacle to the creation of 'class'. Traditional attitudes were evident also in many other occupations. Among the silk weavers of Coventry, for example, where 'the good masters and the good men were always looking for ways . . . to impose their own standards upon the minority who flouted them',[85] among the small workshops and small masters of the Birmingham and Sheffield metal trades, among the growing army of railwaymen, and in those semi-independent mill communities where paternalism still flourished and class relations were so recognizably of the traditional kind that they won the approval of reactionary anti-industrialists like Gaskell.[86]

Consciousness of the numerous finely graded classes of traditional society, where everyone knew their proper station and what distinguished them from the ranks beneath, had scarcely diminished. We noted in Chapter 3 how engineers' labourers cherished their tiny pay differential and regarded themselves as superior to bricklayers' labourers. Bricklayers' labourers looked down in turn upon general labourers. The permanent general labourers condescended to the casual labourers, and the casuals joined in the general contempt for Irish and female workers. Some of the aristocratic factory cotton spinners took their ale in a reserved part of the public house and many superior domestic servants dined alone, waited upon by lesser servants. Social gradations of this kind were evident through all the ranks of the working classes. At their upper end they shaded imperceptibly into the middle classes by way of the ascending ranks of shop assistants (butchers', grocers', and drapers' assistants, in that order), upper domestic servants, superior craftsmen, and operative masters. Although by the 1830s there was far more talk of 'class' than there had been in eighteenth-century England, most workers still thought in terms of this plural society and would have resented historians' attempts to steamroller them into an undifferentiated working class.

Many of the more skilled workers combined some of these traditional attitudes with a calculated appreciation of the advantages of industrialization and the elevating properties of education, temperance, and Methodism. It was from among such workers that most trade unionists were drawn, so it is hardly surprising that the unions showed little inclination to give a lead to other workers in the manner that would have fallen to them in a society moving decisively towards class polarization. The more enduring unions, as we saw in Chapter 6, reflected the elitism and pragmatism of their members. Their chief priority was usually to safeguard the status of skilled workers and their attitudes towards the unorganized were dominated by the fear that the unskilled might somehow enter the skilled trades and diminish their standing.

Among the other reasons why it is probably incorrect to speak of 'a working class' in the first half of the nineteenth century are the widespread chauvinist contempt for foreigners (regardless of their class), the bellicose patriotism that extended to a deep affection for reactionaries like the Duke of Wellington, and the extent of working class participation alongside other classes in the Anti-Corn Law League, the anti-poor law agitation, the factory movement, and similar campaigns. Some of these campaigns were led by 'governors' who found the ideas of class struggle and liberal individualism equally repugnant, who shared the workers' sense of betrayal after 1832, and who were prominent among those who had no intention of abdicating traditional responsibilities to the poor. The retreat from the 'making of class' after 1848 and the social equipoise of the following decades are, of course, further indications of the limits to the previous advance.

Suggestions for further reading are on page 403.

8

WORKING-CLASS MOVEMENTS, 1850–1888: NEW MODEL UNIONISM TO THE REVIVAL OF SOCIALISM

1 · *Mid-century changes in working-class movements; trade union strength and membership, 1850–1888*

There *were* perceptible changes in the character of working-class movements around the middle of the nineteenth century, although their extent is often exaggerated. It was not that an heroic era of mass movements to overthrow industrial capitalism came to an end at this time. Nor does the mid-century mark the beginning of a schism among the working classes whereby the labour aristocracy embraced class collaboration and quietly abandoned the mass of workers. But the changes were in these directions. Skilled workers had always dominated trade unionism and usually looked first to their own sectional interests, but some among them had thrown themselves into attempts to mobilize all labour in the general unionism of 1829–34 and in Chartism. Moreover, both of these movements manifested a greater degree of working-class consciousness than was to be seen for long after 1850 and Chartism had been a mass movement in a way that trade unionism could not claim to be until the very end of the nineteenth century. There were, in addition, several advances in trade union organization that can be dated from around mid-century: unions became more efficient, increasingly skilled at presenting a favourable public image, and more accepted by the middle and upper classes.

They also grew: by 1888 there were some three-quarters of a million trade unionists, about 5 per cent of the labour force or 10 per cent of adult male workers. They were still out-numbered three to one by domestic servants; but compared with mid-century, when membership was probably fewer than a quarter of a million, the proportion of all workers who were organized had increased substantially. And whether judged by numbers, efficiency, or strength the British movement compared impressively with trade unionism elsewhere. In 1884 the Parliamentary Committee of the TUC commented that there was really little point in British unions participating in international congresses until foreign workmen were better organized.

This long-term expansion of unionism was frequently interrupted. In the early 1870s unemployment fell to below 2 per cent and union membership doubled to a million or more. But much of this advance was ephemeral like that of 1824–5 (above, p. 198), and in the depression of the late 1870s 'hundreds of little societies . . . went down before the tide of adversity'.[1] Even so, membership probably did not fall below half a million in the late 1870s whereas in the 1842 slump it was as low as 100,000. Unions were more soundly organized and their membership was no longer quite so vulnerable to trade cycle depressions. Their strength was still concentrated in the more prosperous parts of Britain and they were weakest in those districts where population growth had not been accompanied by industrialization and where labour was consequently abundant. Glasgow and its environs accounted for two-thirds of Scotland's trade unionists in 1892 and over half of the English total was in five northern counties.[2] Distribution of union membership between different kinds of employment was also uneven. A handful of major occupations accounted for the greater part of all unionists and in many other occupations organization had hardly begun.

Table 8·1   *Trade union membership in 1888*

Metals, Engineering, Shipbuilding	190,000
Mining and Quarrying	150,000
Textiles	120,000
Building	90,000
Transport	60,000
Clothing	40,000
Printing and Paper	30,000
Others	70,000
TOTAL	750,000

Source: H. A. Clegg, A. Fox, and A. F. Thompson, *A History of British Trade Unions since 1889*, (Oxford, 1964), p. 1.

Fitters, turners, pattern-makers, and the other skilled engineering workers were prominent among the organized workers. The Amalgamated Society of Engineers, 12,000 strong within a year of its foundation and Britain's largest union, was quickly put to the test when employers resisted its attempts to ban overtime and piece-work. For three months in 1852 much of London and Lancashire engineering was at a standstill and the dispute ended with the ASE totally beaten. More remarkable than its defeat, however, was that the union survived with its membership and privileges largely intact. Membership expanded to 21,000[3] in 1860, 44,000 in 1875, and 54,000 by 1888. The ASE was the prototype of what the Webbs termed the 'new model' trade unions and its establishment was accompanied by a strengthening of the cautious policies that largely explained the survival of its predecessor (the Journeymen Steam Engine Makers Society) since 1826. Before long the ASE became a symbol of permanency and respectability. Its constitution and policies were widely copied, its virtues were much publicized, and its officers played a major part in managing the crisis that threatened all trade unions in the late 1860s when the legal position of their funds, their public acceptance, and the prospect of further legal advance seemed all to be in jeopardy.

By no means all engineers enrolled in the ASE. There were separate unions for men deemed insufficiently skilled for admittance and there were unions that competed with the ASE in certain occupations or particular districts. The largest of the overlapping unions was the United Society of Boilermakers and Iron-Shipbuilders with about one-fifth as many members as the ASE in 1860 and half as many by the late 1880s. And although engineering was one of the most unionized occupations, a great many skilled and semi-skilled engineering workers – the majority still in 1888 – belonged to no union at all.

Building craftsmen also had a prominent place in the trade union world of the second half of the nineteenth century, although their organization lost momentum after 1870 and their relative importance then declined. In 1888 around 90,000 building craftsmen were organized and they comprised about one in eight of all trade unionists. The Amalgamated Society of Carpenters and Joiners was the largest of the builders' unions at this time with 25,000 members. This union had a symbolic role similar to that of the ASE; and its secretary, Robert Applegarth, contributed more than any other trade unionist towards the successful resolution of the trade union crisis in the late 1860s. The ASCJ was begun in 1860 after a long and bitter dispute in the London building trade where the men had demanded a nine-hour day and the employers had responded by trying to break their unions. The London building unions were not crushed, but neither did they win a nine-hour day and their failure (and a handsome subsidy from the ASE during the course of the struggle) underlined the strategic advantages of large national unions. William Allan, secretary of the Engineers, helped to launch the ASCJ and its constitution was closely modelled upon that of the ASE. There were numerous other building unions: the market conditions that gave each district a virtual monopoly of local building encouraged the survival of both small unions and small employers. There were many competing and overlapping unions also, just as there were in the engineering trades. And here too the majority of potential unionists remained unorganized: there were more than a quarter of a million carpenters and joiners in 1891 but only about 40,000 of them were union members.

At this time the miners could boast a far greater degree of organization: a third or more of the hewers had been enrolled by 1888 and miners accounted for perhaps a fifth of all trade unionists. But mine unionism had long been characterized by sudden upheavals and violent collapse and its new-found strength at the end of the eighties exaggerates its previous importance. The miners, of course, lacked the scarcity value that was the basis of craft unionism but demand for coal (and hence for miners) was buoyant in the second half of the century and the large size of many collieries and several other aspects of mining (above, p. 195) were favourable to organization.[4] At times organization advanced rapidly.

But large employers were also powerful and they were not universally resented. In some places, and especially in parts of South Wales, the coal-owners were respected as community leaders upon whose enterprise and capital everyone depended.[5] Growing output, moreover, meant a sizable inflow of migrants to the coalfields – Irishmen to the west of Scotland, Englishmen to the Welsh valleys – and differences between them and the indigenous population were an obstacle to effective combination. Another obstacle to successful mine unionism was that the isolation of mining communities and the differences in coal markets hampered co-operation between the miners of different districts. At various times federal associations were begun that attempted to combine the strengths of all mine unions. But their functions were restricted by these difficulties and effective industrial action occurred mostly at the level of individual pit societies and among combinations of societies from one coalfield. Yet another handicap arose from the intense competition for sales between coalfields: wages were a high proportion of total cost and isolated attempts to resist wage reductions when prices were falling almost always (and almost inevitably) resulted in defeat. At most times before 1888, and in most places other than Northumberland, Durham, and Fife, the forces impeding strong and continuous organization had the upper hand.

The chief function of the early national federations of mine unions was parliamentary lobbying, especially for improved mine safety. The importance attached to parliamentary activity was one of the distinguishing features of mine unionism. It derived from the exceptional danger in underground work, from parliament's willingness to regulate mine conditions and, in time, from the concentration of working-class votes in the coalfield constituencies.[6] The greatest single restraint upon the activities of the national federations was the conflict of interests between the unions in coalfields that readily conceded the necessity for wages to be ruled by the price of coal and those that gave first priority to obtaining an acceptable minimum wage. Northumberland and Durham dominated the former category. Attitudes there, and in other export coalfields, were shaped by the fear that if wages were not reduced with falling prices, then overseas markets would be lost and employment threatened. Miners on fields serving the home market had a far greater prospect of successfully resisting wage-cuts. The north-eastern hewers combined caution on the minimum wage issue with generally conciliatory attitudes to employers and opposition to demands for an eight-hour day. They themselves worked fewer than eight hours and they believed that a reduction in the hours of ancillary mine workers would raise costs, endanger coal exports, disrupt their own preferred shift arrangements, and possibly reduce earnings. Northumberland and Durham was by far the largest and most advanced of Britain's coalfields at mid-century. The skill of the north-eastern hewers, their long traditions of organization, and their cautiously defensive attitudes explain the comparative stability of trade unionism in the north-east during the following forty years.

Even the miners of Northumberland and Durham had been left largely unorganized after the collapse of the Miners Association of Great Britain in 1848. Recovery came in the late 1850s and Alexander Macdonald's National Miners Association (1858) helped to secure the Coal Mines Regulation Act (1860) that provided for improved mines inspection and allowed the men of each pit to appoint their own checkweighman.[7] The Yorkshire Miners Association (1858), the Northumberland Miners Association (1863), and numerous other local associations and unions were sporadically active in the 1860s, while at the national level the National Miners Association (transformed into the National Miners Union in 1863) lobbied for further parliamentary concessions. Macdonald's preference for political lobbying, and his anxiety to appease employers and the public, were eventually challenged by more militant leaders clamouring for joint industrial action. This group broke away from Macdonald in 1869 to form the Amalgamated Association of Miners. But the trade cycle turned down in 1873 and the Amalgamated Association of Miners was soon a victim of its own militancy. By 1879 many other miners' organizations had also been swept aside. In the recovery, Lancashire, Yorkshire, and some of the midland districts – all supplying the home market and resentful of the hegemony of Northumberland and Durham – made progress towards an alliance based upon demands for a minimum wage and an eight-hour day. This progress came to fruition with the creating of the Miners Federation of Great Britain during the great expansion of mine unionism that occurred at the end of the 1880s.

Cotton workers were also among the early beneficiaries of government regulation of working conditions and they too put considerable emphasis upon parliamentary activity. Another feature they shared with the miners, one that both facilitated organization and encouraged parliamentary activity, was residential concentration in communities where they accounted for a large part of the population. When the franchise was extended in 1867 and 1884 this advantage was put to good effect, especially in those Lancashire constituencies where neither Liberals nor Conservatives had a firm hold.

   Their readiness to barter votes for concessions from either party, and their calculated manipulation of parliament's concern for 'defenceless women and children' (above, pp. 214–15), were part of a practical opportunism that characterized most of the activities of the cotton unions. Their attitude towards employers was conciliatory, and they never forgot that it was necessary to keep Lancashire competitive in its far-flung markets. This approach to industrial relations was based upon shrewd calculation of the operatives' long-term interests: the benefits that might safely be extracted from each innovation were carefully calculated and then pursued with great skill and tenacity. The cotton unions were also well to the fore in the general enthusiasm for appointing full-time salaried officials and for putting union administration upon a more professional basis in other ways. Complex and constantly changing lists of piece-work payments necessitated negotiators of considerable intellect and mathematical skill.[8] A further distinguishing feature of the cotton unions, perhaps the most obvious of all, was the considerable number of females among their membership.

   Each cotton union represented a distinct occupational group and was an amalgamation of smaller district societies. The separate unions joined forces in the Factory Acts Reform Committee (1871) and its successor the United Textile Factory Workers Association, but at this level activity was largely confined to parliamentary lobbying. The strongest union was that of the well-paid male spinners. Like other cotton workers the spinners engaged in both collective bargaining and parliamentary activity, but they relied also (and fundamentally) upon their ability to control entry to their occupation. Only those who had worked alongside a spinner as a piecer were admitted: each spinner was restricted to two (sometimes three) piecers, and not all piecers (and no female piecers) were promoted. The piecers were encouraged to join spinners' societies but in an inferior capacity and at a nominal subscription. In 1850 the separate district societies of spinners were not formally associated although they assisted each other at times of crisis. There was a great deal of mutual assistance in the long Preston dispute that began in October 1853, for example, and in the same year these links were formalized by the establishment of the Amalgamated Association of Operative Cotton Spinners. Several of the district societies did not join the amalgamation at first and until the 1870s its functions were minimal. Eventually, however, the Operative Cotton Spinners encroached rather more upon the autonomy of district societies and by 1888 membership reached 17,000, about 90 per cent of those eligible to join.

   By this time far more weavers than spinners were organized. But the 40,000 organized weavers represented only about a quarter of all weavers. Many women had became weavers in the early cotton mills and there was never an opportunity for the men to exclude them as they were excluded from factory spinning. Thus whereas the spinners' societies relied a great deal upon restrictions on entry, the weavers' societies were open to all and forced to rely far more upon collective bargaining, strikes, and parliamentary lobbying. A loose amalgamation of district weavers' societies, the North Lancashire Powerloom Weavers Association, was established in 1858 and by 1884 there were 38,000 organized weavers, over half of them females. The status of these female weavers bore some resemblance to that of the organized piecers – they paid a lower union contribution than male weavers and were excluded from union management. There were several other organized or partly organized cotton occupations besides the spinners and weavers. Together they accounted for about a quarter of the industry's labour-force in 1888 and for about one in eight of all British trade unionists.

The cotton operatives together with the organized engineering and ship-building workers, miners, and building workers comprised over two-thirds of the trade union world in 1888. Printing was another occupation with a significant number of trade unionists (over 20,000 in 1888) and one where the unions had a considerable influence in some centres. There were also substantial numbers of unionists scattered throughout occupations that were otherwise still largely unorganized: at the upper end of the tailoring trades, for example, where most of the Amalgamated Society of Tailors' 14,000 members were concentrated; in parts of the iron and steel industry; on the railways where there were some 22,000 unionists in a labour force of about 200,000; and among male operatives in the footwear and lace industries. In addition, there were numerous minor occupations of a craft or supervisory kind that were strongly organized but whose contribution to trade union membership was numerically insignificant: the London bookbinders and gold-beaters for example, and many of the skilled metal working trades of Sheffield where there were still gild-like societies that could assemble their membership in one room for the annual general meeting. Elsewhere unionism remained weak or non-existent. Some occupations felt particular obstacles to combination more than others; small masters and the sub-contract system, which meant considerable social mobility and a blurring of the distinction between masters and men, were especial obstacles in London's East End and the Birmingham metal trades, for example, and the wool and worsted operatives were handicapped by having so few males among their number. But the main reasons why so many workers remained unorganized were still, by and large, those that were noted when discussing the limits to trade unionism before 1850 (above, pp. 194–7).

Agriculture and female employment, two sections that were still almost entirely unorganized in 1888, are worth describing as particular examples of areas where trade unionism made little headway. There had been several attempts at agricultural combination before Joseph Arch launched the

National Agricultural Labourers Union in 1872 but none made much progress. Helped along by an unusually tight labour market, by resentment at the threat to child earnings in the 1870 Education Act, by outside assistance, and by its own momentum, Arch's union grew rapidly and soon boasted 100,000 members. It succeeded especially in the labour-intensive corn counties of the south, the midlands, and East Anglia where farms were largest and 'Hodge' and his master furthest apart. 'Captain Swing' had found his recruits in much the same areas.

Outside help was probably crucial to this expansion because few able organizers came forward from the ranks of village labourers. Arch himself – lay preacher, one-time independent contract worker, and 'champion hedgecutter of England' – was a far from typical labourer. A great deal of help came from non-conformist ministers, especially from Primitive Methodists. Certain prominent Anglicans, including Canon Girdlestone and the Bishop of Manchester, also backed the labourers, but church and chapel in most places were on opposing sides. There was help too from distant trade unions and from local craftsmen and other individuals. But all this was not enough. The trade cycle turned down and the farmers combined to resist the union. A great lock-out began in Suffolk in March 1874 and Arch suffered a resounding defeat. Weakened and demoralized, the union resolved to challenge the farmers less often and to concentrate instead upon emigration and friendly society activities and the political campaign for land reform and the vote. Squabbles between the NALU and some of its smaller rivals contributed to the collapse. One of these rivals, the Kent Union which was prudently led and also helped by Kent's prosperous market gardening, continued to expand after 1874. But elsewhere there was little left of agricultural trade unionism by 1880.

Organization had probably accelerated farm labourers' wage increases in the early 1870s, but the increases were mainly a consequence of the favourable market conditions that permitted the labourers' organization. The union also affected wages indirectly by encouraging labour mobility, but in this respect also its influence merely supplemented other influences that were already at work.[9] By 1879 wage levels were probably not much different from what they would have been without the NALU. However, the union could fairly claim at least a part in helping to take the franchise to the agricultural labourer in 1884 and in taking Arch to Westminster. In the circumstances it is perhaps remarkable that even as much as this was achieved. Most labourers were poor, deferential, and untutored in the ways of trade unionism. The bolder souls among them soon left for the towns and the emigration ports. Farm labourers had very little scarcity value; indeed, they were grossly under-employed. Moreover, their employers were not accustomed to being challenged and the threat of a strike, even of union recruitment, was strongly resented. The offending labourer risked everything – his employment, his cottage, his allotment, and claims to parish poor rates and charities.[10]

Except among the cotton operatives, women's trade unionism at the end of the 1880s was no further advanced than that of the agricultural labourers. Drake's figures for 1886 show 30,100 women trade unionists in the cotton industry, 4,500 in the other textile industries, 1,300 in the clothing trades, and 1,100 elsewhere.[11] Women's unionism was strongest in the cotton industry chiefly because male workers there believed that women were less of a threat within the union than they would be if they were left unorganized. Female factory operatives were also more easily unionized than women who worked at out-work or domestic service, and many of the cotton workers were the daughters, nieces, or wives of their organizers. Some of the printers came to share the view of the cotton operatives and some trades councils attempted (without much success) to organize women in separate unions. But the attitudes of most male unionists to women workers before 1888 ranged between indifference and hostility. A recent commemorative survey of trade union banners noted that while women frequently appeared on these banners as symbols of virtue, or as tearful widows comforted by union death benefits, they almost never appeared as workers. Women might have organized themselves of course, but they did not. Organization, especially initial organization, entailed at least an element of rebelliousness and women were conditioned to be submissive and to regard work as of secondary importance to the home and family. Even if they had been bolder and if male unionists had been more helpful, organization would still have been difficult because in those restricted employments considered suitable for them women's labour was exceptionally abundant and the working environment unfavourable to organization.

The beginning of continuous and independent women's trade unionism is usually dated from Emma Paterson's Women's Protective and Provident League of 1874. The founder members of the Women's Protective and Provident League were mostly middle-class. At least one male representative of the London Trades Council also attended the inaugural meeting but Mrs Paterson's especial invitation to 'women engaged in trade' seems to have been entirely ignored. The League offered secretarial assistance and in other ways encouraged women's organization. It emphasized friendly society activities, advocated peaceful relations with employers, and its title was carefully drafted to exclude the words 'trade union', 'lest storms of opposition . . . be aroused'. The TUC was uncertain how to respond to this hybrid institution. Attempts to expand trade unionism could hardly be rebuffed openly but the TUC could (and did) object to 'middle-class ladies' purporting to represent working-class women. In 1875, however, Mrs Paterson and another female representative attended the TUC as delegates of operating unions of working women: they were the first female delegates.[12] This innovation was not markedly successful. The women's leaders determined to undermine the discrimination that confined women to 'women's work' by resisting proposals to reduce women's hours and other legislative measures that assumed feminine inferiority. Their stance was short-sighted because such motions were usually advanced not with the intention of further restricting female employment, but in the hope that if parliament protected females the same concessions could be more easily won for men. So feminist obstruction served to reinforce existing male prejudice.

The League was no more successful at the workplace. Its active members struggled to overcome the apathy of working women. They succeeded in calling an inquiry into conditions at the army clothing factory in Pimlico, and they perhaps also helped to prepare the ground for later progress. But the few women's unions that were launched were small and ineffective, and in 1886, when Emma Paterson died, their membership totalled only a few thousands. Her death was in some respects a turning-point at which several of the League's less successful policies were jettisoned. The new policies – more militant, less feminist, and more accommodating to male trade unionists – were a part of the 'new unionism' that will be described in Chapter 9.

II · *'New model' union characteristics; other unions; trades councils*

We turn now to those 'new model' union characteristics that are so often cited as the distinguishing features of unionism between mid-century and 1888 and which receive particular emphasis in interpretations that see the period as a 'gap' between 'the British labour movement's "revolutionary" period' and late nineteenth-century 'new unionism'.[13] Three, at least, of these characteristics have already been mentioned: most accounts suggest that by contemporary standards 'new model' unions like the ASE and the ASCJ were large, efficient, and concentrated power in the hands of full-time head office officials. Among other characteristics commonly associated with such unions were an acceptance of liberal economic tenets, emphasis upon friendly society activities, and the desirability of good relations with employers. The ASE claimed to 'endeavour at all times to prevent strikes', and similar sentiments provided the theme for a poem read (and well received) at a Boilermakers and Iron Ship-Builders Society dinner in 1872:[14]

> Capital and Labour seem
> By our Maker joined
> . . .
> Up the hill of progress bright
> March we on in tether.

The political ambitions of these 'new model' unions were largely restricted to trade union affairs and were pursued through the existing parties with little thought of independent working-class representation. Indeed, some unions were anxious to give the impression that they avoided political controversy of almost any kind. William Newton claimed in 1850 that the Engineers meetings excluded political discussion, and in 1887 when the refractory John Burns was arrested at Trafalgar Square (below, pp. 274–5) the ASE solemnly denounced 'his and any other politics'.

Such unions naturally made light of characteristics and interests that were common to all wage-earners. Their first concern was to maintain the craft's traditional work and to safeguard craft status by regulating labour supply. These preoccupations tended to obscure any consciousness of wider affinities. Such attitudes have been the despair of class-conscious historians and caused H. A. Turner to declare that 'trade union development is as much to be understood in terms of the clash or coincidence of sectional interests among workers, as in terms of the evolution of any general struggle between wage earners at large and employers'.[15] The unskilled workers, social inferiors as well as potential competitors, were patronized and repressed. The Boilermakers and Iron Ship-Builders, for example, responded to attempts by their assistants to organize with complaints of the need to 'get the labourers to keep their places . . . the helper ought to be subservient and do as the mechanic tells him'.[16] Initial unionization among the unskilled was in some cases directed more against the craftsmen (their immediate employers) than against the common capitalist employer, and the craftsmen did not hesitate to recruit 'blacklegs' to brush aside the challenge.

These 'new model' union characteristics tell us a great deal about trade unionism between 1850 and 1888. But in three important respects they are misleading. First, the implied transition (or as H. A. Turner puts it, 'retreat'[17]) from an era of open unionism did not occur. There was some change in this direction (above pp. 204–5, 250), but craft exclusiveness, political quiescence, and conciliatory attitudes towards employers were all marked characteristics of trade unionism in the first half of the nineteenth century. This is abundantly evident from what was said of craft unions in Chapters 6 and 7, and needs no further elaboration. Secondly, the standard 'new model' union characteristics are a poor guide also to events after 1850. Even model 'new model' unions like the ASE and ASCJ were less influenced by 'new model' characteristics than they liked to pretend. Thirdly, union membership extended far beyond the membership of 'new model' unions.

The difference between the 'new model' unions as they were and the image of themselves that they succeeded in foisting upon some politicians and large parts of the public is evident, first, in their attitude to strikes. Certain 'new model' unions were remarkably free of strikes, but few, if any, willingly abandoned the strike weapon. The ASE, whose secretary declared before the Royal Commission on Trade Unions (1867–9) that strikes were 'the very last thing that we would think of encouraging', had in the previous thirteen years distributed 179 separate grants to support strikes by other unions.[18] And the ASCJ, as we saw earlier, was established not least because the London building dispute of 1859–60 demonstrated the greater ability of large national amalgamations to sustain local strikes. If 'new model' policies resulted in fewer strikes than would otherwise have occurred the outcome derived less from any self-denying ordinance than from enlightened self-interest and the exploitation of more subtle alternatives to striking. Above all, the new model unions reinforced traditional craft caution towards action that could easily rebound to the employers' advantage. Officials in London head offices made a calmer and more calculated appraisal of events than those close to a dispute, and the delay that occurred while they completed their deliberations provided an opportunity for tempers to cool, for indefensible positions to be quietly abandoned, and for compromise to be effected.[19] Such tactics were a curb upon strikes but they by no means amounted to their renunciation.

It is sometimes said that extensive 'new model' friendly society benefits also reduced strikes because officials were reluctant to jeopardize the cherished funds from which came pensions and sick benefits as well as strike pay. The existence of these funds probably did discourage strikes, but not only because unions feared depletion of their friendly society reserves. Major battles were costly, and the knowledge that a union had sufficient funds to sustain and survive a prolonged struggle earned that union a healthy respect. Friendly society benefits also reinforced strike discipline. Those with pensions and other claims at stake were less likely to leave the union or to 'blackleg' when it instructed them to stop working. Similar qualifications should be attached to claims that union emigration schemes (above, p. 205) were a substitute for more aggressive trade policies. Emigration and the threat of emigration were used as bargaining ploys, and strike leaders were the more resolute when they knew that if they were later victimized the union would arrange their emigration.

The main alternative to the strike was the rule book. Where employers were prepared to accept craft regulation of labour supply and workshop practice the union could usually secure its interests without resort to striking and at the same time consolidate its public image by boasting of a distaste for unseemly conflict. Individual employers who resisted these impositions could be discreetly boycotted – 'a bad employer should be defeated by quietly withdrawing the men one by one'.[20] Employers, of course, knew better than the public the limits to 'new model' moderation. They knew that if they themselves combined and effectively challenged craft job-control, as the engineering employers did in 1852, they would be bitterly resisted. A Manchester employer in 1868 declared the Engineers to be 'very nice people if they have their own way, but if they have not they will fight, and they can fight anything and anybody, they are so strong'.[21]

The supposed 'new model' acceptance of orthodox economic dogma also requires qualification. These unions recognized mutual interests with employers but they never forgot that their interests could conflict, and the spirit of monopoly and restriction that was the basis of craft unionism was not easily reconcilable with contemporary economic thought. Above all else the 'new model' unions were opportunists and shrewd practitioners of the art of public relations. Their leaders, and middle-class sympathizers like Frederic Harrison, emphasized avoidance of strikes while drawing a discreet veil over the less acceptable of the practices that served in their place.[22] They paid lip-service to establishment views, and particularly to those parts of the economic creed that lent respectability to their policies and aspirations, but they followed no coherent or consistent political theory.

'New model' union constitutions were also not quite as they are often imagined. Despite their size, their London headquarters, and their full-time salaried officials, each 'new model' union branch continued to enjoy what Postgate in 1923 described as 'an amount of power which would surprise a modern trade unionist'.[23] Publicity, finance, and the sanctioning of strikes were all the prerogative of head office, but wage demands, negotiation with employers, control of hours and apprenticeships, and indeed most aspects of workshop practice, were left in the hands of local officers. Very little effort was made, for example, to even out the enormous variation in the 'standard rate' of wages in different towns that was noted in Chapter 3. This division of responsibilities facilitated public relations by allowing the branches to operate the more restrictive trade practices while head office spokesmen dwelt upon the union contribution to industrial harmony and its friendly society activities. The friendly society activities, moreover, were in many cases based upon unsound actuarial assumptions and constitute an important qualification to the 'new model' reputation for administrative efficiency.[24]

The 'new model' reputation for sectionalism and exclusiveness was certainly deserved, but the period was not lacking in demonstrations of union solidarity in which the 'new model' unions took a significant part. During major disputes, and especially those in which the right of combination appeared under challenge, the unions drew together as they had done earlier to express their outrage at the Tolpuddle sentences. The Engineers received £5,000 from other societies during the 1852 lock-out; London unions sent a similar sum to the striking Preston cotton operatives in 1853–4; and the great London building strike of 1859–60 provoked a massive demonstration of solidarity in which unions of every kind subscribed over £23,000.

The third major respect in which the 'new model' characteristics are a misleading guide to the nature of trade unionism between 1850 and 1888 is largely apparent in the earlier survey of organized occupations. The prominent role of 'new model' unions at the time of the 1867–9 Royal Commission on Trade Unions, their publicity-seeking London head offices, and their durability have left an exaggerated impression of their importance. There were numerous small unions of skilled or semi-skilled men that made no pretence to be part of 'new model' unionism. George Potter, a member of a small society of London carpenters, acted as spokesman for these smaller and more militant unions. He publicized their activities in his newspaper, the *Beehive*, and openly challenged the conciliatory 'new model' leaders.[25] There were also, long before 1888, sporadic outbursts of militancy and eruptions of organization among the unskilled, especially in the prosperous early 1870s when many dockers, gas workers, and builders' labourers were first organized. The brief flowering of agricultural trade unionism described earlier was a part of this advance. At this time some of the 'new model' unions were themselves disturbed by rank and file unrest, most of all in the successful nine-hour day campaign of 1871–2 that was led by engineers in the north-east. This campaign embraced trade unionists of every description and many workers who were not previously organized.

Several of the larger unions also cannot be counted as part of 'new model' unionism. Some miners' unions had certain characteristics in common with the 'new model' craft unions but even the cautious unionism of Northumberland and Durham differed from the 'new model' stereotype in several respects. Hewers were too large a part of the mine labour force, too close in status to the lesser miners, and entry to their ranks was too open for them to constitute an 'aristocracy of labour'. And because miners exercised less control than craftsmen over labour supply the 'new model' alternatives to striking were less available to them. Some textile unions also differed significantly from the 'new model' stereotype, notably the cotton weavers with their low subscriptions, modest benefits, and open recruiting.

Another consequence of preoccupation with the activities of the 'new model' unions is that trades councils – other than the London Trades Council which for a time was dominated by 'new model' unions – have received less attention from historians than they deserve. Trades councils were a means of facilitating mutual aid among the organized workers of a town:* typically they began as *ad hoc* associations called together at a time of crisis. Some branches of 'new model' unions affiliated to trades councils but they drew much of their

* The term usually describes associations that were open to all organized workers in a town. Co-operative and political societies might also affiliate. Some trades councils, however, were restricted to workers in allied trades. The various building unions, for example, might form a building trades council.

support from the smaller unions who were less capable than 'new model' unions of managing local disputes without outside assistance.[26] A number of trades councils had been formed in the first half of the century and the first to achieve continuous organization was that begun at Liverpool in 1848. Soon after other trades councils were begun in Edinburgh, Sheffield, and Glasgow, and then in London at the time of the 1860 building dispute. By 1875 trades councils had been established in every sizable town. At a time when there were still many small unions, and as yet no Labour Party to co-ordinate and act as spokesman for local working-class interests and organizations, trades councils had a significant role. They displayed some of the characteristics of the 'new model' unions but their activities are also evidence of a more fraternal side of trade unionism. At Edinburgh, for example, the trades council set about encouraging unionism among the unskilled in 1867 and succeeded in promoting a labourers' union; Aberdeen, Glasgow, and Liverpool trades councils were similarly active in the 1880s; Sheffield and Birmingham gave particular attention to conditions in the unorganized sweated trades; and several councils sponsored a general union for female workers. Besides these industrial activities most trades councils also participated extensively in local politics and, as we shall see below, they had an important role in the creation of the Trades Union Congress.

III · *Political activities, 1850–75; the Junta and its policies; working-class radicalism in the 1860s; the Royal Commission on Trade Unions, 1867–9, and the legislation of 1871–5; the* TUC; *the working-class vote*

There was considerable trade union political activity between 1850 and 1888. Working-class political activity *in total* during these years was probably less than had taken place in the first half of the century, and the earlier activity was certainly more radical. But the unions did not have a very prominent role in the early campaigning. After 1850 they dominated working-class political activity. The period is divided by the crisis in trade union affairs that began with the 'Sheffield Outrages' (1866), the judicial ruling in the case of Hornby v. Close (1867), and the appointment of the Royal Commission on Trade Unions in 1867. By 1875 the crisis had been resolved in the unions' favour.

Compared with unions elsewhere those in Britain had an enviable status long before 1875. Robert Applegarth boasted to Karl Marx's International Working Men's Association (Basle, 1869) that 'we in England have no need to creep into holes and corners lest a policeman should see us . . . we meet in open daylight and organize ourselves, and treat of any questions which affect us without fear'.[27] Nevertheless, there were four major legal disabilities that the unions were anxious to remove. Repeal of the Combination Acts had allowed workmen to organize, negotiate, and strike over issues of hours and wages, free of the threat of prosecution for criminal conspiracy. But intimidation, molestation, obstruction, and threats were all offences, so conducting a strike might be legally precarious. Secondly, the unions felt the need for redress against embezzling officials. Some of them sought protection by registering under the Friendly Societies Act of 1855, but the Hornby *v.* Close case of 1867, in which the Boilermakers Society attempted to recover £24 from the treasurer of their Bradford branch, established that trade unions were not entitled to the protection of this act. More resented than this disability was the Master and Servant law by which employers and workmen could take action for breach of the contract of employment. This legislation could be used in ways that severely qualified the right to strike. Moreover, workmen allegedly in breach of contract were tried under the criminal law but employers were tried under the civil law. The 'servant' might find himself imprisoned, the 'master' could only be made to pay arrears or damages. An amending act of 1867 removed some of the more objectionable features of this legislation but fell short of satisfying union demands. The other chief cause of resentment, felt particularly by those in hazardous occupations, was the law governing liability for accidents at work which enabled employers to escape the consequences of injury to workmen caused by the action of another employee. The unions also attempted to extend the law relating to other aspects of safety at work, and that on working hours, education, and the payment of wages in 'truck'. In addition they sought a further extension of the franchise to give working men greater influence over the law-makers.

All of these issues were pursued with some enthusiasm after the London building dispute of 1859–60. This dispute had several enduring consequences: it was the occasion of the foundation of both the ASCJ and the London Trades Council (LTC) as we noted earlier, and it also fostered solidarity among unionists and sharpened demands for the vote. London, of course, was the headquarters of the 'new model' amalgamated unions and the LTC was soon controlled by their officers. Robert Applegarth and William Allan, secretaries respectively of the ASCJ and the ASE, were the leading figures; Daniel Guile, secretary of the Friendly Society of Ironfounders, Edwin Coulson, secretary of the Operative Bricklayers Society, and George Odger, a skilled shoemaker, gave them close support. This group met frequently and took an active interest in all trade union affairs. They were alike in opinion and temperament, they enjoyed the valuable support of a small group of radical lawyers and literary men (the positivists and christian socialists), they wielded considerable power on their own account as leaders of powerful unions, and they took a particular interest in political questions.

Thus the 'Junta', as the Webbs labelled the closely-knit group, came to act as 'an informal cabinet of the trade union world'.[28] It was the main influence behind the Manhood Suffrage and Vote by Ballot Association (1862) and the National Reform League (1865) which successively worked to extend the franchise, to make working-class opinion known to politicians, and for the election of men sympathetic to working-class interests. The Junta could reasonably claim part of the credit for the Reform Act of 1867 and for several legislative advances on safety and other matters. These political activities were of a very different character to the threats and ultimatums of militant Chartism, but they were certainly not confined to advancing the interests of labour aristocrats. The Junta worked for 'a levelling down of all political privileges, and the opening out of educational and social opportunities to all classes of the community'.[29] It also concerned itself with the principles and issues of the American Civil War and organized a massive demonstration to welcome the Italian patriot Garibaldi to London in 1864.

There was also at this time a great deal of political activity among the less aristocratic unions – among the coal and cotton unions and in the provincial trades councils. London, however, with its working men's radical and republican clubs, was the centre of working-class radicalism and it was there most of all that the Junta's lead was challenged. George Potter argued that the National Reform League was too much influenced by middle-class liberals and too concerned not to offend middle-class susceptibilities. In 1866, after being eased out of the LTC following a quarrel with the Junta over their advice to striking Staffordshire ironworkers, Potter set up a new London Working Men's Association which campaigned vigorously on parliamentary reform and demanded in particular that extension of the franchise should not exclude the lodger population by being limited to male householders. In the mid-1860s rising unemployment swelled the demand for political reform. There was a serious reform riot at Hyde Park in July 1866 and for a short time it seemed possible that London's radical and republican clubs might provide the springboard for a broader radical advance.

Industrial unrest at this time, combined with bad trade and union pressure to change the Master and Servant law, prompted public criticism of the unions. This was the background to the crisis set off by the 'Sheffield Outrages'. The final 'outrage' was the destruction of a non-unionist's house by gunpowder in October 1866. Critics of the unions naturally made the most of this event and called for a full inquiry into union activities. The Junta, anxious to establish that such incidents were unrepresentative of trade union behaviour, joined in the demands for an inquiry. Union anxieties were further aggravated by news of the Hornby *v.* Close decision. In 1867 the government announced a Royal Commission that was to enquire both into the events at Sheffield and trade unionism generally. Fears that the unions were to be put on trial were somewhat mollified by the government's even-handed approach to the inquiry. Thomas Hughes, Frederic Harrison, and the Earl of Lichfield, who were known to be sympathetic to the unions, were among the commissioners, and union representatives were invited to attend the proceedings. The Junta and Potter's faction both sent representatives, but Potter's man was expelled after an indiscreet speech. The Junta, ably represented by Applegarth and in collusion with Harrison and Hughes, presented an account of the movement emphasizing the more acceptable features of the 'new model' unions. This impression prevailed over considerable evidence of questionable restrictive practices and what was little short of systematic terrorism in the Sheffield metal trades and Manchester brickmaking. Shortly after this Potter ceased to attack the Junta. He still resented their assumptions and priorities but he doubtless recognized their skilful manipulation of the Royal Commission and appreciated the necessity for unions to stand together during the crisis. Moreover, the *Beehive* was in difficulties and in need of London Trades Council cash.

The Commission reported in 1869. The majority report contained no recommendations that would have clearly worsened the unions' legal status and the recommendations of the minority report, signed by Harrison, Hughes, and the Earl of Lichfield, were almost identical to union demands. The government, of course, was not compelled to act upon either report but in the same year it introduced a stopgap act whose effect was to nullify the implications of the Hornby *v.* Close decision. Then, in 1871, two further acts were passed. The first gave union funds the same legal protection as the funds of friendly societies. The second, however, the Criminal Law Amendment Act, effectively endorsed existing law which made strikers liable to prosecution for intimidation, molestation, and obstruction. The unions were far from pleased by this, and those that made most use of the strike weapon were naturally the most resentful; George Potter took a leading part in the agitation that followed. Resentment was aggravated by the imprisonment of striking London gas workers for breaking their contracts of employment and by sentences of hard labour upon sixteen farm labourers' wives for intimidation of 'blacklegs'. The protest campaign reached its peak in unprecedented union activity during the 1874 general election when working-class votes had a substantial role in the rejection of the Liberal government. During the election campaign Conservative candidates had appeared the more responsive to trade union pressure.

Instead of immediately repealing the Criminal Law Amendment Act, as unionists had hoped, the Conservatives began a fresh enquiry, the Royal Commission on Labour Laws (1874). Most unionists saw this as a breach of faith or a delaying tactic and although two working men were invited to join the Commission, itself a significant step,[30] many unions refused their co-operation. No substantial change in the law was recommended and thus union suspicions appeared confirmed. But the government ignored the Commission's recommendations and in 1875 introduced the Conspiracy and Protection of Property Act by which the Criminal Law Amendment Act was repealed and peaceful picketing made clearly legal. Violence and intimidation remained offences but the threat of charges for conspiracy was lifted; henceforth unionists could not be prosecuted for doing what an individual might do lawfully. In the same year the government dealt with another major cause of union discontent when it introduced the Employers and Workmen Act which removed the remaining inequalities of the Master and Servant legislation.

This concluded a period of remarkable legislative advance that had begun with the 1867 Reform Act. The legality of trade unions was now assured, their funds were protected against theft or embezzlement, they had considerable latitude in the conduct of strikes, and they had maintained (or at least for a long time it was assumed that they had maintained) their curiously privileged legal position whereby they could not be sued for damages. The initial threat to their position had served to bring unions together and the successful campaign to persuade the 1867–9 Royal Commission and the public of their respectability succeeded handsomely. The contrast between the titles of the Employers and Workmen Act and the Master and Servant law it replaced was a reflection of the unions' enhanced status. It is easy, of course, to overestimate the importance of the law compared to that of market forces: shortly before this legal triumph was complete the trade cycle turned down and many unions that celebrated in 1875 had disappeared by 1880. Even so, the rapidity of legal advance that occurred between 1867 and 1875, and the thawing of official and public attitudes towards the unions, were exceptional.

The most enduring consequence of co-operation between unions during the crisis years was the Trades Union Congress. The TUC was an annual meeting of unions and kindred associations to discuss questions of common interest, to formulate political demands, and to exert political pressure. Three years after the initial meeting a small 'Parliamentary Committee' was appointed that remained in existence between the annual meetings. It is important to appreciate how limited were these functions and what the TUC did *not* do. Collective bargaining and industrial action remained the prerogative of individual unions. From time to time there were proposals that the TUC should intervene directly in industrial disputes, organize joint industrial action, or become either a vast federation or one big union. But such proposals found little support. Unions could leave the TUC at will and they could adopt or disregard Congress recommendations as they saw fit.

The TUC was a logical extension of the trades councils. Several trades councils had extended their political activities to the national stage. Glasgow Trades Council, for example, took up the vexed question of the Master and

Servant law in the early 1860s, called a national conference, lobbied parliament, and helped to bring about the amending act of 1867. The Sheffield Trades Council was similarly active in 1866–7 when it attempted to create a national amalgamation of trades councils (the United Kingdom Alliance of Organized Trades) that would arrange mutual aid during strikes and lock-outs. Sheffield's initiative received considerable backing from George Potter and shortly after it foundered in the reaction to the 'Sheffield Outrages' Potter himself had called a national conference to consider the union response to the forthcoming Royal Commission.

Each of these attempts at national association was among the immediate antecedents of the TUC. In the event, however, an initiative by Manchester and Salford Trades Council in 1868 proved the most significant. Its president and secretary, dissatisfied with the Junta's response to the Royal Commission and offended by the patronizing treatment of artisans at the annual meeting of the Social Science Association, issued invitations to a 'Congress of Trade Unions'. This inaugural meeting at Manchester was modestly attended. Those present were mainly provincial unionists, among them several critics of the Junta. Only two delegates came up from London and one of these was George Potter. The Junta, seeing the arrangements as a challenge and an unnecessary duplication of its own efforts, sent no representive and ignored conciliatory gestures. The second TUC however, held at Birmingham in 1869, was much better supported. The Junta remained unenthusiastic, but grudgingly accepted an invitation to make arrangements for the following Congress. Not long after this a mellowing George Potter made his peace with the Junta and factional interests were further eclipsed by common resentment of the 1871 Criminal Law Amendment Act. In this way the more obvious divisions among trade union leaders had been patched up by the end of 1871. Members of the Junta continued to wield enormous influence both within and outside the TUC but it now ceased to operate as a distinct body.[31] And the TUC – less moderate and less conciliatory than the Junta – took over as the chief spokesman of organized labour.

It was the TUC Parliamentary Committee that had directed the union campaign which influenced the 1874 election. This occasion apart, however, the influence of the working-class vote in the 1860s and 1870s was less than might be expected in a country that was more industrialized and more urbanized than any other and where, after 1867, the working classes commanded a very substantial part of the urban vote.[32] There were many MPs who were sympathetic to labour, but until the 1874 election there were no working men in parliament and then there were only two. The National Reform League (1865–9), Potter's LWMA (1866), and the TUC's Labour Representation League (1869) each made some attempt to increase the number of working-class MPs and to use the working-class vote to this end, but they found only half-hearted support and they had few successes. Only a handful of working men stood in the 1868 election and they were decisively beaten. Some working-class candidates helped the Conservatives in 1874 by splitting the Liberal vote and Thomas Burt and Alexander Macdonald succeeded at Morpeth and Stafford where the Liberals allowed them a clear run against Conservatives, but none of those that stood independently were elected. Working men made rather more headway in local politics both within and (less often) independently of the existing parties, but the overwhelming impression is that the impact of the new working-class vote was not easily distinguished from that of other voters.

The main reason for this is that working-class voters attached more significance to the differences between Liberals and Conservatives than to those between themselves and other classes. Few of them were disposed to support a working-class candidate who was neither Liberal nor Conservative, or necessarily to prefer a working-class Liberal or Conservative over candidates of the accustomed kind. This, no doubt, was because workers were not ostracized by the existing political parties and were not previously so badly treated that their first inclination was to use their new votes against the ruling classes. Both parties courted the working-class vote and allowed working men some influence in the selection of candidates and policy-making. Such concessions were willingly made because at this time working-class political ambitions were neither sufficiently pressing nor sufficiently distinct to prevent their easy accommodation. 'What do you say to the elections in the factory districts?' asked Engels of Marx in 1868. 'Everywhere the working class is the rag, tag and bobtail of the official parties. . . . Not a single working-class candidate had the ghost of a chance but my Lord Tom Noddy or any *parvenu* snob could have the workers' votes with pleasure.'[33]

How did the workers dispose of their votes? With the notable exception of the years between the passing of the Criminal Law Amendment Act and its repeal – on which issue the Conservatives were far more accommodating – the majority of working-class votes went to the Liberal party. We noted earlier that by the 1840s many of the more skilled workers had accepted the permanence of the new industrial order and some elements of orthodox liberalism: in the more favourable economic climate after 1850 these attitudes were adopted by many others. The Liberals came to be less closely identified with factory employers – factories anyway had become less resented – and to some extent they succeeded in diverting working-class hostility towards the great landowners. Gladstone made known his appreciation of the unions' more positive virtues, his advocacy of franchise reform brought him enormous popular support, and in the 1868 general election campaign the National Reform League and the Liberals co-operated closely. The Liberals, moreover, were the party of non-conformity and temperance and on these grounds they enjoyed considerable working-class support. Their support was almost certainly strongest among the more skilled workers, and especially among trade unionists.

But there was always a substantial minority of working-class Conservative voters. Some voted Conservative (as many others voted Liberal) from deference to the political views of their employers. In Lancashire's factory towns, it was said, workmen voted 'by mills and wards in the spirit in which schoolboys play cricket or football by "houses" or "forms" '.[34] In addition, the Conservative championing of factory reform before 1850 was not entirely forgotten and the Liberals' conciliatory attitude towards Roman Catholic Ireland consolidated native working-class support for 'Church and Crown'. Lancashire, which was a particular bastion of working-class Conservatism, had both especial cause to remember the factory reform campaign and far more than the average proportion of Irish immigrants. The Conservatives, moreover, were less bound than Liberals by the sometimes harsh dictates of political economy and Disraeli's 'Tory Democracy' struck a responsive chord. Links with the drink trade and the Anglican church helped to secure the allegiance of many among those working men who were neither abstainers nor non-conformists, and the reputation of being the party of patriotism won support in garrison and shipbuilding towns. There was a substantial working-class Conservative vote also in most places that sought protection from foreign competition to improve employment.[35]

IV · *Politics 1875–88, the Lib-Lab alliance; criticism from the left and the background to 'new unionism'*

The alliance between trade unionism and Liberalism was speedily restored after the passing of the Conspiracy and Protection of Property Act (1875), and the first trade unionist MPs were in almost every respect members of the parliamentary Liberal Party. At the TUC also, and in local politics, the prevailing priorities and principles of the unions were Liberal. Union support was given at a price and the price was sometimes disputed, particularly by those unions that had been most critical of the Junta. There were threats and hard bargaining, but until the twentieth century the partnership was very close and before the 1880s its fundamentals were not seriously questioned.

Political objectives after 1875 were more diverse than they had been in the third quarter of the century. The strengthening of working-class political representation and further extensions of the franchise remained long-term ambitions. The campaign for an employers' liability act also continued, along with demands for improved safety legislation, for more stringent inspection of mines and factories, and in support of Samuel Plimsoll's attempts to improve the safety and status of merchant seamen. Trades councils took up each of

271

these questions and concerned themselves particularly with education, 'sweating', and poor law administration. Many of them became involved also in local issues: the Sheffield Trades Council, for example, was anxious to prevent allegedly inferior items being passed off as hand-made Sheffield goods, and Manchester and Salford took considerable interest in plans for the proposed Manchester Ship Canal.

These activities helped to secure numerous worthwhile reforms. Particularly important was the Reform Act of 1884 which enfranchised many rural workers. Over a third of working men were still without a vote for one reason or another,* but these were now the exceptions. More votes brought increased competition for working-class support: the Conservatives proffered protection and imperialism and the Liberals countered with guarantees of continuing cheap food and a shift from orthodox liberalism towards 'new liberal' collectivism. In 1880 an employers' liability act had been passed. Certain categories of employment and certain kinds of accidents were excluded from the act and any employer and his workmen could 'contract-out'. These were serious omissions, but the act was undeniably a step in the right direction. There were also in these years several piecemeal legislative advances affecting safety and working conditions. The number of mines and factory inspectors was increased, and the first working-class factory inspector began his rounds in 1882. Elsewhere too working men were moving into positions of influence; on to the school-boards for example, and the magistrates' benches (1885). The TUC by this time was accustomed to being annually fêted by municipal authorities, to the courteous attention of the national press, and a respectful audience from government ministers. And in 1886 Henry Broadhurst MP, secretary of the TUC Parliamentary Committee and a recent colleague of the Prince of Wales, sundry lords, knights, and bishops on the Royal Commission on the Housing of the Working Classes, received the invitation to join Gladstone's government that enabled him to sub-title his autobiography *From a Stonemason's Bench to the Treasury Bench*.

Substantial as it was, this progress came to be considered unsatisfactory in certain quarters. Criticism arose partly from the nature of the advance; the gains were the fruits of political alliance and to those who were not closely involved they appeared to come effortlessly. Moreover, there undoubtedly had been a loss of momentum after the parliamentary victories of 1867–75 and the more optimistic expectations aroused then were disappointed. There was particular criticism of the continuing poor representation of working men in parliament: the two miners elected in 1874 were not reinforced until 1880 (by Henry Broadhurst) and in 1890 there were still only eight working-class MPs.

* Many domestic servants, soldiers, policemen and others who were neither householders nor tenants, those who had accepted poor relief, those without a year of stable residence when the register was prepared. In 1910 about 60 per cent of adult males were registered voters.

The T U C and its Parliamentary Committee had not exerted themselves unduly to accelerate this advance and those who urged a separate 'labour party', independent of the Liberals, had been largely disregarded. The Labour Representation League (above, p. 269) was defunct by 1880 and the Labour Electoral Committee (set up in 1886) went about its work without significantly diminishing the Lib-Lab commitment. Moreover, the T U C clung resolutely to its limited political role, carefully avoiding all but the least contentious issues.

To some extent the criticisms were justified. The T U C probably could have used the potential strength of the unions more effectively and might have improved its amateur administration. Like most of its member unions the T U C underestimated the value of white-collar skills and tried to manage with whatever administrative talent it found among its elected officials. It operated with a tiny budget, with only one full-time salaried official, and its officers were preoccupied with the affairs of their own unions.[36] But the scope for independent political action, and for industrial co-operation between unions, was less than critics of the T U C allowed. The T U C remained a loose affiliation largely because its member unions continued to be jealous of their independence and far more concerned for themselves than for other unions or unorganized workers. Many of them had trouble enough imposing cohesion upon their independent-minded branches and when the Parliamentary Committee canvassed the opinion of all unions on a proposal to establish a federation of trade unions (1879) fewer than half a dozen bothered to reply.[37] The T U C, that is, was about as effective as its independent and introspective membership permitted.

Besides offending the majority of unions who were satisfied with the Lib-Lab alliance, any decisive move towards political independence would also have offended the Liberal Party and almost certainly resulted in even fewer unionists finding their way to parliament. Working men who had to stand against Liberals as well as Conservatives normally came last in the poll. Worsening economic conditions also limited the T U C's field of manoeuvre: in the mid-1870s the economic climate became less favourable to union advance. Over a million unionists and more than 150 separate societies were represented at the Sheffield Congress of 1874; at Edinburgh five years later fewer than half as many unionists and only 92 societies were represented.[38] Thrown onto the defensive, unions became less willing than ever to yield sectional advantage.

Who then were the critics of the trade union leadership, and what influences swelled their protest in the mid-1880s and prepared the way for 'new unionism'? Part of the answer to these questions can be found in the revival of socialism in Britain. In 1880 virtually no British working men could be described as socialists and middle-class and upper-class socialists were very few and very eccentric.[39] In 1881, however, H. M. Hyndman, a disciple of

Marx, helped to found the Democratic Federation which adopted a socialist programme in 1884 and changed its name to the Social Democratic Federation. From its start the SDF was handicapped by factiousness and by strategic miscalculations. Some members dreamt of leading mass uprisings, others favoured peaceful change. The majority of them dismissed trade unions as bastions of Liberal capitalism, a minority plotted their infiltration.[40] A few trade unionists joined, including Burns and Mann of the ASE, but attacks on unionism and upon Gladstonian Liberalism alienated many others and the total SDF membership (predominantly middle-class) never exceeded 1,000 in the 1880s. The Fabian Society, founded in 1884, was even smaller and more emphatically middle-class. Fabians were socialists of the kind prepared to work for gradual reform within constitutional bounds. They were less seen among the workers than were members of the SDF, but they were also less contemptuous of unionism and the Lib-Lab alliance. Not surprisingly, the two organizations soon fell to squabbling over the feasibility and propriety of instigating violent change. Tentative and discordant although it was, the socialist revival encouraged working-class critics of orthodox trade unionism. Socialism flattered them by assurances of their crucial role in social change, it encouraged talk of government intervention and an independent labour party, and gave order and a philosophy to their unstructured criticisms.

Even before the socialist revival began, employers and politicians as well as trade unionists had begun to question current solutions to economic distress.[41] Prolonged bad trade undermined confidence in *laissez-faire*, and government intervention came to be regarded as less of a heresy. The changed intellectual climate provided a more favourable environment for radical attacks on the union establishment and is another part of the background to 'new unionism'. Heavy unemployment prompted trade union radicals and middle-class socialists to launch a campaign demanding an eight-hour day. This claim represented far more than an attempt to spread available employment and was to assume considerable symbolic importance. The socialists championed it because it included a veiled attack upon liberalism (it implied government intervention), and thus also upon establishment trade unionism. The campaign was designed to appeal equally to unorganized workers and to rank and file unionists. Both were threatened by unemployment and unionists were resentful of attempts to increase work intensity in response to foreign competition. London, where the SDF was strongest and where the unskilled were suffering particularly from unemployment, saw the most serious manifestations of discontent.[42] Hyndman, Burns, and Mann led a series of unemployment protest meetings and in February 1886 the SDF lost control of a large gathering which for several hours ran wild through the West End, a worse riot than that of 1866. Propertied London was more disturbed than at any time since Chartism. In November of the following year there was the

'Bloody Sunday' episode when police and soldiers dispersed an attempt to hold a banned meeting in Trafalgar Square. Incidents like these brought the socialists considerable publicity.

The TUC saw little evidence of the coming turmoil until the 1886 meeting at Hull which began with a Presidential[43] address advocating the eight-hour day and deploring the gap between unionists and the unskilled. The following Congress began with another radical introductory address, which included an unequivocal call for an independent labour party, and was remarkable also for the first appearance of Keir Hardie, representing the Ayrshire miners. Hardie launched a bitter attack upon Broadhurst and, by implication, upon several of the Liberal principles that he and most other delegates held dear. The attack was easily dismissed, but the struggle between 'new unionism' and old unionism had clearly commenced.

v · *The reformist tradition; the retreat from class consciousness and the re-awakening of the 1880s; the labour aristocracy; social mobility, 1850–88*

The course of the struggle between 'new' and old unionism was to have significant repercussions upon working-class consciousness. In 1888, however, it was only beginning and we have yet to consider the extent of class consciousness, and other questions relating to 'class', in the preceding forty years.

Although there was little change in the political attitudes of trade unionists around mid-century (above, p. 260) there was, of course, a rather more significant change in the attitudes of the great majority of workers who were not trade unionists. This change is immediately obvious if we consider again two questions that were discussed in Chapter 7 – how close was working-class revolution and was there *a* working-class?* From the 1850s the prospect of revolution, never very great earlier in the century, receded significantly. Working-class radicalism survived, but those who advocated fundamental change now had far less influence upon the mass of workers. In 1884 the SDF was established and there was again some talk of bloody revolution in Britain. But the SDF was numerically insignificant and its attacks on Gladstone repulsed many even of the more 'extremist' working men of London's radical clubs. Working-class consciousness, which reached a peak during the Chartist campaigns, declined at the same time as revolutionary threats: 'the English proletariat', wrote Engels to Marx in 1858, 'is becoming more and more bourgeois ... this most bourgeois of all nations is apparently aiming ultimately at the possession of a bourgeois aristocracy and a bourgeois proletariat *as well* as a bourgeoisie.'[44]

---

* On the definition of 'working class' see above, p. 245.

Some influences that might at first appear to have been conducive to greater working-class consciousness continued in the second half of the century. Residential segregation, industrialization, and the size of the average business unit still increased, and trade unions grew stronger and combined together at the TUC. But these trends did not necessarily increase class consciousness. The owner-occupying, shareholding, working-class Lancashire Tories, eager 'to rise out of the wage-earning class and accustomed to adopting the views of the local mill-owners and landlords',[45] are evidence that the advance of the urban factory system was by no means synonymous with increased class consciousness. Larger business units required hierarchies of overlookers, foremen, and clerks who were not clearly working-class or middle-class. And trade union expansion occurred with no lessening of the sectional spirit that had been one of the obstacles to the creation of 'class' before 1850.

Several other forces inhibiting class consciousness continued to be influential after 1850. Religion maintained a very considerable hold until the end of the century[46] and there was no slackening in the determination of churches and charitable bodies to go among the poor. Domestic service, whose stultifying effect upon the development of class consciousness we noted earlier, did not begin to decline in importance until the 1880s and by that time the proportion of manual workers in the labour force (the part in which working-class consciousness was most likely to develop) had probably already begun to fall as the numbers in other service occupations – the teachers, clerks, policemen, shop assistants, postmen and the rest – grew rapidly. Many in the expanding service occupations worked almost as closely with their employers as domestic servants and most of them were conservative and deferential. Real wages, moreover, had begun to rise around mid-century and continued to improve into the 1890s.

By the 1880s there were signs of increasing working-class consciousness. There was the criticism of the Lib-Lab alliance noted above and the accelerated introduction of new manufacturing techniques was reducing differences among the working classes by multiplying the number of semi-skilled workers and undermining the status of engineers and other 'labour aristocrats'. There was even a revolt against middle-class control and patronage in the working men's club movement.[47] However, there was still a very long way to go before all the ground lost since 1848 could be reclaimed. Workers' voting patterns were still determined more by religion and sectional advantage than by class, and it was in 1889 that Engels described the British class structure as divided into 'innumerable gradations each recognized without question, each with its own pride ... its inborn respect for its "betters" and "superiors"'.[48]

Engel's 'innumerable gradations' deserve emphasis, particularly when discussing the 'labour aristocracy'. In the past this group received more than their share of attention from historians, who sometimes assumed it to represent all organized workers. Its size and distinguishing characteristics are now more generally acknowledged, but there are dangers that old misconceptions are being replaced by others that exaggerate the distinction between the labour aristocracy and other classes and the homogeneity within their respective ranks.

The upper boundary of the labour aristocracy was not well defined – indeed, contemporaries sometimes classified artisans among the lower middle classes.[49] Many white-collar workers earned no more than the better-paid labour aristocrats and many of them were the sons and daughters of labour aristocrats.[50] The dividing line between the labour aristocrats and other workers was equally obscure. In certain traditional occupations, and a few new ones, where the labour force consisted of only aristocrats and unskilled labourers it was absolutely clear. But in most occupations, and in the wider working-class community, there were numerous workers of intermediate social status: painters, warehousemen, many railway workers and miners, and most male factory hands all fell into this category. The aristocratic society men naturally claimed that they were a clear cut above non-society men who did similar work, but in fact there was little between them in many cases. Trade unionism everywhere advanced and retreated with the trade cycle, and in high-wage districts non-union tradesmen (and many semi-skilled workers) were paid more than fully-fledged aristocrats received in less prosperous districts. Entry to the labour aristocracy was also not as difficult as it is sometimes said to have been. Apprenticeship was on the wane in the second half of the century and numerous 'mates', 'helpers', and self-proclaimed 'tradesmen' who picked up a trade (including Robert Applegarth, leader of the Junta) were admitted into 'aristocratic' societies. Differences between labour aristocrats and other workers were obscured also, of course, by the distinctions that existed within every occupational group between the thrifty, temperate, chapel-going men and all the various stages of lesser respectability.[51]

There are two other misconceptions concerning the labour aristocracy. The first, the supposition that it somehow sprang into existence at about the time of the Great Exhibition, has been touched upon already. The labour aristocracy was perhaps becoming rather more distinguishable at this time: there were fewer opportunities to become 'master craftsmen', more skilled workers were joining exclusive unions and friendly societies, craft unions were becoming rather more sober and circumspect, and the craft wage-differential may have begun to increase very slightly. But the skilled workers of the 1820s were in most respects very little different from those of the 1860s, and the distinctions between them and other workers did not change significantly over this period.

The other misconception is the supposition that in the second half of the century the labour aristocracy was somehow responsible for diverting less-skilled workers from a far more militant path than that they actually followed. This belief is sometimes accompanied by the further supposition that the labour aristocrats themselves were induced (or 'bribed') to embrace reformism by increases in their living standards significantly greater than those obtained by other workers. The latter argument rests upon very flimsy evidence because skilled workers were wedded to reformism long before differentials widened and the increase in differentials added very little to their already substantial advantages.[52] The overall influence of the labour aristocrats, and of the institutions they established, was doubtless to encourage conciliatory and reformist attitudes. But there is little reason for assuming that the labour aristocracy imposed its values upon other workers – indeed it is frequently criticized for ignoring the unorganized – or that these other classes were necessarily any more inclined than the labour aristocracy to adopt a militant stance. There was little revolutionary potential anywhere among the working classes and the mid-century decline in political radicalism among non-union workers was far more a consequence of the Chartist failure to extract concessions by threats, and of rising real wages, than of any change in the influence of the labour aristocracy. Most workers remained either apolitical or reformist in the following decades because they did not feel that they were oppressed, because they respected the classes above them, because they were not seriously dissatisfied with the pace of material and political advance, and because their grievances could usually be remedied by constitutional means. The labour aristocracy, and indeed the middle classes, had very similar attitudes for very similar reasons.

Whether the mid-century retreat from class consciousness was accompanied by greater or less social mobility we cannot be certain. There is rather more evidence about social mobility in these years than for the first half of the century (above, pp. 245–6) but it is equally difficult to interpret.[53] For this period, as for the years before 1850, historians have relied heavily on evidence of the rate of movement from the working classes to the upper reaches of the social hierarchy and particularly upon evidence of the number of poor men who became industrial employers. The evidence suggests that social mobility of this kind probably declined in the second half of the century as the increasing size of industrial units placed greater obstacles in the paths of talented workers seeking to emulate the self-made men of the early industrial revolution.[54] Moreover, opportunities to move from the bottom to the top of the social hierarchy in other spheres were perhaps also declining (in England and Wales if not in Scotland) as the grammar schools raised financial barriers to poor scholars. The second half of the century has been described as the most difficult time for a poor boy to make his way to Oxford or Cambridge.[55]

But there is far more to social mobility than counting the number of self-made industrialists. And even this issue is by no means resolved. Against the points marshalled by Perkin there is considerable local evidence of the persistence of opportunities by which working men could enter the employing classes if they began in more promising sectors than steel manufacture.[56] At Edinburgh there was little or no increase between 1871 and 1901 in the size of firms engaged in masonry, joinery, painting, engineering, and shoemaking. In Lancashire the average size of mills had increased, but credit was plentiful, plant, space, and power could each be hired, and some three-quarters of those who were weaving employers in 1912 were said to have risen from 'the operative classes or from classes earning no more than the operative'.[57] Moreover, by the last quarter of the century the greatest opportunities of dramatic social mobility were proably not in manufacturing industry but in the faster-growing service sector. The accelerated promotion of working men into influential government and administrative offices that was noted earlier gives some indication of the opportunities in one part of this sector. So many union leaders experienced social mobility of this kind that their elevation has recently been treated as of major significance in nineteenth-century trade union history.[58]

Promotion into the lower middle classes was a far more common experience than mobility of the 'rags to riches' kind. Demand for white-collar labour increased rapidly from the 1870s and a substantial part of the demand was met from the working classes. Many individuals made the transition, but it probably more often occurred over a generation as workers' sons and daughters entered lower middle-class employment from school. Indications of the magnitude of this population 'drawn from the manual working-class into the ranks of independent workers, shop assistants, clerks, teachers, and other occupations'[59] can be seen, among other places, in Hugh McLeod's figures which show that 40 to 50 per cent of white-collar grooms who were married in various Birmingham and London churches around the turn of the century were the sons of working-class fathers.[60] The Webbs had such men in mind when they drew attention to the increased opportunities for advancement in the bureaucracies of the larger late nineteenth-century industrial undertakings, opportunities which they regarded as more than adequate compensation for the lesser chance of working men becoming industrial employers.[61] Such mobility was helped by compulsory elementary schooling and by the expansion in technical education.

Most working-class social mobility probably took place *within* the working classes. Mobility of this kind took several different forms. The greater part of the geographical mobility described in Chapter 5 embraced movement to better-paid work, and the countless farm labourers who found secure and relatively well-paid employment on the railways, in urban police forces, and elsewhere in Britain and overseas were outstanding among those who advanced in this way.[62] At the same time their daughters were flocking to become domestic servants in the towns where they became familiar with middle-class manners and increased their eligibility by sufficient for many of them to marry men of higher status than their fathers. Migration and emigration both increased in the second half of the century and there was also a decline in the proportion of jobs demanding the minimum of skill (above, pp. 30, 146–7). It was because better-paid work accounted for a significantly growing proportion of all employment that Bowley and other wage historians assessed the rise in real wages after 1850 at far above the average of the increase in individual occupations (above, p. 74). Some workers improved their standing without spatial or occupational mobility. They did so by 'self-help': by saving and insuring; by devoting a part of their increased incomes to clothing, cleanliness, the home, and their children's education; and by joining friendly societies, co-operative societies, and trade unions. The expansion and growing influence of working-class institutions, and their gradual acceptance by government and employers, was a part of the wider process of social mobility.

When these various aspects of social mobility are considered together the impression is that the total perhaps increased in the second half of the century. Social mobility was possibly one of the causes of social equipoise. The enormous variety of experience in this respect has been hardly touched upon. There were, of course, losers as well as gainers and those labour aristocrats whose status was reduced by changes in technology were probably prominent among the losers. The labour aristocrats' status may have been further reduced, and they may have been pushed closer towards working-class consciousness, by the increased number of lower middle-class employees. Hobsbawm sees this development 'driving a wedge of white-collar workers . . . between the labour aristocrats and the "masters", reducing their relative social position, and limiting their chances of promotion'.[63] There are, however, several reasons for suggesting that the influence of this development was probably not substantial. First, the lower middle classes were a rag-bag of heterogeneous occupational groups.[64] Such a 'class' was probably not sufficiently co-ordinated to have been felt as a serious threat by labour aristocrats. Secondly, the type of artisan social mobility that the lower middle classes were most likely to have impeded was not of crucial importance. Labour aristocrats looked first to improvements in status and respectability within the artisan class.[65] Thirdly, whatever impediment the expansion of the lower middle classes imposed upon artisan aspirations was probably outweighed by the greater opportunities it provided for their children. The social mobility of their own kin would hardly cause artisan resentment of the class they were entering or encourage artisans to feel a greater affinity with the unskilled. They were more likely to feel that their whole family had advanced in status and respectability.

VI · *Industrial relations; collective bargaining before 1860; the Nottingham Hosiery Board and the expansion of collective bargaining; the weaknesses of British industrial relations*

One sign of improved class relations after mid-century was the great enthusiasm for formal collective bargaining arrangements whose purpose was to avoid industrial conflict. This section attempts to answer questions about industrial relations procedures in the nineteenth century. How did workers and employers resolve differences that arose between them? What were the consequences for industrial efficiency? And do developments in industrial relations before 1890 contain any clues to the causes of either the breakdown in relations before the First World War or Britain's more recent industrial relations problems?

The majority of workers were not much affected by formal collective bargaining at any time in the nineteenth century.[66] After 1860, however, a substantial minority came to be influenced by joint negotiating boards, conciliation and arbitration agreements, and other procedures designed to prevent disputes and to settle differences without resort to strike or lock-out. The main reason why there was so little institutionalized collective bargaining before 1860 was that few workers were then members of strong trade unions. Most forms of collective bargaining required major concessions from employers: they had usually to recognize a trade union and implicitly sanction its existence, they had also to surrender their absolute power at the workplace and, very often, to negotiate with strangers representing their own workmen. Employers, therefore, were not inclined to accept collective bargaining until they encountered opposition strong enough to force them to the negotiating table. Unions like the GNCTU and the Operative Builders (above pp. 201–3) were too weak to compel employers to negotiate. Moreover, they had insufficient hold over their members to ensure that agreements would be respected and the changes they sought were too sweeping to be suitable subjects for collective bargaining. The early craftsmen's unions were stronger and more respected, but many of them were very small and the majority of their members worked in small undertakings where there were adequate informal relations with the employer.

For these reasons there was little formal collective bargaining before mid-century. The Scottish cotton masters and the northern carpet manufacturers allowed workers' representatives to attend annual discussions on piece-rates in the 1830s and there were elementary arbitration and conciliation arrangements in the Potteries. In the 1850s parts of the shipbuilding, printing, and silk trades, as well as pottery manufacture, were covered by boards of arbitration, and the National Association of United Trades (above p. 204) publicized such arrangements and helped to spread the practice of calling upon barristers or other acceptable third parties to settle disputes. But the first conciliation and arbitration board of lasting importance was that established in the Nottingham hosiery trade in 1860.

Another feature of early industrial relations was the very limited extent of government intervention. Measures providing for compulsory arbitration were enacted as late as 1824. But such matters were coming to be considered outside the government's responsibility. The legislation of 1824 remained unused and the government subsequently did very little either to protect the weaker party in industrial disputes or to prevent the two sides pursuing their respective ends regardless of the public interest. It could have done far more: the French government, for example, combined severe restrictions upon trade unions with considerable intervention in industrial relations. At this time few British trade unions would have resisted government intervention. Most unions were too weak to force employers to negotiate and they were prominent among those calling for compulsory arbitration and conciliation.

The Nottingham Hosiery Board of 1860 was the inspiration of A. J. Mundella, a hosiery employer. It consisted of equal numbers of employers and workmen under Mundella's chairmanship, and was greatly assisted by a committee of two employers and two workmen which investigated disputes (and often settled them) before they came before the board. Mundella's initiative was significant in several respects: the board brought harmony to an industry notorious for strife, it continued to operate successfully for many years after the period of initial euphoria, and its success ensured that it was widely imitated. It was notable too for placing more emphasis upon conciliation than upon arbitration: the chairman's casting vote could resolve deadlocks but both sides regarded its use as a regrettable last resort. Other hosiery manufacturing districts and the Nottingham lace trade were among the first to adopt similar arrangements, and in the mid-1860s they spread to the Wolverhampton and Worcestershire building trades. Several coalfields were also influenced by Mundella's example and in 1869 the North of England Iron and Steel Board was established. This proved to be probably the most successful and enduring of all nineteenth-century conciliation and arbitration institutions. In the 1870s collective bargaining spread rapidly wherever trade unionism had a hold: the extension of the franchise; the good impression created by the unions at the 1867–9 Royal Commission; the Conspiracy and

Protection of Property Act of 1875; the increase in company and union size, and the tendency of both unions and employers to combine on a district or trade basis, all gave impetus to the expansion. Numerous employers and unions, several trades councils, and even George Potter, recorded their approval of collective bargaining and called for its extension.[67] Those seeking to terminate a dispute or establish a joint board could by this time call upon a whole corps of trusted conciliators with a record of successful intervention and considerable subtlety in important details like seating arrangements and the timing of refreshments.

This expansion, which continued in the 1880s, saw a great assortment of collective bargaining procedures although some variation on the Nottingham hosiery model remained the most popular arrangement. Certain trade unions and trades councils at times engaged in collective bargaining on demarcation disputes and similar issues in which employers were not directly involved. Another form of collective bargaining fixed wages by product-prices according to a 'sliding scale'. The last arrangement was adopted particularly in industries like mining and iron and steel manufacture that were subject to violent fluctuations in prices and demand and to the labour unrest that tended to accompany such fluctuations. Some sliding scale arrangements (such as that operating on the north-east coalfield) were operated with the support of strong unions, but some others (that covering the South Wales coalfield for example) were imposed upon weak or unorganized workers and, by providing a seemingly automatic wages-regulator, helped to keep labour weak. Most of the handful of profit-sharing schemes that appeared before 1890 were also found in the coal and iron and steel industries and these, quite clearly, were introduced partly in the hope of driving a wedge between the men and their unions.[68]

Why did unions and employers take to collective bargaining with such enthusiasm? Most collective bargaining was welcomed by the unions, much of it was initiated by them, and on balance it brought them considerable benefit: the inaugural TUC (1868) approved a paper on collective bargaining and at the Bradford meeting twenty years later a resolution in favour of its extension was carried almost unanimously. The sliding scale arrangements that were introduced to a union's disadvantage were exceptions to the general pattern.[69] Besides the fundamental prize of recognition and negotiating rights, most collective bargaining brought unions several other advantages. The measure of employer approval implicit in collective bargaining was a stimulus to recruitment and so was the fact that the union in effect negotiated on behalf of unorganized workers as well as their members. Collective bargaining was also recognition that unions might prevent strikes, an acknowledgement welcome both for its own sake and because public approval prepared the way for further legislative advance. By lessening strife, collective bargaining also increased union life-expectancy and reduced a major drain on the funds available for pensions and other benefits. Union leaders appreciated also that centralized bargaining increased their own status and diminished the power of those recalcitrant branches whose inclination to fight blindly, and without regard to cost, had so often proved fatal in the past.

On their side, employers soon realized that collective bargaining had more advantages than the settlement of disputes without loss of output. Experience of working together fostered goodwill among the workers' representatives and a readiness to understand the employer's viewpoint. And while union officials drove a hard bargain, employers found them pragmatic and business-like, not without regard for the company's long-run survival, and usually prepared to reach a compromise and see that it was maintained. These qualities offered certain advantages over dealings with unorganized workers, who were perhaps weaker and less articulate than union spokesmen but who were also more emotive and more likely to disrupt output with lightning strikes and sporadic guerrilla warfare. Collective bargaining on a town or district basis had the additional attraction that it did not directly impinge upon the employer's managerial prerogatives within his own workshop. Moreover, in bargaining of this kind he and his immediate competitors made identical concessions and to this extent union gains did not worsen his competitive standing. In addition, of course, employers who met together to negotiate with the unions had ample opportunity to remove some of the sting from their concessions by arranging a collective adjustment of prices.

These various advantages were obviously appreciated most by employers who stood to lose most from disruption of output: those that is, in parts of the market where labour was strong, where production was heavily capitalized, and where great fluctuations in demand necessitated constant changes in wages. Employers had less incentive to accept collective bargaining arrangements where workers were unorganized or weakly organized, or where wages accounted for a large part of total costs and thus bore a large part of the cost of strikes. A similar variety of attitudes existed among trade unionists. By and large, the weaker and non-craft unions were keener to initiate and maintain collective bargaining than unions whose recognition and survival were not in doubt and whose interests could be protected by craft rules. Cotton weavers, for example, put far more emphasis upon collective bargaining than the aristocratic spinners.

Collective bargaining arrangements worked best when trade was buoyant and in the 'honeymoon' period after they were established, especially if they were established in the wake of costly strife. When prices were falling, and wages with them, both sides were likely to be more impatient of the restrictions that such arrangements imposed. Rank and file unionists then became particularly resentful of restraints upon their freedom to strike against wage cuts and employers were aware that rising unemployment and falling orders enabled them to reduce wages and withstand strikes at little cost and with every prospect of victory. Employers were generally less inclined to combine together than workers[70] and several collective bargaining agreements were ended by employers breaking loose during trade depressions.[71] There were also certain 'issues of principle' upon which collective bargaining was apt to founder because they were regarded as non-negotiable by one side or the other. Many employers considered discussion of profit levels improper; unions felt similarly about their 'rights' to certain work, and the skilled unions reacted strongly to almost any serious threat to craft privileges.

Although collective bargaining was doubtless a great advance on more primitive methods of settling disputes, by the 1880s there were signs of certain shortcomings that later proved important. Two of these shortcomings were associated with the transfer of collective bargaining from the workshop (where disputes originated) to periodic meetings of delegates representing the workmen and employers of a whole city or larger area. This arrangement was encouraged by the dearth of industrial or plant unions in Britain, and by the strength of craft unionism which emphasized the similarities among fellow-craftsmen (wherever they worked) and the differences between craftsmen and their unskilled workmates. It was encouraged also by employers for reasons already noted. The first adverse consequence of collective bargaining of this kind was that it tended to give rise to rank and file frustration caused by the delays in resolving grievances that were inseparable from such arrangements and by a sense of isolation from those acting on their behalf. Unions seldom appointed anyone to act for members in everyday dealings with management and many union negotiators were full-time officials. These officials developed great expertise in bargaining and in the technical intricacies of production. Such skills were necessary if they were to safeguard rank and file interests – but in acquiring them there was a danger that union officials would lose contact with those they were representing. In short, the form of collective bargaining that developed in Britain tended to create what E. H. Phelps Brown has described as the 'gap at shopfloor level',[72] a gap that shop stewards and unofficial workmen's representatives were eventually to fill, in some cases with distinctly unfavourable consequences. This problem was not yet serious in 1890 because most collective bargaining was still restricted to a city or locality, but it was to become serious as the scale of bargaining widened. The other adverse consequence of the way centralized collective bargaining developed was that because bargaining took place away from the workshop, because it allowed wage increases to be granted with little loss of competitiveness, and because it facilitated offsetting wage increases by price increases, it occurred without much emphasis being attached to the desirability of linking improvements in money wages to increases in physical productivity.

A further potential weakness in British industrial relations was the continuing low level of government intervention. In 1867 and 1872 two acts were introduced which, like the legislation of 1824 (above, p. 282), included elements of compulsion. But they were almost entirely ignored and have little significance except as the last feeble nineteenth-century gesture in the direction of compulsory conciliation and arbitration backed by legal sanctions. We can see here, of course, the influence of *laissez-faire*. But *laissez-faire* had not prevented widespread government intervention in other areas and by the 1880s it was everywhere in retreat. Perhaps more important, therefore, in determining the government's negative approach to industrial relations was the absence of any pressing reasons for it to act otherwise at this time. Industrial unrest was not a major threat to public safety, public welfare, or public order. Most areas of employment that were much afflicted by disputes sooner or later established voluntary collective bargaining and on the whole these arrangements functioned satisfactorily. There was no strong evidence that British industrial relations compared badly with those in countries where the government and courts were more active, and the unions' readiness to compromise on most issues, and their regard for the burden that strikes imposed upon their own funds and members' pockets, restricted the number and duration of disputes. Moreover, the unions still gave considerable regard to the consequences of their actions upon the public. The scale of individual outbreaks was also restricted by the virtual absence of political strikes, by the prevalence of local collective bargaining, and by the strongly sectionalist tendencies that discouraged the 'sympathy strike' and prevented the TUC co-ordinating strike action on a national scale. The limits to mechanization and to economic integration generally at this time were further restraints upon the economic disruption that strikes could cause. For all of these reasons the government saw little need to adopt a more positive approach to industrial relations. In some respects collective bargaining in the second half of the nineteenth century had worked all too well.

VII · *Contribution of unions and other working-class movements to working-class welfare, 1850–88; unions and productivity; the union performance; the effect of unionism upon unorganized workers*

What were the consequences of trade unionism upon its members' living standards between 1850 and 1888? And what was its influence upon those outside its ranks? In Chapter 6 it was suggested that the contribution of trade unionism to working-class welfare before 1850 was not great. In the second half of the century the influence of the unions was far more substantial, although the friendly societies, the co-operative societies, the temperance and charity crusades and similar movements, taken together, probably still made a greater contribution to working-class welfare.

Friendly societies had a more restricted role than the unions but they had far more members. Whereas no more than 10 per cent of adult males were unionists in 1888, the great majority (probably 80 per cent or more) belonged to a friendly society.[73] Friendly societies continued to offer a combination of insurance, respectability, and club fellowship. Their convivial activities were declining by the 1880s, but the sheer size of the increasingly important nationwide affiliated orders (the Oddfellows, the Manchester Unity, and the Foresters), and their gradual understanding of actuarial science, were removing some of the uncertainty from working-class insurance. The co-operative movement was less important than the friendly societies, but had grown rapidly in the second half of the century with the expansion of Rochdale-type co-operative retailing (above, p. 210). By 1890 membership was not far short of a million, or about the same number as there were trade unionists. Some leading figures in the co-operative movement were active in Liberal politics and individual societies occasionally gave credit to those on strike and found jobs for strike victims. But the co-operative movement's chief function was providing groceries and its place in members' lives hardly compares with that occupied by the unions. Apart from a few rather half-hearted trade union attempts at co-operative production, and some similar schemes initiated by middle-class idealists, there was little co-operative activity after 1850 of which Robert Owen would have been proud. Few workers seem to have had much interest in becoming their own boss and most attempts at co-operative production appear to have been incompetent.[74]

Perhaps the most remarkable aspect of the union influence upon working-class welfare is how little it has been seriously considered. Too many union histories are mainly descriptive and in many others the analysis stops short of this central question. Some accounts, without broaching the issue directly, convey the impression that the unions were responsible for the greater part of all advances in working-class welfare: 'the union is known by its fruits', wrote the Countess of Warwick in her preface to Joseph Arch's autobiography (1898). 'We have only to compare the condition of the agricultural labourer before the Union was started with his condition today to see that these fruits are manifold.' This claim is obviously exaggerated. But how much influence was wielded by societies more formidable than the National Agricultural Labourers Union?

By combining the bargaining strength of individual workers, by controls upon labour supply, and by their willingness to accept (and relieve) unemployment among their members in preference to reducing the standard rate, some unions were able to exercise a considerable influence on wages in the second half of the nineteenth century. Working hours and working conditions were also improved by combination and we saw earlier how the unions were instrumental in securing legislation on safety at work and the removal of the most onerous legal restraints upon their activities. They had a part too in securing the franchise extensions that made governments more mindful of working-class interests and accelerated public spending upon health, education, and other collective services. In addition, of course, they continued to provide friendly society facilities, libraries, lectures, labour market information, and other aids to security and status.

But is this influence measurable? Much of it clearly cannot be measured. Who could put a figure upon the benefits that workers derived from the extension of the franchise? The unions' effect upon wages might appear to be more measurable but, in fact, there are many difficulties in quantifying even this part of their influence. The size of the increase in the differential between craftsmen's wages and labourers' wages that occurred after 1840, for example, was doubtless in part the result of organization among the craftsmen – but it was the result also of the influence of several other market forces that tended either to widen or to reduce the differential.

Another approach sometimes used in an attempt to measure the union influence upon wages is to examine the relative shares of labour and capital in the national income. The figures available show remarkably little long-term change until after the First World War and contain no evidence that labour's share increased in step with increased unionization.[75] Their implication would seem to be that the union impact upon pay was far less than most trade union historians suppose. Economists point out that when employers have substantial control over prices they can fairly easily defend profits from the consequences of union ability to raise wages. In times of buoyant demand higher wages are easily met by raising prices. In less prosperous times, when prices are less easily raised, the unions are weaker, less likely to press for wage increases, and more easily beaten. Moreover, should unions succeed in raising wages at the expense of profits, their success is likely to cause a fall in investment that will in turn reduce employment and wages and thus tend to restore the original ratio between pay and profits. Similarly, exceptional rises in profits may temporarily disturb the long-term ratio but higher profits will then tend to encourage greater investment with associated increases in employment and wages.[76]

These suggested mechanisms, theoretical although they are, appear to lend some plausibility to the apparent stability of labour's share of the national income. But economists also put emphasis upon what is termed the 'impact effect' of unionism. They suggest that in most labour markets (and especially in those where customary influences are strong) many unorganized workers are paid less than the 'economic wage': that is, less than employers could afford to pay with existing technology and without reducing their profits below the average market rate. In such cases initial organization might be expected to have a considerable once and for all 'impact effect' on wage rates, and on the relative shares of labour and profit, as wages are raised to what the market will bear.[77] Given the great influence of custom in the British labour market of the nineteenth century, and given the long-term union expansion into districts and occupations previously unorganized, it might reasonably be expected that labour's share of the national income should have increased despite the stabilizing influences that have been noted.

There are, in fact, good reasons for treating statistics that profess to show how the national income was divided in the nineteenth century with considerable reservation. Above all, there is the obvious fact that disaggregation of the national income into factor shares is bedevilled by formidable statistical and methodological difficulties.[78] At a time when trade unionists' pay was a very small proportion of the national income (probably well under 5 per cent for most of the nineteenth century) the margin of error in the final figures is more than sufficient to obscure a considerable increase in their share of the total. Worth noting also is that working hours were falling and working-class children were being withdrawn from the labour force: holding steady labour's share of the national income was a minor achievement in itself. There are too, of course, various ways in which the unions could, and probably did, improve their members' pay without necessarily affecting the proportion of the national income that went to labour. Clearly they could affect the way that total pay was divided between organized and unorganized workers: craft wage differentials and other union wage advantages dependent upon excluding outsiders were met at least partly from the pockets of excluded workers. Encouraging a proportion of their members to emigrate; securing wage increases in return for the cessation of restrictive practices; and successfully demanding increases that stimulated employers to introduce sufficient improvement in methods to restore profit levels, were other ways in which trade unionists' pay might be increased without necessarily affecting the ratio of total pay to total profits.

Clearly neither the overall influence of unions upon members' welfare, nor their influence upon wages alone, can be measured. Their influence was certainly far greater than might be deduced by examining the available statistics of long-term changes in labour's share of the national income and it was doubtless greater in the decades after 1850 than it had been earlier in the century. We must remember, however, that organized workers were still a small minority in the labour force and that their union strength was still more a consequence of their relatively strong market position than its cause. Wages of unionists and non-unionists alike continued to be determined largely by far stronger forces: by fundamental changes in the demand for different categories of labour and especially by the long-term increase in productivity.

Improved productivity was the chief source of increases in real wages, outweighing by far the consequences of any union redistribution of the national income. So far union influence upon wages has been discussed as if the size of the total national income was determined exogenously. But unions can clearly affect the total sum available for redistribution. We need, therefore, to examine the effect of unionism upon productivity. Before 1850 unions were too weak to have had much influence on productivity. After 1850, however, their influence was greater and allegations that unions impeded economic progress became more common, particularly when the public became especially aware of foreign competition. The poor showing of British products at the 1867 Paris Exhibition, for example, helped to swell the chorus of anti-unionism provoked by the 'Sheffield Outrages'. Strikes drew particular attention. But loss of output by strikes was not very great and the more persistent and informed complaints were of impediments to efficient working that were backed by the threat of disruption should management attempt their removal.

Among these impediments were restrictions upon the employment of women, unskilled labour, apprentices, and men from outside the district. There were also restrictions, explicit or tacit, on the amount of effort expended: the Manchester Bricklayers Association decreed (1869) that 'any man found running or working beyond a regular speed shall be fined 2s 6d'.[79] Perhaps most resented of all were the restrictions unions placed on mechanization. Some unions attempted an outright ban upon certain machines: cases of the masons refusing to handle machine-finished stone, and carpenters machine-made window frames, were cited before the 1867–9 Royal Commission. More common were instances in which the use of machinery was accepted subject to stringent conditions. Unions might insist that a machine which did the work of skilled men should be manned by skilled men, whether or not their skills were necessary. Or that if it could do the work of four men working by hand then it should be operated by four men, even if the Americans and Germans managed with two. Similarly, they might insist that machine operatives should receive the same piece-rates as handworkers, notwithstanding the greater productivity the machine made possible. The Sheffield unions, notoriously unsympathetic to change, drove several employers to the Birmingham district where labour was more co-operative,[80] and a spokesman from the boot and shoe manufacturers summed up employers' frustrations in an attack upon the unions cited by the Webbs:

The men working the machines exercise all their ingenuity in making machine work as expensive as hand labour. There exists . . . a tacit

understanding that only so much work shall be done within a certain time
. . . . The unions are engaged in a gigantic conspiracy to hinder and retard
the development of labour-saving appliances in this country . . . . It seems to
be a settled policy with the men not to try to earn as much money as possible
per week, but as much as possible per job, in other words to keep the costs of
production as high as possible.[81]

That, of course, was one side of the account. There was another side also,
part of which was indicated in discussing the employers' enthusiasm for
collective bargaining arrangements because they brought order and certainty
to industrial relations. Clearly, a distinction must be drawn between
inefficiency caused by the unions and that which arose from labour force
characteristics no less obvious among unorganized workers. The unions had a
considerable part in the introduction and operation of successful collective
bargaining arrangements[82] and there is evidence that union leaders sometimes
acted as a check upon rank and file members who were less disposed to accept
new methods and more determined to defend traditional privileges. The
Northumberland and Durham mining unions and the Lancashire cotton
unions, in particular, appear to have been well aware of the long-term
consequences of intransigence over methods of working. British trade unions
did not pursue industrial chaos for political ends,[83] and in 1880 the
characteristics of organized labour in parts of Europe were still regarded as
more damaging to economic efficiency than the shortcomings of the British
unions. When Frenchmen spoke of 'the English disease' at this time they had
in mind not bad industrial relations but tuberculosis.

Even militancy sometimes had beneficial consequences for industrial
efficiency. If unions pressed for more wages in an orderly fashion and without
at the same time resisting changes in methods they could (if unwittingly) be the
cause of increased productivity by encouraging employers to search for ways
of offsetting their impositions and by forcing the least efficient among them
out of business. We can note too union claims that they improved labour
quality by insisting upon apprenticeship, by helping to bring about improved
education, and by shortening the working day and thus reducing fatigue. The
employers' share of responsibility must also be taken into account in any
attempt to put allegations of union obstructiveness into perspective. Many
disputes over the introduction of machinery could have been avoided by
greater subtlety on the employers' part, by greater understanding of the
workmen's proprietorial feelings towards their work, and greater willingness
to compensate for its removal. Some employers, including the boot and shoe
manufacturers who were so loud in their denunciation of union 'conspiracy'
(above, p. 290), were equally guilty of attempting to monopolize the benefits
of technical advance.[84]

Where does all this leave us? Clearly unions retarded economic growth in certain ways between 1850 and 1888: in other ways they assisted growth. Their retarding influences may have become dominant by the end of the period: the unions, that is, were possibly reducing the rate of increase in the size of the national cake at the same time as they were winning a larger slice of it for their members. Even so, their influence upon productivity was probably still of no great consequence as the great majority of workers were not members of trade unions. There was cause for concern that union influence upon economic efficiency was growing and might well become formidable. But in 1888 such anxieties were still mainly about what might happen in the future.

Two other questions concerning the union influence on working-class living standards remain to be answered. First, could the unions have achieved much more for their members? It is sometimes alleged that more militant policies would have brought greater benefits, that the unions were too anxious to win public and official approval, too willing to collaborate with employers and Liberal politicians, and over-concerned to safeguard their friendly society funds. Such charges are a main theme of K. Burgess's book, *The Origins of British Industrial Relations* (1975).

Claims such as these rely too much upon exaggerated notions of union docility and of the options available to union leaders. Those who believe that the 'new model' unions were as docile as they appeared before the 1867–9 Royal Commission on Trade Unions merely testify to the effectiveness (and durability) of the Junta's public relations campaign. The 'new model' leaders undoubtedly missed some opportunities: they would have been content to accept the 1867 Reform Act without the 'lodger clause', they were less concerned than George Potter at the restrictions upon strikes in the 1871 Criminal Law Amendment Act, and were slow to appreciate the opportunities that created the 'nine hours' movement of the early 1870s. At most times, however, much greater militancy would probably have been counter-productive. Legislative gains depended upon public approval which was earned by acquiring a reputation for respectability. The history of militant Chartism, and the contrast between its meagre results and the achievements of the 'new model' unions, point unequivocally in this direction. And while the blustering representative of George Potter's unions succeeded only in being expelled from the proceedings of the Royal Commission on Trade Unions, the more subtle 'new model' approach was brilliantly successful. The case for co-operation with the established political parties was touched upon earlier: it was evident not only in the concessions it yielded but also in the electoral fate of working men who stood as independent 'labour' candidates. It is easy to overlook the vulnerability of most unions in the second half of the century, to forget the numerous unorganized craftsmen and semi-skilled workers that could be called upon to replace unionists on strike. Fear of defeat was a constant check upon militancy, and it was felt especially after 1873 when economic conditions worsened and union membership fell by half despite the caution that Burgess and others have condemned.[85]

The remaining question concerns the influence of the unions upon the welfare of unorganized workers between 1850 and 1888. Some accounts see the unionists in the role of pathfinders, removing legal obstacles so that less fortunate workers could eventually profit by the union example and lightening their sufferings meanwhile with a stream of legislative victories. Others, however, portray the unionists selfishly increasing their already substantial advantages (often at the expense of the unorganized) and ignoring lesser workers other than at times when they were a threat to union privileges. There is much to be said for both views. The unions were doubtless motivated primarily by concern for their own members, but many of the legislative advances they helped to obtain, those affecting safety at work for example, undoubtedly benefited most workers. In addition, their cultivation of public opinion prepared the way for subsequent union expansion, and their administrative, financial, and tactical innovations showed others how they might survive in a still hostile environment. And although unionists maintained their differentials partly by excluding unskilled labour, the influence of custom upon differentials resulted in a substantial proportion of union wage increases trickling down to the unskilled.[86] Reductions in hours won by the unions were also likely to be shared by the unskilled because many tasks required skilled and unskilled men to work together. Even when union gains had no immediate effect on the conditions of unorganized workers, their victories established a precedent that made it easier for others to eventually achieve the same advantages. There was also, of course, a certain amount of direct assistance from trade unionists to agricultural labourers and other unskilled workers who were attempting to organize.

But it cannot be denied that such direct assistance from unionists to the unorganized was more the exception than the rule. What might appear to have been the most obvious way of helping other workers – encouraging them to join existing unions – was precluded by the nature of craft unionism. Labour aristocrats believed that the majority of workers were incapable of 'scientific unionism', that their recklessness and indiscipline would make disastrous inroads into union funds if entry barriers were lowered. Thus whatever deliberate help unionists offered the less-skilled workers was mainly directed towards assisting them to form unions of their own. And help of this kind was restricted not only by artisan indifference, but also by perceived and actual conflicts of interest of the kind especially evident where artisans employed their own helpers. It is not surprising, therefore, that some of the less-skilled workers who began to organize at the end of the 1880s looked first for help not to the established unions, but to the socialists.[87] And against the favourable influences of unionism upon the pay of unorganized workers that we have noted must be set the possibly adverse consequences of unionism upon economic growth (slight as it still was), the consequences of overcrowding in the unskilled sector of the labour market due to union exclusiveness, and the unemployment caused by strikes. Unemployment inevitably accompanied strikes, and whereas the comparatively affluent strikers drew their strike benefit and looked forward to the fruits of victory, their unskilled helpers had no strike pay and no direct interest in the outcome of the dispute: 'He has no voice in the organization of these demonstrations, is powerless to prevent them, has no claims upon the funds by which they are supported, and is ever the heaviest sufferer by them.'[88]

On balance the unions probably assisted unorganized workers more than they harmed them. Their exclusiveness and their failure to do much to encourage organization stand out on the debit side – but these shortcomings are probably of less consequence than is often supposed. How much more could the unions have done? And at how much cost to what was being achieved? Attempts by union leaders to remove entry barriers would have encountered formidable rank and file opposition. Such attempts would have undermined the craft-consciousness that was the basis of union cohesiveness and seriously diluted the scarcity value of members' labour that was the basis of union strength. Those like H. A. Turner who write as if only artisan indifference prevented the successful organization of the unskilled give too little weight to these obstacles.[89] Most of all they underestimate the fundamental obstacle of the abundance of unskilled workers, a weakness rediscovered whenever trades councils and middle-class sympathizers attempted to establish labourers' unions. In fact, the most obvious candidates for union membership were not the unskilled workers but the majority of carpenters, printers, engineers, and other artisans who were still outside the unions in 1890 and whose non-organization can hardly be attributed to artisan aloofness. The unions had difficulties enough in organizing fellow artisans. It is unlikely that more 'class-conscious' attitudes would have resulted in many more of the unskilled being successfully organized.

Suggestions for further reading are on pages 403–4.

9

WORKING-CLASS MOVEMENTS, 1889-1914:
'NEW UNIONISM' TO TRIPLE ALLIANCE

I · *Trade union strength and membership, 1889–1914*

The two outstanding developments in the period from 1889 to the First World War were an accelerated growth in trade union membership and the spreading and strengthening of the radicalizing process whose beginnings have already been described. The first of these developments took union membership from about 5 per cent of the labour force (1888) to not far short of one worker in four on the eve of the First World War. The second was marked particularly by the advance of 'new unionism', by the strengthening of independent political attitudes, and by the establishment of the Labour Party. These years were remarkable also for outbreaks of serious labour unrest, most of all in 1910–14.

The increase in membership came mainly in two brief advances. The first of these occurred in 1888–91 and more than doubled membership. Before the end of 1892 membership was falling and it continued to fall until 1895–6 when

Table 9·1   *Great Britain: trade union membership,*
1888–1914 (membership at year end) (thousands)

1888	750 (est.)	1902	2,013
1889	n/a	1903	1,994
1890	n/a	1904	1,967
1891	n/a	1905	1,997
1892	1,576	1906	2,210
1893	1,559	1907	2,513
1894	1,530	1908	2,485
1895	1,504	1909	2,477
1896	1,608	1910	2,565
1897	1,731	1911	3,139
1898	1,752	1912	3,416
1899	1,911	1913	4,135
1900	2,022	1914	4,145
1901	2,025		

Sources: Mitchell and Deane, *Abstract of British Historical Statistics*, p. 68; Clegg, Fox, and Thompson, *A History of British Trade Unions since 1889*, I p. 1.

economic conditions improved and a gradual expansion began that carried the total to two million by 1900. Another period of unsettled economic conditions and relative stagnation in union membership then set in and was not decisively ended until 1910 when the second advance began. This swelled the number of trade unionists by two-thirds in three years. If adult male workers alone are considered, between a third and a half by this time were organized. These unionists comprised what was still by far the strongest labour movement in the world.

Table 9·2 *Trade union membership in 1913:*
Britain, Germany, France, USA

	Union Membership (millions)	Population (millions)
Britain	4.1	40.7 (1911)
Germany	3.3	64.9 (1910)
France	1.1 (est.)	39.1 (1911)
USA	2.6	92.0 (1910)

Sources: Mitchell and Deane, op. cit.; B. R. Mitchell, *European Historical Statistics, 1750–1970,* (1975); *Historical Statistics of the United States: Colonial Times to 1970,* (Washington 1975), Part I; C. M. Cipolla (ed.), *The Emergence of Industrial Societies,* (1973), I, p. 117.

Because many semi-skilled and unskilled workers were organized for the first time, for the most part in newly established unions, the years after 1888 are conventionally described as the period of 'new unionism'. In fact, however, more than half of the increase in membership was in occupations whose organization was already well underway when 'new unionism' began. Of these, the coal-miners were the most successful in maintaining their relative standing. Their share of total union membership was rather greater in 1913 than it had been in 1888 and their influence within the movement had increased more than proportionately. Between these dates the mine labour force expanded rapidly and the unions had succeeded in increasing the organized proportion to over 80 per cent. In many districts organization of the hewers was virtually complete by 1913.

Table 9·3   *Trade union membership by occupation, 1888–1913 (thousands)*

	1888 Members	Proportion of total Trade Unionists (per cent)	1913 Members	Proportion of total Trade Unionists (per cent)
Metals, Engineering, Shipbuilding	190	25	546	13
Mining and Quarrying	150	20	921	22
Textiles	120	16	523	13
Building	90	12	236	6
Transport	60	8	694	17
Clothing	40	5	106	3
Printing and Paper	30	4	85	2
Others	70	9	1,024	25
All Unions	750		4,135	

Sources: Clegg, Fox, and Thompson, op. cit. pp. 1, 488; *Eighteenth Abstract of Labour Statistics* (*Parl. Papers* xxix, 1926). Most of the other trade union statistics that appear in the text are taken from these two works and the following sources: Mitchell and Deane, op. cit.; Webbs, *History of Trade Unionism*; *Seventeenth Abstract of Labour Statistics* (*Parl. Papers* lxi, 1914–16); *Report of the Chief Registrar of Friendly Societies for 1913*, (*Parl. Papers* lxxvi, 1914).

Not long after it was founded the Miners Federation of Great Britain (1888–9) was engaged in the greatest of all nineteenth-century stoppages and the first to be resolved by ministerial intervention.[1] In 1893, when the trade cycle was falling, over 300,000 miners ceased work for sixteen weeks rather than submit to a 25 per cent reduction in wages. The outcome was perhaps less favourable than the men's leaders claimed.[2] But some progress was made towards the principle of a minimum wage, one of the two major demands upon which the Federation had been established, and despite serious disorders in parts of the West Riding[3] the Federation emerged with its reputation considerably enhanced. Shortly after this the miners' influence at the TUC was enormously strengthened by the introduction of block-voting[4] and on the industrial front the Federation set about extending its influence into Scotland and South Wales. The Welsh miners lost a long and bitter strike against the sliding scale in 1898, but both Scotland and South Wales were inside the Federation by the end of the century and in 1908 the Miners' Eight Hours Act secured the affiliation of Northumberland and Durham. The strike that led to the passing of the Mines (Minimum Wage) Act four years later – the greatest of all the pre-war disputes – was thus a national stoppage involving not far short of a million miners.

Unions recruiting among the engineers, shipbuilders, and other metal workers managed to increase their membership almost threefold between 1888 and 1913, sufficient to raise organization in these occupations from around 15 per cent to around 25 per cent. This was well short of the miners' expansion, however, and it meant a relative decline within the union world (Table 9·3). The Amalgamated Society of Engineers suffered a particular decline in influence. Its difficulties arose from the undermining of the skilled engineer's status by machinery whose operation required neither skill nor versatility. Employers, becoming acutely conscious of foreign competition, combined new technology with other practices that were felt to be incompatible with craft traditions: work study, greater division of labour, and extended piece-work. The ASE therefore faced a choice of either coming to terms with these innovations by accepting some loss of privilege and admitting semi-skilled 'machinists', or of clinging to as much as possible of their accustomed status by resisting change. The second alternative entailed defending a position that would become increasingly untenable and also invited the hostility of both the hard-pressed employers and the public. But its members' short-term interests, its structure, its rules, and its past, all pushed the ASE in this direction. Half-hearted attempts to relax entry restrictions were rendered ineffective by branch officials and the rank and file.

The Engineers' inflexibility was evident in their refusal to join the Federation of Engineering and Shipbuilding Trades (1890), in the continued proliferation of demarcation disputes,[5] and in their relations with employers. It was evident most of all in the great lock-out of 1897–8 that was fought over resistance to new methods. This struggle, one of the biggest nineteenth-century disputes and perhaps the most significant, lasted from July 1897 until January 1898. It ended with the ASE thoroughly beaten. Little help had come from other unions during the stoppage – too many of them had known ASE condescension in the past. But two other influences contributed more substantially to the defeat. The first of these was employer solidarity: the cost of ASE restrictions was sufficient to unite the employers and cause them to regard the battle as one they could not afford to lose. The second was the intrinsic weakness of the ASE position: by this time a substantial part of the skilled engineers' work was within the capacity of less-skilled, non-union men and in many works they took the places of locked-out engineers.

Building craftsmen also suffered a relative decline in influence. Some of their difficulties were similar to those that troubled the engineers: new materials like steel and concrete and the greater use of machine-made fittings threatened parts of their employment. A greater difficulty in their case, however, was that the building cycle was distinctly unfavourable after 1903. In the 1890s the building unions had expanded at least as fast as unionism as a whole: in the following decade they lost more than a third of their members. They made up lost ground just before the war, but at the end of this recovery the proportion of all building workers in the unions was still only about 20 per cent. The great majority of these were craftsmen and in some of the more prosperous centres most craftsmen were organized. Over the country as a whole, however, the majority even of these more skilled workers were still outside the unions. Only about 30 per cent of bricklayers and masons were unionized in 1913, and no more than 40 per cent of carpenters and joiners.

Cotton unions fared better than the building unions but their share of all unionists also fell. This was partly because employment in the mills was not expanding very rapidly in these years, and partly because the most powerful of the cotton unions, the (male) Operative Cotton Spinners, had already enrolled most of its potential membership before 1890. Even so, the cotton unions still accounted for almost one unionist in ten in 1913 and for half of all female unionists. Like the miners, and partly for similar reasons, they had been involved in major disputes on the falling trade cycle of the early 1890s. The famous Brooklands Agreement of March 1893 then succeeded in restoring the industry's good industrial relations record for a further fifteen years. Cotton workers had also in common with the miners an increased political influence through the introduction of block-voting at the TUC in 1895.

The cotton weavers illustrate how difficult it is to categorize unions as unequivocally 'old' or 'new': they were long-established but shared certain characteristics (their 'openness' and their members' lack of skill) with the classic 'new' unions of 1889–91. If we ignore such niceties and use union membership among miners, engineers, shipbuilders, other metal workers, building workers, cotton workers, printers, and boot and shoe operatives as a rough guide to the numerical importance of the older unions, we find that at the end of 1892 (*after* the initial 'new' union advance) the old unions still accounted for about two-thirds of all unionists. The proportion was not much different in 1910 and it was still more than half in 1913. These proportions, which leave out of account many of the smaller old unions and many white-collar unionists and others who cannot be even roughly categorized as either 'old' or 'new', provide a clear indication of the numerical limitations of 'new unionism'.

Its limitations can be seen also in the conspicuous failure of attempts to organize farm labourers and women workers. They were still largely unorganized in 1914, and for much the same reasons that prevented their organization before the 1880s (above, pp. 256–9). Of the two, the women had made most progress. There were fewer than 50,000 female trade unionists in 1888, more than twice this number five years later, and around 432,000 by the end of 1913. This obviously represented a considerable increase in their contribution to the movement. But more than 90 per cent of female workers remained unorganized and 90 per cent of all unionists were male. Moreover, almost half the female unionists were the second-class members of male-dominated cotton unions (above, pp. 255–6, 258), and not far short of half the rest were teachers and national or local government employees.

Table 9·4   *Female trade unionists, 1910 and 1913 (thousands) (membership at year end)*

	1910	1913
Cotton	151	214
Other textiles	32	46
Teaching	48	65
National and Local Government	18	24
Shop Assistants, etc.	6	21
Tailoring, Clothing, Boot and Shoe	9	25
Paper, Printing, Food, Drink, Tobacco	5	8
All other occupations	10	28

Source: *Eighteenth Abstract of Labour Statistics* (*Parl. Papers* xxix, 1926), pp. 178–9.

What progress had occurred can be ascribed partly to more tolerant male attitudes. In occupations where new methods were eroding distinctions between men's work and women's work and forcing the men to reconsider their traditional policy of exclusion, tolerance was distinctly in the men's own interest. Male attitudes changed also in response to the changes in the women's movement mentioned in Chapter 8. In the 1890s doctrinal opposition to 'discriminatory' factory reform was discarded and at the same time the women adopted less conciliatory attitudes towards the employers, a change of tack symbolized in the translation of the Women's Protective and Provident League into the Women's Trade Union League (1891). The leaders of women's unionism continued to be drawn mainly from the middle and upper classes. Lady Dilke was prominent after Emma Paterson died and in 1903 she was succeeded by Mary Macarthur, the daughter of a prosperous Scottish draper. Besides launching women's unions and assisting their growth, the WTUL lobbied MPs and male unionists and demanded to be heard whenever the welfare of working women was under discussion. Mary

Macarthur was particularly influential in the sweated industries campaign that led to the Trade Boards Act of 1909.[6]

The history of farm workers' trade unionism between 1888 and 1914 is quickly told. In 1888 Arch's union had fewer than 4,000 members. The expansion of 1889–92 then took the membership of agricultural unions to some 50,000. This, however, was still a minuscule proportion of the labourers and the ending of 'new' union euphoria brought a speedy return towards the position in 1888. A more sustained recovery began in 1906 with the establishment of the Eastern Counties Agricultural Labourers Union, the forerunner of the present National Union of Agricultural Workers. At the end of 1913 this union and the other farm unions together were about 21,000 strong. An equal number of agricultural labourers may have been enrolled in general labour unions, but organization was obviously still considerably less than that briefly achieved by Joseph Arch in 1872–4.

Clearly 'new unionism' drew little strength from either women workers or farm labourers. Its main strength was among semi-skilled workers in the larger towns. Gas workers, dockers, and seamen were the most prominent occupations.[7] Their unions were 'new' both in the sense that most were started in 1888–90 and because they contrasted with the longer-established unions in a number of other ways. They drew upon occupations previously not organized, they imposed few entry restrictions, and several were begun and led by middle-class, or artisan, socialists. These characteristics can be seen, for example, in the Dock, Wharf, Riverside, and General Labourers Union (1889), one of the more successful 'new' unions and the progenitor of the Transport and General Workers Union (1922). This particular 'new' union was established in the wake of the great London dock strike.[8] Its 'open' entry policy was proclaimed in its title and Tom Mann, a socialist and a pungent critic of his own Amalgamated Society of Engineers, was its first president. At the peak of the initial 'new' union expansion (1890–1) the Dock, Wharf, Riverside, and General Labourers Union claimed over 50,000 members and the total 'new' union membership exceeded 350,000, perhaps a quarter of all unionists.[9]

But the expansion could not be sustained. By 1892 'new' union membership was falling and by 1896 it was less than a tenth of all unionists. There was some recovery after this but in 1910 'new' unionists were still a smaller proportion of all unionists than they had been in 1890–1. The hopes and expectations of 1889–90 had so far been disappointed. The more substantial 'new' union advance came between 1910 and the war. Virtually every union prospered in these years and the 'new' union gains far outstripped most others. The Gas-workers and General Labourers, for example, had 32,000 members in 1910 and 135,000 by the end of 1913; the Workers Union, a latter-day (1898) 'new' union and another creation of Tom Mann, advanced from 5,000 to 91,000 in the same years. The majority of the unskilled were still unorganized even in 1914, but a substantial proportion of them were now within the movement and trade unionism had at last ceased to be largely the preserve of a privileged minority.

Two other broad categories of unionists – who were neither 'old' nor 'new' – helped to reduce the dominance of coal, cotton, and the crafts. The first of these was the white-collar unionists, the other was the railwaymen. Organization in the rapidly growing lower middle-class occupations began in the 1870s and 1880s. Several grades of post office workers were being recruited at that time and the National Union of Elementary School Teachers (established 1870) had 14,000 members by 1888. The following few years saw unionism expanding upwards towards the lower middle classes as well as downwards towards the unskilled: the National Amalgamated Union of Shop Assistants (1891), the Second Division Clerks Association (1890), the Postmen's Federation (1891), the Tax Clerks Association (1892), and the Musicians Union (1893) were all started at this time. White-collar unions continued to grow in the first decade of the new century when unionism as a whole stagnated.[10] They then shared fully in the general expansion of 1910–13[11] and by the end of 1913 their total strength was probably not far short of half a million.[12] Each white-collar union had particular interests of its own – the shop assistants, for example, were concerned especially with working hours – but many of them had characteristics in common. A considerable number recruited exclusively in the public sector where there was no close contact with employers of the kind that elsewhere reinforced white-collar antipathy towards organization and caused unionism to be regarded as tantamount to treason. Weakness and reluctance to embark upon the more proletarian forms of industrial action were other common characteristics. And these inhibitions, reinforced by awareness that public sector employers might be particularly susceptible to political pressure, encouraged heavy reliance on parliamentary lobbying.

The last of these characteristics was also one of the distinguishing features of railway unionism. By the end of 1913 there were 300,000 organized railwaymen (excluding the Railway Clerks). Their main union, the Amalgamated Society of Railway Servants, had been founded in 1871, but the railways cannot be considered well organized until after 1910. Until the late 1880s the ASRS was a fairly typical union of the old kind: it recruited from among the better-paid railwaymen, its subscriptions and friendly society benefits were both high, and for the most part (and in most districts) it was conciliatory towards employers. Much the same could be said of what became the second railway union, the Associated Society of Locomotive Engineers and Firemen which broke away from the ASRS in 1880 to pursue sectional interests. From the late 1880s this pattern changed. First, the General Railway

Workers Union was established to cater for those who were neglected by the ASRS or dissatisfied with its cautious and sectional policies. But the General Railway Workers fared no better than most other 'new' unions (between 1889 and 1895 its membership fell from 14,000 to 4,000) and the more important change occurred within the ASRS. During the 1890s the ASRS modified several of its 'new model' characteristics and set about recruiting among railwaymen of every grade. By 1900 it was 62,000 strong. Besides attempting to raise wages the ASRS concentrated particularly on three issues: the long railway working day, compensation for those injured at work, and union recognition.

Recognition was the most important of these issues. The railway companies, traditionally paternalist, expected more loyalty than was compatible with union membership. They claimed too that unionism jeopardized passenger safety.[13] These attitudes were stiffened by financial difficulties arising from the combination of poor productivity, rising costs, and government regulation of rates.[14] Recognition was the crucial issue in 1907 when what threatened to be the first national railway strike was averted by Lloyd George's intervention and the introduction of collective bargaining procedures that entailed tacit recognition of the unions. Thus the railwaymen became the second body of organized workers (after the miners) to threaten industrial action so harmful to the community that the government felt compelled to intervene and enforce compromise.[15] The employers participated in the new arrangements with great reluctance and the government's failure to fulfil promises of some relaxation in rates regulation increased their intransigence.[16] The railwaymen, more conscious now of their strength, pushed for further concessions and in 1911 came out on strike. Again the government intervened, this time inducing a return to work by emphasizing the consequences of strike action at a time when war with Germany appeared imminent and by replacing the existing conciliation boards with arrangements more to the unions' liking. This concession reinforced other influences favourable to recruitment in the years before the war. In 1910 less than one railwayman in three was in the unions: by the end of 1913 over three-quarters of them were organized.

Railwaymen were at the heart of another significant development that was particularly evident just before the war. This was the tendency for unions to become ever larger and to join their strength with that of other unions in the same or kindred occupations. In 1913, before they combined with the General Railway Workers Union and the United Pointsmen and Signalmen to create the National Union of Railwaymen, the Railways Servants themselves had already nearly three times as many members as the biggest union of 1888. Many other unions, the smaller ones especially, lost their identity in larger organizations. Increased company size and employer organization, the tendency towards nation-wide collective bargaining, and the growing importance of unions whose membership was not restricted by entry barriers, were all conducive to an increase in average union size. There was recognition too, particularly among the newer unions, that larger unions and combinations of unions often enjoyed a more than proportionate increase in strength. This was one of the incentives behind the alliances being formed shortly before the war. Ben Tillett and Tom Mann in 1910 put together the National Transport Workers Federation around the dockers' and seamen's unions, and by 1914 plans were agreed for a Triple Alliance whereby the Miners, the Railwaymen, and the Transport Workers might arrange for their agreements to terminate simultaneously and to strike in sympathy if any one of them fell into dispute. This alliance, embracing some 1.5 million workers, contained potential coercive power of a magnitude quite undreamt of in 1888.

II · *The 'new' union advance, 1889–91*

What caused the 'new unionism' advance of 1889–91? So far as its immediate timing is concerned, the crucial influence was the trade cycle. There were several relatively good years within the period conventionally labelled the 'great depression' (1873–96) and conditions in 1888–90 were exceptionally favourable to labour. Such expansion could not have occurred in the mid-1880s when unemployment was around 10 per cent. By 1888, however, unemployment had fallen to below 5 per cent and by 1889 to only 2 per cent.[17] Substantial trade union expansion was almost inevitable in these conditions. And the expansion was bound to have some effect on occupations that were previously unorganized, despite the unwillingness of existing unions to lower their entrance barriers.

In such circumstances a single dramatic victory can play a catalytic role. The Bryant and May matchgirls' strike in the summer of 1888 probably came too early to have this effect and the matchgirls themselves were probably too unlike the workers who had the best prospect of becoming successful 'new' unionists. In the following summer, however, there were two significant victories. The London gas-workers, led from East Ham by Will Thorne, won a reduction in their working day from twelve hours to eight without a fight and without loss of pay. Shortly after this the London waterfront was convulsed by the five-week strike for the 'dockers' tanner'. Daily demonstrations, the successful appeal to public opinion, and the intervention of Cardinal Manning ensured this strike exceptional publicity. Many other previously unorganized workers were now inspired to start unions of their own, trades councils intensified their missionary activities, and the Women's Protective and Provident League began recruiting tours in the provinces. Even the most unpromising trade union material was affected by the organizing mania. Domestic servants, for example, launched the London and Provincial

Domestic Servants Union at a crowded Kensington meeting. There were so many new unions that George Tuthill's East End weaving shop, where most trade union banners were made, turned out more banners in 1889 than in any year before or since.[18]

To some extent this was similar to what had happened on a smaller scale in the prosperous years of the early 1870s and in previous economic booms.[19] But whereas the advance of the early 1870s was mainly a function of the trade cycle alone, that of 1889–91 rested also upon more enduring influences. One of these was the exceptional number of workers that were overdue for organization. Improved education and the extended franchise had raised expectations and self-respect, swelling the numbers who looked to trade unionism as a logical next step in their emancipation. Technical change had a similar influence by elevating many to semi-skilled status. More capital-intensive production, greater division of labour, and the spread of continuous production processes also made it increasingly possible for less-skilled workers to inflict expensive stoppages and thus increased their bargaining strength. The gas stokers, who were helped as well by the exceptional prosperity of the gas industry, are a particularly good example of workers whose organization awaited only suitable trade conditions and determined leadership.[20]

The ground for expansion had been prepared also by developments earlier in the 1880s. By the changing attitude to poverty, the unemployment protests, and the socialist revival that were described in previous chapters. An account of conditions in the docks had appeared in one of the early volumes of Charles Booth's poverty survey shortly before the dockers' strike and helped to put public opinion on their side. As economic conditions improved socialist agitators turned from organizing unemployment protests to trade union organization. The matchgirls, for example, were aroused and led by Annie Besant (of birth-control fame); the gas stokers and dockers were similarly assisted by John Burns, Tom Mann, and Ben Tillett. Karl Marx's daughter, Eleanor, was active in several disputes and found time also to help the gas workers' leader (Will Thorne) to learn to read and write. In these ways socialist leadership and the impetus derived from the earlier protest movements carried 'new unionism' beyond the point it would have reached with the assistance of favourable economic conditions alone.

Socialism had some influence too in shaping 'new' union characteristics. Clearly unskilled workers could not set about organizing themselves into exclusive unions of the kind favoured by the labour aristocracy. Far more vulnerable to substitution, they set out to recruit as many as possible of those who might be 'blacklegs'. Their weakness was also largely responsible for them acquiring a reputation for militancy and violence. Flamboyant talk and bold tactics were thought necessary to arouse and retain men who had little union experience and none of the labour aristocrats' quiet confidence. They lacked also the craftsmen's alternatives to striking (the rule book and the 'strike in detail') and when they did strike their relative abundance encouraged employers to take on non-union men and thus raised the likelihood of fighting on the picket lines. Emphasis upon political activity[21] was another natural accompaniment to industrial weakness, and the initial eschewal of friendly society activities by the 'new' unions was perhaps not surprising given their members' low incomes. To this extent the characteristics of 'new unionism' were dictated by circumstances. But the socialists strengthened and sharpened each of these characteristics and subtly manipulated them to their own ends. Blind protests were garnished with the jargon of class warfare and put into the context of an ideological critique of capitalism; *ad hoc* demands took their place in a programme of reform that gave priority to the eight-hour day and an independent labour party; and repeated emphasis upon working-class solidarity made open unionism a virtue as well as a necessity. Moreover, the disparagement of the sectional spirit and of the Lib-Lab alliance that was implicit in such sentiments provided the main thrust of a wide-ranging attack upon the established unions. These were castigated for their 'utter callousness' towards the less-skilled, dismissed as mere 'coffin clubs' compared with the 'fighting' 'new' unions, and ridiculed in numerous other ways.[22] In John Burns' famous caricature of 'old' and 'new' union delegates at the 1890 TUC for example:

> Physically the 'old' unionists were much bigger than the 'new' .... A great number of them looked like respectable city gentlemen; wore very good coats, large watch chains, and high hats and in many cases were of such splendid build and proportions that they presented an aldermanic, not to say a magisterial form and dignity. Amongst the 'new' delegates not a single one wore a tall hat. They looked workmen; they were workmen.[23]

John Burns' presence at the 1890 TUC is one indication of the 'new' union impact upon the wider trade union world. The previous year an eight-hour day motion had been defeated and the London dockers were scarcely mentioned although they were on strike while Congress met. In 1890, however, there was a sizable 'new' unionist presence at Congress for the first time. Burns, Mann, and Tillett now joined Hardie in attacking the Lib-Lab stalwarts. Many other delegates new to Congress (of various political complexions) were not averse to supporting parts of the socialist programme and numerous socialist-inspired resolutions were carried, including the demand for an eight-hour day by legal enactment. Burns himself was elected to the Parliamentary Committee and later boasted that out of sixty resolutions passed by Congress, 'forty-five were nothing more or less than direct appeals to the State and Municipalities of this country to do for the workmen what trade unionism . . . has proved itself incapable of doing'.[24] 'New unionism' was not quite so triumphant as this claim suggests – but there was every justification for claiming a remarkable success. In the same year Broadhurst resigned from the post of secretary to the Parliamentary Committee, which he had held, except for one short break, since 1875, an event of considerable symbolic importance.

III · *The employers' counter-attack and the 'new' union retreat; the ILP and 'new' unionist political activity in the 1890s*

It was probably in 1890 or 1891 that the distinction between 'new' and 'old' unionists was most marked and their mutual animosity greatest. From that time onwards the differences diminished as the 'new' unions abandoned or modified some of their distinguishing characteristics and as certain of these same characteristics were adopted by the older unions.

The 'new' union retreat was the more significant of these developments. The earlier advance of 'new unionism' had been quite sufficient to excite expectations that the entire trade union movement might be radically and rapidly transformed. But, like most watersheds in British labour history, that of 1889–90 proved to be less important than it at first promised. An exceptionally tight labour market, the employers' unpreparedness, and the momentum generated by initial success had brought far more members than the 'new' unions could retain. The employers soon recovered and began a counter-attack. By the end of 1891 they were being assisted by rising unemployment. And public opinion, which had been favourable to 'new unionism' when the London dock strike began, was soon repulsed by reports of violence, intimidation, and socialist involvement. The South Metropolitan Gas Company, one of the companies that conceded the first significant 'new' union victory in June 1889, ousted Thorne's union eight months later and Tillett's Dock, Wharf, Riverside, and General Labourers Union was quietly driven from the Thames hardly more than a year after the dockers' 'tanner' had been won. Shortly before this Tillett had been decisively beaten at Southampton and the National Union of Dock Workers had the worst of a long strike at Liverpool. The shipping companies responded to 'new unionism' with an organization of their own, the Shipping Federation. First established as a counterweight to Havelock Wilson's National Amalgamated Union of Sailors and Firemen, the Shipping Federation was soon drawn into conflict with other waterfront unions by its militant opposition to the closed shop. Most such conflicts were resolved to the employers' advantage. The greatest clash was at Hull in 1893, when Tillett's union suffered a further humiliating defeat.[25] In the following year the Sailors' and Firemen's Union was dissolved.

Numerous other 'new' unions had disappeared by this time and the survivors, almost without exception, were significantly reduced in strength. Most 'new' unions were vulnerable to 'black-legging' and few had the resources and discipline to hold out against determined opposition. The more militant unions, those most likely to provoke counter-attack, had been among the first to go. 'New' union membership was halved and the weakest and least-skilled recruits – women workers, for example, and casual labourers – were disproportionate among the victims. Prominent among the surviving 'new' unionists were those workers that were described earlier as having been overdue for organization in 1888: they were better-paid, more regularly employed, and considerably less dispensable than the genuinely unskilled labourers. Many of them worked for local authorities. Public sector employers were comparatively tolerant towards unionism, not much troubled by fears that unionization would reduce efficiency, and readily influenced by workmen's votes.

Rid of their least-skilled members, the surviving 'new' unions now found it possible to pursue more subtle policies. They avoided disputes if they could and offered their co-operation in establishing conciliation and arbitration procedures. They ceased to recruit indiscriminately, seeking instead to consolidate membership in the least vulnerable occupations and in those places where employers were least hostile. Will Thorne, for example, in 1892 advised members of his Gas-workers and General Labourers to avoid strikes. The union meanwhile made cautious progress among municipal gas-workers and quietly ignored the women and general labourers that it had welcomed in 1889–90. By this time the Gas workers were also paying sickness and funeral benefits out of substantially increased weekly contributions. Much of what the old unionists had said of the likely consequences of 'open' unionism and confrontation had been proved correct. Conscious of this, and aware that survival depended upon sectional and exclusive tactics not dissimilar to those the socialists so roundly condemned, the 'new' unions also became less critical of the trade union establishment. Economic conditions became rather less hostile to 'new unionism' when the trade cycle improved in the mid-1890s, but until 1910 'new' unionist industrial policy remained, in E. J. Hobsbawm's words, 'cautious, limited, conservative, and sectional'.[26]

There were political set-backs too, the most formidable of which came in 1894–5 at the hands of the old unionists. Until this time 'new' unionist strength at Congress, thanks to TUC standing orders, was quite disproportionate to its modest share of union membership. Each delegate's vote counted equally, to the obvious disadvantage of the larger (and older) unions. Moreover, the trades councils – which had for long been partially ignored by many of the established unions – were entitled to send their own delegates to Congress regardless of the dual representation this entailed. The foundation of the Independent Labour Party by Keir Hardie in 1893 intensified fears of eventual socialist domination and the Parliamentary Committee resolved that it was time the 'new' unions were cut down to size. This they did in 1894 by amending standing orders to make delegates' voting strength proportional to the number of their constituents and to exclude trades council delegates entirely. Moreover, in an amendment aimed chiefly at Keir Hardie (who by now had abandoned the pit for politics and journalism) they ruled that henceforth only salaried trade union officers, or bona fide members working at their trade, could represent a union. These moves were easily defended on the grounds that they removed anomalies and made standing orders more democratic. But the Parliamentary Committee had been motivated primarily by determination to weaken its political enemies.[27] And although the amendments could almost certainly have been pushed through under the old standing orders, the Parliamentary Committee ruled that the 1895 vote to confirm the amendments should be taken under the new standing orders that were being voted upon. It was, as the Webbs described it, something of a *coup d'état*.[28] The trades councils (who had created the T U C) were understandably incensed[29] and 'new' union influence at Congress was considerably diminished. The other major 'new' union setback on the political front also occurred in 1895. In the general election of that year Keir Hardie, the only working-class M P not prepared to work with the Liberals, lost the seat he had won at West Ham in 1892.[30] The other twenty-seven candidates of the new Independent Labour Party were also unsuccessful.

But the employers' counter-attack and worsening economic conditions could not curtail 'new' unionist political activity as decisively as they restricted activities at the workplace. To some extent, in fact, industrial retreat encouraged activists to devote more of their attention to political organization. Certainly there was little prospect of industrial success when the Independent Labour Party (IL P) had been founded in 1893. This event was a major step towards an independent political party capable of weaning workers from the Liberals. The IL P programme was considerably influenced by Fabian thinking but carefully avoided their preference for patient permeation of Liberalism rather than establishing a rival party. Even more care was taken to distinguish the IL P from the Social Democratic Federation whose revolutionary overtones, doctrinaire inflexibility, and disapproving attitude towards the unions condemned it to political impotency. Willingness to accommodate union foibles, to sacrifice principle for expediency, won recruits and helped IL P members to positions of influence in individual unions, on trades councils, and in local politics. The IL P was also associated with the renaissance of the working-class radical press, and particularly with

Robert Blatchford's *Clarion* which attempted to make the socialist case attractive to working men. In the short run of course, as the ILP soon discovered, the way ahead was far from easy. The 1894–5 reversal at the TUC and the disastrous showing in the 1895 election was a double blow from which the new party had hardly fully recovered in 1900. It had only some 6,000 members at this date, many of whom were middle class. They were vociferous and energetic, but they had not yet succeeded in winning over working-class support.

'New' unionist political advance in the 1890s was most evident at the level of the trades councils and in municipal politics. Trades councils were an obvious means of encouraging mutual assistance between workers and furthering other socialist ambitions. At this level members of the ILP, the SDF, and the Fabian Society suspended their doctrinal differences and worked together to advance working-class interests and to weaken the Lib-Lab alliance. Working-class representation in local politics (Lib-Lab as well as 'new' unionist) increased substantially in the early 1890s. School boards and poor law boards, the campaign to induce councils to insert a 'fair wages' clause in their contracts, and those for the municipalization of gasworks, waterworks, and tramways, were the main spheres in which 'new' unionists made their mark. They were probably most successful in London: at Poplar, for example, where many paupers had cause to be grateful for the work of George Lansbury and Will Crooks; at West Ham too, where Will Thorne's organization (which earlier had helped Keir Hardie to Westminster) succeeded in 1898 in capturing independent labour's first municipality. This victory was followed by the introduction of an eight-hour day, a 30s minimum wage, and two weeks' holiday for council employees.[31]

At the TUC the 1895 revision of standing orders proved to be a temporary reversal rather than a complete rout. Patient work by socialist activists among the rank and file (particularly among younger members) brought fresh 'new' unionist delegates to Congress and by the end of the decade there was again substantial pressure in favour of a legal eight-hour day and urging Congress to promote joint industrial action and to put its weight behind attempts to create a working-class political party. Moves to establish a federation that would provide financial assistance to member unions involved in disputes came to fruition in 1899 when the General Federation of Trade Unions was launched with the blessing of Congress. In the same year Congress approved an ILP suggestion (by no means the first) that the unions, the co-operative societies, the Fabian Society, the SDF, and the ILP should confer together 'with a view to securing united political action'. In contrast to several earlier moves of this kind, which either proved abortive or produced organizations that quickly served the Lib-Lab cause, this initiative led to the conference of February 1900 at which it was agreed, in the words of Keir Hardie's resolution, to establish 'a distinct Labour group in Parliament who shall have their own whips and agree upon their policy'. This conference established the Labour Representation Committee and marks the beginning of the Labour Party.

IV · *The old unions move to the left*

While the 'new' unions were shedding some of their distinguishing characteristics the old unions were cautiously modifying their own practices. Several influences edged the older unions in the direction of 'new unionism' during the 1890s. First there were the initial 'new' unionist successes which inspired and strengthened the radical element within the older unions. This element was strengthened too by the great expansion of old unionism in 1888–91. Many new recruits were younger men, less wedded to traditional ways than existing members and more willing to contemplate change. These influences survived the 'new' union retreat because sufficient had been achieved to demonstrate that trade unionism was capable of more than its leaders had envisaged and because 'new' unionist political activity still flourished despite the industrial defeats. The displacement of the SDF as the main socialist influence by the reformist ILP also encouraged old unionists to look rather more favourably upon the socialist case. The ILP was less offensive towards the Lib-Lab establishment than the SDF and less openly challenging. Union leaders were conscious too that socialist influence among their rank and file, however muted, could result in unofficial action, the appearance of irritating 'ginger' groups, and even the establishment of rival unions. These threats were another inducement to modify craft union policy.

The old unionists also felt the growing disenchantment with *laissez-faire*. They had mounting evidence of the practical benefits of municipal socialism, and heavy unemployment in 1892–5 encouraged them to reconsider their opposition to demands for the eight-hour day. The growing influence of the miners and railwaymen among those conventionally regarded as old unionists was probably another contribution to these shifting political attitudes. Both groups had a long history of seeking improvement by political pressure and wildly fluctuating earnings put the Miners Federation alongside the socialists in demanding a minimum wage. The social status of coal-miners, moreover, was very little superior to that of many of the 'new' unionists.

Dissatisfaction with the returns from union support for the Liberal Party was another of the influences that brought 'old' and 'new' unionism closer together. The years up to 1892 had seen a steady flow of acceptable legislation, including the Fair Wages Resolution and the introduction of free elementary schooling (both brought in by the Conservatives in 1891). But the Liberal administration of 1892–5, preoccupied with Ireland, did little to tackle unemployment or in response to rising working-class expectations on other issues. The elderly Gladstone resigned in 1894 and his successor (Lord Rosebery) had little of Gladstone's charisma. The Conservatives then won the 1895 election with a majority sufficient to remove immediate anxieties over the disposition of working-class votes. They introduced the Workmen's Compensation Act of 1897, a significant gain,[32] but their overall legislative record on matters that concerned the unions was unimpressive. This slackening in the flow of ameliorative legislation, at a time of rising expectations and when labour was advancing in local politics, was naturally resented. It focused attention on the shortcomings of the Liberal opposition, upon the meagre working-class representation at Westminster, and, of course, upon the possibility of improving that representation outside the confines of the Liberal Party. The number of Lib-Lab MPs had increased only from eight to eleven in the decade after 1889 when union membership had more than doubled. If the priorities of the Liberal Party leaders had prevailed many more trade union candidates might have been adopted. But Joseph Chamberlain's campaign to give the constituency rank and file a greater influence over MPs and in the selection of candidates had increased the power of middle-class constituency activists who proved to be less willing than the party leaders to accommodate working-class political ambitions. One of their objections was that few working men could contribute anything towards the considerable cost of electioneering and attending Parliament. It was provincial short-sightedness of this kind that denied Keir Hardie the Liberal candidature he sought at Mid-Lanark in 1888 and helped to push him into the socialist camp.[33]

The changes at the workplace mentioned earlier – mechanization, the 'speed-up', greater division of labour, and 'scientific management' – were important also. They had already begun to diminish the status gap between skilled and less-skilled workers in the 1880s and in the 1890s became a more general cause of artisan discontent as the factory system spread and more employers sought to raise productivity in response to overseas competition.[34] Alfred Williams, at the Swindon railway works, complained of 'the speeding-up of late years', of tighter discipline, and of new machines 'well-suited to hustle'.[35] In 1896 John Anderson, a moderate of the old school who had earlier beaten-off a challenge from Tom Mann, was displaced as ASE general secretary by George Barnes, a militant and a socialist. The great dispute over workshop methods began in the following year.

The employers' counter-attack, which reached its peak with the defeat of the ASE, was another influence that reduced differences between old and 'new' unionism. It began as a response to the early 'new' unionist successes and to the violence and militancy associated with 'new unionism'. The older unions at that time were not under attack. By the mid-nineties, however, several developments had combined to make a substantial part of old unionism feel similarly threatened. Employers found that in practice it was not easy to confine their militancy to dealings with 'new' unionists. Moreover, the old unions to some extent invited the employers' attention by adopting 'new' unionist characteristics. New machines and methods had an important role in this process. Craftsmen were inclined to regard such innovations more as evidence of employer militancy than as a consequence of growing foreign competition while employers were inclined to interpret traditional craft job-protection as part of the extension of 'new unionism'. In 1896 the engineering employers combined on a national scale and resolved to demonstrate their determination to be masters of their own workshops. The subsequent ASE defeat caused many lesser unions to consider their own vulnerability.

Certain legal developments also made it appear that the counter-attack had been extended to unionism as a whole. Picketing clearly played a far more crucial role in 'new' unionist strikes than those where only skilled workers were involved. The employers accordingly turned to the law to restrain picketing that was allegedly outside the provisions of the 1875 Conspiracy and Protection of Property Act. Many trade unionists agreed that 'new' unionist picketing sometimes went beyond both the letter and the spirit of this act. But the appearance of employers combining together to use the law against trade unions, and in particular a case of 1896 (Lyons *v*. Wilkins) which appeared to threaten peaceful picketing, caused even moderate union leaders to fear that one of the victories of the 1870s was in jeopardy. A further cause for concern was the development in commercial law of a practice whereby unregistered companies could be sued for damages arising from the action of their officers. A case of 1893 (Temperton *v*. Russell) suggested that this device (the 'representative action') might be applied as readily to the unions, who had for long regarded themselves as exempt from claims for damages. As the old unionists thus came to feel that they too were threatened by the employers they became increasingly aware of mutual interests with those who had first come under attack.

v · *The labour movement at the turn of the century*

What was the effect of 'new unionism' by 1900? So far the account has concentrated upon the changes that occurred. But the limits to change must also be noted. In the context of how much had happened by 1891, and the expectations of continuing change at that time, unionism in 1900 might be regarded as remarkably little different from unionism in the mid-1880s. The 'new' unionist expansion was soon turned back and several of its distinguishing characteristics were quickly muted. Almost every proposal to ease entry to the older unions met bitter rank and file resistance, and the limited moderation of craft exclusiveness that did take place was as much the consequence of unavoidable technical change as of new-found fraternalism. Shipyard craftsmen, building craftsmen, and many other skilled workers still acted as if intent on proving that their main quarrel was with each other.[36] Similar sectional priorities kept the Northumberland and Durham miners outside the Miners Federation and caused the ASE to leave the TUC in 1898.

There had been rather more change in the political sphere, but here too there was abundant evidence of the resilience of traditional attitudes and of the hesitant and tenuous nature of the commitment to an independent political stance. Independent labour offered some sort of challenge to Lib-Labism almost everywhere by the end of the decade, but in most places (as in Sheffield) 'the long, hard road from Liberalism to Socialism . . . had only just been entered'.[37] The general election results of 1900 showed fairly conclusively that dissatisfaction over the number of working men selected as Liberal candidates was not yet sufficient to have much influence on the outcome of elections. In most places where the Liberals' hold upon working-class votes was weakest – in Lancashire for example, and parts of London – the Conservatives, not independent labour, were still their chief rivals. The Conservatism of Lancastrian unionists was among the obstacles to the TUC taking a more active political role[38] and James Mawdsley, secretary of the Operative Cotton Spinners and a Conservative candidate at Oldham in 1899, condemned the new Labour Representation Committee as 'an attempt to saddle another organization upon the shoulders of that patient carrier of burthens – the British workman'.[39]

The Cotton Spinners' indifference to attempts to establish an independent political party was shared by many other unions. Indeed, it was largely because TUC leaders recognized how contentious was this issue that they took such care to disassociate Congress from its management. Ensuring that the new party would be neither the protégé nor the responsibility of the TUC was an act of self-preservation. Member unions could either support or ignore the Labour Representation Committee as they chose while Congress itself was relieved of divisive pressure and left free to follow its customary non-contentious role. The conference that established the LRC was poorly supported. Most unions who were opposed to an independent party failed to attend because they expected its deliberations to prove abortive. Had sufficient socialists been resolved upon establishing a socialist labour party this expectation would doubtless have proved correct. But Keir Hardie and the other ILP representatives were aware that the price of union co-operation was to suppress anything that smacked of socialist dogma or precluded co-operation with the Liberals. Thus Hardie's successful resolution was carefully worded to avoid mentioning socialism and included the proviso that Labour MPs should be 'willing to co-operate with any party which for the time being may be engaged in promoting legislation in the direct interest of Labour'.

Hardie's compromise resolution underlines the extent that 'new' unionist political progress during the 1890s had been dependent upon a simultaneous ideological retreat. From the mid-1890s onwards what was usually understood by 'socialism' in Britain was a constitutional reformism that was opportunist, pragmatic, lacking in ideological perspective, and not easily distinguished from advanced Liberalism.[40] The retreat was recognition that in practical terms the socialism of the SDF had no prospect of winning mass support. Unionists had welcomed socialists for their energies and their organizing ability. They worked with them for so long as their respective interests coincided. But there were never many doctrinaire converts among the working classes. The career of John Burns, perhaps the most able of the socialist 'new' union organizers, epitomizes the ideological transition of the 1890s. In 1886, then a member of the SDF, he won notoriety as 'the man with the red flag' at Trafalgar Square, denouncing the House of Commons and calling for revolution. By 1892, no longer in the SDF, he entered the House of Commons himself as independent labour member for Battersea. Shortly after he began co-operating with the Liberals in furthering practical reforms and before long was openly contemptuous of the 'cranks, fools, and faddists' who persisted in the unfruitful pursuit of class war and revolution.[41]

VI · *Taff Vale; political developments, 1901–06; the 1906 election; Liberal social reforms, 1906–14*

The Taff Vale judgement of 1901 gave renewed impetus to radical influences and helped to ensure the survival and growth of the Labour Representation Committee.[42] Following a strike on the Taff Vale railway in South Wales the Taff Vale Company sued the Amalgamated Society of Railway Servants for damages and was eventually awarded £23,000. The earlier development of the 'representative action' (above, p. 313) had raised some doubt about the unions' legal status, but in 1900 it was still generally believed that the acts of 1871 and 1875 exempted unions from claims for damages. Taff Vale made it clear that the unions' privileged exemption from collective responsibility was over.

Although fears that industrial action would now jeopardize every penny of union funds proved exaggerated,[43] the majority of working-class leaders regarded Taff Vale as a fundamental challenge to union rights and a major obstacle to industrial activity. Memories of the ASE defeat were still fresh and militants could claim that the judiciary had now joined the employers in attacking unions. Liberal politicians protested at the decision less strenuously than they might have done, and the Conservative government did no more than eventually (in 1903) appoint the Royal Commission on Trade Disputes. The membership of this Commission was so little to the unions' liking that they refused their co-operation. All this made workers more conscious of common interests and far keener to establish an independent working-class presence at Westminster. Unions once hostile or indifferent to the L R C now flocked to affiliate: in two years support more than doubled.[44] 'The Taff Vale case', wrote G. D. H. Cole, 'created the Labour Party.'[45]

The period between Taff Vale and the 1906 election was one of considerable unemployment, stagnation in union membership, little industrial unrest, and union preoccupation with the consequences of Taff Vale. There were some significant legislative advances in these years: the 1901 Factory and Workshop Act, the inclusion of agricultural labourers within the terms of the 1897 Workmen's Compensation Act, and the Unemployed Workmen's Act of 1905 which had some importance as a step towards acceptance of state responsibility for providing work and unemployment relief.[46] The most significant political development, however, was the partial closing of the gap between Liberal and Labour that had been opened by the establishment of the L R C and then widened by Taff Vale. The crucial move in this rapprochement was the electoral pact of 1903 whereby the two parties agreed not to oppose each other in a number of constituencies. This deal was an obvious and sensible move by the L R C. There were no substantial differences in the programmes of the two parties and the political views of the great majority of L R C supporters (and potential supporters) were very similar to those of the Liberal Party. Moreover, working-class support for the Liberals was such that the L R C still had little prospect of winning many seats without Liberal co-operation.[47] At the same time, however, the arrangement imposed yet greater strain upon the fragile alliance of trade unionists and socialists that had created the L R C. Some on the left were profoundly uneasy about the initial compromise that went into this creation and the S D F had left the alliance in 1902 to recover its doctrinal purity.

These factional strains were temporarily eclipsed by the highly favourable performance at the 1906 election when the pact with the Liberals paid handsome dividends. The L R C – or Labour Party as it decided to call itself on the eve of the election – put up fifty candidates. Thirty-two of these, the majority of whom were elected, enjoyed a clear run against Conservatives. Two other Labour candidates overcame unofficial Liberal opposition, and three won against Liberal Party candidates. In all there were now twenty-nine Labour M Ps.[48] Many of the gains were made in Lancashire where the Liberals were relatively weak and therefore willing to stand aside in the hope that Labour candidates would take sufficient working-class votes to defeat Conservatives. Labour's triumph owed something also to the general swing away from the Conservatives. This was the 'free trade' election and the Conservatives were divided whereas Liberals and Labour were steadfast for cheap food. The number of Lib-Lab M Ps also increased (to twenty-four) but the Labour Party now accounted for the majority of working-class MPs. The new parliament was the first to contain a sizable working-class representation[49] and the increase in Labour and Lib-Lab strength (from a combined total of fifteen MPs in 1905 to over fifty in 1906) was regarded as no less sensational than the Liberal 'landslide'. Working-class expectations were raised accordingly.

There followed a flood of favourable legislative and administrative measures greater even than that of 1867–75. It was as if the Liberals – who had shown few signs of willingness to embark on such sweeping social reform while in opposition – had suddenly sensed the threat that eventually overtook them and were determined to spare no effort to retain working-class support. An early measure was an act that removed the consequences of the Taff Vale ruling by giving unions complete immunity from claims for damages. At first the government had proposed to act upon the report of the Royal Commission on Trade Disputes which appeared in 1906 with proposals that fell some way short of union demands.[50] But many Liberal candidates had earlier pledged their unqualified support to the unions and so the government now met their demands in full. In the same year John Burns was made President of the Local Government Board with a seat in the Cabinet, local authorities were enabled (and encouraged) to provide meals for needy schoolchildren, and another Workmen's Compensation Act was introduced that provided compensation for industrial diseases for the first time and extended cover to an additional six million workers. The new administration also showed itself to be more conciliatory than its predecessor in its dealings with unions of government employees. During the following year Lloyd George attempted to impose a similar conciliatory spirit upon the railway companies (above, p. 303) and legislation was introduced on school clinics and child medical inspection. Addressing the 1907 conference of South Wales miners William Abraham ('Mabon') declared that 'never before during any session of Parliament has such a crop of beneficial industrial and social measures been passed'.[51]

There was far more still to come. In 1908 the miners got their eight-hour day; the report of the Royal Commission on the Poor Laws was anticipated by a non-contributory old-age pension scheme; and the Children's Act was introduced to protect the young from negligent baby-minders, drunken parents, and other harmful influences. The following year saw provision for the first Trade Boards, which went some way towards conceding the demand for a minimum wage, and also plans for employment exchanges, a measure recommended by the Royal Commission on the Poor Laws (1905–9) in the hope that unemployment would be reduced by improved market information and greater labour mobility. The unions at first feared that these exchanges might be used to supply strike-breakers and cheap labour. But they were won over when Winston Churchill invited their assistance in planning and administrating the scheme. To pay for old-age pensions (which soon cost almost as much as the army), and for other social legislation in preparation, Lloyd George introduced his 'People's Budget' of 1909. His proposals, designed (as he put it) to 'wage implacable warfare against poverty and squalidness', were hailed in the presidential address to the 1909 TUC as 'the greatest financial reform of modern times'.[52] The budget provoked the *Daily Mail* to denounce the 'Plundering of the Middle Classes' in its heaviest type and became the cause of constitutional crisis when it was rejected by the House of Lords.

The Liberals took heavy losses in the first 1910 election,[53] but they survived the crisis and in 1911 introduced sickness and unemployment insurance schemes. Neither scheme was comprehensive: sickness insurance (providing free medical care and 10s a week) covered almost all wage-earners but not children or non-working wives and unemployment insurance was initially provided only for workers in trades (like engineering and building) that were especially afflicted by cyclical unemployment. Even so, in the context of the existing poor laws Beveridge's description of the scheme as 'a daring adventure' was justified. These schemes and the 1908 old-age pension scheme are the basis for claims that by 1914 the Liberals, prodded by the unions and the Labour Party, had laid the foundations of the post-1945 'welfare state'. Labour reservations about certain aspects of national insurance, and particularly the fear that it would remove a chief incentive to join a union, were dispelled by designating unions and existing friendly societies as 'approved societies' and thus incorporating their welfare activities within the state scheme. This device – which amounted almost to an official injunction to join a union or friendly society – was among the causes of the great pre-war increase in trade union membership. In the same year as the National Insurance Act a House of Commons resolution introduced payment of MPs, a measure particularly welcome at a time when union financial support for the Labour Party had been placed in jeopardy by the Osborne judgement (see below, p. 324). The Mines (Minimum Wage) Act was passed in 1912, and in 1913 an act was introduced that effectively reversed the Osborne judgement.

VII · *Strife, 1908–14, the causes of unrest*

At first it might seem surprising that the great labour unrest that dominated the years before the war should have occurred at the same time as the remarkable legislative advances just described. But workers' living standards consist of a great deal more than what had been affected by Liberal social reform. And the unrest, as we shall see, arose from several causes besides discontent over living standards.

Table 9·5 *Unemployment and working days lost by stoppages, 1891–1914*

	Unemployment (per cent)	Days Lost (thousands)		Unemployment (per cent)	Days Lost (thousands)
1891	3.5	6,810	1903	4.7	2,320
1892	6.3	17,380	1904	6.0	1,460
1893	7.5	30,440	1905	5.0	2,370
1894	6.9	9,510	1906	3.6	3,020
1895	5.8	5,700	1907	3.7	2,150
1896	3.3	3,560	1908	7.8	10,790
1897	3.3	10,330	1909	7.7	2,690
1898	2.8	15,260	1910	4.7	9,870
1899	2.0	2,500	1911	3.0	10,160
1900	2.5	3,090	1912	3.2	40,890
1901	3.3	4,130	1913	2.1	9,800
1902	4.0	3,440	1914	3.3	9,880

Sources: Mitchell and Deane, op. cit. pp. 64, 72; Pelling, *History of British Trade Unionism* (1963 edn.), pp. 261–2. The 'days lost' figures for 1891 and 1892 are for Great Britain and Ireland. After 1892 the figures are of days lost in disputes involving unions with headquarters in Great Britain and Northern Ireland. Unemployment figures are of 'all unions making returns'.

Table 9·5 shows that after two periods in the 1890s when the number of working days lost by strikes was high there was almost a decade of relative tranquillity in which the number of days lost averaged less than three million per annum. This quiescence was decisively broken in 1908, a year of bad trade and high unemployment. In September that year proposals to reduce cotton workers' wages provoked greater resentment than even the Brooklands Agreement could accommodate and precipitated a seven-week strike. The Tyneside engineering and shipbuilding trades were also afflicted by strikes against wage cuts and these stoppages were prolonged by rank and file militancy after union leaders had negotiated settlements. There were fewer demands for wage cuts in 1909 and the unrest seemed to have abated except on the coalfields where the introduction of the Eight Hours Act was disrupting working arrangements and increasing employers' sensitivity to falling productivity. The following year, however, showed that the earlier strikes were more than a temporary interruption of the long industrial peace. There were major disputes in the Clyde and Tyne shipyards, there was a strike of railwaymen in the north-east, and the cotton mills were stopped again. There was also a great deal more unrest in the coalfields. The hewers of Northumberland and Durham stopped work on 1 January when the Eight

319

Hours Act became operative there and some were still out three months later despite the efforts of their unions and independent conciliators to get them back.[54] There was trouble too over payment for working the hard places, or 'abnormal places', where a hewer's wages might be very low if the difficulties he contested were not adequately compensated by higher piece-rates.

The 'abnormal places' issue was the background to the great Cambrian dispute that started in the autumn of 1910. This strike began with disagreement over the rates to be paid for working a new seam at Tonypandy and continued when the Rhondda miners refused to accept terms agreed by their leaders. By the time they returned to work the following August the Rhondda had seen repeated clashes between police and strikers and attempts to supplant existing mine unionism by industrial unionism dedicated to class war and the revolutionary strike. In the course of 1911 uncompromising belligerency of this kind erupted in many other places. Unemployment had by now fallen sufficiently for the unskilled to resume the short-lived advance they had begun at the end of the 1880s and they joined the unrest inspired by long-restrained frustrations and with the militant example of the miners before them. As in 1889–90, and for similar reasons, their organization and industrial activity proceeded with an explosive, self-sustaining, momentum. Clashes with police and 'blacklegs', and the intermingling of strikers and town mobs, were seen again, this time on a far greater scale. The slightest reason for ceasing work now became sufficient. Tried methods of conciliation and arbitration were increasingly brushed aside, and almost every strike raised expectations and helped to spark off others. In many instances unskilled workers acted spontaneously. Some 15,000 women all over Bermondsey, for example, simply left their work demanding better pay and conditions and in September there was even a 'strike' of schoolchildren.

The 1911 turbulence reached its peak in the course of a long, hot summer. There was a major strike of seamen in June. Dock workers up and down the country then came out in support of the seamen and in pursuit of their own demands. Carters, tramwaymen, and other transport workers joined in, and on 18 August, after unofficial action that began in Liverpool, the first national railway strike commenced. Liverpool was one of the places where strikes had spilled over into general rioting and on 15 August two men were shot dead by troops. That same week, on the second day of the railway strike and during the closing stages of the Cambrian dispute, troops shot and killed two of a crowd attacking a train at Llanelli. In the mining valleys not far away angry mobs had been terrorizing the Jewish population (above, p. 185). Some older unionists, including most of the TUC Parliamentary Committee, had serious misgivings about the temper of the unrest. But younger and more militant delegates to the 1911 TUC resolved that 'no effort shall be spared by the forces of organized labour to arouse and maintain the discontent of underpaid workers'.[55]

In terms of days lost 1912 was the worst year. The national miners strike that began at the end of February arose, in the main, out of the same grievance (the abnormal places) that had provoked the Cambrian dispute. It was resolved, after five weeks, when the government intervened with minimum wage legislation. There were many other disputes in the first half of 1912, particularly in the major ports. The London dockers came out in May over the working of the agreement that concluded their 1911 strike. The port employers, still smarting from that defeat, were in an uncompromising mood and the dispute was prolonged until the end of July, by which time the men were ready for unconditional surrender. During the battle the National Transport Workers Federation (established in 1910 to combine the strength of dockers and seamen throughout the country) failed abysmally in an attempt to rally support for the London men. This was the last of the great pre-war strikes and its outcome appears to have dissipated some of the impatience and high expectations that had built up in the spring and summer of 1911. The unrest, however, was not yet finished. There were numerous lesser strikes, including those that swept through the previously little-troubled Birmingham and Black Country metal trades in 1913 (the midlands 'prairie fire'). Union membership moreover, particularly among the unskilled, continued to advance rapidly. In 1913 a long and hard-fought strike in Dublin, led by the revolutionary James Larkin, held the attention of British unionists and helped to keep alive expectations of still greater clashes to come. The creation of the Triple Alliance, which brought together three groups of workers who had taken a prominent role in the unrest, appeared to many to be an obvious preparation for just such a clash. But war with Germany intervened before their collective strength could be put to the test.

How is the pre-war labour unrest to be explained? The state of the trade cycle was one of the more important general influences and throws particular light upon differences between the initial unrest of 1908 and the far greater outbreak of 1910–14. During 1908 unemployment was higher than at any time since the mid-1880s.[56] The strikes of that year, not surprisingly, came mainly in response to demands for wage cuts. They were largely restricted to workers who were already well organized, they occurred without any expansion in union membership, some were prolonged and bitter (as defensive strikes on a falling trade cycle tend to be), and in time they died away as unionists became reconciled to adverse conditions and postponed further action until there was greater prospect of success. By 1910 economic conditions were becoming more propitious for strike action and throughout most of the second round of unrest unemployment was almost as low as it was at the time of the 1889–91 advance.[57] The 1910–14 unrest was therefore of a more opportunist character.

There were more strikes each year than occurred in 1908 and many of them were quickly settled by higher wages. Moreover, the labour market had become sufficiently tight for newly organized (and even unorganized) workers to take a prominent part and for strife to occur alongside very rapid increase in union membership. The 1908 unrest, in short, was analogous to that of 1892–3 (above, pp. 297, 299) while the strikes of 1910–14 had far more in common with those of 1888–91 (above, pp. 304–5). The trade cycle then is our starting-point. But much remains still to be explained. Why, for example, were these years so much more disturbed than other years of exceptionally high, or exceptionally low, unemployment? And why were some occupations so much more disturbed than others?

Stagnant or falling real wages from the mid-1890s (Table 3·1, above) are another part of the explanation. The unrest did not begin until well after real wages had ceased to rise, but this is not surprising because it took time for workers to become conscious of change. The change, after all, was not great nor did it occur in all occupations. Information on short-term movements in real wages was less recorded and less discussed than it is today, and the longer-term trend was obscured by fluctuations in earnings arising from unemployment, by changing spending patterns, and by spasmodic improvement in money wages. As Knowles emphasized in his investigation of strikes, and as the strike waves of 1892–3 and 1908 both testify, British unions normally reacted far more quickly to cuts in money wages (even when prices were also falling) than to falls in real wages brought about by rising prices.[58] After 1908, however, the accumulation of minor changes began to be felt. Coalfield agitators, for example, complained of 'a very serious rise in the cost-of-living'.[59]

Perhaps more important than the movement in real wages was an increasing consciousness and resentment of income inequalities. Education by this time was probably more influential in sharpening critical faculties and raising expectations than in instilling deference. The poverty surveys and disclosures of the alarmingly high proportion of Boer War recruits that had been found to be medically unfit were among other causes of the increase in 'felt' poverty. Changes in middle-class and upper-class spending habits contributed also. The early decline in middle-class fertility facilitated greater expenditure upon dining out, motoring, holidays, and other forms of conspicuous consumption at a time when miners and unskilled workers – the two groups most prominent in the unrest – had hardly begun to enjoy the benefits of smaller families. Aristocratic circles were shedding their inhibitions and behaving more ostentatiously, an indulgence symbolized by the demise of the rectitudinous Queen Victoria and the succession of the twenty-stone playboy Prince Edward. Upper-class extravagance was widely reported in the new popular press and so was the obvious contrast between their dissipation and the poverty revealed by successive social surveys. And the impression that other classes were growing wealthier while workers' living standards were under pressure may have been based upon more than changing expenditure patterns and rising expectations: we noted earlier some evidence of a change of this kind in the statistics of national income distribution (above, p. 115).

This consciousness of relative impoverishment partially eclipsed the new Liberal social reforms. Most trade unionists were in any event less impressed by these reforms than were the Labour and Liberal MPs who voted them through Parliament. Looking after the aged, the poor, and the sick was all very well: but the first concern of able-bodied workmen was their own wages. Certain of the reforms, especially those concerned with child welfare, also entailed more inspectors of various kinds and other unwelcome interference in working-class lives. Others, proposals for state pensions and health insurance in particular, had for long been opposed by the greater part of the friendly society movement on the grounds that they were incompatible with the spirit of self-help, a threat to friendly society independence, and unfair competition for working-class savings.[60] Moreover, working-class expectations had been so raised by the 1906 election that the shortcomings of subsequent reform received nearly as much attention as the reforms themselves. The miners, for example, complained that their eight-hour day was exclusive of winding times and disrupted work patterns, that their minimum wage was a district minimum and not the national minimum they had sought. Workers of every kind resented the new health contributions, and trade unionists grumbled that their hard-earned pennies were subsidizing the improvident poor. Many socialists resented parts of the Liberal reform programme because they felt that sickness and unemployment relief should have been met entirely from taxes upon the rich. Some of them dismissed all relief and piecemeal reform as unacceptable substitutes for social reconstruction.

These socialist attitudes were part of a continuing dissatisfaction over the outcome of their alliance with the unions that also has a place among the explanations of the pre-war unrest. Socialists derided reform less because of its nature than because it came from the Liberals, or as the fruit of political co-operation. The absence of a distinct Labour Party policy, and the upstaging of its working-class MPs by Lloyd George and Winston Churchill, marked the failure of socialist strategy. The socialists had hoped that workers would eventually contribute their votes and their subscriptions to a socialist crusade. But the Labour Party remained untrammelled by principles. As they came to appreciate the enduring nature of working-class pragmatism, socialists increasingly regretted the ideological sacrifices that had been made to secure union co-operation. In 1908, when there was heavy unemployment and the 1906 election euphoria was fading fast, Ben Tillett denounced Labour MPs as 'toadies' and 'hypocrites' in a pamphlet that asked *Is the Labour Party a Failure?* The affiliation of the Miners Federation of Great Britain in 1908 had in some ways heightened socialist frustration. The miners had been the only major union still withholding support from the Labour Party and by joining they broke up the Lib-Lab group of MPs and brought the majority of them (at the next election) under the Labour whip. But their transition was largely devoid of political conviction: their MPs, and most of their other leaders, continued to think and act like Liberals. Thus their affiliation reinforced the alliance between Labour and Liberals that socialists found so unpalatable.

Had the Labour Party continued the advance it began so dramatically at the 1906 election its critics might have been more tolerant of its ideological limitations. But there were rather less Labour MPs in 1914 than the combined strength of miners' and Labour MPs in 1906. This record – which contrasted with the advance in local government – fuelled the mood of disillusionment and frustration. The position after the 1910 elections was especially frustrating because the Liberal government was dependent on Labour and Irish Nationalist support. But this situation offered Labour no useful coercive advantage because most Labour MPs had been assisted to their seats by the electoral pact with the Liberals.[61] Labour MPs had no real alternative to ignoring socialist taunts and supporting the Liberals in office. The party was further embarrassed by the Osborne judgment of 1909. W. V. Osborne, a railwayman and a Liberal, had successfuly objected to being forced to contribute to the Labour Party through his trade union subscription. This was a serious blow because the party depended heavily upon union levies. The judgement, which in effect prohibited union expenditure upon anything other than strictly trade objectives, was not reversed until 1913[62] and it obviously strengthened critics of the Labour Party and all those who sought more certain and more immediate gains by industrial action.

These critics were not a substantial proportion of union membership. Most rank and file members took little interest in the doings of the Labour Party and were certainly not given to weighing the relative merits of political and industrial activity. Many of their leaders found altruistic satisfaction in the Lib-Lab reforms and they understood, and made allowances for, the various constraints upon the Labour Party. But the small number of politically active unionists who were critics of the Labour Party, and of the trade union establishment, was reinforced by the slow rate of political advance. The party's lack-lustre performance, its failure to impart a sense of purpose or to attain much hold upon the working-class imagination, strengthened the resolve of this group and eased their attempts to move the rank and file in the direction of industrial action.

Some militants became converts to syndicalism when it was introduced from Europe and America in 1910. Tom Mann returned from Australia in that year and became the chief advocate of syndicalism in Britain. He had an active part in most of the major disputes and in the drive to combine union strength in great industrial unions and federations. Syndicalism looked to the eventual replacement of capitalist employment by workers' control. Beyond this its long-term aims were less clearly defined than the means of obtaining them. Capitalist employers were to be brought to their knees by strikes. Their ultimate collapse, syndicalists preached, would be achieved by the general strike and almost any strike would contribute to this end by weakening the 'class enemy' and heightening workers' consciousness of mutual interests. Syndicalists were highly critical of the existing trade union structure whose multitudinous societies reflected consciousness of separate (and often conflicting) interests and they rejected state socialism as scarcely preferable to capitalism. They rejected parliamentary methods too – the class struggle, they believed, would be fought-out on the factory floor.

Those who held these views influenced the temper and scale of the pre-war unrest. Wherever serious discontent smouldered they were to be found encouraging workers to see their grievances as part of a wider class struggle and urging them to seek redress at once, by strike action, and if necessary in defiance of their official leaders. They eagerly endorsed the suspicion that real wages were falling, they proclaimed the failure of the Labour Party and orthodox unionism to provide a remedy, and on several occasions they forced official leaders to adopt aggressive postures for fear that their members might otherwise follow the militant intruders. Once battle was joined syndicalists sought to prolong and widen disputes by urging rejection of all attempts at compromise and inciting other workers to sympathetic action. They had most success among South Wales miners and sections of the railwaymen and dockers, particularly at the time of the Cambrian dispute and during the 1912 miners' strike. They could also claim some influence in the moves that led to the formation of the National Union of Railwaymen, the Transport Workers Federation, and the Triple Alliance.

Syndicalists and socialists together helped to expose one of the limitations of British industrial relations procedures by encouraging demands for 'minimum living wages' and by raising other 'issues of principle' that were not easily encompassed within the pragmatic give and take of voluntary collective bargaining. The weaknesses in British industrial relations described in Chapter 8 had become of some consequence by this time and are another part of the explanation of the pre-war strife. After 1890 the government more often offered advice and conciliation during disputes, but the absence of any means of enforcement was still the outstanding characteristic of official industrial relations policy when the pre-war strikes began.[63] 'New unionism' had earlier raised momentary doubts about the adequacy of this policy and prompted the Royal Commission on Labour (1891–4). But that unrest subsided before the

Commission reported and the majority report declared relations to be at their best when both sides were well organized and negotiation was facilitated by voluntary collective bargaining procedures. The legislative outcome of this inquiry, the Conciliation Act of 1896,[64] was consequently hardly more than an endorsement of the government's long-standing negative policy and its more recent practice of encouraging voluntary bargaining through the good offices of the Labour Department of the Board of Trade.[65] The government was now also forced to make occasional *ad hoc* interventions in disputes when other means of reaching a settlement had failed and the national economy or public safety were exceptionally threatened. But intervention of this kind was by no means a conscious and considered departure from the preferred official policy. Ministers approached the two sides without any means of enforcement at their disposal – and that they had to intervene at all in this fashion was a logical (if unforeseen and unwelcome) consequence of the absence of positive policy.

In 1909 Winston Churchill, then President of the Board of Trade, toyed with proposals to introduce compulsory arbitration. The strikes of the previous year, the miners' reaction to the Eight Hours Act of 1908, and the unrest that followed in 1910–14 caused many others to question the adequacy of existing government policy. By this time, however, the government probably would not have found it easy to regulate industrial relations in the public interest.[66] Such changes might well have been introduced without difficulty before 1890 when the unions were weak, when many of them were still seeking recognition, and when union leaders were anxious to demonstrate their claims that unionism was responsible and public spirited.[67] If a positive industrial relations policy had been introduced at that time, and administered judiciously, unions might have become sufficiently accustomed to legal constraints, and sufficiently convinced of their long-term benefits, to resist the temptation to cast them aside when they became strong enough to do so. It was perhaps still not too late to introduce such a policy after the 'new' union eruption, and had that outburst been more sustained this might have been the recommendation of the Royal Commission on Labour.[68] But Taff Vale (1901) encouraged unionists to believe that they could not be sure of fair treatment from the courts, and labour's growing industrial and political strength permitted a more cavalier attitude towards the public interest and encouraged demands for complete freedom from legal restraint. The report of the Royal Commission on Trade Disputes (1906) was rejected out of hand by the TUC. And far from attempting to act upon the report, the government (and the opposition) surrendered to political expediency by granting unions complete freedom from civil liability.[69]

The increasing resort to last-minute ministerial intervention in major disputes almost encouraged strong unions to eschew compromise and override voluntary collective bargaining. They did so in the expectation that the government, mindful of its communal responsibilities and lacking the means to impose a settlement, would eventually introduce concessions by legislation or persuade the employers to back down. This prospect was also an encouragement to smaller unions to join together in alliances sufficiently powerful to hold the community to ransom. These developments in industrial relations posed ominous threats to economic efficiency, to the health, safety, and comfort of the public, and ultimately to democratic government. They led eventually to the general strike of 1926 and since 1960 have again become a preoccupation of politicians and economists.

The other main weakness in British industrial relations–the 'gap at shopfloor level' (above, p. 285)–did not become a serious cause of unrest until well into the new century. Until 1908, in fact, the spread of formal collective bargaining–favoured both by employers and unions and encouraged by the costly stoppages of 1892–3 and 1897–8–almost certainly contributed to industrial tranquillity.[70] But whereas in 1890 few joint negotiating boards covered employment beyond a city and its environs, by 1914 numerous trades negotiated upon a county or regional basis and some boards governed an entire industry. Each step towards nation-wide collective bargaining shifted the decision-making process further from the shop floor. Thus unionists found themselves bound by national or regional agreements whose origins were (to them) obscure, which too often did not recognize local customs, and which failed to deal expeditiously with local grievances. Such grievances might simmer for months while the issues percolated through successively more distant negotiations and union members grew resentful of their leaders' pledge not to strike before every stage of collective bargaining had been exhausted. The duration of these agreements and their curbs upon the size and incidence of wage changes were also resented, especially when the cost of living began to rise.[71] Enforcement fell mainly upon union officials who had the power to fine or threaten errant members and control over strike pay. The impression that union officials were 'doing the bosses' work for them' helped to open up rifts between the men and their leaders.[72] Younger trade unionists, who had more quickly forgotten (or never knew) the costs of the 1890s strikes, became especially impatient with what appeared to them as excessive union caution. Tangible evidence of their impatience was not substantial before 1908–merely a sprinkling of unofficial strikes and employers' complaints that shop stewards were exceeding their duties and short-circuiting agreed procedures. After 1908 however, and especially in 1911–13, it was evident in the influence that socialist and syndicalist agitators could wield over men partially alienated from their official leaders and in the unofficial and spontaneous nature of much of the unrest.

Some of these general causes of the pre-war unrest were far more apparent

327

in certain occupations than in others. Shortcomings in formal collective bargaining procedures, for example, can hardly have been responsible for much of the unrest among unskilled workers because so few of them were covered by such procedures. In their case a growing consciousness of poverty, rising prices, and the tightening labour market, were far more important. Nor can such shortcomings explain the railwaymen's discontent because one of their two chief grievances was the employers' refusal to grant recognition.[73] In some other occupations moreover, in iron and steel making for example, long-established collective bargaining procedures continued to function reasonably satisfactorily throughout the pre-war years. The engineering industry exhibited yet another pattern: there the nature of collective bargaining gave rise to considerable discontent but to relatively few major strikes. This was perhaps in part a consequence of the comprehensiveness of the employers' victory in 1897–8, and in part due to the fact that new methods of work and payment (resented although they were for their erosion of craft status) in many cases increased real wages.

The miners, who took the most prominent part in the pre-war strife, were particularly affected by some of the influences that have been described. Coal prices and mine wages rose to exceptional levels during the Boer War and the miners were naturally resentful when their earnings subsequently fell. They had a leading place in the minimum wage campaign, as we noted earlier, and they were also the first organized workers to disrupt economic activity sufficiently to force the government to become involved in their disputes. Having once tasted this power the miners were emboldened by the belief that they could bring the government into industrial relations almost at will. The coal-masters, moreover, conscious that labour productivity was falling and finding little compensation in coal prices, were more inclined than most British employers to resist union demands[74]. The miners of South Wales felt these pressures more than other miners. Earnings and productivity in South Wales suffered exceptionally from the introduction of the Eight Hours Act[75] and the Welsh coal-masters, accustomed to dealing with weak unions, were inclined to meet the new militancy head-on. Dependence upon the competitive export market stiffened their resistance while the men, whose erratic piece-rate earnings reflected the contorted geology of the South Wales field, had become more vociferous than other miners in demanding a minimum wage regardless of output. This coalfield also saw a considerable combination movement among colliery companies[76] and suffered exceptionally from mine accidents.[77] For these reasons the South Wales miners acquired a special reputation for militancy. They distinguished themselves by making the transition from Lib-Lab to Labour in 1908 with some political conviction[78] and it was in South Wales that syndicalists gained their greatest influence over British workers.

It is impossible to give an entirely satisfactory explanation of the pre-war unrest, either as a whole or in any particular occupation. Workers were motivated by a great variety of influences, many of which were far less measurable than movements in wages, prices, and unemployment. The majority of workers outside the mining and transport sectors failed to respond to similar influences for reasons that are equally obscure. Once the unrest was underway it became self-sustaining and self-reinforcing on an unprecedented scale. The popular press gave national publicity to each major dispute and increased the sense of shared grievances. Political agitators did the same. Each concession gained by militancy was an encouragement to others to act similarly, if only in an attempt to restore disturbed differentials. Moreover, labour unrest was one of a number of crises that seemed likely to come to a head at this time: there was the constitutional crisis on the role of the House of Lords, provoked in part by sweeping social reform; protestant Ulster was threatening armed resistance to Home Rule; there was the suffragettes' campaign; there was labour unrest abroad; and the growing international tension that preceded the First World War. Just as labour unrest in one industry or district was encouraged by similar events elsewhere, so these larger crises may have been mutually reinforcing.

VIII · *Prospect of revolution or revolutionary strike, 1910–14; class consciousness and the making of class, 1889–1914*

George Dangerfield, in *The Strange Death of Liberal England*, emphasized the associations between these various pre-war crises and implied that the war averted an impending clash between capital and labour of possibly revolutionary proportions.[79] Industrial action was frequently accompanied by violence in these years, syndicalists were attempting to engage the unions in class war, and the Triple Alliance raised the prospect of an almighty confrontation from which the government could hardly stand aside.

In fact, the prospects were less alarming than Dangerfield supposed. Most of the violence that occurred was no more than the predictable consequence of initial organization among the unskilled and even in the coal industry syndicalism had little support outside South Wales.[80] At the time of the 1912 coal strike *The Economist* (30 March 1912) doubted whether as many as one-tenth of the miners had any clear conception of what syndicalists stood for. The Transport Workers Federation, the NUR, and the Triple Alliance each owed something to syndicalist influence, and their creation was certainly consistent with syndicalist ambitions. But the coincidence between these ambitions and those of the majority of unionists stopped far short of creating giant amalgamations to wage revolutionary strikes. The amalgamation movement, moreover, by no means transformed British unionism in the way syndicalists intended. Motions in favour of amalgamation were passed at the 1910 and 1911 Trades Union Congresses, but when unions separately considered the implications of such moves the great majority of them, including the South Wales miners, chose to preserve the autonomy that safeguarded their sectional interests.[81]

Syndicalists, in fact, had no more success than revolutionary socialists in weaning the mass of British working men from political apathy or in diverting the politically conscious minority from constitutional reform. These attitudes had prevailed over even the watered-down socialism that the ILP brought to the Labour Party. Their persistence was among the reasons why working-class revolution was less of a possibility in Britain than where workers' political organization had preceded industrial organization and given unions an ideological perspective.[82] The lack of a significant revolutionary impulse is evident in many aspects of the pre-war unrest. Many disputes were quickly settled by wage advances or by union recognition. The mine leaders' decided to return to work in 1912 despite a majority vote in favour of staying out, and in the same year the Transport Workers Federation failed in its attempt to spread the London dockers' strike. There was no response to James Larkin's appeal for sympathetic strike action in 1913 and before the strike was over he was denouncing British union leaders as cowards and traitors.

Perhaps most significant was the contrast between what alarmists suspected was the purpose of the Triple Alliance and the cautious and pragmatic intentions of its leaders.[83] The Alliance was neither a declaration of class war nor a manifestation of revolutionary urge for amalgamation. Prominent among the reasons for its establishment was the unemployment and expense that had resulted from unsynchronized strike action by its constituent unions – the 1912 miners' strike, for example, had cost the Railway Servants £94,000 in out-of-work benefits. In addition, the Alliance was a means of tightening union discipline and an effective riposte to the militants at work among the rank and file.[84] Clearly it was intended also to improve wages and conditions by marshalling greater pressure against employers and the government. But the political implications of this strategy, its revolutionary potential in particular, were certainly not sought and barely even contemplated. Even industrial objectives appear to have taken second place to preserving the right of each union to act (or not act) independently: there was absolutely no obligation to come to each other's assistance. It is hardly surprising, therefore, that after the war the Triple Alliance was to demonstrate a paralysing reluctance to do anything that jeopardized sectional interests. In 1926, when the government confronted the unions with the choice of giving way or persisting in a course that was now decreed to be insurrectionary, the limits to union ambitions were abundantly clear. Threatened with victory of a kind they had never sought, union leaders opted for surrender.

The pragmatic and conciliatory attitudes of the unions were generally reciprocated and this also helped to make a revolutionary explosion unlikely. Employers obviously differed enormously in their response to unions: the railway and shipping companies, for example, were for long as uncompromisingly hostile as the majority of employers in the United States and Europe. Exceptional instances of union militancy or union obstructiveness, and initial organization in occupations where employers were not accustomed to combination, could also provoke an authoritarian reaction. For the most part, however, the response of British employers to unionism was a grumbling acceptance. The majority were willing to co-operate in operating formal collective bargaining long before the pre-war unrest began, and even at the time of Taff Vale very few employers seemed anxious to press the unions to the point where they would have needed to fight the system to survive.[85]

British governments by this time were more favourably disposed towards unions than British employers. The government forced the railway companies to accept collective bargaining and an increasing reluctance to provide military and police protection for 'blackleg' labour was among the reasons why the ship-owners also were becoming more conciliatory before 1914.[86] In 1891 half a dozen unionists and several labour sympathizers had been appointed to the Royal Commission on Labour (1891–4) and so many were appointed to the Labour Department of the Board of Trade that employers questioned the department's supposed impartiality.[87] Invitations to participate in managing the labour exchanges scheme (1909) and national insurance (1911) were among the other ways in which the unions came to have a not insubstantial part in administering labour affairs.

Working-class revolution appears to have been as far off in the troubled years before 1914 as it was in the second half of the nineteenth century. Working-class consciousness, however, definitely grew stronger from the late 1880s. In 1890 Engels wrote joyfully of the British working class 'newly awakened from its forty-years' sleep'. The developments that marked subsequent progress in the making of class have each been mentioned. There were, in particular, 'new unionism', the employers' counter-attack; the establishment of the GFTU and the Labour Party; Taff Vale; an increasing resentment of relative poverty, and the pre-war industrial unrest that brought class interests more into the open and allowed millions of workers to experience the camaraderie of industrial action. The five-fold increase in the number of unionists between 1890 and 1914; the movement's extension into occupations and districts that were previously unorganized; the continuing expansion of semi-skilled occupations; and the associated decline of the craftsmen and their distinctive status each had obvious consequences for class consciousness. Some of the divisions between employer and employed that were noted in previous chapters continued to widen after 1890 as companies grew bigger, and by 1914 organized religion, with its emphasis upon communal interests and the distinctions between the respectables and the disreputables of whatever class, was fast losing influence.

Working-class consciousness was therefore more pervasive by the early twentieth century than at any time previously. But was there sufficient class consciousness, sufficient homogeneity, and sufficient hostility towards other classes for the working class (as defined on p. 245 above) to be regarded as having come into existence? The contrast between the heady expectations of early 'new unionism' and the distinctly limited change that had taken place by 1900 was emphasized earlier. At that time, it seems, class was still in the making. And progress in the following years was certainly not sufficient to put the matter beyond doubt. 'Insular, aristocratic, philistinely selfish' was Lenin's summing-up of English unions just before the war[88] – a partial judgement, but one that syndicalists and socialists who were struggling to overcome these obstacles would have accepted with little qualification.[89] The ASE by this time had found it advantageous to leave and rejoin the TUC three times and the most recent (1912) of a number of moves towards recruiting unskilled engineering workers met the usual rank and file opposition and was soon abandoned. The Operative Cotton Spinners still accepted their piecer assistants as fellow unionists only on terms that underlined the piecers' inferiority, and the building craftsmen agreed to admit labourers to conciliation boards subject to conditions that have been likened to 'the safeguards of ascendancy in a multi-racial society'.[90] Until the *Daily Citizen* was begun in 1913 (in response to the militant propaganda of the *Daily Herald*) the labour movement lacked even its own newspaper, each attempt to begin one having foundered upon sectional apathy. The relative indifference of many trade unionists to social reforms intended to benefit those outside the union ranks[91] and the incessant squabbling between the co-operative movement and the unions acting for its employees are also significant. It was clear too, long before 1914, that the GFTU (above, p. 310) would never enjoy the support of more than a minority of the movement. Few of the larger unions joined the Federation: they felt strong enough to look after themselves and disinclined to surrender their autonomy.[92] The GFTU, in fact, became something of a prop to small, sectional, societies that otherwise might have lost their separate identity in larger unions. It never co-ordinated sympathy strikes and so widespread were suspicions that its funds might be misused that they were dispensed with the greatest parsimony and the Federation did all it could to discourage conflict. This was not far from the opposite of the militant and class-conscious role that some had envisaged for the GFTU when it was launched.

On the political front too there is considerable evidence of similar implication. The miners' unions did not affiliate to the Labour Party until 1908. 45 per cent of miners voted against affiliation,[93] and after the Trade Union Act of 1913 40 per cent of them voted against a political levy to support the Labour Party. Given the choice between Liberal and other candidates, the majority of all working men still voted Liberal. Socialist politics had made most headway where Lib-Labism was least firmly entrenched but the usual alternative to a conscious Lib-Labism was an unthinking political conservatism of the kind that Alfred Williams complained of in his workmates, 'if you should be at the pains of pointing-out anything for their benefit they will tell you that you are mad, or curse you for a socialist. Anyone at the works who holds a view different from that of the crowd is called a socialist'.[94] Robert Roberts emphasized similar attitudes in pre-war Salford where Hyndman Hall (home of the SDF) was said to have 'about as much political impact on the neighbourhood as the nearby gasworks', where the class struggle 'was apolitical' and took place 'entirely within their own society', and where few bothered to listen to street politicians because they were not conscious of any connection between themselves and 'the proletariat'.[95] A. L. Rowse's working-class Cornish neighbours appear to have felt much the same. Oxford-bound after the First World War Rowse acquired an interest in Labour politics, but until then his father had voted Liberal 'as all the china-clay workers voted Liberal, because the china-clay captains were Liberal'.[96]

The effect of social mobility on class consciousness and the overall direction of social mobility are no clearer for these years than for earlier decades. But there is no particular reason for supposing that the trends described in Chapter 8 changed in a manner conducive to a hardening of class lines. The rate of internal geographical mobility fell towards the end of the century but there was at least some compensation in the numbers leaving to better themselves abroad. After 1890, moreover, working-class social mobility benefited from the fall in middle-class fertility and from substantial improvement in technical and secondary education.[97] The erosion of the social status of skilled workers probably accelerated, but perhaps by no more than the rate at which their sons and daughters joined the lower middle classes.[98] J. Ramsay MacDonald, the illegitimate son of a ploughman and a servant girl who later became a schoolteacher and eventually Prime Minister, and D. H. Lawrence who left his father's colliery cottage for a desk in Edwardian Nottingham, were following routes whose initial stages were taken by a great many others. There was sufficient social mobility of this kind for very few families, however poor, to have been quite without middle-class relatives and virtually none whose proletarian consciousness was not qualified by the prospect of their children's advancement. Robert Roberts' 'classic slum' home was familiar with the servant-keeping difficulties of suburban aunts and Stella Davies's numerous relatives included (besides the impeccably proletarian) a manager of a co-operative clothing factory, a chemist, and Uncle Sept who began in a very small way buying and cleaning entrails and finished with a food processing and restaurant business.[99] Even Beatrice Webb had northern relatives sufficiently humble to merit social investigation.[100]

Working-class consciousness was clearly less advanced by 1914 than the dramatic events of 1889–91 had seemed to promise. At the same time it was indisputably more advanced than it had been in the 1880s. Whether a single working class could yet be said to exist in 1914 is a question that cannot be answered in other than a subjective fashion and one that hangs a great deal upon how 'class' is defined. Measured against E. P. Thompson's definition (above, p. 245) the working class appears still to have been in the making when the pre-war unrest began. In the industrial sphere there was still too much sectionalism, too little solidarity, and too few signs of trade union consciousness being translated into class consciousness. In the political sphere there were still too many working men who were either lacking in political consciousness of any kind or who were adherents of some form of Lib-Labism. It is quite legitimate, of course, to define class less rigorously. If a 'working class' requires only that considerable numbers be born and bred in working-class districts, that they work with their hands, and follow working-class leisure pursuits, then Britain obviously had a 'working class' long before 1914. G. Stedman Jones, for example, has claimed 'something akin to a remaking of the working class' between 1870 and 1900 (in London at least) with considerable emphasis in his account upon the mass pursuit of proletarian forms of leisure.[101] But the 'class' he describes – politically conservative and manifesting little militancy, hostility, or solidarity – is a decidedly feeble form of 'class'.[102]

A working class of a less feeble kind certainly existed sometime between 1910 and 1939. But the inter-war years, and especially the years from the Armistice to the general strike, probably have a stronger claim to class consciousness of this kind than the pre-war period. By 1920 there were twice the number of unionists there had been in 1914, sectionalism had been further eroded, and class consciousness was being consolidated by economic adversity and exceptionally persistent and widespread industrial unrest. The Labour Party, moreover, was no longer in any danger of losing its identity within the Liberal Party, it had accepted socialism (nominally at least), and could depend upon a very considerable proportion of working-class votes.

IX · *Working-class movements and working-class living standards, 1889–1914*

From what has been said it is clear that the unions affected working-class living standards far more after 1890 than they had done earlier and that their influence by this time considerably outweighed that of the friendly societies and other movements. After 1890, and particularly after 1906, the unions acquired a voice in determining certain aspects of central and local government policy. Thus their influence on living standards was increasingly felt beyond the workplace. It was still subject to the trade cycle and other limitations, but the combination of increased industrial strength, growing influence over governments, and the increasing activities of governments, was reducing these restraints.

What of union performance? How much weight should be allowed to claims that substantial opportunities were missed through excessive caution? The overall position in this respect was probably not greatly dissimilar to that in the pre-1889 period which was discussed in some detail in Chapter 8. That is, some opportunities doubtless were missed but there were fewer options available than critics of the unions were prepared to concede. 'New unionism' certainly showed that the unions had not done everything possible to advance working-class interests. But its rapid collapse, and the counter-attack it provoked, showed also how easily industrial militancy could rebound. The political record was not a bad one, plodding and uninspiring although Lib-Labism undoubtedly appeared. Socialists resented the lack of political independence and the rank and file were often impatient at the rate of advance. But a great deal was achieved and the best part of it came from Lib-Lab co-operation. More determined attempts to establish an independent political identity would have meant fewer concessions from the Liberals and might have delayed the emergence of the Labour Party or brought about its early collapse. In this context there is a significant contrast between the pragmatic achievements of Lib-Labism and the generally futile activities of the SDF.[103]

By 1914, in fact, the advantages that unions denied their members by too much caution, and the costs they inflicted upon non-members by their exclusiveness, may have been far smaller than the consequences of the union influence upon industrial efficiency. Strikes had become increasingly costly. As unions and companies grew larger, and as collective bargaining agreements came to cover many more workers, the numbers who might be directly involved in a single dispute increased proportionately. And the number of those who lost employment as a consequence of other workers' strikes increased more than proportionately as economic activity became more capital intensive, more specialized, and more interdependent. The annual statistics of days lost per worker by striking–it still averaged under

335

two days in 1910–14 and was only four days in 1912 – were thus increasingly inadequate as an indication of the total cost of stoppages. The miners now had the capacity to put a stranglehold upon considerable areas of economic activity and their leaders appeared to be increasingly prepared to use the hardship they could inflict upon the community as a means of coercing employers and the government: 'In less than a week,' boasted one of the coalfield militants (1912), 'we can paralyse the nation, bring the government to its knees and make it beg us to resume work.'[104] Workers had no natural immunity against such hardship: the disruption to milk and food supplies in the summer of 1911 probably helped to cause the exceptional infant mortality of that year,[105] and the 1912 miners' strike was calculated to have reduced industrial earnings by 12 per cent and to have made 60 per cent of iron and steel workers unemployed within three weeks.[106]

But union rules on manning and recruiting, their undermining of employers' authority, resistance to new machines and methods, and other on-the-job restrictive practices that were backed by the threat of strikes, remained the more serious long-term obstacle to greater efficiency. 'New unionism' was associated with the systematic extension of the old practice of deliberately restricting output (ca' canny) in the hope that what was left undone would provide work for the unemployed. Often it did, at least in the short run. But employers complained bitterly that by raising costs its long-term effect would be that markets, wages, profits, and employment would all be lost together. These fears were prominent at the time of the 1890s counter-attack. The South Metropolitan Gas Company, for example, claimed that unionization had temporarily raised labour costs by up to a third and that once rid of the union it was able to invest in new machinery and to pay above-average wages as well as running a profit-sharing scheme.[107]

The great engineering dispute of 1897–8 over union resistance to workshop changes provoked a prolonged discussion on trade unionism and its effect upon output. That the normally individualistic and comparatively easy-going British engineering employers should join together and confront the mighty ASE in the aggressive fashion of Krupp or Carnegie is one indication of the importance that had become attached to union restrictions. The purpose of their Federation, said its president, Colonel Dyer, was 'to obtain the freedom to manage their own affairs which had proved so beneficial to American manufacturers as to enable them to compete . . . in what was formerly an English monopoly'.[108] Another spokesman for the Federation announced that during the strike the output of certain categories of comparatively inexperienced operatives was between a fifth and a half greater than that of the ASE men they had replaced.[109] After the strike one manufacturer claimed that he could sell in Germany products that previously had been exported from Germany to Britain.[110] What the employers' victory meant in gains such as this, in greater freedom to invest and adopt new methods, is incalculable. But it seems likely that a different outcome would have resulted in British engineering in 1918 being even less prepared than it was for the challenges of the inter-war economy and that the subsequent unemployment and suffering would have been that much greater. There were other strikes in the 1890s whose outcomes were regarded as similarly crucial to British competitiveness. One of the biggest was that of 1895 in the boot and shoe industry where union restrictions were held largely to blame for the ability of Chicago manufacturers, paying well above English wages, to compete successfully with Northampton and Leicester-made boots in the home market.[111]

The whole question of unionism and economic efficiency was given another thorough airing early in the new century, this time against the background of the Taff Vale case and in the context of the controversy over tariff reform. The unions were particularly criticized in a series of articles in *The Times* that was later published as *Trade Unionism and British Industry*.[112] Evidence was produced showing how several of the Sheffield trades, much of the glass industry, parts of the printing trade, and the manufacture of iron and steel, tinplate, and other products had been impeded by union restrictions upon recruiting or union resistance to the introduction and efficient operation of machinery. At Sheffield, it was said, 'everything new must be fought for with the unions'.[113] There were complaints too that the extension of municipal employment (free of competitive restraints and in an atmosphere sympathetic to the unions) was setting new standards in low productivity, that workshop discipline had suffered because unionism diminished the fear of sackings, and that other priorities were neglected as managers found it necessary to spend an ever growing proportion of their time upon labour issues. Yet another category of charges concerned the extension of union control of labour supply to obstructing technical instruction on the supposition that it was intended to 'flood the market': the Birmingham gun trade, desperately in need of trained youths, encountered this objection and so did several Sheffield trades.[114]

Against all this criticism must be set evidence that the unions continued to exercise some favourable influences upon productivity in the various ways described in Chapter 8: by curbing spontaneous strikes, for example, and by assisting the operation of collective bargaining arrangements. The unions are certainly entitled to some of the credit for the long period of industrial tranquillity that began in 1898, and it remained true that a great deal of indiscipline, indolence, and resistance to machinery for which they were blamed might possibly have been no less evident in their absence.[115] The high proportion of the pre-war labour unrest that was unofficial is significant in this respect. Political agitators and their disruptive activities were no more welcome to the average union leader than to employers.

Employers continued to have a share of responsibility for poor industrial relations. Attempts to increase productivity were invariably disruptive. In some cases they increased workloads, they were almost sure to be resented at a time when there was considerable fear of unemployment, and they called for more managerial tact and sensitivity than was usual in British industry. One critic of the unions cited by Pratt went on to attribute superior American labour productivity to 'the splendid handling of their men which American employers show' and their 'greater willingness to encourage their men to share in the benefits and profits of improved methods and machinery'.[116] The government too must take some part of the blame, both because of its failure to introduce a framework of industrial relations law and because the unconditional surrender of 1906 (above, p. 326) put the unions in a position where responsible behaviour required a greater sacrifice of short-term interests.

What was the net effect of these influences? Here again there can be no certain answers but only impressions and probabilities. It was suggested earlier that unionism was possibly already a restraint upon productivity in the 1880s, although its influence then was still not great. By 1900, however, unionism was probably among the more serious impediments to improved economic efficiency and a significant handicap in international competition. E. H. Phelps Brown, in accounting for Britain's poor productivity record at this time, gave as one of the causes 'the changed attitude of the worker', the 'withholding of co-operation', and 'increased resistance to management'.[117] E. J. Hobsbawm has argued similarly.[118] The union influence had become far more widespread and less easily resisted at a time when British manufacturers were struggling to keep abreast of American and German competitors whose labour was less unionized and more easily disciplined.[119] Taff Vale caused the unions to tread warily for a few years but in 1906 they succeeded in removing this constraint. Greatly increased union influence called for leaders of an appropriate calibre. It required men far-sighted enough to accept that increased power carried with it increased responsibility, men who could recognize both the importance of economic growth to long-term advance in working-class living standards and that union behaviour would significantly affect the rate of growth. The leaders of British unionism in 1914 lacked these qualities. Union impediments to efficiency were probably still by no means so great that they offset all the very substantial political and industrial benefits that unionism brought to the working classes. But they were becoming considerable, they were still growing, and with hindsight it is clear that the unions were already on a course that, if continued, would eventually make them one of the main constraints upon British living standards.

Suggestions for further reading are on pages 404–5.

CONCLUSION

The labour force of 1815 presents a remarkable contrast with that of a century later. By 1914 Britain's workforce was larger, more productive, and better paid. There were fewer children at work and workers had moved to the towns and into industrial and tertiary employment. The working week was shorter, the workplace less dangerous, and the urban environment much healthier. At the beginning of the nineteenth century there had been very few trade unionists and the working classes had little political influence. By 1914 almost a quarter of the labour force was organized, most workmen had the vote, and the Labour Party had began to make its presence felt at Westminster. These are among the more important of the changes that have been described.

One of the distinguishing characteristics of British labour, although one that is often overlooked, was its relative affluence. Some workers were wretchedly poor, but there were few places overseas, and none in Europe, where working-class living standards were above those in Britain. International comparisons, and comparisons of wages in different parts of Britain, suggest that industrialization was usually associated with relatively favourable working-class living standards. Urban squalor detracted significantly from the high wages and employment opportunities of the industrial centres in the first half of the nineteenth century. But most urban squalor was not the direct result of industrialization, and the advantages of the manufacturing districts were always sufficient to attract large numbers of migrants from elsewhere in Britain.

One reason why rural living standards remained comparatively low was that the rural population increased more rapidly than rural employment. A close association between population pressure and poverty can be seen also in every household that struggled to raise a large family on low wages and in the way that high rates of natural increase maintained the flow of recruits to some of the most crowded parts of the labour market. The nineteenth-century belief that demographic pressures were an important cause of working-class distress deserves more serious consideration than historians have usually been willing to concede.

Another distinguishing characteristic of British labour was its high quality. In most respects labour productivity in Britain compared well with that in

339

Europe until at least the end of the nineteenth century. British workers were by no means as workshy as the architects of the 1834 Poor Law Amendment Act supposed. They responded readily to cash incentives and were willing to take up new occupations, to adopt new work patterns, and to move about the country in response to changing job opportunities. There was an abundance of inherited skill in Britain and the shortcomings of working-class education appear to have had little effect on labour productivity. British labour was also conciliatory towards employers. Strikes, arson, machine smashing, and politically motivated violence have been highlighted in the literature, but they were not often serious impediments to industrial advance in the nineteenth century. The high quality of British labour was one of the chief causes of high wage levels in Britain.

How much did trade unionism contribute to working-class living standards? There is little agreement among historians on this important issue. To some it is self-evident that improvement in working-class living standards came largely as a consequence of working-class pressure, but others give prominence to claims that numerous opportunities to advance working-class interests were lost because unions were over-cautious and too concerned with their sectional interests. Contemporaries frequently claimed that unionism was a serious obstacle to greater economic efficiency. The conclusions of Chapters 8 and 9 were that the unions made an increasing contribution to working-class welfare throughout the nineteenth century and that by the Edwardian period their contribution had become substantial. Unions advanced the living standards of non-members as well as unionists, and their achievements were probably as great as could be expected in the circumstances. For most of the nineteenth century unionism did not seriously reduce labour productivity. By 1914, however, the advantages it brought to workers may have been significantly offset by the union influence upon labour productivity.

Despite industrialization, urbanization, and the widening gulf between employers and workers, the persistence of harmonious class relations and the remarkably slow development of working-class consciousness are two of the major themes in nineteenth-century British labour history. British working-class movements were pragmatic and constitutional. They adopted what most suited them from Owenism, liberalism, and socialism; but there was no significant commitment to any political philosophy until the years immediately before the First World War. Why this should have been so was considered in the last three chapters. The remarkable diversity in every aspect of working-class life and the keen consciousness of sectional interests are important parts of the explanation. Any analysis of labour history which treats workers *en masse*, or divides them in some simple fashion between the 'politically conscious' and the 'lumpenproletariat' or between the 'labour aristocracy' and 'the rest', courts the obvious danger of playing down the diversity of working-class experience and thus exaggerating working-class consciousness.

Among the clearest evidence of muted class consciousness is the pattern of working-class voting. Political activists made repeated attempts to launch an independent working-class party and after the 1867 Reform Act working-class votes could have made such a party a formidable rival to the Liberals and Conservatives. Yet there was no substantial support for an independent party until the Labour Representation Committee was established in 1900. The LRC, moreover, would never have secured sufficient initial support from trade unions if it had pursued a class-conscious programme, and the support necessary to sustain the new party would probably have been unavailable on any terms had it not been for the Taff Vale judgement of 1901. Two years after Taff Vale the LRC entered into formal alliance with the Liberals and even in 1914 it was not yet certain that the Labour Party (as the LRC had become) could command a majority of working-class votes or that it was yet much more than a substantial pressure group within the Liberal Party.

Unless otherwise indicated, the place of publication in works cited is London.

Part I · The Labour Market, Incomes and Consumption

Introduction

1 J. Burnett, *Plenty and Want: A Social History of Diet in England*, (1966), p. 149; F. Engels, *The Condition of the Working Class in England*, ed. W. O. Henderson and W. H. Chaloner (Oxford 1958), p. 278.

2 *The Times*, 20–24 Jan. 1862.

1 · *Work and Workers*

3 Calculations based upon figures of working population in P. Deane and W. A. Cole, *British Economic Growth, 1688–1959*, (Cambridge 1967), p. 143.

4 See, for example, B. Inglis, *Poverty and the Industrial Revolution*, (1972 edn.), p. 30.

5 *A True Account of the Island of England* (c. 1500), (Camden Society XXXVII, 1847), pp. 24–5.

6 F. Collier, *The Family Economy of the Working Classes in the Cotton Industry, 1784–1833*, (Manchester 1964), p. 2.

7 Collier, op. cit. p. 2. See also I. Pinchbeck and M. Hewitt, *Children in English Society*, (1969), I, pp. 310–311; O. J. Dunlop, *English Apprenticeship and Child Labour*, (1912), p. 101; N. McKendrick (ed.), *Historical Perspectives*, (1974), p. 158.

8 In 1851, 42,000 children under ten were employed, in 1871 22,000. B. R. Mitchell and P. Deane, *Abstract of British Historical Statistics*, (Cambridge 1962), p. 59.

9 D. V. Glass, 'Changes in Fertility in England and Wales, 1851 to 1931', in *Political Arithmetic*, ed. L. Hogben (1938), p. 210. This figure, like those for earlier dates, is probably an underestimate. A substantial number of children had part-time jobs. In 1902 it was estimated that some 253,000 schoolchildren were employed in some capacity outside school hours. M. W. Thomas, *Young People in Industry, 1750–1945*, (1945), p. 143.

10 By 1911 the proportion of children under fifteen in the population of England and Wales has been reduced to 31 per cent; in 1881 it was 36 per cent.

11 Some of the children themselves, and their parents, were unenthusiastic about restrictive legislation; and one sign that the government was determined to make the act of 1833 effective can be seen in the search for a reliable way of ascertaining the age of children as it was realized that baptismal certificates of sufficient vintage were securing employment for others besides their rightful bearers. It was recommended, for example, that children's teeth should be examined as a more reliable guide to age. Henry Ashworth complained that 'a mill-owner, if he employs his time properly, should have something else to do than be running about and examining children's teeth'. R. Boyson, *The Ashworth Cotton Enterprise*, (Oxford 1970), p. 174.

12 In 1815 only about a quarter of all children had attended school, by mid-century the proportion was about half. E. H. Phelps Brown, *The Growth of British Industrial Relations*, (1959), p. 43. What is meant by 'attending school' is, of course, open to a variety of interpretations. Some accounts put the proportion of children attending school in 1850 at well over half.

13 A survey of 1833–4 suggested that about half of all children in cotton factories were employed by operatives. S. Pollard, *The Genesis of Modern Management*, (1968 edn.), p. 58.

14 Factory apprentices employed by the Gregs at Quarry Bank, by Smalley of Holywell, and by Samuel Oldknow of Mellor, for example – 'no one ever had owt to complain of at Mellor'. G. Unwin, *Samuel Oldknow and the Arkwrights*, (Manchester 1924), pp. 173–4.

15 Pinchbeck and Hewitt, *Children in English Society*, I, p. 257.

16 M. A. Bienefeld, *Working Hours in British Industry* (1972), pp. 30–2. It was authoritatively stated that children in cotton factories in the 1820s worked longer hours than adult carpenters, masons, bricklayers, blacksmiths, or millwrights. J. H. Clapham, *An Economic History of Modern Britain*, (Cambridge 1950), I, 377.

17 Clapham, loc. cit. p. 376.

18 The campaign to regulate factory hours and conditions is discussed in Chapter 6. There was some international co-operation among reformers, and those abroad made much of Britain's initiative. In the extent of factory legislation on child employment, and in effectiveness of enforcement, Britain had a clear lead over other countries until at least the 1870s. The United States had little effective legislation of this kind until after the Civil War. There, and in some other countries, child employment was curbed far more by compulsory education than by factory legislation. So far as can be ascertained from the census material, in 1900 a slightly greater proportion of the child population was at work in the United States than in England and Wales. L. Horner, *On the Employment of Children in Factories and Other Works in the United Kingdom and some Foreign Countries*, (1840); A Redgrave and J. A. Redgrave, *Labour, Wages, Production in the Cotton, Woollen, and Flax Factories in France and Belgium*, (1873); H. Grebing, *The History of the German Labour Movement*, (1969 edn.), p. 18; W. I. Trattner, *Crusade for the Children*, (Chicago 1970), Chap. 1; A. R. Sanderson, 'Child Labor

Legislation and the Labor Force Participation of Children', *Journal of Economic History*, XXIV (1974), pp. 297–9.

19 H. A. Turner, *Trade Union Growth, Structure, and Policy*, (1962), p. 257.

20 There were an estimated 400 or 500 climbing boys in late eighteenth-century London and less than 400 in London in 1841. G. L. Phillips, *England's Climbing Boys*, (Cambridge Mass. 1949), p. 3.

21 *Children's Employment Commission: First Report (Mines)*, (*Parl. Papers* XV, 1842), pp. 38–9; C. Booth 'On Occupations of the People of the United Kingdom, 1801–81', *Journal of the Royal Statistical Society* XLIX (1886), 353, 374.

22 *Children's Employment Commission: First Report (Mines)*, p. 255.

23 Ibid. p. 71; Keir Hardie at one time worked as a trapper.

24 *Return of the Number of Persons Employed in Cotton, Woollen, Worsted, Flax and Silk Factories in the United Kingdom*, (*Parl. Papers* XLV, 1836).

25 According to the Hammonds three-quarters of the children were piecers. J. L. and B. Hammond, *The Town Labourer*, (1966 edn.), p. 159.

26 *Children's Employment Commission, Second Report*, (*Parl. Papers* XIII, 1843), p. 195.

27 Ibid. p. 10. While ascertaining these facts the investigator was interrupted by the mother's exhortations: 'mind your work', 'take care', 'make haste', 'now, Anne, get on'. The *Fifth Report* of this Commission commented 'against no person do the children require so much protection as against their parents'.

28 The Gangs Act prohibited the employment of children under eight in work gangs of the kind that farmers engaged for short periods on a sub-contract basis. It also discouraged the 'gang system' in other ways.

29 *Employment of School Children (Committee)* (*Parl. Papers* XXV, 1902), appendix p. 281.

30 Clapham, *An Economic History of Modern Britain*, I, p. 566.

31 *Census of England and Wales, 1911*, Vol. X. Table 24; N. J. Smelser, *Social Change in the Industrial Revolution*, (1959), p. 202.

32 Glass in *Political Arithmetic*, p. 210. Bedfordshire and Hertfordshire were at one time considered 'the most ignorant counties in England', *Morning Chronicle*, 5 April 1850.

33 *Employment of Children, Young Persons, and Women in Agriculture: Second Report*, (*Parl. Papers* XIII, 1968–9), p. ix.

34 Ibid.

35 Ibid. *Fourth Report*, (*Parl. Papers*, XIII, 1870), pp. 5–26.

36 The census figures, particularly the early figures, almost certainly underestimate female employment. Casual work like baby-minding, midwifery, and taking in lodgers were under-enumerated and treatment of the employment of the wives of farmers, blacksmiths, publicans, and other craftsmen and tradesmen was inconsistent.

37 See, for example, E. Richards, 'Women in the British Economy since about 1700: An Interpretation', *History*, LIX (1974); J. W. Scott and L. A. Tilly, 'Women's Work and the Family in Nineteenth Century Europe', *Comparative Studies in Society and History*, XVII (1975), pp. 41–2.

38 M. Hewitt, *Wives and Mothers in Victorian Industry*, (1958), p. 3. Many

departments of central and local government and a great many private employers, including some of those regarded as particularly enlightened, required women to retire when they married.

39 In 1844, according to one report, a little over one-sixth of women in the cotton mills were married. In the second half of the century the proportion was about a quarter. C. Bray, *The Industrial Employment of Women*, (1857), p. 3; Hewitt, op. cit. pp. 14–17.

40 W. Hasbach, *A History of the English Agricultural Labourer* (1908 edn.), pp. 224–5; C. S. Orwin and B. I. Felton, 'A Century of Wages and Earnings in Agriculture', *Journal of the Royal Agricultural Society*, XCII (1931), p. 241.

41 *Census of England and Wales, 1911, General Report*, pp. 108–9, 162.

42 Ibid. p. 162.

43 According to one estimate, women's employment in engineering grew more than twice as fast as men's employment between 1891 and 1911. S. Meacham, *A Life Apart: The English Working Class, 1890–1914*, (1977), p. 103.

44 B. S. Rowntree and M. Kendall, *How the Labourer Lives*, (1913).

45 Lady F. Bell, *At the Works*, (1907), p. 178; *Census of England and Wales 1911, General Report* p. 158.

46 *Census of England and Wales, 1911, General Report* p. 158, Diagram XXXII.

47 Most of those affected by the Mines Act of 1842 were in Lancashire, Yorkshire, South Wales, and the east of Scotland. I. Pinchbeck, *Women Workers and the Industrial Revolution, 1750–1850*, (1930), p. 244.

48 Cited by M. Drake in *Nineteenth Century Society*, ed. E. Wrigley (Cambridge 1972), p. 7.

49 See, for example, R. S. Schofield, 'Dimensions of Illiteracy, 1750–1850', *Explorations in Economic History*, X (1972–3), p. 443.

50 Quoted in Smelser, *Social Change in the Industrial Revolution*, p. 232.

51 Quoted in B. Drake, *Women in Trade Unions*, (1921), p. 6.

52 Ibid. p. 16.

53 F. Dovring, 'The Transformation of European Agriculture', in *The Cambridge Economic History of Europe*, ed. H. J. Habakkuk and M. Postan (Cambridge 1965), VI, pp. 604–5; C. M. Cipolla, *The Economic History of World Population*, (1970), p. 29.

54 Mitchell and Deane, *Abstract of British Historical Statistics*, p. 187; Deane and Cole, *British Economic Growth, 1688–1959*, p. 143.

55 Mitchell and Deane, op. cit. pp. 187–8, 199, 204, 211; Clapham, *An Economic History of Modern Britain*, I, pp. 72–3.

56 Clapham, loc. cit. I, 73; *Census of Great Britain, 1841 (Parl. Papers* XXVII, 1844), pp. 31, 36.

57 A. Redford, *Labour Migration in England, 1800–1850*, (Manchester 1964 edn.), p. 129.

58 P. Mathias in *British Agriculture, 1875–1914* ed. P. J. Perry, (1973), p. vii.

59 A. Marshall, *Principles of Economics*, (1920 edn.), p. 276.

60 Deane and Cole, *British Economic Growth, 1688–1959*, p. 143.

61 Ibid. p. 142.

Notes to Chapter 2

2 · *Population: Births and Deaths*

1 E. A. Wrigley, 'Family Limitation in pre-Industrial England', *Economic History Review*, XIX (1966).

2 D. V. Glass and E. Grebenik, 'World Population, 1800–1950', in *The Cambridge Economic History of Europe*, ed. H. J. Habakkuk and M. Postan (Cambridge 1965), VI, pp. 108, 124.

3 Ibid. p. 107.

4 In the West African state of Niger, for example, the death-rate in the 1960s was similar to that of Britain a century earlier. But the birth-rate was more than 50 per cent higher than it was in mid-nineteenth-century Britain, and the rate of natural increase was more than twice as great. *United Nations' Statistical Yearbook*, (1972), p. 89.

5 On European population growth at this time see E. A. Wrigley, *Population and History*, (1969), pp. 152–4.

6 Glass and Grebenik, loc. cit. pp. 103–4; J. T. Krause, 'Changes in English Fertility and Mortality, 1781–1850', *Economic History Review*, XI (1958–9), p. 67.

7 The census of fertility (1911) collected information on births to all women alive in 1911 and thus records part of the fertility history of earlier decades.

8 J. W. Innes, *Class Fertility Trends in England and Wales, 1876–1934*, (Princeton 1938), Chap. 3; W. A. Armstrong, 'The Interpretation of the Census Enumerators' Books for Victorian Towns', in *The Study of Urban History*, ed. H. J. Dyos (1968), p. 83; D. J. Loschky and D. F. Krier, 'Income and Family Size in Three Eighteenth Century Lancashire Parishes', *Journal of Economic History*, XXIX (1969).

9 Redford, *Labour Migration in England, 1800–1850*, pp. 56–7.

10 Bray, *The Industrial Employment of Women*, pp. 9–10.

11 R. Q. Gray, 'Thrift and Working-Class Mobility in Victorian Edinburgh' in *Social Class in Scotland: Past and Present*, ed. A. A. MacLaren (Edinburgh 1976), p. 130.

12 A. Briggs (ed.), *Chartist Studies*, (1959), p. 12.

13 M. Hewitt, *Wives and Mothers in Victorian Industry*, (1958), p. 94.

14 See, for example, M. Anderson, *Family Structure in Nineteenth Century Lancashire*, (Cambridge 1971), pp. 68–9; Hewitt, op. cit. pp. 93–6; R. Smith, 'Early Victorian Household Structure', *International Review of Social History*, XV (1970), pp. 78, 83.

15 *Labour of Children in the Mills and Factories*, (*Parl. Papers* XV, 1831–2), p. 132.

16 The birth-controllers favoured a sponge pessary, 'as large as a green walnut or small apple', that was to be doused in warm water before use. Place mentioned *coitus interruptus* in his handbills, but as an inferior alternative to the sponge pessary. Another traditional method of birth-control was prolonged suckling: the 1871 *Report of the Registrar General on Births, Deaths, and Marriages* (*Parl. Papers*, XX, 1873) p. 226, observed that poor mothers delayed weaning 'even to eighteen months and two years . . . with the hope that it may prevent a rapid recurrence of pregnancy'. How extensive was this practice, and how far the reduction in births thus secured was offset by a reduction in infant mortality, are interesting questions. Abortion may also have been a common working-class practice. Desire for abortion must have arisen fairly often given the element of risk

entailed in *coitus interruptus*, and abortion had the advantage over some other methods of restraint that it did not require male co-operation. Place believed that abortion was widespread and hoped that the methods he advocated would lead to its decline. On abortion see A. McLaren, 'Women's Work and Regulation of Family Size: The Question of Abortion in the Nineteenth Century', *History Workshop*, IV (1977), pp. 73–4; Glass in *Political Arithmetic*, p. 279; and above, pp. 36, 52.

17 A. McLaren, *Birth Control in Nineteenth Century England*, (1978), p. 64.

18 J. Peel, 'Contraception and the Medical Profession', *Population Studies*, XVIII (1964–5), p. 136.

19 In 1885 H. A. Allbutt, a doctor, published a pamphlet that included disastrously misleading advice on the incidence of the 'safe period'. Two years later his name was removed from the Medical Register, not because he had offered false advice, but because he had dared to mention such matters at all. Peel, loc. cit. pp. 135–6.

20 H. J. Habakkuk, *Population Growth and Economic Development since 1750*, (Leicester 1971), p. 54.

21 Farm labourers, however, were by no means immune from urban middle-class influence. Probably one of the ways in which the middle-class example was disseminated was through domestic servants, who would have become conscious of changes in middle-class practices and attitudes. Many domestic servants were country girls.

22 Phelps Brown, *Growth of British Industrial Relations*, pp. 6–7.

23 Glass in *Political Arithmetic*, p. 205.

24 McLaren, *Birth Control in Nineteenth Century England*, p. 227. Improved contraceptive techniques, however, may have had a significant influence upon the level of illegitimate births, which also fell at this time.

25 The increase in the proportion of women who had never married at age forty-five to fifty-four years was from 13.1 per cent in 1871 to 16.3 per cent in 1911. Emigration probably had some part too in raising the average age at marriage within the years when a woman was likely to have children. *Report of the Royal Commission on Population*, (1949), pp. 22–3.

26 For a detailed account see J. A. Banks, *Prosperity and Parenthood*, (1954).

27 Habakkuk, op. cit. pp. 59–65.

28 E. M. Elderton, *Report on the English Birthrate*, Part I (1914).

29 This campaign encountered a combination of socialist and moral opposition very similar to that which confronted the early birth-control campaign (above, p. 37). There was also opposition from social imperialists concerned to ensure sufficient population to settle and defend the Empire, and from eugenists who feared that the curbing of the birth-rate of the more respectable classes, while that of the lower working classes continued largely unabated, amounted to 'race suicide'. For recent accounts of the developments see McLaren, *Birth Control in Nineteenth Century England*, and F. D'Arcy, 'The Malthusian League and the Resistance to Birth Control Propaganda in late-Victorian Britain', *Population Studies*, XXXI (1977).

30 J. A. Banks and O. Banks, 'The Bradlaugh-Besant Trial and the English Newspapers', *Population Studies*, VIII (1954–5), p. 24.

31 Deaths, like births, were initially under-registered and perhaps by enough to obscure a fall in the crude death-rate between 1838 and 1860.

32 A. H. Gale, *Epidemic Diseases*, (1959), p. 138; *Sanitary Condition of the Labouring Population*, (*Parl. Papers House of Lords* XXVI, 1842), p. 159.

33 Anderson, *Family Structure*, p. 34.

34 M. D. George, *London Life in the Eighteenth Century*, (1925), p. 26.

35 Ibid. p. 25.

36 Glass and Grebenik, loc. cit. pp. 68–9; Cipolla, *Economic History of World Population*, p. 85.

37 'I shall be 36 next month and you know that is getting an old man at our trade', fork grinder to Sheffield doctor in the 1860s. J. C. Hall, 'Effects of Certain Sheffield Trades on Life and Health', *Transactions of the National Association for the Promotion of Social Science*, (1865), p. 394.

38 P. E. H. Hair, 'Mortality from Violence in British Coal Mines, 1800–50', *Economic History Review*, XXI (1968), pp. 545, 554, 560–1; *Report of H. M. Chief Inspector of Mines and Quarries for 1966*, p. 48; *Supplement to Sixty-fifth Report of the Registrar General*, Pt. II, p. xciv.

39 One in 200 shunters was killed at work each year at the end of the century and one in 12 was killed or injured. T. Oliver (ed.), *Dangerous Trades*, (1902), p. 200.

40 Hall, loc. cit. p. 394.

41 Oliver, *Dangerous Trades*, pp. 135, 505.

42 E. L. Collis and M. Greenwood, *The Health of the Industrial Worker*, (1921), pp. 31–2; Oliver, op. cit. pp. 17, 160.

43 A. L. Baxter in *Life and Labour of the People in London*, ed. C. Booth (1903 edn.), Ser. II, Vol. IV, p. 285.

44 Baxter, loc. cit.; Oliver, *Dangerous Trades*, p. 146.

45 *Supplement to the Sixty-fifth Report of the Registrar General*, Pt. II, pp. xlvii, clxxxii.

46 Hall, loc. cit. pp. 386–8.

47 Oliver, *Dangerous Trades*, p. 384.

48 *Supplement to the Sixty-fifth Report of the Registrar General*, Pt. II, pp. xcii, cvi, cxx–cxxi.

49 Hair, loc. cit. pp. 545, 560; Oliver, *Dangerous Trades*, p. 523.

50 A. L. Baxter, loc. cit. p. 285.

51 Hair, loc. cit. pp. 550–3.

52 For more details on safety legislation see Oliver, *Dangerous Trades*, Chap. 2; Collis and Greenwood, *Health of the Industrial Worker*, Chap. 2; B. L. Hutchins and A. Harrison, *A History of Factory Legislation*, (1903).

53 Oliver, *Dangerous Trades*, Chap. 3.

54 Ibid. pp. 518, 523 and Chap. 3. passim.

55 *Sanitary Condition of the Labouring Population*, pp. 154, 157, 159.

56 *Annual Report of the Registrar of Births, Deaths, and Marriages*, (*Parl. Papers* XV, 1900), p. 122.

57 W. P. D. Logan, 'Mortality in England and Wales from 1848 to 1947', *Population Studies*, IV (1950–1), Table 1.

58 Lady F. Bell, *At The Works*, (1907), p. 194.

59 *Local Government Board: Supplementary Report on Infant and Child Mortality* (*Parl. Papers* xxxix, 1910), pp. 87–8.

60 Miners' housing is discussed in Chapter 3. Abstracts from the *Supplementary Reports on Infant and Child Mortality* (*Parl. Papers* xxxix, 1910), pp. 63–7 indicate the main sanitary problems:

> 'The defects of sanitation which are specially associated with excessive infant mortality come under one of three heads . . . (1) Conservancy methods of disposal of excreta, (2) Inefficient scavenging of domestic refuse, and still worse inefficient scavenging when the contents of pail-closets and privies have to be emptied, (3) Unpaved or unmade road and back streets, and unpaved back yards of dwellings. All these lead to dirtiness of the environment of the house, to treading of dirt, often of excretal origin, into the house. . . . A large part of the densely populated parts of the counties of Durham and Glamorgan and certain parts of Lancashire, Staffordshire and Yorkshire, are in a profoundly lower condition as regards elementary sanitation than other parts of England. . . . The contents of midden privies have to be thrown out on the ground in many districts. . . . In many instances the contents have to be conveyed through the dwellings in baskets, to be emptied into the cart in the street.'

61 Ibid. p. 108; Hewitt, *Wives and Mothers*, pp. 107, 110–22. On this point see also p. 19 above. The Potteries was another district where high infant mortality was found in conjunction with considerable employment of married women.

62 'They go back at the end of fourteen days [Manchester midwife, 1833], three weeks they think a great bit.' Quoted in Hewitt, op. cit. p. 126. Dosing babies with 'Godfrey's cordial' and other opium or morphia 'quieteners' was most widespread in areas where mothers worked. See, for example, Pinchbeck, op. cit. p. 274; C. Aspin (ed.), *Manchester and the Textile Districts in 1849*, (Helmshore 1972), pp. 24–32.

63 A late nineteenth-century survey discovered that working-class babies in Liverpool who were weaned before three months were twenty-two times more likely than breast-fed babies to die from diarrhoea. Oliver, *Dangerous Trades*, p. 85.

64 Logan, loc. cit. Table 2A.

65 Ibid. Table 7B.

66 Ibid. Tables 6 and 7. In 1848–72 tuberculosis accounted for over a third of all deaths of males aged 24–44.

67 Consumption of infected milk, however, could also confer a degree of protection, and one possible reason for the eventual decline in tuberculosis deaths is that the railways were taking more infected milk into the great cities.

68 C. Creighton, *A History of Epidemics in Britain*, (1894), II, Chap. IX.

69 A recent biographer suggests that Albert perhaps died from some other cause. H. D. Bennett, *King Without a Crown*, (1977).

70 According to one estimate London at one time may have needed as much as a third of the natural increase of provincial England to offset its excess of mortality. E. A. Wrigley, 'A Simple Model of London's Importance in Changing English Society and Economy, 1650–1750', *Past and Present*, xxxvii (1967), pp. 46–7.

71 E. E. Lampard, in *The Victorian City: Images and Realities*, eds. H. J. Dyos and M. Wolff (1973), I, pp. 13–14.

72 Clapham, *An Economic History of Modern Britain*, II, pp. 440, 446.

73 T. McKeown and R. G. Record, 'Reasons for the Decline in Mortality in England and Wales during the Nineteenth Century', *Population Studies*, XVI (1962–3).

74 The following headings and sub-headings appeared in Chadwick's 1842 *Report on the Sanitary Condition of the Labouring Population*: Pecuniary Burdens created by the Neglect of Sanitary Measures; Cost of Disease as compared with the Cost of Prevention; Cost of Remedies for Sickness and of Mortality which is Preventable.

75 A writer in the *Edinburgh Review* (1850) described cholera as 'in truth a health inspector who speaks through his interpreter, the Registrar General, in a language which reaches all ears'. In Australia, unaffected by cholera, sanitary reformers half-wished for such an epidemic to rouse public opinion. A. Briggs, 'Cholera and Society in the Nineteenth Century', *Past and Present*, XIX (1961), p. 85. A recent study of the first epidemic – R. J. Morris, *Cholera 1832: The Social Response to an Epidemic*, (1976) – suggests that cholera perhaps had a rather less influential role in public health improvements than has generally been assumed.

76 B. Harrison, *Drink and the Victorians: The Temperance Question in England, 1815–72*, (1971), p. 299.

77 Elderton, *Report on the English Birthrate*, pp. 136–9. On the level of abortion, and the increased use of lead-based abortifacients, see also McLaren, *Birth Control in Nineteenth Century England*, pp. 242, 248; Women's Co-operative Guild, *Maternity: Letters from Working Women*, (1915), p. 15; P. Knight, 'Women and Abortion in Victorian and Edwardian England', *History Workshop*, IV (1977), pp. 60, 67; R. Sauer, 'Infanticide and Abortion in Nineteenth Century Britain', *Population Studies*, XXXII (1978).

78 See, for example, *Report on the Inter-Departmental Committee on Physical Deterioration*, (*Parl. Papers* XXXII, 1904), pp. 50–1.

79 Mothers always had an incentive to declare that a baby who died soon after delivery had been stillborn because a stillborn baby required no funeral. At the turn of the century burying a baby cost more than a labourer earned in a week and a baby who died soon after birth was not likely to be insured. M. S. Pember Reeves, *Round About a Pound a Week*, (1913), pp. 69–70.

80 'The sanitary authorities within the following administrative counties and in the following districts are most urgently called upon to perform more completely their primary duties.' A list of place names followed. *Report on Infant and Child Mortality*, (*Parl. Papers* XXXIX, 1910), p. 77.

81 A certain amount was achieved by simple measures like impressing upon mothers the inadvisability of taking babies into their own beds. On Saturday nights, when mothers were most likely to have been drinking, deaths from smothering increased substantially. M. Greenwood, W. J. Martin, and W. T. Russell, 'Deaths by Violence, 1837–1937', *Journal of the Royal Statistical Society*, CIV (1941), pp. 154, 164. On the campaign to reduce infant mortality see C. Dyhouse, 'Working-Class Mothers and Infant Mortality in England, 1895–1914', *Journal of Social History*, XII (1978–9).

82 Infant mortality in England and Wales fell from 154 per 1,000 in 1900 to 105 per 1,000 in 1914. Several European countries also experienced a fall in infant mortality at this time. Any explanation of the fall in Britain will have to be set in an international context.

83 Population grew faster in the industrializing districts, but almost entirely as a consequence of migration from the rural districts and the fact that the migrants included a more than proportionate number of men and women in their procreative years.

84 Quoted in W. Beveridge, *Unemployment: A Problem of Industry*, (1930), p. 69.

85 F. Clifford, 'The Labour Bill in Farming', *Journal of the Royal Agricultural Society*, 2nd ser. xi (1875), p. 125.

86 Differences in male and female living standards, and the extent to which working-class husbands could escape the consequences of large families are discussed in Chapter 4. R. M. Titmuss noted that the 'typical working-class mother of the 1890's' experienced ten pregnancies and spent about fifteen years in a state of pregnancy and in nursing a child during its first year. He considered that women's living standards had subsequently benefited more from falling fertility than from increases in working-class earnings. *Essays on The Welfare State*, (1958), pp. 90–7.

3 · *Wages and Living Standards*

1 N. McKendrick (ed.), *Historical Perspectives*, (1974), p. 168.

2 T. S. Ashton, 'Changes in Standards of Comfort in Eighteenth-Century England', *Proceedings of the British Academy*, xli (1955), p. 174. Ashton discusses diet at this time in some detail.

3 'Custom ... has rendered leather shoes a necessity of life in England. ... In France they are necessities neither to men nor to women.' A. Smith, *Wealth of Nations*, ed. R. H. Campbell and A. S. Skinner (Oxford 1976), ii, p. 870.

4 See, for example, P. Deane, *The First Industrial Revolution*, (Cambridge 1965), pp. 6–7.

5 Estimated from statistics of building and farm wages in E. H. Phelps Brown and S. V. Hopkins, 'Seven Centuries of the Prices of Consumables, compared with Builders' Wage-rates', *Economica*, xxiii (1956); A. L. Bowley, *Wages in the United Kingdom in the Nineteenth Century* (Cambridge 1900); *British Labour Statistics: Historical Abstract, 1886–1968*, (HMSO 1971).

6 G. D. H. Cole, *A Short History of the British Working-Class Movement, 1789–1947*, (1948 edn.), p. 24.

7 G. J. Barnsby, 'The Standard of Living in the Black Country during the Nineteenth Century', *Economic History Review*, xxiv (1971), p. 233.

8 T. P. O'Neill, 'Poverty in Ireland, 1815–45', *Folk Life*, xi (1973), pp. 26–7.

9 For a fuller, but strongly 'pessimist', account of the history of the debate see the article by B. Inglis in *Encounter*, Sept. 1971.

10 T. S. Ashton in *Capitalism and the Historians*, ed. F. A. Hayek (1954), p. 146.

11 Boyson, *The Ashworth Cotton Enterprise*, Chap. 10.

12 M. W. Flinn, 'Trends in Real Wages, 1750–1850', *Economic History Review*, xxvii (1974).

13 E. P. Thompson, *The Making of the English Working Class*, (1968 edn.), p. 268.

14 Cole, *Short History of the British Working-Class Movement*, p. 131.
15 G. H. Wood, *A Glance at Wages and Prices since the Industrial Revolution*, (Manchester 1900), p. 7; G. H. Wood, *Wages in the Cotton Trade*, (1910), p. 147; W. T. Layton, 'Changes in the Wages of Domestic Servants during Fifty Years', *Journal of the Royal Statistical Society*, LXXI (1908), p. 523. There is more than one view on building wages: compare, for example, the figures of E. H. Phelps Brown and S. V. Hopkins in *Economica*, XXIII (1956) with those of R. S. Tucker in *Journal of the American Statistical Association*, XXXI (1936).
16 P. Gaskell, *Artisans and Machinery* (1836), p. 334.
17 Thompson, *Making of the English Working Class*, p. 231.
18 On this theme see E. P. Thompson, 'Time, Work-Discipline, and Industrial Capitalism', *Past and Present*, XXXVIII (1967).
19 W. Cooke Taylor, who was no pessimist, declared that middle-class Ardwick 'knows less about Ancoats than it does about China and feels more interest in the condition of New Zealand than of Little Ireland', *Notes of a Tour in the Manufacturing Districts of Lancashire*, (1842), p. 160.
20 F. Engels, *The Condition of the Working Class in England*, (Oxford 1958), ed. W. O. Henderson and W. H. Chaloner, p. 312.
21 C. J. Erickson, 'Agrarian Myths of English Immigrants' in *In the Trek of the Immigrants*, ed. O. F. Ander (Rock Island, Illinois 1964); W. H. G. Armytage, *Heavens Below: Utopian Experiments in England, 1560–1960*, (1961).
22 M. Anderson, *Family Structure in Nineteenth-Century Lancashire*, (Cambridge 1971). See also the same author's contribution in *Household and Family in Past Time*, ed. P. Laslett and R. Wall (Cambridge 1972).
23 'Ah con allus get four looms,' J. B. Priestley, *English Journey*, (1934), p. 275. The optimists' case does not extend to claiming that industrialization encouraged female emancipation in any general sense at this time. Those wives who followed their employment to the factory were outnumbered by others who simply withdrew from the labour market. The transition from the dual role of housewife and domestic industrial worker to that of mere housewife, no matter how much it was welcomed by the women concerned, must be counted a retrogressive step in this context.
24 Indeed, some families probably sought work in a number of mills quite deliberately, because in that way they reduced the risk that all would be unemployed together. Horner, *On the Employment of Children in Factories*, p. 29.
25 'Their earnings, and the comparatively agreeable nature of the occupations, present a constant temptation for girls and young women to enter the factory rather than engage in domestic service.' D. Chadwick, 'Wages in Manchester and Salford, and the Manufacturing Districts of Lancashire, 1839–59', *Journal of the Royal Statistical Society*, XXIII (1860), p. 7. On this point see also L. Faucher, *Manchester in 1844*, (1844), p. 40.
26 See, for instance, Gaskell, *Artisans and Machinery*, pp. 7, 25, 165, 217.
27 'It appears that, of all employment to which children are subjected, those carried on in the factories are among the least laborious.' Report of 1833, quoted by I. Pinchbeck and M. Hewitt, *Children in English Society*, II (1973), p. 403.

28 Gaskell, op. cit. pp. 141, 163; Engels, *The Condition of the Working Class in England*, pp. 194–5.

29 R. K. Webb, 'Working Class Readers in Early Victorian England', *English Historical Review*, LXV (1950), p. 350; E. G. West, 'Literacy and the Industrial Revolution', *Economic History Review*, XXXI (1978); George, *London Life in the Eighteenth Century*, Chap. 1; M. I. Thomis, *Responses to Industrialization: The British Experience, 1780–1850*, (Newton Abbot 1976), pp. 25, 77–8, 146–8.

30 Ashton in *Capitalism and the Historians*, p. 36.

31 Engels, *The Condition of the Working Class in England*, p. 64.

32 Gaskell, *Artisans and Machinery*, Chap. 1.

33 Pinchbeck, *Women Workers and the Industrial Revolution*, p. 241.

34 B. F. Duckham, 'Serfdom in Eighteenth Century Scotland', *History*, LIV (1969).

35 Engels, *The Condition of the Working Class in England*, p. 12.

36 T. S. Ashton, *The Industrial Revolution, 1760–1830*, (1958 edn.), p. 161; P. Mathias, *The First Industrial Nation*, (1969), pp. 6–7; M. I. Thomis, *The Town Labourer and the Industrial Revolution*, (1974), pp. 148, 158.

37 J. Caird, *English Agriculture in 1850–51*, (1852), p. 513.

38 Ibid. p. 514.

39 A. Briggs, *Victorian Cities*, (1963), p. 113; Engels, *The Condition of the Working Class in England*, pp. 64, 155; E. J. Hobsbawm, 'History and the "Dark Satanic Mills"' in *Labouring Men*, (1968 edn.), p. 117.

40 See among others, G. J. Barnsby, in *Economic History Review*, XXVI (1973), pp. 515–16; S. G. Checkland, *The Rise of Industrial Society in England, 1815–1885*, (1964), pp. 228–9; H. Perkin, *The Origins of Modern English Society, 1780–1880*, (1969), p. 414; J. Strang in *Journal of the Royal Statistical Society*, XX (1857), p. 312.

41 Cole, op. cit. p. 140.

42 Ibid. p. 266.

43 G. H. Wood, 'Real Wages and the Standard of Comfort since 1850', *Journal of the Royal Statistical Society*, LXXII (1909), pp. 99–101.

44 G. J. Barnsby, *Economic History Review*, XXVI (1973), pp. 515–16.

45 It also arises partly from Barnsby's failure to make realistic allowance for the effect upon average incomes of changes in occupational structure. On the declining level of Black Country wages relative to wages elsewhere in Britain, see E. H. Hunt, *Regional Wage Variations in Britain, 1850–1914*, (Oxford 1973), pp. 31, 33, 158–9; E. Hopkins, 'Small Town Aristocrats of Labour and their Standard of Living, 1840–1914', *Economic History Review*, XXVIII (1975), and above, pp. 101–2.

46 Mitchell and Deane, *Abstract of British Historical Statistics*, pp. 64–5. Coppock (in the *Economic History Review*, XVII [1964–5] p. 394) gives higher figures than Mitchell and Deane for the years after 1873. Trade unionists may have been over-represented in the volatile export occupations, but they were grossly under-represented among the unskilled whose wages were also considerably affected by short-time and unemployment.

47 J. W. F. Rowe, *Wages in the Coal Industry*, (1923).

48 *Sums Received and Expended for the Purposes of the Metropolitan Police*, (*Parl. Papers* XLVI, 1851), p. 15.

49 A. E. Musson, *The Typographical Association*, (Oxford 1954), pp. 162–3; S. Pollard, *A History of Labour in Sheffield* (Liverpool 1959), pp. 339–40.

50 G. H. Wood, *Wages in the Cotton Trade*, p. 147; Phelps Brown and Hopkins, loc. cit. p. 314.

51 Unemployment in these years, on average, was lower than it was when wages rose fastest. Mitchell and Deane, *Abstract of British Historical Statistics*, pp. 64–5; Coppock, loc. cit. p. 394. Bowley suggested that if no allowance is made for changing occupational structure, average real wages fell by about 4 or 5 per cent between the late 1890s and 1913. *The Change in the Distribution of the National Income, 1880–1913*, (Oxford 1920), pp. 19–20.

52 *Working Class Rents and Retail Prices*, (*Parl. Papers* LXVI, 1913), p. xiii.

53 A. Briggs, 'The Political Scene' and M. Laski, 'Domestic Life' in *Edwardian England, 1901–14*, ed. S. Nowell-Smith (1964), pp. 62, 206. Even if real wages fell by as much as the 13 per cent Marghanita Laski claims, it would have set them back only as far as the level of the late 1880s when they were already some 40 or 50 per cent or more above wages in 1850. Breast-feeding among the working classes probably was declining at this time but largely in imitation of middle-class fashion.

54 E. Hopkins, 'Working Conditions in Victorian Stourbridge', *International Review of Social History*, XIX (1974); Pollard, *Labour in Sheffield*, p. 211. See also, D. A. Reid, 'The Decline of Saint Monday, 1766–1876', *Past and Present*, LXXI (1976).

55 O. J. Dunlop and R. D. Denman, *English Apprenticeship and Child Labour*, (1912), pp. 99, 175; S. and B. Webb, *Industrial Democracy*, (1920 edn.), p. 352; Hopkins, loc. cit. p. 409.

56 E. P. Thompson, in *Past and Present*, XXXVIII, p. 85; M. A. Bienefeld, *Working Hours in British Industry*, (1972), p. 20; Webbs, *Industrial Democracy*, p. 352.

57 The working week in factories was not, however, sufficiently above the average, and there were not sufficient factory workers, to justify writing, as Bienefeld has done (op. cit. p. 7), of a 'massive move into the factories' increasing the hours of 'the majority of the working population'.

58 *Factory Commission Report* (*Parl. Papers*, XX, 1833, D2), p. 44.

59 A. Redgrave and J. A. Redgrave, *Labour, Wages, Production in the Cotton, Woollen, and Flax Factories in France and Belgium*, (1873).

60 J. H. Clapham, *The Economic Development of France and Germany, 1815–1914*, (Cambridge 1936 edn.), p. 405; H. A. Clegg, A. Fox, and A. F. Thompson, *A History of British Trade Unions since 1889*, (Oxford 1964), I, p. 243; A. Shadwell, *Industrial Efficiency: A Comparative Study of Industrial Life in England, Germany, and America*, (1906), II, pp. 81, 103; E. H. Phelps Brown and M. H. Browne, *A Century of Pay*, (1968), pp. 55–6, 171–3.

61 J. Walvin, *The People's Game*, (1975), p. 74.

62 C. Booth (ed.), *Life and Labour of the People in London*, Final Volume (1903), p. 50.

63 D. N. Paton, J. C. Dunlop, and E. M. Inglis, *A Study of the Diet of the Labouring Classes in Edinburgh*, (Edinburgh n.d.), pp. 28, 32.

64 On the rate at which wheaten bread came to dominate consumption see E. J. T.

Collins, 'Dietary Change and Cereal Consumption in Britain in the Nineteenth Century', *Agricultural History Review*, XXIII (1975).

65 *Morning Chronicle*, 26 Dec. 1849; J. Arch, *Joseph Arch: The Story of His Life*, (1898), p. 101.

66 M. K. Ashby, *Joseph Ashby of Tysoe, 1859–1919*, (Cambridge 1961), pp. 36–7.

67 *Sixth Report of the Medical Officer of the Privy Council*, (*Parl. Papers*, XXVIII, 1864); R. Hutchison, 'On the Dietary of the English Agricultural Labourer in Contrast to the Scottish', *Transactions of the Highland and Agricultural Society*, 4th ser. III (1870–1). See also T. C. Barker, J. C. McKenzie, and J. Yudkin (eds.), *Our Changing Fare*, (1966), p. 79.

68 T. E. Kebbel, *The Agricultural Labourer*, (1893) pp. 56–7.

69 A. Wilson Fox, 'Agricultural Wages in England and Wales during the last Fifty Years', *Journal of the Royal Statistical Society*, LXVI (1903), p. 295.

70 *Wages, Earnings, and Conditions of Employment of Agricultural Labourers*, (*Parl. Papers* XCVII, 1905), pp. 227–8.

71 The more skilled of the urban workers, and the miners, were far better fed. See Pollard, *History of Labour in Sheffield*, pp. 25, 107–8, 180; E. Dückershoff, *How the English Workman Lives*, (1899), pp. 30–1, 38.

72 P. Mathias, *Retailing Revolution*, (1967), pp. 24–5.

73 Phelps Brown, *Growth of British Industrial Relations*, pp. 19–20.

74 Barker, McKenzie, and Yudkin, *Our Changing Fare*, p. 137.

75 See, for example, H. H. Mann, 'Life in an Agricultural Village in England', *Sociological Papers*, I (1904); B. S. Rowntree and M. Kendall, *How the Labourer Lives*, (1913).

76 See, for example, F. G. Heath, *Peasant Life in the West of England*, (1883), pp. 314–5; Dückershoff, *How the English Workman Lives*, p. 37. E. A. M. Roberts has recently defended the culinary reputation of the wives of Barrow and Lancaster in *Working-Class Barrow and Lancaster, 1890–1930*, (Lancaster 1976), p. 23.

77 On the reduction in adulteration of food see J. Burnett, *Plenty and Want: A Social History of Diet in England*, (1966), Chap. 10.

78 T. R. Gourvish's figures, however, show a 15 per cent fall in Glasgow rents between 1810 and 1831. 'The Cost of Living in Glasgow in the Early Nineteenth Century', *Economic History Review*, XXV (1972), p. 73.

79 Pollard, *A History of Labour in Sheffield*, pp. 18–20.

80 Arch, *Joseph Arch*, p. 57.

81 Boyson, *The Ashworth Cotton Enterprise*, pp. 116–18. This company history shows photographs and plans of the Ashworth cottages.

82 Armytage, *Heavens Below*, pp. 251–4; E. Gauldie, *Cruel Habitations: A History of Working-Class Housing, 1780–1918*, (1974), pp. 62–3. The site, alas, is now engulfed by a greater Bradford but the houses, the fine church, and magnificent literary institute can still be seen.

83 *Morning Chronicle*, 28 Jan. 1850.

84 'For the labour we had to get people from all parts; we took any who would come and put them into huts and various dwelling houses, wherever we could locate them for the time being.' (South Wales manager). *Organization and Rules of Trades Unions*, (*Parl. Papers* XXXIX, 1867–68), Fifth Report, evidence, p. 95.

85 *Committee of Council on Education: Minutes*, (*Parl. Papers* XLV, 1847), pp. 97–8.
86 G. R. Porter quoted in J. Burnett, *A Social History of Housing, 1815–70*, (Newton Abbot 1978), p. 88.
87 *Victoria County History of Leicestershire*, IV, p. 263; S. D. Chapman (ed.), *The History of Working-Class Housing*, (Newton Abbot 1971), p. 228; J. H. Treble, 'The Place of Irish Catholics in the Social Life of the North of England, 1829–51', (unpublished Ph.D. thesis, University of Leeds 1968), p. 158.
88 Chapman (ed.), op. cit. pp. 24, 172.
89 Ibid. pp. 182–4; Burnett, *Social History of Housing*, p. 61.
90 In 1861 over a third of families in Scotland lived in one-room households, *Census of Scotland 1861*, (*Parl. Papers* L, 1862), p. xxxii.
91 On improvement in working-class housing see Chapman (ed.), *The History of Working-Class Housing*, pp. 154–5, 159; W. G. Rimmer, 'Working Men's Cottages in Leeds, 1770–1840', *Thoresby Society Publications*, XLVI (1960); Thompson, *Making of the English Working Class*, p. 354; A. Sutcliffe, 'Working-class Housing in Nineteenth Century Britain', *Bulletin of the Society for the Study of Labour History*, XXIV (1972), p. 40.
92 Chapman (ed.), op. cit. pp. 188–9.
93 *Royal Commission on the Housing of the Working Classes*, (*Parl. Papers* XXX, 1884–5), p. 4.
94 The figures are for England and Wales and show 'overcrowding' in dwellings of fewer than five rooms. Sculleries and closets were not counted as rooms, kitchens were counted. *Census of England and Wales 1911: General Report*, (*Parl. Papers* XXXV, 1917–18), p. 174; (*Parl. Papers* LXXXI, 1914–16), Summary Table 67.
95 Shadwell, *Industrial Efficiency*, I, p. 77; Roberts, *Working Class Barrow and Lancaster*, p. 31.
96 *Forty-Second Annual Report of the Local Government Board, Part III*, (*Parl. Papers* XXXI, 1913), p. L.
97 Gauldie, *Cruel Habitations*, p. 81.
98 Builders in Leeds, however, discovered a loophole that exempted plans already approved. Chapman (ed.), op. cit. pp. 117–19.
99 On improvements in rural housing in the second half of the century see, for example, Clapham, *An Economic History of Modern Britain*, II, p. 512; A. Wilson Fox, in *Journal of the Royal Statistical Society*, LXVI (1903), p. 309; Burnett, *A Social History of Housing*, pp. 132–3.
100 B. S. Rowntree, *Land and Labour: Lessons from Belgium*, (1910), pp. 458–9. B. S. Rowntree, *Poverty: A Study of Town Life*, (1901 edn.), p. 161. Belgian housing was perhaps, on average, rather better than English housing.
101 Only 2.3 per cent of Londoners lived in rooms shared by four persons or more in 1911. A. Shadwell, 'Housing', in *Encyclopaedia Britannica*, 11th edn. (Cambridge, 1910); *Census of England and Wales, 1911*, (*Parl. Papers* XXXV, 1917–18), p. 177.
102 Shadwell, 'Housing', loc. cit. For the comments of a coal-miner on the superiority of English over German housing see Dückershoff, op. cit. Chap. 4. For details of higher rent in Germany, see Shadwell, *Industrial Efficiency*, II, pp. 186–98.
103 R. Palmer, *The Water Closet: A New History*, (Newton Abbot 1973), p. 65. There are still hotels in France that boast *'confort anglais'*.

104 Mitchell and Deane, *Abstract of British Historical Statistics*, pp. 472–5; H. W. Singer, 'An Index of Urban Land Rents and House Rents in England and Wales, 1845–1914', *Econometrica*, IX (1941), p. 230.

105 Chapman (ed.), *The History of Working-Class Housing*, p. 85. Some 45 per cent of Scotland's population were still living in one or two rooms in 1911. Scottish rooms were larger than those in England but this went only a little way to compensate for higher rates of 'overcrowding'.

106 Gauldie, *Cruel Habitation*, pp. 87, 248; Burnett, *Social History of Housing*, p. 144.

107 Chapman (ed.), *The History of Working-Class Housing*, p. 26. In York, Rowntree calculated, rent took about 15 per cent of the average working-class wage. Rowntree, *Poverty: A Study of Town Life*, p. 165.

108 Chapman (ed.), op. cit. p. 25; G. Stedman Jones, *Outcast London*, (Oxford 1971), p. 176.

109 On the situation in London see Stedman Jones, op. cit. Chap. 8.

110 W. Ashworth, *The Genesis of Modern British Town Planning*, (1954), p. 84.

111 Rowntree, *Poverty: A Study of Town Life*, p. 166.

112 Shadwell, *Industrial Efficiency*, I, pp. 77–92.

113 G. J. Crossick, 'Social Structure and Working-Class Behaviour: Kentish London, 1840–80', (unpublished Ph.D. thesis, University of London 1976), pp. 348, 353–4.

114 Chapman (ed.), *The History of Working-Class Housing*, pp. 11, 41; Sutcliffe, loc. cit. p. 47.

115 Several writers have recently noted how insubstantial was working-class pressure for housing reform before 1900. See for example Gaudie, *Cruel Habitations*, p. 17; McLaren, op. cit. p. 175; A. S. Wohl, *The Eternal Slum: Housing and Social Policy in Victorian London*, (1977), pp. 319–20.

116 *Royal Commission on the Housing of the Working Classes* (*Parl. Papers* XXXI, 1884–5), p. 5.

117 *Royal Commission on Labour,* (*Parl. Papers* XXXVI, i, 1892), para. 13,458.

118 K. Maiwald, 'An Index of Building Costs in the United Kingdom, 1845–1938', *Economic History Review*, VII (1954–5), p. 189.

119 *Morning Chronicle*, 21 Dec. 1849.

120 Ibid. 18 Mar. 1850.

121 E. H. Phelps Brown and S. V. Hopkins, 'Seven Centuries of Building Wages', *Economica*, XXII (1955), p. 202.

122 Rowntree, *Poverty: A Study of Town Life*, pp. 111–12.

123 E. J. Hobsbawm, *Labouring Men*, (1968), pp. 290–5.

124 K. G. J. C. Knowles and D. J. Robertson, 'Differences between the Wages of Skilled and Unskilled Workers, 1880–1950', *Bulletin of the Oxford University Institute of Statistics*, XIII (1951), p. 111; Phelps Brown and Hopkins, in *Economica*, (1955), p. 204. See also H. A. Turner, 'Trade Unions, Differentials, and the Levelling of Wages', *Manchester School of Economic and Social Studies*, XX (1952).

125 G. Routh, 'Civil Service Pay, 1875 to 1950', *Economica*, XXI (1954).

126 J. A. Banks, *Prosperity and Parenthood* (1954), p. 48; B. G. Orchard, *The Clerks of Liverpool* (Liverpool 1871), p. 20. In 1851 only 10,000 persons, equivalent to less than one occupied male in 500, were assessed for tax on incomes over £300.

127 See Banks, *Prosperity and Parenthood*, p. 105; Orchard, op. cit. pp. 26–7, 51.

128 Orchard, op. cit.

129 Perkin, *The Origins of Modern English Society*, pp. 417–18.

130 Banks, *Prosperity and Parenthood*, p. 112.

131 Routh, in *Economica*, XXI (1954), pp. 208–10.

132 For a much fuller discussion of regional differential see Hunt, *Regional Wage Variations in Britain, 1850–1914* from which most of the detail that follows is taken.

133 *Report of the Fair Wages Committee*, (*Parl. Papers* XXXIV, 1908), p. 14.

134 Caird, *English Agriculture in 1850–51*, p. 513.

135 *Royal Commission on Labour*, (*Parl. Papers* XXXV, 1893–4), Summary Report by A. Wilson Fox, p. 25; *British and Foreign Trade and Industrial Conditions*, (*Parl. Papers* LXVII, 1903), p. 210.

136 Pinchbeck, *Women Workers and the Industrial Revolution*, p. 177.

137 On this theme generally, and on the illustrations that follow see, C. A. Foley, 'The Employment of Women', *Economic Journal*, IV (1894), p. 188; S. Webb, 'The Alleged Differences in the Wages Paid to Men and to Women for Similar Work', *Economic Journal*, I (1891), pp. 645–50; V. Gollancz (ed.), *The Making of Women*, (1917), Appendix A; E. Cadbury, M. C. Matheson and G. Shann, *Women's Work and Wages*, (1906), p. 120; G. C. Allen, *The Industrial Development of Birmingham and the Black Country, 1860–1927*, (1929), p. 168; *Royal Commission on the Housing of the Working Classes*, (*Parl. Papers* XXX, 1884–5), para. 7106.

138 Gollancz (ed.), op. cit. p. 179.

139 See, for example, S. Webb, loc. cit. p. 645; C. Black (ed.), *Married Women's Work*, (1915), p. 131; A. L. Bowley, 'Wages in the Worsted and Woollen Manufactures', *Journal of the Royal Statistical Society*, LXV (1902), p. 109.

140 Quoted in Gollancz (ed.), *The Making of Women*, p. 195.

141 *Royal Commission on Labour: Employment of Women*, (*Parl. Papers* XXXVII, 1893–4), p. 174.

142 S. Webb, loc. cit. p. 642.

143 S. Webb, loc. cit. pp. 637–8; *Wages of the Manual Labour Classes*, (*Parl. Papers* LXXXIIIii, 1893–4), p. xxxii; Clegg, Fox, and Thompson, *A History of British Trade Unions since 1889*, I, pp. 480–2.

144 *Report of the War Cabinet Committee on Women in Industry*, (*Parl. Papers* XXXI, 1919), pp. 32, 67; *Morning Chronicle*, 21 Jan. 1850; Bowley, loc. cit. (1902), p. 116; Pinchbeck, op. cit. p. 193.

145 *Women in Industry*, (*Parl. Papers* XXXI, 1919), p. 67.

146 See, for example, B. L. Hutchins and A. Harrison, *A History of Factory Legislation*, (1903), p. 261.

147 *Morning Chronicle*, 28 Nov. 1849, 5 April 1850; Pinchbeck, *Women Workers and the Industrial Revolution*, pp. 231–2; Hutchins and Harrison, op. cit. p. 262; Booth (ed.), *Life and Labour*, I. Vol. IV, pp. 259–60, 281.

148 In Hutchins and Harrison, op. cit. pp. 283–4.

149 R. H. Tawney, *Minimum Rates in the Tailoring Industry*, (1915), p. 80; M. E. Bulkley, *Minimum Rates in the Boxmaking Industry*, (1915), pp. 88–9.

150 See, among others, *Royal Commission on Labour: Employment of Women*, (*Parl. Papers* XXXV, 1894), p. 483; Booth (ed.), *Life and Labour*, Ser. II, Vol. IV, p. 224; Women's Industrial Council, *Women's Wages in England in the Nineteenth Century*, (1906), pp. 7–8; *Women in Industry*, (*Parl. Papers* XXXI, 1919), p. 69.

151 On domestic servants' wages and allowances at this time see D. Marshall, *The English Domestic Servant in History*, (1949), p. 18; J. Burnett, *Useful Toil*, (1974), pp. 159–61.

152 Layton in *Journal of the Royal Statistical Society*, LXXI (1908), p. 523.

153 J. F. C. Harrison, *The Early Victorians, 1832–51*, (1971), p. 45.

154 J. W. Scott and L. A. Tilley, 'Women's Work and the Family in Nineteenth Century Europe', *Comparative Studies in Society and History*, XVII (1975), p. 40.

155 'My first holiday was three days (William Lanceley, 1870). . . . Our cottage homes and food were no comparison to what we had left behind.' Burnett, *Useful Toil*, p. 187. On this theme see also Booth (ed.), *Life and Labour*, Ser. II, Vol. IV, p. 219; G. Bourne, *Change in the Village*, (1966 edn.), p. 55; M. M. Bird, *Women at Work*, (1911), p. 109.

156 Among many examples see the *Morning Chronicle*, 21 Mar. 1850; Hewitt, *Wives and Mothers*, pp. 77–8; *Factory Commission Report*, (*Parl. Papers* XX D2, 1833), pp. 8–9; T. M. McBride, *The Domestic Revolution: The Modernization of Household Service in Britain and France, 1820–1920*, (New York, 1976), p. 92.

157 *Sanitary Condition of the Labouring Population*, (*House of Lords Papers* XXVI, 1842), p. 187; Boyson, *The Ashworth Cotton Enterprise*, p. 162.

158 N. Rosenberg, 'Anglo-American Wage Differences in the 1820's', *Journal of Economic History*, XXVII (1967), p. 222; J. E. Handley, *The Navvy in Scotland*, (Cork 1970), p. 168.

159 M. G. Mulhall, *Dictionary of Statistics*, (1899), p. 579.

160 P. Uselding, 'Wages and Consumption Levels in England and on the Continent in the 1830's', *Journal of European Economic History*, IV (1975), p. 512.

161 Engels, *The Condition of the Working Class in England*, p. 299.

162 See, for example, Rosenberg, loc. cit. p. 222; Mulhall, *Dictionary of Statistics*, p. 579; D. R. Adams, 'Some evidence on English and American Wages Rates, 1790–1830', *Journal of Economic History*, XXX (1970), p. 510; Phelps Brown and Browne, *A Century of Pay*, p. 164. On Australian living standards in the 1840s see W. A. Cole and P. Deane in *Cambridge Economic History of Europe*, VI, p. 35.

163 Phelps Brown and Browne, *A Century of Pay*, pp. 159, 165. It is worth noting that Ireland was a part of the UK at that time and wages there, especially unskilled wages, were below British levels.

164 *Industrial Classes (Foreign Countries)*, (*Parl. Papers* LXVI, 1870, LXVIII, 1871, LXII, 1872).

165 Ibid. (*Parl. Papers* LXVI, 1870, p. 13; LXVIII, 1871, p. 518).

166 Ibid. (*Parl. Papers* LXVI, 1870, p. 516; LXVIII, 1871, pp. 66, 686; LXII, 1872, pp. 9, 103).

167 US Consular Reports, 1884–5, *Labor in Europe*, (3 vols.), I, p. 177.

168 A. Fryer, *Cost of Living in Various Countries*, (Stockport 1886).

169 Phelps Brown and Browne, *A Century of Pay*, pp. 159, 165.

170 Ibid., pp. 159–61.

171 *Cost of Living in German Towns*, (*Parl. Papers* CVIII, 1908), p. iii; *Cost of Living in French Towns*, (*Parl. Papers* XCI, 1909), p. xlvi.

172 Barker, McKenzie, and Yudkin (eds.), *Our Changing Fare*, pp. 90–1.

173 L. Stone, 'Literacy and Education in England, 1640–1900', *Past and Present*, XLII (1969); E. G. West, 'Literacy and the Industrial Revolution', *Economic History Review*, XXXI (1978).

174 Faucher, *Manchester in 1844*, pp. 82–3.

175 T. Brassey, *Lectures on the Labour Question*, (1878), p. 13.

176 *Industrious Class (Foreign Countries)*, (*Parl. Papers* LXII, 1872), pp. 168–71.

177 See, for example, Shadwell, *Industrial Efficiency*, II, p. 135; S. and B. Webb, *Industrial Democracy*, p. 413; S. Pollard, 'British and World Shipbuilding, 1890–1914: A Study in Comparative Costs', *Journal of Economic History*, XVII (1957).

178 See G. W. Hilton, 'The British Truck System in the Nineteenth Century', *Journal of Political Economy*, LXV (1957), p. 246; W. R. Lambert, 'Drink and Work Discipline in Industrial South Wales 1800–1870', *Welsh History Review*, VII (1974–5), p. 300. On this theme generally see S. Pollard, *The Genesis of Modern Management* (1968).

179 On working-class thrift see B. Supple, 'Legislation and Virtue: An Essay on Working Class Self-Help and the State in the early Nineteenth Century', in McKendrick (ed.), *Historical Perspectives*.

180 As indicated above (p. 344) the proportion of children 'educated' before the 1880s cannot be calculated precisely. Among other problems there is that of assessing the educational value of Sunday-schooling and other part-time instruction. Some historians would put the proportion educated at mid-century well above 50 per cent, and R. K. Webb in *English Historial Review*, LVX (1950), pp. 349–350 has estimated that at least two-thirds of the labour force could read by 1840.

181 On the ease of recruiting police constables at this time see J. P. Martin and G. Wilson, *The Police: A Study in Manpower* (1969), p. 12. The *General Report* of the 1891 census commented that 'the increased diffusion of education has apparently flooded the country with candidates for clerkships', and went on to note 'frequent complaints of difficulty in getting clerical employment'. (*Parl. Papers* CVI, 1893–4), p. 41.

182 The chief deficiency of British schooling so far as economic needs were concerned was in the supply of chemists, technicians, managers, engineers, and others of the higher echelons. Two of the shortcomings of working-class education had some bearing upon their supply: first there was the failure to impart sufficient basic knowledge to serve as a foundation for the more advanced studies necessary for these occupations and, second, the fact that in England and Wales (although not in Scotland) very few ·talented working-class children were educated to a level where their academic qualifications alone secured them a place among the scientists and managers. But the discussion above is restricted to the education of those who entered working-class occupations.

183 On mechanics institutes see M. Tylecote, *The Mechanics' Institutes of Lancashire and Yorkshire before 1851*, (Manchester 1957); S. F. Cotgrove, *Technical Education and Social Change*, (1958), Chaps. 1, 3.

184 'The advantages derived from the vast increase of wealth have principally fallen into the hands of those by whose enterprise and industry the interests of our manufacturing power have been directed. . . . On every hand the sides of the hills are adorned with the commodious dwellings of the master manufacturers manifesting wealth and comfort'–cotton manufacturer (1842) cited in A. J. Taylor (ed.), *The Standard of Living in Britain in the Industrial Revolution*, (1975), p. xxxvi. On this theme see also Perkin, *The Origins of Modern English Society*, Chap. 5.

185 These variables have been strangely neglected in the standard of living debate. P. Mathias and P. O'Brien explore some aspects of the topic for the years up to 1810 in their article, 'Taxation in Britain and France, 1715–1810: A Comparison of the Social and Economic Incidence of Taxes Collected for the Central Governments', *Journal of European Economic History*, v (1976).

186 A. H. Imlah, *Economic Elements in the Pax Britannica*, (Cambridge Mass. 1958), p. 101.

187 Mitchell and Deane, *Abstract of British Historical Statistics*, pp. 398, 416–17, 420.

188 Perkin, *The Origins of Modern English Society*, p. 414; Deane and Cole, *British Economic Growth*, p. 247.

189 Deane and Cole, op. cit. p. 247; S. B. Saul, *The Myth of the Great Depression, 1873–96*, (1969), p. 33.

190 Deane and Cole, op. cit. p. 247.

191 Imlah, *Economic Elements in the Pax Britannica*, p. 101.

192 Phelps Brown and Browne, *A Century of Pay*, p. 118.

193 Ibid. pp. 190–1.

4 · Poverty

1 M. E. Rose, *The Relief of Poverty, 1834–1914* (1972), p. 15.

2 C. Booth (ed.), *Life and Labour of the People in London* (1902–3 edn.), Ser I, vol. I, p. 33; vol. II, Chap. 2.

3 Rowntree, *Poverty: A Study of Town Life*, p. 111.

4 Ibid. p. 117.

5 A. L. Bowley and A. R. Burnett-Hurst, *Livelihood and Poverty* (1915).

6 Rowntree, *Poverty: A Study of Town Life*, pp. 300–1.

7 'Professional vagrants', said Mayhew, 'come to town as regularly as noblemen every winter'. *Morning Chronicle*, 11 Jan. 1850. See also, R. Vorspar, 'Vagrancy and the New Poor Law in late-Victorian and Edwardian England', *English Historical Review*, XCII (1977), p. 62.

8 S. B. Rowntree, *Poverty and Progress: A Second Social Survey of York*, (1941), p. 461. Another Rowntree survey, that of rural poverty, considerably overestimated the proportion in poverty by comparing 1913 prices with 1907 wages. B. S. Rowntree and M. Kendall, *How the Labourer Lives*, (1913); G. E. Mingay, 'The Course of Agricultural Labourers' Earnings' in *The Long Debate on Poverty*, Institute of Economic Affairs (1972), p. 50.

9 For some indication of sources of subsidiary income and the diverse other ways of supplementing pay from the husband's chief employment, see E. Roberts,

'Working-Class Standards of Living in Barrow and Lancaster, 1890–1914', *Economic History Review*, xxx (1977).

10 Liverpool Economic and Statistical Society, *How the Casual Labourer Lives*, (Liverpool 1909), p. xxxiii.

11 'A family living upon the scale allowed for in the estimate must never spend a penny on railway fare or omnibus. . . . They must never purchase a halfpenny newspaper. . . . They must write no letters to absent children, for they cannot afford to pay the postage. . . . The children must have no pocket money for dolls, marbles, or sweets. . . . Should a child fall ill, it must be attended by the parish doctor; should it die, it must be buried by the parish.' Rowntree, *Poverty: A Study of Town Life*, pp. 133–4.

12 See, for example, H. H. Mann, 'Life in an Agricultural Village in England', *Sociological Papers*, I (1904), which found 38 per cent of working-class families in primary poverty at Ridgemont (Beds.). Rowntree and Kendal's conclusions (in *How the Labourer Lives*, adjusted to correct their comparison of 1913 prices with 1907 earnings) suggest that farm labourers' earnings were below the poverty line level in almost half of English counties.

13 M. Anderson, *Family Structure in Nineteenth Century Lancashire*, (Cambridge 1971), pp. 29–32; W. A. Armstrong, *Stability and Change in an English County Town*, (Cambridge 1974), p. 51; J. Foster, *Class Struggle and the Industrial Revolution*, (1974), pp. 95–6.

14 W. Ashworth, while agreeing that the proportion in poverty fell between 1850 and the end of the century, has suggested (*An Economic History of England, 1870–1939* (1960), p. 252) that the living standards of those beneath the poverty line may have fallen because they suffered particularly from rising rents and coal prices and from deterioration in the quality of bread and certain other cheap foodstuffs. His speculation almost certainly cannot be applied to the rural poor because their rents rose very little (above, p. 95). It would be surprising too if the urban poor were net losers from the sum of changes after 1850. They spent more upon food than upon coal and rent, and food prices fell considerably. They also gained as much as any class from the suppression of adulteration and from improvements in public health.

15 London School of Economics, *New Survey of London Life and Labour*, (1932), III, Chap. 6.

16 Rowntree, *Poverty and Progress*, p. 461.

17 Booth (ed.), *Life and Labour*, Ser. I, Vol. I, p. 147. Much poverty was obviously the consequence of a combination of influences over which individuals had no control and their own shortcomings. E. P. Hennock has shown that Booth himself was less disturbed by his findings, and that he distinguished less clearly between the different causes of poverty, than has usually been supposed. E. P. Hennock, 'Poverty and Social Theory in England: The Experience of the Eighteen-eighties', *Social History*, I (1976).

18 Rowntree, *Poverty: A Study of Town Life*, p. 120.

19 G. S. Jones, *Outcast London*, (Oxford 1971), p. 96.

20 W. H. Beveridge, *Full Employment in a Free Society*, (1944), pp. 312–3. Mitchell and Deane, *Abstract of British Historical Statistics*, pp. 64–5 show slightly

different figures. We noted earlier that trade unionists were over-represented in occupations particularly susceptible to cyclical unemployment. But those workers who were more likely than trade unionists to fall below the poverty line were easily replaceable and quickly dismissed whenever trade slackened. Thus they probably suffered at least as much trade cycle unemployment as the unionists.

21 Pollard, *Labour in Sheffield*, pp. 126, 164.

22 Rowntree, *Poverty: A Study of Town Life*, p. 120.

23 J. A. Hobson, *Problems of Poverty*, (1891), p. 22; C. Booth, *The Aged Poor in England and Wales*, (1894), p. 420; P. Thane (ed.), *The Origins of British Social Policy*, (1978), p. 45. Booth soon appreciated that a substantial amount of poverty was a consequence of old age and he became a leading advocate of non-contributory state pensions.

24 B. L. Hutchins, 'Statistics of Women's Life and Employment', *Journal of the Royal Statistical Society*, LXXII (1909), p. 231.

25 There were far more unmarried mothers in the nineteenth century than is often supposed. In the middle of the century some 6 per cent of births in England and Wales were registered as illegitimate. Richard Jefferies, in *The Toilers of the Field* (1894), pp. 135–7, described how in many districts country girls with bastard children experienced little disapproval from their own class. Pre-nuptial pregnancy was so commonplace that the clergyman's wife in one village offered a prize of a piece of furniture to the first wife who failed to bear a child before she was nine months married.

26 'This is not only acquiesced in by the wife, but felt by her to be right. . . . The important practical fact is . . . that the labourer eats meat or bacon almost daily, whilst his wife and children may eat it but once a week.' Dr. E. Smith (1862–3) quoted in T. C. Barker, D. J. Oddy, and J. Yudkin, *The Dietary Surveys of Dr Edward Smith, 1862–3*, (1970), p. 32.

27 Woman at York to one of Rowntree's assistants. *Poverty: A Study of Town Life*, p. 55.

28 It may, in fact, help to explain both the greater absenteeism of female workers due to sickness and the higher than average incidence of deaths from tuberculosis among women in the third quarter of the century that was noted in Chapter 2. The subsequent marked fall in female tuberculosis mortality may have occurred partly because improved diet (the consequence of rising real wages) and improved poor law medical services proved most beneficial to those who previously had been most deprived.

29 Families with little storage space and those whose homes were filled with mice and hungry children probably had no better alternative to buying food in small quantities at the corner shop in any event, because only there could they buy just so much food as was needed for the next meal.

30 It was made possible by burial club, collecting society, or insurance company pay-outs. Management expenses took up to half of collecting society subscriptions, making them a peculiarly expensive form of saving. For details see P. H. J. H. Gosden, *Self-Help: Voluntary Associations in Nineteenth Century Britain*, (1973), Chap. 5.

31 The prospect of 'being put away properly' was a great comfort and in every sense the last occasion anyone wished to be marred by stinting. A pauper funeral ranked high among working-class fears and one of the attractions of the Salvation Army, it was said, was the quasi-military funeral with uniforms and a band that was promised to those who enlisted.

32 J. S. Curl in *The Victorian Celebration of Death*, (Newton Abbot 1972), p. 9 cites the case of a house-painter's widow who resolved to spend no more on her husband's funeral than she could afford. She quickly relented when her relations and neighbours made clear that the proposed economies would be tantamount to admission that she and her husband had been living in sin.

33 R. Moore, *Pitmen, Preachers, and Politics* (Cambridge 1974), p. 147.

34 Phelps Brown, *Growth of British Industrial Relations*, p. 21. A considerable proportion of wives, one in three at Middlesbrough (Lady F. Bell, *At the Works*, (1907), p. 78), were ignorant of their husbands' earnings. Poverty investigators frequently noted that what wives reported as expenditure on drink and tobacco appeared suspiciously little. See, for example, C. Booth *et al*, *Family Budgets*, (1896), p. 12.

35 'First came the question of the husband's keep. In every working-class family this is the first charge on the income, taking precedence even of rent. . . .' 'It would appear that it is upon the non-wage earning members of the working-class that the burden of poverty falls with the most crushing effect.' A. M. Martin, A. L. Bowley and A. R. Burnett-Hurst cited in L. Davidoff, 'The Employment of Married Women in England, 1850–1950', (unpublished M.A. thesis, University of London 1956), p. 154.

36 Rowntree, *Poverty: A Study of Town Life*, pp. 132, 142, 165. National figures of alcohol consumption per head were just past their peak at the time of Rowntree's survey. After 1900 consumption fell sharply.

37 *Morning Chronicle*, 21, 25, 28 Dec. 1849.

38 In Mayhew's day, however, when other thirst quenchers (not least unboiled water) were still suspect, there was at least some substance to the claims of those who allegedly took beer for the sake of their health.

39 In 1842 it was made illegal to pay miners in a public house. It became illegal to pay any workmen in a public house in 1883.

40 Some working-class women drank of course, and there are several accounts of respectable women being more often seen in pubs after 1890. But the typical nineteenth-century pub was a male domain. When chapel missions visited the mining districts wives were reported running through the streets, still wearing their aprons, crying with joy at the news of a drinking man's conversion. Moore, *Pitmen, Preachers, and Politics*, p. 146.

41 Cited in K. D. Brown (ed.), *Essays in Anti-Labour History*, (1974), p. 140.

42 *Ardrossan and Saltcoats Herald*, 12 Nov. 1886, cited in F. Reid, 'Keir Hardie's conversion to Socialism', in *Essays in Labour History, II, 1886–1923* eds. A. Briggs and J. Saville (1971), pp. 29, 33.

43 Rowntree, *Poverty: A Study of Town Life*, pp. 119–20.

44 Bowley and Burnett-Hurst, *Livelihood and Poverty*, pp. 46–7.

45 N. McCord, 'The Poor Law and Philanthropy' in *The New Poor Law in the Nineteenth Century*, ed. D. Fraser (1976), p. 97.

46 H. Bosanquet (ed.), *Social Conditions in Provincial Towns*, (1912), p. 58.

47 C. B. Hawkins, *Norwich: A Social Survey* (1910), p. 264.

48 Dr Barnardo's charitable work was initiated by his concern for children orphaned in London's East End by the 1866 cholera epidemic.

49 John Bewick's widow (see above, p. 3) received almost 20s a week.

50 G. M. Young (ed.), *Early Victorian England* (Oxford 1934), II, pp. 319–22.

51 Ibid., pp. 320–1.

52 Some part of the apparent expansion in charitable activity may have been illusory in that it arose from growing residential segregation causing a greater proportion of all donations to be channelled through formal charitable institutions.

53 On the proliferation of charitable activity in the East End, 'the land of the ever-simmering soup cauldron', see 'Home of Good Causes', Chap. 8 in C. Bermant, *Point of Arrival: A Study of London's East End*, (1975).

54 Young (ed.), *Early Victorian England*, II, p. 343; on the consequences of the Mansion House Fund see, among others, J. Harris, *Unemployment and Politics: A Study in English Social Policy, 1886–1914*, (Oxford 1972), p. 111; Jones, *Outcast London*, p. 299.

55 On the history of the COS see C. L. Mowat, *The Charity Organization Society, 1869–1913*, (1961). Mowat was the grandson of Charles Loch who was Secretary of the COS between 1875 and 1914.

56 Settlement might be acquired in a number of ways including by parentage (that is, the child acquired a claim on the father's parish), by birth in the parish, by marriage (females acquired a claim on their husband's parish), and by apprenticeship, long residence, or employment in the parish. Those requiring assistance could be removed to their parish of settlement. Changes in the law relating to removal and settlement and its effect upon labour mobility are discussed in Chapter 5.

57 Deaths from starvation were not unknown in England and Wales. Doubtless some deaths occurred through failure to establish a claim to parish relief or because relief was too tardy – but such cases were exceptional. On this point see, among others, D. V. Glass, *Numbering the People*, (Farnborough 1973), pp. 146–7. Until near the end of the nineteenth century there was no other country where central or local government took such an active role in poor relief as in England and Wales. On the chief features of poor relief in other countries during the nineteenth century see: *Poor Laws in Foreign Countries*, (*Parl. Papers* LXV, 1875); *Royal Commission on the Poor Laws: Foreign and Colonial System of Poor Relief* (*Parl. Papers* LV, i, 1910); S. Mencher, *Poor Law to Poverty Program: Economic Security Policy in Britain and the United States*, (Pittsburg 1967); G. V. Rimlinger, *Welfare Policy and Industrialization in Europe, America, and Russia*, (New York 1971).

58 Most such pre-1834 unions of parishes were of all the parishes within one town. At the beginning of the nineteenth century there were about 400 workhouses in all and a survey of 1802 suggests that about 8 per cent of paupers were then

workhouse residents. M. Blaug, 'The Myth of the Old Poor Law and the Making of the New', *Journal of Economic History*, XXIII (1963), p. 157.

59 *Discouraging* geographical mobility, in the interests of law and order, was one of its original aims.

60 Mitchell and Deane, *Abstract of British Historical Statistics*, pp. 5–6, 410, 469; J. D. Marshall, *The Old Poor Law, 1795–1834*, (1968), p. 26.

61 Clapham, *An Economic History of Modern Britain*, I, p. 364; N. Gash, 'Rural Unemployment, 1815–34', *Economic History Review*, VI (1935–6), pp. 90–1.

62 Mark Blaug has suggested that bias of this kind was crucially important in the selection of facts from the enormous volume of evidence that the commissioners accumulated but failed to analyse. M. Blaug, 'The Poor Law Report Reexamined', *Journal of Economic History*, XXIV (1964).

63 The 1834 report, in fact, made little attempt to analyse the causes of poverty and failed to appreciate their complexity. Chadwick, who later emphasized the contribution of sickness, at this time assumed that influences other than idleness, excessive births, and improvidence were of secondary importance.

64 D. A. Baugh, 'The Cost of Poor Relief in South-East England, 1790–1834', *Economic History Review*, XXVIII (1975).

65 D. Ashforth, 'The Urban Poor Law', in *The New Poor Law*, ed. Fraser, pp. 133–5.

66 N. McCord, 'The Implementation of the 1834 Poor Law Amendment Act on Tyneside', *International Review of Social History*, XIV (1969).

67 See, for instance, P. Searby, 'The Relief of the Poor in Coventry, 1830–63', *Historical Journal*, XX (1977).

68 A. Digby, 'The Labour Market and the Continuity of Social Policy after 1834: The Case of the Eastern Counties', *Economic History Review*, XXVIII (1975), pp. 71–3.

69 *The New Poor Law*, ed. Fraser, p. 18.

70 In the decade up to 1834 relief averaged around £6.5 million p.a. and in the decade after 1836 (when prices were somewhat higher on average) it had fallen to around £4.75 million p.a. Mitchell and Deane, *Abstract of British Historical Statistics*, pp. 410, 471.

71 Rose, *The Relief of Poverty*, p.15.

72 There was a very rapid expansion of the friendly society movement in the decade after 1834 and contemporaries were in no doubt that the expansion was a direct consequence of the new poor law. Gosden, *Self-Help: Voluntary Associations in Nineteenth Century Britain* (1973), pp. 69–71.

73 M. E. Rose, 'The New Poor Law in an Industrial Area', in *The Industrial Revolution*, ed. R. M. Hartwell, (Oxford 1970), pp. 135–6. See also Fraser (ed.), *The New Poor Law*, pp. 19–20, 139; D. Roberts, 'How Cruel was the Victorian Poor Law?', *Historical Journal*, VI (1963), p. 104.

74 The superiority of workhouse diets to those of many rural labourers in the low-wage south was a recurring theme in the *Morning Chronicle* survey of 1849–50 – 'The wonder is that every labourer in the land is not eager to pauperize himself'. (26 Jan. 1850).

75 In parts of rural Wales for example. D. Williams, *The Rebecca Riots*, (Cardiff 1955), p. 140.

76 A. Paterson, 'The Poor Law in Nineteenth-Century Scotland', in *The New Poor Law*, ed. Fraser, pp. 16, 178; C. S. Loch, 'Poor Relief in Scotland', *Journal of the Royal Statistical Society*, LXI (1898), p. 330; Mitchell and Deane, *Abstract of British Historical Statistics*, pp. 6, 416, 424.

77 Webbs, *Industrial Democracy*, Appendix III; Rose, *Relief of Poverty*, pp. 15, 53.

78 Mitchell and Deane, op. cit. p. 410.

79 The rule enforcing silence at meals, for example, was relaxed in the 1840s. And there had been no way of preventing the able-bodied from enjoying some of the concessions that were introduced for sick and elderly paupers.

80 The Boer War recruiting disclosures strengthened demands for social reform by enlisting the support of those concerned to remove a source of military weakness. On the fitness of Boer War volunteers, and the subsequent Inter-departmental Committee on Physical Deterioration, see B. B. Gilbert, 'Health and Politics: The British Physical Deterioration Report of 1904', *Bulletin of the History of Medicine*, XXXIX (1965).

81 Critics of the poor law also sought change in the way poverty was relieved. They considered that most of the poor were 'deserving' and entitled therefore to generous treatment. For the 'undeserving' poor however – vagrants and the incorrigibly idle – they demanded far more rigorous treatment. Those who were disinclined to work regularly and used to living rough had long been a particular nuisance to the poor law authorities because they found the workhouse an acceptable alternative to earning a living. To deal with them special 'casual wards' had been introduced with conditions even less 'less eligible' than those elsewhere in the workhouse. 'New liberals' and 'socialists', unimpeded by traditional liberal regard for individual freedoms and individual responsibilities, urged that the 'residual' class should be forcibly removed to penal labour colonies of the kind that existed in several European countries. There they would be reformed and in the meantime prevented both from harming the employment prospects of the deserving poor and from fathering a new generation of degenerates. On proposals for labour colonies and other means of treating the residuum see Harris, *Unemployment and Politics*, Chap. 3, and Jones, *Outcast London*, Part III.

82 This was a more radical departure from existing policy than the temporary public relief works at the time of the Lancashire cotton famine. Both measures implicitly acknowledged that unemployed workmen were not necessarily workshy.

5 · *Migrants, Emigrants, Immigrants*

1 Cited in A. J. Youngson Brown, 'Trade Union Policy in the Scots Coalfields, 1855–85', *Economic History Review*, VI (1953–4), p. 40.

2 Booth (ed.), *Life and Labour*, Ser. I, vol. III, pp. 86, 98.

3 The direction of migration, the question of optimum migration levels and the relative contribution of migration and natural increase to population redistribution are discussed in Hunt, *Regional Wage Variations in Britain, 1850–1914*, Chaps. 6 and 7.

4 The London area is defined here as London, the counties that adjoin it, Sussex, and Hertfordshire.

5 N. H. Carrier and J. R. Jeffery, *External Migration: A Study of the Available Statistics*, (HMSO 1953), pp. 92–3.

6 Between 1850 and 1914 the French farm labour force increased by over one million. At the same time the British farm labour force contracted by approaching half a million.

7 A. F. Weber, *Growth of Cities*, (New York 1899), p. 250.

8 E. E. Lampard, 'The Urbanizing World' in *The Victorian City: Images and Realities*, ed. H. J. Dyos and M. Wolff (1973), I, p. 15.

9 Some migration streams that *were* economically motivated also tended to cancel out one another, particularly when local demand for labour favoured one sex far more than the other. Lancashire in the 1880s, for example, lost more males than it gained, but gained far more females than it lost. The same was true of many residential areas that attracted domestic servants. Several coalfields, on the other hand, attracted men in large numbers but were net losers of females. Migration of this type could produce massive disparity in the numbers of males and females in an area – at Edinburgh and Leith in 1851 there were 65,000 females aged twenty and over but only 47,000 males.

10 See, for example, A. B. Hill, 'Internal Migration and its Effects upon the Death-Rates', *Medical Research Council Reports*, No. 95 (1925), pp. 22–3; A. Constant, 'The Geographical Background of Inter-Village Population Movements in Northamptonshire and Huntingdonshire, 1754–1943', *Geography*, XXXIII (1948).

11 *Poor Inquiry (Ireland)* (*Parl. Papers* XXXIV, 1836), Appendix G, p. xxvi. For other claims of this kind see pp. xxvi–viii, 66 of the same report.

12 W. S. Shepperson, *British Emigration to North America*, (Oxford 1957), p. 48. A further reason why there were so few poor-law emigrants was that the authorities, anxious to settle and strengthen the Empire, would seldom subsidize emigration to the United States.

13 Professor Beesley quoted in C. J. Erickson, 'The Encouragement of Emigration by British Trade Unions, 1850–1900', *Population Studies*, III (1949–50), p. 256.

14 An investigation of long-term mobility in Northamptonshire and Huntingdonshire, for example, noted a sharp rise following the completion of the line between Peterborough and Northampton in 1845. Constant, loc. cit.

15 M. C. F. Morris, *The British Workman, Past and Present*, (1928), pp. 80–1.

16 T. Wood, *Autobiography*, (1956), p. 15.

17 Ashby, *Joseph Ashby*, pp. 160–1. P. J. Perry has stressed the impact of the bicycle on short distance mobility in Dorset. P. J. Perry, 'Working-Class Isolation and Mobility in Rural Dorset, 1837–1936', *Institute of British Geographers, Transactions*, XLVI (1969), pp. 133–4.

18 Mitchell and Deane, *Abstract of British Historical Statistics*, p. 60. The increase between 1901 and 1911 remains after allowance is made for the disturbing effect of the Boer War upon employment.

19 See, for example, Booth (ed.), *Life and Labour*, Ser. I, vol. III, pp. 133, 138. This survey (ibid. p. 139) also cited an investigation which found that 80 per cent of migrants from villages to London and other towns were aged between fifteen and twenty-five.

20 *Census of England and Wales 1891: General Report*, (*Parl. Papers* CVI, 1893–4), p. 40.
21 Another reason for greater female mobility, of course, is that women more often moved at marriage. With regard to emigration, however, males were distinctly the more mobile sex.
22 Booth (ed.), *Life and Labour*, Ser. I, vol. III, p. 75.
23 F. Clifford, 'The Labour Bill in Farming', *Journal of the Royal Agricultural Society*, XI (1875), p. 125.
24 *Morning Chronicle* report on the rural population of Berkshire, Buckinghamshire, Oxfordshire, and Wiltshire, 31 Oct. 1849.
25 F. Thompson, *Lark Rise to Candleford* (1948 edn.), p. 30.
26 For details of rural-urban living costs see Hunt, *Regional Wage Variations in Britain, 1850–1914*, Chap. 2.
27 B. Kerr, 'The Dorset Agricultural Labourer, 1759–1850', *Proceedings, Dorset Natural History and Archaeological Society*, LXXXIV (1962), p. 176.
28 Booth (ed.), *Life and Labour*, Ser. I, vol. III, pp. 131–3.
29 Erickson, in *Population Studies*, III (1949–50); Hobsbawm, *Labouring Men*, Chap. 4.
30 R. Samuel (ed.), *Village Life and Labour* (1975), p. 240.
31 *Poor Inquiry (Ireland)*, (*Parl. Papers* XXXIV, 1836), Appendix G, pp. xxvi-xxviii.
32 For a fuller discussion of these points and evidence of spatial differences in migration responses to wage differences see Hunt, op. cit. Chap. 7.
33 A. L. Rowse, *A Cornish Childhood* (1975 edn.), pp. 35, 39, 52. This village was therefore an exception to the pattern noted earlier in which southern migrants tended to make for London. Cornwall was distinguished by the very high proportion of its migrants who went overseas. My colleague Dudley Baines has calculated that between 1861 and 1901 over half of male Cornish-born migrants left for destinations outside England and Wales.
34 Engels, *The Condition of the Working Class in England*, p. 107; W. H. G. Armytage, *Four Hundred Years of English Education*, (Cambridge 1970), p. 116.
35 Engels, op. cit. pp. 139, 241.
36 Steamships made the crossing faster and far cheaper. In the mid-1820s it was possible to cross from Belfast to Glasgow for only fourpence. The introduction of steamships thus probably had a greater direct impact upon migration from Ireland than the introduction of railways had upon internal mobility (above, p. 151).
37 In 1851 75 per cent of the Irish-born in England and Wales, and 55 per cent of the natives, were aged twenty and above. On these points see J. H. Clapham, 'Irish Immigration into Great Britain in the Nineteenth Century', *Bulletin of the International Committee of Historical Sciences*, V (1933), p. 603; J. A. Jackson, *The Irish in Britain*, (1963), Table VIII; R. Lawton, 'Irish Immigration to England and Wales in the mid-Nineteenth Century', *Irish Geography*, IV (1959); M. W. Flinn (ed.), *Scottish Population History*, (Cambridge 1977), p. 456.
38 J. Denvir, *The Irish in Britain*, (1892), pp. 390, 392, 433–4.
39 Ibid. p. 430.
40 The proportion of Irish-born in Scotland's population was considerably above

their proportion in the population of England and Wales throughout the nineteenth century.

41 Clapham, loc. cit. p. 604; *Report on the Diminution in the Number of Migratory Labourers from Ireland*, (*Parl. Papers* LXII, 1884).

42 *Report on Migratory Agricultural Labourers* (*Parl. Papers* CI, 1900), p. 20; *Second Report on the Wages, Earnings and Conditions of Employment of Agricultural Labourers* (*Parl. Papers* XCVII, 1905), p. 139.

43 Engels, *Condition of the Working Class in England*, p. 105.

44 M. D. George, *London Life in the Eighteenth Century*, (1925), p. 105; W. A. Armstrong, *Stability and Change in an English County Town*, (Cambridge 1974), p. 124; O. Handlin, *Boston's Immigrants*, (Cambridge Mass. 1959), p. 114; T. Dillon, 'The Irish in Leeds, 1851–61', *Publications of the Thoresby Society*, LIV (1973), p. 13; *Victoria County History of Leicestershire*, IV (1958), p. 263; Burnett, *A Social History of Housing*, p. 89.

45 *Poor Inquiry (Ireland)*, *Appendix G*, (*Parl. Papers* XXXIV, 1836), p. 24.

46 Ibid. pp. x–xi, 57.

47 *Poor Inquiry (Ireland)*, *Appendix G*, pp. xiii, 48.

48 Denvir, *The Irish in Britain*, p. 299.

49 See, for example, N. Glazer and D. P. Moynihan, *Beyond the Melting Pot: The Negroes, Puerto Ricans, Jews, Italians, and Irish of New York City*, (Cambridge Mass. 1963), p. 257.

50 Quoted in Chapman (ed.), *The History of Working-Class Housing*, p. 202.

51 A. Redford, *Labour Migration in England, 1800–50*, (Manchester 1964), p. 157.

52 C. Creighton, *A History of Epidemics in Britain*, (1894), II, p. 207.

53 George, *London Life in the Eighteenth Century*, p. 124.

54 *Poor Inquiry (Ireland)*, *Appendix G*, p. xxiv.

55 Ibid. p. 11; *Destitute Irish (Liverpool)*, (*Parl. Papers* LIV, 1847), p. 2.

56 See, for examples, C. Richardson, 'The Irish in Victorian Bradford', Urban History Society Conference Paper (1969), p. 3 n. 17; George, op. cit. pp. 122–3; Fraser (ed.), *The New Poor Law*, p. 145.

57 See, for example, George, op. cit. p. 122.

58 There was a great variety in the way that poor law authorities treated Irish-born applicants for relief, particularly before the settlement laws were relaxed. Some towns granted them settlements after only six weeks, some followed a policy of wholesale repatriation, and Bristol claimed the right to treat all Irish as aliens.

59 *Poor Inquiry (Ireland)*, *Appendix G*, pp. 14, 110.

60 J. E. Handley, *The Irish in Scotland, 1798–1845*, (Cork 1945), p. 59.

61 H. J. M. Johnston, *British Emigration Policy, 1815–1830*, (Oxford 1972), pp. 101, 104; Redford, *Labour Migration in England*, pp. 165–6; *Morning Chronicle*, 18 Dec. 1849; K. Smith, *The Malthusian Controversy*, (1951), p. 313.

62 Richardson, loc. cit. p. 8.

63 W. O. Henderson (ed.), *Engels: Selected Writings*, (1967), p. 95.

64 Elderton, *Report on the English Birthrate*, I, p. 70.

65 The Irish of Clare Market were described in Booth's London survey as 'violent and drunken, but not criminal'. Booth (ed.), *Life and Labour*, Ser. III, vol. II, p. 178.

66 At Newburyport (Massachusetts) Irish immigrants were well represented among

those of humble origin who were sufficiently thrifty to join the ranks of owner-occupiers. S. Thermstrom, *Poverty and Progress* (Cambridge, Mass. 1964), p. 156. What perhaps confused commentators was the mistaken assumption that those as ready as many Irish were to seek charity or poor law assistance were therefore also destitute. Many Irish harvesters who applied for assistance did so after having sent back their savings via the post office or a trusted friend, and in the hope that the poor law officials would order (and pay for) their removal to Ireland. Redford, *Labour Migration in England*, pp. 148–9.

67 *Poor Inquiry (Ireland), Appendix G*, p. 5.

68 See, for example, R. D. Lobban, 'The Irish Community in Greenock in the Nineteenth Century', *Irish Geography*, VI (1971), pp. 279–80.

69 See, for example, Richardson, loc. cit. pp. 3, 7; George, *London Life in the Eighteenth Century*, p. 116.

70 *Poor Inquiry (Ireland), Appendix G*, p. iii.

71 Redford, *Labour Migration in England*, pp. 151–2.

72 J. E. Handley, *The Irish in Modern Scotland*, (Cork 1947), p. 319.

73 See, for example, L. H. Lees, *Exiles of Erin: Irish Migrants in Victorian London*, (Manchester 1979), pp. 99, 118; Richardson, loc. cit. p. 9. There is, unfortunately, no work on immigrants in Britain comparable with Stephan Thermstrom's studies of Newburyport and Boston.

74 *Poor Inquiry (Ireland), Appendix G*, p. 5.

75 *Morning Chronicle*, 21 Mar. 1850.

76 Cited in W. M. Walker, 'Irish Immigrants in Scotland: Their Priests, Politics and Parochial Life', *Historical Journal*, xv (1972), p. 662. On the similarity of the Irish employment pattern in Glasgow at mid-century and at the end of the century, see J. H. Treble, 'The Market for Unskilled Male Labour in Glasgow, 1891–1914', in *Essays in Scottish Labour History*, ed. I. MacDougall (Edinburgh 1978), p. 121.

77 Denvir, *The Irish in Britain*, p. 252.

78 Not least their urban background and a hierarchy of Jewish occupations within which they could advance. But they made impressive progress also where their route was more difficult and in certain respects (language for example) they faced the greater obstacles.

79 O. Handlin, *The Newcomers*, (Cambridge Mass. 1959), p. 26. See also, S. Thermstrom, *The Other Bostonians*, (Cambridge Mass. 1973), Chaps. 6, 7, and pp. 253–4; Glazer and Moynihan, *Beyond the Melting Pot*, p. 256; D. R. Esslinger, *Immigrants and the City*, (Port Washington N.Y. 1975), pp. 88–9, 120.

80 Lobban, loc. cit. p. 279. See also Lees, *Exiles of Erin*, p. 201.

81 Thermstrom, *The Other Bostonians*, Chap. 7.

82 The hope that domicile in Britain would be temporary rested partly on the belief that home rule for Ireland, when it came, would somehow transform the Irish economy. T. P. O'Connor, MP, declared in the House of Commons in 1912, 'Never more after an Irish Parliament comes into existence will any Irishman leave Ireland'.

83 Quoted in Redford, *Labour Migration in England*, p. 159.

84 Ibid. p. 159. Interestingly enough, some of the immigrants themselves also appear to have believed that their presence was detrimental to native living standards. A

common theme in appeals that English workers should support demands for Irish home rule was that home rule would encourage immigrants to return to Ireland and thus improve English living standards. See, for example, J. H. Treble, O'Connor, O'Connell, and the Attitudes of Irish Immigrants towards Chartism in the North of England, 1838–48', in *The Victorians and Social Protest*, ed. J. Butt and I. F. Clarke (Newton Abbot 1973), p. 47.

85 For examples see Hunt, *Regional Wage Variations in Britain, 1850–1914*, p. 297.

86 J. Treble, 'The Attitude of the Roman Catholic Church towards Trade Unionism in the North of England, 1833–42', *Northern History*, v (1970), p. 112.

87 H. M. Pelling, *A History of British Trade Unionism*, (1963), pp. 47–8.

88 H. A. Turner, *Trade Union Growth, Structure, and Policy*, (1962), pp. 48, 145.

89 On this episode generally see Treble, in *Northern History*, v (1970).

90 F. C. Mather, 'The Railways, the Electric Telegraph, and Public Order during the Chartist Period, 1837–48', *History*, xxxviii (1953), p. 42.

91 T. Coleman, *The Railway Navvies*, (1968 edn.), p. 94. In 1841 about one railway navvy in ten was Irish.

92 See, for example, Redford, *Labour Migration in England*, p. 147; Handley, *The Irish in Scotland, 1798–1845*, pp. 46–7; *Poor Inquiry (Ireland), Appendix G*, pp. xliv-v.

93 B. M. Kerr, 'Irish Seasonal Migration to Great Britain, 1800–38', *Irish Historical Studies*, iii (1942–3), p. 376.

94 Youngson Brown, in *Economic History Review*, vi (1953–4), pp. 38–9.

95 A. Campbell and F. Reid, 'The Independent Collier in Scotland', and A. Campbell, 'Honourable Men and Degraded Slaves', in *Independent Colliers: The Coalminer as Archetypal Proletarian Reconsidered*, ed. R. Harrison (1978).

96 *Poor Inquiry (Ireland), Appendix G*, pp. iv, 20, 73.

97 Thompson, *Making of the English Working Class*, p. 480.

98 J. Werly, 'The Irish in Manchester, 1832–49', *Irish Historical Studies*, xviii (1972–3), pp. 345–7.

99 Dillon, loc. cit. pp. 1, 7–10; Richardson, loc. cit. pp. 3–4, 9. See also C. G. Pooley, 'The Residential Segregation of Migrant Communities in mid-Victorian Liverpool', *Institute of British Geographers, Transactions*, new series, ii (1977), pp. 364, 379; Lees, *Exiles of Erin*, p. 63.

100 Lobban, in *Irish Geography*, vi (1971), p. 277; R. D. Lobban, 'The Migration of Highlanders into Lowland Scotland, (c. 1750–1890)', (unpublished Ph.D. thesis, University of Edinburgh 1969), pp. 173–4, 279–80, 289–90, 296.

101 Lobban, in *Irish Geography*, vi (1971), p. 279.

102 Handlin, *Boston's Immigrants*, pp. 176–7.

103 A. E. Dingle and B. H. Harrison, 'Cardinal Manning as Temperance Reformer', *Historical Journal*, xii (1969), pp. 496–500.

104 Thermstrom, *The Other Bostonians*, p. 161; Handlin, *Boston's Immigrants*, p. 133.

105 W. J. Fishman, *East End Jewish Radicals, 1875–1914*, (1975), p. 78.

106 Quoted in Jackson, *The Irish in Britain*, p. 116.

107 See, for example, Handley, *The Irish in Modern Scotland*, pp. 117–19.

108 Richardson, loc. cit. p. 4; Dillon, loc. cit. p. 9.

109 A 1912 survey described them as 'the roughest and lowest element of the people

... mainly settled in two poor districts. ... Gay, irresponsible, idle, and quarrelsome, they seem by nature unfitted for the controlled life of a large town. ... They contribute abnormally to the work of the police court and fill the workhouses and charitable institutions.' F. G. D'Aeth in *Social Conditions in Provincial Towns*, ed. H. Bosanquet (1912), p. 38.

110 Lobban, in *Irish Geography*, VI (1971), p. 278.

111 Roberts, *The Classic Slum*, pp. 22–3.

112 Jackson, *The Irish in Britain*, p. 82.

113 Handley, *Irish in Modern Scotland*, p. 319; Thompson, *Making of the English Working Class*, pp. 473–5. Among others who have put forward similar views see W. H. Marwick, *Economic Developments in Victorian Scotland*, (1936), p. 132.

114 *Poor Inquiry (Ireland), Appendix G*, p. xxxvii.

115 Ibid. p. xxxvi.

116 Ibid. pp. xxvii, xxix, 28–9; Handley, *The Irish in Scotland, 1798–1845*, p. 104.

117 The natural increase in population was over three times as great as immigration even in the famine decade.

118 See, for example, D. F. MacDonald, *Scotland's Shifting Population, 1770–1850*, (Glasgow 1937), p. 78; Flinn (ed.), *Scottish Population History*, p. 453.

119 *Poor Inquiry (Ireland), Appendix G*, pp. xlv, 38.

120 *Census of Great Britain 1851*, (*Parl. Papers* LXXXVIIIi, 1852–3), p. 526.

121 Ibid. (*Parl. Papers* LXXXVIIIii, 1852–3), p. 737.

122 Thompson, *Making of the English Working Class*, p. 473.

123 The appendix to the 1834 Report shows that outside the large towns much of this work was still done by natives even in Lancashire. *Poor Inquiry (Ireland), Appendix G*, pp. 71, 90–1.

124 J. H. Treble, 'Irish Navvies in the North of England, 1830–50', *Transport History*, VI (1973), pp. 229–30.

125 *Poor Inquiry (Ireland), Appendix G*, p. xlvi. The Highlanders were probably more successful in maintaining part of their traditional work against Irish competition than this comment suggests. See T. M. Devine, 'Temporary Migration and the Scottish Highlands in the Nineteenth Century', *Economic History Review*, XXXII (1979).

126 *Poor Inquiry (Ireland), Appendix G*, p. 70.

127 Ibid. p. 71.

128 See, for example, Lobban in *Irish Geography*, VI (1971), p. 274.

129 The same attitudes were evident in New England when Irish immigrants were recruited for the cotton mills. The work then lost status and Yankee girls were less easily recruited. See, for example, Handlin, *Boston's Immigrants*, p. 73.

130 *Poor Inquiry (Ireland), Appendix G*, p. 21.

131 Ireland, that is, was reducing its Malthusian crisis by exporting it to Britain, and with the consequence of delaying the solution of Britain's milder version of the same crisis. Nineteenth-century America had far more need of immigrants than nineteenth-century Britain, but I have suggested elsewhere that the rural labour of low-wage Britain was in a position analogous to that of southern negroes in the United States between the Civil War and the 1920s. Both suffered because employment opportunities elsewhere within the country were taken up by

immigrants. In the United States the restriction of immigration in the 1920s was accompanied by a substantial quickening in the northward flow of black labour.

132 V. D. Lipman, *Social History of the Jews in England, 1850–1950*, (1954), pp. 65–6.

133 Largely, but by no means entirely. The Jewish rate of natural increase was probably well above the average.

134 Not only were most of the immigrants poor but they contained a more than proportionate number of adult males. Over half of the Russians and Poles who arrived in 1893 were men, a quarter were women, and only 20 per cent were children. *Volume and Effects of Recent Immigration from Eastern Europe*, (*Parl. Papers* LXVIII, 1894), p. 10.

135 Including, that is, 'Irish' workers born in London. For details and sources of the numbers and dispersion of the Jewish population see Hunt, *Regional Wage Variations in Britain, 1850–1914*, pp. 305–8. The estimate of 110,000 Jews in London at the end of the century given there is probably too low.

136 Lipman, *Social History of the Jews*, p. 102.

137 Ibid. pp. 106–7.

138 Booth (ed.), *Life and Labour*, Ser. I, vol. IV, p. 60; *Report of the Chief Inspector of Factories and Workshops*, (*Parl. Papers* XXVI, 1888), p. 95.

139 Cited in B. Gainer, *The Alien Invasion: The Origins of the Aliens Act of 1905*, (1972), p. 43.

140 Ibid. p. 61; J. Arch, *Joseph Arch: The Story of his Life*, (1898), p. 255.

141 *St. James's Gazette* (1887) cited in J. A. Garrard, *The English and Immigration, 1880–1910*, (1971), pp. 25–6.

142 On this theme generally see Gainer, *The Alien Invasion*, pp. 105–7; Garrard, op. cit. pp. 26, 199.

143 S. Webb, *The Decline in the Birthrate*, (1907), pp. 16–17.

144 L. P. Gartner, *The Jewish Immigrant in England, 1870–1914*, (Detroit 1960), p. 156. See also Fishman, *East End Jewish Radicals*, p. 216.

145 Lipman, *Social History of the Jews*, p. 106.

146 Gartner, op. cit. p. 159.

147 Ibid.

148 See, for example, C. Russell and H. S. Lewis, *The Jew in London*, (1900), p. 176.

149 *Volume and Effects of Recent Immigration from Eastern Europe*, (*Parl. Papers* LXVIII, 1894), p. 45.

150 Ibid. pp. 61–2.

151 On this topic generally see Lipman, *Social History of the Jews*, p. 34; Gartner, *The Jewish Immigrant in England*, pp. 183–6.

152 'No Englishman could have perpetrated such a horrible crime . . . it must have been done by a Jew.' Fishman, *East End Jewish Radicals*, p. 73.

153 Fishman, *East End Jewish Radicals*, pp. 106, 224–5, 259, 300. See also Gainer, op. cit. pp. 22, 100–1.

154 'Drink figures as the cause of poverty to a much greater extent everywhere else than in Whitechapel. . . . This is no doubt to be explained by the Jewish population, who, whatever their faults may be, are very sober.' Booth (ed.), *Life and Labour*, Ser. I, vol. 1, p. 148. Modest expenditure on alcohol left more to spend

on food and may be another reason for the comparative good health of the Jewish immigrant community.

155 *Select Committee on Emigration and Immigration (Foreigners)*, (*Parl. Papers* x, 1889), para. 1469; Gainer, *The Alien Invasion*, p. 15.

156 B. Webb, *My Apprenticeship* (1946 edn.), p. 283. On Burnett's 1887 report on sweating, and reactions to it, see Gainer, op. cit. Chap. 5. On Beatrice Webb's experiences as a sweated worker ('do you want a plain 'and?') see 'Pages from a Work-Girl's Diary', *The Nineteenth Century*, xxiv, (Sept. 1888). She proved a poor seamstress but the shrewd Jewish mistress promoted her to supervising the outworkers, 'She's got the voice and manner to deal with that bloody lot.' (*My Apprenticeship*, 1946 edn. p. 38).

157 On these points see, for example, *Volume and Effects of Recent Immigration*, pp. 84, 86, 132; Booth (ed.), *Life and Labour*, Ser. I, vol. IV, p. 211; Russell and Lewis, *The Jew in London*, pp. 70–2.

158 There were also, of course, some very prosperous Jewish immigrants who brought capital, trade connections, and highly specialist knowledge as well as their talent. Ludwig Mond the chemist for example (one of the founders of Brunner, Mond), and merchants like Sir Jacob Behrens of Bradford – but we are concerned mainly with the contributions of more humble men. On the various points mentioned here see Gartner, op. cit. pp. 74–5, 84–93; Lipman, op. cit. p. 114; Russell and Lewis, op. cit. pp. 72–3; A. R. Rollin, 'The Jewish Contribution to the British Textile Industry', *Transactions of the Jewish Historical Society of England*, xvii (1951–2).

159 See, for example, *Volume and Effects of Recent Immigration*, pp. 90–1; *Royal Commission on Alien Immigration*, (*Parl. Papers* ix, 1903), Report, p. 19.

160 Fishman, *East End Jewish Radicals*, p. 47.

161 'Odd Jews who strayed into the village were driven out at once. Very early in the century one did venture to set up a small second-hand clothing store. Ignored by the police, thugs arrived, carried his stock into the road and set fire to it.' Roberts, *The Classic Slum*, p. 171; G. Alderman, 'The Anti-Jewish Riots of August 1911 in South Wales', *Welsh History Review*, vi (1972–3).

162 The Aliens Act of 1905 came into operation in January 1906. Under this Act authorities could turn back immigrants who were diseased or insane, those with criminal records, and those who seemed likely to become a public charge. The Act was not vigorously enforced and its provisions were easily evaded. Those who travelled cabin class, for example, and all those on boats with fewer than twenty steerage-class passengers were allowed in unchecked. However, the act was not repealed by the new Liberal government and it probably deterred some potential immigrants and diverted many others to the United States. For detailed accounts of the Act and its enforcement, see Gainer, *The Alien Invasion* and Garrard, *The English and Immigration*.

163 W. H. Wilkins, *The Alien Invasion* (1892), Appendix G.

164 *Select Committee on Emigration and Immigration (Foreigners)*, (*Parl. Papers* x, 1889), para. 1491.

165 Gainer, op. cit. p. 31.

166 Ibid. p. 96.

167 Ibid. p. 138; Fishman, *East End Jewish Radicals*, pp. 76–7.

Part II · Working-Class Movements

6 · *Working-Class Movements, 1815–1850.*
(I) Trade Unionism and Other Movements.

1 S. and B. Webb, *The History of Trade Unionism*, (1920 edn.), p. 1.

2 These shortcomings, in fact, are less apparent in the Webbs' original work than in that of historians who have followed them and simplified or emphasized parts of their account.

3 H. A. Turner, *Trade Union Growth, Structure, and Policy*, (1962), p. 51.

4 Webbs, *History of Trade Unionism*, pp. 748–9.

5 G. D. H. Cole, *A Short History of the British Working Class Movement*, (1948), p. 85.

6 E. J. Hobsbawm, *Labouring Men*, (1968), p. 278; H. Perkin, *The Origins of Modern English Society, 1780–1880*, (1969), p. 395; A. E. Musson, *Trade Union and Social History*, (1974), pp. 125–6.

7 Musson, *Trade Union and Social History*, pp. 130–1.

8 Webbs, *History of Trade Unionism*, p. 182.

9 Luddism embraced also the Lancashire handloom weavers' loom-smashing of 1812 and the Yorkshire croppers' violent resistance to the shearing-frame and gigmill in the same year. These geographically separate activities seem, however, to have had little in common besides their tactics. There are various accounts of how Luddism acquired its name. Most concern a Leicestershire youth, Ned Ludlam. It is said that when he was told by his father to square his needles (a technical term) he took a large hammer and beat them to a heap.

10 Cut-out hosiery was a logical and enterprising response to trade crisis but was seen by the knitters as cheap expediency and as a cause of further loss of status. Note that midland Luddism, the main Luddite activity, was not resistance to new machines. Similar frames were in use two centuries earlier.

11 Luddism eventually declined as a result of arrests and betrayals, despair, the introduction of a law making frame breaking a capital offence, and a temporary improvement in trade.

12 The name 'Swing' probable came from the swinging-stick of the flail used in hand-threshing.

13 D. J. V. Jones, *Before Rebecca*, p. 97; M. I. Thomis, *The Luddites*, (Newton Abbot 1970), p. 133.

14 J. L. and B. Hammond, *The Town Labourer*, (1966 edn.), p. 143.

15 D. Bythell, *The Handloom Weavers*, (Cambridge 1969), p. 193; Turner, *Trade Union Growth, Structure, and Policy*, p. 68; M. I. Thomis, *The Town Labourer and the Industrial Revolution*, (1974), p. 138.

16 Webbs, *History of Trade Unionism*, p. 77.

17 Thomis, *The Town Labourer and the Industrial Revolution*, p. 138.

18 For an example see, N. McCord, 'The Seamen's Strike of 1815 in North-East England', *Economic History Review*, xxi (1968).

19 W. H. Marwick, 'Early Trade Unionism in Scotland', *Economic History Review*, v (1934–5), p. 89. Some early writers were less than certain that the Combination

Acts applied only in England and Wales. There were certainly no prosecutions under the Acts in Scotland.

20 So called because the marchers, who hoped to present a reform petition to the Prince Regent, each carried a blanket to use on the way to London.

21 The name was a propaganda device that associated the bloodshed at St Peter's Field (eleven died) with the infinitely bloodier Battle of Waterloo four years earlier. The meeting, like the Blanketeers meeting, was ordered to close by the magistrates after it had begun.

22 The Acts prohibited most meetings of over fifty people. They also gave magistrates powers to search private houses for arms; prohibited drilling and military training; strengthened the law against blasphemous and seditious libel; and increased the stamp duty on cheap publications. The effect of these acts is often overrated. The decline in popular radicalism soon after 'Peterloo' was due mainly to an upturn in the trade cycle, cheaper food, and dissension among radical leaders. D. Read, *Peterloo: the 'Massacre' and its Background*, (Manchester 1958), pp. 151–63.

23 There was a heightened consciousness of shared interests at the time of repeal, aroused by employers' attempts to restore legal restraints. Workers' 'defence associations' were established in several towns. The Act of 1824 was followed by another in 1825 which made some concessions to employers.

24 Webbs, *History of Trade Unionism*, p. 115.

25 The initial moves towards what became the National Association of United Trades for the Protection of Labour were made before this. See R. G. Kirby and A. E. Musson, *The Voice of the People: John Doherty, 1798–1854*, (Manchester 1975), Chap. 6.

26 W. H. Oliver, 'The Consolidated Trades' Union of 1834', *Economic History Review*, XVII (1964–5), pp. 85–6. The figure is for April 1834, about the time of the Tolpuddle protest campaign.

27 The convicted labourers were transported nevertheless, but the remainder of their sentence was remitted in 1836 and in 1838 they were brought back to England.

28 Webbs, *History of Trade Unionism*, pp. 153, 168.

29 Turner, *Trade Union Growth, Structure, and Policy*, pp. 169, 192.

30 See A. E. Musson, *British Trade Unions, 1800–75*, (1972) and Chaps. 1 and 2 in his *Trade Union and Social History*, (1974).

31 Quoted in Cole, *A Short History of the British Working-Class Movement*, p. 173.

32 Webbs, *History of Trade Unionism*, p. 178.

33 The Webbs stressed this point and with good reason. But note that transport changes had an influence on the timing of this development (above, p. 150) and that emigration was sometimes used as part of an aggressive trade policy (above, p. 261). Some schemes (that of the potters for example) were designed to escape industrialization by creating agrarian communes in the American wilderness.

34 Webbs, *History of Trade Unionism*, p. 199; H. M. Pelling, *A History of British Trade Unionism*, (1963 edn.), p. 57.

35 A. J. Taylor, 'The Miners' Association of Great Britain and Ireland, 1842–8', *Economica*, XXII (1955), p. 52.

36 P. H. J. H. Gosden, *The Friendly Societies in England, 1815–1875*, (Manchester 1961), p. 16.

37 'Were you to have a Parliament chosen, next year, by universal suffrage and vote by ballot,' he wrote in 1835, 'it would be most probably the least efficient, most turbulent and worst public assembly that has yet ruled this country.' Quoted in J. Butt (ed.), *Robert Owen: Prince of Cotton Spinners*, (Newton Abbot 1971), p. 12.

38 The same is true of the numerous trade unions who later included some variation of this declaration on their banners.

39 The last co-operative village, at Queenswood in Hampshire, collapsed in 1846. On the Owenite communes see W. H. G. Armytage, *Heavens Below: Utopian Experiments in England, 1560–1960*, (1961), and Chap. 3 in S. Pollard and J. Salt (eds.), *Robert Owen: Prophet of the Poor*, (1971).

40 W. W. Rostow, *British Economy of the Nineteenth Century*, (Oxford 1948), p. 124.

41 The Merthyr demonstrators were easily placated by half-promises that wage-cuts would be restored. On these various riots see G. Rudé, 'English Rural and Urban Disturbances on the Eve of the First Reform Bill, 1830–1831', *Past and Present*, xxxvii (1967); D. J. V. Jones, *Before Rebecca: Popular Protests in Wales, 1793–1835*, (1973), Part iii; S. Thomas, *The Bristol Riots*, (Bristol 1974).

42 R. G. Kirby and A. E. Musson, *The Voice of the People: John Doherty, 1798–1854*, (Manchester 1975), p. 346.

43 Quoted in N. C. Edsall, *The Anti-Poor Law Movement, 1834–44*, (Manchester 1971), p. 179.

44 Their attitudes may have been influenced also by allegations that the poor law migration schemes were designed to supply pauper children to facilitate the relay system that was restricting the benefits of the 1833 Factory Act.

45 For a fuller account of this and similar incidents see Edsall, op. cit. Chaps. 4 and 5.

46 There were times after 1838 when it was very active: in 1841–2 especially when the authorities made fresh attempts to bring the north of England into line.

7 · *Working-Class Movements, 1815–1850.*
(II) · *Chartism, Revolution, and the Making of Class*

 1 J. T. Ward, *Chartism*, (1973), p. 117.

 2 Ibid. p. 118.

 3 D. Read, 'Chartism in Manchester' in *Chartist Studies*, ed. A. Briggs (1959), pp. 45–9.

 4 Mather (in *Chartist Studies*, p. 383) gives the number killed as twenty-two, Ward (op. cit. p. 134) puts it at fourteen.

 5 F. C. Mather, *Chartism*, (1965), p. 16.

 6 Briggs (ed.), *Chartist Studies*, p. 301; Cole, *A Short History of the British Working-Class Movement*, p. 112; Ward, op. cit. p. 158.

 7 Bands of enthusiasts spread the stoppages, sometimes by removing the plugs from works boilers. One historian has claimed that these strikes represent Britain's first general strike. F. C. Mather, 'The General Strike of 1842', in *Provincial Labour History*, ed. J. H. Porter (Exeter 1972).

 8 D. Read in *Chartist Studies*, p. 60.

9 On this aspect of the movement see B. Harrison, 'Teetotal Chartism', *History*, LVIII (1973).

10 D. J. V. Jones, *Chartism and the Chartists*, (1975), p. 55; A. Wilson, 'Chartism in Glasgow' in *Chartist Studies*, p. 281.

11 Ward, *Chartism*, p. 160.

12 Ibid. pp. 155, 185.

13 See J. MacAskill, 'The Chartist Land Plan' in *Chartist Studies*.

14 Between 12,000 and 20,000 according to the government and *The Times*. Even the *Northern Star* could not bring itself to claim more than 250,000.

15 Ward, op. cit. p. 216; Jones, *Chartism and the Chartists*, p. 169.

16 Bythell, *The Handloom Weavers*, pp. 215–6, 228–30; D. J. Rowe, 'Chartism and the Spitalfields Silk-weavers', *Economic History Review*, XX, (1967); J. K. Edwards, 'Chartism in Norwich', *Yorkshire Bulletin of Economic and Social Research*, XIX (1967); R. P. Pugh in *Chartist Studies*, Chap. 6.

17 D. J. Rowe, 'The Chartist Convention and the Regions', *Economic History Review*, XXII (1969).

18 Briggs (ed.), *Chartist Studies*, pp. 260, 359.

19 Ibid. p. 294.

20 Jones, *Chartism and the Chartists*, p. 26.

21 At the 1839 convention there were no delegates from rural areas. Their absence, and the far from democratic way in which delegates were selected, gave rise to the obvious jibe that the 'People's Parliament' that had been convened to demand parliamentary reform was as much in need of reform as the House of Commons. A few rural areas saw considerable Chartist activity. Parts of rural Wales, for example, especially those parts where there had been organized resistance to the new poor law and those where anti-Anglicanism was strongest.

22 J. Rule, 'Methodism and Chartism among the Cornish Miners', *Bulletin of the Society for the Study of Labour History*, XXII (1971). Primitive Methodists, by contrast, were in many places among the Chartist organizers. On the north-east coalfields, for example, where militant Chartism made few converts among the more conservative of the Methodists. W. H. Maehl, 'Chartist Disturbances in Northeastern England, 1839', *International Review of Social History*, VIII (1963); D. J. Rowe, 'Some Aspects of Chartism on Tyneside', ibid. XVI (1971), p. 34.

23 For other reasons, and on the initial weakness of 'physical force' Chartism in London, see D. J. Rowe, 'The Failure of London Chartism', *Historical Journal*, XI (1968); I. J. Prothero, 'Chartism in London', *Past and Present*, XLIV (1969); I. J. Prothero, 'London Chartism and the Trades', *Economic History Review*, XXIV (1971).

24 Not all of them were indifferent of course: there were other Irish leaders besides O'Connor, including Bronterre O'Brien, and some of them were extreme 'physical force' Chartists. However, the only town where significant numbers of Irish Roman Catholic immigrants supported Chartism was Barnsley.

25 For more detailed accounts of the attitudes of the Irish immigrant population see J. H. Treble, 'O'Connor, O'Connell and the Attitudes of Irish Immigrants towards Chartism in the North of England, 1838–48' in *The Victorians and Social Protest*, ed. J. Butt and I. F. Clark (Newton Abbot 1973).

26 Webbs, *A History of Trade Unionism*, p. 175.
27 Ibid. p. 177.
28 Ward, *Chartism*, p. 177. After the 'plug plot' strikes the Journeymen Steam Engine and Machine Makers had censured one of their members for 'impropriety of conduct during the late excitement'. The *Compositors' Chronicle* proudly recorded its members' aloofness from 'the prevailing mania', and the secretaries of seven Sheffield unions wrote to the newspapers dissociating themselves from the strikes. *Chartist Studies*, ed. Briggs, p. 4; Musson, *Trade Union and Social History*, p. 131; Webbs, *History of Trade Unionism*, p. 176.
29 Webbs, *History of Trade Unionism*, p. 175.
30 See in particular Prothero, in *Past and Present*, XLIV (1969).
31 See, for example, Read on Manchester and Wilson on Glasgow in *Chartist Studies*, pp. 43–4, 252.
32 Cited in Perkin, *Origins of Modern English Society*, p. 236.
33 F. C. Mather in *Chartist Studies*, pp. 401–3.
34 Some considered that Chartism was a consequence of education having raised workers' expectations. But those who argued this way were probably a minority.
35 See, for example, M. Vicinus (ed.), *Suffer and be Still*, (Bloomington Indiana 1972), p. 175.
36 Edsall, *The Anti-Poor Law Movement*, pp. 188–9.
37 On this theme generally see Mather in *Chartist Studies*, pp. 398–9.
38 In September 1845 O'Connor claimed that England could support a peasant population of 300 million. Shortly after there appeared the potato blight that showed eight million peasants were too many for his native Ireland.
39 Hobsbawm, *Labouring Men*, p. 381.
40 F. Engels, *The Condition of the Working Class in England*, ed. W. O. Henderson and W. H. Chaloner, (Oxford 1958), p. 259.
41 Read in *Chartist Studies*, pp. 49, 63; Edwards in *Yorkshire Bulletin of Economic and Social Research*, XIX (1967), p. 98; Rowe in *International Review of Social History*, XVI (1971), p. 36.
42 Quoted in F. C. Mather, *Public Order in the Age of the Chartists*, (Manchester 1959), pp. 40–1.
43 Jones, *Chartism and the Chartists*, p. 158.
44 Mather, *Public Order in the Age of the Chartists*, Chap. 6.
45 Quoted in Ward, *Chartism*, p. 128.
46 Ibid. p. 204.
47 E. P. Thompson, *The Making of the English Working Class*, (1968), p. 194.
48 Quoted in G. A. Williams, *Artisans and Sans Culottes*, (1968), p. 8.
49 On this theme see G. F. E. Rudé, *The Crowd in History* (New York 1964), pp. 51, 229, 245; E. J. Hobsbawm, *The Age of Revolution, 1789–1848*, (1962), p. 103.
50 Ironically, the revolutionary excesses in France that led to exaggerated fears of insurrection in Britain and to curbs on British freedoms (above, p. 198), were accompanied by more repressive, more effective, and more enduring measures against combination than Britain ever saw. Despite the Combination Acts British workers enjoyed greater freedom of organization than most workers in Europe.
51 Hobsbawm, *Age of Revolution*, p. 104; G. A. Williams, op. cit. p. 102.

52 Thompson, *Making of the English Working Class*, pp. 194, 660.

53 Ibid. Postscript to 1968 edn. p. 916.

54 See, for example, Thomis, *The Luddites*, pp. 120–2; R. A. Church and S. D. Chapman, 'Gravener Henson and the Making of the English Working Class', in *Land, Labour and Population in the Industrial Revolution*, ed. E. L. Jones and G. E. Mingay (1967), p. 144; M. I. Thomis and P. Holt, *Threats of Revolution in Britain, 1789–1848*, (1977), p. 3. E. P. Thompson (*Making of the English Working Class*, p. 604) earlier went far closer towards claiming that Luddism was a revolutionary movement. He considered that while Luddism was never a 'wholly conscious revolutionary movement', it 'continually trembled on the edge of ulterior revolutionary objectives'.

55 J. Dinwiddy, 'Luddism and Politics in the Northern Counties', *Social History*, IV (1979), pp. 55, 59.

56 Thomis, *The Luddites*, pp. 84, 113–4; F. O. Darvall, *Popular Disturbances and Public Order in Regency England*, (Oxford 1934), p. 315.

57 Darvall, op. cit. p. 261.

58 Thompson, *Making of the English Working Class*, p. 733.

59 For a detailed account of 'Peterloo' see Read, *Peterloo: The 'Massacre' and its Background*.

60 On two other conspiracies that occurred in 1820, at Bonnymuir and Strathaven in Scotland, see Thomis and Holt, *Threats of Revolution in Britain*, Chap. 3.

61 Hobsbawm describes 1830–2 as 'the only period in the nineteenth century when the analysis of British politics in such terms is not wholly artificial'. *Age of Revolution, 1789–1848*, p. 139.

62 'The object of these movements was not revolutionary . . . nobody demanded the land', E. J. Hobsbawm and G. Rudé, *Captain Swing*, (1969), p. 16. See also G. Rudé, 'English Rural and Urban Disturbances on the Eve of the First Reform Bill, 1830–1', *Past and Present*, XXXVII (1967).

63 Rudé, in *Past and Present*, XXXVII (1967), pp. 98–9.

64 Thomis and Holt, op. cit. Chap. 4.

65 Rudé, in *Past and Present*, XXXVII (1967), pp. 98–9.

66 Jones, *Before Rebecca*, pp. 195–6.

67 The historian of the 'Peterloo massacre' has commented, 'perhaps only in peace-loving England could a death-roll of only eleven persons have been so described'. Read, *Peterloo*, preface.

68 In April 1834, for example, after pitched fighting and the killing of a rioter by a 'blackleg', Oldham was in turmoil. But the trouble stopped there and within a week the town was quietly back at work. Webbs, *History of Trade Unionism*, p. 152. On the confinement of the Merthyr riots (June 1831) see D. J. V. Jones, *Before Rebecca*, Chap. 6.

69 Landes' observation also suggests another source of relatively high labour productivity in Britain. D. S. Landes in *The Cambridge Economic History of Europe*, ed. H. J. Habakkuk and M. Postan, VI (Cambridge 1966), p. 419.

70 In Paris in June 1832 for example – see G. Rudé, *The Crowd in History*, p. 245. On how reaction to this epidemic in Britain revealed 'the underlying stability' (p. 213) of British society in 1832, see R. J. Morris, *Cholera 1832: The Social Response to*

an Epidemic (1976). There were cholera riots in Britain. But they were of a non-political nature, directed usually at hospitals, doctors, or burial grounds.

71 Engels was twenty-two when he landed. Much later, in the preface to the English edition of *Condition of the Working Class*, he dismissed his forecast of coming revolution as a consequence of 'youthful ardour'.

72 Apart from anything else, his cotton-manufacturing family was not pleased by his political activities. Neither were the Prussian police.

73 'At the bar of world opinion I shall charge the English middle-classes with mass-murder, wholesale robbery and all the other crimes in the calendar. . . . These chaps will have good cause to remember me.' Engels to Marx, 19 Nov. 1844. Quoted in Engels, *Condition of the Working Class*, p. xxiii.

74 A. Briggs, *Victorian Cities*, (1963), p. 113.

75 R. N. Salaman, *The History and Social Influence of the Potato*, (Cambridge 1949), p. 542; R. Boston, *British Chartists in America*, (Manchester 1971), p. 85.

76 Perkin, *The Origins of Modern English Society*, p. 355; Thomis, *The Town Labourer and the Industrial Revolution*, p. 181.

77 On this point and on Methodism and revolution generally, see E. J. Hobsbawm, 'Methodism and the Threat of Revolution in Britain', *History Today*, VII (1957).

78 Thompson, *Making of the English Working Class*, pp. 9–10.

79 In 1851 only 5 per cent of London industrial employers employed twenty or more persons. Lees, op. cit. p. 89.

80 M. Tylecote, *The Mechanics' Institutes of Lancashire and Yorkshire* (Manchester 1957), pp. 262–3. Most comment on social mobility in the first half of the nineteenth century concerns itself only with mobility of the 'rags to riches' kind. We really know very little about social mobility at this time: in a book published to mark the bi-centenary of Robert Owen's birth one contributor described Owen as 'one of the very few self-made manufacturers of the Industrial Revolution', while another wrote that he 'operated in what might be described as the Golden Age of the self-made man'. S. Pollard and J. Salt (eds.), *Robert Owen: Prophet of the Poor*, (1971), pp. x, 160.

81 Engels, *Condition of the Working Class*, p. 9.

82 Thompson, *Making of the English Working Class*, p. 12.

83 Mather, *Chartism*, pp. 31–2; Pelling, *History of British Trade Unions*, p. 13; Musson, *Trade Union and Social History*, p. 5; R. Currie and R. M. Hartwell, 'The Making of the English Working Class?', *Economic History Review*, XVIII (1965).

84 *Morning Chronicle*, 21 Dec. 1849.

85 J. Prest, *The Industrial Revolution in Coventry*, (Oxford 1960), p. 55.

86 P. Gaskell, *Artisans and Machinery*, (1836), p. 90.

8 · *Working-Class Movements, 1850–1888:*
New Model Unionism to the Revival of Socialism

1 Webbs, *History of Trade Unionism*, p. 349.

2 Ibid. pp. 425–7, 741–3.

3 This figure, and most of those on union membership that follow, is taken from Appendix VI of the Webbs' *History of Trade Unionism*.

4 Among them was the safety clause in the 1887 Coal Mines Regulation Act that

prohibited men with less than two years' mining experience working at the coal-face unless accompanied by an experienced miner. This rule made it far more difficult for employers to introduce 'blacklegs' during strikes.

5 P. Stead, 'The Welsh Working Class', *Llafur*, I (1973).

6 The first two trade union MPs (elected 1874) and five of the eight trade union MPs in 1889 were miners.

7 There had been recurrent complaints of hewers being credited with less than full measure for coal sent to the surface.

8 The weavers were selecting officials by competitive examination as early as the 1860s. A spinners' union examination described by the Webbs consisted of papers in arithmetic and technical calculations, an essay paper, and a searching oral test in which examiners assumed the parts of recalcitrant employers. Among the questions set for candidates seeking to be Secretary of the Bolton and District Spinners (1895) was the following: Q8. 'Assuming a rim shaft to be making 680 revolutions per minute, with a 20-inch rim, a $11\frac{1}{2}$-inch tin roller pulley, a 6-inch tin roller, and spindle wharves 13/16ths of an inch in diameter, what will be the number of revolutions of the spindle per minute, after allowing 1/16th of an inch to the diameter of the tin roller and spindle wharves for slipping of bands?' S. and B. Webb, *Industrial Democracy*, (1920), pp. 197–8.

9 For some details of the numbers involved, and of Arch's exaggerated claims for union-sponsored emigration, see R. V. Clements, 'Trade Unions and Emigration, 1840–80', *Population Studies*, IX (1955–6), p. 173.

10 An old woman of Chesterton (Cambridgeshire) whose son had joined the union was told by the Guardians that she should not expect to draw relief from both the Chesterton Union and the Labourers Union. A. J. Peacock, 'The Revolt of the Field in East Anglia', in *The Luddites and other Essays*, ed. L. M. Munby (1971), pp. 166–7.

11 B. Drake, *Women in Trade Unions*, (1921), Table 1. These figures take no account of organization among teachers and professional workers.

12 The Lancashire cotton operatives were always represented by men.

13 Turner, *Trade Union Growth, Structure, and Policy*, p. 169.

14 *First Report on the Organization and Rules of Trade Unions*, (*Parl. Papers* XXXII, 1867), Evidence, Q.826; J. B. Jefferys, *Labour's Formative Years* (1948), pp. 48–9.

15 Turner, *Trade Union Growth, Structure, and Policy*, p. 168.

16 Clegg, Fox, and Thompson, *A History of British Trade Unions since 1889*, (Oxford 1964), p. 132.

17 Turner, *Trade Union Growth, Structure, and Policy*, p. 192.

18 *Royal Commission on Trade Unions*, (*Parl. Papers* XXXII, 1867), Q 826; W. H. Fraser, *Trade Unions and Society*, (1974), p. 69.

19 'What is the state of trade at present, and what reasons have you for anticipating that at the time when the notice expires the state of trade will be such as to induce your employers to concede the advance asked for?' Question on official application to ASE head-office for permission to strike.

20 Webbs, *History of Trade Unionism*, p. 199. For illustrations of 'the strike in detail' see their *Industrial Democracy*, pp. 167–9.

21 Clegg, Fox, and Thompson, *A History of British Trade Unions*, p. 9.

22 Harrison, who did a great deal to establish the 'new model' union image, was himself appalled by some of these practices. He conceded privately that there existed 'a sort of general selfishness' among unions and declared that the masons 'deserve all that was ever said of them and are as mere organs of class tyranny'. Cited in H. W. McCready, 'British Labour and the Royal Commission on Trade Unions, 1867–9', *University of Toronto Quarterly*, XXIV (1954–5), pp. 396–7.

23 R. W. Postgate, *The Builders' History*, (1923), p. 156.

24 Because many unions did not distinguish between their friendly society reserves and funds used to finance strikes, and because they reserved the right to vary benefits, to raise subscriptions, and to make occasional levies upon members, they cannot be strictly described as actuarially unsound. There is no doubt, however, that they made unsound assumptions whose consequences would have been more serious but for the income that accrued from continual expansion in membership. For an introduction to the issues see P. Thane, A. E. Musson, and C. G. Hanson, 'Craft Unions, Welfare Benefits, and the Case for Trade Union Law Reform, 1867–75', *Economic History Review*, XXIX (1976).

25 George Potter was portrayed rather unfairly by the Webbs. For a more sympathetic account of his work and influence, see B. C. Roberts, *The Trades Union Congress, 1868–1921*, (1958).

26 By 1875 the ASCJ and the ASE had both withdrawn from the London Trades Council and very few provincial ASE branches were affiliated to their local trades council.

27 Cited in A. Briggs, *Victorian People*, (1954), p. 185. French and German unions at this time had only recently reached a position roughly equivalent with that enjoyed by British unions at the repeal of the Combination Acts nearly half a century earlier.

28 Webbs, *History of Trade Unionism*, p. 245.

29 Ibid. p. 241.

30 One of these declined the invitation. The only previous appointment of a working-man to a Royal Commission was that of Robert Applegarth in 1871 to the Royal Commission on the Contagious Diseases Act.

31 Its demise was partly a consequence of Applegarth's resignation from the ASCJ in order to accept appointment to the Royal Commission on Contagious Diseases.

32 The 1867 Reform Act increased the francise by over 80 per cent and more than doubled the urban electorate.

33 W. O. Henderson (ed.), *Engels: Selected Writings*, (1967), pp. 96–7.

34 Frederic Harrison cited by P. Joyce, 'The Factory Politics of Lancashire in the Late Nineteenth Century', *Historical Journal*, XVIII (1975), p. 526.

35 In 1874 Frederic Harrison described Conservative working men as made up of 'a sprinkling of the skilled and the mass of the unskilled and rough'. There were, of course, many exceptions to all of these generalizations. The cotton spinners, for example, were far stronger supporters of the Conservative party than their less 'aristocratic' workmates. For other, very fragmentary, information on working-class voting, see G. S. Jones, *Outcast London*, (Chap. 19); G. S. Jones, 'Working-Class Culture and Working-Class Politics in London, 1870–1900', *Journal of*

Social History, VII (1973–4), pp. 482–3; Roberts, *Classic Slum* (1973 edn.), p. 167; R. Greenall, 'Popular Conservatism in Salford, 1868–1886', *Northern History*, IX (1974); H. M. Pelling, *Popular Politics and Society in Late Victorian Britain*, (1968), Chap. 3.

36 Broadhurst, secretary of the Parliamentary Committee between 1875 and 1890 except for one short break, became an MP in 1880 and combined his nominally 'full-time' TUC duties with those to his constituents.

37 Webbs, *History of Trade Unionism*, p. 356.

38 Roberts, *The Trades Union Congress, 1868–1921*, p. 379. There is some double-counting in these figures arising from unionists being represented by both unions and trade councils.

39 'Marx's death in London (1883) would have passed unnoticed by *The Times* had not the Paris correspondent sent a paragraph on his European reputation.' H. M. Pelling, *The Origins of the Labour Party*, (Oxford 1965), p. 14.

40 William Morris led the greatest schism when he founded the Socialist League in 1884. The SDF was characterized also by endearing upper-class dottiness. The Countess of Warwick, for example, once ordered a private train to carry her home from an SDF convention. Hyndman himself was a patriot, an imperialist, an old Etonian, and a passable cricketer. He cheerfully played the Stock Exchange to finance revolution and once set out to persuade Disraeli to have the Conservative Party adopt a Marxist programme.

41 The great popularity in radical circles of Henry George's *Progress and Poverty* (1879) when socialist propaganda had scarcely begun shows the extent of existing dissatisfaction. His book, which advocated a 'single tax' on land, helped to prepare the ground for SDF and Fabian propaganda.

42 On the situation in London, see G. S. Jones, *Outcast London*.

43 At this time the TUC President was normally a union official of the town where Congress was held. Presidents held office for only a year.

44 Quoted in Hobsbawm, *Labouring Men*, p. 302.

45 K. Burgess, *The Origins of British Industrial Relations*, (1975), pp. 243–5; Webbs, *Industrial Democracy*, p. 260.

46 Pollard, *Labour in Sheffield*, p. 117.

47 R. N. Price, 'The Working Men's Club Movement and Victorian Social Reform Ideology', *Victorian Studies*, XV (1971–2).

48 *Marx and Engels on Britain* (Moscow 1953), pp. 522–3. When Engels's *The Condition of the Working Class in England* was first translated (1887) he withdrew his original dedication 'to the English Workingman'. For another visitor's comments on class relations in Britain at this time see G. von Schulze-Gaevernitz, *Social Peace: A Study of the Trade Union Movement in England*, (1890, translated 1893), pp. xix-xx.

49 Hobsbawm, *Labouring Men*, pp. 273–4.

50 Ibid. p. 274; R. Q. Gray, *The Labour Aristocracy in Victorian Edinburgh*, (Oxford 1976), pp. 110, 130–1; G. Crossick (ed.), *The Lower Middle Class in Britain, 1870–1914*, (1977), p. 36.

51 See, for example, R. Roberts on Salford where each street and every family had its social rating (*The Classic Slum*, p. 17) or Moore on the Durham miners: 'The

Methodists did not share leisure-time activities with their non-Methodist workmates . . . [they were] divided from the bosses as workers, but united with them as "respectable" men.' R. Moore, *Pitmen, Preachers and Politics*, (Cambridge 1974), p. 176.

52 The differential between building labourers' wages and building craftsman's wages was approximately stable from the fifteenth century to the First World War, see above, p. 99. Lower-paid workers were probably more than compensated for the slight widening in craft differentials by the greater benefit they derived from the post-1870 fall in the price of basic foodstuffs (above, p. 114). Low-paid workers spent a relatively high proportion of their incomes on basic foodstuffs.

53 The neglect of this important aspect of labour history was noted in Chapter 7. Recently it has received more attention but the issues can never be analysed with as much rigour as historians in America are applying to similar questions because the quantitative evidence at their disposal is not available in Britain.

54 See especially Perkin, *The Origins of Modern English Society*, pp. 425–7. John Rule gives a useful short account of this process in one industry, and Charlotte Erickson's work on steel and hosiery entrepreneurs emphasizes the low proportion from working-class origins and a possible decline in this proportion in the second half of the century. J. Rule, 'The British Fisherman, 1840–1914', *Bulletin of the Society for the Study of Labour History*, XXVII (1973); C. J. Erickson, *British Industrialists: Steel and Hosiery, 1850–1950*, (Cambridge 1959), pp. 13, 56, 121, 129.

55 Perkin, op. cit. p. 426.

56 Buckley (on Aberdeen), Crossick (on south-east London), and Gray (on Edinburgh) have each noted such opportunities. K. D. Buckley, *Trade Unionism in Aberdeen, 1878–1900* (Edinburgh 1955), p. 25; G. J. Crossick, 'Social Structure and Working-Class Behaviour: Kentish London, 1840–80', pp. 86–7; Gray, *The Labour Aristocracy in Victorian Edinburgh*, pp. 128, 131; Gray, 'Thrift and Working-Class Mobility in Victorian Edinburgh' in *Social Class in Scotland: Past and Present*, ed. A. A. MacLaren (Edinburgh 1976), pp. 135–6.

57 S. J. Chapman and F. J. Marquis, 'The Recruiting of the Employing Classes from the Ranks of the Wage Earners in the Cotton Industry', *Journal of the Royal Statistical Society*, LXXV (1912), p. 296.

58 Burgess, *Origins of British Industrial Relations*. The theme illustrated in the title of Henry Broadhurst's autobiography, *From a Stonemason's Bench to the Treasury Bench*, (1901), was repeated in the titles of autobiographies by several other working-men who were similarly successful in the late nineteenth and early twentieth centuries. Among them were G. Edwards, *From Crow Scaring to Westminster*, (1922); J. Hodge, *Workman's Cottage to Windsor Castle*, (1931); G. N. Barnes, *From Workshop to War Cabinet*, (1924).

59 A. L. Bowley, *The Change in the Distribution of the National Income, 1880–1913*, (Oxford 1920), p. 12.

60 H. McLeod, 'White Collar Values and the Role of Religion' in *The Lower Middle Class in Britain, 1870–1914*, ed. G. Crossick (1977), p. 84.

61 Webbs, *Industrial Democracy*, p. 547.

62 On urban workmen's low regard for farm labourers see, for example, A. Williams, *Life in a Railway Factory* (1969 edn.), p. 279. Some emigrant Cornish miners later returned with sufficient capital to buy farms. P. J. Perry, *British Farming in the Great Depression, 1870–1914*, (Newton Abbot 1974), p. 63.

63 Hobsbawm, *Labouring Men*, p. 297.

64 On this point see Crossick (ed.), op. cit. pp. 18, 44–45.

65 G. Crossick, 'The Labour Aristocracy and its Values: A Study of mid-Victorian Kentish London', *Victorian Studies*, XIX (1975–6), p. 305.

66 Over three-quarters of all workers remained outside formal collective bargaining arrangements at the end of the nineteenth century.

67 Many of the trade unions formed at this time included on their banners the exhortation, 'Come let us reason together.'

68 R. A. Church, 'Profit-sharing and Labour Relations in England in the Nineteenth Century', *International Review of Social History*, XVI (1971).

69 Even these were not in every case as detrimental to unionism as employers hoped: the 'automatic regulator' was seldom found mutually satisfactory for long and knowledge that the scale would eventually be re-negotiated helped to hold unions together. J. H. Porter notes that few of the sliding scale arrangements ran for more than two or three years, and J. W. F. Rowe has drawn attention to changes in the basis of coal-mining sliding-scales. J. H. Porter, 'Wage Bargaining under Conciliation Agreement, 1860–1914', *Economic History Review*, XXII (1970), pp. 467–8; J. W. F. Rowe, *Wages in the Coal Industry*, (1923), Chaps. 3 and 4. Sliding scales also protected weak unions from the usually unfavourable consequences of set-battles over wage reductions during the downward phase of the trade cycle.

70 The railways and parts of the iron, coal, and building industries were the significant exceptions to this generalization.

71 The essential features of the short history of the first national employers' association, the National Federation of Associated Employers of Labour, were similar to those of many smaller employer organizations. It was begun in 1873 in response to union initiatives (the establishment of the TUC and the successful public relations campaign after 1867) and became defunct within a decade.

72 E. H. Phelps Brown, *The Growth of British Industrial Relations: A Study from the Standpoint of 1906–14*, (1959), p. xxxiv.

73 Gosden, *Self-Help*, pp. 91–2; C. G. Hanson, 'Welfare before the Welfare State' in *The Long Debate on Poverty*, (Institute of Economic Affairs 1972), pp. 122–3. Exact figures of friendly society membership are not available because a large part of the membership was in unregistered societies and because many belonged to more than one society. Some societies offered only meagre benefits, but the figures cited appear to exclude membership of the 'collecting societies' that offered only death benefits.

74 'The ideal of the control of industry by the workers concerned had the supreme detriment *that it would not work.*' Webb, *My Apprenticeship*, p. 324. Chapter 7 of this part of Beatrice Webb's autobiography and also Appendix E, 'Why the Self-Governing Workshop has failed' contain much of interest on co-operative production. The more successful enterprises were those that appointed able managers at the going managerial rate and allowed them a free hand to hire and

fire and to employ whatever methods they considered most efficient. Those, that is, that came closest to normal capitalism. The factories that manufactured goods for sale in co-operative shops (they employed some 20,000 by 1914) appear to have been reasonably efficient. Their administration, however, represented not workers' control, but consumers' control.

75 See, for example, Deane and Cole, *British Economic Growth, 1688–1959,* (Cambridge 1967), p. 247; E. H. Phelps Brown and P. E. Hart, 'The Share of Wages in National Income', *Economic Journal,* LXII (1952), p. 276.

76 To these highly generalized accounts there are many theoretical qualifications and numerous observed exceptions. Several commentators have drawn attention to a rise in labour's share in the 'great depression' years (1873–96) apparent in some statistical series (see above, pp. 114–15) and qualify the account given above by noting that unions are likely to bitterly resist cuts in money wages even when prices are falling and their market position is weak. In prolonged periods of poor trade, therefore, profit may fall by more than it is possible for employers to reduce money wages.

77 'When they come into action for the first time, they raise the rate of pay relative to other rates; and in subsequent movements it retains, though very likely it does not improve on, this higher ranking. In this impact effect we may well have the measure of the bargaining power of trade unionism.' E. H. Phelps Brown, *The Economics of Labor,* (New Haven and London 1962), p. 180.

78 Among these difficulties may be noted the disparity between actual and recorded profits; the difficulty of distinguishing between income from capital and income earned by entrepreneurial labour; the considerable shortcomings of aggregate wage statistics; and the changing importance of central and local government activities that employed considerable labour but made little 'profit'. The distinction between the proportion of 'labour's share' that went to wages and that which went to salaries raises yet more difficulties.

79 Webbs, *Industrial Democracy,* p. 304.

80 G. C. Allen, *The Industrial Development of Birmingham and the Black Country, 1860–1917,* (1929), p. 67.

81 Webbs, *Industrial Democracy,* pp. 397–8. The article they cited was published in 1892.

82 It was noted earlier that such arrangements may have eventually impeded economic growth because they gave insufficient attention to the desirability of matching increased wages with increased wealth. However, in 1888 this problem was still mainly in the future, and the unions, of course, were participating in arrangements that were approved also by government and employers.

83 Lord Brabazon, in Paris shortly after the Commune, wondered whether industry could possibly flourish 'where communism is the dream of the workman, where armed Revolution, not against forms of government only, but against property and capital, is of periodic occurrence'. *Industrial Classes (Foreign Countries) Further Reports,* (*Parl. Papers,* LXII, 1872), p. 33.

84 Webbs, *Industrial Democracy,* pp. 398–402; E. Brunner, 'The Origins of Industrial Peace: The Case of the British Boot and Shoe Industry', *Oxford Economic Papers,* N.S. I (1949), p. 253.

85 Several of the weaknesses of the 'missed opportunities' thesis are evident within Burgess's account, although their implications appear to have been overlooked. His secondary thesis of 'betrayal' by union leaders is partly contradicted by the same evidence. Union officials, overworked and underpaid (Webbs, *History of Trade Unionism*, p. 588), were by no means as stupid or as sycophantic as Burgess suggests. A particular weakness of his interpretation is the treatment of collective bargaining arrangements, which are described as though they were invariably introduced for the exclusive advantage of employers and union officials and at the expense of the majority of unionists. *Origins of British Industrial Relations*, (especially pp. viii–ix, 32, 111, 175, 181, 185–6, 196–7).

86 Hunt, *Regional Wage Variations in Britain, 1850–1914*, p. 341.

87 See, for example, E. P. Thompson in Briggs and Saville (eds.), *Essays in Labour History*, p. 295.

88 'A Working Man', in *Working Men and Women*, (1879), pp. 112–13. On some occasions unions distributed strike pay to non-members. The labourers were included in union payments for a time during the 1859–60 building dispute, and it was sometimes found prudent to buy the goodwill of any workmates with sufficient skill to 'blackleg'. But such cases were exceptional: the unorganized workers normally went hungry and drew upon their savings or petitioned the parish and local charities.

89 H. A. Turner, *Trade Union Growth, Structure, and Policy*.

9 · *Working-Class Movements, 1889–1914: 'New Unionism' to Triple Alliance*

1 Gladstone, greatly concerned at the effect of the stoppage upon the economy, directed the Foreign Secretary, Lord Rosebery, to get the two sides to reach agreement.

2 The owners re-opened the pits at the old rates. But by reducing the supply of coal, and thus increasing its price, the dispute presented the owners with a perfectly acceptable alternative to wage reductions.

3 These disorders, which were roundly condemned by union leaders, culminated in the Featherstone 'massacre', in which two were killed. On this incident see R. G. Neville, 'The Yorkshire Miners and the 1893 Lockout: The Featherstone "Massacre"', *International Review of Social History*, XXI (1976).

4 That is, voting according to the membership represented by each delegate. Previously voting had been by a show of hands with the vote of each delegate carrying equal weight.

5 In 1898 the Engineers disaffiliated from the TUC rather than accept the ruling of its Parliamentary Committee on a trivial case of alleged 'blacklegging' that had been raised by the Gateshead Co-operative Smiths Society.

6 This Act provided for hours and wages regulation in a number of trades that were notorious for low pay and the poor working conditions of their numerous female employees.

7 As E. J. Hobsbawn pointed out some years ago, many dockers – the stevedores, cranemen, lightermen, grain and coal-porters, etc. – had a considerable degree of immunity from the competition of unskilled and inexperienced labour. Some of the gas-workers were so far removed from unskilled labourers that their

previously unorganized status is perhaps more remarkable than their organization after 1888. *Labouring Men*, pp. 161, 187, 207–9.

8 It was based upon and absorbed Ben Tillett's Tea Operatives and General Labourers Association (1887).

9 Clegg, Fox and Thompson, *A History of British Trade Unions*, pp. 82–3.

10 The Shop Assistants for example grew from 7,500 members in 1900 to 22,500 in 1910. One of the Shop Assistants' leaders, Margaret Bondfield, was later the first woman cabinet minister.

11 The first stirrings of organization among university lecturers occurred at this time. H. Perkin, *Key Profession: The History of the Association of University Teachers*, (1969), Chap. 2.

12 *The Eighteenth Abstract of Labour Statistics* (*Parl. Papers* XXIX, 1926) shows 480,000 unionists in the following four categories in 1913: shop assistants etc., banking and insurance, national and local government, teaching.

13 'You might as well have a Trade Union . . . in the Army, where discipline has to be kept at a very high standard, as have it on the railways.' Sir George Findlay, General Manager of the London and North-Western, quoted by the Webbs, *History of Trade Unionism*, p. 525.

14 Rates regulation prevented the companies following the example of many other employers by recognizing the unions and buying industrial peace with concessions met from higher prices. The North-Eastern Railway, whose profits were more satisfactory than those of most railway companies, was comparatively tolerant towards unionism.

15 The 1893 coal dispute was not the only previous occasion when the government had intervened in disputes. On other such occasions however, the 1893 Hull Dock strike for example, less was at risk and the government was not nearly so ready to enforce a settlement.

16 G. Alderman, 'The Railway Companies and the Growth of Trade Unionism', *Historical Journal*, XIV (1971), pp. 142–6.

17 Unemployment among trade unionists whose unions made returns. Mitchell and Deane, *Abstract of British Historical Statistics*, p. 64.

18 J. Gorman, *Banners Bright*, (1973), pp. 12, 53.

19 More recent organization, in less prosperous years, had also anticipated 'new unionism': the Liverpool dockers, for example, had been active in 1879–80 (when Roman Catholics and protestants were briefly in alliance) and the Knights of Labour, an American general union, enjoyed some success in the Black Country and elsewhere in the mid-1880s. In fact, few of the occupations newly organized in 1889–91 were *entirely* new to unionism.

20 E. J. Hobsbawm, 'British Gas-Workers, 1873–1914', *Labouring Men*, pp. 159–62.

21 The rules of the National Union of Gas-workers and General Labourers included among the union's objects 'to secure the return of members of the union to vestries, school boards, boards of guardians, municipal bodies, and to Parliament'. Webbs, *Industrial Democracy*, pp. 147–8.

22 T. Mann and B. Tillett, *The 'New' Trades Unionism*, (1890), p. 3; Webbs, *History of Trade Unionism*, p. 406. 'Coffin clubs' was an allusion to the old unions' friendly society activities.

23 Quoted in Postgate, *The Builders' History*, p. 343. There were, however, a few 'new' unions in which the socialists had little influence. The Tyneside and National Labour Union, for example, was Lib-Lab in politics and followed conciliatory policies from the outset.

24 Webbs, *History of Trade Unionism*, pp. 408–9.

25 1893 also saw the establishment of the National Free Labour Association by William Collison, an ex-union official who had suffered from 'new' union tactics. Collison, with others who shared the employers' resentment at the militancy, violence, and socialism associated with 'new unionism', aimed to provide 'free' labour where ever it was requested. The practical influence of the NFLA was not great, probably far less than that of the Shipping Federation. On Collison and the NFLA see Saville, 'Trade Unions and Free Labour: The Background to the Taff Vale Decision' in *Essays in Labour History*, I, and G. Alderman, 'The National Free Labour Association', *International Review of Social History*, XXI (1976).

26 Hobsbawm, 'General Labour Unions in Britain, 1889–1914', *Labouring Men*, Chap. 10. This is by far the best general account of the 'new' union retreat.

27 James Mawdsley, whose Cotton Spinners benefited considerably from the introduction of block-voting, commented in 1895, 'We saw that Congress was losing whatever influence it had, and we were determined to pull it back again into the old paths.' Cited in Clegg, Fox, and Thompson, *A History of British Trade Unions*, p. 259.

28 Webbs, *History of Trade Unionism*, p. 562.

29 It was largely because of this exclusion that Scottish trades councils took the lead in establishing the Scottish TUC in 1897.

30 John Burns and Havelock Wilson were also elected as independent candidates in 1892. But once elected Wilson quickly reached an understanding with the Liberals, and Burns' transition from revolutionary to Liberal cabinet minister was well underway by 1895.

31 The 'new' unionists also gained considerable influence at Battersea. On the extension of 'direct employment' there, and on Battersea's municipal housing, electric lighting, libraries, and baths, see C. Wrigley, 'Liberals and the Desire for Working Class Representatives in Battersea, 1886–1922', in *Essays in Anti-Labour History*, ed. K. D. Brown (1974).

32 It left seamen, agricultural labourers, and some other occupations still unprotected, but it removed many of the shortcomings of the 1880 Employers' Liability Act.

33 Hardie was affected by other influences also at this time and F. Reid has argued that his socialism pre-dated the Liberal snub. However, he went on to contest the election (unsuccessfully) as an independent labour candidate under the slogan 'a vote for Hardie is a vote for Gladstone', F. Reid, 'Keir Hardie's Conversion to Socialism' in *Essays in Labour History, II, 1886–1923*; Pelling, *The Origins of the Labour Party*, p. 65.

34 Only 5 per cent of British engineering and boilermaking workers were on piece-rates in 1886 but by 1906 the proportion was 27.5 per cent. Hobsbawm in *Essays in Labour History*, I, p. 136.

35 A. Williams, *Life in a Railway Factory*, (1969 edn.), pp. 139, 150, 183, 267, 307.

36 Clegg, Fox, and Thompson, op. cit. pp. 128–33, 153; Postgate, *The Builders' History*, Chap. 15; P. W. Kingsford, *Builders and Building Workers*, (1973), p. 168.
37 J. Mendelson, W. Owen, S. Pollard, and V. M. Thornes, *The Sheffield Trades and Labour Council, 1858–1958*, (Sheffield 1958), p. 46.
38 Webbs, *Industrial Democracy*, p. 271.
39 Cited in P. F. Clarke, *Lancashire and the New Liberalism*, (Cambridge 1971), p. 90.
40 'British Socialism is not Utopian. . . . It trusts to no sudden changes, it needs no beginnings afresh, it works under the conditions it has found, its constructive methods are chiefly adaptation and re-arrangement.' J. Ramsay MacDonald and Keir Hardie, on 'The ILP's Programme', *The Nineteenth Century*, XLV (Jan. 1899), p. 25. Lenin dismissed the ILP as the 'independent of socialism party'.
41 Roberts, *The Trades Union Congress, 1868–1921*, p. 153.
42 The LRC performance in the 1900 general election had been decidedly unimpressive. Only two LRC candidates were elected, one of whom, Richard Bell, went over to the Liberals in 1904.
43 There were a few similar cases but employers were not eager for an all-out attack. Even the railway companies made less of the opportunity than they could have done. See, for example, Phelps Brown, *A Century of Pay*, p. 189; Clegg, Fox, and Thompson, op. cit. pp. 362–3. The Webbs (*History of Trade Unionism*, pp. 601–2) calculated that all such cases cost the trade union movement, in damages and legal expenses together, only some £200,000 of which £42,000 arose from the Taff Vale case. The ASE paid out more than twice this amount in strike benefits during the 1897–8 dispute.
44 Clegg, Fox, and Thompson, op. cit. p. 375.
45 Cole, *Short History of the British Working-Class Movement*, p. 291.
46 On the campaign leading to the Unemployed Workmen's Act, in which the SDF had a significant part, see K. D. Brown, *Labour and Unemployment, 1900–14* (Newton Abbot 1971). The Act provided for the establishment of distress committees empowered to collect information, to direct labour, and to relieve unemployment in various ways and (within limits) at the taxpayers' expense. The Act was largely permissive and was soon supplanted by other measures.
47 R. E. Dowse, *Left in the Centre: The ILP, 1893–1940*, (1966), p. 11. Each of the five existing LRC MPs (there were three by-election gains in 1902–3) had been elected with Liberal support or Liberal connivance.
48 H. M. Pelling estimates that without the electoral pact Labour might have won no more than a dozen seats. *Popular Politics and Society in late Victorian Britain*, (1968), p. 110.
49 The overall strength of the parties was: Liberals (including Lib-Labs) 400; Conservatives 157; Irish Nationalists 83; Labour 29. The Labour Party polled 330,000 out of 5,627,000 votes cast.
50 The report recommended further legislative measures to safeguard peaceful picketing, that unions should have immunity from claims for damages arising from unofficial action, and that union friendly society funds should be immune from any awards for damages.
51 Cited by P. Stead, 'Working-Class Leadership in South Wales, 1900–20', *Welsh History Review*, VI (1972–3), pp. 332–3.

52 Roberts, *The Trades Union Congress, 1868–1921*, p. 221.
53 Election results, 1910:

First election		Second election	
Liberals	275	Liberals	272
Conservatives	273	Conservatives	272
Irish Nationalists	82	Irish Nationalists	84
Labour	40	Labour	42

54 The northeast hewers had opposed the eight-hours campaign from the start (see above, p. 254). When the Northumberland representatives to the Fourth International Miners' Congress (Brussels, 1893) moved an amendment whose effect was to nullify a motion demanding a legal eight hours day, a French observer, unaware of the niceties of British union politics, assumed that they were anarchists. R. P. Arnot, *The Miners: A History of the Miners Federation of Great Britain, 1889–1910*, (1949), p. 172.
55 Roberts, *The Trades Union Congress, 1868–1921*, p. 241.
56 Table 9·5 (above, p. 319) and Mitchell and Deane, op. cit. pp. 64–5.
57 Ibid.
58 K. G. J. C. Knowles, *Strikes: A Study in Industrial Conflict*, (Oxford 1952), pp. 223, 227. P. N. Stearns comments that French workmen were more interested than British workmen in food and its cost, and that they reacted sooner and more emphatically to change in the cost of living. 'National Character and European Labor History', *Journal of Social History*, IV (1970–1), pp. 102–3.
59 *The Miners' Next Step*, (Tonypandy 1912), p. 7.
60 Until the mid-1890s this was the view of most friendly societies. By 1900, however, a substantial part of the movement was coming to favour state pensions. In part this was because the societies shared the general change in attitudes towards poverty and state intervention, and in part it was a consequence of their financial embarrassment. Falling mortality from infectious diseases was leaving more members to draw benefits in old age when they were likely to suffer prolonged illness or to be incapable of work through senility. The friendly societies had not anticipated this development and each of them was reluctant to make the necessary adjustment to contributions and benefits because they feared losing their share of new, young, recruits. State pensions would obviously ease the burden of maintaining elderly members of friendly societies. Even so, half of the societies that answered a 1908 question from the Chief Registrar of Friendly Societies on the consequences of a non-contributory pension considered that their interests would be harmed by the introduction of state pensions. On the working-class reaction to social reform generally see Pelling, *Popular Politics and Society*, Chap. 1; B. B. Gilbert, 'The Decay of Nineteenth Century Provident Institutions and the Coming of Old Age Pensions in Great Britain', *Economic History Review*, XVII (1964–5); and Gosden, *Self-Help*, Chap. 9.
61 Forty of the forty-two successful Labour candidates at the second 1910 election were unopposed by Liberals.
62 The act that reversed the Osborne judgement was far from entirely acceptable to union leaders. It required unions to secure the consent of a majority of their

members by ballot before imposing a political levy and provided that members could 'contract out'. However, the proceeds of the political levy had to be spent on politics, whereas previously the unions had given the Labour Party as much, or as little, as they considered appropriate. An unsought consequence of this act, therefore, was greater and more certain trade union assistance for the Labour Party.

63 The Fair Wages resolution of 1891 which encouraged public authorities to boycott firms that paid exceptionally badly, and the Trade Boards Act of 1909 that introduced what amounted almost to compulsory collective bargaining in a number of low-wage occupations, were not significant departures from the policy of allowing and encouraging voluntary collective bargaining. Rather they were attempts to provide a substitute for voluntary collective bargaining in trades where the absence of unions prevented its spontaneous appearance.

64 The Act provided that the Board of Trade could appoint an arbitrator at the request of both sides to a dispute or a conciliator at the request of either side, and that it might enquire into the circumstances of any dispute.

65 A. J. Mundella (President of the Board of Trade in 1886 and 1892–4) established a 'bureau of labour statistics' within the Board of Trade in 1886. This organization collected statistics on disputes and unemployment and by 1893, when it became the 'Labour Department', had extended its activities to enquiring into the circumstances of disputes and to encouraging negotiation and permanent collective bargaining procedures. In time the department acquired a cadre of expert and experienced conciliation officers, one or more of whom were involved in attempts to settle virtually every major dispute. G. R. Askwith became the best known of these officers: he was appointed Chief Industrial Commissioner in 1911 and had a leading part in attempts to quell the pre-war unrest. The Labour Department made full use of the limited powers granted by the 1896 Conciliation Act. On its activities after 1896 see R. Davidson, 'Social Conflict and Social Administration: The Conciliation Act in British Industrial Relations', in *The Search for Wealth and Stability*, ed. T. C. Smout (1979).

66 Compulsory arbitration was introduced during the First World War. But conditions then, of course, were very exceptional.

67 At that time many employers probably would have resented such infringements upon their freedom to deal with workers as they saw fit. But governments always found employers easier to persuade than employees.

68 The TUC Parliamentary Committee showed some enthusiasm for compulsory state intervention in the late 1890s and as late as 1903, after Taff Vale, accepted that unions should not be entirely free of liability for damage arising from their activities. Clegg, Fox, and Thompson, *A History of British Trade Unions*, p. 265; Pelling, *Popular Politics and Society*, pp. 76–7.

69 A. V. Dicey commented that this enactment gave the unions 'a freedom from civil liability for the commission of even the most heinous wrong . . . a privilege and protection not possessed by any other persons or body of persons.' Cited in D. F. MacDonald, *The State and the Trade Unions*, (1976), p. 61. The Webbs, more sympathetic to organized labour yet aware also of the potentially harmful

consequences of its unfettered power, wrote of 'an extraordinary and unlimited immunity . . . which most lawyers, as well as all employers, regard as nothing less than monstrous'. *History of Trade Unionism*, p. 606.

70 It had a major part in particular, alongside the inhibiting influences of the Taff Vale judgement and memories of the cost and hardships of the earlier disputes, in accounting for the extraordinarily low level of unrest between 1899 and 1907 (Table 9·5 above).

71 The Brooklands agreement (above, p. 299), for example, allowed wages to be varied only once each year and never by more than 5 per cent.

72 For an example see the Webbs, *Industrial Democracy*, pp. 207–8.

73 The other was the reduction in their money wages relative to what other workers received. Their employers, as we noted earlier, were made more intransigent by their inability to raise prices. Phelps Brown, *Growth of British Industrial Relations*, pp. 298–300.

74 Mitchell and Deane, op. cit. p. 483. In explaining the pre-war unrest Phelps Brown put considerable emphasis on the plight of coal employers 'caught between rising costs and insufficiently rising prices' (*Growth of British Industrial Relations*, p. 334). But other sources raise some doubts about the level of coal profits – see, for example, R. Gregory, *The Miners and British Politics, 1906–14*, (Oxford 1968), pp. 180–1; Burgess, *Origins of British Industrial Relations*, pp. 152–3, 215; D. H. Aldcroft (ed.), *British Industry and Foreign Competition, 1875–1914*, (1968), p. 43.

75 R. Walters, 'Labour Productivity in the South Wales Steam-Coal Industry, 1870–1914', *Economic History Review*, XXVIII (1975), pp. 287–8.

76 Briggs and Saville (eds.), *Essays in Labour History*, II, p. 96.

77 On the relationship between mine accidents and the temper of industrial relations see Knowles, *Strikes*, pp. 187–8. H. S. Jevons, in *The British Coal Trade*, (1915), p. 124, gives the following death-rates from colliery accidents per 1,000 employed (1901–10): S. Wales 1.78; Lancashire 1.57; Scotland 1.49; North Wales 1.42; Midlands 1.29; Northumberland and Durham 1.08; Yorkshire 1.03.

78 Pelling, *Popular Politics and Society*, pp. 111–13.

79 G. Dangerfield, 'The great General Strike of 1914, forestalled by some bullets at Sarajevo', *The Strange Death of Liberal England*, (1966 edn.), p. 351.

80 See, among others, Webbs, *History of Trade Unionism*, p. 659; Roberts, *The Trades Union Congress, 1868–1921*, pp. 252–3; R. Holton, *British Syndicalism, 1900–1914: Myths and Realities*, (1976), p. 202.

81 Roberts, *The Trades Union Congress, 1868–1921*, p. 243; J. Lovell, *British Trade Unions, 1875–1933*, (1977), p. 47; Pelling, *Popular Politics and Society*, pp. 157–9.

82 On this theme see E. M. Kassalow, *Trade Unions and Industrial Relations: An International Comparison*, (New York 1969).

83 P. S. Bagwell, 'The Triple Industrial Alliance, 1913–1922' in *Essays in Labour History* II (1971); G. A. Phillips, 'The Triple Industrial Alliance in 1914', *Economic History Review*, XXIV (1971).

84 Roberts, *The Trades Union Congress, 1868–1921*, p. 268; Holton, op. cit. p. 205.

85 On the conciliatory attitudes of British employers see, among others, Phelps Brown and Browne, *A Century of Pay*, pp. 188–9; Phelps Brown, *Growth of British Industrial Relations*, p. 269; Clegg, Fox, and Thompson, loc. cit. pp. 362–3; P. N.

Stearns, *Lives of Labour: Work in a Maturing Industrial Society*, (1975), pp. 181–2;
A. Shadwell, *Industrial Efficiency: A Comparative Study of Industrial Life in
England, Germany, and America* (1906), II, p. 311.

86 G. Alderman, 'The National Free Labour Association', *International Review of
Social History*, XXI (1976), p. 326; R. Bean, 'Employers' Associations in the Port
of Liverpool, 1890–1914', *International Review of Social History*, XXI (1976),
pp. 381–2.

87 E. Wigham, *Strikes and the Government, 1893–1974*, (1976), pp. 2–15. The job of
first Labour Commissioner was initially offered to Tom Mann. It was then given
to Llewellyn Smith, who had helped Annie Besant organize the 1888 matchgirls'
strike.

88 Cited in *Marxism Today*, (July 1970), p. 208.

89 Ben Tillett ascribed the 1912 dockers' defeat to 'a lack of class loyalty and class-
conscience'. Cited in P. Thompson, *The Edwardians: The Remaking of British
Society*, (1975), p. 233.

90 Phelps Brown, *Growth of British Industrial Relations*, p. 149.

91 The trade boards for example, and some of the changes proposed in the Webbs'
minority poor law report. Roberts, *The Trades Union Congress, 1868–1921*, pp.
216–7, 221; Clegg, Fox, and Thompson, op. cit. pp. 397–8.

92 They remained indifferent to the trades councils for exactly the same reasons. By
1913 the proportion of union membership affiliated to trades councils had fallen
to 36 per cent. In 1895 it has been 45 per cent.

93 The Lancashire miners favoured affiliation to the Labour Party long before 1908.
But mainly because they found their antipathy towards Irish Roman Catholics
incompatible with the Liberal Party's support for Irish home rule. Pelling, *Popular
Politics and Society*, p. 113.

94 Williams, *Life in a Railway Factory*, p. 306.

95 Roberts, *Salford: The Classic Slum*, pp. 16, 28.

96 Rowse, *A Cornish Childhood*, p. 55.

97 Nine out of ten trade union secretaries who were asked in 1911 whether
opportunities to move into the managerial classes were as great as formerly replied
affirmatively and cited technical education as a main cause of mobility. Chapman
and Marquis, loc. cit. 306.

98 According to Bowley, between 1881 and 1911 the number of male workers in
'middle-class' occupations rose by 72 per cent while the number in 'working-class'
occupations rose by 41 per cent. Over the same years the number of female
workers in 'middle-class' occupations rose by 168 per cent while the number in
working-class occupations rose by only 24 per cent. A. L. Bowley, *Wages and
Income in the United Kingdom since 1860*, (Cambridge 1937), Appendix E.

99 R. Roberts, *A Ragged Schooling*, (Manchester 1976), p. 21; C. S. Davies, *North-
Country Bred*, (1963), pp. 43–6, 122.

100 B. Webb, *My Apprenticeship*, p. 131.

101 G. S. Jones, 'Working-Class Culture and Working-Class Politics in London,
1870–1900', *Journal of Social History*, VII (1973–4).

102 Jones's accounts appears, in any event, to discount rather heavily the widespread
striving for respectability, the petty snobberies, and the struggling for social

advantage that others have noted. See, for example, S. Meacham, *A Life Apart: The English Working Class, 1890–1914*, (1977), pp. 27, 90, 98; Roberts, *The Classic Slum*, Chap. 1; M. M. Bird, *Women at Work*, (1911), pp. 16–22.

103 Kassalow, *Trade Unions and Industrial Relations*, (p. 40) draws attention also to the contrast with the achievements of militant working-class parties in Europe.

104 Quoted in E. Halévy, *History of the English People*, (1952 edn.) VI, p. 465.

105 J. M. Winter, 'The Impact of the First World War upon Civilian Health in Britain', *Economic History Review*, XXX (1977), pp. 493–4.

106 Knowles, *Strikes*, p. 272.

107 E. A. Pratt (ed.), *Trade Unionism and British Industry*, (1904), p. 64; R. A. Church, 'Profit Sharing and Labour Relations in England in the Nineteenth Century', *International Review of Social History*, XVI (1971), pp. 10–11.

108 Cited in Pelling, *History of British Trade Unionism* (1963 edn.), p. 112.

109 E. J. Hobsbawm, *Labour's Turning Point, 1880–1900*, (1974), p. 157.

110 Pratt, op. cit. pp. 43–5. See also R. O. Clarke, 'The Dispute in the British Engineering Industry, 1897–8: An Evaluation', *Economica*, XXIV (1957), pp. 135–7.

111 Brunner, in *Oxford Economic Papers*, I (1949), pp. 251–2.

112 *Trade Unionism and British Industry*, ed. E. A. Pratt (1904). See also A. L. Levine, *Industrial Retardation in Britain, 1880–1914*, (1967), Chap. 5.

113 Pratt, op. cit., pp. 136–7, 143.

114 Ibid. pp. 124–5; Pollard, *Labour in Sheffield*, p. 212. Some time before this the unions had succeeded in inserting a sweeping exclusion into the 1889 Technical Education Act prohibiting instruction in 'the practice of any trade, industry, or employment'.

115 At one point in his critique of the unions Edwin Pratt (op. cit. p. 45) touched upon this possibility and in doing so appeared to cast some doubt over parts of his overall thesis: 'while the leaders of the men employed in the engineering trades are beginning to see more clearly how the interests of the employed are bound up with those of the employers, and to understand the real nature of the conditions which the latter have to face, these newer ideas and this broader knowledge have not yet permeated the general mass of the men.' Elsewhere in the same work there is evidence that might be taken to imply that 'ca' canny' was less universally a consequence of unionism than Pratt believed. On this last point see also Levine, op. cit. p. 84.

116 Pratt, op. cit. p. 186. The report of the *Mosely Industrial Commission to the USA*, (Manchester 1903, p. 7) also drew attention to this point.

117 Phelps Brown and Browne, *A Century of Pay*, pp. 181–90.

118 'It is at least possible that certain groups of workers now began systematically to allow their output to sink unless held up by incentives, or else that the weakening of older forms of labour discipline or tradition produced the same result', Hobsbawm, *Labouring Men*, pp. 350–1.

119 Unionism elsewhere was also not so rigidly organized along craft lines and for this reason it was rather more willing to accept technical change and less likely to embark on demarcation disputes.

FURTHER READING

Only the more essential works are listed. Most of the other books and articles that have been cited in the notes will be found useful and many of the books listed below contain more specialist bibliographies. Books with no indicated place of publication were published in London.

Reference
British Labour Statistics: Historical Abstracts, 1886–1968 (HMSO 1971)
Mitchell, B. R. and Deane, P. *Abstract of British Historical Statistics* (Cambridge 1962)

1 · *Work and Wages*
Bythell, D. *The Sweated Trades: Outwork in Nineteenth Century Britain* (1978)
Cadbury, E., Matheson, M. C. and Shann, G. *Women's Work and Wages* (1906)
Davidoff, L. 'Mastered for Life: Servant and Wife in Victorian and Edwardian England', *Journal of Social History* VII (1973–4)
Deane, P. and Cole, W. A. *British Economic Growth, 1688–1959* (Cambridge 1967)
Hartwell, R. M. 'The Service Revolution' in *Fontana Economic History of Europe* ed. C. M. Cipolla III (1973)
Hewitt, M. *Wives and Mothers in Victorian Industry* (1958)
Neff, W. *Victorian Working Women* (1929)
Pinchbeck, I. *Women Workers and the Industrial Revolution, 1750–1850* (1930)
Pinchbeck, I. and Hewitt, M. *Children in English Society* I (1969) II (1973)
Pollard, S. 'Labour in Great Britain' in *Cambridge Economic History of Europe* ed. P. Mathias and M. M. Postan VII, Part I (1978)
Richards, E. 'Women in the British Economy since about 1700: An Interpretation', *History* LIX (1974)
Thomas, M. W. *Young People in Industry, 1750–1945* (1945)

2 · *Population: Births and Deaths*
Banks, J. A. *Prosperity and Parenthood* (1954)
Collis, E. L. and Greenwood, M. *The Health of the Industrial Worker* (1921)
Flinn, M. W. *British Population Growth, 1700–1850* (1970)
Flinn, M. W. (ed.) *Scottish Population History* (Cambridge 1977)

Habakkuk, H. J. *Population Growth and Economic Development since 1750* (Leicester 1971)

Hair, P. E. H. 'Mortality from Violence in British Coal Mines, 1800–50', *Economic History Review* XII (1968)

Logan, W. P. D. 'Mortality in England and Wales from 1848 to 1947', *Population Studies* IV (1950–1)

McKeown, T. and Record, R. G. 'Reasons for the Decline in Mortality in England and Wales during the Nineteenth Century', *Population Studies* XVI (1962–3)

McLaren, A. *Birth Control in Nineteenth Century England* (1978)

Mitchison, R. *British Population Change since 1860* (1977)

Oliver, T. (ed.) *Dangerous Trades* (1902)

Report of the Royal Commission on Population (HMSO 1949)

Wrigley, E. A. *Population and History* (1969)

3 · *Wages and Living Standards*

Ashworth, W. *The Genesis of Modern British Town Planning* (1954)

Bienefeld, M. A. *Working Hours in British Industry* (1972)

Burnett, J. *Plenty and Want: A Social History of Diet in England* (1966)

Burnett, J. *A Social History of Housing, 1815–1970* (Newton Abbot 1978)

Bythell, D. *The Handloom Weavers* (Cambridge 1969)

Bythell, D. 'The History of the Poor', *English Historical Review* LXXXIX (1974)

Chapman, S. D. (ed.) *The History of Working-Class Housing* (Newton Abbot 1971)

Collier, F. *The Family Economy of the Working Classes in the Cotton Industry, 1784–1833* (Manchester 1964)

Cotgrove, S. F. *Technical Education and Social Change* (1958)

Engels, F. *The Condition of the Working Class in England* ed. W. O. Henderson and W. H. Chaloner (Oxford 1958)

Flinn, M. W. (ed.) *Report on the Sanitary Condition of the Labouring Population of Great Britain, 1842* (1965)

Flinn, M. W. 'Trends in Real Wages, 1750–1850', *Economic History Review* XXVII (1974)

Hayek, F. A. (ed.) *Capitalism and the Historians* (1954)

Hobsbawm, E. J. *Labouring Men* (1968) Chapters 5, 6, 7, 17

Hunt, E. H. *Regional Wage Variations in Britain, 1850–1914* (Oxford 1973)

Knowles, K. G. J. C. and Robertson, D. J. 'Differences between the Wages of Skilled and Unskilled Workers, 1880–1950', *Bulletin of the Oxford University Institute of Statistics* XIII (1951)

McBride, T. M. *The Domestic Revolution: The Modernization of Household Service in England and France, 1820–1920* (New York 1976)

Phelps Brown E. H. and Hopkins, S. V. 'Seven Centuries of the Prices of Consumables, compared with Builders' Wage Rates', *Economica* XXIII (1956)

Phelps Brown, E. H. and Browne, M. H. *A Century of Pay* (1968)

Pollard, S. *A History of Labour in Sheffield* (Liverpool 1959)

Pollard, S. 'Factory Discipline and the Industrial Revolution', *Economic History Review* XVI (1963–4)

Pollard, S. *The Genesis of Modern Management* (1968)

Reid, D. A. 'The Decline of Saint Monday, 1766–1876', *Past and Present* LXXI (1976)

Stone, L. 'Literacy and Education in England, 1640–1900', *Past and Present* XLII (1969)

Sutcliffe, A. 'Working-Class Housing in Nineteenth Century Britain', *Bulletin of the Society for the Study of Labour History* XXIV (1972)

Taylor, A. J. *The Standard of Living in Britain in the Industrial Revolution* (1975)

Thomis, M. I. *The Town Labourer and the Industrial Revolution* (1974)

Thomis, M. I. *Responses to Industrialization: The British Experience, 1780–1850* (Newton Abbot 1976)

Thompson, E. P. 'Time, Work-Discipline, and Industrial Capitalism', *Past and Present* XXXVIII (1967)

Thompson, E. P. *The Making of the English Working Class* (1968)

Webb, S. 'The Alleged Differences in the Wages Paid to Men and to Women for Similar Work', *Economic Journal* I (1891)

West, E. G. *Education and the Industrial Revolution* (1975) Chap. 18

West, E. G. 'Literacy and the Industrial Revolution', *Economic History Review* XXXI (1978)

4 · *Poverty*

Blaug, M. 'The Myth of the Old Poor Law and the Making of the New', *Journal of Economic History* XXIII (1963)

Blaug, M. 'The Poor Law Report Re-examined', *Journal of Economic History* XXIV (1964)

Bowley, A. L. and Burnett-Hurst, A. R. *Livelihood and Poverty* (1915)

Checkland, S. G. and E. O. A. (eds.), *The Poor Law Report of 1834* (1974)

Digby, A. 'The Labour Market and the Continuity of Social Policy after 1834: The Case of the Eastern Counties', *Economic History Review* XXVIII (1975)

Fraser, D. *The Evolution of the British Welfare State* (1973)

Fraser, D. (ed.) *The New Poor Law in the Nineteenth Century* (1976)

Gilbert, B. B. 'The Decay of Nineteenth Century Provident Institutions and the Coming of Old Age Pensions in Great Britain', *Economic History Review* XVIII (1964–5)

Gosden, P. H. J. H. *Self-Help: Voluntary Associations in Nineteenth Century Britain* (1973)

Hay, J. R. *The Origins of the Liberal Welfare Reforms, 1906–14* (1975)

Institute of Economic Affairs, *The Long Debate on Poverty* (1972)

Jones, G. S. *Outcast London* (Oxford 1971)

Lascelles, E. C. P. 'Charity' in *Early Victorian England* ed. G. M. Young (Oxford 1934)

Marshall, J. D. *The Old Poor Law, 1795–1834* (1968)

Pember Reeves, M. S. *Round about a Pound a Week* (1913)

Roberts, D. *The Victorian Origins of the British Welfare State* (1960)

Rose, M. E. *The Relief of Poverty, 1834–1914* (1972)

Rowntree, B. S. *Poverty: A Study of Town Life* (1901)

Rowntree, B. S. and Kendall, M. *How the Labourer Lives* (1913)
Thane, P. 'Women and the Poor Law in Victorian and Edwardian England', *History Workshop* VI (1978)

5 · *Migrants, Emigrants, Immigrants*
Carrier, N. H. and Jeffery, J. R. *External Migration: A Study of the Available Statistics* (HMSO 1953)
Erickson, C. J. 'The Encouragement of Emigration by British Trade Unions, 1850–1900', *Population Studies* III (1949–50)
Gainer, B. *The Alien Invasion: The Origins of the Aliens Act of 1905* (1972)
Garrard, J. A. *The English and Immigration, 1880–1910* (1971)
Gartner, L. P. *The Jewish Immigrant in England, 1870–1914* (Detroit 1960)
Hobsbawm, E. J. *Labouring Men* (1968) Chapter 4
Jackson, J. A. *The Irish In Britain* (1963)
Lampard, E. E. 'The Urbanizing World' in *The Victorian City: Images and Realities* I ed. H. J. Dyos and M. Wolff (1973)
Lees, L. H. *Exiles of Erin: Irish Migrants in Victorian London* (Manchester 1979)
Lipman, V. D. *Social History of the Jews in England, 1850–1950* (1954)
Lobban, R. D. 'The Irish Community in Greenock in the Nineteenth Century', *Irish Geography* VI (1971)
Macdonald, D. F. *Scotland's Shifting Population, 1770–1850* (Glasgow 1937)
Redford, A. *Labour Migration in England, 1800–1850* (Manchester 1964)
Richardson, C. 'Irish Settlement in mid-Nineteenth Century Bradford', *Yorkshire Bulletin of Economic and Social Research* XX (1968)
Saville, J. *Rural Depopulation in England and Wales, 1851–1951* (1957)
Shepperson, W. S. *British Emigration to North America* (Oxford 1957)

6 · *Working-Class Movements, 1815–1850: (I) Trade Unionism and Other Movements*
Butt, J. (ed.) *Robert Owen: Prince of Cotton Spinners* (Newton Abbot 1971)
Edsall, N. C. *The Anti-Poor Law Movement, 1834–44* (Manchester 1971)
George, M. D. 'The Combination Laws Re-considered', *Economic History* I (1927)
Gosden, P. H. J. H. *The Friendly Societies in England, 1815–1875* (Manchester 1961)
Hobsbawm, E. J. *Labouring Men* (1968) Chapters 2, 8
Musson, A. E. *British Trade Unions, 1800–75* (1972)
Oliver, W. H. 'The Consolidated Trades' Union of 1834', *Economic History Review* XVII (1964–5)
Pelling, H. M. *A History of British Trade Unionism* (1976)
Pollard, S. 'Nineteenth Century Co-operation: From Community Building to Shopkeeping', in *Essays in Labour History* ed. A. Briggs and J. Saville I (1967)
Pollard, S. and Salt, J. (eds.) *Robert Owen: Prophet of the Poor* (1971)
Taylor, A. J. 'The Miners' Association of Great Britain and Ireland, 1842–8', *Economica* XXII (1955)
Thomis, M. I. *The Luddites* (Newton Abbot 1970)
Thomis, M. I. *The Town Labourer and the Industrial Revolution* (1974)

Further Reading

Turner, H. A. *Trade Union, Growth, Structure, and Policy* (1962)

Tylecote, M. *The Mechanics' Institutes of Lancashire and Yorkshire before 1851* (Manchester 1957)

Ward, J. T. *The Factory Movement, 1830–55* (1962)

Ward, J. T. (ed.) *Popular Movements, c. 1830–50* (1970)

Webb, S. and B. *The History of Trade Unionism* (1920)

7 · *Working-Class Movements, 1815–1850 (II):*
Chartism, Revolution, and the Making of Class

Briggs, A. (ed.) *Chartist Studies* (1959)

Briggs, A. 'The Language of "Class" in Early Nineteenth Century England' in *Essays in Labour History* ed. A. Briggs and J. Saville I (1967)

Hobsbawm, E. J. 'Methodism and the Threat of Revolution in Britain', *History Today* VII (1957)

Hobsbawm, E. J. *The Age of Revolution, 1789–1848* (1962)

Hobsbawm, E. J. *Labouring Men* (1968), Chapters 3, 8

Hobsbawm, E. J. and Rudé G. F. E. *Captain Swing* (1969)

Jones, D. J. V. *Before Rebecca: Popular Protests in Wales, 1793–1835* (1973)

Jones, D. J. V. *Chartism and the Chartists* (1975)

Mather, F. C. 'The Railways, the Electric Telegraph, and Public Order during the Chartist Period, 1837–48', *History* XXXVIII (1953)

Mather, F. C. *Public Order in the Age of the Chartists* (Manchester 1959)

Mather, F. C. *Chartism* (1965)

Morris, R. J. *Class and Class Consciousness in the Industrial Revolution, 1780–1850* (1979)

Perkin, H. *The Origins of Modern English Society, 1780–1880* (1969)

Rowe, D. J. 'The Chartist Convention and the Regions', *Economic History Review* XXII (1969)

Rudé, G. F. E. *The Crowd in History; A Study of Popular Disturbances in France and England, 1730–1848* (New York 1964)

Stevenson, J. *Popular Disturbances in England, 1700–1870* (1979)

Thomis, M. I. and Holt, P. *Threats of Revolution in Britain, 1789–1848* (1977)

Thompson, E. P. *The Making of the English Working Class* (1968)

Ward, J. T. *Chartism* (1973)

Williams, G. A. *Artisans and Sans Culottes* (1968)

8 · *Working-Class Movements, 1850–1888:*
New Model Unionism to the Revival of Socialism

Allen, V. L. *Trade Unions and the Government* (1960)

Bagwell, P. S. *Industrial Relations* (Dublin 1974)

Buckley, K. D. *Trade Unionism in Aberdeen, 1878–1900* (Edinburgh 1955)

Clements R. V. 'British Trade Unions and Popular Political Economy, 1850–75', *Economic History Review* XIV (1961–2)

Clinton, A. 'The History of Trades Councils', *Bulletin of the Society for the Study of Labour History* XXIX (1974)

Crossick, G. 'The Labour Aristocracy and its Values: A Study of mid-Victorian Kentish London', *Victorian Studies* XIX (1975–6)

Fraser, W. H. *Trade Unions and Society: The Struggle for Acceptance, 1850–80* (1974)

Gray, R. Q. *The Labour Aristocracy in Victorian Edinburgh* (Oxford 1976)

Hobsbawm, E. J. *Labouring Men* (1968) Chapters 12, 15, 16

Jones, G. S. *Outcast London* (Oxford 1971)

Lovell, J. *British Trade Unions, 1875–1933* (1977)

Lovell, J. and Roberts, B. C. *A Short History of the TUC* (1968)

Macdonald, D. F. *The State and the Trade Unions* (1976)

Pelling, H. M. *A History of British Trade Unionism* (1976)

Perkin, H. J. *The Origins of Modern English Society, 1780–1880* (1969)

Pollard, S. 'Trade Unions and the Labour Market, 1870–1914', *Yorkshire Bulletin of Economic and Social Research* XVII (1965)

Porter, J. H. 'Wage Bargaining under Conciliation Agreements, 1860–1914', *Economic History Review* XXIII (1970)

Roberts, B. C. *The Trades Union Congress, 1868–1921* (1958)

Saville, J. 'Trades Councils and the Labour Movement to 1900', *Bulletin of the Society for the Study of Labour History* XIV (1967)

Sharp, I. G. *Industrial Conciliation and Arbitration in Great Britain* (1950)

Turner, H. A. *Trade Union Growth, Structure, and Policy* (1962)

Webb, S. and B. *Industrial Democracy* (1920)

Webb, S. and B. *The History of Trade Unionism* (1920)

9 · *Working-Class Movements, 1889–1914: 'New Unionism' to Triple Alliance*

Alderman, G. 'The Railway Companies and the Growth of Trade Unionism', *Historical Journal* XIV (1971)

Bagwell, P. S. 'The Triple Industrial Alliance, 1913–1922' in *Essays in Labour History 1886–1923* ed. A. Briggs and J. Saville II (1971)

Clegg, H. A., Fox, A. and Thompson, A. F. *A History of British Trade Unions since 1889,* I (Oxford 1964)

Dangerfield, G. *The Strange Death of Liberal England* (1936)

Drake, B. *Women in Trade Unions* (1921)

Hobsbawm, E. J. *Labouring Men* (1968) Chapters 9, 10

Lewenhak, S. *Women and Trade Unions* (1977)

Macdonald, D. F. *The State and the Trade Unions* (1976)

Meacham, S. 'English Working-Class Unrest before the First World War', *American Historical Review* LXXVII (1972)

Meacham, S. *A Life Apart: The English Working Class, 1890–1914* (1977)

Moore, R. *Pitmen, Preachers, and Politics* (Cambridge 1974)

Pelling, H. M. *The Origins of the Labour Party* (Oxford 1965)

Pelling, H. M. *Popular Politics and Society in late Victorian Britain* (1968)

Pelling, H. M. *A History of British Trade Unionism* (1976)

Pelling, H. M. *A Short History of the Labour Party* (1978)

Further Reading

Phelps Brown, E. H. *The Growth of British Industrial Relations: A Study from the Standpoint of 1906–14* (1959)

Phillips, G. A. 'The Triple Industrial Alliance in 1914', *Economic History Review* XXIV (1971)

Porter, J. H. 'Wage Bargaining under Conciliation Agreements, 1860–1914', *Economic History Review* XXIII (1970)

Pratt, E. A. (ed.) *Trade Unionism and British Industry* (1904)

Roberts, B. C. *The Trades Union Congress, 1868–1921* (1958)

Saville, J. 'Trade Unions and Free Labour: The Background to the Taff Vale Decision' in *Essays in Labour History* ed. A. Briggs and J. Saville I (1967)

Webb, S. and B. *Industrial Democracy* (1920)

Wigham, E. *Strikes and the Government, 1893–1974* (1976)

INDEX

INDEX

D

E

F

Y